Lecture Notes in Computer Science 7118

Commenced Publication in 1973
Founding and Former Series Editors:
Gerhard Goos, Juris Hartmanis, and Jan van Leeuwen

Ali Miri   Serge Vaudenay (Eds.)

Selected Areas in Cryptography

18th International Workshop, SAC 2011
Toronto, ON, Canada, August 11-12, 2011
Revised Selected Papers

Springer

Volume Editors

Ali Miri
Ryerson University
Department of Computer Science
Toronto, ON, Canada
E-mail: ali.miri@ryerson.ca

Serge Vaudenay
Ecole Polytechnique Fédérale de Lausanne
Lausanne, Switzerland
E-mail: serge.vaudenay@epfl.ch

ISSN 0302-9743 e-ISSN 1611-3349
ISBN 978-3-642-28495-3 ISBN 978-3-642-28496-0 (eBook)
DOI 10.1007/978-3-642-28496-0
Springer Heidelberg Dordrecht London New York

Library of Congress Control Number: 2012931441

CR Subject Classification (1998): E.3, D.4.6, K.6.5, F.2.1-2, C.2, H.4.3

LNCS Sublibrary: SL 4 – Security and Cryptology

Typesetting: Camera-ready by author, data conversion by Scientific Publishing Services, Chennai, India

Printed on acid-free paper

Springer is part of Springer Science+Business Media (www.springer.com)

Preface

The 18th International Conference on Selected Areas in Cryptography (SAC 2011) was held August 11–12, 2011 in Toronto, Canada. SAC is an annual event held in co-operation with the International Association for Cryptologic Research (IACR). There were 72 participants from 18 countries. Previous events in this series were held at Queen's University (1994, 1996, 1998, 1999, and 2005), Carleton University (1995, 1997, and 2003), Fields Institute (2001), Memorial University of Newfoundland (2002), Concordia University (2006), University of Ottawa (2007), Mount Allison University (2008), University of Calgary (2009), and University of Waterloo (2000, 2004, and 2010).

The objective of the conference is to present cutting-edge research in the designated areas of cryptography and to facilitate future research through an informal and friendly workshop setting. The SAC conference series has established itself as a premier international forum for information, discussion and exchange of ideas in cryptographic research. The themes for SAC 2011 were:

- Design and analysis of symmetric key primitives and cryptosystems, including block and stream ciphers, hash functions, and MAC algorithms
- Efficient implementation of symmetric and public key algorithms
- Mathematical and algorithmic aspects of applied cryptology
- Cryptographic tools and methods for securing clouds

The conference received 92 submissions which went through a careful doubly-anonymous review process aided by 40 Program Committee members and 68 external sub-reviewers. Each paper was reviewed by at least three reviewers, and submissions that were co-authored by a member of the Program Committee received two or more additional reviews. Our invited talks were given by:

- Kristin Lauter (Microsoft Research) — "Cryptographic Techniques for Securing the Cloud"
- Alfred Menezes (University of Waterloo) — "Another Look at Tightness"

This volume represents the revised version of the 23 accepted contributed papers which were presented at the conference along with two invited papers.

The submission and review process was done using the *iChair* Web-based software system developed by Thomas Baignères and Matthieu Finiasz.

We would like to thank the authors of all submitted papers, whether their submission was published or could not be accommodated. Moreover, Program Committee members and external sub-reviewers put a tremendous amount of work into the review process and we would like to thank them for their time and effort. We would also like to acknowledge and thank the work done by the conference Publicity and Publication Chair, Atefeh Mashatan.

August 2011

Ali Miri
Serge Vaudenay

SAC 2011

The 18th International Conference on
Selected Areas in Cryptography

Ryerson University
Toronto, Ontario, Canada
August 11-12, 2011

Organized by

Department of Computer Science, Ryerson University
Ecole Polytechnique Fédérale de Lausanne (EPFL)

In Cooperation with

The International Association for Cryptologic Research (IACR)

SAC Organizing Board

Carlisle Adams (Chair)	University of Ottawa, Canada
Roberto Avanzi	Qualcomm CDMA Technologies GmbH, Germany
Orr Dunkelman	Weizmann Institute of Science, Israel
Liam Keliher	Mount Allison University, Canada
Doug Stinson	University of Waterloo, Canada
Nicolas Theriault	Universidad del Bío-Bío, Chile
Mike Jacobson	University of Calgary, Canada
Vincent Rijmen	Graz University of Technology, Austria
Amr Youssef	Concordia University, Canada

SAC 2011 Organizing Committee

Co-chairs

Ali Miri	Ryerson University, Canada
Serge Vaudenay	EPFL, Switzerland

Publicity and Publication Chair

Atefeh Mashatan	EPFL, Switzerland

Program Committee

Carlisle Adams	University of Ottawa, Canada
Mikhail J. Atallah	Purdue University, USA
Thomas Baignères	CryptoExperts, France
Feng Bao	Institute for Infocomm Research, Singapore
Lejla Batina	Radboud University Nijmegen, The Netherlands and K.U. Leuven, Belgium
Alex Biryukov	University of Luxembourg, Luxembourg
Ian Blake	University of British Columbia, Canada
Anne Canteaut	INRIA, France
Christophe Doche	Macquarie University, Australia
Orr Dunkelman	Weizmann Institute of Science, Israel
Pierre-Alain Fouque	Ecole Normale Supérieure, France
Steven Galbraith	University of Auckland, New Zealand
Catherine H. Gebotys	University of Waterloo, Canada
Guang Gong	University of Waterloo, Canada
Anwar Hasan	University of Waterloo, Canada
Howard Heys	Memorial University, Canada
Thomas Johansson	Lund University, Sweden
Antoine Joux	University of Versailles, France
Pascal Junod	HEIG-VD, Switzerland
Seny Kamara	Microsoft Research, USA
Liam Keliher	Mount Allison University, Canada
Stefan Lucks	Bauhaus Universität Weimar, Germany
Atefeh Mashatan	EPFL, Switzerland
Barbara Masucci	Università di Salerno, Italy
Mitsuru Matsui	Mitsubishi Electric Corporation, Japan
Kanta Matsuura	University of Tokyo, Japan
Willi Meier	FHNW, Switzerland
Kaisa Nyberg	Aalto University, Finland
Thomas Peyrin	NTU, Singapore
Vincent Rijmen	K.U. Leuven and TU Graz, Belgium, Austria
Greg Rose	Qualcomm, Australia
Rei Safavi-Naini	University of Calgary, Canada
Taizo Shirai	Sony Corporation, Japan
Doug Stinson	University of Waterloo, Canada
Willy Susilo	University of Wollongong, Australia
Nicolas Thériault	Universidad del Bío-Bío, Chile
Ruizhong Wei	Lakehead University, Canada
Michael Wiener	Irdeto, Canada
Adam Young	MITRE Corp, USA
Amr Youssef	Concordia University, Canada

External Reviewers

Rodrigo Abarzúa
Zahra Aghazadeh
Hadi Ahmadi
Kazumaro Aoki
Roberto Avanzi
Masoud Barati
Aslı Bay
Murat Cenk
Sherman S.M. Chow
Stelvio Cimato
Paolo D'Arco
Vanesa Daza
Giancarlo De Maio
Junfeng Fan
Xinxin Fan
Anna Lisa Ferrara
Matthieu Finiasz
Ewan Fleischmann
Christian Forler
Clemente Galdi
Benoît Gérard
Michael Gorski
Robert Granger
Matthew Green
Johann Groszschaedl
Jian Guo
Jason Hinek
Man Ho Au
Honggang Hu
Xinyi Huang
Sebastiaan Indesteege
Takanori Isobe
Kimmo Järvinen
Jeremy Jean
Marcio Juliato
Aleksandar Kircanski
Simon Knellwolf
Miroslav Knezevic
Gaëtan Leurent
Julio López
Alexander May
Carlos Moreno
Shiho Moriai
James Muir
Ashkan Namin
Maria Naya-Plasencia
Christophe Negre
Kenji Ohkuma
Roger Oyono
Pascal Paillier
Chris Peikert
Mohammad Reza Reyhanitabar
Arnab Roy
Sumanta Sarkar
Pouyan Sepehrdad
Kyoji Shibutani
Claudio Soriente
Martijn Stam
Petr Sušil
Tomoyasu Suzaki
Ashraful Tuhin
Jalaj Upadhyay
Yongge Wang
Gaven Watson
Ralf-Philipp Weinmann
Yanjiang Yang
Jingwei Zhang
Chang-An Zhao

Sponsoring Institutions

Faculty of Engineering, Architecture, and Science, Ryerson University
Department of Computer Science, Ryerson University
Fields Institute
Certicom

Table of Contents

Selected Areas in Cryptography 2011

Cryptanalysis of Hash Functions

Boomerang Distinguishers on MD4-Family — First Practical Results on Full 5-Pass HAVAL 1
Yu Sasaki

Improved Analysis of ECHO-256 19
Jérémy Jean, María Naya-Plasencia, and Martin Schläffer

Provable Chosen-Target-Forced-Midfix Preimage Resistance 37
Elena Andreeva and Bart Mennink

Security in Clouds

On CCA-Secure Somewhat Homomorphic Encryption 55
Jake Loftus, Alexander May, Nigel P. Smart, and Frederik Vercauteren

Efficient Schemes for Anonymous Yet Authorized and Bounded Use of Cloud Resources 73
Daniel Slamanig

Invited Paper I

Group Law Computations on Jacobians of Hyperelliptic Curves 92
Craig Costello and Kristin Lauter

Bits and Randomness

Cryptographic Analysis of All 4 × 4-Bit S-Boxes 118
Markku-Juhani O. Saarinen

The Cryptographic Power of Random Selection 134
Matthias Krause and Matthias Hamann

Proof of Empirical RC4 Biases and New Key Correlations 151
Sourav Sen Gupta, Subhamoy Maitra, Goutam Paul, and Santanu Sarkar

Cryptanalysis of Ciphers I

Combined Differential and Linear Cryptanalysis of Reduced-Round PRINTcipher 169
Ferhat Karakoç, Hüseyin Demirci, and A. Emre Harmancı

Practical Attack on the Full MMB Block Cipher 185
Keting Jia, Jiazhe Chen, Meiqin Wang, and Xiaoyun Wang

Conditional Differential Cryptanalysis of Trivium and KATAN 200
Simon Knellwolf, Willi Meier, and María Naya-Plasencia

Cryptanalysis of Ciphers II

Some Instant- and Practical-Time Related-Key Attacks on KTANTAN32/48/64 213
Martin Ågren

Analysis of the Initial and Modified Versions of the Candidate 3GPP Integrity Algorithm 128-EIA3 230
Thomas Fuhr, Henri Gilbert, Jean-René Reinhard, and Marion Videau

New Insights on Impossible Differential Cryptanalysis 243
Charles Bouillaguet, Orr Dunkelman, Pierre-Alain Fouque, and Gaëtan Leurent

Cryptanalysis of Public-Key Cryptography

A Unified Framework for Small Secret Exponent Attack on RSA 260
Noboru Kunihiro, Naoyuki Shinohara, and Tetsuya Izu

Cipher Implementation

Very Compact Hardware Implementations of the Blockcipher CLEFIA 278
Toru Akishita and Harunaga Hiwatari

Invited Paper II

Another Look at Tightness 293
Sanjit Chatterjee, Alfred Menezes, and Palash Sarkar

New Designs

Duplexing the Sponge: Single-Pass Authenticated Encryption and Other Applications 320
Guido Bertoni, Joan Daemen, Michaël Peeters, and Gilles Van Assche

Blockcipher-Based Double-Length Hash Functions for Pseudorandom Oracles 338
Yusuke Naito

ASC-1: An Authenticated Encryption Stream Cipher 356
Goce Jakimoski and Samant Khajuria

Mathematical Aspects of Applied Cryptography

On Various Families of Twisted Jacobi Quartics 373
Jérôme Plût

Improved Three-Way Split Formulas for Binary Polynomial Multiplication 384
Murat Cenk, Christophe Negre, and M. Anwar Hasan

Sublinear Scalar Multiplication on Hyperelliptic Koblitz Curves 399
Hugo Labrande and Michael J. Jacobson Jr.

Faster Hashing to $\mathbb{G}_2$ 412
Laura Fuentes-Castañeda, Edward Knapp, and Francisco Rodríguez-Henríquez

Author Index 431

Boomerang Distinguishers on MD4-Family: First Practical Results on Full 5-Pass HAVAL

Yu Sasaki

NTT Information Sharing Platform Laboratories, NTT Corporation
3-9-11 Midori-cho, Musashino-shi, Tokyo 180-8585 Japan
sasaki.yu@lab.ntt.co.jp

Abstract. In this paper, we study a boomerang attack approach on MD4-based hash functions, and present a practical 4-sum distinguisher against the compression function of the full 5-pass HAVAL. Our approach is based on the previous work by Kim *et al.*, which proposed the boomerang distinguisher on the encryption mode of MD4, MD5, and HAVAL in the related-key setting. Firstly, we prove that the differential path for 5-pass HAVAL used in the previous boomerang distinguisher contains a critical flaw and thus the attack cannot work. We then search for new differential paths. Finally, by using the new paths, we mount the distinguisher on the compression function of the full 5-pass HAVAL which generates a 4-sum quartet with a complexity of approximately 2^{11} compression function computations. As far as we know, this is the first result on the full compression function of 5-pass HAVAL that can be computed in practice. We also point out that the 4-sum distinguisher can also be constructed for other MD4-based hash functions such as MD5, 3-pass HAVAL, and 4-pass HAVAL. Our attacks are implemented on a PC and we present a generated 4-sum quartet for each attack target.

Keywords: boomerang attack, 4-sum distinguisher, hash, HAVAL.

1 Introduction

Hash functions are taking important roles in various aspects of the cryptography. After the breakthrough by Wang *et al.* [26,27] and through the SHA-3 competition [20], cryptanalysis against hash functions have been improved significantly.

The boomerang attack, which was proposed by Wagner [22], is a tool for the cryptanalysis against block-ciphers. At FSE2011, Biryukov *et al.* applied the boomerang attack for hash functions, and showed that a zero-sum distinguisher could be constructed on them [3], where zero-sum is a set of messages whose XOR is 0 and the XOR of their corresponding outputs is also 0. Lamberger and Mendel independently applied the boomerang attack on SHA-2 and obtained a significant improvement on the 4-sum distinguisher against its reduced-step compression function [10], where a k-sum is a set of k paired initial-values and messages such that the XOR of their outputs is 0. It seems that the boomerang attack is potentially very powerful against hash functions, and thus more investigation is required to understand their impact deeply. Note that at CRYPTO2007,

A. Miri and S. Vaudenay (Eds.): SAC 2011, LNCS 7118, pp. 1–18, 2012.

Joux and Peyrin proposed an (amplified) boomerang attack for SHA-1 [7]. They used the idea of the boomerang attack for the message modification technique in the collision attack, which the purpose is different from our research.

The boomerang attack on hash functions does not always discuss the security as the hash function. As done in [10], it often discusses the security of the compression function or the internal block-cipher. Although they do not impact to the security of the hash function immediately, such analyses are useful from several viewpoints; 1) The progress of the cryptanalysis, in other words, the security margin can be measured, 2) The attack could be used as a tool for different purposes in the future, e.g., a pseudo-collision attack on MD5 [4]. 3) The attack on a building-block may invalidate the security proof for the hash function. Specifically, hash functions using the PGV modes tend to have the reduction security by assuming the ideal behavior of the internal block-cipher.

MD4, which was proposed by Rivest in 1990 [13], is a hash function that is used as a base of various hash functions. MD4 has an interesting property in its message expansion. The sketch of its computation is as follows;

- Divide an input message block M into several message words $m_0, m_1, \ldots, m_{N_S-1}$.
- Iteratively apply a round function N_R times, where the round function consists of N_S steps.
- For N_S steps in each round, each of m_0 to m_{N_S-1} is used exactly once.
- The order of message words, in other words, the permutation of the message-word index may change for different rounds.

We call this type of the message expansion *message-words permutation*. MD4, MD5 [14], and HAVAL [32] are examples using the message-words permutation.

MD4, MD5, and HAVAL are now known to be vulnerable against various attacks. For example, Van Rompay *et al.* found collisions of 3-pass HAVAL in 2003 [21], and Wang *et al.* found collisions of MD4, MD5, and 3-pass HAVAL in 2004 [25,27]. The complexity of collision attacks were optimized to 2 for MD4 [18], 2^{10} for MD5 [29], 2^7 for 3-pass HAVAL [19,24], 2^{36} for 4-pass HAVAL [28,31], and 2^{123} for 5-pass HAVAL [31], where the unit of the complexity is one computation of the compression function. Note that, only the theoretical result is known for 5-pass HAVAL, and thus real collisions have not been found yet.

Theoretical preimage attacks are also presented. For example, [1,6,11] for MD4, [17] for MD5, [2,16] for 3-pass HAVAL, and [16] for 4-pass HAVAL. For 5-pass HAVAL, only the attack on 158-steps out of 160-steps is known [15].

Several researchers evaluated the security of the building block for these hash functions. Examples which analyzed full steps are [4,5] for MD5 and [8,9,30] for HAVAL. Among them, the work by Kim *et al.* [8,9], which applied the boomerang attack to distinguish their encryption modes from a random permutation in the related-key setting, is very powerful. They successfully distinguished these encryption modes with 2^6 queries for MD4, $2^{11.6}$ queries for MD5, and $2^{9.6}$ queries for 4-pass HAVAL. These attacks were implemented and an example of the boomerang quartet was presented for MD5. In addition, Kim *et al.* claimed that 5-pass HAVAL could also be distinguished with 2^{61} queries and the attack

Table 1. Comparison of the attack complexity

Attack	Target	MD4 (Time	Ref.)	MD5 (Time	Ref.)	HAVAL-3 (Time	Ref.)	HAVAL-4 (Time	Ref.)	HAVAL-5 (Time	Ref.)
Collision	Hash Function	2	[18]	2^{10}	[29]	2^{7}	[19,24]	2^{36}	[28,31]	2^{123}	[31]
Boomerang	Block-Cipher	2^{6}	[9]	$2^{11.6}$	[9]		-	$2^{9.6}$	[9]	2^{61}	[9]
Boomerang	Compress. Func.	-		2^{10}	Ours	2^{4}	Ours	2^{11}	Ours	2^{11}	Ours

was partially verified by implementing it for reduced-round variants. Note that although Kim *et al.* pointed out the vulnerability of the MD4-based structure against the boomerang attack, the analysis on 5-pass HAVAL is still infeasible.

Our Contributions

In this paper, we study the boomerang attack approach on MD4-based hash functions. We use the differential path for the boomerang attack to construct the 4-sum distinguisher on the compression function, while Kim *et al.* [9] used the boomerang path to distinguish its encryption mode from a random permutation. For both of our approach and the one in [9], the core of the attack is the existence of the differential path suitable for the boomerang attack. However, because the attack scenario is different, the procedure to optimize the attack is quite different. We first collect various techniques for the boomerang attack on hash functions from several papers (mainly [3,9,10]), and summarize the attack framework.

We then revisit the differential path for the boomerang attack against 5-pass HAVAL in [9]. On the contrary to the authors' claim, we prove that the differential path in [9] contains a critical flaw and thus the attack cannot work.

We then search for new differential paths for the boomerang attack and construct the attack procedure optimized for attacking the compression function. Finally, by using the new paths, we mount the distinguisher on the full compression function of 5-pass HAVAL which generates a 4-sum quartet with a complexity of 2^{11} compression function computations. The attack complexity is summarized in Table 1. As far as we know, this is the first result on the full 5-pass HAVAL that can be computed in practice. The attack is implemented on a PC and we present a generated 4-sum quartet.

Note that as long as the good boomerang differential path is available, 4-sum distinguishers can be constructed on the compression function. Then, with the differential paths in [9], we attack MD5, 3-pass HAVAL, and 4-pass HAVAL with a complexity of 2^{10}, 2^{4} and 2^{11} compression function computations, respectively. We present generated 4-sums in Appendix B.

Paper Outline

We describe the specification of HAVAL and clarify the terminology in Sect. 2. We summarize previous work in Sect. 3. We give a summary of techniques for the boomerang attack on hash functions in Sect. 4. We demonstrate a dedicate attack on 5-pass HAVAL in Sect. 5. Finally, we conclude this paper in Sect. 6.

Table 2. Word-wise rotation $\phi_{x,y}$ of HAVAL

	x_6	x_5	x_4	x_3	x_2	x_1	x_0		x_6	x_5	x_4	x_3	x_2	x_1	x_0		x_6	x_5	x_4	x_3	x_2	x_1	x_0
	↓	↓	↓	↓	↓	↓	↓		↓	↓	↓	↓	↓	↓	↓		↓	↓	↓	↓	↓	↓	↓
$\phi_{3,1}$	x_1	x_0	x_3	x_5	x_6	x_2	x_4	$\phi_{4,1}$	x_2	x_6	x_1	x_4	x_5	x_3	x_0	$\phi_{5,1}$	x_3	x_4	x_1	x_0	x_5	x_2	x_6
$\phi_{3,2}$	x_4	x_2	x_1	x_0	x_5	x_3	x_6	$\phi_{4,2}$	x_3	x_5	x_2	x_0	x_1	x_6	x_4	$\phi_{5,2}$	x_6	x_2	x_1	x_0	x_3	x_4	x_5
$\phi_{3,3}$	x_6	x_1	x_2	x_3	x_4	x_5	x_0	$\phi_{4,3}$	x_1	x_4	x_3	x_6	x_0	x_2	x_5	$\phi_{5,3}$	x_2	x_6	x_0	x_4	x_3	x_1	x_5
-				-				$\phi_{4,4}$	x_6	x_4	x_0	x_5	x_2	x_1	x_3	$\phi_{5,4}$	x_1	x_5	x_3	x_2	x_0	x_4	x_6
-				-				-				-				$\phi_{5,5}$	x_2	x_5	x_0	x_6	x_4	x_3	x_1

Table 3. Message-words permutation. The first column shows the round numbers.

	index for each round																															
1	0	1	2	3	4	5	6	7	8	9	10	11	12	13	14	15	16	17	18	19	20	21	22	23	24	25	26	27	28	29	30	31
2	5	14	26	18	11	28	7	16	0	23	20	22	1	10	4	8	30	3	21	9	17	24	29	6	19	12	15	13	2	25	31	27
3	19	9	4	20	28	17	8	22	29	14	25	12	24	30	16	26	31	15	7	3	1	0	18	27	13	6	21	10	23	11	5	2
4	24	4	0	14	2	7	28	23	26	6	30	20	18	25	19	3	22	11	31	21	8	27	12	9	1	29	5	15	17	10	16	13
5	27	3	21	26	17	11	20	29	19	0	12	7	13	8	31	10	5	9	14	30	18	6	28	24	2	23	16	22	4	1	25	15

2 Preliminaries

2.1 Specification of HAVAL

HAVAL [32] uses a narrow-pipe Merkle-Damgård structure. An input message M is padded to be a multiple of the block-size (1024 bits), and then divided into message blocks $(M_0, M_1, \ldots, M_{L-1})$. Then, chaining variable H_i starting from the pre-specified initial value H_0 is iteratively updated by the compression function CF; $H_{i+1} \leftarrow \mathrm{CF}(H_i, M_i)$, for $i = 0, 1, \ldots, L-1$. Finally, H_L is the hash value of M. HAVAL can produce a hash value of smaller sizes by using the output tailoring function. Because our attack target is the compression function, we omit the description for the padding and the output tailoring function.

The size of chaining variables is 256 bits. Inside the compression function, M_i is divided into thirty-two 32-bit message words $(m_0, m_1, \ldots, m_{31})$. Three algorithms are prepared for HAVAL; 3-pass, 4-pass, and 5-pass. The number of rounds for 3-pass, 4-pass, and 5-pass are 3 rounds (96 steps), 4 rounds (128 steps), and 5 rounds (160 steps), respectively.

Let us denote a 256-bit state before step j by p_j and denote p_j by eight 32-bit variables $Q_{j-7} \| Q_{j-6} \| Q_{j-5} \| Q_{j-4} \| Q_{j-3} \| Q_{j-2} \| Q_{j-1} \| Q_j$. The step function R_j computes Q_{j+1} as follows:

$$Q_{j+1} \leftarrow (Q_{j-7} \ggg 11) + (\Phi_j(\phi_{x,y}(Q_{j-6}, Q_{j-5}, \ldots, Q_j)) \ggg 7) + m_{\pi(j)} + k_j,$$

where $\phi_{x,y}$ is a word-wise rotation for x-pass HAVAL in round y defined in Table 2, and $\pi(j)$ is shown in Table 3.

2.2 Technical Terminologies

In this paper, we discuss *differences* of several computations. Let us consider the two computations $H_{i+1} \leftarrow \mathrm{CF}(H_i, M_i)$ and $H'_{i+1} \leftarrow \mathrm{CF}(H'_i, M'_i)$. The message difference, input chaining-variable difference, and output difference are defined as $M_i \oplus M_i'$, $H_i \oplus H_i'$, and $H_{i+1} \oplus H_{i+1}'$, respectively. Similarly, the difference of two computations is defined as XOR of corresponding states.

The transition of the difference of internal state is described by several terms such as *differential path*, *differential trail*, and *differential characteristic*. As far as we know, the term *differential characteristic* was firstly used in the context of the symmetric-key cryptography. However, in the context of the hash function analysis, the term *differential path* seems to be used more frequently e.g., [26,27]. To follow this convention, in this paper, we use the term *differential path*.

When the input and output differences are fixed, we often consider all possible differential paths connecting them. A set of all possible differential paths is called *a differential* or *multiple-paths*. In this paper, we use the term *differential*.

3 Related Work

3.1 Boomerang Attack

The boomerang attack was proposed by Wagner [22] as a tool for attacking block-ciphers. The attack is a chosen-plaintext and adaptively chosen-ciphertext attack. It can be regarded as a type of the second-order differential attack. In this attack, the attacker divides the target cipher E into two parts E_1 and E_2 such that $E(\cdot) = E_2 \circ E_1(\cdot)$. Let us denote the differential for E_1 by $\Delta \rightarrow \Delta^*$ and for E_2 by $\nabla^* \rightarrow \nabla$. The differences $\Delta, \Delta^*, \nabla^*$, and ∇ are chosen by the attacker at offline. The attack procedure is as follows;

1. The attacker first prepares a plaintext P^1 and compute $P^2 \leftarrow P^1 \oplus \Delta$.
2. P^1 and P^2 are passed to the encryption oracle and the attacker obtains the corresponding ciphertexts C^1 and C^2.
3. The attacker prepares the paired ciphertexts $C^3 \leftarrow C^1 \oplus \nabla$ and $C^4 \leftarrow C^2 \oplus \nabla$, and passes them to the decryption oracle.
4. Finally, the attacker checks whether or not P^3 and P^4 has the difference Δ.

Assume that the probability for the differentials for E_1 and E_2 are p and q, respectively. Then, $\Pr[P^3 \oplus P^4 = \Delta]$ is expressed as p^2q^2. In the end, we can conclude that if E can be divided into two parts with a high-probability differential, the boomerang attack is very efficient.

For a long time, it was assumed that the differentials for E_1 and E_2 can be chosen independently. In 2009, Murphy pointed out that this was not sufficient, and discovered several examples of this case for DES and AES [12].

3.2 Boomerang Distinguishers for Hash Functions

In 2011, Biryukov *et al.* pointed out that the zero-sum distinguisher can be constructed by applying the boomerang attack on hash functions [3]. In the boomerang attack, $P^1 \oplus P^2 = \Delta$ and $P^3 \oplus P^4 = \Delta$. Therefore, $P^1 \oplus P^2 \oplus P^3 \oplus P^4 = \Delta \oplus \Delta = 0$. Similarly, $C^1 \oplus C^2 \oplus C^3 \oplus C^4 = \nabla \oplus \nabla = 0$. Hence, by starting from a pair of plaintexts P^1 and P^2 such that $P^1 \oplus P^2 = \Delta$, the attacker finds a zero-sum quartet with a complexity of $(p^2q^2)^{-1}$. [3] considered the attack starting from the border state between E_1 and E_2, and optimized the attack by applying the message modification technique [26,27]. [3] also computed the complexity to find a zero-sum in a random function for n-bit output. They explained that by starting from two paired plaintexts (resp. ciphertexts) with pre-specified differences, the complexity to find a zero-sum quartet of ciphertexts (resp. plaintexts) is $2^{\frac{n}{2}}$. Note that [3] considered the differential path rather than the differential for their attack. In fact, to apply the message modification technique, considering a differential path is much easier than a differential. Also note that [3] considered the observation by Murphy [12]. They had to give up combining the best differential paths for E_1 and E_2 due to their dependency.

In 2011, Lamberger and Mendel independently applied the boomerang 4-sum for the SHA-2 compression function [10]. They claimed that the complexity for finding a 4-sum quartet in a random function without any limitation on the input is $2^{\frac{n}{3}}$ by using the generalized birthday attack [23].

3.3 Boomerang on Encryption Modes of MD4, MD5, and HAVAL

Kim *et al.* applied the boomerang attack approach on the encryption modes of MD4, MD5, and HAVAL in the related-key model [9]. They proposed boomerang distinguishers with 2^6 queries for MD4, $2^{11.6}$ queries for MD5, and $2^{9.6}$ queries for 4-pass HAVAL. These attacks were verified by the machine experiment. Furthermore, they proposed differential paths for 5-pass HAVAL, and claimed that the boomerang distinguisher with 2^{61} queries was possible. They also claimed that this distinguisher was partially verified with an experiment on a reduced-round variant which was truncated for the first and the last several rounds.

Our attack framework is close to the one discussed in Sect. 3.2, but use the differential paths in [9] as a tool. In fact, we use the same paths as [9] for MD5 and 4-pass HAVAL. However, we need new differential paths for 5-pass HAVAL due to the flaw which we will point out in Sect. 5.

4 Summary of Boomerang Attack on Hash Function

Because various techniques for the boomerang attack on hash functions are distributed in several papers, we summarize the attack framework. Therefore, most of the contents in this section were originally observed by [3,9,10].

The attack can be divided into five phases; 1) message differences (ΔM), 2) differential paths and sufficient conditions (DP), 3) contradiction between two paths (CP), 4) message modification (MM), and 5) amplified probability (AP). We explain each phase with several observations specific to message-words permutation hash functions.

4.1 Message Differences (ΔM)

A generic strategy for an N_R-round hash function is illustrated in Fig. 1. For $N_R = 4$, the first two and last two rounds are regarded as E_1 and E_2, respectively.

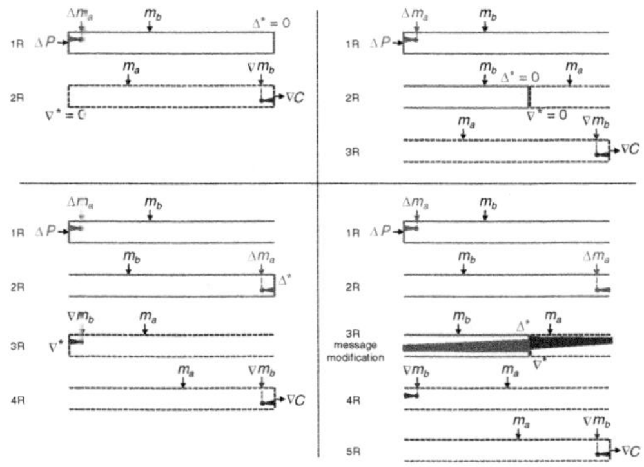

Fig. 1. Strategies for differential path

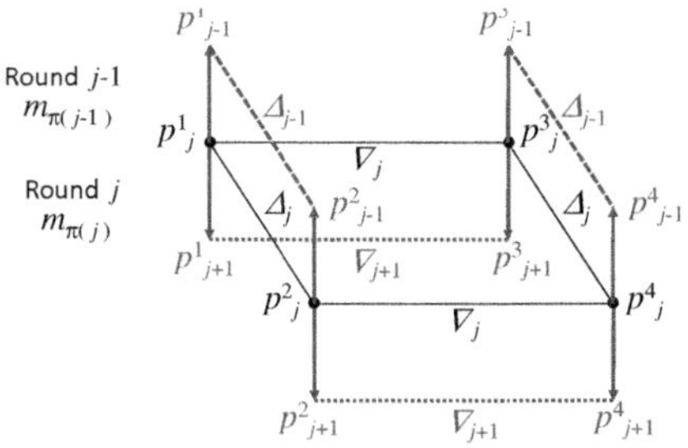

Fig. 2. Message search procedure

For E_1, we search for the message word which appear in an early step in the first round and in a late step in the second round. Then, the message difference is propagated until the beginning and end of E_1. The same strategy is applied for E_2. Because the differential paths for both of E_1 and E_2 are short, they are satisfied with high probability even without the message modification technique.

For $N_R = 5$, we extend the differential paths for the 4-round attack by a half more round. As shown in Fig. 1, the paths become long and hard to satisfy by the naive search. Wang *et al.* showed that the differential path for one round can be satisfied for free by the message modification technique [26,27]. Hence, with these techniques, 5 rounds can be attacked. In this paper, we denote the differential path between the end of round 2 and the beginning of round 4 by *inside path*, and the differential paths in round 1 and round 5 by *outside paths*.

4.2 Differential Paths and Sufficient Conditions (DP)

Based on the strategy in Fig. 1, we construct differential paths and conditions for chaining variables. These procedures are basically the same as the ones for previous collision attacks. We only list the differences of the path search procedure between the collision and boomerang attacks.

- If the feed-forward operation is performed by a modular addition ($H = P \boxplus C$), the attacker should introduce the additive difference among a quartet. in such a case, the difference for the quartet is defined as $(H^4 \boxminus H^3) \boxminus (H^2 \boxminus H^1) = H^1 \boxminus H^2 \boxminus H^3 \boxplus H^4$.
- The number of conditions must be minimized because setting x more conditions will increase the complexity by a factor of 2^{2x} rather than 2^x.
- In the middle round, we apply the message modification, and thus even complicated paths can be satisfied. However, by taking into account the Phase CP, the paths should be simplified around the border of two paths.

- If active-bit positions are concentrated around the MSB in both of E_1 and E_2 for the optimization, the risk of the contradiction of two paths will increase.

4.3 Contradiction between Two Paths (*CP*)

As Murphy pointed out [12], differential paths for E_1 and E_2 are not independent, and thus we need to check that any contradiction does not occur. As far as we know, no systematic method is known to check the contradiction. However, it can be said that the attacker at least needs to check the following conditions.

Condition 1. E_1 and E_2 do not require to fix the same bit to different values.
Condition 2. E_1 (resp. E_2) does not require to fix the value of an active bit for E_2 (resp. E_1).

The first case is obviously in contradiction. In the second case, even if the condition is satisfied between one pair, say P^1 and P^2, the condition is never satisfied for the other pair P^3 and P^4 due to the difference between P^1 and P^3.

As discussed in Sect. 4.2, if many bits are activated or active-bit positions are concentrated around MSB, the contradiction comes to occur more easily. Regarding HAVAL, due to the large word-size (32 bits) and the different rotation constants in forward and backward, the contradiction is less likely to occur. If the word size is smaller or if the similar rotation constants are used such as BLAKE, the contradiction seems to occur with a high probability.

If the contradiction occurs, rotating the path for either E_1 or E_2 by several bits may avoid the contradiction (though the efficiency becomes worse).

4.4 Message Modification (*MM*)

Let us denote a quartet of texts at step j forming the boomerang structure by $(p_j^1, p_j^2, p_j^3, p_j^4)$. The difference for E_1 is denoted by Δ, which is considered between p_1 and p_2 and between p_3 and p_4. The difference for E_2 is denoted by ∇, which is considered between p_1 and p_3 and between p_2 and p_4. We call conditions on the path for E_1 Δ-conditions, and for E_2 ∇-conditions.

The message search procedure is described in Fig. 2. The attack starts from the state at the border between E_1 and E_2. Let us denote this step by b. First, we set a chaining-variables quartet $(p_b^1, p_b^2, p_b^3, p_b^4)$ so that both of Δ- and ∇-conditions are satisfied. We then perform the backward computation for E_1 and forward computation for E_2 as shown in Alg. 1 and Alg. 2, respectively.

These procedures are computed until the inside path is ensured to be satisfied with probability of 1. This often occurs before all message words are fixed by the above procedure. Therefore, towards the outside paths, we do as follows.

- Assume that several message-words are not determined even after the inside path are ensured. Then, we never modify the message-words and chaining-variables related to the inside path, and compute the outside paths by randomly choosing the message-words not used for the inside path.

This enables us to iterate the outside computation with keeping the inside path satisfied. Hence, the complexity for satisfying the inside path can be ignored.

Algorithm 1. Message search procedure for step j in the backward direction
Input: Inside differential path and a chaining-variables quartet $(p^1_{j+1}, p^2_{j+1}, p^3_{j+1}, p^4_{j+1})$
Output: A message-words quartet $(m^1_{\pi(j)}, m^2_{\pi(j)}, m^3_{\pi(j)}, m^4_{\pi(j)})$ and a chaining-variables quartet $(p^1_j, p^2_j, p^3_j, p^4_j)$

1: Choose the value of p^1_j to satisfy conditions (Δ-conditions) for p^1_j. Then, compute $m^1_{\pi(j)}$ by solving equation R_j.
2: Compute $m^2_{\pi(j)}$, $m^3_{\pi(j)}$, and $m^4_{\pi(j)}$ with the specified differences ΔM and ∇M.
3: Compute p^3_j with $m^3_{\pi(j)}$ and check if all conditions (Δ-conditions) for p^3_j are satisfied. If so, compute p^2_j and p^4_j. If not, repeat the procedure with different p^1_j.

Algorithm 2. Message search procedure for step j in the forward direction
Input: Inside differential path and a chaining-variables quartet $(p^1_j, p^2_j, p^3_j, p^4_j)$
Output: A message-words quartet $(m^1_{\pi(j)}, m^2_{\pi(j)}, m^3_{\pi(j)}, m^4_{\pi(j)})$ and a chaining-variables quartet $(p^1_{j+1}, p^2_{j+1}, p^3_{j+1}, p^4_{j+1})$

1: Choose the value of p^1_{j+1} to satisfy conditions (∇-conditions) for p^1_{j+1}. Then, compute $m^1_{\pi(j)}$ by solving R_j.
2: Compute $m^2_{\pi(j)}$, $m^3_{\pi(j)}$, and $m^4_{\pi(j)}$ with the specified differences ΔM and ∇M.
3: Compute p^2_{j+1} and check if all conditions (∇-conditions) for p^2_{j+1} are satisfied. If so, compute p^3_{j+1} and p^4_{j+1}. If not, repeat the procedure with different p^1_{j+1}.

4.5 Amplified Probability (AP)

Amplified probability is the probability that each outside path results in the 4-sum. We consider the differential to estimate this probability. This is often estimated by an experiment. Alg. 3 shows how to compute the amplified probability AP^{Back} for the first round (from step $j-1$ to step 0). The amplified probability for the final round AP^{For} is similarly computed. Note that as long as the operation (usually either XOR or the modular addition) used to compute the 4-sum in this experiment and used in the feed-forward is identical, the success probability after the feed-forward is preserved as $AP^{Back} \times AP^{For}$.

5 4-Sum Distinguisher on 5-Pass HAVAL

We start from pointing out the flaw of the previous differential path (Sect. 5.1), and construct new differential paths (Sect. 5.2). We then explain the attack based on the discussion in Sect. 4 and finally show the experimental results.

Algorithm 3. Evaluation of the amplified probability
Input: Outside differential path
Output: Amplified probability of the outside differential path

1: Randomly choose a chaining-variables quartet $(p^1_j, p^2_j, p^3_j, p^4_j)$ and message-words used in steps $j-1$ to 0 with appropriate message differences ΔM and ∇M.
2: Compute this quartet until step 0 and check whether the 4-sum is constructed.
3: Repeat the above for an enough amount of times, and calculate the probability.

Table 4. Differential path and conditions for 5-pass HAVAL [9]. e_z represents that only z-th bit has a difference.

j	Output diff. at step j $(\Delta Q_{j-7}, \ldots, \Delta Q_j)$	Equation for Φ_j $\Phi_j(\phi_{5,3}(Q_{j-6}, \ldots, Q_j))$	Conditions on 20th bit for $\Phi_j = 0$
	$(0,0,0,0,0,0,0,e_{20})$		
70	$(0,0,0,0,0,0,e_{20},0)$	$\Phi_{70}(Q_{68}, Q_{64}, \Delta Q_{70}, Q_{66}, Q_{67}, Q_{69}, Q_{65})$	$Q_{69} = 0$
71	$(0,0,0,0,0,e_{20},0,0)$	$\Phi_{71}(Q_{69}, Q_{65}, Q_{71}, Q_{67}, Q_{68}, \Delta Q_{70}, Q_{66})$	$Q_{67}Q_{68} \oplus Q_{71} = 0$
72	$(0,0,0,0,e_{20},0,0,0)$	$\Phi_{72}(\Delta Q_{70}, Q_{66}, Q_{72}, Q_{68}, Q_{69}, Q_{71}, Q_{67})$	$Q_{68} = 0$
73	$(0,0,0,e_{20},0,0,0,0)$	$\Phi_{73}(Q_{71}, Q_{67}, Q_{73}, Q_{69}, \Delta Q_{70}, Q_{72}, Q_{68})$	$Q_{72}Q_{69} \oplus Q_{67} = 0$
74	$(0,0,e_{20},0,0,0,0,0)$	$\Phi_{74}(Q_{72}, Q_{68}, Q_{74}, \Delta Q_{70}, Q_{71}, Q_{73}, Q_{69})$	$Q_{73} \oplus Q_{71} \oplus Q_{72}Q_{69} = 0$
75	$(0,e_{20},0,0,0,0,0,0)$	$\Phi_{75}(Q_{73}, Q_{69}, Q_{75}, Q_{71}, Q_{72}, Q_{74}, \Delta Q_{70})$	$Q_{71} = 1$
76	$(e_{20},0,0,0,0,0,0,0)$	$\Phi_{76}(Q_{74}, \Delta Q_{70}, Q_{76}, Q_{72}, Q_{73}, Q_{75}, Q_{71})$	$Q_{73} = 0$
77	$(0,0,0,0,0,0,0,e_9)$	$\Phi_{77}(Q_{75}, Q_{71}, Q_{77}, Q_{73}, Q_{74}, Q_{76}, Q_{72})$	-

5.1 Proving Flaw of Previous Differential Path

We point out that the differential path for the third round in [9] cannot work. Note that the verifying experiment by [9] is for the reduced-round variants which are truncated for the first and the last several rounds [9, Sect. 4.2]. Hence, our claim does not contradict to the partial verification by [9].

The differential path during 8 steps (steps 70-77) in the third round is shown in Table 4. The authors claimed that the path could be satisfied with a probability of 2^{-7}. The necessary and sufficient condition for satisfying this path with a probability of 2^{-7} is that the difference in Q_{70} will not propagate through Φ_j. Φ_j for these steps is a bit-wise Boolean function expressed as

$$\Phi_j(x_6, x_5, x_4, x_3, x_2, x_1, x_0) = x_1x_2x_3 \oplus x_1x_4 \oplus x_2x_5 \oplus x_3x_6 \oplus x_0x_3 \oplus x_0.$$

Conditions to achieve the path were not explained in [9]. We first derive the necessary and sufficient conditions to achieve the path, which are shown in Table 4.

Proof. For steps 70, 75, and 76, we have conditions $Q_{69} = 0$, $Q_{71} = 1$, and $Q_{73} = 0$. Then, the left-hand side of the condition for step 74 becomes $0 \oplus 1 \oplus (Q_{72} \cdot 0) = 1$, which contradicts to the condition that this value must be 0. □

We verified the above proof with a small experiment;

1. Randomly choose the values of Q_{63} to Q_{70} and $m_{\pi(70)}$ to $m_{\pi(77)}$.
2. Set $Q'_z \leftarrow Q_z$ for $z = 63, 64, \ldots, 70$. Then compute $Q'_{70} \leftarrow Q_{70} \oplus \texttt{0x00100000}$.
3. Compute until step 77 and check whether or not the path is satisfied.

With 2^{30} trials, the differential path in Table 4 was not satisfied. This contradicts to the claim in [9], which the path is satisfied with a probability 2^{-7}.

5.2 Constructing New Differential Paths

We reconstruct the attack based on the strategy explained Sect. 4.1. For Phase ΔM, we confirmed that the message differences in [9] ($\Delta m_2 = \texttt{0x80000000}$,

Table 5. Boomerang path construction for 5-pass HAVAL

	index for each round																															
1	0	1	②	3	④	5	6	7	8	9	10	11	12	13	14	15	16	17	18	19	20	21	22	23	24	25	26	27	28	29	30	31
		← Δ|															constant															
2	5	14	26	18	11	28	7	16	0	23	20	22	1	10	④	8	30	3	21	9	17	24	29	6	19	12	15	13	②	25	31	27
														constant															| Δ →			
3	19	9	④	20	28	17	8	22	29	14	25	12	24	30	16	26 |	31	15	7	3	1	0	18	27	13	6	21	10	23	11	5	②
							message modification									|							message modification								
4	24	④	0	14	②	7	28	23	26	6	30	20	18	25	19	3	22	11	31	21	8	27	12	9	1	29	5	15	17	10	16	13
	← ∇|																constant															
5	27	3	21	26	17	11	20	29	19	0	12	7	13	8	31	10	5	9	14	30	18	6	28	24	②	23	16	22	④	1	25	15
														constant															| ∇ →			

$\Delta m_x = 0$ for $x \neq 2$, $\nabla m_4 =$ 0x80000000, $\nabla m_x = 0$ for $x \neq 4$) match the strategy in Fig. 1, and thus we use the same message differences. This is described in Table 5.

For Phase *DP*, we need to specify how the differences will propagate to chaining variables. We describe our path search algorithm in Appendix A. The searched paths and conditions for chaining variables are given in Table 6.

For Phase *CP*, the overlap of the conditions and active-bit positions in Table 6 must be checked. According to Table 6, the conditions 1 and 2 described in Sect. 4.3 are satisfied. Note that as long as the step function is similar to MD4, MD5, or HAVAL, the active bit positions and conditions for Δ and ∇ tend to be different due to the asymmetric rotation constants in forward and backward directions. In fact, for all differential paths in [9] and ours, the best differential paths which were independently computed could be combined.

5.3 Attack Procedure

In Phase *MM*, we optimize the attack complexity based on the strategy in Sect. 4.4. The detailed procedure is given in Alg. 4.

As shown in Table 5 the inside path starts from step 60 and ends at step 97. Several words ($w_2, w_{25}, w_{31}, w_{27}, w_{24}, w_4$) are used twice and we need a special attention. However, as shown in Table 6, conditions are set only on Q_{58} to Q_{93}, and thus, the second-time use of these words outside of Q_{58} to Q_{93} always succeed for any value. Hence, these values are chosen for satisfying conditions for Q_{58} to Q_{93}. After we satisfy all conditions for Q_{58} to Q_{93}, 4 message words w_{19}, w_{11}, w_5, and w_2 are still unfixed. Therefore, we can iterate the outside path search without changing the inside path up to 2^{128} times, which is enough to satisfy the outside paths.

The complexity of the message modification for satisfying the inside path (up to Step 3 in Alg. 4) is negligible. Hence, the attack complexity is only the iterative computations for satisfying the outside paths (Steps 4–11 in Alg. 4). This complexity is evaluated by considering the amplified probability in Phase *AP*, which will be explained in the following section.

Algorithm 4. Attack procedure with the message modification

Input: Entire differential paths and conditions

Output: A quartet of (H_{i-1}, M_{i-1}) satisfying the 4-sum property

1: Randomly choose the values of p^1_{80}, p^2_{80}, p^3_{80} and p^4_{80} so that the differences and conditions (both of Δ and ∇) in Table 6 can be satisfied. Note that, choosing p^x_{80} means choosing eight 32-bit variables Q^x_{80}, Q^x_{79}, Q^x_{78}, Q^x_{77}, Q^x_{76}, Q^x_{75}, Q^x_{74}, and Q^x_{73}.

2: Apply the backward computation in Alg. 1 to obtain p^1_{65}, p^2_{65}, p^3_{65} and p^4_{65}. This fixes chaining variables up to Q^x_{58} and message words from $m_{\pi(79)}$ to $m_{\pi(65)}$.

3: Apply the forward computation in Alg. 2 to obtain p^1_{93}, p^2_{93}, p^3_{93} and p^4_{93}. This fixes chaining variables up to Q^x_{93} and message words from $m_{\pi(80)}$ to $m_{\pi(92)}$.
`//End of the message modification for the inside path`

4: **while** a 4-sum quartet of the compression function output is not found **do**

5: Randomly choose the values of message-words quartet for $m_{\pi(93)} = m_{11}$, $m_{\pi(94)} = m_5$, and $m_{\pi(95)} = m_2$ with the message difference on m_2, and compute a chaining-variables quartet until p^1_{98}, p^2_{98}, p^3_{98} and p^4_{98}.

6: Randomly choose the values of message-words quartet for $m_{\pi(64)} = m_{19}$, and compute a chaining-variables quartet until p^1_{60}, p^2_{60}, p^3_{60} and p^4_{60}.

7: Compute a chaining-variables quartet until p^1_0, p^2_0, p^3_0 and p^4_0 in backward and p^1_{160}, p^2_{160}, p^3_{160} and p^4_{160} in forward.

8: **if** $(p^1_0 \boxplus p^1_{160}) \boxminus (p^2_0 \boxplus p^2_{160}) \boxminus (p^3_0 \boxplus p^3_{160}) \boxplus (p^4_0 \boxplus p^4_{160}) = 0$ **then**

9: **return** $(p^1_0, p^2_0, p^3_0, p^4_0)$ and (M^1, M^2, M^3, M^4)

10: **end if**

11: **end while**

Algorithm 5. Differential path search algorithm for E_1 from step 60 to step 79

Input: Message difference ΔM, where $\Delta m_2 =$ 0x80000000 and $\Delta m_x = 0$ for $x \neq 2$

Output: Differences of each chaining variable between step 60 and step 79

1: Initialize $tempHD \leftarrow 0$

2: **for** $x = 53$ **to** 60 **do**

3: $Q_x \leftarrow$ a randomly chosen value

4: $Q'_x \leftarrow Q_x$

5: **end for**

6: **for** $x = 60$ **to** 79 **do**

7: $m_{\pi(x)} \leftarrow$ a randomly chosen value

8: $m'_{\pi(x)} \leftarrow m_{\pi(x)} \oplus \Delta M$

9: Compute Q_{x+1} and Q'_{x+1}

10: $tempHD \leftarrow tempHD + HW(Q_{x+1} \oplus Q'_{x+1})$

11: **if** $tempHD > 10$ **then**

12: goto step 1

13: **end if**

14: **end for**

15: **print** $Q_y \oplus Q'_y$ for $y = 61, 62, \ldots, 80$

Table 6. New differential paths and conditions for 5-Pass HAVAL. $[z] = 0, [z] = 1$ are conditions on the value of z-th bit of the chaining variable. For the first and last several steps, we do not fix a particular difference for the amplified probability. The difference is considered in XOR. In some cases, we need conditions on the sign of the difference. $[z] = 0+, [z] = 1-$ mean the value is first fixed to 0 (resp. 1) and change to 1 (resp. 0) after the difference is inserted.

Path for E_1 with Δm_2 = 0x80000000				Path for E_2 with ∇m_4 = 0x80000000				
j	ΔQ_j	Conditions on Q_j	Δm	j	∇Q_j	Conditions on Q_j	∇m	$m_{\pi(j)}$
-7	AP	AP		-7				m_1
-6	AP	AP		-6				m_0
-5	AP	AP	0x80000000	-5				m_2
-4				-4				m_3
...	...	...	...	...	...	...	...	...
52				52				m_{13}
53			0x80000000	53				m_2
54				54				m_{25}
55				55				m_{31}
56				56				m_{27}
57				57				m_{19}
58		[31]=0		58				m_9
59		[31]=0		59				m_4
60		[31]=0		60				m_{20}
61	0x80000000			61				m_{28}
62		[31]=0		62				m_{17}
63		[31]=0		63				m_8
64		[31,24]=0		64				m_{22}
65		[24]=0		65				m_{29}
66		[24,20]=0		66				m_{14}
67	0x01000000	[20]=0		67				m_{25}
68		[24,20]=0		68				m_{12}
69	0x00100000	[24]=0		69				m_{24}
70		[24,20,17]=0		70				m_{30}
71		[20,17]=0		71				m_{16}
72		[24,20,17]=0		72				m_{26}
73	0x00020000	[17]=1−		73				
74		[20,17]=0		74	0x00000001	[0]=1−		
75		[17,9]=0		75		[18]=0		
76		[17,9]=0		76		[18]=0		start
77	0x00000200	[9]=0+		77		[18,0]=0		step
78		[17,10,9]=0		78	0x00040000	[21]=0,[18]=0+		
79	0x00000400	[10]=1−		79		[21]=0,[18]=1		
80				80		[21,18]=0		
81				81		[21,18,14]=0		m_{31}
82				82	0x00200000	[14]=0		m_{15}
83				83		[21]=1,[14]=0		m_7
84				84	0x00004000	[21]=0		m_3
85				85		[21]=0,[14]=1		m_1
86				86		[14]=0		m_0
87				87		[14,10]=0		m_{18}
88				88		[10]=0		m_{27}
89				89		[10]=0		m_{13}
90				90	0x00000400			m_6
91				91		[10]=1		m_{21}
92				92		[10]=1		m_{10}
93				93		[10]=1		m_{23}
94				94				m_{11}
95				95				m_5
96				96				m_2
97				97				m_{24}
98				98			0x80000000	m_4
99				99				m_0
...	...	...	...	...	...	...	...	...
156				156				m_{22}
157				157	0x80000000	AP	0x80000000	m_4
158				158	AP	AP		m_1
159				159	AP	AP		m_{25}
160				160	AP	AP		m_{15}

Table 7. Experimental results for the amplified probability

Direction	Number of trials	Number of obtained 4-sums	Amplified probability
Back	1,000,000	53,065	$2^{-4.24}$
For	1,000,000	37,623	$2^{-4.73}$
Total	1,000,000	1,975	$2^{-8.98}$

Table 8. An example of the boomerang quartet for the full 5-pass HAVAL

H_i^1	0x6ad6913b	0x52831497	0x42e2afea	0x042171e8	0x05c66540	0xf6308a5d	0x69b242bb	0xfeadf2df
M_i^1	0x55f408ea	0xade29473	0x5cd48f01	0x862fac29	0xb59b9103	0xdfe1dff3	0x44aaff68	0xa5716cc8
	0xd9b3c72a	0x9d9907bb	0x263e9a6f	0x0d81dbdd	0x1a1d1f69	0x35a88db0	0xb50f50b3	0xcb85d403
	0xe2898bd5	0x3dc4e64c	0x48a696ae	0x1568e06b	0x286a00c5	0x236529bd	0x8bb673fd	0x481411ed
	0xb2117cb1	0xe6911e8d	0x5816e997	0x1a8fc1d3	0xc5dda128	0x43e5f428	0xcf1e861f	0xf5258b98
H_{i+1}^1	0x50b484bf	0x9d28c720	0xc2a5ab4d	0x5aec2d4b	0x63659cae	0x0023f316	0xa02276be	0xeab5fb84
H_i^2	0x6ad6913b	0x52831497	0x42e2afea	0x042171e8	0x05c66540	0xf6308e5d	0x69b242bb	0xfeae32df
M_i^2	0x55f408ea	0xade29473	0xdcd48f01	0x862fac29	0xb59b9103	0xdfe1dff3	0x44aaff68	0xa5716cc8
	0xd9b3c72a	0x9d9907bb	0x263e9a6f	0x0d81dbdd	0x1a1d1f69	0x35a88db0	0xb50f50b3	0xcb85d403
	0xe2898bd5	0x3dc4e64c	0x48a696ae	0x1568e06b	0x286a00c5	0x236529bd	0x8bb673fd	0x481411ed
	0xb2117cb1	0xe6911e8d	0x5816e997	0x1a8fc1d3	0xc5dda128	0x43e5f428	0xcf1e861f	0xf5258b98
H_{i+1}^2	0xfa15769c	0x6ed1b19a	0x405b263b	0x57cd6359	0xd8688750	0xcdc3c9d3	0xa3dc7fd8	0x2e59f283
H_i^3	0xb70b5251	0x851d041a	0x7a5f5fad	0x98626bb1	0x9d739cbc	0x67bc3181	0xe48e4cac	0xeeb57f26
M_i^3	0x55f408ea	0xade29473	0x5cd48f01	0x862fac29	0x359b9103	0xdfe1dff3	0x44aaff68	0xa5716cc8
	0xd9b3c72a	0x9d9907bb	0x263e9a6f	0x0d81dbdd	0x1a1d1f69	0x35a88db0	0xb50f50b3	0xcb85d403
	0xe2898bd5	0x3dc4e64c	0x48a696ae	0x1568e06b	0x286a00c5	0x236529bd	0x8bb673fd	0x481411ed
	0xb2117cb1	0xe6911e8d	0x5816e997	0x1a8fc1d3	0xc5dda128	0x43e5f428	0xcf1e861f	0xf5258b98
H_{i+1}^3	0x9ce945d5	0xcfc2b6a3	0xfa225b10	0xef2d2714	0x7b12d42a	0x71af9a3a	0x1afe80af	0xdbbd87cb
H_i^4	0xb70b5251	0x851d041a	0x7a5f5fad	0x98626bb1	0x9d739cbc	0x67bc3581	0xe48e4cac	0xeeb5bf26
M_i^4	0x55f408ea	0xade29473	0xdcd48f01	0x862fac29	0x359b9103	0xdfe1dff3	0x44aaff68	0xa5716cc8
	0xd9b3c72a	0x9d9907bb	0x263e9a6f	0x0d81dbdd	0x1a1d1f69	0x35a88db0	0xb50f50b3	0xcb85d403
	0xe2898bd5	0x3dc4e64c	0x48a696ae	0x1568e06b	0x286a00c5	0x236529bd	0x8bb673fd	0x481411ed
	0xb2117cb1	0xe6911e8d	0x5816e997	0x1a8fc1d3	0xc5dda128	0x43e5f428	0xcf1e861f	0xf5258b98
H_{i+1}^4	0x464a37b2	0xa16ba11d	0x77d7d5fe	0xec0e5d22	0xf015becc	0x3f4f70f7	0x1eb889c9	0x1f617eca
4-sum	0x00000000	0x00000000	0x00000000	0x00000000	0x00000000	0x00000000	0x00000000	0x00000000

Table 9. An example of the boomerang quartet for MD5

H_i^1	0x7ad51bee	0x68a07529	0x5369e5f1	0x62f52251				
M_i^1	0x58df0f5e	0x678b3525	0x03105c08	0xa068f82a	0x21ead339	0xe6e2ea9c	0x5cf986e1	0x9890fd27
	0xcf8a438f	0x2cecb915	0x44935dfe	0xf06f103f	0x72d5b376	0x9688dfed	0x7b2ae2f6	0xe9256628
H_{i+1}^1	0x1de7b79a	0x6e573e2a	0x0ef900e3	0xc72985ef				
H_i^2	0xfad51bee	0x68a07529	0xd369e5f1	0xe2f52251				
M_i^2	0x58df0f5e	0x678b3525	0x83105c08	0xa068f82a	0x21ead339	0xe6e2ea9c	0x5cf986e1	0x9890fd27
	0xcf8a438f	0x2cecb915	0x44935dfe	0xf06f103f	0x72d5b376	0x9688dfed	0x7b2ae2f6	0xe9256628
H_{i+1}^2	0x03d5ae50	0x722a5685	0x361b13a1	0x75a3a89d				
H_i^3	0x97e364fe	0xb191e24c	0xdec0361f	0x6a8d3d9f				
M_i^3	0x58df0f5e	0x678b3525	0x03105c08	0xa068f82a	0x21ead339	0xe6e2ea9c	0x5cf986e1	0x9890fd27
	0xcf8a438f	0x2cecb915	0x44935dfe	0x706f103f	0x72d5b376	0x9688dfed	0x7b2ae2f6	0xe9256628
H_{i+1}^3	0x3af600aa	0xb748a94d	0x9a4f4f11	0xcec19f3d				
H_i^4	0x17e364fe	0xb191e24c	0x5ec0361f	0xea8d3d9f				
M_i^4	0x58df0f5e	0x678b3525	0x83105c08	0xa068f82a	0x21ead339	0xe6e2ea9c	0x5cf986e1	0x9890fd27
	0xcf8a438f	0x2cecb915	0x44935dfe	0x706f103f	0x72d5b376	0x9688dfed	0x7b2ae2f6	0xe9256628
H_{i+1}^4	0x20e3f760	0xbb1bc1a8	0xc17161cf	0x7d3bc1eb				
4-sum	0x00000000	0x00000000	0x00000000	0x00000000				

Table 10. An example of the boomerang quartet for 3-pass HAVAL

H_i^1	0x8af103dd	0x89952e4e	0xba8ba930	0xb1681125	0x8bf68d12	0x11f454da	0x31babeaf	0x1c684f37
M_i^1	0x14c97b03	0x03021d0b	0x6e0a398b	0x12acd59d	0xa0e58017	0x56a25710	0x31381427	0x193906fa
	0xa97fe484	0x9228f3e7	0x3d307061	0x7ea148a1	0xcf1cf1f5	0x2b250fb8	0xd874f573	0xb71f7585
	0xb277563c	0xdb382652	0x1068c5fc	0x12cd8ceb	0x290580bf	0xc95cca2a	0x931d8c52	0xc835f9e8
	0x3ef066f9	0x098a53d0	0xf25db814	0xdb003165	0x31779903	0x4ebc57a0	0x9060622a	0x24c0bf29
H_{i+1}^1	0x9b18b769	0x01959420	0x480cea32	0x7c38cf17	0x70323bda	0xd46e06e9	0x09d05ae3	0xd315f8f6
H_i^2	0x8af103dd	0x89952e4e	0xba8ba930	0xb1681125	0x8bf68d12	0x11f454da	0x31babeaf	0x1c684b37
M_i^2	0x94c97b03	0x03021d0b	0x6e0a398b	0x12acd59d	0xa0e58017	0x56a25710	0x31381427	0x193906fa
	0xa97fe484	0x9228f3e7	0x3d307061	0x7ea148a1	0xcf1cf1f5	0x2b250fb8	0xd874f573	0xb71f7585
	0xb277563c	0xdb382652	0x1068c5fc	0x12cd8ceb	0x290580bf	0xc95cca2a	0x931d8c52	0xc835f9e8
	0x3ef066f9	0x098a53d0	0xf25db814	0xdb003165	0x31779903	0x4ebc57a0	0x9060622a	0x24c0bf29
H_{i+1}^2	0x2ab0c721	0xda378441	0x99789481	0xaf2db9cb	0x900971d1	0xdfa8ec61	0x122c330e	0xa77c26af
H_i^3	0x6ca48418	0x6711d760	0x52670414	0x4dfe762f	0xf9bae1d5	0x7a9a2074	0x4518e6bf	0x6acec54d
M_i^3	0x14c97b03	0x03021d0b	0x6e0a398b	0x12acd59d	0xa0e58017	0xd6a25710	0x31381427	0x193906fa
	0xa97fe484	0x9228f3e7	0x3d307061	0x7ea148a1	0xcf1cf1f5	0x2b250fb8	0xd874f573	0xb71f7585
	0xb277563c	0xdb382652	0x1068c5fc	0x12cd8ceb	0x290580bf	0xc95cca2a	0x931d8c52	0xc835f9e8
	0x3ef066f9	0x098a53d0	0xf25db814	0xdb003165	0x31779903	0x4ebc57a0	0x9060622a	0x24c0bf29
H_{i+1}^3	0x7ccc37a4	0xdf123d32	0xdfe84516	0x18cf3421	0xddf6909d	0x3d13d283	0x9d2e82f3	0x217c6f0c
H_i^4	0x6ca48418	0x6711d760	0x52670414	0x4dfe762f	0xf9bae1d5	0x7a9a2074	0x4518e6bf	0x6acec14d
M_i^4	0x94c97b03	0x03021d0b	0x6e0a398b	0x12acd59d	0xa0e58017	0xd6a25710	0x31381427	0x193906fa
	0xa97fe484	0x9228f3e7	0x3d307061	0x7ea148a1	0xcf1cf1f5	0x2b250fb8	0xd874f573	0xb71f7585
	0xb277563c	0xdb382652	0x1068c5fc	0x12cd8ceb	0x290580bf	0xc95cca2a	0x931d8c52	0xc835f9e8
	0x3ef066f9	0x098a53d0	0xf25db814	0xdb003165	0x31779903	0x4ebc57a0	0x9060622a	0x24c0bf29
H_{i+1}^4	0x0c64475c	0xb7b42d53	0x3153ef65	0x4bc41ed5	0xfdcdc694	0x484eb7fb	0xa58a5b1e	0xf5e29cc5
4-sum	0x00000000	0x00000000	0x00000000	0x00000000	0x00000000	0x00000000	0x00000000	0x00000000

Table 11. An example of the boomerang quartet for 4-pass HAVAL

H_i^1	0x564187b3	0x5af775fb	0x10136ca0	0x8a9ffa0c	0x3edeecd0	0xd2e74f6c	0x15576f1c	0x70de0eb7
M_i^1	0x8bc2d93c	0xc9e9f4eb	0xd4e85905	0x39828bfb	0x6aefef32	0xc3284793	0x0ed3477d	0x7e8a91f9
	0x84963793	0x263a6675	0xafa8892c	0x340904ff	0xaccb5103	0xf3bac932	0xbe1f0ae4	0x93c377c1
	0x48142ead	0x5b911f1b	0xe5693f5f	0xd1c28e92	0x11b24646	0xac7dd73d	0x745b0c46	0x5ca1756c
	0xdfb80fbd	0x88cee1fd	0x7bd6c417	0x43ab29df	0xfdb5d87a	0x3569ce43	0xc7dc1347	0x462ef5da
H_{i+1}^1	0x910e3d63	0x83c406ec	0x464230f7	0x3bfc4d84	0x14fddff2	0x5092bf5f	0x07cd2ad3	0x31c0e36a
H_i^2	0x564187b3	0x5af775fb	0x10136ca0	0x8a9ffa0c	0x3edeecd0	0xd2e74b6c	0x15572f1c	0x70e24eb7
M_i^2	0x8bc2d93c	0xc9e9f4eb	0x54e85905	0x39828bfb	0x6aefef32	0xc3284793	0x0ed3477d	0x7e8a91f9
	0x84963793	0x263a6675	0xafa8892c	0x340904ff	0xaccb5103	0xf3bac932	0xbe1f0ae4	0x93c377c1
	0x48142ead	0x5b911f1b	0xe5693f5f	0xd1c28e92	0x11b24646	0xac7dd73d	0x745b0c46	0x5ca1756c
	0xdfb80fbd	0x88cee1fd	0x7bd6c417	0x43ab29df	0xfdb5d87a	0x3569ce43	0xc7dc1347	0x462ef5da
H_{i+1}^2	0xe6b6ce20	0x3260de7a	0x681aa45d	0x277995cd	0x9d4959bc	0xaec251c2	0x41446efa	0x75cf2b80
H_i^3	0xaf8abf6d	0xd2aafd4c	0xc7f01506	0xfd258be0	0x299edd95	0xa561cfbc	0x61175f52	0xec8049a0
M_i^3	0x8bc2d93c	0xc9e9f4eb	0xd4e85905	0x39828bfb	0x6aefef32	0xc3284793	0x0ed3477d	0x7e8a91f9
	0x84963793	0x263a6675	0xafa8892c	0x340904ff	0xaccb5103	0xf3bac932	0xbe1f0ae4	0x93c377c1
	0x48142ead	0xdb911f1b	0xe5693f5f	0xd1c28e92	0x11b24646	0xac7dd73d	0x745b0c46	0x5ca1756c
	0xdfb80fbd	0x88cee1fd	0x7bd6c417	0x43ab29df	0xfdb5d87a	0x3569ce43	0xc7dc1347	0x462ef5da
H_{i+1}^3	0xea57751d	0xfb778e3d	0xfe1ed95d	0xae81df58	0x7fbdd0b7	0x230d3faf	0x538d1b09	0xad631e53
H_i^4	0xaf8abf6d	0xd2aafd4c	0xc7f01506	0xfd258be0	0x299edd95	0xa561cbbc	0x61171f52	0xec8489a0
M_i^4	0x8bc2d93c	0xc9e9f4eb	0x54e85905	0x39828bfb	0x6aefef32	0xc3284793	0x0ed3477d	0x7e8a91f9
	0x84963793	0x263a6675	0xafa8892c	0x340904ff	0xaccb5103	0xf3bac932	0xbe1f0ae4	0x93c377c1
	0x48142ead	0xdb911f1b	0xe5693f5f	0xd1c28e92	0x11b24646	0xac7dd73d	0x745b0c46	0x5ca1756c
	0xdfb80fbd	0x88cee1fd	0x7bd6c417	0x43ab29df	0xfdb5d87a	0x3569ce43	0xc7dc1347	0x462ef5da
H_{i+1}^4	0x400005da	0xaa1465cb	0x1ff74cc3	0x99ff27a1	0x08094a81	0x813cd212	0x8d045f30	0xf1716669
4-sum	0x00000000	0x00000000	0x00000000	0x00000000	0x00000000	0x00000000	0x00000000	0x00000000

5.4 Experimental Results

By following the algorithm in Alg. 3, we evaluated the amplified probability for the first and last several rounds. The results are shown in Table 7. According to our experiments, $AP^{Back} = 2^{-4.24}$, $AP^{For} = 2^{-4.73}$, and the entire success probability is $2^{-8.98}$, which matches $AP^{Back} \times AP^{For} = 2^{-8.97}$. The attack complexity is for $2^{8.98}$ iterations of Steps 4–11 in Alg. 4. Because we compute quartets, the complexity is approximately $2^{11}(\approx 4 \times 2^{8.98})$ compression function computations. Finally, we implemented our 4-sum distinguisher on 5-pass HAVAL. An example of the generated 4-sum quartet is presented in Table 8.

6 Concluding Remarks

We studied the boomerang attack approach on hash functions. We proved that the previous differential path on 5-pass HAVAL contained a flaw. We then constructed the new path and proposed the 4-sum distinguisher on the compression function with a complexity of approximately 2^{11} computations. We implemented the attack and showed an example of the 4-sum quartet. As far as we know, this is the first feasible result on the full compression function of 5-pass HAVAL.

References

1. Aoki, K., Sasaki, Y.: Preimage Attacks on One-Block MD4, 63-Step MD5 and More. In: Avanzi, R.M., Keliher, L., Sica, F. (eds.) SAC 2008. LNCS, vol. 5381, pp. 103–119. Springer, Heidelberg (2009)
2. Aumasson, J.-P., Meier, W., Mendel, F.: Preimage Attacks on 3-Pass HAVAL and Step-Reduced MD5. In: Avanzi, R.M., Keliher, L., Sica, F. (eds.) SAC 2008. LNCS, vol. 5381, pp. 120–135. Springer, Heidelberg (2009)
3. Biryukov, A., Nikolić, I., Roy, A.: Boomerang Attacks on BLAKE-32. In: Joux, A. (ed.) FSE 2011. LNCS, vol. 6733, pp. 218–237. Springer, Heidelberg (2011)
4. den Boer, B., Bosselaers, A.: Collisions for the Compression Function of MD-5. In: Helleseth, T. (ed.) EUROCRYPT 1993. LNCS, vol. 765, pp. 293–304. Springer, Heidelberg (1994)
5. Dobbertin, H.: The Status of MD5 after a Recent Attack. CryptoBytes The technical newsletter of RSA Laboratories, a division of RSA Data Security, Inc. 2(2) (Summer 1996)
6. Guo, J., Ling, S., Rechberger, C., Wang, H.: Advanced Meet-in-the-Middle Preimage Attacks: First Results on Full Tiger, and Improved Results on MD4 and SHA-2. In: Abe, M. (ed.) ASIACRYPT 2010. LNCS, vol. 6477, pp. 56–75. Springer, Heidelberg (2010)
7. Joux, A., Peyrin, T.: Hash Functions and the (Amplified) Boomerang Attack. In: Menezes, A. (ed.) CRYPTO 2007. LNCS, vol. 4622, pp. 244–263. Springer, Heidelberg (2007)
8. Kim, J.-S., Biryukov, A., Preneel, B., Lee, S.-J.: On the Security of Encryption Modes of MD4, MD5 and HAVAL. In: Qing, S., Mao, W., López, J., Wang, G. (eds.) ICICS 2005. LNCS, vol. 3783, pp. 147–158. Springer, Heidelberg (2005)

9. Kim, J., Biryukov, A., Preneel, B., Lee, S.: On the Security of Encryption Modes of MD4, MD5 and HAVAL. Cryptology ePrint Archive, Report 2005/327 (2005); In: Qing, S., Mao, W., López, J., Wang, G. (eds.) ICICS 2005. LNCS, vol. 3783, pp. 147–158. Springer, Heidelberg (2005)
10. Lamberger, M., Mendel, F.: Higher-Order Differential Attack on Reduced SHA-256. Cryptology ePrint Archive, Report 2011/037 (2011), `http://eprint.iacr.org/2011/037`
11. Leurent, G.: MD4 is Not One-Way. In: Nyberg, K. (ed.) FSE 2008. LNCS, vol. 5086, pp. 412–428. Springer, Heidelberg (2008)
12. Murphy, S.: The Return of the Cryptographic Boomerang. IEEE Transactions on Information Theory 57(4), 2517–2521 (2011)
13. Rivest, R.L.: The MD4 Message Digest Algorithm. In: Menezes, A., Vanstone, S.A. (eds.) CRYPTO 1990. LNCS, vol. 537, pp. 303–311. Springer, Heidelberg (1991), also appeared in RFC 1320 `http://www.ietf.org/rfc/rfc1320.txt`
14. Rivest, R.L.: Request for Comments 1321: The MD5 Message Digest Algorithm. The Internet Engineering Task Force (1992)
15. Sakai, Y., Sasaki, Y., Wang, L., Ohta, K., Sakiyama, K.: Preimage Attacks on 5- Pass HAVAL Reduced to 158-Steps and One-Block 3-Pass HAVAL. Industrial Track of ACNS 2011 (2011)
16. Sasaki, Y., Aoki, K.: Preimage Attacks on 3, 4, and 5-Pass HAVAL. In: Pieprzyk, J.P. (ed.) ASIACRYPT 2008. LNCS, vol. 5350, pp. 253–271. Springer, Heidelberg (2008)
17. Sasaki, Y., Aoki, K.: Finding Preimages in Full MD5 Faster than Exhaustive Search. In: Joux, A. (ed.) EUROCRYPT 2009. LNCS, vol. 5479, pp. 134–152. Springer, Heidelberg (2009)
18. Sasaki, Y., Wang, L., Ohta, K., Kunihiro, N.: New Message Difference for MD4. In: Biryukov, A. (ed.) FSE 2007. LNCS, vol. 4593, pp. 329–348. Springer, Heidelberg (2007)
19. Suzuki, K., Kurosawa, K.: How to Find Many Collisions of 3-Pass HAVAL. In: Miyaji, A., Kikuchi, H., Rannenberg, K. (eds.) IWSEC 2007. LNCS, vol. 4752, pp. 428–443. Springer, Heidelberg (2007)
20. U.S. Department of Commerce, National Institute of Standards and Technology: Federal Register Vol. 72, No. 212/Friday, November 2, 2007/Notices (2007)
21. Van Rompay, B., Biryukov, A., Preneel, B., Vandewalle, J.: Cryptanalysis of 3-Pass HAVAL. In: Laih, C.-S. (ed.) ASIACRYPT 2003. LNCS, vol. 2894, pp. 228–245. Springer, Heidelberg (2003)
22. Wagner, D.: The Boomerang Attack. In: Knudsen, L.R. (ed.) FSE 1999. LNCS, vol. 1636, pp. 156–170. Springer, Heidelberg (1999)
23. Wagner, D.: A Generalized Birthday Problem. In: Yung, M. (ed.) CRYPTO 2002. LNCS, vol. 2442, pp. 288–303. Springer, Heidelberg (2002)
24. Wang, X., Feng, D., Yu, X.: An Attack on Hash Function HAVAL-128. Science in China (Information Sciences) 48(5), 545–556 (2005)
25. Wang, X., Lai, X., Feng, D., Chen, H., Yu, X.: Cryptanalysis of the Hash Functions MD4 and RIPEMD. In: Cramer, R. (ed.) EUROCRYPT 2005. LNCS, vol. 3494, pp. 1–18. Springer, Heidelberg (2005)
26. Wang, X., Yin, Y.L., Yu, H.: Finding Collisions in the Full SHA-1. In: Shoup, V. (ed.) CRYPTO 2005. LNCS, vol. 3621, pp. 17–36. Springer, Heidelberg (2005)
27. Wang, X., Yu, H.: How to Break MD5 and Other Hash Functions. In: Cramer, R. (ed.) EUROCRYPT 2005. LNCS, vol. 3494, pp. 19–35. Springer, Heidelberg (2005)

28. Wang, Z., Zhang, H., Qin, Z., Meng, Q.: Cryptanalysis of 4-Pass HAVAL. Crptology ePrint Archive, Report 2006/161 (2006)
29. Xie, T., Liu, F., Feng, D.: Could the 1-MSB Input Difference be the Fastest Collision Attack for MD5? Cryptology ePrint Archive, Report 2008/391 (2008)
30. Yoshida, H., Biryukov, A., De Cannière, C., Lano, J., Preneel, B.: Non-Randomness of the Full 4 and 5-Pass HAVAL. In: Blundo, C., Cimato, S. (eds.) SCN 2004. LNCS, vol. 3352, pp. 324–336. Springer, Heidelberg (2005)
31. Yu, H., Wang, X., Yun, A., Park, S.: Cryptanalysis of the Full HAVAL with 4 and 5 Passes. In: Robshaw, M.J.B. (ed.) FSE 2006. LNCS, vol. 4047, pp. 89–110. Springer, Heidelberg (2006)
32. Zheng, Y., Pieprzyk, J., Seberry, J.: HAVAL — One-Way Hashing Algorithm with Variable Length of Output. In: Zheng, Y., Seberry, J. (eds.) AUSCRYPT 1992. LNCS, vol. 718, pp. 83–104. Springer, Heidelberg (1993)

A Differential Path Search Algorithm for 5-Pass HAVAL

Our path search algorithm is semi-automated and minimizes the Hamming distance of the entire inside path. We independently searched for the path for E_1 (steps 60 – 79) with $\Delta m_2 =$ `0x80000000` and path for E_2 (steps 98 – 73) with $\nabla m_4 =$ `0x80000000`. Conditions and contradiction of two paths were later checked by hand. We only explain the algorithm for E_1 in Alg. 5. $HW(\cdot)$ returns the Hamming weight of the input variable.

After an enough number of iterations of Alg. 5, we obtained the path in Table 6 whose $tempHD$ is 6.

B Examples of Boomerang Quartet

The differential paths in [9] can be used to construct a 4-sum on the compression function. We show the generated 4-sums for MD5, 3-pass HAVAL, and 4-pass HAVAL. The amplified probability to satisfy the entire path is approximately 2^{-8} for MD5, 2^{-2} for 3-pass HAVAL, and 2^{-9} for 4-pass HAVAL.

Improved Analysis of ECHO-256*

Jérémy Jean[1], María Naya-Plasencia[2], and Martin Schläffer[3]

[1] Ecole Normale Supérieure, France
[2] FHNW, Windisch, Switzerland
[3] IAIK, Graz University of Technology, Austria

Abstract. ECHO-256 is a second-round candidate of the SHA-3 competition. It is an AES-based hash function that has attracted a lot of interest and analysis. Up to now, the best known attacks were a distinguisher on the full internal permutation and a collision on four rounds of its compression function. The latter was the best known analysis on the compression function as well as the one on the largest number of rounds so far. In this paper, we extend the compression function results to get a distinguisher on 7 out of 8 rounds using rebound techniques. We also present the first 5-round collision attack on the ECHO-256 hash function.

Keywords: hash function, cryptanalysis, rebound attack, collision attack, distinguisher.

1 Introduction

ECHO-256 [1] is the 256-bit version of one of the second-round candidates of the SHA-3 competition. It is an AES-based hash function that has been the subject of many studies. Currently, the best known analysis of ECHO-256 are a distinguisher on the full 8-round internal permutation proposed in [13] and improved in [10]. Furthermore, a 4-round collision attack of the compression function has been presented in [4]. A previous analysis due to Schläffer in [14] has been shown to be incorrect in [4], but it introduced an alternative description of the ECHO round-function, which has then been reused in several analyses, including this paper. The best results of this paper are a collision attack on the hash function reduced to 5 rounds and a distinguisher of the compression function on 7 rounds. Additionally, we cover two more attacks in the Appendix. The complexities of previous results and our proposed attacks are reported in Table 1.

Apart from the improved attacks on ECHO-256, this paper also covers a number of new techniques. The merging process of multiple inbound phases has been improved to find solutions also for the hash function, where much less freedom is available in the chaining input. For the hash function collision attack on 5

* This work was supported in part by ANR/SAPHIR II, by the French DGA, by the NCCR-MICS under grant number 5005-67322, by the ECRYPT II contract ICT-2007-216646, by the Austrian FWF project P21936 and by the IAP Programme P6/26 BCRYPT of the Belgian State.

A. Miri and S. Vaudenay (Eds.): SAC 2011, LNCS 7118, pp. 19–36, 2012.

Table 1. Best known cryptanalysis results on ECHO-256

Rounds	Time	Memory	Generic	Type	Reference
8	2^{182}	2^{37}	2^{256}	Internal Permutation Distinguisher	[13]
8	2^{151}	2^{67}	2^{256}	Internal Permutation Distinguisher	[10]
4	2^{52}	2^{16}	2^{256}	Compression Function Collision	[4]
5	2^{112}	$2^{85.3}$	2^{128}	Hash Function Collision	Section 3
6	2^{193}	2^{128}	2^{256}	Compression Function Collision	Section 4
7	2^{193}	2^{128}	2^{240}	Compression Function Distinguisher	Section 4

rounds, we use subspace differences which collide with a high probability at the output of the hash function. Additionally, we use multiple phases also in the outbound part to reduce the overall complexity of the attacks. For the 7-round compression function distinguisher, we use the new techniques and algorithms introduced in [10, 11].

Outline. The paper is organized as follows. In Section 2, we describe the 256-bit version of the ECHO hash function and detail an alternative view that has already been used in several analysis [4, 14]. In particular, we emphasize the SuperMixColumns and SuperSBox transformations that ease the analysis. In Section 3, we provide a collision attack on this hash function reduced to 5 rounds and a distinguisher of the 7-round compression function in Section 4.

In the extended version of this paper [5], we describe a chosen-salt collision attack on the 6-round compression function and a chosen-salt distinguisher for the compression function reduced to 7 rounds. We also improve the result from [4] into a collision attack on the 4-round ECHO-256 hash function.

2 ECHO-256 Description

ECHO is an iterated hash function and the compression function of ECHO updates an internal state described by a 16×16 matrix of GF (2^8) elements, which can also be viewed as a 4×4 matrix of 16 AES states. Transformations on this large 2048-bit state are very similar to the one of the AES, the main difference being the equivalent S-Box called BigSubWords, which consists in two AES rounds. The diffusion of the AES states in ECHO is ensured by two *big* transformations: BigShiftRows and BigMixColumns (Figure 1).

At the end of the permutation, the BigFinal operation adds the current state to the initial one (feed-forward) and, in the case of ECHO-256, adds its four columns together to produce the new chaining value. In this paper, we only focus on ECHO-256 and refer to the original publication [1] for more details on both ECHO-256 and ECHO-512 versions. Note that the keys used in the two AES rounds are an internal counter and the salt, respectively: they are mainly introduced to break the existing symmetries of the AES unkeyed permutation [7]. Since we are not

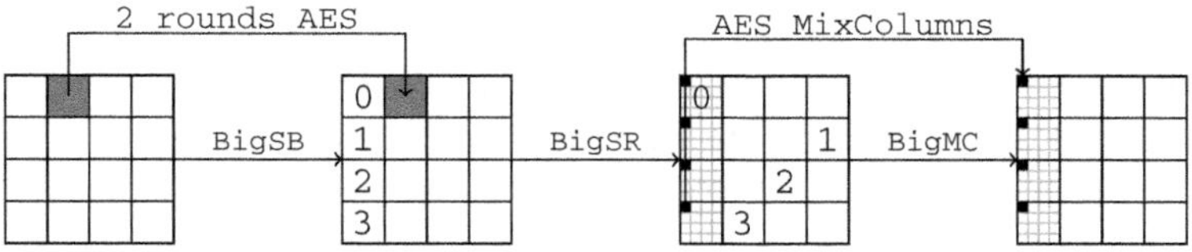

Fig. 1. One round of the ECHO permutation. Each of the 16 cells is an AES state.

using any property relying on symmetry and adding constants does not change differences, we omit these steps in the following.

Two versions of the hash function ECHO have been submitted to the SHA-3 contest: ECHO-256 and ECHO-512, which share the same state size and round function, but inject messages of size 1536 or 1024 bits respectively in the compression function. Note that the message is padded by adding a single 1 followed by zeros to fill up the last message block. The last 18 bytes of the last message block always contain the 2-byte hash output size, followed by the 16-byte message length. Focusing on ECHO-256 and denoting f its compression function, H_i the i-th output chaining value, $M_i = M_i^0 \mid\mid M_i^1 \mid\mid M_i^2$ the i-th message block composed of three chunks of 512 bits each M_i^j and $S = [C_0C_1C_2C_3]$ the four 512-bit ECHO-columns constituting state S, we have ($H_0 = IV$):

$$C_0 \leftarrow H_{i-1}, \qquad C_1 \leftarrow M_i^0, \qquad C_2 \leftarrow M_i^1, \qquad C_3 \leftarrow M_i^2.$$

AES. We recall that one round, among the ten ones, of the AES-128 permutation is the succession of four transformations: SubBytes (**SB**), ShiftRows (**SR**), MixColumns (**MC**) and AddRoundKey (**AK**). We refer to the original publication [15] for further details.

Notations. We consider each state in the ECHO internal permutation, namely after each elementary transformations. We start with S_0, where the IV and the message are combined and end the first round after eight transformations in S_8. To refer to the AES-state at row i and column j of a particular ECHO-state S_n, we use the notation $S_n[i, j]$. Additionally, we introduce *column-slice* to refer to a thin column of size 16×1 of the ECHO state. The process of merging two lists L_1 and L_2 into a new list L is denoted $L = L_1 \bowtie L_2$. In the event that the merging should be done under some relation t, we use the operator $\bowtie_{|t|}$, where $|t|$ represents the size of the constraint to be verified in bits. Finally, in an AES-state, we consider four diagonals (from 0 to 3): diagonal $j \in [0, 3]$ will be the four elements $(i, i + j \pmod 4)$, with $i \in [0, 3]$.

2.1 Alternative Description

For an easier description of some of the following attacks, we use an equivalent description of one round of the ECHO permutation. First, we swap the BigShiftRows transformation with the MixColumns transformation of the second AES round. Second, we swap SubBytes with ShiftRows of the first AES round. Swapping these operations does not change the computational result of ECHO and similar alternative descriptions have already been used in the analysis of AES. Hence, one round of ECHO results in the two transformations SuperSBox (SB-MC-SB) and SuperMixColumns (MC-BMC), which are separated just by byte-shuffling operation. The SuperSBox has first been analyzed by Daemen and Rijmen in [2] to study two rounds of AES and has been independently used by Lamberger et al. in [6] and Gilbert and Peyrin in [12] to analyze AES-based hash functions. The SuperMixColumns has been first introduced by Schläffer in [14] and reused in [4]. We refer to those articles for further details as well.

3 Attack on the 5-Round ECHO-256 Hash Function

In this section, we use a sparse truncated differential path and the properties of SuperMixColumns to get a collision attack on 5 rounds of the ECHO-256 hash function. The resulting complexity is 2^{112} with memory requirements of $2^{85.3}$. We first describe the truncated differential path (a truncated differential path only considers whether a byte of the state is active or not) and show how to find conforming input pairs. Due to the sparse truncated differential path, we are able to apply a rebound attack with multiple inbound phases to ECHO. Since at most one fourth of each ECHO state is active, we have enough freedom for two inbound phases and are also able to fully control the chaining input of the hash function.

3.1 The Truncated Differential Path

In the attack, we use two message blocks where the first block does not contain differences. For the second message block, we use the truncated differential path given in Figure 2. We use colors (red, yellow, green, blue, cyan) to describe different phases of the attack and to denote their resulting solutions. Active bytes are denoted by black color, and active AES states contain at least one active byte. Hence, the sequence of active AES states for each round of ECHO is as follows:

$$5 \xrightarrow{r_1} 16 \xrightarrow{r_2} 4 \xrightarrow{r_3} 1 \xrightarrow{r_4} 4 \xrightarrow{r_5} 16.$$

Note that in this path, we keep the number of active bytes low, except for the beginning and end. Therefore, we have enough freedom to find many solutions. We do not allow differences in the chaining input (blue) and in the padding (cyan). The last 16 bytes of the padding contain the message length and the two bytes above contain size of the hash function output. Note that the AES states containing the chaining values (blue) and padding (cyan) do not get mixed with other AES states until the first BigMixColumns transformation. Since the lower half of the state (row 2 and 3) is truncated to compute the final hash value, we force all differences to be in the lower half of the message: the feed-forward will then preserve that property.

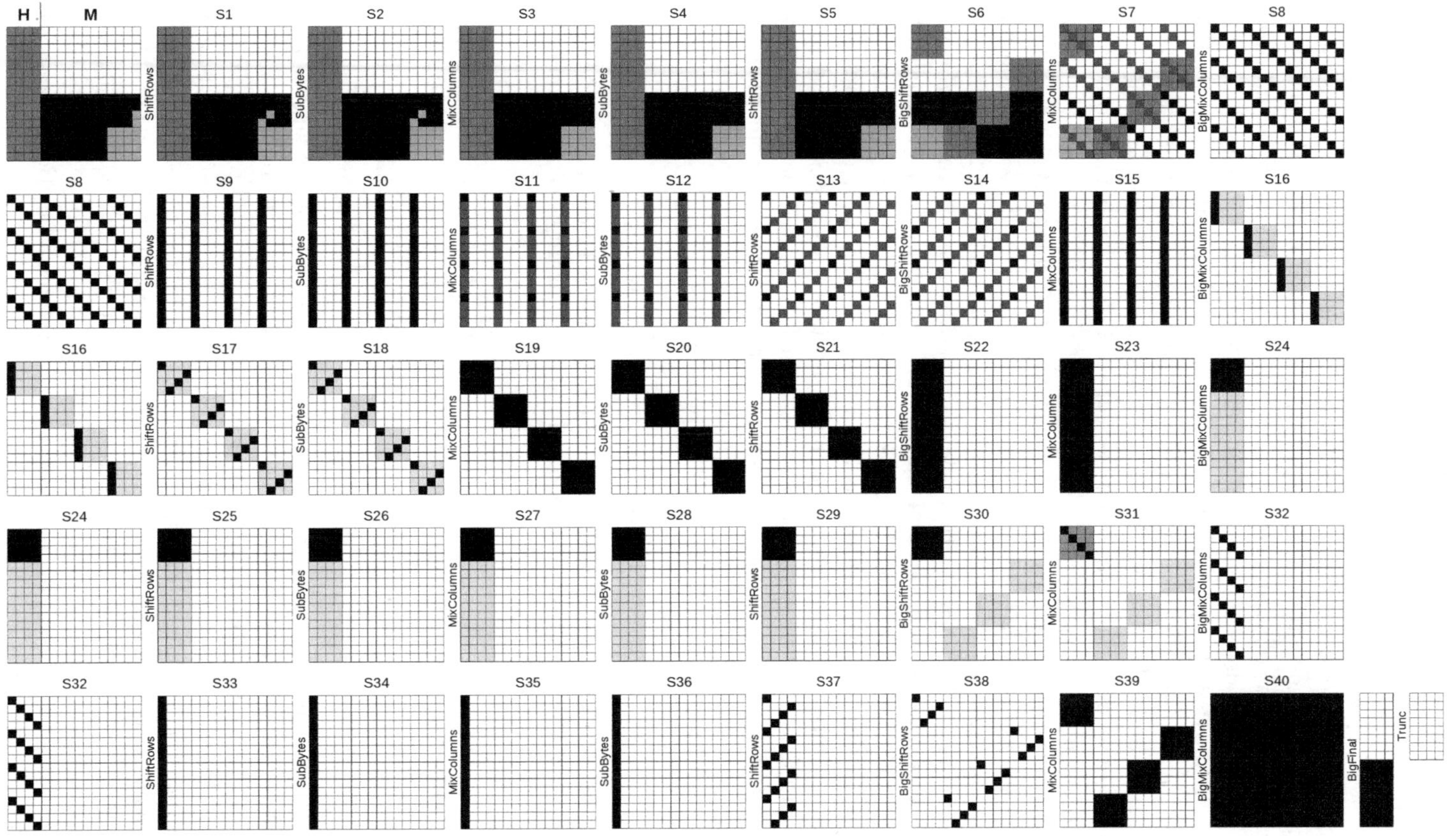

Fig. 2. The truncated differential path to get a collision for 5 rounds of ECHO-256. Black bytes are active, blue and cyan bytes are determined by the chaining input and padding, red bytes are values computed in the red inbound phase, yellow bytes in the yellow inbound phase and green bytes in the outbound phase.

3.2 Colliding Subspace Differences

In the following, we show that the resulting output differences after 5 rounds lie in a vector space of reduced dimension. This can be used to construct a distinguisher for 5 rounds of the ECHO-256 hash function. However, due to the low dimension of the output vector space, we can even extend this subspace distinguisher to get a collision attack on 5 rounds of the ECHO-256 hash function.

First, we need to determine the dimension of the vector space at the output of the hash function. In general, the dimension of the output vector space is defined by the number of active bytes prior to the linear transformations in the last round (16 active bytes after the last SubBytes), combined with the number of active bytes at the input due to the feed-forward (0 active bytes in our case). This would results in a vector space dimension of $(16+0) \times 8 = 128$. However, a weakness in the combined transformations SuperMixColumns, BigFinal and the output truncation reduces the vector space to a dimension of 64 at the output of the hash function for the truncated differential path in Figure 2.

We can move the BigFinal function prior to SuperMixColumns, since BigFinal is a linear transformation and the same linear transformation $\mathbf{M_{SMC}}$ is applied to all columns in SuperMixColumns. Then, we get 4 active bytes at the same position in each AES state of the 4 resulting column-slices. To each active column-slice C_{16}, we first apply the SuperMixColumns multiplication with $\mathbf{M_{SMC}}$ and then, a matrix multiplication using $\mathbf{M_{trunc}} = [I_8 \mid 0_8]$ which truncates the lower 8 rows. Since only 4 bytes are active in C_{16}, these transformations can be combined into a transformation using a reduced 4×8 matrix $\mathbf{M_{comb}}$ applied to the reduced input C_4, which contains only the 4 active bytes of C_{16}:

$$\mathbf{M_{trunc}} \cdot \mathbf{M_{SMC}} \cdot C_{16} = \mathbf{M_{comb}} \cdot C_4,$$

The multiplication with zero differences of C_{16} removes 12 columns of $\mathbf{M_{SMC}}$ while the truncation removes 8 rows of $\mathbf{M_{SMC}}$. For example, considering the first active column-slice leads to:

$$\mathbf{M_{trunc}} \cdot \mathbf{M_{SMC}} \cdot \begin{bmatrix} a\,0\,0\,0\,b\,0\,0\,0\,c\,0\,0\,0\,d\,0\,0\,0 \end{bmatrix}^{\mathrm{T}} = \underbrace{\begin{bmatrix} 4&6&2&2&6&5&3&3 \\ 2&3&1&1&4&6&2&2 \\ 2&3&1&1&2&3&1&1 \\ 6&5&3&3&2&3&1&1 \end{bmatrix}^{\mathrm{T}}}_{\mathbf{M_{comb}}} \cdot \begin{bmatrix} a\,b\,c\,d \end{bmatrix}^{\mathrm{T}}$$

Analyzing the resulting matrix $\mathbf{M_{comb}}$ for all four active column-slices shows that in each case, the rank of $\mathbf{M_{comb}}$ is two, and not four. This reduces the dimension of the vector space in each active column-slice from 32 to 16. Since we have four active columns, the total dimension of the vector space at the output of the hash function is 64. Furthermore, column $i \in \{0,1,2,3\}$ of the output hash value depends only on columns $4i$ of state S_{38}. It follows that the output difference in the first column $i=0$ of the output hash value depends only on the four active differences in columns 0, 4, 8 and 12 of state S_{38}, which we denote by a, b, c and d. To get a collision in the first column of the hash function output, we get the following linear system of equations:

$$\mathbf{M_{comb}} \cdot \begin{bmatrix} a\, b\, c\, d \end{bmatrix}^{\mathrm{T}} = \begin{bmatrix} 0\,0\,0\,0\,0\,0\,0\,0 \end{bmatrix}^{\mathrm{T}}.$$

Since we cannot control the differences a, b, c and d in the following attack, we need to find a solution for this system of equations by brute-force. However, the brute-force complexity is less than expected due to the reduced rank of the given matrix. Since the rank is two, 2^{16} solutions exist and a random difference results in a collision with a probability of 2^{-16} instead of 2^{-32} for the first output column. Since the rank of all four output column matrices is two, we get a collision at the output of the hash function with a probability of $2^{-16\times 4} = 2^{-64}$ for the given truncated differential path.

3.3 High-Level Outline of the Attack

To find input pairs according to the truncated differential path given in Figure 2, we use a rebound attack [9] with multiple inbound phases [6, 8]. The main advantage of multiple inbound phases is that we can first find pairs for each inbound phase independently and then, connect (or merge) the results. Furthermore, we also use multiple outbound phases and separate the merging process into three different parts which can be solved mostly independently:

1. **First Inbound between S_{16} and S_{24}:** find 2^{96} partial pairs (yellow and black bytes) with a complexity of 2^{96} in time and 2^{64} memory.
2. **First Outbound between S_{24} and S_{31}:** filter the previous solutions to get 1 partial pair (green, yellow and black bytes) with a complexity of 2^{96} in time and 2^{64} memory.
3. **Second Inbound between S_7 and S_{14}:** find 2^{32} partial pairs (red and black) for each of the first three BigColumns and 2^{64} partial pairs for the last BigColumn of state S_7 with a total complexity of 2^{64} in time and memory.
4. **First Part in Merging the Inbound Phases:** combine the 2^{160} solutions of the previous phases according to the 128-bit SuperMixColumns condition given in [4]. We get 2^{32} partial pairs (black, red, yellow and green bytes between state S_7 and S_{31}) with complexity 2^{96} in time and 2^{64} memory.
5. **Merge Chaining Input:** repeat from Step 1 for 2^{16} times to get 2^{48} solutions for the previous phases. Compute 2^{112} chaining values (blue) using 2^{112} random first message blocks. Merge these solutions according to the overlapping 20 bytes (red with blue/cyan) in state S_7 to get $2^{48} \times 2^{112} \times 2^{-160} = 1$ partial pair with complexity 2^{112} in time and 2^{48} memory.
6. **Second Part in Merging the Inbound Phases:** find one partial solution for the first two columns of state S_7 according to the 128-bit condition at SuperMixColumns between S_{14} and S_{16} with complexity 2^{64} in time and memory.
7. **Third Part in Merging the Inbound Phases:** find one solution for all remaining bytes (last two columns of state S_7) by fulfilling the resulting 192-bit condition using a generalized birthday attack with 4 lists. The complexity is 2^{64} in time and memory to find one solution, and $2^{85.3}$ in time and memory to find 2^{64} solutions [16].

8. **Second Outbound Phase to Get Collisions:** in a final outbound phase, the resulting differences at the output of the hash function collide with a probability of 2^{-64} and we get one collision among the 2^{64} solutions of the previous step.

The total time complexity of the attack is 2^{112} and determined by Step 5; the memory complexity is $2^{85.3}$ and determined by Step 7.

3.4 Details of the Attack

In this section, we describe the each phase of the collision attack on 5 rounds of ECHO-256 in detail. Note that some phases are also reused in the attacks on the compression function of Section 4.

First Inbound between S_{16} and S_{24}. We first search for internal state pairs conforming to the truncated differential path in round 3 (yellow and black bytes). We start the attack by choosing differences for the active bytes in state S_{16} such that the truncated differential path of SuperMixColumns between state S_{14} and S_{16} is fulfilled (Section 2.1). We compute this difference forward to state S_{17} through the linear layers.

We continue with randomly chosen differences of state S_{24} and compute backwards to state S_{20}, the output of the SuperSBoxes. Since we have 64 active S-boxes in this state, the probability of a differential is about $2^{-1 \times 64}$. Hence, we need 2^{64} starting differences but get 2^{64} solutions for the inbound phase in round 3 (see [9]). We determine the right pairs for each of the 16 SuperSBox between state S_{17} and S_{20} independently. Using the Differential Distribution Table of the SuperSBoxes, we can find one right pair with average complexity one. In total, we compute 2^{96} solutions for this inbound phase with time complexity 2^{96} and memory complexity of at most 2^{64}. For each of these pairs, differences and values of all yellow and black bytes in round 3 are determined.

Second Outbound between S_{24} and S_{31}. In the outbound phase, we ensure the propagation in round 4 of the truncated differential path by propagating the right pairs of the previous inbound phase forwards to state S_{31}. With a probability of 2^{-96}, we get four active bytes after MixColumns in state S_{31} (green) conforming to the truncated path. Hence, among the 2^{96} right pairs of the inbound phase between S_{16} and S_{24} we expect to find one such right pair.

The total complexity to find this partial pair between S_{16} and S_{31} is then 2^{96}. Note that for this pair, the values and differences of the yellow, green and black bytes between states S_{16} and S_{31} can be determined. Furthermore, note that for any choice of the remaining bytes, the truncated differential path between state S_{31} and state S_{40} is fulfilled.

Second Inbound between S_7 and S_{14}. Here, we search for many pairs of internal states conforming to the truncated differential path between states S_7 and S_{14}. Note that we can independently search for pairs of each BigColumn of state S_7, since the four BigColumns stay independent until they are mixed by the following BigMixColumns transformation between states S_{15} and S_{16}. For each BigColumn, four SuperSBoxes are active and we need at least 2^{16} starting differentials for each one to find the first right pair.

The difference in S_{14} is already fixed due to the yellow inbound phase but we can still choose at least 2^{32} differences for each active AES state in S_7. Using the rebound technique, we can find one pair on average for each starting difference in the inbound phase. Then, we independently iterate through all 2^{32} starting differences for the first, second and third column and through all 2^{64} starting differences for the fourth column of state S_7. We get 2^{32} right pairs for each of the first three columns and 2^{64} pairs for the fourth column. The complexity to find all these pairs is 2^{64} in time and memory.

For each resulting right pair, the values and differences of the red and black bytes between states S_7 and S_{14} can be computed. Furthermore, the truncated differential path in backward direction, except for two cyan bytes in the first states, is fulfilled. In the next phase, we partially merge the right pairs of the yellow and red inbound phase. But first, we recall the conditions for this merge.

First Part in Merging the Inbound Phases. For each pair of the previous two phases, the values of the red, yellow and black bytes of state S_{14} and S_{16} are fixed. These two states are separated by the linear SuperMixColumns transformation: taking the first column-slice as an example, we get

$$\mathbf{M_{SMC}} \cdot [A_0\ x_0\ x_1\ x_2\ A_1\ x_3\ x_4\ x_5\ A_2\ x_6\ x_7\ x_8\ A_3\ x_9\ x_{10}\ x_{11}]^{\mathrm{T}}$$
$$= [B_0\ B_1\ B_2\ B_3\ y_0\ y_1\ y_2\ y_3\ y_4\ y_5\ y_6\ y_7\ y_8\ y_9\ y_{10}\ y_{11}]^{\mathrm{T}},$$

where $\mathbf{M_{SMC}}$ is the SuperMixColumns transformation matrix, A_i the input bytes determined by the red inbound phase and B_i the output bytes determined by the yellow inbound phase. All bytes x_i and y_i are free to choose. As shown by Jean and Fouque [4], we only get a solution with probability 2^{-8} for each column-slice due to the low rank of the $\mathbf{M_{SMC}}$ matrix. In [4] (Appendix A), the 8-bit condition for that particular column-slice that ensures the system to have solutions has been derived and is given as follows:

$$2 \cdot A_0 + 3 \cdot A_1 + A_2 + A_3 = 14 \cdot B_0 + 11 \cdot B_1 + 13 \cdot B_2 + 9 \cdot B_3. \qquad (1)$$

Similar 8-bit conditions exist for all 16 column-slices. In total, each right pair of the two (independent) inbound phases results in a 128-bit condition on the whole SuperMixColumns transformation between states S_{14} and S_{16}.

Remember that we have constructed one pair for the yellow inbound phase and in total, $2^{32} \times 2^{32} \times 2^{32} \times 2^{64} = 2^{160}$ pairs for the red inbound phase. Among these 2^{160} pairs, we expect to find 2^{32} right pairs which also satisfy the 128-bit condition of the SuperMixColumns between states S_{14} and S_{16}. In the following, we show how to find all these 2^{32} pairs with a complexity of 2^{96}.

First, we combine the $2^{32} \times 2^{32} = 2^{64}$ pairs determined by the two first BigColumns of state S_7 in a list L_1 and the $2^{32} \times 2^{64} = 2^{96}$ pairs determined by the last two BigColumns of state S_7 in a list L_2. Note that the pairs in these two lists are independent. Then, we separate Equation (1) into terms determined by L_1 and terms determined by L_2:

$$2 \cdot A_0 + 3 \cdot A_1 = A_2 + A_3 + 14 \cdot B_0 + 11 \cdot B_1 + 13 \cdot B_2 + 9 \cdot B_3. \quad (2)$$

We apply the left-hand side to the elements of L_1 and the right-hand side to elements of L_2 and sort L_1 according to the bytes to be matched.

Then, we can simply merge (join) these lists to find those pairs which satisfy the 128-bit condition imposed by the SuperMixColumns and store these results in list $L_{12} = L_1 \bowtie_{128} L_2$. This way, we get $2^{64} \times 2^{96} \times 2^{-128} = 2^{32}$ right pairs with a total complexity of 2^{96}. We note that the memory requirements can be reduced to 2^{64} if we do not store the elements of L_2 but compute them online. The resulting 2^{32} solutions are partial right pairs for the black, red, yellow and green bytes between state S_7 and S_{31}.

Merge Chaining Input. Next, we need to merge the 2^{32} results of the previous phases with the chaining input (blue) and the bytes fixed by the padding (cyan). The chaining input and padding overlap with the red inbound phase in state S_7 on $5 \times 4 = 20$ bytes. This results in a 160-bit condition on the overlapping blue/cyan/red bytes. To find a pair verifying this condition, we first generate 2^{112} random first message blocks, compute the blue bytes of state S_7 and store the results in a list L_3.

Additionally, we repeat 2^{16} times from the yellow inbound phase but with other starting points[1] in state S_{24}. This way, we get $2^{16} \times 2^{32} = 2^{48}$ right pairs for the combined yellow and red inbound phases, which also satisfy the 128-bit condition of SuperMixColumns between states S_{14} and S_{16}. The complexity is $2^{16} \times 2^{96} = 2^{112}$. We store the resulting 2^{48} pairs in list L_{12}.

Next, we merge the lists according to the overlapping 160-bits ($L_{12} \bowtie_{160} L_3$) and get $2^{48} \times 2^{112} \times 2^{-160} = 1$ right pair. If we compute the 2^{112} message blocks of list L_3 online, the time complexity of this merging step is 2^{112} with memory requirements of 2^{48}. For the resulting pair, all differences between states S_4 and S_{33} and all colored byte values (blue, cyan, red, yellow, green and black) between states S_0 and S_{31} can be determined.

Second Part in Merging Inbound Phases. To completely merge the two inbound phases, we need to find according values for the white bytes. We use Figure 3 to illustrate the second and third part of the merge inbound phase. In this figure, we only consider values and therefore, do not show active bytes (black). Furthermore, all brown and cyan bytes have already been chosen in one of the previous steps. In the second part of the merge inbound phase, we only choose values for the gray and light-gray bytes. All other colored bytes show steps of the following merging phase.

We first choose random values for all remaining bytes of the two first columns in state S_7 (gray and light-gray) and independently compute the columns forward

[1] Until now, we have chosen only 2^{96} out of 2^{128} differences for this state.

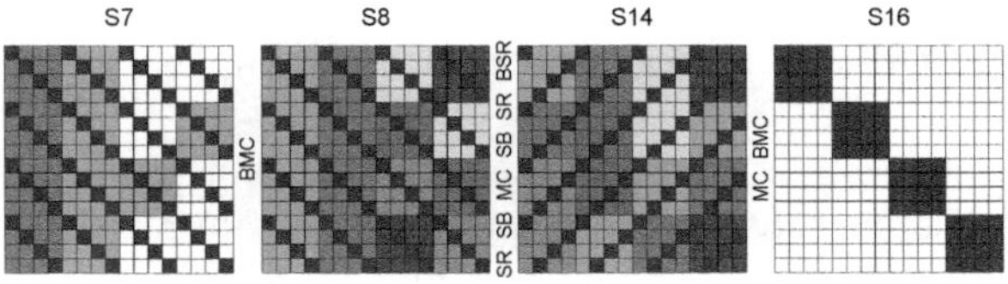

Fig. 3. States used to merge the two inbound phases with the chaining values. The merge inbound phase consists of three parts. Brown bytes show values already determined (first part) and gray values are chosen at random (second part). Green, blue, yellow and red bytes show independent values used in the generalized birthday attack (third part) and cyan bytes represent values with the target conditions.

to state S_{14}. Note that we need to try $2^{2\times 8+1}$ values for AES state $S_7[2,1]$ to also match the 2-byte (cyan) and 1-bit padding at the input in AES state $S_0[2,3]$. Then, all gray, light-gray, cyan and brown bytes have already been determined either by an inbound phase, chaining value, padding or just by choosing random values for the remaining free bytes of the two first columns of S_7. However, all white, red, green, yellow and blue bytes are still free to choose.

By considering the linear SuperMixColumns transformation, we observe that in each column-slice, 14 out of 32 input/output bytes are already fixed and 2 bytes are still free to choose. Hence, we expect to get 2^{16} solutions for this linear system of equations. Unfortunately, also for the given position of already determined 14 bytes, the linear system of equations does not have a full rank. Again, we can determine the resulting system using the matrix $\mathbf{M_{SMC}}$ of SuperMixColumns. As an example, for the first column-slice, the system is given as follows:

$$\mathbf{M_{SMC}} \cdot [A_0\ L_0\ L_1\ L_2\ A_1\ L'_0\ L'_1\ L'_2\ A_2\ x_6\ x_7\ x_8\ A_3\ x_9\ x_{10}\ x_{11}]^{\mathrm{T}}$$
$$= [B_0\ B_1\ B_2\ B_3\ y_0\ y_1\ y_2\ y_3\ y_4\ y_5\ y_6\ y_7\ y_8\ y_9\ y_{10}\ y_{11}]^{\mathrm{T}}.$$

The free variables in this system are $x_6, \ldots, x_{11}$ (green). The values A_0, A_1, A_2, A_3, B_0, B_1, B_2, B_3 (brown) have been determined by the first or second inbound phase and the values L_0, L_1, L_2 (light-gray) and L'_0, L'_1, L'_2 (gray) are determined by the choice of arbitrary values in state S_7. We proceed as before and determine the linear system of equations which needs to have a solution:

$$\begin{bmatrix} 3&1&1&3&1&1 \\ 2&3&1&2&3&1 \\ 1&2&3&1&2&3 \\ 1&1&2&1&1&2 \end{bmatrix} \cdot \begin{bmatrix} x_6\ x_7\ x_8\ x_9\ x_{10}\ x_{11} \end{bmatrix}^{\mathrm{T}} = \begin{bmatrix} c_0\ c_1\ c_2\ c_3 \end{bmatrix}^{\mathrm{T}}. \qquad (3)$$

The resulting linear 8-bit equation to get a solution for this system can be separated into terms depending on values of L_i and on L'_i, and we get $f_1(L_i) + f_2(L'_i) + f_3(a_i, b_i) = 0$, where f_1, f_2 and f_3 are linear functions. For all other 16 column-slices and fixed positions of gray bytes, we get matrices of rank three as well. In total, we get 16 8-bit conditions and the probability to find a solution for a given choice of gray and light-gray values in states S_{14} and S_{16} is 2^{-128}.

However, we can find a solution to these linear equations using the birthday effect and a meet-in-the-middle attack with a complexity of 2^{64} in time and memory.

We start by choosing 2^{64} values for each of the first (gray) and second (light-gray) BigColumns in state S_7. We compute these values independently forward to state S_{14} and store them in two lists L and L'. We also separate all equations of the 128-bit condition into parts depending only on values of L and L'. We apply the resulting functions f_1, f_2, f_3 to the elements of lists L_i and L'_i, and merge two lists $L \bowtie_{128} L'$ using the birthday effect.

Third Part in Merging Inbound Phases. We continue with a generalized birthday match to find values for all remaining bytes of the state (blue, red, green, yellow, cyan and white of Figure 3). For each column in state S_{14}, we independently choose 2^{64} values for the green, blue, yellow and red columns, and compute them independently backward to S_8. We need to match the values of the cyan bytes of state S_7, which results in a condition on 24 bytes or 192 bits. Since we have four independent lists with 2^{64} values in state S_8, we can use the generalized birthday attack [16] to find one solution with a complexity of $2^{192/3} = 2^{64}$ in time and memory.

In more detail, we need to match values after the BigMixColumns transformation in the backward direction. Hence, we first multiply each byte of the four independent lists by the four multipliers of the InvMixColumns transformation. Then, we get 24 equations containing only XOR conditions on bytes between the target value and elements of the four independent lists, which can be solved using a generalized birthday attack.

To improve the average complexity of this generalized birthday attack, we can start with larger lists for the green, blue, yellow and red columns in state S_{14}. Since we need to match a 192-bit condition, we can get $2^{3 \cdot x} \times 2^{-192} = 2^x$ solutions with a time and memory complexity of $\max\{2^{64}, 2^x\}$ (see [16] for more details). Note that we can even find solutions with an average complexity of 1 using lists of size 2^{96}. Each solutions of the generalized birthday match results in a valid pair conforming to the whole 5-round truncated differential path.

Second Outbound Phase to Get Collisions. For the collision attack on 5 rounds, we start the generalized birthday attack of the previous phase with lists of size $2^{85.3}$. This results in $2^{3 \cdot 85.3} \times 2^{-192} = 2^{64}$ solutions with a time and memory complexity of $2^{85.3}$, or with an average complexity of $2^{21.3}$ per solution. These solutions are propagated outwards in a second, independent outbound phase. Since the differences at the output collide with a probability of 2^{-64}, we expect to find one pair which collides at the output of the hash function. The time complexity is determined by merging the chaining input and the memory requirements by the generalized birthday attack. To summarize, the complexity to find a collision for 5 rounds of the ECHO-256 hash function is given by about 2^{112} compression function evaluations with memory requirements of $2^{85.3}$.

4 Distinguisher on the 7-Round ECHO-256 Compression Function

In this section, we detail our distinguisher on 7 rounds in the known-salt model. First, we show how to obtain partial solutions that verify the path from the state S_6 to S_{23} with an average complexity of 2^{64} in time, as we obtain 2^{64} solutions with a cost of 2^{128}. These partial solutions determine also the values of the blue bytes (in Figure 4). Next, we show how to do the same for the yellow part of the path from S_{30} to S_{47}. Finally, we explain how to merge these partial solutions for finding one that verifies the whole path.

4.1 Finding Pairs between S_6 and S_{23}

We explain here how to find 2^{64} solutions for the blue part with a cost of 2^{128} in time and 2^{64} in memory. This is done with a stop-in-the-middle algorithm similar to the one presented in [11] for improving the time complexity of the ECHO-256 distinguisher. This algorithm has to be adapted to this particular situation, where all the active states belong to the same BigColumn.

We start by fixing the difference in S_8 to a chosen value, so that the transition between S_6 and S_8 is verified. We fix the difference in the active diagonals of the two AES-states $S_{23}[0,0]$ and $S_{23}[3,1]$ to a chosen value.

From state S_8 to S_{13}, we have four different SuperSBox groups involved in the active part. From states S_{16} to S_{22}, we have 4×4 SuperSBox groups involved (4 per active AES state). Those 16 groups, as well as the 4 previous ones, are completely independent from S_{16} to S_{22} (respectively from S_8 to S_{13}). From the known difference in S_8, we build four lists of values and differences in S_{13}: each list corresponds to one of the four SuperSBox groups. Each list is of size 2^{32} because once we know the input difference, we try all the possible 2^{32} possible values and then we can compute the values and differences in S_{13} (as we said, the four groups are independent in this part of the path). In the sequel, those lists are denoted L_A^0, L_A^1, L_A^2 and L_A^3.

There are 64 bits of differences not yet fixed in S_{23}. Each active diagonal only affects the AES state where it is in, so we can independently consider 2^{32} possible differences for one diagonal and 2^{32} differences for the other. We can now build the 16 lists corresponding to the 16 SuperSBox groups as we did before, but considering that: the 8 lists corresponding to 8 groups of the two AES states $S_{16}[0,0]$ and $S_{16}[3,0]$, as they have their differences in S_{22} already fixed, have a size of 2^{32} (corresponding to the possible values for each group). These are the lists $L_{0,0}^i$ and $L_{3,0}^i$, with $i \in [0,3]$ that represents the ith diagonal of the state. But the lists $L_{1,0}^i, L_{2,0}^i$, with $i \in [0,3]$, as they do not have yet the difference fixed, have a size of 2^{32+32} each, as we can consider the 2^{32} possible differences for each not fixed diagonal independently. Next, we go through the 2^{64} possible differences of the two first diagonals (diagonals 0 and 1) of the active AES state in S_{15}. For each one of these 2^{64} possible differences:

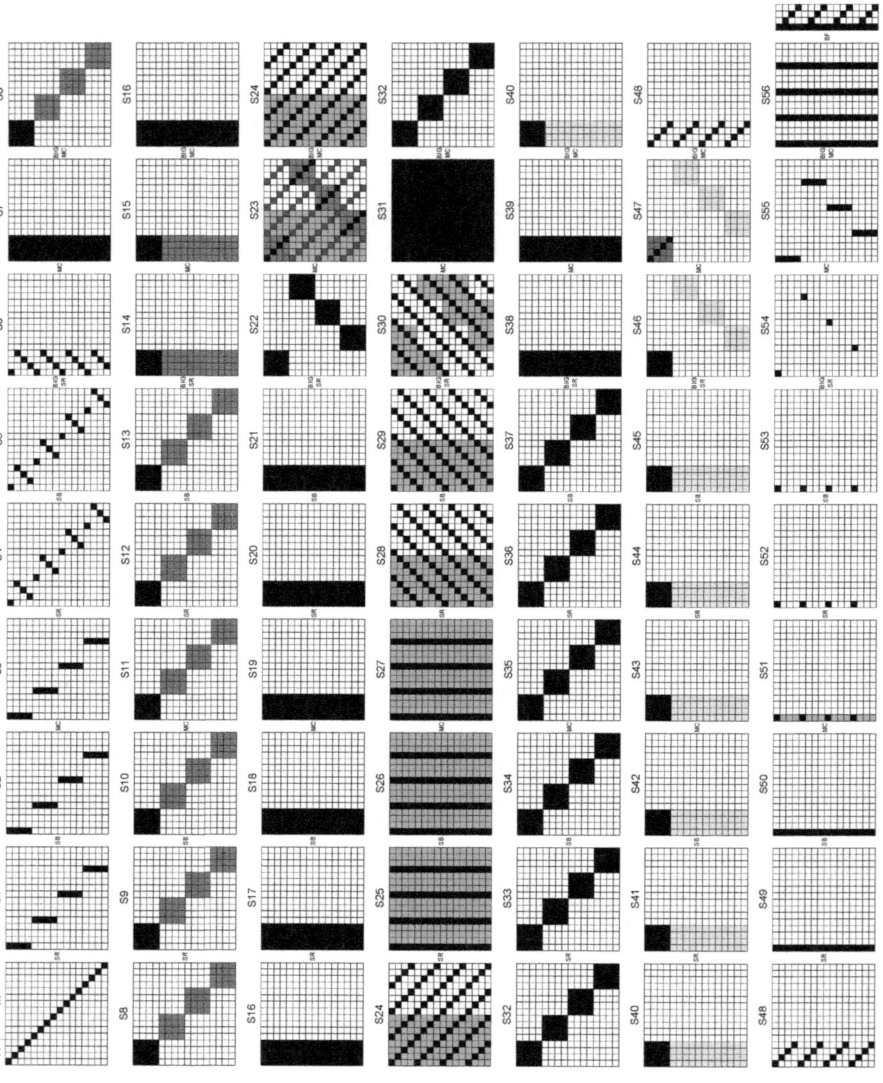

Fig. 4. Differential path for the seven-round distinguisher

– The associated differences in the two same diagonals in the four active AES states of S_{16} can be computed. Consequently, we can check in the previously computed ordered lists $L^i_{j,0}$ with $j \in [0,3]$ and $i \in [0,1]$ where we find this difference[2]. For $j \in \{0,3\}$, on average, we obtain one match on each one of the lists $L^0_{0,0}$, $L^1_{0,0}$, $L^0_{3,0}$ and $L^1_{3,0}$. For $j \in \{1,2\}$, we obtain 2^{32} matches, one for each of the 2^{32} possible differences in the associated diagonals in S_{23}. That is 2^{32} matches for $L^0_{1,0}$ and $L^1_{1,0}$, where a pair of values formed

[2] i is either 0 or 1 because we are just considering the two first diagonals.

by one element of each list is only valid if they were generated from the same difference in S_{23}. Consequently, we can construct the list $L_{1,0}^{0,1}$ of size 2^{32} where we store the values and differences of those two diagonals in the AES state $S_{16}[1,0]$ as well as the difference in S_{23} from which they were generated. Repeating the process for $L_{2,0}^{0}$ and $L_{2,0}^{1}$, we construct the list $L_{2,0}^{0,1}$ of size 2^{32}. We can merge the lists $L_{1,0}^{0,1}$, $L_{2,0}^{0,1}$ and the four fixed values for differences and values obtained from the matches in the lists $L_{0,0}^{0}$, $L_{0,0}^{1}$, $L_{3,0}^{0}$ and $L_{3,0}^{1}$, corresponding to the AES states $S_{16}[0,0]$ and $S_{16}[3,0]$. This generates the list $L^{0,1}$ of size 2^{64}. Each element of this list contains the values and differences of the two diagonals 0 and 1 of the four active AES states in S_{16}. As we have all the values for the two first diagonals in the four AES states, for each one of these elements, we compute the values in the two first diagonals of the active state in S_{15} by applying the inverse of BigMixColumns. We order them according to these values.

- Next, we go through the 2^{64} possible differences of the two next diagonals (diagonals 2 and 3) of the active AES state in S_{15}. For each one of these 2^{64} possible differences:
  - All the differences in the AES state $S_{13}[0,0]$ are determined. We check in the lists L_A^0, L_A^1, L_A^2 and L_A^3 if we find a match for the differences. We expect to find one in each list and this determines the values for the whole state $S_{15}[0,0]$ (as the elements in these lists are formed by differences and values). This means that the value of the active AES state in S_{15} is also completely determined. This way, we can check in the previously generated list $L^{0,1}$ if the correct value for the two diagonals 0 and 1 appears. We expect to find it once.
  - As we have just found a valid element from $L^{0,1}$, it determines the differences in the AES states $S_{23}[1,0]$ and $S_{23}[2,0]$ that were not fixed yet. Now, we need to check if, for those differences in S_{23}, the corresponding elements in the four lists $L_{1,0}^{i}$, $L_{2,0}^{i}$ for $i \in [2,3]$ that match with the differences fixed in the diagonals 2 and 3 of S_{15}[3], satisfy the values in S_{15} that were also determined by the lists L_A^i. This occurs with probability 2^{-64}.

All in all, the time complexity of this algorithm is $2^{64} \cdot (2^{64} + 2^{64}) = 2^{129}$ with a memory requirement of 2^{64}. The resulting expected number of valid pairs is $2^{64} \cdot 2^{64} \cdot 2^{64} \cdot 2^{-64} \cdot 2^{-64} = 2^{64}$.

4.2 Finding Pairs between S_{30} and S_{47}

In quite the same way as the previous section, we can find solutions for the yellow part with an average cost of 2^{64}. To do so, we take into account the fact that the MixColumns and BigMixColumns transformations commute. So, if we exchange their positions between states S_{39} and S_{40}, we only have one active AES state in S_{39}. We fix the differences in S_{47} and in two AES states, say $S_{32}[0,0]$ and

[3] We expect one match per list.

$S_{32}[1,1]$, and we still have 2^{32} possible differences for each of the two remaining active AES states in S_{32}. Then, the lists L_A^i are generated from the end and contain values and differences from S_{40}. Similarly, the lists $L_{j,j}^i$ contain values and differences from S_{38}. We can apply the same algorithm as before and obtain 2^{64} solutions with a cost of 2^{128} in time and 2^{64} in memory.

4.3 Merging Solutions

In this section, we explain how to get a solution for the whole path. As explained in our Section 4.1, we can find 2^{64} solutions for the blue part, that have the same difference for the active AES states of columns 0 and 1 in S_{23}. We obtain 2^{64} solutions from a fixed value for the differences in S_8 and the AES states $S_{23}[0,0]$ and $S_{23}[3,1]$. Repeating this process for the 2^{32} possible differences in S_8, we obtain in total 2^{96} solutions for the blue part with the same differences in the columns 0 and 1 in S_{23}. The cost of this step is 2^{160} in time and 2^{96} in memory.

The same way, using the algorithm explained in Section 4.2, we can also find 2^{96} solutions for the yellow part, that have the same difference value for the AES active states of columns 0 and 1 in S_{32} (we fix the difference value of this two columns in S_{32}, and we try all the 2^{32} possible values for the difference in S_{47}). The cost of this step is also 2^{160} in time and 2^{96} in memory.

Now, from the partial solutions obtained in the previous steps, we want to find a solution that verifies the whole differential path. For this, we want to merge the solutions from S_{23} with the solutions from S_{32}. We know that the differences of the columns 0,1 of S_{24} and S_{31} are fixed. Hence, from S_{24} to S_{31}, there are four AES states for which we know the input difference and the output difference, as they are fixed[4]. We can then apply a variant of the SuperSBox [3, 6] technique in these four AES states: it fixes the possible values for the active diagonals of those states.

The differences in the other four AES states in S_{24} that are fixed are associated to other differences that are not fixed[5]. There are 2^{64} possible differences, each one associated to 2^{32} solutions for S_{32}-S_{47} given by the solutions that we found in the second step. For each one of these 2^{64} possible differences, one possible value is associated by the SuperSBox. When computing backwards these values to state S_{24}, as we have also the values for the other four AES states of the columns 0 and 1 that are also fixed (in the third step), we can compute the values for these two columns in S_{23}, and we need 32×2 bit conditions to be verified on the values. So for each one of the 2^{64} possible differences in S_{31}, we obtain $2^{96-64} = 2^{32}$ that verify the conditions on S_{23}. In total, we have $2^{64+32} = 2^{96}$ possible partial matches.

For each of the 2^{64} possible differences in S_{31}, its associated 2^{32} possible partial matches also need to verify the 128-bit condition in S_{30}-S_{32} at the SuperMixColumns layer [4] and the remaining 2×32 bit conditions on the values

[4] $S_{24}[0,0]$, $S_{24}[0,1]$, $S_{24}[1,1]$, $S_{24}[3,0]$ correspond to $S_{31}[0,0]$, $S_{31}[0,1]$, $S_{31}[1,0]$, $S_{31}[3,1]$, respectively.

[5] $S_{24}[1,0]$, $S_{24}[2,0]$, $S_{24}[2,1]$, $S_{24}[3,1]$ correspond to $S_{31}[1,3]$, $S_{31}[2,2]$, $S_{31}[2,3]$, $S_{31}[3,2]$.

of S_{23}. Since for each of the 2^{64} differences we have 2^{32} possible associated values in S_{32}, the probability of finding a good pair is $2^{96-128-64+32} = 2^{-64}$.

If we repeat this merging procedure 2^{64} times, namely for 2^{32} differences in the columns 0 and 1 of S_{23} and for 2^{32} differences in the columns 0 and 1 of S_{32}, we should find a solution. We then repeat the procedure for the cross product of the 2^{32} solutions for each side. As we do not want to compute them each time that we use them, as it would increase the time complexity, we can just store the $2^{64+32+32} = 2^{128}$ solutions for the first part and use the corresponding ones when needed, while the second part is computed in sequence. The complexity would be: $2^{192} + 2^{192} + 2^{96+64}$ in time and 2^{128} in memory. So far, we have found a partial solution for the differential part for rounds from S_6 to S_{48}. We still have the passive bytes to determine and the condition to pass from S_{50} to S_{51} to verify. This can be done exactly as in the second and third part of the merge inbound phase of Section 3.4 with no additional cost.

Moreover, since we can find x solutions with complexity $\max\{x, 2^{96}\}$ in time and 2^{96} memory for the (independent) merge inbound phase, we can get $x < 2^{193}$ solutions with time complexity $2^{193} + \max\{x, 2^{96}\} \sim 2^{193}$ and 2^{128} memory. We need only 2^{96} of these solutions to pass the probabilistic propagation in the last round from S_{50} to S_{51}. Hence, we can find a complete solution for the whole path with a cost of about 2^{193} in time and 2^{128} in memory. Furthermore, with a probability of 2^{-128}, the input and output differences in S_0 and S_{48} collide in the feed-forward and BigFinal transformation. Therefore, we can also generate free-start collisions for 6 rounds of the compression function with a time complexity of $2^{193} + 2^{128} \sim 2^{193}$ and 2^{128} memory.

5 Conclusions

In this work, we have presented new results on the second-round candidate of the SHA-3 competition ECHO-256 that improve considerably the previous published cryptanalysis. Our analysis are based on multi-inbound rebound attacks and are summarized in Table 1. The main results are a 5-round collision of the hash function and a 7-round distinguisher of its compression function. All of our results take into account the condition observed in [4], which is needed to merge the results of multiple inbound phases, and satisfy it. The 7-round distinguisher on the compression function uses the stop-in-the-middle algorithms proposed in [10].

References

1. Benadjila, R., Billet, O., Gilbert, H., Macario-Rat, G., Peyrin, T., Robshaw, M., Seurin, Y.: SHA-3 proposal: ECHO. Submission to NIST (updated) (2009), http://crypto.rd.francetelecom.com/echo/doc/echo_description_1-5.pdf
2. Daemen, J., Rijmen, V.: Understanding Two-Round Differentials in AES. In: De Prisco, R., Yung, M. (eds.) SCN 2006. LNCS, vol. 4116, pp. 78–94. Springer, Heidelberg (2006)

3. Gilbert, H., Peyrin, T.: Super-Sbox Cryptanalysis: Improved Attacks for AES-Like Permutations. In: Hong, S., Iwata, T. (eds.) FSE 2010. LNCS, vol. 6147, pp. 365–383. Springer, Heidelberg (2010)
4. Jean, J., Fouque, P.-A.: Practical Near-Collisions and Collisions on Round-Reduced ECHO-256 Compression Function. In: Joux, A. (ed.) FSE 2011. LNCS, vol. 6733, pp. 107–127. Springer, Heidelberg (2011)
5. Jean, J., Naya-Plasencia, M., Schläffer, M.: Improved Analysis of ECHO-256. Cryptology ePrint Archive, Report 2011/422 (2011), `http://eprint.iacr.org/`
6. Lamberger, M., Mendel, F., Rechberger, C., Rijmen, V., Schläffer, M.: Rebound Distinguishers: Results on the Full Whirlpool Compression Function. In: Matsui, M. (ed.) ASIACRYPT 2009. LNCS, vol. 5912, pp. 126–143. Springer, Heidelberg (2009)
7. Van Le, T., Sparr, R., Wernsdorf, R., Desmedt, Y.G.: Complementation-Like and Cyclic Properties of AES Round Functions. In: Dobbertin, H., Rijmen, V., Sowa, A. (eds.) AES 2005. LNCS, vol. 3373, pp. 128–141. Springer, Heidelberg (2005)
8. Matusiewicz, K., Naya-Plasencia, M., Nikolić, I., Sasaki, Y., Schläffer, M.: Rebound Attack on the Full LANE Compression Function. In: Matsui, M. (ed.) ASIACRYPT 2009. LNCS, vol. 5912, pp. 106–125. Springer, Heidelberg (2009)
9. Mendel, F., Rechberger, C., Schläffer, M., Thomsen, S.S.: The Rebound Attack: Cryptanalysis of Reduced Whirlpool and `Grøstl`. In: Dunkelman, O. (ed.) FSE 2009. LNCS, vol. 5665, pp. 260–276. Springer, Heidelberg (2009)
10. Naya-Plasencia, M.: How to Improve Rebound Attacks. In: Rogaway, P. (ed.) CRYPTO 2011. LNCS, vol. 6841, pp. 188–205. Springer, Heidelberg (2011)
11. Naya-Plasencia, M.: How to Improve Rebound Attacks. Cryptology ePrint Archive, Report 2010/607 (2010) (extended version), `http://eprint.iacr.org/`
12. Peyrin, T.: Improved Differential Attacks for ECHO and Grøstl. In: Rabin, T. (ed.) CRYPTO 2010. LNCS, vol. 6223, pp. 370–392. Springer, Heidelberg (2010)
13. Sasaki, Y., Li, Y., Wang, L., Sakiyama, K., Ohta, K.: Non-Full-Active Super-Sbox Analysis: Applications to ECHO and Grøstl. In: Abe, M. (ed.) ASIACRYPT 2010. LNCS, vol. 6477, pp. 38–55. Springer, Heidelberg (2010)
14. Schläffer, M.: Subspace Distinguisher for 5/8 Rounds of the ECHO-256 Hash Function. In: Biryukov, A., Gong, G., Stinson, D.R. (eds.) SAC 2010. LNCS, vol. 6544, pp. 369–387. Springer, Heidelberg (2011)
15. National Institute of Standards, Technology (NIST): Advanced E.D.F.-G.D.F.ncryption Standard (FIPS PUB 197) (November 2001), `http://www.csrc.nist.gov/publications/fips/fips197/fips-197.pdf`
16. Wagner, D.: A Generalized Birthday Problem. In: Yung, M. (ed.) CRYPTO 2002. LNCS, vol. 2442, pp. 288–303. Springer, Heidelberg (2002)

Provable Chosen-Target-Forced-Midfix Preimage Resistance

Elena Andreeva and Bart Mennink

Dept. Electrical Engineering, ESAT/COSIC and IBBT
Katholieke Universiteit Leuven, Belgium
{elena.andreeva,bart.mennink}@esat.kuleuven.be

Abstract. This paper deals with definitional aspects of the herding attack of Kelsey and Kohno, and investigates the provable security of several hash functions against herding attacks.

Firstly, we define the notion of chosen-target-forced-midfix (CTFM) as a generalization of the classical herding (chosen-target-forced-prefix) attack to the cases where the challenge message is not only a prefix but may appear at any place in the preimage. Additionally, we identify four variants of the CTFM notion in the setting where salts are explicit input parameters to the hash function. Our results show that including salts without weakening the compression function does not add up to the CTFM security of the hash function.

Our second and main technical result is a proof of CTFM security of the classical Merkle-Damgård construction. The proof demonstrates in the ideal model that the herding attack of Kelsey and Kohno is optimal (asymptotically) and no attack with lower complexity exists. Our security analysis applies to a wide class of narrow-pipe Merkle-Damgård based iterative hash functions, including enveloped Merkle-Damgård, Merkle-Damgård with permutation, HAIFA, zipper hash and hash-twice hash functions. To our knowledge, this is the first positive result in this field.

Finally, having excluded salts from the possible tool set for improving narrow-pipe designs' CTFM resistance, we resort to various message modification techniques. Our findings, however, result in the negative and we demonstrate CTFM attacks with complexity of the same order as the Merkle-Damgård herding attack on a broad class of narrow-pipe schemes with specific message modifications.

Keywords: Herding attack; Chosen-target-forced-midfix; Provable security; Merkle-Damgård.

1 Introduction

Hash functions are an important cryptographic primitive finding numerous applications. Most commonly, hash functions are designed from a fixed input length compression function to accommodate messages of arbitrary length. The most common domain extender is the Merkle-Damgård (MD) iteration [8,16], which has long been believed to be a secure design choice due to its collision security reduction. Recently, however, several results cast doubt on its security with

A. Miri and S. Vaudenay (Eds.): SAC 2011, LNCS 7118, pp. 37–54, 2012.

respect to other properties. The MD design was showed to not preserve either second preimage or preimage properties [3]. Moreover, the indifferentiability attack of Coron et al. [7], the multicollision attack of Joux [12] and the herding attack of Kelsey and Kohno [13] exposed various weaknesses of the MD design.

The herding attack of Kelsey and Kohno, also known as the chosen-target-forced-prefix (CTFP) attack, considers an adversary that commits to a hash value y for a message that is not entirely under his control. The adversary then demonstrates abilities to incorporate an unknown challenge prefix as part of the original preimage corresponding to the committed value y. While for a random oracle the complexity of such an attack is $\Theta(2^n)$ compression function calls for y of length n bits, the herding attack on Merkle-Damgård takes about $\sqrt{n}2^{2n/3}$ compression function executions for a preimage message of length $O(n)$ as demonstrated by Kelsey and Kohno [13]. A more precise attack bound was obtained by Blackburn et al. [6].

Several other hash functions have been analyzed with respect to resistance to herding attacks. In [2], Andreeva et al. showed applications of the herding attack to dither hash functions, and in [1] they generalized the herding attack of [13] to several multi-pass domain extenders, such as the zipper hash and the hash twice design. Gauravaram et al. [9,10] concluded insecurity against herding attacks for the MD designs where an XOR tweak is used in the final message block.

While this topic has generated significant interest, many important questions still remain unanswered. All research so far focused on negative results, being generalized herding attacks on hash function designs, but it is not known whether one can launch herding attacks with further improved complexity against the MD design. The task becomes additionally complicated by the lack of formal security definitions for herding to accommodate the objectives of a proof based approach. Apart from wide-pipe designs, no scheme known yet is secure against herding attacks, nor is it clear how to improve the MD design without enlarging its state size. Some of the possible directions are to either use randomization (salts) or to apply certain message modification techniques.

Our Contributions. In this work we address the aforementioned open problems. Firstly, we develop a formal definition for security against herding attacks. Neven et al. first formalize the notion of chosen-target-forced-prefix security (as the random-prefix preimage problem) in [17]. Our new notion of chosen-target-forced-midfix (CTFM) security extends his notion by enabling challenges of not only prefix type but also as midfixes and suffixes. We achieve this by giving the adversary the power to output an "order"-defining mixing function g together with his response, which fixes the challenge message at a selected by the adversary position in the preimage message.

In addition, we investigate the notion of salted CTFM. Depending on when the salt value is generated and who is in control of it, four variants of the salted notion emerge in the setting where randomness (salt) is used. One of the variants serves no practical purposes because it forces an adversary to commit to a hash value for an unknown salt, where the salt is defined as an input parameter to the hash function. Although the other three variants are plausible from a practical perspective, we show that they do not attribute to an improved CTFM resistance. This is true for the case where the salt is added in such a way that the cryptographic strength of the compression function is not compromised on some other level, i.e. collision or preimage resistance.

Our main technical contribution is to exhibit a CTFM security proof for the MD domain extender. While until now the research in this area has been focusing on finding herding attacks against hash function designs, we are the first to provide a security upper bound for a hash function design. In more detail, we upper bound the strength of a CTFM attacker in finding in the ideal model a preimage for the MD design, and show that the herding attack described by Kelsey and Kohno is optimal (asymptotically). Using new proof techniques we prove that at least approximately $2^{2n/3}/L^{1/3}$ compression function queries are needed for a CTFM attack, where n is size of the commitment y and L is the maximal allowed length of the preimage in blocks. To the best of our knowledge, there has not been a positive result of this form before. Due to its generic nature, the new security techniques introduced in this work not only apply to the MD design, but directly carry over to a broad spectrum of domain extenders derived from MD, including strengthened MD, MD with a distinct final transformation and HAIFA [5]. Additionally, the bound implies optimality of the attacks on hash twice and the zipper hash function performed by Andreeva et al. [1].

We explore further the question of whether a simple tweak on the narrow-pipe MD construction would allow us to prove optimal CTFM security. Excluding randomness or salting from the set of available tools, we investigate tweaks that modify the message inputs by simple message modification techniques like the XOR operation. These schemes can be viewed as MD type domain extenders with a more sophisticated padding. Our findings, however, result in the negative and we demonstrate CTFM attacks on a class of schemes of this form. The attack particularly applies also to the MD with checksum design, therewith providing a simple and elegant alternative to the attack by Gauravaram et al. [10].

2 Preliminaries

By $x \xleftarrow{\$} \mathcal{X}$ we denote the uniformly random sampling of an element from a set $\mathcal{X}$. By $y \leftarrow \mathsf{A}(x)$ and $y \xleftarrow{\$} \mathsf{A}(x)$, we denote the assignment to y of the output of a deterministic and randomized algorithm A, respectively, when run on input x. For a function f, by $\mathsf{rng}(f)$ we denote its range. By *Func(n+m,n)*, for $m, n \geq 1$, we denote the set of compression functions $f : \{0,1\}^n \times \{0,1\}^m \to \{0,1\}^n$. As of now, we assume $m = \Theta(n)$.

A hash function $\mathcal{H} : \{0,1\}^* \to \{0,1\}^n$ is a function that maps an arbitrarily long input to a digest of n bits, internally using a compression function $f \in$ *Func(n+m,n)*. In this work we distinguish between a general hash function design $\mathcal{H}$, and the notion of an iterated hash function which is a specific type of hash function that executes the underlying compression function in an "iterated" way. Let $\mathsf{pad} : \{0,1\}^* \to (\{0,1\}^m)^*$ be an injective padding function. Let $\mathsf{iv} \in \{0,1\}^n$ be a fixed initial value. We define the iterated hash function $\mathcal{IH}$ as follows:

$$\begin{aligned} \mathcal{IH}(M) = h_l, \text{ where: } & (M_1, \ldots, M_l) \leftarrow \mathsf{pad}(M); \\ & h_0 \leftarrow \mathsf{iv}; \\ & h_i \leftarrow f(h_{i-1}, M_i) \text{ for } i = 1, \ldots, l. \end{aligned} \quad (1)$$

One may include a special final transformation, but we note that this would not result in any added value against the herding attack. The general iterative principle of $\mathcal{IH}$ is followed by a wide range of existing modes of operations, including the traditional (strengthened) MD design [8,16], enveloped MD (includes final transformation) [4], MD with permutation (includes final transformation) [11], HAIFA [5] and the zipper hash design [15].

3 Chosen-Target-Forced-Midfix Preimage Resistance

An adversary for a hash function is a probabilistic algorithm with oracle access to underlying compression function f. Queries to f are stored in a query history $\mathcal{Q}$. In the remainder, we assume that $\mathcal{Q}$ always contains the queries required for the attack, and we assume that the adversary does not make trivial queries, i.e. queries to which the adversary already knows the answer in advance. In this work we consider information-theoretic adversaries only. This type of adversary has unbounded computational power, and its complexity is measured by the number of queries made to its oracles.

The goal of an attacker in the original herding attack [13] against a hash function $\mathcal{H}$ is to successfully commit to a hash digest without knowing the prefix of the preimage message in advance. In the first phase of the attack, the adversary makes an arbitrary amount of queries to f. Then, he commits to a hash digest y, and receives challenge prefix P. After a second round of compression function calls, the adversary outputs a response R such that $\mathcal{H}(P\|R) = y$. In this form the power of the adversary is limited significantly. In particular, if the hash function is defined so as to process the message blocks in reverse order, the success probability of the adversary is limited to the preimage advantage. We generalize the original attack by introducing the chosen-target-forced-midfix (CTFM) attack. In the CTFM attack, the challenge P does not necessarily need to be a prefix, but can technically occur at any place in the preimage message. The generalized attack mainly differs from the original one in the fact that the adversary not only outputs a bit string R, but also an "order"-defining function g such that $\mathcal{H}(g(P, R)) = y$. We note that the attack is trivial for some choices of g (e.g. if it is defined by the identity function on its second argument). Below we give a concrete specification of g.

Definition 1. *Let $\mathcal{H} : \{0,1\}^* \to \{0,1\}^n$ be a hash function design employing compression function $f \in$ Func(n+m,n). Let p denote the length of the forced* *midfix, and denote by $L \geq 1$ the maximal length of the forged preimage in blocks. Let $\mathcal{A}$ be a chosen-target-forced-midfix (CTFM) finding adversary for this hash function. The advantage of $\mathcal{A}$ is defined as*

$$\mathbf{Adv}_{\mathcal{H}}^{\mathsf{ctfm}}(\mathcal{A}) = \mathbf{Pr}\Big(f \xleftarrow{\$} Func(n{+}m,n),\ (y, st) \leftarrow \mathcal{A}^f,\ P \xleftarrow{\$} \{0,1\}^p,$$
$$(g, R) \leftarrow \mathcal{A}^f(P, st)\ :\ \mathcal{H}^f(g(P,R)) = y \wedge \big|\mathsf{rng}(g)\big| \leq 2^{Lm}\Big).$$

By $\mathbf{Adv}_{\mathcal{H}}^{\mathsf{ctfm}}(q)$ we denote the maximum advantage, taken over all adversaries making q queries to their oracle.

The function g can technically be any function as long as its range is at most 2^{Lm}, but for some choices of g the definition becomes irrelevant. For instance, if the mutual information between P and $g(P,R)$ is 0, the CTFM attack is trivial. More generally, the attack becomes easier if the function g is allowed to split P into parts. However, this type of functions does not correspond to any practically relevant CTFM attacks. Therefore, in the remainder, we restrict g to satisfy that $g(P, R_1 \| R_2) = R_1 \| P \| R_2$, where R_1, R_2 are of arbitrary length.

The chosen-target-forced-prefix attack of Kelsey and Kohno is covered for g restricted to R_1 being the empty string. The variant of the herding attack by Andreeva et al. [1] on the zipper hash function can be seen as a chosen-target-forced-suffix attack, with R_2 being the empty string.

The value p defines the size of the challenge P, and plays an important role in the security results. A smaller value of p allows for higher success probability in guessing P in the first phase of the attack. A larger value of p limits the number of "free" queries of the adversary, the adversary needs to make at least $\lceil p/m \rceil$ compression function queries for incorporating the challenge P, where m is the message block size.

4 Salted-Chosen-Target-Forced-Midfix Preimage Resistance

In this section we discuss the salted variant of CTFM, which we denote by SCTFM. Depending on whether the challenger generates the salt value S or the adversary himself, and at which stage of the game the salt is chosen, four salted variants of CTFM emerge. We view the salt as an explicit input parameter of size $s \geq 1$ to the hash function $\mathcal{H}$, which is not integrated at an internal compression function level, but processed at the higher (iteration) hash function $\mathcal{H}$ level. We define $\mathsf{enc}_i : \{0,1\}^s \times \{0,1\}^n \times \{0,1\}^m \to \{0,1\}^{n+m}$ to take inputs S, chaining value h_{i-1} and message block M_i, where i varies between 1 and L (which is the maximum length of the preimage) to provide a possible function diversification. The function enc_i is a bijection on h_{i-1} and M_i and we denote its inverse function by enc_i^{-1}. More concretely,

$$\mathsf{enc}_i(S, h_{i-1}, M_i) = (h'_{i-1}, M'_i) \wedge \mathsf{enc}_i^{-1}(S, h'_{i-1}, M'_i) = (h_{i-1}, M_i).$$

We can view the functions enc_i as keyed permutations on the chaining value and message block inputs to the compression function, where the key is the salt S.

Our choice of this encoding function is guided by a simple security objective. Let us define f'_i as $f'_i(S, h_{i-1}, M_i) = f(\mathsf{enc}_i(S, h_{i-1}, M_i))$ for $i = 1, \ldots, L$. We choose enc_i to be a bijection on h_{i-1} and M_i to provide the full set of valid input points for the function f. Any deviation from this would weaken the cryptographic strength of f, i.e. by allowing an adversary to easily launch collision attacks on the encoding function as a way to circumvent collision computations on f. If enc_i is not a bijection on its variable inputs (notice that once chosen the salt is fixed), then the function f would be working only with a restricted set of its domain points.

We provide the definitions of SCTFM security for the four variants indexed by $j = 1, 2, 3, 4$.

Definition 2. *Let $\mathcal{H} : \{0,1\}^* \to \{0,1\}^n$ be a salted hash function design and p, L be as in Def. 1. Let s denote the size of the salt and let $\mathsf{enc} = \{\mathsf{enc}_i\}_{i=1}^{L}$ be the family of encoding functions as described above. Let $\mathcal{B}$ be a salted-chosen-target-forced-midfix (SCTFM) finding adversary for this hash function. For $j \in \{1, 2, 3, 4\}$ the advantage of an adversary $\mathcal{B}$ is defined as*

$$\mathbf{Adv}_{\mathcal{H}}^{\mathsf{sctfm}}(\mathcal{B}) = \mathbf{Pr}\Big(\mathsf{E}_j \;:\; \mathcal{H}^{f,\mathsf{enc}}(g(P,R),S) = y \;\wedge\; \big|\mathsf{rng}(g)\big| \leq 2^{Lm} \;\wedge\; |S| = s\Big).$$

By $\mathbf{Adv}_{\mathcal{H}}^{\mathsf{sctfm}}(q)$ we denote the maximum advantage, taken over all adversaries making q queries to their oracle. The events E_j ($j = 1, 2, 3, 4$) are illustrated by the following four game experiments:

j	E_j
1	$f \xleftarrow{\$} \mathit{Func(n{+}m,n)},\ (y, S, st) \leftarrow \mathcal{B}^f,\ P \xleftarrow{\$} \{0,1\}^p,\ (g, R) \leftarrow \mathcal{B}^f(P, st)$
2	$f \xleftarrow{\$} \mathit{Func(n{+}m,n)},\ S \xleftarrow{\$} \{0,1\}^s,\ (y, st) \leftarrow \mathcal{B}^f(S),\ P \xleftarrow{\$} \{0,1\}^p,\ (g, R) \leftarrow \mathcal{B}^f(P, st)$
3	$f \xleftarrow{\$} \mathit{Func(n{+}m,n)},\ (y, st) \leftarrow \mathcal{B}^f,\ P \xleftarrow{\$} \{0,1\}^p,\ S \xleftarrow{\$} \{0,1\}^s,\ (g, R) \leftarrow \mathcal{B}^f(P, S, st)$
4	$f \xleftarrow{\$} \mathit{Func(n{+}m,n)},\ (y, st) \leftarrow \mathcal{B}^f,\ P \xleftarrow{\$} \{0,1\}^p,\ (g, R, S) \leftarrow \mathcal{B}^f(P, st)$

We provide a discussion on the adversarial abilities for the four SCTFM security notions in comparison with the standard CTFM definition and also to the relevance of salted definitions in practice.

Variants 1, 2 and 4. We will compare the strength of a SCTFM adversary $\mathcal{B}$ in variant 1, 2 or 4 with a CTFM adversary $\mathcal{A}$. Notice first that in a (non-salted) CTFM security game, $\mathcal{A}$ can gain advantage in the precomputation phase (the phase before the challenge midfix is known) only by skillfully preparing some computations for f, such that they are consistent with the evaluation of the function $\mathcal{H}$ in order to compute y. Overall, $\mathcal{A}$ can only exploit f. On the other hand, a SCTFM adversary $\mathcal{B}$ (for either of the variants) encounters the additional problem that he has to handle the encoding functions enc_i which may differ each message block. With respect to the advantage of $\mathcal{A}$, $\mathcal{B}$'s advantage would differ only in the case $\mathcal{B}$ loses control over the outputs of the enc_i function (which are inputs to f), i.e. in the case when he does not know the salt value.

But in each of these three variants the SCTFM adversary $\mathcal{B}$ knows the salt and has control over the inputs to f (as is the case with $\mathcal{A}$) before his commitment to y, and thus his advantage will be the same as the advantage of $\mathcal{A}$. In variant 1, the SCTFM adversary is in full control of the salt value and in variant 2 he knows the salt before committing to y, therefore he can prepare the respective computations for f. Notice that, although in variant 4 the salt value is revealed by the $\mathcal{B}$ in the second stage of the game, he is still in full control of the salt value and his advantage is optimal when he chooses the salt S in the first phase of the attack, does the respective computations for f, and then reveals S only in the second phase.

This analysis comes to show that the SCTFM adversary has the same computational advantage as a CTFM adversary in variants 1, 2 and 4. The conclusion is that salting in these variants does not help build more secure CTFM hash functions $\mathcal{H}$ and one can do as good without additionally increasing the efficiency and complexity of $\mathcal{H}$.

Variant 3. As opposed to the previous variants, here the SCTFM adversary $\mathcal{B}$ does not have control over the salt value before his commitment to y. In this scenario, $\mathcal{B}$ may lose control over the precomputation, because he is forced to use an unknown salt. This is the case for example when a Merkle-Damgård scheme is used where the salt is XORed with each chaining value. The Kelsey and Kohno attack would fail for such a scheme since the precomputed diamond does not contain the correct salt value, unless the adversary guessed it correctly in advance.

Variant 3, however, is not a valid notion because it does not reflect any real world uses of salts with hash functions. More concretely, variant 3 says that the SCTFM adversary first commits to some value y and only then is challenged on the randomness S, which means that he needs to make his precomputations and commitment without knowing or being able to learn the actual input parameter of the hash function. It is clear that such scenario fails not only from the point of view of adversarial abilities, but from a more practical point. The commitment simply does not make sense since one challenges the committer to make his best guess at the salt value. The salt shall be available at the point of hash computation, because it is an explicit input parameter to the hash function. This is the case with examples of salted hashing, such as password salted hashing and randomized hashing.

We exhibited 4 variants of salted hashing, where 3 of them have equivalent complexity as in the non-salted setting and one does not make it for a meaningful salted definition. As opposed to variant 3, the rest of the salted variants attribute to plausible security definitions. However, the clear conclusion we want to draw here is that salts do not help prevent CTFM attacks and one shall aim at non-salted solutions. We want to elaborate that this is a conclusion drawn for a reasonable encoding function. A different encoding function might lead to weakening the cryptographic strength of the compression function.

5 CTFM Resistance of Merkle-Damgård Design

We consider the resistance of the traditional Merkle-Damgård design against the chosen-target-forced midfix attack. This Merkle-Damgård hash function is an iterated hash function as in (1) with the following padding function:

$$\mathsf{pad}(M) = M\|10^{-|M|-1 \bmod m}, \tag{2}$$

splitted into blocks of length m. As demonstrated by Kelsey and Kohno [13] and Blackburn et al. [6], one can obtain a CTFM preimage of length $O(n)$ in about $\sqrt{n}2^{2n/3}$ compression function executions. When larger preimages are allowed, the elongated herding attack of [13] results in faster attacks: for $0 \leq r \leq n/2$, one can find a CTFP preimage of length $L = O(n+2^r)$ in approximately $\sqrt{n}2^{(2n-r)/3}$ queries. As we will demonstrate, this is (asymptotically) the best possible result. In Thm. 1 we derive an upper bound on $\mathbf{Adv}_{\mathrm{MD}}^{\mathsf{ctfm}}(q)$ that holds for any q, and we consider the limiting behavior in Cor. 1, in which we show that at least $2^{2n/3}/L^{1/3}$ queries are needed for an attack to succeed. After Cor. 1 we explain why the same or similar analysis applies to a wide class of MD based functions.

Theorem 1. *For any integral threshold $t > 0$, we have*

$$\mathbf{Adv}_{MD}^{\mathsf{ctfm}}(q) \leq \frac{(L-1)tq}{2^n} + \frac{m2^{\lceil p/m \rceil}q}{2^p} + \left(\frac{q^2 e}{t2^n}\right)^t + \frac{q^3}{2^{2n}}.$$

Proof. See Sect. 5.1. □

The bound of Thm. 1 includes a parameter t used to bound multiple events in the security analysis, and the bound holds for any integral t. Notice that for larger value of t, the first factor of the bound becomes large, while for small values the third term becomes large. Therefore, it is of importance to find a balance for this value t. Recall that, as explained in the beginning of this section, an adversary has a higher success probability if larger preimages are allowed. Consequently, the optimum for t partially depends on the allowed length L. In Cor. 1 we analyze the limiting behavior of the bound of Thm. 1.

Notice that the bound of Thm. 1 contains a term that not directly depends on n, the second term. This term essentially represents the "guessing probability" of the attacker: $\mathcal{A}$ may succeed guessing P in advance. If $p = |P|$ is very small, this factor dominates the bound. Therefore, it only makes sense to evaluate this bound for p being "large enough", and we have to put a requirement on p. Although the requirement looks complicated at first sight, it is satisfied by any relevant value of p. In particular, it is satisfied for $p \geq 2n/3$ for $L = O(n)$ preimages and even for lower values of p when L becomes larger.

Corollary 1. *Let* $L = O(2^{n/2})$ *and let* p *be such that* $\frac{2^{\lceil p/m \rceil} 2^{2n/3}}{L^{1/3} 2^p} = O(1)$ *for* $n \to \infty$. *For any* $\varepsilon > 0$, *we obtain* $\lim_{n\to\infty} \mathbf{Adv}_{MD}^{\mathsf{ctfm}}\left(2^{n(2/3-\varepsilon)}/L^{1/3}\right) = 0$.

Proof. The bound of Thm. 1 holds for any $t \geq 1$. As $L = O(2^{n/2})$, there exists a constant c such that $L \leq c2^{n/2}$. We put $t = \frac{2^{n/3}}{(L/c)^{2/3}} \geq 1$. Without loss of generality, t is integral (one can tweak c a little bit to get integral t). From Thm. 1:

$$\mathbf{Adv}_{\mathrm{MD}}^{\mathsf{ctfm}}(q) \leq \frac{L^{1/3} c^{2/3} q}{2^{2n/3}} + \frac{m 2^{\lceil p/m \rceil} q}{2^p} + \left(\frac{(L/c)^{2/3} q^2 e}{2^{4n/3}}\right)^{\frac{2^{n/3}}{(L/c)^{2/3}}} + \frac{q^3}{2^{2n}}.$$

For any $\varepsilon > 0$, we obtain:

$$\mathbf{Adv}_{\mathrm{MD}}^{\mathsf{ctfm}}\left(\frac{2^{n(2/3-\varepsilon)}}{L^{1/3}}\right) \leq \frac{c^{2/3}}{2^{n\varepsilon}} + \frac{m}{2^{n\varepsilon}} \frac{2^{\lceil p/m \rceil} 2^{2n/3}}{L^{1/3} 2^p} + \left(\frac{e}{c^{2/3} 2^{2n\varepsilon}}\right)^{\frac{2^{n/3}}{(L/c)^{2/3}}} + \frac{1}{L 2^{3n\varepsilon}}.$$

All terms approach 0 for $n \to \infty$ (notice that for the second term we have $m = \Theta(n)$, and for the third term its exponent is ≥ 1). □

Although the security analysis of Thm. 1 and Cor. 1 focuses on the original Merkle-Damgård (MD) hash function, a very similar analysis can be directly derived for a broad class of MD based iterative hash functions, including MD with length strengthening [14], enveloped MD [4], MD with permutation [11] and HAIFA [5]. Indeed, a CTFP attack against strengthened MD is provably harder than an attack against plain MD due to the presence of the length encoding at the end, and a similar remark applies to HAIFA. For enveloped MD and MD with permutation, and in general for any MD based function with final transformation, one can use security properties of the final transformation to show the adversary knows only a limited amount of state values y' which propagate to the commitment y through the final transformation, and we can analyze the success probability with respect to each of these possible commitments y'.[1] The security analysis furthermore applies to the hash twice hash function (where the padded message is simply hashed twice) and the zipper hash function (where the padded message is hashed once forward, and once in the opposite direction) [15], therewith demonstrating the (asymptotic) optimality of the attacks deployed by Andreeva et al. [1]. Indeed, a CTFM attack for zipper or hash twice is provably harder than an attack for MD, but the attacks of Andreeva et al. are of similar complexity as the attack of Kelsey and Kohno on MD.

5.1 Proof of Thm. 1

We introduce some definitions for the purpose of security analysis of MD against the CTFM attack. We consider adversaries making $q = q_1 + q_2$ queries to their

[1] In detail for enveloped MD and MD with permutation, the condition on event $\neg \mathsf{E}_2$ in the proof of Thm. 1 guarantees the adversary to know at most 2 such values y'. The final success probability is then at most 2 times as large.

random oracle f. Associated to the queries made in the attack we consider a directed graph (V, A). A compression function execution $f(h_{i-1}, M_i) = h_i$ corresponds to an arc $h_{i-1} \xrightarrow{M_i} h_i$ in the graph. The graph is initialized as $(\{\mathsf{iv}\}, \emptyset)$. We denote by $(V(j), A(j))$ (for $j = -q_1, \ldots, q_2$) the subgraph of (V, A) after the j-th query. Hence, after the first phase of the attack we are left with graph $(V(0), A(0))$.

A path $h_i \xrightarrow{M_{i+1}} h_{i+1} \cdots \xrightarrow{M_l} h_l$ in a graph is called "v-tail" (for "valid tail") if $M_{i+1}\| \cdots \|M_l$ forms the suffix of a correctly padded message. Formally, it is v-tail if there exists $M_i \in (\{0,1\}^m)^*$ such that

$$M_i\|M_{i+1}\| \cdots \|M_l\|M_{l+1} \in \mathsf{rng}(\mathsf{pad}).$$

Intuitively, it means that $h_i \to h_l$ is formed by a valid sequence of message blocks and can possibly occur at the end of a hash function execution. Notice that the v-tail property of a path carries over to its sub-suffixes. For two state values $h_i, h_l \in \{0,1\}^n$, we define

$$\mathsf{dist}_{h_i \to h_l}(j) = \big\{0 \le k < \infty \;\big|\; (V(j), A(j)) \text{ contains v-tail } h_i \longrightarrow h_l \text{ of length } k\big\}.$$

For a $P \in \{0,1\}^p$, a path $h_i \xrightarrow{M_{i+1}} h_{i+1} \cdots \xrightarrow{M_k} h_k$ is called "P-comprising" if $M_{i+1}\| \cdots \|M_k$ contains P as a substring.

Proof of Thm. 1. Let $\mathcal{A}$ be any CTFM adversary making $q_1 + q_2$ queries to its random function f. In other words, at a high level the attack works as follows: (1) the adversary makes q_1 queries to f, (2) he commits to digest y, (3) he receives a random challenge $P \xleftarrow{\$} \{0,1\}^p$, (4) he makes q_2 queries to f, and (5) he responds with R_1, R_2 such that $\mathcal{H}(R_1\|P\|R_2) = y$ and $\big|R_1\|P\|R_2\big| \le Lm$. Denote by $\mathbf{Pr}\left(\mathsf{suc}_{\mathcal{A}}(j)\right)$ for $j = -q_1, \ldots, q_2$ the success probability of $\mathcal{A}$ after the j-th query. Obviously, $\mathbf{Adv}^{\mathsf{ctfm}}_{\mathrm{MD}}(\mathcal{A}) = \mathbf{Pr}\left(\mathsf{suc}_{\mathcal{A}}(q_2)\right)$. In the first phase of the attack, the adversary arbitrarily makes q_1 queries to f, and then outputs a commitment y. Consequently, he receives challenge $P \xleftarrow{\$} \{0,1\}^p$. Consider the following event E_0:

$$\mathsf{E}_0 : \; (V(0), A(0)) \text{ contains a } P\text{-comprising path.}$$

E_0 captures the event of $\mathcal{A}$ "guessing" P in the first phase of the attack. We will split the success probability of the attacker, using the fact that he either did or did not guess P in the first phase. In other words, we can write $\mathbf{Pr}\left(\mathsf{suc}_{\mathcal{A}}(q_2)\right) \le \mathbf{Pr}\left(\mathsf{suc}_{\mathcal{A}}(q_2) \mid \neg\mathsf{E}_0\right) + \mathbf{Pr}\left(\mathsf{E}_0\right)$. However, for the purpose of the analysis we introduce two more events $\mathsf{E}_1, \mathsf{E}_2$. Let $t > 0$ be any integral threshold.

$$\mathsf{E}_1 : \; \alpha_1 > t, \text{ where } \alpha_1 = \max_{0 \le k \le L} \big|\{h \in V(q_2) \mid k = \min \mathsf{dist}_{h \to y}(q_2)\}\big|,$$

$$\mathsf{E}_2 : \; \alpha_2 > 2, \text{ where } \alpha_2 = \max_{h \in V(q_2)} \big|\{h' \in V(q_2) \mid (h', h) \in A(q_2)\}\big|.$$

E_1 sorts all nodes in $V(q_2)$ in classes with elements at (minimal) distance $0, 1, 2, \ldots, L$ from y, and considers the class with the maximal number of nodes.

E_2 considers the event that $\mathcal{Q}$ contains a multi-collision of more than two compression function executions. By basic probability theory, we have

$$\begin{aligned}\mathbf{Pr}\left(\mathsf{suc}_{\mathcal{A}}(q_2)\right) &\leq \mathbf{Pr}\left(\mathsf{suc}_{\mathcal{A}}(q_2) \mid \neg\mathsf{E}_0 \wedge \neg\mathsf{E}_1\right) + \mathbf{Pr}\left(\mathsf{E}_0 \vee \mathsf{E}_1\right), \\ &\leq \mathbf{Pr}\left(\mathsf{suc}_{\mathcal{A}}(q_2) \mid \neg\mathsf{E}_0 \wedge \neg\mathsf{E}_1\right) + \mathbf{Pr}\left(\mathsf{E}_0 \vee \mathsf{E}_1 \mid \neg\mathsf{E}_2\right) + \mathbf{Pr}\left(\mathsf{E}_2\right), \\ &\leq \mathbf{Pr}\left(\mathsf{suc}_{\mathcal{A}}(q_2) \mid \neg\mathsf{E}_0 \wedge \neg\mathsf{E}_1\right) + \mathbf{Pr}\left(\mathsf{E}_0 \mid \neg\mathsf{E}_2\right) \\ &\qquad + \mathbf{Pr}\left(\mathsf{E}_1 \mid \neg\mathsf{E}_2\right) + \mathbf{Pr}\left(\mathsf{E}_2\right), \end{aligned} \tag{3}$$

and we consider the probabilities on the right hand side separately.

- $\mathbf{Pr}\left(\mathsf{suc}_{\mathcal{A}}(q_2) \mid \neg\mathsf{E}_0 \wedge \neg\mathsf{E}_1\right)$. By $\neg\mathsf{E}_0$, P is not contained in $(V(0), A(0))$ yet, but it may be contained partially and hence the adversary will at least need to make 1 compression function execution. It may be the case that the adversary makes calls to the compression function for multiple strings P, and it may be the case that after he queried for P, he knows multiple paths of different length including P, but this does not violate the analysis. In general, the suffix R_2 of the attack covers at most $L-1$ message blocks. At any time in the attack, there are at most
$$|\{h \in V(q_2) \mid \mathsf{dist}_{h\to y}(q_2) \cap \{0,\ldots,L-1\}|$$
possible nodes for which a hit results in a collision. By $\neg\mathsf{E}_1$, this set is upper bounded by $(L-1)t$. As the adversary makes at most $q_2 \leq q$ compression function calls that may result in success, the total probability is upper bounded by $\frac{(L-1)tq}{2^n}$;
- $\mathbf{Pr}\left(\mathsf{E}_0 \mid \neg\mathsf{E}_2\right)$. Notice that $\neg\mathsf{E}_2$ implies that all nodes in $(V(q_2), A(q_2))$, as well as all nodes in $(V(0), A(0))$, have at most 2 incoming arcs. We consider the probability that there exists a P-comprising path. The existence of such path implies the existence of an arc that supplies the last bit of P. Consider any arc $h_{j-1} \xrightarrow{M_j} h_j$, and let $M_j^{(i)}$ for $i = 1,\ldots,m$ denote the m-th bit. Now, we can analyze the probability that $P \xleftarrow{\$} \{0,1\}^p$ is included as a substring of a path in $(V(0), A(0))$, with $M_j^{(i)}$ corresponding to the last bit of P. Then, $\mathbf{Pr}\left(\mathsf{E}_0 \mid \neg\mathsf{E}_2\right)$ is upper bounded by this probability summed over all i and the number of arcs. We consider the probability for different values of i:
  - $i \geq p$. P is integrally captured in M_j as $M_j^{(i-p+1)} \| \ldots \| M_j^{(i)} = P$. This happens with probability $1/2^p$ for predetermined M_j and random P;
  - $i < p$. The first i bits of M_j correspond to the last i bits of P, and that the first $p-i$ bits of P are a suffix of any path ending in h_{j-1}. Let $\beta = \lceil (p-i)/m \rceil$. As by $\neg\mathsf{E}_2$ there are at most 2^β paths of length β blocks to h_{j-1}, we can upper bound the probability by $\frac{1}{2^i} \cdot \frac{2^\beta}{2^{p-i}} = \frac{2^\beta}{2^p}$.

  Now, we can sum over all possible values of i and the number of queries q_1. We obtain
$$\mathbf{Pr}\left(\mathsf{E}_0 \mid \neg\mathsf{E}_2\right) \leq \begin{cases} \frac{(m+p-1)q_1}{2^p} & \text{if } p \leq m, \\ \frac{m2^{\lceil p/m \rceil}q_1}{2^p} & \text{if } p > m. \end{cases}$$
  In both cases, we derive upper bound $\frac{m2^{\lceil p/m \rceil}q}{2^p}$, given $q_1 \leq q$;

- **Pr** $(\mathsf{E}_1 \mid \neg\mathsf{E}_2)$. Let k^* be minimal such that the maximum is achieved, and let $h_1, \dots, h_{\alpha_1}$ be all nodes with distance k^* from y. Consider the subgraph $(\overline{V}, \overline{A})$ of $(V(q_2), A(q_2))$ consisting of all[2] paths $h_i \to y$ of length k^* edges (for $i = 1, \dots, \alpha_1$). By ways of an elaborate case distinction (see App. A), one can show that for each node h in $(\overline{V}, \overline{A})$, all paths to y are of the same length. This in particular implies that the h_i's $(i = 1, \dots, \alpha_1)$ have no ingoing edge, and that y has no outgoing edge. Therefore, we can classify the nodes in the subgraph into sets: $\alpha_1^{k^*} = \alpha_1$ at distance k^* from y, $\alpha_1^{k^*-1}$ at distance $k^* - 1$, etc., $\alpha_1^0 = 1$ at distance 0. Notice that $\alpha_1^0, \dots, \alpha_1^{k^*-1} < \alpha_1^{k^*}$ by definition, but it can be the case that $\alpha_1^{i-1} > \alpha_1^i$ (for $1 < i < k^*$) for technical reasons. By $\neg\mathsf{E}_2$, $\mathcal{Q}$ does not contain any 3-way collisions, but only 2-way collisions. The number of 2-way collisions between the nodes at distances i and $i-1$ equals $\max\{\alpha_1^i - \alpha_1^{i-1}, 0\}$. Consequently, the described subgraph, and hence $(V(q_2), A(q_2))$ itself, contains at least

$$\sum_{i=1}^{k^*} \max\{\alpha_1^i - \alpha_1^{i-1}, 0\} \geq \alpha_1^{k^*} - \alpha_1^0 = \alpha_1 - 1 \geq t$$

2-way collisions. Thus, the probability is upper bounded by $\binom{q}{t}\left(\frac{q}{2^n}\right)^t \leq \left(\frac{q^2 e}{t 2^n}\right)^t$, where the inequality holds due to Stirling's approximation ($x! \geq (x/e)^x$ for any x);
- **Pr** (E_2). The occurrence of E_2 implies the presence of a 3-way collision in $\mathcal{Q}$, which exists with probability at most $q^3/2^{2n}$ only [18].

From equation (3) and above upper bounds on the three probabilities, we obtain:

$$\mathbf{Adv}_{\mathrm{MD}}^{\mathsf{ctfm}}(\mathcal{A}) = \mathbf{Pr}\left(\mathsf{suc}_{\mathcal{A}}(q_2)\right) \leq \frac{(L-1)tq}{2^n} + \frac{m 2^{\lceil p/m \rceil} q}{2^p} + \left(\frac{q^2 e}{t 2^n}\right)^t + \frac{q^3}{2^{2n}}.$$

As this holds for any adversary making q queries, this completes the proof.

6 On Optimally CTFM Resistant Iterated Hash Functions

Knowing that irrespectively of adding a salt or not, the original MD design of Sect. 5 does not withstand the CTFM attack, a natural question arises: is it possible to secure the MD design by ways of a simple tweak? Naturally, wide-pipe designs offer optimal CTFM security, but they require a larger state size, which accounts for an efficiency loss. Note that modes of operation that use the chaining values in an advanced way (e.g. by adding a final compression function call with the checksum of the chaining values) implicitly belong to the set of wide-pipe designs. Another direction may be to tweak the way the message is

[2] In case of multiple paths of the same length starting from a node h_i, one arbitrarily chooses a path.

processed by the mode of operation, which is captured by considering the iterated hash function design of (1) with a more sophisticated padding.

In this section, we launch a CTFM attack against a wide class of iterated hash functions that differ from the original MD design only in the way the message is processed. More detailed, we consider the standard iterated hash function design of (1), with the difference that it employs a sophisticated padding function s-pad satisfying some criteria. This padding function s-pad may be depending on the standard padding function pad, and generally does. The attack covers a wide spectrum of hash functions, and in particular provides an efficient and elegant alternative to the attacks proposed by Gauravaram et al. [10] on several MD designs using checksums.

We describe the attack on the base of one representative example hash function. A generic version of it can be directly extracted from the attack description. Further, we consider three similar hash functions and a comparison with the attack of [10].

Let pad be the padding function of (2). Let $M \in \{0,1\}^*$ and denote $\mathsf{pad}(M) = M_1\|\cdots\|M_l$. We define a sophisticated padding function $\mathsf{s\text{-}pad}_1 : \{0,1\}^* \to (\{0,1\}^m)^*$ on M as follows.

$$\mathsf{s\text{-}pad}_1(M) = M_1 \Big\| \bigoplus_{i=1}^{1} M_i \Big\| M_2 \Big\| \bigoplus_{i=1}^{2} M_i \Big\| \cdots \Big\| M_l \Big\| \bigoplus_{i=1}^{l} M_i .$$

For simplicity, denote by N_i for $i = 1, \ldots, 2l$ the i-th block of $\mathsf{s\text{-}pad}_1(M)$. Let $\mathcal{IH}_1$ be defined as an iterated hash function of (1) accommodated with the advanced padding function $\mathsf{s\text{-}pad}_1$. We will describe a CTFM attack against $\mathcal{IH}_1$, but before that we briefly recall the attack of Kelsey and Kohno against the MD hash function. Denote by $\kappa \geq 1$ the size of the diamond we will use.

1. The adversary constructs a diamond of κ levels. He randomly generates 2^κ state values $h_0^{(1)}, \ldots, h_0^{(2^\kappa)}$, and dynamically finds $2^{\kappa-1}$ compression function collisions by varying the message values. The same procedure is applied to the resulting $2^{\kappa-1}$ state values $h_1^{(1)}, \ldots, h_1^{(2^{\kappa-1})}$ until one node $h_\kappa^{(1)}$ is left;
2. The adversary commits to this state value $y := h_\kappa^{(1)}$ and receives challenge P. Without loss of generality P is of length a multiple of m, and he computes the path $\mathsf{iv} \xrightarrow{P} h_{p'}$;
3. The adversary finds a message M_{hit} such that $f(h_{p'}, M_{\text{hit}}) = h_0^{(j)}$ for some $j \in \{1, \ldots, 2^\kappa\}$.

The resulting forgery is formed by $P\|M_{\text{hit}}\|M_{\text{diam}}$, where M_{diam} denotes the message string that labels the path $h_0^{(j)} \to h_\kappa^{(1)}$. Phase 1 of the attack requires about $\sqrt{\kappa}2^{(n+\kappa)/2}$ work [13,6], the work for phase 2 is negligible and phase 3 takes about $2^{n-\kappa}$ amount of work. The message is of length $\lceil p/m \rceil + 1 + \kappa$ blocks.

The construction of the diamond (phase 1) is correct due to the independent character of the message blocks: given a string $M_i\|\cdots\|M_l$ of message blocks, one can arbitrarily change one block while still having a valid string of message blocks. Thus, when constructing the diamond one can vary the message blocks independently for obtaining collisions. For the sophisticated padding function $\mathsf{s\text{-}pad}_1$ this is not possible. If for a given padded message one changes N_{2i-1} for $i \in \{1,\ldots,l-1\}$, the values taken by the checksum blocks $N_{2i},\ldots,N_{2i+2},\ldots,N_{2l}$ should change as well. At first sight, this makes the construction of the diamond impossible, but by additionally changing N_{2i+1}, one can "stabilize" the values $N_{2i+2},\ldots,N_{2l}$ and only the blocks N_{2i-1},N_{2i},N_{2i+1} get affected (in case $i=l$ only N_{2i-1},N_{2i} get affected). Based on this observation the attack is defined as follows. Notice, the adversary decides on the length of the forgery in advance: $p'+2\kappa+2$.

1. The adversary constructs a diamond of κ levels.
   – He fixes constants $C_0,C_1,\ldots,C_\kappa \in \{0,1\}^m$ in advance. These constants represent

$$C_0 = \bigoplus_{i=1}^{p'+2} M_i, \qquad C_i = M_{p'+2i+1} \oplus M_{p'+2i+2} \text{ for } i=1,\ldots,\kappa. \tag{4}$$

   The adversary does not know the blocks M_i yet, but will choose them so as to comply with (4);
   – He randomly generates 2^κ state values $h_0^{(1)},\ldots,h_0^{(2^\kappa)}$, and dynamically finds collisions of the following form for $j=1,\ldots,2^{\kappa-1}$

$$\begin{array}{l} h_0^{(2j-1)} \xrightarrow{C_0} \xrightarrow{M_{p'+3}^{(2j-1)}} \xrightarrow{C_0 \oplus M_{p'+3}^{(2j-1)}} \xrightarrow{C_1 \oplus M_{p'+3}^{(2j-1)}} \\ \qquad\qquad\qquad\qquad\qquad\qquad\qquad\qquad h_1^{(j)}. \\ h_0^{(2j)} \xrightarrow{C_0} \xrightarrow{M_{p'+3}^{(2j)}} \xrightarrow{C_0 \oplus M_{p'+3}^{(2j)}} \xrightarrow{C_1 \oplus M_{p'+3}^{(2j)}} \end{array}$$

   These collisions can indeed by dynamically found, simply by varying the $M_{p'+3}$-blocks (recall that C_0,C_1 are fixed constants). The corresponding blocks $M_{p'+4}$ are computed as $M_{p'+4}=C_1 \oplus M_{p'+3}$ by (4);
   – The same procedure is applied to the resulting $2^{\kappa-1}$ state values $h_1^{(1)}$, $\ldots,h_1^{(2^{\kappa-1})}$, where the arcs are labeled by $C_0 \oplus C_1$, $M_{p'+5}$, $C_1 \oplus M_{p'+5}$ and $C_2 \oplus M_{p'+5}$, respectively. Finally, one node $h_\kappa^{(1)}$ is left;
2. The adversary commits to this state value $y := h_\kappa^{(1)}$ and receives challenge P. Without loss of generality P is of length a multiple of m, and he defines $M_1,\ldots,M_{p'}$ to be the first corresponding blocks. Denote $C_{-1} = \bigoplus_{i=1}^{p'} M_i$. In accordance to the padding function $\mathsf{s\text{-}pad}$ he computes the path $\mathsf{iv} \xrightarrow{M_1} \cdots \xrightarrow{M_{p'}} \xrightarrow{C_{-1}} h_{2p'}$;
3. The adversary finds a message $M_{p'+1}$ such that

$$h_{2p'} \xrightarrow{M_{p'+1}} \xrightarrow{C_{-1}\oplus M_{p'+1}} \xrightarrow{C_{-1}\oplus M_{p'+1}\oplus C_0} h_0^{(j)}$$

   for some $j \in \{1,\ldots,2^\kappa\}$.

The resulting forgery is formed by $P\|M_{p'+1}\|M_{p'+2}\|M_{\text{diam}}$, where $M_{p'+2} = C_{-1} \oplus M_{p'+1} \oplus C_0$ by (4) and M_{diam} denotes the message string of 2κ blocks that labels the path $h_0^{(j)} \to h_\kappa^{(1)}$. By construction, because the values $C_0, \ldots, C_\kappa$ have been fixed in advance, the path $\mathsf{iv} \longrightarrow h_\kappa^{(1)}$ is in accordance with the padding function $\mathsf{s\text{-}pad}$. Phase 1 of the attack requires about $4 \cdot \sqrt{\kappa} 2^{(n+\kappa)/2}$ work, the work for phase 2 is negligible and phase 3 takes about $3 \cdot 2^{n-\kappa}$ amount of work. The message is of length $\lceil p/m \rceil + 2 + 2\kappa$ blocks.

We notice that the same approach can be applied to the following example hash functions. Consider the following advanced padding functions $\mathsf{s\text{-}pad}_k(M) : \{0,1\}^* \to (\{0,1\}^m)^*$ for $k = 2, 3, 4$:

$$\mathsf{s\text{-}pad}_2(M) = M_1 \Big\| M_2 \Big\| M_1 \oplus M_2 \Big\| M_3 \Big\| M_2 \oplus M_3 \Big\| \cdots \Big\| M_l \Big\| M_{l-1} \oplus M_l,$$

$$\mathsf{s\text{-}pad}_3(M) = \mathsf{rotate}_{m/2}(\mathsf{pad}(M)),$$

$$\mathsf{s\text{-}pad}_4(M) = \mathsf{pad}(M) \Big\| \bigoplus_{j=1}^{l} M_j,$$

where the function $\mathsf{rotate}_{m/2}$ rotates the bit string by $m/2$ places (a half message block). We define by $\mathcal{IH}_k$ for $k = 2, 3, 4$ the standard iterated hash function of (1) accommodated with the advanced padding function $\mathsf{s\text{-}pad}_k$. Notice that for $\mathcal{IH}_4$, any change of M_i can be corrected by M_{i+1} to keep the final checksum invariant. Now, the attacks are described in a similar manner. For $\mathcal{IH}_2$, the complexity is the same as for $\mathcal{IH}_1$. The complexities for $\mathcal{IH}_3, \mathcal{IH}_4$ are half as large. For each of the functions $\mathcal{IH}_k$ the optimum is achieved for $\kappa = n/3$. By tweaking the proof of Thm. 1, asymptotic tightness of this bound can be proven. We notice that Gauravaram et al. [10] describe a generalized herding attack against a class of MD based hash functions using checksums at the end (such as $\mathcal{IH}_4$). The attack described in this section carries over to many of these designs, therewith providing an elegant alternative. These attacks are of the same complexity, although our attack renders shorter messages in case $n/3 < m$. The cause of this difference is the fact that the attack of Gauravaram et al. sets the value of the final checksum at the end while in our attack it is essentially fixed by the adversary in advance.

We leave the existence of narrow-pipe hash functions that achieve optimal security against the CTFM attack as an open problem.

7 Conclusions

We introduced and formalized the notion of a chosen-target-forced-midfix (CTFM) attack as a generalization of the classical herding attack of Kelsey and Kohno [13]. The new notion allows the adversary to include the challenge P at any place in the forged preimage. Hence, it enables arguing the security of hash functions which for example process the message in reverse order and which were otherwise trivially secure against the herding attack. Additionally, we investigated the CTFM security of salted hash functions showing that adding a salt value without weakening the compression function does not improve the CTFM security of the hash function.

As a main technical contribution of the paper we provided a formal security proof of the MD design against the CTFM attack, and showed that the attack of Kelsey and Kohno [13] is (asymptotically) the best possible. This proof directly applies to a wide class of MD based domain extenders, and implies optimality of other herding attacks, such as those of Andreeva et al. [1] and Gauravaram et al. [10].

In the quest for optimally CTFM secure narrow-pipe MD designs, we analyzed the possibility of message modification as a tool to increase CTFM security. Our result shows however, that such techniques applied to a wide class of narrow-pipe iterated hash function designs do not block CTFM attacks. An open research question that emerges from these observations is to construct a narrow-pipe iterated hash functions that achieves optimal security against the CTFM attacks.

Acknowledgments. This work has been funded in part by the IAP Program P6/26 BCRYPT of the Belgian State (Belgian Science Policy), in part by the European Commission through the ICT program under contract ICT-2007-216676 ECRYPT II, and in part by the Research Council K.U.Leuven: GOA TENSE. The first author is supported by a Ph.D. Fellowship from the Flemish Research Foundation (FWO-Vlaanderen). The second author is supported by a Ph.D. Fellowship from the Institute for the Promotion of Innovation through Science and Technology in Flanders (IWT-Vlaanderen).

References

1. Andreeva, E., Bouillaguet, C., Dunkelman, O., Kelsey, J.: Herding, Second Preimage and Trojan Message Attacks Beyond Merkle-Damgård. In: Jacobson Jr., M.J., Rijmen, V., Safavi-Naini, R. (eds.) SAC 2009. LNCS, vol. 5867, pp. 393–414. Springer, Heidelberg (2009)
2. Andreeva, E., Bouillaguet, C., Fouque, P.-A., Hoch, J., Kelsey, J., Shamir, A., Zimmer, S.: Second Preimage Attacks on Dithered Hash Functions. In: Smart, N.P. (ed.) EUROCRYPT 2008. LNCS, vol. 4965, pp. 270–288. Springer, Heidelberg (2008)
3. Andreeva, E., Neven, G., Preneel, B., Shrimpton, T.: Seven-Property-Preserving Iterated Hashing: ROX. In: Kurosawa, K. (ed.) ASIACRYPT 2007. LNCS, vol. 4833, pp. 130–146. Springer, Heidelberg (2007)
4. Bellare, M., Ristenpart, T.: Multi-Property-Preserving Hash Domain Extension and the EMD Transform. In: Lai, X., Chen, K. (eds.) ASIACRYPT 2006. LNCS, vol. 4284, pp. 299–314. Springer, Heidelberg (2006)
5. Biham, E., Dunkelman, O.: A framework for iterative hash functions – HAIFA. Cryptology ePrint Archive, Report 2007/278 (2007)
6. Blackburn, S., Stinson, D., Upadhyay, J.: On the complexity of the herding attack and some related attacks on hash functions. Des. Codes Cryptography (to appear, 2011)

7. Coron, J.-S., Dodis, Y., Malinaud, C., Puniya, P.: Merkle-Damgård Revisited: How to Construct a Hash Function. In: Shoup, V. (ed.) CRYPTO 2005. LNCS, vol. 3621, pp. 430–448. Springer, Heidelberg (2005)
8. Damgård, I.: A Design Principle for Hash Functions. In: Brassard, G. (ed.) CRYPTO 1989. LNCS, vol. 435, pp. 416–427. Springer, Heidelberg (1990)
9. Gauravaram, P., Kelsey, J.: Linear-XOR and Additive Checksums Don't Protect Damgård-Merkle Hashes from Generic Attacks. In: Malkin, T. (ed.) CT-RSA 2008. LNCS, vol. 4964, pp. 36–51. Springer, Heidelberg (2008)
10. Gauravaram, P., Kelsey, J., Knudsen, L., Thomsen, S.: On hash functions using checksums. International Journal of Information Security 9(2), 137–151 (2010)
11. Hirose, S., Park, J.H., Yun, A.: A Simple Variant of the Merkle-Damgård Scheme with a Permutation. In: Kurosawa, K. (ed.) ASIACRYPT 2007. LNCS, vol. 4833, pp. 113–129. Springer, Heidelberg (2007)
12. Joux, A.: Multicollisions in Iterated Hash Functions. Application to Cascaded Constructions. In: Franklin, M. (ed.) CRYPTO 2004. LNCS, vol. 3152, pp. 306–316. Springer, Heidelberg (2004)
13. Kelsey, J., Kohno, T.: Herding Hash Functions and the Nostradamus Attack. In: Vaudenay, S. (ed.) EUROCRYPT 2006. LNCS, vol. 4004, pp. 183–200. Springer, Heidelberg (2006)
14. Lai, X., Massey, J.L.: Hash Functions Based on Block Ciphers. In: Rueppel, R.A. (ed.) EUROCRYPT 1992. LNCS, vol. 658, pp. 55–70. Springer, Heidelberg (1993)
15. Liskov, M.: Constructing an Ideal Hash Function from Weak Ideal Compression Functions. In: Biham, E., Youssef, A.M. (eds.) SAC 2006. LNCS, vol. 4356, pp. 358–375. Springer, Heidelberg (2007)
16. Merkle, R.C.: One Way Hash Functions and DES. In: Brassard, G. (ed.) CRYPTO 1989. LNCS, vol. 435, pp. 428–446. Springer, Heidelberg (1990)
17. Neven, G., Smart, N., Warinschi, B.: Hash function requirements for Schnorr signatures. Journal of Mathematical Cryptology 3(1), 69–87 (2009)
18. Suzuki, K., Tonien, D., Kurosawa, K., Toyota, K.: Birthday Paradox for Multi-Collisions. In: Rhee, M.S., Lee, B. (eds.) ICISC 2006. LNCS, vol. 4296, pp. 29–40. Springer, Heidelberg (2006)

A Appendum to Proof of Thm. 1

We show that the graph $(\overline{V}, \overline{A})$ defined in Thm. 1 does not contain a node with two paths of different lengths to y. Recall that $(\overline{V}, \overline{A})$ is constructed in the following manner. k^* is the minimal value for which there are the maximum number of nodes, α_1 with distance k^* to y. For each of the α_1 nodes $h_1, \ldots, h_{\alpha_1}$, we take any path of length k^* to y, and add it to $(\overline{V}, \overline{A})$. By definition, for each $i = 1, \ldots, \alpha_1$, there does not exist a path $h_i \to y$ of length shorter than k^* arcs. We show that for any node $h \in \overline{V}$, all paths to y are of the same length. The proof is done by contradiction: we will show that the existence of an h contradicting aforementioned property implies the existence of a path $h_i \to y$ (for some i) of length strictly shorter than k^* arcs. Notice that this result in particular implies that the h_i's $(i = 1, \ldots, \alpha_1)$ have no ingoing edge, and that y has no outgoing edge.

Suppose there exists $h \in \overline{V}$ such that for some $M_1, M_2 \in (\{0,1\}^m)^*$ with $|M_1| < |M_2|$ the paths $h \xrightarrow{M_1} y$ and $h \xrightarrow{M_2} y$ are included in $(\overline{V}, \overline{A})$. If the path

$h \xrightarrow{M_2} y$ is a subpath of any $h_i \to y$ for some i, one can replace this subpath by $h \xrightarrow{M_1} y$ to obtain a path $h_i \to y$ of length strictly shorter than k^* arcs, rendering contradiction. Thus, we assume that $h \xrightarrow{M_2} y$ is not integrally included as a subpath of any $h_i \to y$. We split up the path $h \xrightarrow{M_2} y$ intro three parts. Let $i \in \{1, \ldots, \alpha_1\}$ be such that the first edge of $h \xrightarrow{M_2} y$ is included in the path $h_i \to y$. Let $M_2^{(1)}$ be the maximal prefix of M_2 such that $h \xrightarrow{M_2^{(1)}} h^{(1)}$ (for some $h^{(1)}$) is a subpath of $h_i \to y$. Secondly, identify the edge leaving[3] $h^{(1)}$ in the path $h \xrightarrow{M_2} y$, and let i' be such that this edge is included in the path $h_{i'} \to y$. Let $M_2^{(2)}$ be of maximal length such that $M_2^{(1)} \| M_2^{(2)}$ is a prefix of M_2 and $h^{(1)} \xrightarrow{M_2^{(2)}} h^{(2)}$ (for some $h^{(2)}$) is a subpath of $h_{i'} \to y$. Thus, we splitted $h \xrightarrow{M_2} y$ into

$$h \xrightarrow{M_2^{(1)}} h^{(1)} \xrightarrow{M_2^{(2)}} h^{(2)} \xrightarrow{M_2^{(3)}} y, \tag{5}$$

where $|M_2^{(1)}|, |M_2^{(2)}| > 0$ and $|M_2^{(3)}| \geq 0$ and

$$h_i \xrightarrow{M_3} h \xrightarrow{M_2^{(1)}} h^{(1)} \xrightarrow{M_4} y, \qquad h_{i'} \xrightarrow{M_5} h^{(1)} \xrightarrow{M_2^{(2)}} h^{(2)} \xrightarrow{M_6} y, \tag{6}$$

for some $M_3, M_4, M_5, M_6 \in (\{0,1\}^m)^*$. Here, $M_2^{(1)}$ and $M_2^{(2)}$ are of maximal possible length, i.e. the first arcs of $h^{(1)} \xrightarrow{M_4} y$ and $h^{(1)} \xrightarrow{M_2^{(2)}} h^{(2)}$ are different and the first arcs of $h^{(2)} \xrightarrow{M_6} y$ and $h^{(2)} \xrightarrow{M_2^{(3)}} y$ are different.

If $h^{(1)} = h$, the path $h_i \xrightarrow{M_3} h \xrightarrow{M_4} y$ is in $(V(q_2), A(q_2))$ and of length shorter than k^* blocks, rendering contradiction. Similarly, if $h^{(2)} = h^{(1)}$, a shorter path $h_{i'} \to y$ can be found. Hence, we consider the case $h \neq h^{(1)} \neq h^{(2)}$, and make the following case distinction:

1. $|M_4| \neq |M_2^{(2)} M_6|$. One can combine the two paths described in (6) to obtain either a path $h_i \to y$ or $h_{i'} \to y$ of length strictly shorter than k^* arcs;
2. $|M_4| = |M_2^{(2)} M_6|$. We make the following case distinction:
   a. $|M_6| \geq |M_2^{(3)}|$. This means that $|M_4| \geq |M_2^{(2)} M_2^{(3)}|$ and hence $|M_2^{(1)} M_4| \geq |M_2| > |M_1|$. The path $h_i \xrightarrow{M_3} h \xrightarrow{M_1} y$ is thus strictly shorter than k^* arcs;
   b. $|M_6| < |M_2^{(3)}|$. One can do the same analysis with paths $h^{(2)} \xrightarrow{M_6} y$ and $h^{(2)} \xrightarrow{M_2^{(3)}} y$. But by construction $|M_2^{(3)}| < |M_2| - 2m$ so one will eventually end up with the same problem with $|M_2^{(3)}| = 0$, in which case one will not arrive in case 2b.

Concluding, there does not exist any node in $(\overline{V}, \overline{A})$ which has two paths of different lengths to y.

[3] This edge exists, as $h \xrightarrow{M_2} y$ is not an integral subpath of any path $h_i \to y$.

On CCA-Secure Somewhat Homomorphic Encryption

Jake Loftus[1], Alexander May[2], Nigel P. Smart[1], and Frederik Vercauteren[3]

[1] Dept. Computer Science,
University of Bristol,
Merchant Venturers Building, Woodland Road,
Bristol, BS8 1UB, United Kingdom
{loftus,nigel}@cs.bris.ac.uk
[2] Horst Görtz Institute for IT-Security,
Faculty of Mathematics,
Ruhr-University Bochum, Germany
alex.may@rub.de
[3] COSIC - Electrical Engineering,
Katholieke Universiteit Leuven,
Kasteelpark Arenberg 10,
B-3001 Heverlee, Belgium
fvercaut@esat.kuleuven.ac.be

Abstract. It is well known that any encryption scheme which supports any form of homomorphic operation cannot be secure against adaptive chosen ciphertext attacks. The question then arises as to what is the most stringent security definition which is achievable by homomorphic encryption schemes. Prior work has shown that various schemes which support a single homomorphic encryption scheme can be shown to be IND-CCA1, i.e. secure against lunchtime attacks. In this paper we extend this analysis to the recent fully homomorphic encryption scheme proposed by Gentry, as refined by Gentry, Halevi, Smart and Vercauteren. We show that the basic Gentry scheme is not IND-CCA1; indeed a trivial lunchtime attack allows one to recover the secret key. We then show that a minor modification to the variant of the somewhat homomorphic encryption scheme of Smart and Vercauteren will allow one to achieve IND-CCA1, indeed PA-1, in the standard model assuming a lattice based knowledge assumption. We also examine the security of the scheme against another security notion, namely security in the presence of ciphertext validity checking oracles; and show why CCA-like notions are important in applications in which multiple parties submit encrypted data to the "cloud" for secure processing.

1 Introduction

That some encryption schemes allow homomorphic operations, or exhibit so called *privacy homomorphisms* in the language of Rivest et. al [24], has often been considered a weakness. This is because any scheme which supports homomorphic operations is malleable, and hence is unable to achieve the de-facto security definition for encryption namely IND-CCA2. However, homomorphic encryption schemes do present a number of functional benefits. For example schemes which support a single additive homomorphic operation have been used to construct secure electronic voting schemes, e.g. [9,12].

A. Miri and S. Vaudenay (Eds.): SAC 2011, LNCS 7118, pp. 55–72, 2012.

The usefulness of schemes supporting a single homomorphic operation has led some authors to consider what security definition existing homomorphic encryption schemes meet. A natural notion to try to achieve is that of IND-CCA1, i.e. security in the presence of a lunch-time attack. Lipmaa [20] shows that the ElGamal encryption scheme is IND-CCA1 secure with respect to a hard problem which is essentially the same as the IND-CCA1 security of the ElGamal scheme; a path of work recently extended in [2] to other schemes.

A different line of work has been to examine security in the context of Plaintext Awareness, introduced by Bellare and Rogaway [5] in the random oracle model and later refined into a hierarchy of security notions (PA-0, -1 and -2) by Bellare and Palacio [4]. Intuitively a scheme is said to be PA if the only way an adversary can create a valid ciphertext is by applying encryption to a public key and a valid message. Bellare and Palacio prove that a scheme which possesses both PA-1 (resp. PA-2) and is IND-CPA, is in fact secure against IND-CCA1 (resp. IND-CCA2) attacks.

The advantage of Bellare and Palacio's work is that one works in the standard model to prove security of a scheme; the disadvantage appears to be that one needs to make a strong assumption to prove a scheme is PA-1 or PA-2. The assumption required is a so-called *knowledge assumption*. That such a strong assumption is needed should not be surprising as the PA security notions are themselves very strong. In the context of encryption schemes supporting a single homomorphic operation Bellare and Pallacio show that the Cramer-Shoup Lite scheme [10] and an ElGamal variant introduced by Damgård [11] are both PA-1, and hence IND-CCA1, assuming the standard DDH (to obtain IND-CPA security) and a Diffie–Hellman knowledge assumption (to obtain PA-1 security). Informally, the Diffie–Hellman knowledge assumption is the assumption that an algorithm can only output a Diffie–Hellman tuple if the algorithm "knows" the discrete logarithm of one-tuple member with respect to another.

Rivest et. al originally proposed homomorphic encryption schemes so as to enable arbitrary computation on encrypted data. To perform such operations one would require an encryption scheme which supports two homomorphic operations, which are "complete" in the sense of allowing arbitrary computations. Such schemes are called fully homomorphic encryption (FHE) schemes, and it was not until Gentry's breakthrough construction in 2009 [15,16] that such schemes could be constructed. Since Gentry's construction appeared a number of variants have been proposed, such as [14], as well as various simplifications [27] and improvements thereof [17]. All such schemes have been proved to be IND-CPA, i.e. secure under chosen plaintext attack.

At a high level all these constructions work in three stages: an initial *somewhat* homomorphic encryption (SHE) scheme which supports homomorphic evaluation of low degree polynomials, a process of squashing the decryption circuit and finally a bootstrapping procedure which will give fully homomorphic encryption and the evaluation of arbitrary functions on ciphertexts. In this paper we focus solely on the basic somewhat homomorphic scheme, but our attacks and analysis apply also to the extension using the bootstrapping process. Our construction of an IND-CCA1 scheme however only applies to the SHE constructions as all existing FHE constructions require public keys which already contain ciphertexts; thus with existing FHE constructions the notion of IND-CCA1 security is redundant; although in Section 7 we present a notion of CCA embeddability which can be extended to FHE.

In this paper we consider the Smart–Vercauteren variant [27] of Gentry's scheme. In this variant there are two possible message spaces; one can either use the scheme to encrypt bits, and hence perform homomorphic operations in $\mathbb{F}_2$; or one can encrypt polynomials of degree N over $\mathbb{F}_2$. When one encrypts bits one achieves a scheme that is a specialisation of the original Gentry scheme, and it is this variant that has recently been realised by Gentry and Halevi [17]. We call this the Gentry–Halevi variant, to avoid confusion with other variants of Gentry's scheme, and we show that this scheme is not IND-CCA1 secure.

In particular in Section 4 we present a trivial complete break of the Gentry–Halevi variant scheme, in which the secret key can be recovered via a polynomial number of queries to a decryption oracle. The attack we propose works in a similar fashion to the attack of Bleichenbacher on RSA [8], in that on each successive oracle call we reduce the possible interval containing the secret key, based on the output of the oracle. Eventually the interval contains a single element, namely the secret key. Interesting all the Bleichenbacher style attacks on RSA, [8,21,26], recover a target message, and are hence strictly CCA2 attacks, whereas our attack takes no target ciphertext and recovers the key itself.

In Section 5 we go on to show that a modification of the Smart–Vercauteren SHE variant which encrypts polynomials can be shown to be PA-1, and hence is IND-CCA1. Informally we use the full Smart–Vercauteren variant to recover the random polynomial used to encrypt the plaintext polynomial in the decryption phase, and then we re-encrypt the result to check against the ciphertext. This forms a ciphertext validity check which then allows us to show PA-1 security based on a new lattice knowledge assumption. Our lattice knowledge assumption is a natural lattice based variant of the Diffie–Hellman knowledge assumption mentioned previously. In particular we assume that if an algorithm is able to output a non-lattice vector which is sufficiently close to a lattice vector then it must "know" the corresponding close lattice vector. We hope that this problem may be of independent interest in analysing other lattice based cryptographic schemes; indeed the notion is closely linked to a key "quantum" step in the results of Regev [23].

In Section 6 we examine possible extensions of the security notion for homomorphic encryption. We have remarked that a homomorphic encryption scheme (either one which supports single homomorphic operations, or a SHE/FHE scheme) cannot be IND-CCA2, but we have examples of singlely homomorphic and SHE IND-CCA1 schemes. The question then arises as to whether IND-CCA1 is the "correct" security definition, i.e. whether this is the strongest definition one can obtain for SHE schemes. In other contexts authors have considered attacks involving partial information oracles. In [13] Dent introduces the notion of a CPA+ attack, where the adversary is given access to an oracle which on input of a ciphertext outputs a single bit indicating whether the ciphertext is valid or not. Such a notion was originally introduced by Joye, Quisquater and Yung [19] in the context of attacking a variant of the EPOC-2 cipher which had been "proved" IND-CCA2. This notion was recently re-introduced under the name of a CVA (ciphertext verification) attack by Hu et al [18], in the context of symmetric encryption schemes. We use the term CVA rather than CPA+ as it conveys more easily the meaning of the security notion.

Such ciphertext validity oracles are actually the key component behind the traditional application of Bleichenbacher style attacks against RSA, in that one uses the oracle to recover information about the target plaintext. We show that our SHE scheme which is IND-CCA1 is not IND-CVA, by presenting an IND-CVA attack. In particular this shows that CVA security is not implied by PA-1 security. Given PA-1 is such a strong notion this is itself interesting since it shows that CVA attacks are relatively powerful. The attack is not of the Bleichenbacher type, but is now more akin to the security reduction between search and decision LWE [25]. This attack opens up the possibility of a new SHE scheme which is also IND-CVA, a topic which we leave as an open problem; or indeed the construction of standard additive or multiplicative homomorphic schemes which are IND-CVA.

Finally, in Section 7 we consider an application area of cloud computing in which multiple players submit encrypted data to a cloud computer; which in turn will perform computations on the encrypted data. We show that such a scenario does indeed seem to require a form of IND-CCA2 protection of ciphertexts, yet still maintaining homomorphic properties. To deal with this we introduce the notion of CCA-embeddable homomorphic encryption.

2 Notation and Standard Definitions

For integers z, d reduction of z modulo d in the interval $[-d/2, d/2)$ will be denoted by $[z]_d$. For a rational number q, $\lfloor q \rceil$ will denote the rounding of q to the nearest integer, and $[q]$ denotes the (signed) distance between q and the nearest integer, i.e. $\lfloor q \rceil = q - [q]$. The notation $a \leftarrow b$ means assign the object b to a, whereas $a \leftarrow B$ for a set B means assign a uniformly at random from the set B. If B is an algorithm this means assign a with the output of B where the probability distribution is over the random coins of B.

For a polynomial $F(X) \in \mathbb{Q}[X]$ we let $\|F(X)\|_\infty$ denote the ∞-norm of the coefficient vector, i.e. the maximum coefficient in absolute value. If $F(X) \in \mathbb{Q}[X]$ then we let $\lfloor F(X) \rceil$ denote the polynomial in $\mathbb{Z}[X]$ obtained by rounding the coefficients of $F(X)$ to the nearest integer.

FULLY HOMOMORPHIC ENCRYPTION: A fully homomorphic encryption scheme is a tuple of three algorithms $\mathcal{E} = (\mathsf{KeyGen}, \mathsf{Encrypt}, \mathsf{Decrypt})$ in which the message space is a ring $(R, +, \cdot)$ and the ciphertext space is also a ring $(\mathcal{R}, \oplus, \otimes)$ such that for all messages $m_1, m_2 \in R$, and all outputs $(\mathsf{pk}, \mathsf{sk}) \leftarrow \mathsf{KeyGen}(1^\lambda)$, we have

$$\begin{aligned} m_1 + m_2 &= \mathsf{Decrypt}(\mathsf{Encrypt}(m_1, \mathsf{pk}) \oplus \mathsf{Encrypt}(m_2, \mathsf{pk}), \mathsf{sk}) \\ m_1 \cdot m_2 &= \mathsf{Decrypt}(\mathsf{Encrypt}(m_1, \mathsf{pk}) \otimes \mathsf{Encrypt}(m_2, \mathsf{pk}), \mathsf{sk}). \end{aligned}$$

A scheme is said to be *somewhat* homomorphic if it can deal with only a limited number of addition and multiplications before decryption fails.

SECURITY NOTIONS FOR PUBLIC KEY ENCRYPTION: Semantic security of a public key encryption scheme, whether standard, homomorphic, or fully homomorphic, is captured by the following game between a challenger and an adversary $\mathcal{A}$, running in two stages;

- $(\mathsf{pk}, \mathsf{sk}) \leftarrow \mathsf{KeyGen}(1^\lambda)$.
- $(m_0, m_1, \mathsf{St}) \leftarrow \mathcal{A}_1^{(\cdot)}(\mathsf{pk})$. /* Stage 1 */
- $b \leftarrow \{0, 1\}$.
- $c^* \leftarrow \mathsf{Encrypt}(m_b, \mathsf{pk}; r)$.
- $b' \leftarrow \mathcal{A}_2^{(\cdot)}(c^*, \mathsf{St})$. /* Stage 2 */

The adversary is said to win the game if $b = b'$, with the advantage of the adversary winning the game being defined by

$$\mathrm{Adv}_{\mathcal{A},\mathcal{E},\lambda}^{IND-atk} = |\Pr(b = b') - 1/2|.$$

A scheme is said to be IND-atk secure if no polynomial time adversary $\mathcal{A}$ can win the above game with non-negligible advantage in the security parameter λ. The precise security notion one obtains depends on the oracle access one gives the adversary in its different stages.

- If $\mathcal{A}$ has access to no oracles in either stage then atk=CPA.
- If $\mathcal{A}$ has access to a decryption oracle in stage one then atk=CCA1.
- If $\mathcal{A}$ has access to a decryption oracle in both stages then atk=CCA2, often now denoted simply CCA.
- If $\mathcal{A}$ has access to a ciphertext validity oracle in both stages, which on input of a ciphertext determines whether it would output $\perp$ or not on decryption, then atk=CVA.

<u>LATTICES</u>: A (full-rank) lattice is simply a discrete subgroup of $\mathbb{R}^n$ generated by n linear independent vectors, $B = \{\mathbf{b}_1, \ldots, \mathbf{b}_n\}$, called a basis. Every lattice has an infinite number of bases, with each set of basis vectors being related by a unimodular transformation matrix. If B is such a set of vectors, we write

$$L = \mathcal{L}(B) = \{\mathbf{v} \cdot B | \mathbf{v} \in \mathbb{Z}^n\}$$

to be the resulting lattice. An integer lattice is a lattice in which all the bases vectors have integer coordinates.

For any basis there is an associated fundamental parallelepiped which can be taken as $\mathcal{P}(B) = \{\sum_{i=1}^n x_i \cdot \mathbf{b}_i | x_i \in [-1/2, 1/2)\}$. The volume of this fundamental parallelepiped is given by the absolute value of the determinant of the basis matrix $\Delta = |\det(B)|$. We denote by $\lambda_\infty(L)$ the ∞-norm of a shortest vector (for the ∞-norm) in L.

3 The Smart-Vercauteren Variant of Gentry's Scheme

We will be examining variants of Gentry's SHE scheme [15], in particular three variants based on the simplification of Smart and Vercauteren [27], as optimized by Gentry and Halevi [17]. All variants make use of the same key generation procedure, parametrized by a tuple of integers (N, t, μ); we assume there is a function mapping security parameters λ into tuples (N, t, μ). In practice N will be a power of two, t will be greater than $2^{\sqrt{N}}$ and μ will be a small integer, perhaps one.

$\mathsf{KeyGen}(1^\lambda)$
- Pick an irreducible polynomial $F \in \mathbb{Z}[X]$ of degree N.
- Pick a polynomial $G(X) \in \mathbb{Z}[X]$ of degree at most $N-1$, with coefficients bounded by t.
- $d \leftarrow \mathsf{resultant}(F, G)$.
- G is chosen such that $G(X)$ has a single unique root in common with $F(X)$ modulo d. Let α denote this root.
- $Z(X) \leftarrow d/G(X) \pmod{F(X)}$.
- $\mathsf{pk} \leftarrow (\alpha, d, \mu, F(X))$, $\mathsf{sk} \leftarrow (Z(X), G(X), d, F(X))$.

In [17] Gentry and Halevi show how to compute, for the polynomial $F(X) = X^{2^n}+1$, the root α and the polynomial $Z(X)$ using a method based on the Fast Fourier Transform. In particular they show how this can be done for non-prime values of d (removing one of the main restrictions in the key generation method proposed in [27]).

By construction, the principal ideal $\mathfrak{g}$ generated by $G(X)$ in the number field $K = \mathbb{Z}[X]/(F(X))$ is equal to the ideal with $\mathcal{O}_K$ basis $(d, X-\alpha)$. In particular, the ideal $\mathfrak{g}$ precisely consists of all elements in $\mathbb{Z}[X]/(F(X))$ that are zero when evaluated at α modulo d. The Hermite-Normal-Form of a basis matrix of the lattice defined by the coefficient vectors of $\mathfrak{g}$ is given by

$$B = \begin{pmatrix} d & & & 0 \\ -\alpha & 1 & & \\ -\alpha^2 & & 1 & \\ \vdots & & & \ddots \\ -\alpha^{N-1} & 0 & & 1 \end{pmatrix}, \qquad (1)$$

where the elements in the first column are reduced modulo d.

To aid what follows we write $Z(X) = z_0 + z_1 \cdot X + \ldots + z_{N-1} \cdot X^{N-1}$ and define

$$\delta_\infty = \sup\left\{ \frac{\|g(X) \cdot h(X) \pmod{F(X)}\|_\infty}{\|g(X)\|_\infty \cdot \|h(X)\|_\infty} : g, h \in \mathbb{Z}[X], \deg(g), \deg(h) < N \right\}.$$

For the choice $f = X^N + 1$, we have $\delta_\infty = N$. The key result to understand how the simplification of Smart and Vercauteren to Gentry's scheme works is the following lemma adapted from [27].

Lemma 1. *Let $Z(X), G(X), \alpha$ and d be as defined in the above key generation procedure. If $C(X) \in \mathbb{Z}[X]/(F(X))$ is a polynomial with $\|C(X)\|_\infty < U$ and set $c = C(\alpha) \pmod{d}$, then*

$$C(X) = c - \left\lfloor \frac{c \cdot Z(X)}{d} \right\rceil \cdot G(X) \pmod{F(X)}$$

for

$$U = \frac{d}{2 \cdot \delta_\infty \cdot \|Z(X)\|_\infty}.$$

Proof. By definition of c, we have that $c - C(X)$ is contained in the principal ideal generated by $G(X)$ and thus there exists a $q(X) \in \mathbb{Z}[X]/(F(X))$ such that $c - C(X) = q(X)G(X)$. Using $Z(X) = d/G(X) \pmod{F(X)}$, we can write

$$q(X) = \frac{cZ(X)}{d} - \frac{C(X)Z(X)}{d}.$$

Since $q(X)$ has integer coefficients, we can recover it by rounding the coefficients of the first term if the coefficients of the second term are strictly bounded by $1/2$. This shows that $C(X)$ can be recovered from c for $\|C(X)\|_\infty < d/(2 \cdot \delta_\infty \cdot \|Z(X)\|_\infty)$.

Note that the above lemma essentially states that if $\|C(X)\|_\infty < U$, then $C(X)$ is determined uniquely by its evaluation in α modulo d. Recall that any polynomial $H(X)$ of degree less than N, whose coefficient vector is in the lattice defined in equation (1), satisfies $H(\alpha) = 0 \pmod{d}$. Therefore, if $H(X) \neq 0$, the lemma implies, for such an H, that $\|H(X)\|_\infty \geq U$, and thus we conclude that $U \leq \lambda_\infty(L)$. Since the coefficient vector of $G(X)$ is clearly in the lattice L, we conclude that

$$U \leq \lambda_\infty(L) \leq \|G(X)\|_\infty.$$

Although Lemma 1 provides the maximum value of U for which ciphertexts are decryptable, we will only allow a quarter of this maximum value, i.e. $T = U/4$. As such we are guaranteed that $T \leq \lambda_\infty(L)/4$. We note that T defines the size of the circuit that the somewhat homomorphic encryption scheme can deal with. Our choice of T will become clear in Section 5.

Using the above key generation method we can define three variants of the Smart–Vercauteren variant of Gentry's scheme. The first variant is the one used in the Gentry/Halevi implementation of [17], the second is the general variant proposed by Smart and Vercauteren, whereas the third divides the decryption procedure into two steps and provides a ciphertext validity check. In later sections we shall show that the first variant is not IND-CCA1 secure, and by extension neither is the second variant. However, we will show that the third variant is indeed IND-CCA1. We will then show that the third variant is not IND-CVA secure.

Each of the following variants is only a somewhat homomorphic scheme, extending it to a fully homomorphic scheme can be performed using methods of [15,16,17].

GENTRY–HALEVI VARIANT: The plaintext space is the field $\mathbb{F}_2$. The above KeyGen algorithm is modified to only output keys for which $d \equiv 1 \pmod{2}$. This implies that at least one coefficient of $Z(X)$, say z_{i_0} will be odd. We replace $Z(X)$ in the private key with z_{i_0}, and can drop the values $G(X)$ and $F(X)$ entirely from the private key. Encryption and decryption can now be defined via the functions:

Encrypt(m, pk; r)
- $R(X) \leftarrow \mathbb{Z}[X]$ s.t. $\|R(X)\|_\infty \leq \mu$.
- $C(X) \leftarrow m + 2 \cdot R(X)$.
- $c \leftarrow [C(\alpha)]_d$.
- Return c.

Decrypt(c, sk)
- $m \leftarrow [c \cdot z_{i_0}]_d \pmod{2}$
- Return m.

FULL-SPACE SMART–VERCAUTEREN: In this variant the plaintext space is the algebra $\mathbb{F}_2[X]/(F(X))$, where messages are given by binary polynomials of degree less than N. As such we call this the Full-Space Smart–Vercauteren system as the plaintext space is the full set of binary polynomials, with multiplication and addition defined modulo $F(X)$. We modify the above key generation algorithm so that it only outputs keys for which the polynomial $G(X)$ satisifies $G(X) \equiv 1 \pmod 2$. This results in algorithms defined by:

Encrypt($M(X)$, pk; r)
- $R(X) \leftarrow \mathbb{Z}[X]$ s.t. $\|R(X)\|_\infty \leq \mu$.
- $C(X) \leftarrow M(X) + 2 \cdot R(X)$.
- $c \leftarrow [C(\alpha)]_d$.
- Return c.

Decrypt(c, sk)
- $C(X) \leftarrow c - \lfloor c \cdot Z(X)/d \rceil$.
- $M(X) \leftarrow C(X) \pmod 2$.
- Return $M(X)$.

That decryption works, assuming the input ciphertext corresponds to the evaluation of a polynomial with coefficients bounded by T, follows from Lemma 1 and the fact that $G(X) \equiv 1 \pmod 2$.

CCSHE: This is our ciphertext-checking SHE scheme (or ccSHE scheme for short). This is exactly like the above Full-Space Smart–Vercauteren variant in terms of key generation, but we now check the ciphertext before we output the message. Thus encryption/decryption become;

Encrypt($M(X)$, pk; r)
- $R(X) \leftarrow \mathbb{Z}[X]$ s.t. $\|R(X)\|_\infty \leq \mu$.
- $C(X) \leftarrow M(X) + 2 \cdot R(X)$.
- $c \leftarrow [C(\alpha)]_d$.
- Return c.

Decrypt(c, sk)
- $C(X) \leftarrow c - \lfloor c \cdot Z(X)/d \rceil \cdot G(X)$.
- $C(X) \leftarrow C(X) \pmod{F(X)}$
- $c' \leftarrow [C(\alpha)]_d$.
- If $c' \neq c$ or $\|C(X)\|_\infty > T$ return $\perp$.
- $M(X) \leftarrow C(X) \pmod 2$.
- Return $M(X)$.

4 CCA1 Attack on the Gentry–Halevi Variant

We construct an IND-CCA1 attacker against the above Gentry–Halevi variant. Let z be the secret key, i.e. the specific odd coefficient of $Z(X)$ chosen by the decryptor. Note that we can assume $z \in [0, d)$, since decryption in the Gentry–Halevi variant works for any secret key $z + k \cdot d$ with $k \in \mathbb{Z}$. We assume the attacker has access to a decryption oracle to which it can make polynomially many queries, $\mathcal{O}_D(c)$. On each query the oracle returns the value of $[c \cdot z]_d \pmod 2$.

In Algorithm 1 we present pseudo-code to describe how the attack proceeds. We start with an interval $[L, \ldots, U]$ which is known to contain the secret key z and in each iteration we split the interval into two halves determined by a specific ciphertext c. The choice of which sub-interval to take next depends on whether k multiples of d are sufficient to reduce $c \cdot z$ into the range $[-d/2, \ldots, d/2)$ or whether $k+1$ multiples are required.

ANALYSIS: The core idea of the algorithm is simple: in each step we choose a "ciphertext" c such that the length of the interval for the quantity $c \cdot z$ is bounded by d. Since in

Algorithm 1. CCA1 attack on the Gentry–Halevi Variant

$L \leftarrow 0, U \leftarrow d-1$
while $U - L > 1$ **do**
  $c \leftarrow \lfloor d/(U-L) \rfloor$
  $b \leftarrow \mathcal{O}_D(c)$
  $q \leftarrow (c+b) \mod 2$
  $k \leftarrow \lfloor Lc/d + 1/2 \rfloor$
  $B \leftarrow (k+1/2)d/c$
  if ($k \bmod 2 = q$) **then**
    $U \leftarrow \lfloor B \rfloor$
  else
    $L \leftarrow \lceil B \rceil$
return L

each step, $z \in [L, U]$, we need to take $c = \lfloor d/(U-L) \rfloor$. As such it is easy to see that $c(U-L) \leq d$.

To reduce cL, we need to subtract kd such that $-d/2 \leq cL - kd < d/2$, which shows that $k = \lfloor Lc/d + 1/2 \rfloor$. Furthermore, since the length of the interval for $c \cdot z$ is bounded by d, there will be exactly one number of the form $d/2 + id$ in $[cL, cU]$, namely $d/2 + kd$. This means that there is exactly one boundary $B = (k+1/2)d/c$ in the interval for z.

Define q as the unique integer such that $-d/2 \leq cz - qd < d/2$, then since the length of the interval for $c \cdot z$ is bounded by d, we either have $q = k$ or $q = k+1$. To distinguish between the two cases, we simply look at the output of the decryption oracle: recall that the oracle outputs $[c \cdot z]_d \pmod 2$, i.e. the bit output by the oracle is

$$b = c \cdot z - q \cdot d \pmod 2 = (c+q) \pmod 2 .$$

Therefore, $q = (b+c) \pmod 2$ which allows us to choose between the cases k and $k+1$. If $q = k \pmod 2$, then z lies in the first part $[L, \lfloor B \rfloor]$, whereas in the other case, z lies in the second part $[\lceil B \rceil, U]$.

Having proved correctness we now estimate the running time. The behaviour of the algorithm is easily seen to be as follows: in each step, we obtain a boundary B in the interval $[L, U]$ and the next interval becomes either $[L, \lfloor B \rfloor]$ or $[\lceil B \rceil, U]$. Since B can be considered random in $[L, U]$ as well as the choice of the interval, this shows that in each step, the size of the interval decreases by a factor 2 on average. In conclusion we deduce that recovering the secret key will require $O(\log d)$ calls to the oracle.

The above attack is highly efficient in practice and recovers keys in a matter of seconds for all parameter sizes in [17].

5 ccSHE is PA-1

In this section we prove that the ccSHE encryption scheme given earlier is PA-1, assuming a lattice knowledge assumption holds. We first recap on the definition of PA-1 in the standard model, and then we introduce our lattice knowledge assumption. Once this is done we present the proof.

PLAINTEXT AWARENESS – PA-1: The original intuition for the introduction of plaintext awareness was as follows - if an adversary knows the plaintext corresponding to every ciphertext it produces, then the adversary has no need for a decryption oracle and hence, PA+IND-CPA must imply IND-CCA. Unfortunately, there are subtleties in the definition for plaintext awareness, leading to three definitions, PA-0, PA-1 and PA-2. However, after suitably formalizing the definitions, PA-x plus IND-CPA implies IND-CCAx, for x = 1 and 2. In our context we are only interested in IND-CCA1 security, so we will only discuss the notion of PA-1 in this paper.

Before formalizing PA-1 it is worth outlining some of the terminology. We have a polynomial time adversary $\mathcal{A}$ called a *ciphertext creator*, that takes as input a public key and can query ciphertexts to an oracle. An algorithm $\mathcal{A}^*$ is called a *successful extractor* for $\mathcal{A}$ if it can provide responses to $\mathcal{A}$ which are computationally indistinguishable from those provided by a decryption oracle. In particular a scheme is said to be PA-1 if there exists a successful extractor for any ciphertext creator that makes a polynomial number of queries. The extractor gets the same public key as $\mathcal{A}$ and also has access to the random coins used by algorithm $\mathcal{A}$. Following [4] we define PA-1 formally as follows:

Definition 1 (PA1). *Let $\mathcal{E}$ be a public key encryption scheme and $\mathcal{A}$ be an algorithm with access to an oracle $\mathcal{O}$ taking input* pk *and returning a string. Let $\mathcal{D}$ be an algorithm that takes as input a string and returns a single bit and let $\mathcal{A}^*$ be an algorithm which takes as input a string and some state information and returns either a string or the symbol $\perp$, plus a new state. We call $\mathcal{A}$ a* ciphertext creator, *$\mathcal{A}^*$ a* PA-1-extractor, *and $\mathcal{D}$ a* distinguisher. *For security parameter λ we define the (distinguishing and extracting) experiments in Figure 1, and then define the PA-1 advantage to be*

$$\mathrm{Adv}^{PA\text{-}1}_{\mathcal{E},\mathcal{A},\mathcal{D},\mathcal{A}^*}(\lambda) = \left|\Pr(\mathrm{Exp}^{PA\text{-}1\text{-}d}_{\mathcal{E},\mathcal{A},\mathcal{D}}(\lambda) = 1) - \Pr(\mathrm{Exp}^{PA\text{-}1\text{-}x}_{\mathcal{E},\mathcal{A},\mathcal{D},\mathcal{A}^*}(\lambda) = 1)\right|.$$

We say $\mathcal{A}^*$ is a successful PA-1-extractor for $\mathcal{A}$, if for every polynomial time distinguisher the above advantage is negligible.

$\mathrm{Exp}^{PA\text{-}1\text{-}d}_{\mathcal{E},\mathcal{A},\mathcal{D}}(\lambda)$:
- $(\mathsf{pk},\mathsf{sk}) \leftarrow \mathsf{KeyGen}(1^\lambda)$.
- $x \leftarrow \mathcal{A}^{\mathsf{Decrypt}(\cdot,\mathsf{sk})}(\mathsf{pk})$.
- $d \leftarrow \mathcal{D}(x)$.
- Return d.

$\mathrm{Exp}^{PA\text{-}1\text{-}x}_{\mathcal{E},\mathcal{A},\mathcal{A}^*}(\lambda)$:
- $(\mathsf{pk},\mathsf{sk}) \leftarrow \mathsf{KeyGen}(1^\lambda)$.
- Choose coins $\mathsf{coins}[\mathcal{A}]$ (resp. $\mathsf{coins}[\mathcal{A}^*]$) for $\mathcal{A}$ (resp. $\mathcal{A}^*$).
- $\mathsf{St} \leftarrow (\mathsf{pk}, \mathsf{coins}[\mathcal{A}])$.
- $x \leftarrow \mathcal{A}^{\mathcal{O}}(\mathsf{pk}; \mathsf{coins}[\mathcal{A}])$, replying to the oracle queries $\mathcal{O}(c)$ as follows:
  - $(m, \mathsf{St}) \leftarrow \mathcal{A}^*(c, \mathsf{St}; \mathsf{coins}[\mathcal{A}^*])$.
  - Return m to $\mathcal{A}$
- $d \leftarrow \mathcal{D}(x)$.
- Return d.

Fig. 1. Experiments $\mathrm{Exp}^{PA\text{-}1\text{-}d}_{\mathcal{E},\mathcal{A},\mathcal{D}}$ and $\mathrm{Exp}^{PA\text{-}1\text{-}x}_{\mathcal{E},\mathcal{A},\mathcal{A}^*}$

Note, in experiment $\mathrm{Exp}^{PA\text{-}1\text{-}d}_{\mathcal{E},\mathcal{A},\mathcal{D}}(\lambda)$ the algorithm $\mathcal{A}$'s oracle queries are responded to by the genuine decryption algorithm, whereas in $\mathrm{Exp}^{PA\text{-}1\text{-}x}_{\mathcal{E},\mathcal{A},\mathcal{A}^*}(\lambda)$ the queries are responded to by the PA-1-extractor. If $\mathcal{A}^*$ did not receive the coins $\mathsf{coins}[\mathcal{A}]$ from $\mathcal{A}$ then it would be functionally equivalent to the real decryption oracle, thus the fact that $\mathcal{A}^*$ gets access to the coins in the second experiment is crucial. Also note that the distinguisher acts independently of $\mathcal{A}^*$, and thus this is strictly stronger than having $\mathcal{A}$ decide as to whether it is interacting with an extractor or a real decryption oracle.

The intuition is that $\mathcal{A}^*$ acts as the unknowing subconscious of $\mathcal{A}$, and is able to extract knowledge about $\mathcal{A}$'s queries to its oracle. That $\mathcal{A}^*$ can obtain the underlying message captures the notion that $\mathcal{A}$ needs to know the message before it can output a valid ciphertext.

The following lemma is taken from [4] and will be used in the proof of the main theorem.

Lemma 2. *Let $\mathcal{E}$ be a public key encryption scheme. Let $\mathcal{A}$ be a polynomial-time ciphertext creator attacking $\mathcal{E}$, $\mathcal{D}$ a polynomial-time distinguisher, and $\mathcal{A}^*$ a polynomial-time PA-1-extractor. Let* DecOK *denote the event that all $\mathcal{A}^*$'s answers to $\mathcal{A}$'s queries are correct in experiment $\mathrm{Exp}^{PA\text{-}1\text{-}x}_{\mathcal{E},\mathcal{A},\mathcal{D},\mathcal{A}^*}(\lambda)$. Then,*

$$\Pr(\mathrm{Exp}^{PA\text{-}1\text{-}x}_{\mathcal{E},\mathcal{A},\mathcal{D},\mathcal{A}^*}(\lambda) = 1) \geq \Pr(\mathrm{Exp}^{PA\text{-}1\text{-}d}_{\mathcal{E},\mathcal{A},\mathcal{D}}(\lambda) = 1) - \Pr(\overline{\mathsf{DecOK}})$$

LATTICE KNOWLEDGE ASSUMPTION: Our knowledge assumption can be stated informally as follows: suppose there is a (probabilistic) algorithm $\mathcal{C}$ which takes as input a lattice basis of a lattice L and outputs a vector $\mathbf{c}$ suitably close to a lattice point $\mathbf{p}$, i.e. closer than $\epsilon \cdot \lambda_\infty(L)$ in the ∞-norm for a fixed $\epsilon \in (0, 1/2)$. Then there is an algorithm $\mathcal{C}^*$ which on input of $\mathbf{c}$ and the random coins of $\mathcal{C}$ outputs a close lattice vector $\mathbf{p}$, i.e. one for which $\|\mathbf{c} - \mathbf{p}\|_\infty < \epsilon \cdot \lambda_\infty(L)$. Note that the algorithm $\mathcal{C}^*$ can therefore act as a ϵ-CVP-solver for $\mathbf{c}$ in the ∞-norm, given the coins $\mathsf{coins}[\mathcal{C}]$. Again as in the PA-1 definition it is perhaps useful to think of $\mathcal{C}^*$ as the "subconscious" of $\mathcal{C}$, since $\mathcal{C}$ is capable of outputting a vector close to the lattice it must have known the close lattice vector in the first place. Formally we have:

Definition 2 (LK-ϵ). *Let ϵ be a fixed constant in the interval $(0, 1/2)$. Let $\mathcal{G}$ denote an algorithm which on input of a security parameter 1^λ outputs a lattice L given by a basis B of dimension $n = n(\lambda)$ and volume $\Delta = \Delta(\lambda)$. Let $\mathcal{C}$ be an algorithm that takes a lattice basis B as input, and has access to an oracle $\mathcal{O}$, and returns nothing. Let $\mathcal{C}^*$ denote an algorithm which takes as input a vector $\mathbf{c} \in \mathbb{R}^n$ and some state information, and returns another vector $\mathbf{p} \in \mathbb{R}^n$ plus a new state. Consider the experiment in Figure 2. The LK-ϵ advantage of $\mathcal{C}$ relative to $\mathcal{C}^*$ is defined by*

$$\mathrm{Adv}^{LK\text{-}\epsilon}_{\mathcal{G},\mathcal{C},\mathcal{C}^*}(\lambda) = \Pr[\mathrm{Exp}^{LK\text{-}\epsilon}_{\mathcal{G},\mathcal{C},\mathcal{C}^*}(\lambda) = 1].$$

We say $\mathcal{G}$ satisfies the LK-ϵ assumption, for a fixed ϵ, if for every polynomial time $\mathcal{C}$ there exists a polynomial time $\mathcal{C}^*$ such that $\mathrm{Adv}^{LK\text{-}\epsilon}_{\mathcal{G},\mathcal{C},\mathcal{C}^*}(\lambda)$ is a negligible function of λ.

The algorithm $\mathcal{C}$ is called an LK-ϵ adversary and $\mathcal{C}^*$ a LK-ϵ extractor. We now discuss this assumption in more detail. Notice, that for all lattices, if $\epsilon < 1/4$ then the probability of a random vector being within $\epsilon \cdot \lambda_\infty(L)$ of the lattice is bounded from above by $1/2^n$, and for lattices which are not highly orthogonal this is likely to hold for all ϵ

$\mathrm{Exp}^{LK\text{-}\epsilon}_{\mathcal{G},\mathcal{C},\mathcal{C}^*}(\lambda)$:

- $B \leftarrow \mathcal{G}(1^\lambda)$.
- Choose coins $\mathsf{coins}[\mathcal{C}]$ (resp. $\mathsf{coins}[\mathcal{C}^*]$) for $\mathcal{C}$ (resp. $\mathcal{C}^*$).
- $\mathsf{St} \leftarrow (B, \mathsf{coins}[\mathcal{C}])$.
- Run $\mathcal{C}^{\mathcal{O}}(B; \mathsf{coins}[\mathcal{C}])$ until it halts, replying to the oracle queries $\mathcal{O}(\mathbf{c})$ as follows:
  - $(\mathbf{p}, \mathsf{St}) \leftarrow \mathcal{C}^*(\mathbf{c}, \mathsf{St}; \mathsf{coins}[\mathcal{C}^*])$.
  - If $\mathbf{p} \notin \mathcal{L}(B)$, return 1.
  - If $\|\mathbf{p} - \mathbf{c}\|_\infty > \epsilon \cdot \lambda_\infty(L)$, return 1.
  - Return $\mathbf{p}$ to $\mathcal{C}$.
- Return 0.

Fig. 2. Experiment $\mathrm{Exp}^{LK\text{-}\epsilon}_{\mathcal{G},\mathcal{C},\mathcal{C}^*}(\lambda)$

up to $1/2$. Our choice of T in the ccSHE scheme as $U/4$ is to guarantee that our lattice knowledge assumption is applied with $\epsilon = 1/4$, and hence is more likely to hold.

If the query $\mathbf{c}$ which $\mathcal{C}$ asks of its oracle is within $\epsilon \cdot \lambda_\infty(L)$ of a lattice point then we require that $\mathcal{C}^*$ finds such a close lattice point. If it does not then the experiment will output 1; and the assumption is that this happens with negligible probability.

Notice that if $\mathcal{C}$ asks its oracle a query of a vector which is not within $\epsilon \cdot \lambda_\infty(L)$ of a lattice point then the algorithm $\mathcal{C}^*$ may do whatever it wants. However, to determine this condition within the experiment we require that the environment running the experiment is all powerful, in particular, that it can compute $\lambda_\infty(L)$ and decide whether a vector is close enough to the lattice. Thus our experiment, but not algorithms $\mathcal{C}$ and $\mathcal{C}^*$, is assumed to be information theoretic. This might seem strange at first sight but is akin to a similarly powerful game experiment in the strong security model for certificateless encryption [1], or the definition of insider unforgeable signcryption in [3].

For certain input bases, e.g. reduced ones or ones of small dimension, an algorithm $\mathcal{C}^*$ can be constructed by standard algorithms to solve the CVP problem. This does not contradict our assumption, since $\mathcal{C}$ would also be able to apply such an algorithm and hence "know" the close lattice point. Our assumption is that when this is not true, the only way $\mathcal{C}$ could generate a close lattice point (for small enough values of ϵ) is by computing $\mathbf{x} \in \mathbb{Z}^n$ and perturbing the vector $\mathbf{x} \cdot B$.

MAIN THEOREM:

Theorem 1. *Let $\mathcal{G}$ denote the lattice basis generator induced from the* KeyGen *algorithm of the ccSHE scheme, i.e. for a given security parameter 1^λ, run* $\mathsf{KeyGen}(1^\lambda)$ *to obtain* $\mathsf{pk} = (\alpha, d, \mu, F(X))$ *and* $\mathsf{sk} = (Z(X), G(X), d, F(X))$, *and generate the lattice basis B as in equation* (1). *Then, if $\mathcal{G}$ satisfies the LK-ϵ assumption for $\epsilon = 1/4$ then the ccSHE scheme is PA-1.*

Proof. Let $\mathcal{A}$ be a polynomial-time ciphertext creator attacking the ccSHE scheme, then we show how to construct a polynomial time PA1-extractor $\mathcal{A}^*$. The creator $\mathcal{A}$ takes as input the public key $\mathsf{pk} = (\alpha, d, \mu, F(X))$ and random coins $\mathsf{coins}[\mathcal{A}]$ and returns an integer as the candidate ciphertext. To define $\mathcal{A}^*$, we will exploit $\mathcal{A}$ to build a polynomial-time LK-ϵ adversary $\mathcal{C}$ attacking the generator $\mathcal{G}$. By the LK-ϵ assumption there exists a polynomial-time LK-ϵ extractor $\mathcal{C}^*$, that will serve as the main building block for the PA1-extractor $\mathcal{A}^*$. The description of the LK-ϵ adversary $\mathcal{C}$ is given in Figure 3 and the description of the PA-1-extractor $\mathcal{A}^*$ is given in Figure 4.

LK-ϵ adversary $\mathcal{C}^{\mathcal{O}}(B; \mathsf{coins}[\mathcal{C}])$
- Let $d = B[0][0]$ and $\alpha = -B[1][0]$
- Parse $\mathsf{coins}[\mathcal{C}]$ as $\mu || F(X) || \mathsf{coins}[\mathcal{A}]$
- Run $\mathcal{A}$ on input $(\alpha, d, \mu, F(X))$ and coins $\mathsf{coins}[\mathcal{A}]$ until it halts, replying to its oracle queries as follows:
  - If $\mathcal{A}$ makes a query with input c, then
  - Submit $(c, 0, 0, \dots, 0)$ to $\mathcal{O}$ and let $\mathbf{p}$ denote the response
  - Let $\mathbf{c} = (c, 0, \dots, 0) - \mathbf{p}$, and $C(X) = \sum_{i=0}^{N-1} \mathbf{c}_i X^i$
  - Let $c' = [C(\alpha)]_d$
  - If $c' \neq c$ or $\|C(X)\|_\infty \geq T$, then $M(X) \leftarrow \perp$, else $M(X) \leftarrow C(X) \pmod 2$
  - Return $M(X)$ to $\mathcal{A}$ as the oracle response.
- Halt

Fig. 3. LK-ϵ adversary

PA-1-extractor $\mathcal{A}^*(c, \mathsf{St}[\mathcal{A}^*]; \mathsf{coins}[\mathcal{A}^*])$
- If $\mathsf{St}[\mathcal{A}^*]$ is initial state then
  - parse $\mathsf{coins}[\mathcal{A}^*]$ as $(\alpha, d, \mu, F(X)) || \mathsf{coins}[\mathcal{A}]$
  - $\mathsf{St}[C^*] \leftarrow (\alpha, d, \mu, F(X)) || \mathsf{coins}[\mathcal{A}]$
  - else parse $\mathsf{coins}[\mathcal{A}^*]$ as $(\alpha, d, \mu, F(X)) || \mathsf{St}[\mathcal{C}^*]$
- $(\mathbf{p}, \mathsf{St}[\mathcal{C}^*]) \leftarrow \mathcal{C}^*((c, 0, \dots, 0), \mathsf{St}[\mathcal{C}^*]; \mathsf{coins}[\mathcal{A}^*])$
- Let $\mathbf{c} = (c, 0, \dots, 0) - \mathbf{p}$, and $C(X) = \sum_{i=0}^{N-1} \mathbf{c}_i X^i$
- Let $c' = [C(\alpha)]_d$
- If $c' \neq c$ or $\|C(X)\|_\infty \geq T$, then $M(X) \leftarrow \perp$, else $M(X) \leftarrow C(X) \pmod 2$
- $\mathsf{St}[\mathcal{A}^*] \leftarrow (\alpha, d, \mu, F(X)) || \mathsf{St}[C^*]$
- Return $(M(X), \mathsf{St}[\mathcal{A}^*])$.

Fig. 4. PA-1-extractor

We first show that $\mathcal{A}^*$ is a successful PA-1-extractor for $\mathcal{A}$. In particular, let DecOK denote the event that all $\mathcal{A}^*$'s answers to $\mathcal{A}$'s queries are correct in $\mathrm{Exp}^{PA\text{-}1\text{-}x}_{\mathrm{ccSHE},\mathcal{A},\mathcal{D},\mathcal{A}^*}(\lambda)$, then we have that $\Pr(\overline{\mathsf{DecOK}}) \leq \mathrm{Adv}^{LK\text{-}\epsilon}_{\mathcal{G},\mathcal{C},\mathcal{C}^*}(\lambda)$.

We first consider the case that c is a valid ciphertext, i.e. a ciphertext such that $\mathsf{Decrypt}(c, \mathsf{sk}) \neq \perp$, then by definition of Decrypt in the ccSHE scheme there exists a $C(x)$ such that $c = [C(\alpha)]_d$ and $\|C(X)\|_\infty \leq T$. Let $\mathbf{p}'$ be the coefficient vector of $c - C(X)$, then by definition of c, we have that $\mathbf{p}'$ is a lattice vector that is within distance T of the vector $(c, 0, \dots, 0)$. Furthermore, since $T \leq \lambda_\infty(L)/4$, the vector $\mathbf{p}'$ is the *unique* vector with this property. Let $\mathbf{p}$ be the vector returned by $\mathcal{C}^*$ and assume that $\mathbf{p}$ passes the test $\|(c, 0, \dots, 0) - \mathbf{p}\|_\infty \leq T$, then we conclude that $\mathbf{p} = \mathbf{p}'$. This shows that if c is a valid ciphertext, it will be decrypted correctly by $\mathcal{A}^*$.

When c is an invalid ciphertext then the real decryption oracle will always output $\perp$, and it can be easily seen that our PA-1 extractor $\mathcal{A}^*$ will also output $\perp$. Thus in the case of an invalid ciphertext the adversary $\mathcal{A}$ cannot tell the two oracles apart. The theorem now follows from combining the inequality $\Pr(\overline{\mathsf{DecOK}}) \leq \mathrm{Adv}_{\mathcal{G},\mathcal{C},\mathcal{C}^*}^{LK\text{-}\epsilon}(\lambda)$ with Lemma 2 as follows:

$$\begin{aligned}\mathrm{Adv}_{\mathcal{E},\mathcal{A},\mathcal{D},\mathcal{A}^*}^{PA\text{-}1}(\lambda) &= \Pr(\mathrm{Exp}_{\mathcal{E},\mathcal{A},\mathcal{D}}^{PA\text{-}1\text{-}d}(\lambda)=1) - \Pr(\mathrm{Exp}_{\mathcal{E},\mathcal{A},\mathcal{D},\mathcal{A}^*}^{PA\text{-}1\text{-}x}(\lambda)=1)\\ &\leq \Pr(\mathrm{Exp}_{\mathcal{E},\mathcal{A},\mathcal{D}}^{PA\text{-}1\text{-}d}(\lambda)=1) - \Pr(\mathrm{Exp}_{\mathcal{E},\mathcal{A},\mathcal{D}}^{PA\text{-}1\text{-}d}(\lambda)=1) + \Pr(\overline{\mathsf{DecOK}})\\ &\leq \mathrm{Adv}_{\mathcal{G},\mathcal{C},\mathcal{C}^*}^{LK\text{-}\epsilon}(\lambda)\,.\end{aligned}$$

6 ccSHE Is Not Secure in the Presence of a CVA Attack

We now show that our ccSHE scheme is not secure when the attacker, after being given the target ciphertext c^*, is given access to an oracle $\mathcal{O}_{\mathrm{CVA}}(c)$ which returns 1 if c is a valid ciphertext (i.e. the decryption algorithm would output a message), and which returns 0 if it is invalid (i.e. the decryption algorithm would output $\perp$). Such an "oracle" can often be obtained in the real world by the attacker observing the behaviour of a party who is fed ciphertexts of the attackers choosing. Since a CVA attack is strictly weaker than a IND-CCA2 attack it is an interesting open (and practical) question as to whether an FHE scheme can be CVA secure.

We now show that the ccSHE scheme is not CVA secure, by presenting a relatively trivial attack: Suppose the adversary is given a target ciphertext c^* associated with a hidden message m^*. Using the method in Algorithm 2 it is easy to determine the message using access to $\mathcal{O}_{\mathrm{CVA}}(c)$. Basically, we add on multiples of α^i to the ciphertext until it does not decrypt; this allows us to perform a binary search on the i-th coefficient of $C(X)$, since we know the bound T on the coefficients of $C(X)$.

Algorithm 2. CVA attack on ccSHE

```
C(X) ← 0
for i from 0 upto N − 1 do
    L ← −T + 1, U ← T − 1
    while U ≠ L do
        M ← ⌈(U + L)/2⌉.
        c ← [−c* + (M + T − 1) · α^i]_d.
        if O_CVA(c) = 1 then
            L ← M.
        else
            U ← M − 1.
    C(X) ← C(X) + U · X^i.
m* ← C(X) (mod 2)
return m*
```

If c_i is the ith coefficient of the actual $C(X)$ underlying the target ciphertext c^*, then the ith coefficient of the polynomial underlying ciphertext c being passed to the $\mathcal{O}_{\mathrm{CVA}}$

oracle is given by $M + T - 1 - c_i$. When $M \leq c_i$ this coefficient is less than T and so the oracle will return 1, however when $M > c_i$ the coefficient is greater than or equal T and hence the oracle will return 0. Thus we can divide the interval for c_i in two depending on the outcome of the test.

It is obvious that the complexity of the attack is $O(N \cdot \log_2 T)$. Since, for the recommended parameters in the key generation method, N and $\log_2 T$ are polynomial functions of the security parameter, we obtain a polynomial time attack.

7 CCA2 Somewhat Homomorphic Encryption?

In this section we deal with an additional issue related to CCA security of somewhat homomorphic encryption schemes. Consider the following scenario: three parties wish to use SHE to compute some information about some data they posses. Suppose the three pieces of data are m_1, m_2 and m_3. The parties encrypt these messages with the SHE scheme to obtain ciphertexts c_1, c_2 and c_3. These are then passed to a third party who computes, via the SHE properties, the required function. The resulting ciphertext is passed to an "Opener" who then decrypts the output and passes the computed value back to the three parties. As such we are using SHE to perform a form of multi-party computation, using SHE to perform the computation and a special third party, called an Opener, to produce the final result.

Consider the above scenario in which the messages lie in $\{0, 1\}$ and the function to be computed is the majority function. Now assume that the third party and the protocol are not synchronous. In such a situation the third party may be able to make a copy of the first party's ciphertext and submit it as his own. In such a situation the third party forces the above protocol to produce an output equal to the first party's input; thus security of the first party's input is lost. This example may seem a little contrived but it is, in essence, the basis of the recent attack by Smyth and Cortier [28] on the Helios voting system; recall Helios is a voting system based on homomorphic (but not fully homomorphic) encryption.

An obvious defence against the above attack would be to disallow input ciphertexts from one party, which are identical to another party's. However, this does not preclude a party from using malleability of the underlying SHE scheme to produce a ciphertext c_3, such that $c_3 \neq c_1$, but $\mathsf{Decrypt}(c_1, \mathsf{sk}) = \mathsf{Decrypt}(c_3, \mathsf{sk})$. Hence, we need to preclude (at least) forms of benign malleability, but to do so would contradict the fact that we require a fully homomorphic encryption scheme.

To get around this problem we introduce the notion of *CCA-embeddable homomorphic encryption*. Informally this is an IND-CCA2 public key encryption scheme $\mathcal{E}$, for which given a ciphertext c one can publicly extract an equivalent ciphertext c' for an IND-CPA homomorphic encryption scheme $\mathcal{E}'$. More formally

Definition 3. *An IND-CPA homomorphic (possibly fully homomorphic) public key encryption scheme* $\mathcal{E}' = (\mathsf{KeyGen}', \mathsf{Encrypt}', \mathsf{Decrypt}')$ *is said to be* CCA-embeddable *if there is an IND-CCA encryption scheme* $\mathcal{E} = (\mathsf{KeyGen}, \mathsf{Encrypt}, \mathsf{Decrypt})$ *and an algorithm* Extract *such that*

- KeyGen *produces two secret keys* $\mathsf{sk}', \mathsf{sk}''$*, where* sk' *is in the keyspace of* $\mathcal{E}'$.
- $\mathsf{Decrypt}'(\mathsf{Extract}(\mathsf{Encrypt}(m, pk), \mathsf{sk}''), \mathsf{sk}') = m$.

- *The ciphertext validity check for $\mathcal{E}$ is computable using only the secret key* sk''.
- *CCA1 security of $\mathcal{E}'$ is not compromised by leakage of* sk''.

As a simple example, for standard homomorphic encryption, is that ElGamal is CCA-embeddable into the Cramer–Shoup encryption scheme [10]. We note that this notion of CCA-embeddable encryption was independently arrived at by [7] for standard (singularly) homomorphic encryption in the context of providing a defence against the earlier mentioned attack on Helios. See [7] for a more complete discussion of the concept.

As a proof of concept for somewhat homomorphic encryption schemes we show that, in the random oracle model, the somewhat homomorphic encryption schemes considered in this paper are CCA-embeddable. We do this by utilizing the Naor–Yung paradigm [22] for constructing IND-CCA encryption schemes, and the zero-knowledge proofs of knowledge for semi-homomorphic schemes considered in [6]. Note that our construction is inefficient; we leave it as an open problem as to whether more specific constructions can be provided for the specific SHE schemes considered in this paper.

CONSTRUCTION: Given an SHE scheme $\mathcal{E}' = (\mathsf{KeyGen}', \mathsf{Encrypt}', \mathsf{Decrypt}')$ we construct the scheme $\mathcal{E} = (\mathsf{KeyGen}, \mathsf{Encrypt}, \mathsf{Decrypt})$ into which $\mathcal{E}'$ embeds as follows, where $\mathsf{NIZKPoK} = (\mathsf{Prove}, \mathsf{Verify})$ is a suitable non-malleable non-interactive zero-knowledge proof of knowledge of equality of two plaintexts:

$\mathsf{KeyGen}(1^\lambda)$

- $(\mathsf{pk}_1', \mathsf{sk}_1') \leftarrow \mathsf{KeyGen}'(1^\lambda)$.
- $(\mathsf{pk}_2', \mathsf{sk}_2') \leftarrow \mathsf{KeyGen}'(1^\lambda)$.
- $\mathsf{pk} \leftarrow (\mathsf{pk}_1', \mathsf{pk}_2'), \mathsf{sk} \leftarrow (\mathsf{sk}_1', \mathsf{sk}_2')$.
- Return $(\mathsf{pk}, \mathsf{sk})$.

$\mathsf{Encrypt}(m, \mathsf{pk}; r)$

- $c_1' \leftarrow \mathsf{Encrypt}'(m, \mathsf{pk}_1'; r_1')$.
- $c_2' \leftarrow \mathsf{Encrypt}'(m, \mathsf{pk}_2'; r_2')$.
- $\Sigma \leftarrow \mathsf{Prove}(c_1, c_2; m, r_1', r_2')$.
- $c \leftarrow (c_1', c_2', \Sigma)$.
- Return c.

$\mathsf{Extract}(c)$

- Parse c as (c_1', c_2', Σ).
- Return c_1'.

$\mathsf{Decrypt}(c, \mathsf{sk})$

- Parse c as (c_1', c_2', Σ).
- If $\mathsf{Verify}(\Sigma, c_1', c_2') = 0$ return $\perp$.
- $m \leftarrow \mathsf{Decrypt}'(c_1', \mathsf{sk}_1')$.
- Return m.

All that remains is to describe how to instantiate the NIZKPoK. We do this using the Fiat–Shamir heuristic applied to the Sigma-protocol in Figure 5. The protocol is derived from the same principles as those in [6], and security (completeness, soundness and zero-knowledge) can be proved in an almost identical way to that in [6]. The main difference being that we need an adjustment to be made to the response part of the protocol to deal with the message space being defined modulo two. We give the Sigma protocol in the simplified case of application to the Gentry–Halevi variant, where the message space is equal to $\{0, 1\}$. Generalising the protocol to the Full Space Smart–Vercauteren variant requires a more complex "adjustment" to the values of t_1 and t_2 in the protocol. Notice that the soundness error in the following protocol is only $1/2$, thus we need to repeat the protocol a number of times to obtain negligible soundness error which leads to a loss of efficiency.

Prover		**Verifier**
$c_1 = \mathsf{Encrypt}'(m, \mathsf{pk}_1'; r_1')$		
$c_2 = \mathsf{Encrypt}'(m, \mathsf{pk}_2'; r_2')$		c_1, c_2
$y \leftarrow \{0,1\}$		
$a_1 \leftarrow \mathsf{Encrypt}'(y, \mathsf{pk}_1'; s_1')$		
$a_2 \leftarrow \mathsf{Encrypt}'(y, \mathsf{pk}_2'; s_2')$	$\xrightarrow{a_1, a_2}$	
	$\xleftarrow{e}$	$e \leftarrow \{0,1\}$
$z \leftarrow y \oplus e \cdot m$		
$t_1 \leftarrow s_1 + e \cdot r_1 + e \cdot y \cdot m$		
$t_2 \leftarrow s_2 + e \cdot r_2 + e \cdot y \cdot m$	$\xrightarrow{z, t_1, t_2}$	Accept if and only if
		$\mathsf{Encrypt}'(z, pk_1; t_1) = a_1 + e \cdot c_1$
		$\mathsf{Encrypt}'(z, pk_2; t_2) = a_2 + e \cdot c_2.$

Fig. 5. ZKPoK of equality of two plaintexts

Acknowledgements. All authors were partially supported by the European Commission through the ICT Programme under Contract ICT-2007-216676 ECRYPT II. The first author was also partially funded by EPSRC and Trend Micro. The third author was supported by the Defense Advanced Research Projects Agency (DARPA) and the Air Force Research Laboratory (AFRL) under agreement number FA8750-11-2-0079, and by a Royal Society Wolfson Merit Award. The US Government is authorized to reproduce and distribute reprints for Government purposes notwithstanding any copyright notation thereon. The views and conclusions contained herein are those of the authors and should not be interpreted as necessarily representing the official policies or endorsements, either expressed or implied, of DARPA), AFRL, the U.S. Government, the European Commission or EPSRC.

References

1. Al-Riyami, S.S., Paterson, K.G.: Certificateless Public Key Cryptography. In: Laih, C.-S. (ed.) ASIACRYPT 2003. LNCS, vol. 2894, pp. 452–473. Springer, Heidelberg (2003)
2. Armknecht, F., Peter, A., Katzenbeisser, S.: A cleaner view on IND-CCA1 secure homomorphic encryption using SOAP. IACR e-print 2010/501 (2010), http://eprint.iacr.org/2010/501
3. Baek, J., Steinfeld, R., Zheng, Y.: Formal proofs for the security of signcryption. Journal of Cryptology 20(2), 203–235 (2007)
4. Bellare, M., Palacio, A.: Towards Plaintext-Aware Public-Key Encryption Without Random Oracles. In: Lee, P.J. (ed.) ASIACRYPT 2004. LNCS, vol. 3329, pp. 48–62. Springer, Heidelberg (2004)
5. Bellare, M., Rogaway, P.: Optimal Asymmetric Encryption. In: De Santis, A. (ed.) EUROCRYPT 1994. LNCS, vol. 950, pp. 92–111. Springer, Heidelberg (1995)
6. Bendlin, R., Damgård, I., Orlandi, C., Zakarias, S.: Semi-Homomorphic Encryption and Multiparty Computation. In: Paterson, K.G. (ed.) EUROCRYPT 2011. LNCS, vol. 6632, pp. 169–188. Springer, Heidelberg (2011)
7. Bernhard, D., Cortier, V., Pereira, O., Smyth, B., Warinschi, B.: Adapting Helios for Provable Ballot Privacy. In: Atluri, V., Diaz, C. (eds.) ESORICS 2011. LNCS, vol. 6879, pp. 335–354. Springer, Heidelberg (2011)

8. Bleichenbacher, D.: Chosen Ciphertext Attacks Against Protocols based on the RSA Encryption Standard PKCS #1. In: Krawczyk, H. (ed.) CRYPTO 1998. LNCS, vol. 1462, pp. 1–12. Springer, Heidelberg (1998)
9. Cramer, R., Gennaro, R., Schoenmakers, B.: A Secure and Optimally Efficient Multi-Authority Election Scheme. In: Fumy, W. (ed.) EUROCRYPT 1997. LNCS, vol. 1233, pp. 103–118. Springer, Heidelberg (1997)
10. Cramer, R., Shoup, V.: A Practical Public Key Cryptosystem Provably Secure Against Adaptive Chosen Ciphertext Attack. In: Krawczyk, H. (ed.) CRYPTO 1998. LNCS, vol. 1462, pp. 13–25. Springer, Heidelberg (1998)
11. Damgård, I.B.: Towards Practical Public Key Systems Secure against Chosen Ciphertext Attacks. In: Feigenbaum, J. (ed.) CRYPTO 1991. LNCS, vol. 576, pp. 445–456. Springer, Heidelberg (1992)
12. Damgård, I., Groth, J., Salomonsen, G.: The theory and implementation of an electronic voting system. In: Secure Electronic Voting, pp. 77–99. Kluwer Academic Publishers (2002)
13. Dent, A.: A Designer's Guide to KEMs. In: Paterson, K.G. (ed.) Cryptography and Coding 2003. LNCS, vol. 2898, pp. 133–151. Springer, Heidelberg (2003)
14. van Dijk, M., Gentry, C., Halevi, S., Vaikuntanathan, V.: Fully Homomorphic Encryption Over the Integers. In: Gilbert, H. (ed.) EUROCRYPT 2010. LNCS, vol. 6110, pp. 24–43. Springer, Heidelberg (2010)
15. Gentry, C.: Fully homomorphic encryption using ideal lattices. In: Symposium on Theory of Computing – STOC 2009, pp. 169–178. ACM (2009)
16. Gentry, C.: A fully homomorphic encryption scheme. PhD, Stanford University (2009)
17. Gentry, C., Halevi, S.: Implementing Gentry's Fully-Homomorphic Encryption Scheme. In: Paterson, K.G. (ed.) EUROCRYPT 2011. LNCS, vol. 6632, pp. 129–148. Springer, Heidelberg (2011)
18. Hu, Z.-Y., Sun, F.-C., Jiang, J.-C.: Ciphertext verification security of symmetric encryption schemes. Science in China Series F 52(9), 1617–1631 (2009)
19. Joye, M., Quisquater, J., Yung, M.: On the Power of Misbehaving Adversaries and Security Analysis of the Original EPOC. In: Naccache, D. (ed.) CT-RSA 2001. LNCS, vol. 2020, pp. 208–222. Springer, Heidelberg (2001)
20. Lipmaa, H.: On the CCA1-security of ElGamal and Damgård's ElGamal. In: Lai, X., Yung, M., Lin, D. (eds.) Inscrypt 2010. LNCS, vol. 6584, pp. 18–35. Springer, Heidelberg (2011)
21. Manger, J.: A Chosen Ciphertext Attack on RSA Optimal Asymmetric Encryption Padding (OAEP) as Standardized in PKCS #1 v2.0. In: Kilian, J. (ed.) CRYPTO 2001. LNCS, vol. 2139, pp. 230–238. Springer, Heidelberg (2001)
22. Naor, M., Yung, M.: Public-key cryptosystems provably secure against chosen ciphertext attacks. In: Symposium on Theory of Computing – STOC 1990, pp. 427–437. ACM (1990)
23. Regev, O.: On lattices, learning with errors, random linear codes, and cryptography. In: Symposium on Theory of Computing – STOC 2005, pp. 84–93. ACM (2005)
24. Rivest, R.L., Adleman, L., Dertouzos, M.L.: On data banks and privacy homomorphisms. In: Foundations of Secure Computation, pp. 169–177 (1978)
25. Regev, O.: On lattices, learning with errors, random linear codes, and cryptography. Journal ACM 56(6), 1–40 (2009)
26. Smart, N.P.: Errors Matter: Breaking RSA-Based PIN Encryption with Thirty Ciphertext Validity Queries. In: Pieprzyk, J. (ed.) CT-RSA 2010. LNCS, vol. 5985, pp. 15–25. Springer, Heidelberg (2010)
27. Smart, N.P., Vercauteren, F.: Fully Homomorphic Encryption with Relatively Small Key and Ciphertext Sizes. In: Nguyen, P.Q., Pointcheval, D. (eds.) PKC 2010. LNCS, vol. 6056, pp. 420–443. Springer, Heidelberg (2010)
28. Smyth, B., Cortier, V.: Attacking and fixing Helios: An analysis of ballot secrecy. In: IEEE Computer Security Foundations Symposium – CSF 2011 (to appear, 2011)

Efficient Schemes for Anonymous Yet Authorized and Bounded Use of Cloud Resources

Daniel Slamanig

Carinthia University of Applied Sciences, Primoschgasse 10, 9020 Klagenfurt, Austria
d.slamanig@cuas.at

Abstract. In this paper we introduce *anonymous yet authorized and bounded* cloud resource schemes. Contrary to many other approaches to security and privacy in the cloud, we aim at hiding behavioral information, i.e. *consumption patterns*, of users consuming their cloud resources, e.g. CPU time or storage space, from a cloud provider. More precisely, users should be able to purchase a contingent of resources from a cloud provider and be able to anonymously and unlinkably consume their resources till their limit (bound) is reached. Furthermore, they can also reclaim these resources back anonymously, e.g. if they delete some stored data. We present a definition of such schemes along with a security model and present an instantiation based on Camenisch-Lysyanskaya signatures. Then, we extend the scheme to another scheme providing even more privacy for users, i.e. by even hiding the issued resource limit (bound) during interactions and thus providing full anonymity to users, and present some useful extensions for both schemes. We also support our theoretical claims with experimental results obtained from an implementation that show the practicality of our schemes.

1 Introduction

Cloud computing is an emerging paradigm, but some significant attention remains justifiably focused on addressing security and privacy concerns. Reasons are among others that customers have to trust the security mechanisms and configuration of the cloud provider and the cloud provider itself. Recently, different cryptographic solutions to improve privacy, mainly focusing on private storage, private computations and private service usage have been proposed and will be briefly discussed below.

Storing data encrypted seems to be sine qua non in many cloud storage settings, since cloud providers, having access to the storage infrastructure, can neither be considered as fully trustworthy nor are resistant to attacks. Kamara and Lauter [25] propose several architectures for cryptographic cloud storage and provide a sound overview of recent non-standard cryptographic primitives like searchable encryption and attribute-based encryption, which are valuable tools in this context. Other issues are data privacy and verifiability when outsourcing data and performing computations on these data using the cloud as computation infrastructure. The recent introduction of fully homomorphic encryption [24] is a promising concept for performing arbitrary computation on encrypted

A. Miri and S. Vaudenay (Eds.): SAC 2011, LNCS 7118, pp. 73–91, 2012.

data. Up to now these concepts are far from being practical, although for some practical applications somewhat homomorphic schemes seem to be promising [26]. Another interesting issue from a privacy perspective is to hide user's usage behavior (access patterns and frequencies) when accessing cloud services. More precisely, users may not want the cloud provider to learn how often they use a service or which resources they access. Nevertheless, cloud providers can be assumed to have access restricted to authorized users and additionally users may want to enforce (attribute-based) access control policies. Some approaches to realize this are anonymous credential systems [3], oblivious transfer [6,7] or oblivious RAM [23].

In this paper we discuss an additional aspect, which may be valuable when moving towards privacy friendly cloud computing and seems to be valuable when used in conjunction with the aforementioned approaches. In particular, we focus on the anonymous yet authorized and bounded use of cloud resources like CPU time (e.g. CPU per hour) or storage space. Thereby, we note that in this paper we illustrate our concept by means of the resource storage space. Think for instance of anonymous document publishing services provided by organizations like WikiLeaks or the American Civil Liberties Union (ACLU) who may use third party cloud storage services like Amazon's S3[1] as their document stores. In this example, WikiLeaks or ACLU may wish to store documents in the cloud, but may not want to learn the cloud provider, e.g. Amazon, how much storage they (and their users respectively) store. These organizations may also force their users to respect storage limits, since they will have to pay for the storage, but at the same time provide their users with anonymity. Another example are clients who outsource computations to the cloud and want to hide their pattern.

Our Contribution. We consider a setting where users should be able to register and obtain a resource bound (limit) from a cloud provider (CP) in form of a "partially blindly signed" token. This token includes an identifier, the already consumed resources and the limit, wheres the limit in fact is the only value signed in clear. This limit determines how much of a resource, e.g. CPU time, storage space, a user is allowed to consume. Then, users should be able to consume their resources in an anonymous and unlinkable yet authorized fashion. For instance, if a user wants to consume l resources, he has to convince the CP that he possesses a signed token with a valid identifier (double-spending protection) and that his consumed resources (including l) do not exceed his bound. If this holds, the anonymous user is allowed to consume the resources and obtains an updated signature for a token corresponding to a new identifier and updated consumed resources. Note, due to the anonymity and unlinkability properties, the CP is unable to track how much a user has already consumed, however, can be sure that he solely consumes what he has been granted. Furthermore, a user may also reclaim resources back, e.g. when deleting data or computations did not require the preassigned time, while still hiding the pattern.

We for the first time consider this problem and provide a definition for the concept of anonymous yet authorized and bounded cloud resource schemes along

[1] `http://aws.amazon.com/s3/`

with a security model. Furthermore, we present an efficient instantiation of such schemes and extend the scheme to another scheme providing even more privacy for users and present some useful extensions for both schemes. Our schemes are obtained using recent signature schemes due to Camenisch and Lysyanskaya [11,12] along with efficient zero-knowledge proofs for proving properties of signed messages. We note that many of the approaches discussed subsequently employ similar features of CL signatures as our approach does. But the signer controlled interactive update of signed messages discussed in Section 4.1, which is an important functionality behind our protocols, seems to be novel[2]. Furthermore, we note that we base our concrete scheme on groups of known order and the essential ingredient is the pairing based CL signature scheme [12].

Related Work. Pairing based CL signatures [12] and it's strong RSA based pendant [11] are useful to construct various privacy enhancing cryptographic protocols. Among them are anonymous credential systems [19] and group signatures [12] as well as privacy protecting multi-coupon systems [15,17], anonymous subscriptions [5], electronic toll pricing [4], e-cash systems [9] and n-times anonymous authentication schemes [8] based on compact e-cash or unclonable group identification schemes [21] (which achieve similar goals as in [8]). To solve our problem, the most straightforward solutions seems e-cash, i.e. CP issues k coins to a user and a user can use one coin per resource unit. However, to achieve a suitable granularity this induces a large amount of "small valued coins" which makes this approach impractical. The same holds for compact e-cash schemes [9], where a user can withdraw a wallet of 2^l coins at a time and thus the withdrawal procedure is much more efficient. However, in compact e-cash coins from the wallet can only be spend one by one and the above problem still exists. In divisible e-cash [14,2], which allows a user to withdraw a wallet of value 2^l in a single withdraw protocol, spending a value 2^m for $m \leq l$ can be realized more efficient than repeating the spending 2^m times. However, in the former solution even for a moderate value of $l = 10$ the spending of a single coin requires 800 exponentiations which makes it very expensive. The latter approach is more efficient but statistical, meaning that users can spend more money than withdrawn. Nevertheless, we may consider our scheme as some type of a *divisible* e-cash scheme, since it allows to withdraw a contingent of resources and to spend *arbitrary amounts of these resources* until the contingent is consumed. But we want to mention that we have not designed these schemes with e-cash as an application in mind and do not support usual properties of e-cash schemes such as double-spender identification and spending with arbitrary merchants.

Multi-coupons [15,17] represent a collection of coupons (or coins or tokens) which is issued in a single withdraw protocol and every single coupon of the MC can be spend in an anonymous and unlinkable fashion. But in our scenario, they suffer from the same problem as simple e-cash solutions.

Recently, Camenisch et al. proposed an interesting protocol for unlinkable priced oblivious transfer with rechargeable wallets [7]. This does not exactly

[2] As we were recently informed, the general idea of updating signatures has already been used in independent work [10] based on Boneh-Boyen signatures.

fit our scenario but could be mapped to it. However, [7] do not provide an efficiency analysis in their work and their protocols seem to be quite costly. Their rechargeable wallets are an interesting feature and recharching is also supported by our second scheme in Section 4.4.

2 Definition

2.1 Problem Description and Motivation

In our setting we have a cloud provider (CP) and a set of users U. Our main goal is that users are able to purchase a contingent of resources (we focus on storage space here) and CP does not learn anything about the resource consumption behavior of users. In particular, users can store data at the CP as long as there are still resources from their contingent available. The CP is in any interaction with the user convinced that a user is allowed to consume (or reclaim) resources but cannot identify the user nor link any of the user's actions. Clearly, if the resource is storage space and the data objects contain information on the user, then this may break the anonymity property. Nevertheless, then we can assume that data is encrypted which seems to be sine qua non in many cloud storage settings.

Our main motivation is that it is very likely that only a few large cloud providers will own large portions of the infrastructure of the future Internet. Thus, these cloud providers will eventually be able to link data and information about resource consumption behavior of their consumers (users) allowing them to build extensive dossiers. Since for many enterprises such a transparency can be too intrusive or problematic if these information are available to their competitors we want to hide these information from cloud providers. As for instance argued in [18], activity patterns may constitute confidential business information and if divulged could lead to reverse-engineering of customer base, revenue size, and the like.

2.2 Definition of the Scheme

An anonymous yet authorized and bounded cloud resource scheme is a tuple (`ProviderSetup`, `ObtainLimit`, `Consume`, `Reclaim`) of polynomial time algorithms or protocols between users U and cloud provider CP respectively:

- `ProviderSetup`. On input a security parameter k, this algorithms outputs a key pair sk and pk of a suitable signature scheme and an empty blacklist BL (for double-spending detection).
- `ObtainLimit`. In this protocol a user u wants to obtain a token t for a resource limit of L units from the CP. The user's output is a token t with corresponding signature σ_t issued by CP. The token contains the limit L and the actually consumed resources s (wheres both may be represented by a single value $L' := L - s$). The output of CP is a transcript T_{OL} of the protocol.

- `Consume`. In this protocol user u wants to consume l units from his remaining resources. The user shows value $t.id$ of a token t and convinces the CP that he holds a valid signature σ_t for token t. If the token was not already spend ($t.id$ is not contained in BL), the signature is valid and there are still enough resources left, i.e. $s' + l \leq L$ (or $L' - l \geq 0$), then the user's output is `accept` and an updated token t' for resource limit L and actually consumed resources $s' + l$ (or $L' - l$) with an updated signature $\sigma_{t'}$ from CP. Otherwise the user's output is `reject`. The output of CP is a transcript T_C.
- `Reclaim`. In this protocol user u wants to reclaim l units, e.g. he wants to delete some data of size l. The protocol is exactly the same as the `Consume` protocol. Except for the `accept` case the updated token t' contains $s' - l$ (or $L' + l$) as the actually consumed resources and the transcript is denoted as T_R. We emphasize that u needs to prove by some means that he is allowed to reclaim l resources, e.g. when deleting some data, the user needs prove knowledge of some secret associated with the data during the integration. Otherwise, users could simply run arbitrary many `Reclaim` protocols to illicitly reclaim resources and indirectly improve their actual resource limit (see end of Section 4.3 for a discussion).

2.3 Security Model

We now describe our formal model for the security requirements of an anonymous yet authorized and bounded cloud resource scheme and say such a scheme is secure if it satisfies the properties correctness, unlinkability and unforgeability.

Correctness. If an honest user runs an `ObtainLimit` protocol with an honest CP for resource limit L, then he obtains a token t with corresponding signature σ_t for resource limit L. If an honest user runs a `Consume` or `Reclaim` protocol with an honest CP for value l, then the respective protocol will output `accept` and a valid token-signature pair $(t', \sigma_{t'})$ with $t'.s = t.s \pm l$ (or $t'.L' = t.L' \pm l$). If the limit is explicitly included we additionally require for the `Consume` protocol that $t.s + l \leq t.L$.

Unlinkability. It is required that no collusion of users and the CP can learn the resource consumption habit of an honest user. Note, that this in particular means that issuing and showing of a token cannot be linked. With exception of the issued resource limit, the tokens reveal no information about the actually consumed resources (if the issued limit is not included then there is absolutely no link). Formally, we consider a game and provide the adversary $\mathcal{A}$ with (sk, pk) and BL generated by the `ProviderSetup` algorithm. Furthermore, $\mathcal{A}$ obtains a fixed (large) resource limit L. Then, during the game $\mathcal{A}$ can

- execute `ObtainLimit` protocols (if included w.r.t. resource limit L) with honest users in an arbitrary manner,
- execute `Consume` and `Reclaim` protocols with honest users.

At some point, $\mathcal{A}$ outputs two transcripts T^0_{OL} and T^1_{OL} of previously executed `ObtainLimit` protocols, whereas we require that the sum of all values consumed during all Consume protocols is at most $L - v$. Then, a bit b is secretly and randomly chosen and $\mathcal{A}$ runs a Consume with value at most v (or Reclaim) protocol with the user who was issued his initial token during the ObtainLimit protocol corresponding to T^b_{OL}. Finally, $\mathcal{A}$ outputs a bit b' and we say that $\mathcal{A}$ has won the game if $b = b'$ holds. We require that for every efficient adversary $\mathcal{A}$ the probability of winning the game differs from 1/2 at most by a negligible fraction (the intuition why we require the sum to be $L - v$ and the last Consume is performed with respect to value v at most is to rule out trivial attacks[3]).

Unforgeability. It is required that no collusion of users can spend more tokens (which will be accepted in Consume or Reclaim protocols) than they have been issued. Furthermore, no collusion of users must be able to consume more resources than they have obtained. Formally, we consider a game and provide the adversary $\mathcal{A}$ with a public key pk generated by the ProviderSetup algorithm. Then, during the game $\mathcal{A}$ can

- execute ObtainLimit protocols with an honest CP and
- execute Consume and Reclaim protocols with an honest CP.

At some point, $\mathcal{A}$ specifies a sequence $\mathbf{t} = (t_1, \ldots, t_n)$ of valid tokens (which were not already shown) and at the end of the game the verifier

- outputs a token t' either not contained in $\mathbf{t}$
- or a modified token t'' corresponding to a token t_i in $\mathbf{t}$, whereas it holds that $t''.id \neq t_i.id$ and/or $t''.L \neq t_i.L$ and/or $t''.s \neq t_i.s$ (or if L is not explicitey included $t''.L' \neq t_i.L'$).
- and conducts a Consume or Reclaim protocol with an honest CP.

We require that for every efficient adversary $\mathcal{A}$ the probability that the Consume or Reclaim protocol in the last step terminates with accept is negligible.

3 Preliminaries

An essential ingredient for our construction are honest-verifier zero-knowledge proofs of knowledge (Σ-protocols). We use the notation from [13], i.e. a proof of knowledge of a discrete logarithm $x = \log_g y$ to the base g will be denoted as $PK\{(\alpha) : y = g^\alpha\}$, whereas Greek letters always denote values whose knowledge will be proven. We note, that compositions of single Σ-protocols using conjunctions and disjunctions can be efficiently realized [20]. Furthermore, the non-interactive version of a (composed) proof obtained by applying the Fiat-Shamir transform [22] is denoted as a signature of knowledge or SPK for short.

[3] The adversary could run one single ObtainLimit protocol and run Consume till the user can have no more available resources, i.e. Consume protocols will terminate with reject. Then before going into the challenge phase, the adversary can run another ObtainLimit protocol and output those two transcripts. Obviously, he will be able to assign a Consume protocol to the *correct* user, since one will terminate with reject and the other one with accept.

Bilinear Maps. Let $\mathbb{G}$ and $\mathbb{G}_t$ be two groups of prime order p, let g be a generator of $\mathbb{G}$ and $e : \mathbb{G} \times \mathbb{G} \rightarrow \mathbb{G}_t$ a bilinear map between these two groups. The map e must satisfy the following properties:

1. Bilinear: for all $u, v \in \mathbb{G}$ and $a, b \in \mathbb{Z}_p$ we have $e(u^a, v^b) = e(u, v)^{ab}$.
2. Non-degenerate: $e(g, g) \neq 1$.
3. Computable: there is an efficient algorithm to compute $e(u, v)$ for any $u, v \in \mathbb{G}$.

Though the group operation in $\mathbb{G}$ is in general an additive one, we express both groups using multiplicative notation. This notion is commonly used, since $\mathbb{G}_t$ is always multiplicative and it is more easy to capture the sense of cryptographic protocols.

Pedersen Commitments. Pedersen commitments [30] represent a widely used commitment scheme working in any group $\mathbb{G}$ of prime order p. Let g, h be random generators of $\mathbb{G}$, whereas $\log_g h$ is unknown. To commit to a value $s \in \mathbb{Z}_p$, one chooses $r \in_R \mathbb{Z}_p$ and computes $C(s, r) = g^s h^r$, which unconditionally hides s as long as r is unknown. To open the commitment, one simply publishes $(s, r, C(s, r))$ and one verifies whether $g^s h^r = C(s, r)$ holds. For simplicity, we often write $C(s)$ for a commitment to s instead of $C(s, r)$. We note that the Pedersen commitment inherits an additive homomorphic property, i.e. given two commitments $C(s_1, r_1) = g^{s_1} h^{r_1}$ and $C(s_2, r_2) = g^{s_2} h^{r_2}$ then one is able to compute $C(s_1 + s_2, r_1 + r_2) = C(s_1, r_1) \cdot C(s_2, r_2)$ without either knowing any of the hidden values s_1 or s_2. Furthermore, note that a proof of knowledge $PK\{(\alpha, \beta) : C = g^\alpha h^\beta\}$ of the ability to open a Pedersen commitment can be realized using a proof of knowledge of a DL representation of C with respect to the elements g and h [28].

Range Proofs. An elegant proof that a number hidden within a Pedersen commitment lies in an interval $[a, b]$ in the setting of prime order groups was presented in [27]. Although this proof might be impractical in general, since it requires $O(\log\ b)$ single bit-proofs, it is efficient for the application that we have in mind due to relatively small values of b. The basic idea is to consider for a number $x \in [0, b]$ its binary representation $x = x_0 2^0 + x_1 2^1 + \ldots + x_{k-1} 2^{k-1}$, whereas $x_i \in \{0, 1\}$, $0 \leq i < k$. Thereby, $k = [\log_2\ b] + 1$ represents the number of digits, which are necessary to represent every number within $[0, b]$. Now, in essence one proves that the binary representation of x lies within the interval $[0, 2^k - 1]$. This can be done by committing to each x_i using an Okamoto commitment [29] (essentially a Pedersen bit commitment) along with a proof that this commitment hides either 0 or 1 and demonstrating that for commitments to x and all x_i's it holds that $x = x_0 2^0 + x_1 2^1 + \ldots + x_{k-1} 2^{k-1}$. The concrete range proof is a Σ-protocol for a proof of knowledge

$$PK\{(\alpha_0, \ldots, \alpha_{k-1}) : \bigwedge_{i=0}^{k-1} (C_i = h^{\alpha_i} \vee C_i g^{-1} = h^{\alpha_i})\}$$

or $PK\{(\alpha, \beta) : C = g^\alpha h^\beta \wedge\ (0 \leq \alpha \leq b)\}$ for short.

Camenisch-Lysyanskaya Signature Scheme. Camenisch and Lysyanskaya have proposed a signature scheme in [12] which satisfies the usual correctness and unforgeability properties of digital signatures and is provably secure under the LRSW assumption for groups with bilinear maps, which implies that the DLP is hard (cf. [12]). We present the CL signature scheme below:

Key Generation. Let $\mathbb{G}$ and $\mathbb{G}_t$ be groups of prime order p and $e : \mathbb{G} \times \mathbb{G} \to \mathbb{G}_t$ a bilinear map. Choose $x, y, z_1, \ldots, z_l \in_R \mathbb{Z}_p$. The private key is $sk = (x, y, \{z_i\})$ and the public key is $pk = (X, Y, \{Z_i\}, e, g, \mathbb{G}, \mathbb{G}_t, p)$, whereas $X = g^x$, $Y = g^y$ and $Z_i = g^{z_i}$.

Signing. On input message $(m_0, \ldots, m_l)$, sk and pk, choose $a \in_R \mathbb{G}$, compute $A_i = a^{z_i}$, $b = a^y$, $B_i = (A_i)^y$ and $c = a^{x+xym_0} \prod_{i=1}^{l} A_i^{xym_i}$. Output the signature $\sigma = (a, \{A_i\}, b, \{B_i\}, c)$.

Verification. On input of $(m_0, \ldots, m_l)$, pk and $\sigma = (a, \{A_i\}, b, \{B_i\}, c)$ check whether

- A_i's are formed correct: $e(a, Z_i) = e(g, A_i)$
- b and B_i's are formed correct: $e(a, Y) = e(g, b)$ and $e(A_i, Y) = e(g, B_i)$
- c is formed correct: $e(X, a) \cdot e(X, b)^{m_0} \prod_{i=1}^{l} e(X, B_i)^{m_i} = e(g, c)$

What makes this signature scheme particularly attractive is that it allows a receiver to obtain a signature on committed messages (using Pedersen commitments), while the messages are information-theoretically hidden from the signer (messages here means elements of the message tuple). Additionally, the receiver can randomize a CL signature such that the resulting signature is unlinkable to the original signature. Furthermore, receivers can use efficient zero-knowledge proofs to prove knowledge of a signature on committed messages. We will elaborate on the aforementioned functionalities more detailed in Section 4.1 and will show how to extend this functionality to interactive updates of signatures, the signed commitments and messages respectively.

4 Scheme

In this section we present our scheme along with an optional modification in order to increase the privacy in some settings even further. We start with the presentation of an important observation of CL signatures which is central to our constructions. Then, we first give a high level description followed by a detailed description of the schemes. Additionally, we present an performance evaluation of a prototypical implementation which supports the efficiency of the schemes. Finally, we present some extensions as well as system issues and provide a security analysis of the protocols.

4.1 Interactive Update of Signed Messages

As already noted, CL signatures allow signing of committed messages (using Pedersen commitments), while the signer does not learn anything about them.

Assume that the signer holds a private key $sk = (x, y, z)$ and publishes the corresponding public key $pk = (X, Y, Z, e, g, \mathbb{G}, \mathbb{G}_t, p)$.

Blind Signing. If a receiver wants to obtain a blind signature for message m, he chooses $r \in_R \mathbb{Z}_p$, computes a commitment $C = g^m Z^r$ and sends C along with a signature of knowledge $SPK\{(\alpha, \beta) : C = g^\alpha Z^\beta\}$ to the signer (the ability to open the commitment is necessary for the security of the scheme, cf. [12]). If the verification of the proof holds, the signer computes a signature $\sigma = (a, A, b, B, c)$ for the commitment C by choosing $k \in_R \mathbb{Z}_p$, setting $a = g^k$ and computing $\sigma = (a, a^z, a^y, a^{yz}, a^x C^{kxy})$ and sends σ to the receiver.

Verification. In order to show the signature to a verifier, the receiver randomizes the signature by choosing $\mathsf{r}, \mathsf{r}' \in_R \mathbb{Z}_p$ and computing $\sigma' = (a', A', b', B', c')$ as $\sigma' = (a^\mathsf{r}, A^\mathsf{r}, b^\mathsf{r}, B^\mathsf{r}, c^{\mathsf{r}\mathsf{r}'})$ and sends σ' with the message m along with a signature of knowledge $SPK\{(\gamma, \delta) : v_\sigma^\gamma = \mathbf{v} v_r^\delta\}$ to the verifier. Therefore, both need to compute $v_\sigma = e(c', g)$, $\mathbf{v} = e(X, a') \cdot e(X, b')^m$ and $v_r = e(X, B')$. The verifier checks the proof and checks whether A' as well as b' and B' were correctly formed. Note, that the proof can be conducted by means of a standard DL-representation proof [16], which can easily be seen by rewriting the proof as $SPK\{(\gamma, \delta) : \mathbf{v} = v_\sigma^\gamma (v_r^{-1})^\delta\}$.

Remark. Observe, that we can realize a concept which is similar to partially blind signatures. However, in contrast to existing partially blind signature schemes [1], where the signer can integrate some common agreed upon information in the signature, here, the signer *arithmetically adds* a message to the "blinded message" (hidden in the commitment). Therefore, during the signing, the signer simply updates the commitment to $C' = Cg^{m_S}$ and uses C' instead of C for signing. The receiver then obtains a signature for message $m + m_S$, whereas m_S is determined by the signer and m is hidden from the signer.

Update. The interesting and from our point of view novel part is that a signer can use a somewhat related idea to "update" a randomized signature without showing the message. Assume that a receiver holds a randomized signature σ' for message (m', r) whereas $m' = m + m_S$ and wants the signer to update the signature such that it represents a signature for message $(m' + m'_S, r + 1)$. Since showing m', as within the signature above, would destroy the unlinkability due to both messages are known, the receiver can solely prove that he knows the message in zero knowledge and both can then interactively update the signature. Therefore in the verification the receiver provides a signature of knowledge $SPK\{(\alpha, \beta, \gamma) : v_\sigma^\alpha = \mathbf{v} v_{m'}^\beta v_r^\gamma\}$ to the verifier, whereas $v_\sigma = e(g, c')$, $\mathbf{v} = e(g, a')$, $v_{m'} = e(g, b')$ and $v_r = e(g, B')$, which convinces the signer that the receiver possesses a valid signature for unknown message (m', r). Then, for the update, i.e. to *add* m'_S it is sufficient for the signer to compute $\tilde{C}_{m'+m'_S} = a'^{m'_S} A'$ and send it to the receiver. The receiver computes $C_{m'+m'_S} = (\tilde{C}_{m'+m'_S})^{\mathsf{r}'}$ and provides a signature of knowledge $SPK\{(\alpha, \beta, \gamma) : v_\sigma^\alpha = \mathbf{v} v_{m'}^\beta v_r^\gamma \wedge \tilde{C}_{m'+m'_S} = (C_{m'+m'_S})^\alpha\}$. Note that this proof convinces the signer that the receiver has randomized the commitment of the signer using the same random factor (r')

as within the randomization of the signature. Then, the signer computes the updated signature $\sigma'' = (a^{\tilde{r}}, A'^{\tilde{r}}, b'^{\tilde{r}}, B'^{\tilde{r}}, (c'(C_{m'+m'_S})^{xy})^{\tilde{r}})$ for $\tilde{r} \in \mathbb{Z}_p$ and gives $\sigma'' = (a'', A'', b'', B'', \tilde{c}'')$ to the receiver. The receiver sets $c'' = (\tilde{c}'')^{r'^{-1}}$ and now holds a valid signature for message $(m'+m'_S, r+1)$ which he can in turn randomize. Therefore, observer that in the signature tuple only the last element actually includes the messages and we have $c' = c^{rr'} = (a^x C'^{kxy})^{rr'} = (a^{x+xy(m'+zr)})^{rr'}$ and $(C_{m'+m'_S})^{xy} = (a^{xy(m'_S+z)})^{r}$. By taking these results together we have a well formed signature component $c'' = (a^{x+xy(m'+m'_S+z(r+1))})^{rr'}$. The remaining elements of the signature are easy to verify for correctness.

Remark. This functionality can easily be extended to signatures on arbitrary tuples of messages, will be a building block for our scheme and may also be of independent interest. Note that issuing a new signature in every step without revealing the hidden messages would not work and thus we use this "update functionality".

4.2 High Level Description of the First Scheme

Before presenting the detailed protocols, we provide a high level description. The aim of our construction is to let the user solely prove in each `Consume` protocol that enough resources, i.e. storage space, is available. In this setting, the user does not provide any useful information about the actual consumed space to the verifier, but the verifier learns only the fact that the user is still allowed to consume storage space.

ProviderSetup. The cloud provider generates a key-pair (sk, pk) for the CL signature scheme, publishes pk, initializes an empty blacklist BL and fixes a set $\mathcal{L} = \{L_1, \ldots, L_n\}$ of space limits.

ObtainLimit. A user chooses a limit $L \in \mathcal{L}$ and obtains a CL signature σ_t for a token $t = (C(id), C(s), L)$, whereas the initially consumed storage space s is set to be $s = 1$.

Consume. Assume that the user holds a token $t = (C(id), C(s), L)$ and corresponding signature σ_t. Note, that id (the token-id) and s were signed as commitments and thus the signer is not aware of these values. When a user wants to integrate a data object d, the user computes $C(id')$ for the new token, randomizes the signature σ_t to σ'_t and proves that σ'_t is a valid signature for id and L (by revealing these two elements) and an unknown value s that satisfies $(s + |d|) \in [0, L]$ or equivalently $s \in [0, L - |d|]$, i.e. when integrating the new data object d the user needs to prove that after adding of $|d|$ space units at most L storage space will be consumed. If id is not contained in BL and this proof succeeds, the signature will be updated to a signature for $C(id + id')$, $C(s + |d|)$ and L. Consequently, the provider adds id to BL and the user obtains an updated signature for a token $t' = (C(id + id'), C(s + |d|), L)$. Otherwise, the cloud provider will reject the integration of a new data object.

Reclaim. Assume that the user holds a token $t = (C(id), C(s), L)$ and corresponding signature σ_t. When a user wants to delete a data object d, as above, the user computes $C(id')$ for the new token, randomizes the signature σ_t to σ'_t and "proves" that he is allowed to delete d and that σ'_t is a valid signature for id and L (by revealing these two elements). If id is not contained in BL and the signature is valid, the user obtains a signature for a token $t' = (C(id + id'), C(s - |d|), L)$. Otherwise, the cloud provider will reject to delete d.

4.3 Detailed Description of the First Scheme

ProviderSetup: The cloud provider generates a key-pair for the CL signature scheme to sign tokens of the form $t = (id, s, L)$. More precisely, the cloud provider signs tokens of the form $t = (id, r_{id}, s, r_s, L)$, but we usually omit the randomizers for the ease of presentation. Consequently, the cloud provider obtains the private key $sk = (x, y, z_1, z_2, z_3, z_4)$ and publishes the public key $pk = (X, Y, Z_1, Z_2, Z_3, Z_4, e, g, \mathbb{G}, \mathbb{G}_t, p)$. Furthermore, he initializes an empty blacklist BL and fixes a set $\mathcal{L} = \{L_1, \ldots, L_n\}$ of available limits.

ObtainLimit: A user registers with the cloud provider and obtains a space limit $L_i \in \mathcal{L}$ (we do not fix any concrete protocol for this task here since no anonymity is required). After the user has registered and both have agreed on L_i (which we denote as L below for simplicity), they proceed as depicted in Protocol 1.

1. The user chooses a token-identifier $id \in_R \{0,1\}^{l_{id}}$ and randomizers $r_{id}, r_s \in_R \mathbb{Z}_p$ for the commitments and we let the user start with value $s = 1$. Then, he computes the commitments $C_{id} = g^{id} Z_1^{r_{id}}$ and $C_s = Z_2^s Z_3^{r_s}$ and sends them along with a signature of knowledge
$$SPK\{(\alpha, \beta, \gamma) : \; C_{id} = g^\alpha Z_1^\beta \wedge C_s = Z_2 Z_3^\gamma\} \tag{1}$$
to prove the ability to open the commitments, whereas the second part in the proof also convinces the cloud provider that $s = 1$.
2. If the verification of the signature of knowledge in (1) holds, the cloud provider computes a CL signature for (C_{id}, C_s, L) as follows: He chooses $k \in_R \mathbb{Z}_p$, computes $a = g^k$, $b = a^y$, $A_i = a^{z_i}$, $B_i = A_i^y$ for $1 \leq i \leq 4$ and $c = a^x (C_{id} C_s Z_4^L)^{kxy}$ and sends $\sigma = (a, \{A_i\}, b, \{B_i\}, c)$ to the user.
3. The user verifies whether the signature is valid and if this holds the user is in possession of a valid signature σ for a token $t = (id, s, L)$, whereas the cloud provider is not aware of id and knows that $s = 1$. Furthermore, the user locally randomizes the signature σ to $\sigma' = (a', \{A'_i\}, b', \{B'_i\}, c')$ by choosing $\mathsf{r}, \mathsf{r}' \in \mathbb{Z}_p$ and computing $\sigma' = (a^{\mathsf{r}}, \{A_i^{\mathsf{r}}\}, b^{\mathsf{r}}, \{B_i^{\mathsf{r}}\}, c^{\mathsf{r}\mathsf{r}'})$.

Remark. All further actions are fully anonymous and in practice also unlinkable, since we can assume that one limit will be issued to a quite large number of users (and the limit is the only information that could potentially be used for linking)!

Prot. 1. The `ObtainLimit` protocol

Consume: A user holds a randomized signature $\sigma' = (a', \{A'_i\}, b', \{B'_i\}, c')$ for a token $t = (id, s, L)$ and wants to integrate a data object d. The protocol to integrate a data object and obtain a new token is depicted in Protocol 2.

1. The user sends the randomized signature σ', the "visible part" (id, L) of the token t and a data object d along with a signature of knowledge

$$SPK\{(\alpha, \beta, \gamma, \delta) : v_\sigma^\alpha = \mathbf{v} v_{r_{id}}^\beta v_s^\gamma v_{r_s}^\delta \wedge (0 \leq \gamma \leq 2^{l_L - l_{|d|}} - 1)\} \quad (2)$$

for the validity of the randomized signature containing a proof that still enough space is available to the cloud provider. It must be noted, that the presentation of the proof in (2) represents a shorthand notation for the signature of knowledge

$$SPK\{(\alpha, \beta, \gamma, \delta, \epsilon, \epsilon_1, \ldots, \epsilon_k, \zeta, \zeta_1, \ldots, \zeta_k) : \mathbf{v} = v_\sigma^\alpha (v_{r_{id}}^{-1})^\beta (v_s^{-1})^\gamma (v_{r_s}^{-1})^\delta \wedge$$
$$C = g^\beta Z_1'^\zeta \wedge$$
$$C = \prod_{i=1}^{k} (g^{\epsilon_i} Z_1'^{\zeta_i})^{2^{i-1}} \wedge$$
$$\bigwedge_{i=1}^{k} (C_i = Z_1^{\zeta_i} \vee C_i g^{-1} = Z_1'^{\zeta_i})\}$$

Essentially, besides the DL-representation proof for the validity of the randomized signature, we use an additional commitment $C = g^s Z_1'^r$ to the value s with a new randomizer r computed as

$$r = r_1 2^0 + r_2 2^1 + \ldots + r_k 2^{k-1} \text{ MOD } p$$

for r_i's chosen uniformly at random from $\mathbb{Z}_p$ and the single commitments for the range proof are $C_i = g^{s_i} Z_1'^{r_i}$. It also must be mentioned, that k represents $l_L - l_{|d|}$, the binary length of $L - |d|$. Furthermore, note that in case of $s = 1$, i.e. in the first execution of the `Consume` protocol, it would not be necessary to provide a range proof. However, when performing a range proof, the initial `Consume` protocol is indistinguishable from other protocol executions and thus provides stronger privacy guarantees.

2. The cloud provider checks whether $id \in BL$. If id is not blacklisted, the cloud provider verifies the validity of the signature for the part (id, L) of the token t. Therefore, the cloud provider locally computes the values

$$v_\sigma = e(g, c'),\ v_{r_{id}} = e(X, B_1'),\ v_s = e(X, B_2'),\ v_{r_s} = e(X, B_3') \text{ and}$$

$$\mathbf{v} = e(X, a') \cdot e(X, b')^{id} \cdot e(X, B_4')^L$$

from pk, (id, L) and σ' and verifies the signature of knowledge (2) Additionally, he checks whether the A_i''s as well as b' and B_i''s are correctly formed. A positive verification convinces the cloud provider that enough storage space is available to integrate d and a signature for an updated token t' can be computed in cooperation with the user as follows: Firstly, we need an observation regarding the signature σ'. Note, that the only element of the signature that depends on the message is c', which can be rewritten as

$$c' = (a^{x+xy(id+z_1 r_{id}+z_2 s+z_3 r_s+z_4 L)})^{rr'} = (a^{x+xyid} A_1^{xyr_{id}} A_2^{xys} A_3^{xyr_s} A_4^{xyL})^{rr'}$$

and in order to update a signature for the id-part (to construct a new id for the new token) it is sufficient to update a and A_1. To update the s-part, which amounts to update the currently consumed space, it is sufficient to update A_2 and A_3. The latter update needs to be computed by the cloud provider to be sure that the correct value $|d|$ is integrated and the former one needs to be computed by the user to prevent the cloud provider from learning the new token identifier. Hence, the cloud provider computes $\tilde{C}_{s+|d|} = A_2'^{|d|} A_3'$ and sends $\tilde{C}_{s+|d|}$ to the user, who verifies whether $|d|$ has been used to update the commitment. The user in turn chooses a new identifier and randomizer $id', r_{id'} \in_R \mathbb{Z}_p$, computes $C_{id+id'} = (a'^{id'} A_1'^{r_{id'}})^{r'}$, $C_{s+|d|} = (\tilde{C}_{s+|d|})^{v} = (A_2'^{|d|} A_3')^{r'}$ and sends $(C_{id+id'}, C_{s+|d|})$ along with a signature of knowledge:

$$SPK\{(\epsilon, \zeta, \eta, \phi, \iota, \kappa) : C_{id+id'} = a'^\epsilon A_1'^\zeta \wedge$$
$$\tilde{C}_{s+|d|} = (C_{s+|d|})^\eta \wedge \mathbf{v} = v_\sigma^\eta (v_{r_{id}}^{-1})^\phi (v_s^{-1})^\iota (v_{r_s}^{-1})^\kappa\}$$

to the cloud provider.

Note, that the user additionally to the knowledge of the ability to open the commitments proves that he has randomized the commitment $\tilde{C}_{s+|d|}$ to a commitment $C_{s+|d|}$ using the same randomization factor ($\mathfrak{r}'$) as used to randomize the signature σ without revealing this value. After positive verification of this signature of knowledge, the cloud provider chooses $\tilde{\mathfrak{r}} \in_R \mathbb{Z}_p$ and computes an updated signature

$$\sigma'' = (a'^{\tilde{\mathfrak{r}}}, \{A_i'^{\tilde{\mathfrak{r}}}\}, b'^{\tilde{\mathfrak{r}}}, \{B_i'^{\tilde{\mathfrak{r}}}\}, (c'(C_{id+id'}C_{s+|d|})^{xy})^{\tilde{\mathfrak{r}}}) \quad (3)$$

and sends this updated signature $\sigma'' = (a'', \{A_i''\}, b'', \{B_i''\}, \tilde{c}'')$ to the user. The user sets $c'' = (\tilde{c}'')^{\mathfrak{r}'^{-1}}$ and obtains a valid signature for a token $t' = (id + id', s + |d|, L)$ or more precisely a token $t' = (id + id', r_{id} + r_{id'}, s + |d|, r_s + 1, L)$, which he verifies for correctness (it is quite easy to verify that σ'' is indeed a valid signature). Consequently, the user can randomize σ'' and run a new `Consume` protocol for a data object d' with token $t' = (id + id', s + |d|, L)$.

Prot. 2. The `Consume` protocol

Reclaim: Reclaiming resources, i.e. deleting a data object, is achieved by a slight adaption of the `Consume` protocol. In step 1, instead of the SPK (2) the user provides the subsequent signature of knowledge (the proof that enough space is available is not necessary)

$$SPK\{(\alpha, \beta, \gamma, \delta) : v_\sigma^\alpha = \mathbf{v} v_{r_{id}}^\beta v_s^\gamma v_{r_s}^\delta\}$$

And in step 3, the cloud provider computes $\tilde{C}_{s-|d|} = A_2'^{p-|d|} A_3'$ instead of $\tilde{C}_{s+|d|} = A_2'^{|d|} A_3'$.

Remark. As we have already mentioned, a cloud provider should only perform a `Reclaim` protocol if the user is able to prove the possession of the data object d (and we may assume that only owners delete their data objects). It is not the focus of this paper to provide a solution to this task. However, a quite straightforward solution would be to commit to some secret value for every data object and the cloud provider requires a user to open the commitment or prove knowledge that he is able to open the commitment to delete a data object.

4.4 A Modified Scheme Providing Even More Privacy

In order to increase privacy further, it may be desirable that the initially issued limit L is hidden from the CP during `Consume` or `Reclaim` protocols. We, however, note that if the number of initial tokens associated to CP-defined limits in $\mathcal{L}$ is huge, the respective anonymity sets may be of reasonable size for practical application and this adaption may not be necessary. Nevertheless, we provide an adaption of our protocols which removes the necessity to include L, does only include the available amount of resources (denoted as s) and hides this value s from the CP during any further interactions. We present the modification below:

ProviderSetup. Now, tokens are of the form $t = (id, r_{id}, s, r_s)$ and thus the private key is $sk = (x, y, z_1, z_2, z_3)$ and the public key is $pk = (X, Y, Z_1, Z_2, Z_3, e, g, \mathbb{G}, \mathbb{G}_t, p)$.

ObtainLimit. The user computes commitments $C_{id} = g^{id} Z_1^{r_{id}}$ and $C_s = Z_3^{r_s}$ and provides $SPK\{(\alpha, \beta, \gamma) : C_{id} = g^{\alpha} Z_1^{\beta} \wedge C_s = Z_3^{\gamma}\}$. The element c of the signature is now computed by the CP as $c = a^x (C_{id} C_s Z_2^L)^{kxy}$ and the user can randomize this signature for token $t = (id, r_{id}, L, r_s)$ as usual.

Consume. Here the user only provides id of the actual token and a signature of knowledge

$$SPK\{(\alpha, \beta, \gamma, \delta) : v_\sigma^\alpha = \mathbf{v} v_{r_{id}}^\beta v_s^\gamma v_{r_s}^\delta \wedge (2^{l_{|d|}} - 1 \leq \gamma \leq 2^{l_\mathbf{L}} - 1)\}$$

In this setting $\mathbf{L}$ does not represent a user-specific limit but *the maximum* of all issued limits (or any large enough number), whereas this proof convinces the CP that enough resources to integrate d are still available (note that the local computations of the CP for the verification of the signature in step 2 have to be adapted, which is however straightforward). In step 3, the update of the signature remains identical to the first scheme with the exception that the CP computes the commitment as $\tilde{C}_{s-|d|} = A_2'^{p-|d|} A_3'$, which updates the remaining resources, e.g. in the first run of the `Consume` protocol to $s := L - |d|$.

Reclaim. The reclaim protocol remains identical to the first scheme with the exception that $\tilde{C}_{s+|d|} = A_2'^{|d|} A_3'$.

4.5 Performance Evaluation

In this section we provide a performance evaluation of our first scheme. We have implemented the user's and the cloud provider's parts of the protocols in Java using the `jPBC`[4] library version 1.2.0. This library provides a Java porting of as well as a Java wrapper for the Pairing-Based Cryptography Library (`PBC`)[5]. In particular, we have used the Java PBC wrapper which calls the PBC C library and is significantly faster than the pure Java implementation. All our experiments were performed on an Intel Core 2 duo running at 2.6 GHz with 3GB RAM on Linux Ubuntu 10.10.

As the cryptographic setting we have chosen a symmetric pairing $e : \mathbb{G} \times \mathbb{G} \rightarrow \mathbb{G}_t$ constructed on the supersingular elliptic curve $y^2 = x^3 + x$ over a prime field $\mathbb{F}_q$ where $|q| = 512$ bits and $q \equiv 3 \pmod 4$. The group $\mathbb{G}$ represents a subgroup of $E(\mathbb{F}_q)$ of order $r = 160$ bits. The embedding degree is $k = 2$ and thus $\mathbb{G}_t$ is a subgroup of $\mathbb{F}_{q^2}$ and with our choice of the parameters we obtain a DL security of 1024 bit. For the non-interactive proofs of knowledge we have used the SHA-256 hash function as a single parameter random oracle.

Experiments. For evaluating the computational performance of the client and the server implementation we have taken the average timing from 100 experiments. Therefore we have chosen the resource bounds (limits) as $L = 10^i$ for $i = 3, \ldots, 9$ (see Figure 1). Within every of the 100 experiments per bound, the user has conducted 10 `Consume` as well as 10 `Reclaim` operations with $|d|$ sampled uniformly at random from $[1, 10^{i-2}]$. Figure 1 presents the performance of

[4] `http://libeccio.dia.unisa.it/projects/jpbc/`

[5] `http://crypto.stanford.edu/pbc/`

the ObtainLimit, the Consume and the Reclaim protocols from a computational and bandwidth perspective, whereas point compression for elements in $\mathbb{G}$ is used to reduce the bandwidth consumption. As one can see, all protocols are highly

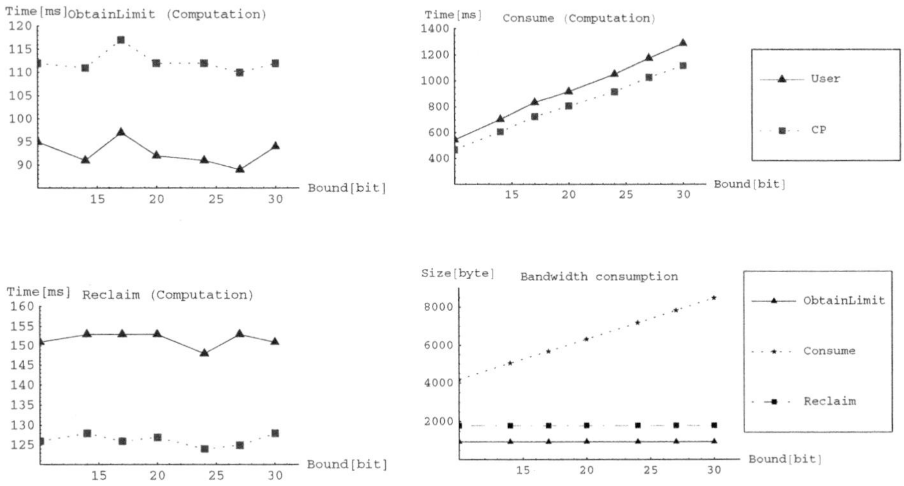

Fig. 1. Experimental results from a Java implementation of our first scheme

efficient from the user's as well as the cloud provider's perspective, both in the computational effort and the bandwdith consumption. This holds, although the code has not been optimized for performance and pre-computations have not been used. Hence, our evaluation shows that from the efficiency point of view our protocols are entirely practical.

4.6 Extensions and System Issues

Below, we present extensions of our schemes and aspects which seem to be important when deploying them for practical applications.

Limited Validity. One could rightly argue that in a large scale cloud the double spending detection of token identifiers using a blacklist (database) does not scale well. In order to overcome this limitation, we can extend our schemes such that a resource limit associated to a token only has a limited validity. Then, before the validity ends a user has to provide the actual token, i.e. the identifier and the available resources (either s and L or solely s in the second scheme) along with the corresponding signature. Then the user runs a new ObtainLimit protocol with the CP. Note that in case of the first scheme users should not end up with a new limit L representing the remaining resources, since this is very likely to be unique. Thus users should take one of the predefined limits. We now sketch how this adaption for the first scheme looks like (for the second one it can be done analogously): The keys of the CP are adapted such that the public key is $pk = (X, Y, Z_1, Z_2, Z_3, Z_4, Z_5, Z_6, e, g, \mathbb{G}, \mathbb{G}_t, p)$. Token are augmented by elements (V, r_V) whereas the former represent the validity period, e.g. a hash computed from an encoding in Unix time. In the `ObtainLimit` protocol the user additionally computes $Z_6^{r_V}$ (and proves knowledge of this DL) and the c part of the signature is adapted to $c = a^x(C_{id}C_s Z_4^L Z_5^V Z_6^{r_V})$ whereas the CP here integrates the validity V. The remainig ideas stay the same with exception that in the `Consume` protocol, the SPK needs to be adapted to

$$SPK\{(\alpha, \beta, \gamma, \delta, \epsilon, \zeta) : v_\sigma^\alpha = \mathbf{v} v_{r_{id}}^\beta v_s^\gamma v_{r_s}^\delta v_V^\epsilon v_{r_V}^\zeta \wedge \\ (0 \leq \gamma \leq 2^{l_L - l_{|d|}} - 1) \wedge (2^{l_{\mathtt{time}}} - 1 \leq \epsilon \leq 2^{l_{\mathbf{p}}} - 1)\}$$

whereas $\mathbf{p}$ represents the maximum validity period and `time` the representation of the actual date and time (in the `Reclaim` protocol we only need the second range proof). For the update of the signature and the token respectively, the user has to additionally compute $C_V = (A_5' A_6'^{r_V'})^{r'}$ and augment the proof of knowledge in step 3 of Protocol 2 to

$$SPK\{(\zeta, \eta, \phi, \iota, \kappa, \lambda, \mu, \nu, \xi) : C_{id+id'} = a'^\zeta A_1'^\eta \wedge C_V = A_5'^\phi A_6'^\iota \wedge \\ \tilde{C}_{s+|d|} = (C_{s+|d|})^\phi \wedge \mathbf{v} = v_\sigma^\phi (v_{r_{id}}^{-1})^\kappa (v_s^{-1})^\lambda (v_{r_s}^{-1})^\mu (v_V^{-1})^\nu (v_{r_V}^{-1})^\xi\}$$

Note that these modifications do influence the overall performance of the `Consume` protocol approximately by a factor of two, which though performs very good in practice when compared with our experimental results.

Elasticity. Clouds extremely benefit from users being able to request resources "on the fly". In our first scheme this can only be achieved by means of requesting additional tokens, i.e. running additional `ObtainLimt` protocols for the required resource, and users have then to manage a list of tokens. The second scheme allows for such updates, whereas we can simply use the `Reclaim` protocol of Section 4.4 (we may denote it as `Recharge` in this case), whereas $|d|$ is simply replaced by the amount of resources to be extended.

Tariff Schemes. If we consider the resource bound as "credits", then the CP can apply different tariff schemes at different points in time. This can simply be realized by using a different weight w_i for tariff scheme i and using $|d|' = |d| \cdot w_i$ instead of $|d|$ in our schemes.

4.7 Security Analysis

Regarding the security we have the following theorem whereas due to space constraints we refer the reader to the full version of this paper for the proof.

Theorem 1. *Assuming that the LRSW assumption in $\mathbb{G}$ (CL signature scheme is secure) and the DL assumption in $\mathbb{G}$ hold (the commitments are secure) and the proofs of knowledge are honest-verifier zero-knowledge, then the anonymous yet authorized and bounded cloud resource scheme presented in section 4.3 is secure with respect to the security model defined in section 2.3.*

5 Conclusion

In this paper we have investigated the problem of anonymous yet authorized and bounded use of cloud resources. We have presented a scheme, it's modification providing even more privacy, have presented extensions valuable for practical application and have supported the efficiency of the proposed scheme by a performance analysis based on a prototypical implementation.

Concluding we present anonymity revocation as an open problem. It is not clear to us how anonymity revocation could be suitably realized in this setting. We argue that it does not seem to be meaningful to use identity escrow within every transaction, i.e. to verifiably encrypt the user's identity. It is absolutely not clear who would have the power to perform anonymity revocation. In contrast, if at all, it seems more suitable to employ techniques like used within e-cash [9] or (n-times) anonymous authentication [9,21]. However, it is not clear to us how to achieve this, since in the aforementioned approaches spend protocols or authentications are atomic and in our setting we do not know in advance how often a user will consume or reclaim resources. We leave this functionality as an open problem for future work.

Acknowledgements. The author would like to thank the anonymous referees for providing valuable and helpful comments on this work as well as Gregory Zaverucha for pointing out prior independent work [10] on signature updates.

References

1. Abe, M., Okamoto, T.: Provably Secure Partially Blind Signatures. In: Bellare, M. (ed.) CRYPTO 2000. LNCS, vol. 1880, pp. 271–286. Springer, Heidelberg (2000)
2. Au, M.H., Susilo, W., Mu, Y.: Practical Anonymous Divisible E-Cash from Bounded Accumulators. In: Tsudik, G. (ed.) FC 2008. LNCS, vol. 5143, pp. 287–301. Springer, Heidelberg (2008)
3. Backes, M., Camenisch, J., Sommer, D.: Anonymous Yet Accountable Access Control. In: WPES, pp. 40–46. ACM (2005)
4. Balasch, J., Rial, A., Troncoso, C., Preneel, B., Verbauwhede, I., Geuens, C.: PrETP: Privacy-Preserving Electronic Toll Pricing. In: 19th USENIX Security Symposium, pp. 63–78. USENIX Association (2010)
5. Blanton, M.: Online Subscriptions with Anonymous Access. In: ASIACCS, pp. 217–227. ACM (2008)
6. Camenisch, J., Dubovitskaya, M., Neven, G.: Oblivious Transfer with Access Control. In: CCS, pp. 131–140. ACM (2009)
7. Camenisch, J., Dubovitskaya, M., Neven, G.: Unlinkable Priced Oblivious Transfer with Rechargeable Wallets. In: Sion, R. (ed.) FC 2010. LNCS, vol. 6052, pp. 66–81. Springer, Heidelberg (2010)
8. Camenisch, J., Hohenberger, S., Kohlweiss, M., Lysyanskaya, A., Meyerovich, M.: How to Win the Clone Wars: Efficient Periodic n-Times Anonymous Authentication. In: CCS, pp. 201–210. ACM (2006)
9. Camenisch, J.L., Hohenberger, S., Lysyanskaya, A.: Compact E-Cash. In: Cramer, R. (ed.) EUROCRYPT 2005. LNCS, vol. 3494, pp. 302–321. Springer, Heidelberg (2005)

10. Camenisch, J., Kohlweiss, M., Soriente, C.: An Accumulator Based on Bilinear Maps and Efficient Revocation for Anonymous Credentials. In: Jarecki, S., Tsudik, G. (eds.) PKC 2009. LNCS, vol. 5443, pp. 481–500. Springer, Heidelberg (2009)
11. Camenisch, J.L., Lysyanskaya, A.: A Signature Scheme with Efficient Protocols. In: Cimato, S., Galdi, C., Persiano, G. (eds.) SCN 2002. LNCS, vol. 2576, pp. 268–289. Springer, Heidelberg (2003)
12. Camenisch, J.L., Lysyanskaya, A.: Signature Schemes and Anonymous Credentials from Bilinear Maps. In: Franklin, M. (ed.) CRYPTO 2004. LNCS, vol. 3152, pp. 56–72. Springer, Heidelberg (2004)
13. Camenisch, J.L., Stadler, M.A.: Efficient Group Signature Schemes for Large Groups. In: Kaliski Jr., B.S. (ed.) CRYPTO 1997. LNCS, vol. 1294, pp. 410–424. Springer, Heidelberg (1997)
14. Canard, S., Gouget, A.: Divisible E-Cash Systems Can Be Truly Anonymous. In: Naor, M. (ed.) EUROCRYPT 2007. LNCS, vol. 4515, pp. 482–497. Springer, Heidelberg (2007)
15. Canard, S., Gouget, A., Hufschmitt, E.: A Handy Multi-Coupon System. In: Zhou, J., Yung, M., Bao, F. (eds.) ACNS 2006. LNCS, vol. 3989, pp. 66–81. Springer, Heidelberg (2006)
16. Chaum, D., Evertse, J.-H., van de Graaf, J.: An Improved Protocol for Demonstrating Possession of Discrete Logarithms and Some Generalizations. In: Price, W.L., Chaum, D. (eds.) EUROCRYPT 1987. LNCS, vol. 304, pp. 127–141. Springer, Heidelberg (1988)
17. Chen, L., Escalante B., A.N., Löhr, H., Manulis, M., Sadeghi, A.-R.: A Privacy-Protecting Multi-Coupon Scheme with Stronger Protection Against Splitting. In: Dietrich, S., Dhamija, R. (eds.) FC 2007 and USEC 2007. LNCS, vol. 4886, pp. 29–44. Springer, Heidelberg (2007)
18. Chen, Y., Paxson, V., Katz, R.H.: What's New About Cloud Computing Security? Tech. Rep. UCB/EECS-2010-5, University of California, Berkeley (2010)
19. Coull, S., Green, M., Hohenberger, S.: Controlling Access to an Oblivious Database Using Stateful Anonymous Credentials. In: Jarecki, S., Tsudik, G. (eds.) PKC 2009. LNCS, vol. 5443, pp. 501–520. Springer, Heidelberg (2009)
20. Cramer, R., Damgård, I.B., Schoenmakers, B.: Proof of Partial Knowledge and Simplified Design of Witness Hiding Protocols. In: Desmedt, Y.G. (ed.) CRYPTO 1994. LNCS, vol. 839, pp. 174–187. Springer, Heidelberg (1994)
21. Damgård, I.B., Dupont, K., Pedersen, M.Ø.: Unclonable Group Identification. In: Vaudenay, S. (ed.) EUROCRYPT 2006. LNCS, vol. 4004, pp. 555–572. Springer, Heidelberg (2006)
22. Fiat, A., Shamir, A.: How to Prove Yourself: Practical Solutions to Identification and Signature Problems. In: Odlyzko, A.M. (ed.) CRYPTO 1986. LNCS, vol. 263, pp. 186–194. Springer, Heidelberg (1987)
23. Franz, M., Williams, P., Carbunar, B., Katzenbeisser, S., Peter, A., Sion, R., Sotakova, M.: Oblivious Outsourced Storage with Delegation. In: Financial Cryptography and Data Security. LNCS, Springer, Heidelberg (2011)
24. Gentry, C.: Fully Homomorphic Encryption using Ideal Lattices. In: STOC, pp. 169–178 (2009)
25. Kamara, S., Lauter, K.: Cryptographic Cloud Storage. In: Sion, R., Curtmola, R., Dietrich, S., Kiayias, A., Miret, J.M., Sako, K., Sebé, F. (eds.) RLCPS, WECSR, and WLC 2010. LNCS, vol. 6054, pp. 136–149. Springer, Heidelberg (2010)
26. Lauter, K., Naehrig, M., Vaikuntanathan, V.: Can Homomorphic Encryption be Practical? Tech. Rep. MSR-TR-2011-58, Microsoft Research (2011)

27. Mao, W.: Guaranteed Correct Sharing of Integer Factorization with Off-Line Shareholders. In: Imai, H., Zheng, Y. (eds.) PKC 1998. LNCS, vol. 1431, pp. 60–71. Springer, Heidelberg (1998)
28. Okamoto, T.: Provably Secure and Practical Identification Schemes and Corresponding Signature Schemes. In: Brickell, E.F. (ed.) CRYPTO 1992. LNCS, vol. 740, pp. 31–53. Springer, Heidelberg (1993)
29. Okamoto, T.: An Efficient Divisible Electronic Cash Scheme. In: Coppersmith, D. (ed.) CRYPTO 1995. LNCS, vol. 963, pp. 438–451. Springer, Heidelberg (1995)
30. Pedersen, T.P.: Non-Interactive and Information-Theoretic Secure Verifiable Secret Sharing. In: Feigenbaum, J. (ed.) CRYPTO 1991. LNCS, vol. 576, pp. 129–140. Springer, Heidelberg (1992)

Group Law Computations on Jacobians of Hyperelliptic Curves

Craig Costello[1,2,3,⋆] and Kristin Lauter[3]

[1] Information Security Institute
Queensland University of Technology, GPO Box 2434, Brisbane QLD 4001, Australia
craig.costello@qut.edu.au
[2] Mathematics Department
University of California, Irvine - Irvine, CA 92697-3875, USA
[3] Microsoft Research
One Microsoft Way, Redmond, WA 98052, USA
klauter@microsoft.com

Abstract. We derive an explicit method of computing the composition step in Cantor's algorithm for group operations on Jacobians of hyperelliptic curves. Our technique is inspired by the geometric description of the group law and applies to hyperelliptic curves of arbitrary genus. While Cantor's general composition involves arithmetic in the polynomial ring $\mathbb{F}_q[x]$, the algorithm we propose solves a linear system over the base field which can be written down directly from the Mumford coordinates of the group elements.

We apply this method to give more efficient formulas for group operations in both affine and projective coordinates for cryptographic systems based on Jacobians of genus 2 hyperelliptic curves in general form.

Keywords: Hyperelliptic curves, group law, Jacobian arithmetic, genus 2.

1 Introduction

The field of curve-based cryptography has flourished for the last quarter century after Koblitz [31] and Miller [44] independently proposed the use of elliptic curves in public-key cryptosystems in the mid 1980's. Compared with traditional group structures like $\mathbb{F}_p^*$, elliptic curve cryptography (ECC) offers the powerful advantage of achieving the same level of conjectured security with a much smaller elliptic curve group. In 1989, Koblitz [32] generalized this idea by proposing Jacobians of hyperelliptic curves of arbitrary genus as a way to construct Abelian groups suitable for cryptography. Roughly speaking, hyperelliptic curves of genus g can achieve groups of the same size and security as elliptic curves, whilst being

⋆ This author acknowledges funding from the Australian-American Fulbright Commission, the Gregory Schwartz Enrichment Grant, the Queensland Government Smart State Ph.D. Fellowship, and an Australian Postgraduate Award.

A. Miri and S. Vaudenay (Eds.): SAC 2011, LNCS 7118, pp. 92–117, 2012.

defined over finite fields with g times fewer bits[1]. At the same time however, increasing the genus of a hyperelliptic curve significantly increases the computational cost of performing a group operation in the corresponding Jacobian group. Thus, the question that remains of great interest to the public-key cryptography community is, under which circumstances elliptic curves are preferable, and vice versa. At the present time, elliptic curves carry on standing as the front-runner in most practical scenarios, but whilst both ECC and hyperelliptic curve cryptography (HECC) continue to enjoy a wide range of improvements, this question remains open in general. For a nice overview of the progress in this race and of the state-of-the-art in both cases, the reader is referred to the talks by Bernstein [4], and by Lange [39].

Cantor [6] was the first to give a concrete algorithm for performing computations in Jacobian groups of hyperelliptic curves over fields of odd characteristic. Shortly after, Koblitz [32] modified this algorithm to apply to fields of any characteristic. Cantor's algorithm makes use of the polynomial representation of group elements proposed by Mumford [46], and consists of two stages: (i) the *composition* stage, based on Gauss's classical composition of binary quadratic forms, which generally outputs an unreduced divisor, and (ii) the *reduction* stage, which transforms the unreduced divisor into the unique reduced divisor that is equivalent to the sum, whose existence is guaranteed by the Riemann-Roch theorem [33]. Cantor's algorithm has since been substantially optimized in work initiated by Harley [24], who was the first to obtain practical explicit formulas in genus 2, and extended by Lange [34,38], who, among several others [43,50,45,49], generalized and significantly improved Harley's original approach. Essentially, all of these improvements involve unrolling the polynomial arithmetic implied by Cantor's algorithm into operations in the underlying field, and finding specialized shortcuts dedicated to each of the separate cases of input (see [35, §4]).

In this paper we propose an explicit alternative to unrolling Cantor's polynomial arithmetic in the composition phase. Our method is inspired by considering the geometric description of the group law and applies to hyperelliptic curves of any genus. The equivalence of the geometric group law and Cantor's algorithm was proven by Lauter [40] in the case of genus 2, but since then there has been almost no reported improvements in explicit formulas that benefit from this depiction. The notable exception being the work of Leitenberger [42], who used Gröbner basis reduction to show that in the addition of two distinct divisors on the Jacobian of a genus 2 curve, one can obtain explicit formulas to compute the required geometric function directly from the Mumford coordinates without (unrolling) polynomial arithmetic. Leitenberger's idea of obtaining the necessary geometric functions in a simple and elementary way is central to the theme of this paper, although we note that the affine addition formulas that result from our description (which do not rely on any Gröbner basis reduction) are significantly faster than the direct translation of those given in [42].

[1] The security argument becomes more complicated once venturing beyond genus 2, where the attacks by Gaudry [17] and others [8,21,48] overtake the Pollard Rho method [47].

We use the geometric description of the group law to prove that the interpolating functions for the composition step can be found by writing down a linear system in the ground field to be solved in terms of the Mumford coordinates of the divisors. Therefore, the composition algorithm for arbitrary genera proposed in this work is immediately explicit in terms of arithmetic in $\mathbb{F}_q$, in contrast to Cantor's composition which operates in the polynomial ring $\mathbb{F}_q[x]$, the optimization of which calls for ad-hoc attention in each genus to unravel the $\mathbb{F}_q[x]$ operations into explicit formulas in $\mathbb{F}_q$.

To illustrate the value of our approach, we show that, for group operations on Jacobians of general genus 2 curves over large prime fields, the (affine and projective) formulas that result from this description are more efficient than their predecessors. Also, when applying this approach back to the case of genus 1, we are able to recover several of the tricks previously explored for merging simultaneous group operations to optimize elliptic curve computations.

The rest of this paper is organized as follows. We briefly touch on some more related work, before moving to Section 2 where we give a short background on hyperelliptic curves and the Mumford representation of Jacobian elements. Section 3 discusses the geometry of Jacobian arithmetic on hyperelliptic curves, and shows that we can use simple linear algebra to compute the required geometric functions from the Mumford coordinates. Section 4 is dedicated to illustrating how this technique results in fast explicit formulas in genus 2, whilst Section 5 generalizes the algorithm for all $g \geq 2$. As we hope this work will influence further progress in higher genus arithmetic, in Section 6 we highlight some further implications of adopting this geometrically inspired approach, before concluding in Section 7. MAGMA scripts that verify our proposed algorithms and formulas can be found in the full version of this paper.

Related Work. There are several high-level papers (e.g. [27,25]) which discuss general methods for computing in Jacobians of arbitrary algebraic curves. In addition, there has also been work which specifically addresses arithmetic on non-hyperelliptic Jacobians from a geometric perspective (e.g. [13,14]).

Khuri-Makdisi treated divisor composition on arbitrary algebraic curves with linear algebra techniques in [29] and [30]. In contrast to Khuri-Makdisi's deep and more general approach, our paper specifically aims to present an explicit algorithm in an implementation-ready format that is specific to hyperelliptic curves, much like his joint work with Abu Salem which applied his earlier techniques to present explicit formulas for arithmetic on $C_{3,4}$ curves [1]. Some other authors have also applied techniques from the realm of linear algebra to Jacobian operations: two notable examples being the work of Guyot *et al.* [23] and Avanzi *et al.* [2] who both used matrix methods to compute the resultant of two polynomials in the composition stage.

Since we have focused on general hyperelliptic curves, our comparison in genus 2 does not include the record-holding work by Gaudry [19], which exploits the Kummer surface associated with curves of a special form to achieve the current outright fastest genus 2 arithmetic for those curve models. Gaudry and Harley's second exposition [20] further describes the results in [24]. Finally, we do not draw comparisons with any work on real models of hyperelliptic curves, which usually result in slightly slower formulas than imaginary hyperelliptic curves, but we note that both Galbraith *et al.* [16] and Erickson *et al.* [11] achieve very competitive formulas for group law computations on real models of genus 2 hyperelliptic curves.

2 Background

We give some brief background on hyperelliptic curves and the Mumford representation of points in the Jacobian. For a more in depth discussion, the reader is referred to [3, §4] and [15, §11]. Over the field K, we use C_g to denote the general ("imaginary quadratic") hyperelliptic curve of genus g given by

$$C_g : y^2 + h(x)y = f(x),$$
$$h(x), f(x) \in K[x], \quad \deg(f) = 2g+1, \quad \deg(h) \leq g, \quad f \text{ monic}, \tag{1}$$

with the added stipulation that no point $(x, y) \in \overline{K}$ simultaneously sends both partial derivatives $2y + h(x)$ and $f'(x) - h'(x)y$ to zero [3, §14.1]. As long as $\mathrm{char}(K) \neq 2g+1$, we can isomorphically transform C_g into $\hat{C}_g$, given as $\hat{C}_g$: $y^2 + h(x)y = x^{2g+1} + \hat{f}_{2g-1}x^{2g-1} + ... + \hat{f}_1 x + \hat{f}_0$, so that the coefficient of x^{2g} is zero [3, §14.13]. In the case of odd characteristic fields, it is standard to also annihilate the presence of $h(x)$ completely under a suitable transformation, in order to obtain a simpler model (we will make use of this in §4). We abuse notation and use C_g from hereon to refer to the simplified version of the curve equation in each context. Although the proofs in §3 apply to any K, it better places the intention of the discussion to henceforth regard K as a finite field $\mathbb{F}_q$.

We work in the Jacobian group $\mathrm{Jac}(C_g)$ of C_g, where the elements are equivalence classes of degree zero divisors on C_g. Divisors are formal sums of points on the curve, and the degree of a divisor is the sum of the multiplicities of points in the support of the divisor. Two divisors are *equivalent* if their difference is a principal divisor, i.e. equal to the divisor of zeros and poles of a function. It follows from the Riemann-Roch Theorem that for hyperelliptic curves, each class D has a unique *reduced* representative of the form

$$\rho(D) = (P_1) + (P_2) + ... + (P_r) - r(P_\infty),$$

such that $r \leq g$, $P_i \neq -P_j$ for $i \neq j$, no P_i satisfying $P_i = -P_i$ appears more than once, and with P_∞ being the point at infinity on C_g. We drop the ρ from hereon and, unless stated otherwise, assume divisor equations involve reduced divisors. When referring to the non-trivial elements in the reduced divisor D, we mean all $P \in \mathrm{supp}(D)$ where $P \neq P_\infty$, i.e. the elements corresponding to the effective part of D. For each of the r non-trivial elements appearing in D, write $P_i = (x_i, y_i)$. Mumford proposed a convenient way to represent such divisors as $D = (u(x), v(x))$, where $u(x)$ is a monic polynomial with $\deg(u(x)) \leq g$ satisfying $u(x_i) = 0$, and $v(x)$ (which is not monic in general) with $\deg(v(x)) < \deg(u(x))$

is such that $v(x_i) = y_i$, for $1 \leq i \leq r$. In this way we have a one-to-one correspondence between reduced divisors and their so-called *Mumford representation* [46]. We use $\oplus$ (resp. $\ominus$) to distinguish group additions (resp. subtractions) between Jacobian elements from "additions" in formal divisor sums. We use $\bar{D}$ to denote the divisor obtained by taking the hyperelliptic involution of each of the non-trivial elements in the support of D.

When developing formulas for implementing genus g arithmetic, we are largely concerned with the frequent case that arises where both (not necessarily distinct) reduced divisors $D = (u(x), v(x))$ and $D' = (u'(x), v'(x))$ in the sum $D \oplus D'$ are such that $\deg(u(x)) = \deg(u'(x)) = g$. This means that $D = E - g(P_\infty)$ and $D' = E' - g(P_\infty)$, with both E and E' being effective divisors of degree g; from hereon we interchangeably refer to such divisors as *full degree* or *degree g* divisors, and we use $\hat{\mathrm{J}}\mathrm{ac}(C_g)$ to denote the set of all such divisor classes of full degree, where $\hat{\mathrm{J}}\mathrm{ac}(C_g) \subset \mathrm{Jac}(C_g)$. In Section 5.2 we discuss how to handle the special case when a divisor of degree less than g is encountered.

3 Computations in the Mumford Function Field

The purpose of this section is to show how to compute group law operations in Jacobians by applying linear algebra to the Mumford coordinates of divisors. The geometric description of the group law is an important ingredient in the proof of the proposed linear algebra approach (particularly in the proof of Proposition 3), so we start by reviewing the geometry underlying arithmetic on Jacobians of hyperelliptic curves.

Since the Jacobian of a hyperelliptic curve is the group of degree zero divisors modulo principal divisors, the group operation is formal addition modulo the equivalence relation. Thus two divisors D and D' can be added by finding a function whose divisor contains the support of both D and D', and then the sum is equivalent to the negative of the complement of that support. Such a function $\ell(x)$ can be obtained by interpolating the points in the support of the two divisors. The complement of the support of D and D' in the support of $\mathrm{div}(\ell)$ consists of the other points of intersection of ℓ with the curve. In general those individual points may not be defined over the ground field for the curve. We are thus led to work with Mumford coordinates for divisors on hyperelliptic curves, since the polynomials in Mumford coordinates are defined over the base field and allow us to avoid extracting individual roots and working with points defined over extension fields.

For example, consider adding two full degree genus 3 divisors $D, D' \in \hat{\mathrm{J}}\mathrm{ac}(C_3)$, with respective supports $\mathrm{supp}(D) = \{P_1, P_2, P_3\} \cup \{P_\infty\}$ and $\mathrm{supp}(D') = \{P_1', P_2', P_3'\} \cup \{P_\infty\}$, as in Figure 1. After computing the quintic function $\ell(x, y) = \sum_{i=0}^{5} \ell_i x^i$ that interpolates the six non-trivial points in the composition phase, computing the x-coordinates of the remaining (four) points of intersection explicitly would require solving

$$\ell_5^2 \cdot \prod_{i=1}^{3}(x - x_i) \cdot \prod_{i=1}^{3}(x - x_i') \prod_{i=1}^{4}(x - \bar{x}_i) = \Big(\sum_{i=0}^{5} \ell_i x^i\Big)^2 - f(x)$$

for $\bar{x}_1$,$\bar{x}_2$,$\bar{x}_3$ and $\bar{x}_4$, which would necessitate multiple root extractions. On the other hand, the exact division $\prod_{i=1}^{4}(x - \bar{x}_i) = \Big(\big(\sum_{i=0}^{5} \ell_i x^i\big)^2 - f(x)\Big) / \Big(\ell_5^2 \cdot \prod_{i=1}^{3}(x - x_i) \cdot \prod_{i=1}^{3}(x - x_i')\Big)$ can be computed very efficiently (and entirely over $\mathbb{F}_q$) by equating coefficients of x.

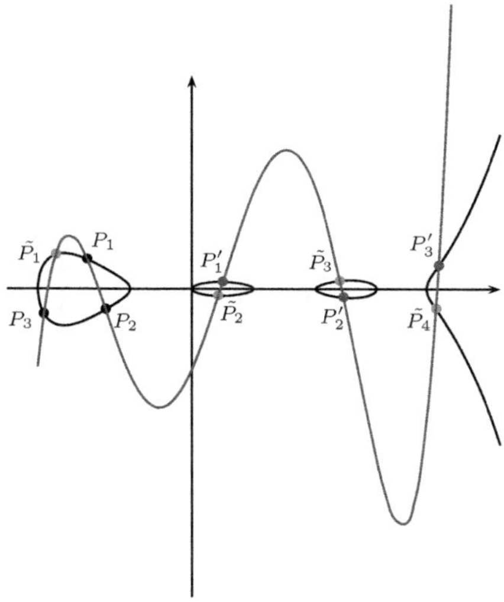

Fig. 1. The *composition* stage of a general addition on the Jacobian of a genus 3 curve C_3 over the reals $\mathbb{R}$: the 6 points in the combined supports of D and D' are interpolated by a quintic polynomial which intersects C in 4 more places to form the unreduced divisor $\tilde{D} = \tilde{P}_1 + \tilde{P}_2 + \tilde{P}_3 + \tilde{P}_4$.

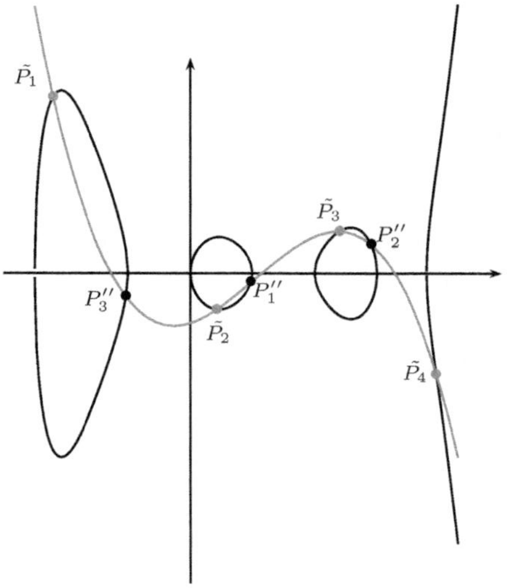

Fig. 2. The *reduction stage*: a (vertically) magnified view of the cubic function which interpolates the points in the support of $\tilde{D}$ and intersects C_3 in three more places to form $\bar{D}'' = (P_1'' + P_2'' + P_3'') \sim \tilde{D}$, the reduced equivalent of $\tilde{D}$.

Whilst the Mumford representation is absolutely necessary for efficient reduction, the price we seemingly pay in deriving formulas from the simple geometric description lies in the composition phase. In any case, finding the interpolating function $y = \ell(x)$ would be conceptually trivial if we knew the (x, y) coordinates of the points involved, but computing the function directly from the Mumford coordinates appears to be more difficult. In what follows we detail how this can be achieved in general, using only linear algebra over the base field. The meanings of the three propositions in this section are perhaps best illustrated through the examples that follow each of them.

Proposition 1. *On the Jacobian of a genus g hyperelliptic curve, the set* $\hat{\mathrm{J}}\mathrm{ac}(C_g)$ *of divisor classes with reduced representatives of full degree g can be described exactly as the intersection of g hypersurfaces of dimension (at most) 2g.*

Proof. Let $D = (u(x), v(x)) = \left(x^g + \sum_{i=0}^{g-1} u_i x^i\,,\, \sum_{i=0}^{g-1} v_i x^i\right) \in \hat{\mathrm{J}}\mathrm{ac}(C_g(K))$ be an arbitrary degree g divisor class representative with $\mathrm{supp}(D) = \{(x_1, y_1), ..., (x_g, y_g)\} \cup \{P_\infty\}$, so that $u(x_i) = 0$ and $v(x_i) = y_i$ for $1 \le i \le g$. Let $\Psi(x) = \sum_{i=0}^{g-1} \Psi_i x^i$ be the polynomial obtained by substituting $y = v(x)$ into the equation for C_g and reducing modulo the ideal generated by $u(x)$. Clearly, $\Psi(x_i) \equiv 0 \bmod \langle u(x)\rangle$ for each of the g non-trivial elements in $\mathrm{supp}(D)$, but since $\deg(\Psi(x)) \le g-1$, it follows that each of its g coefficients Ψ_i must be identically zero, implying that every element $D \in \hat{\mathrm{J}}\mathrm{ac}(C_g)$ of full degree g lies in the intersection of the g hypersurfaces $\Psi_i = \Psi_i(u_0, ..., u_{g-1}, v_0, ..., v_{g-1}) = 0$. On the other hand, each unique $2g$-tuple in K which satisfies $\Psi_i = 0$ for $1 \le i \le g$ defines a unique full degree representative $D \in \hat{\mathrm{J}}\mathrm{ac}(C_g(K))$ (cf. [15, ex 11.3.7]). □

Definition 1 (Mumford ideals). *We call the g ideals* $\langle \Psi_i \rangle$ *arising from the g hypersurfaces* $\Psi_i = 0$ *in Proposition 1 the Mumford ideals.*

Definition 2 (Mumford function fields). *The function fields of* $\hat{\mathrm{J}}\mathrm{ac}(C_g)$ *and* $\hat{\mathrm{J}}\mathrm{ac}(C_g) \times \hat{\mathrm{J}}\mathrm{ac}(C_g)$ *are respectively identified with the quotient fields of*

$$\frac{K[u_0, ..., u_{g-1}, v_0, ..., v_{g-1}]}{\langle \Psi_0, ..., \Psi_{g-1}\rangle} \text{ and } \frac{K[u_0, ..., u_{g-1}, v_0, ..., v_{g-1}, u_0', ..., u_{g-1}', v_0', ..., v_{g-1}']}{\langle \Psi_0, ..., \Psi_{g-1}, \Psi_0', ..., \Psi_{g-1}'\rangle},$$

which we call the Mumford function fields and denote by $K_{\mathrm{DBL}}^{\mathrm{Mum}} = K(\hat{\mathrm{J}}\mathrm{ac}(C_g))$ *and* $K_{\mathrm{ADD}}^{\mathrm{Mum}} = K(\hat{\mathrm{J}}\mathrm{ac}(C_g) \times \hat{\mathrm{J}}\mathrm{ac}(C_g))$ *respectively. We abbreviate and use* Ψ_i, Ψ_i' *to differentiate between* $\Psi_i = \Psi_i(u_0, ..., u_{g-1}, v_0, ..., v_{g-1})$ *and* $\Psi_i' = \Psi_i(u_0', ..., u_{g-1}', v_0', ..., v_{g-1}')$ *when working in* $K_{\mathrm{ADD}}^{\mathrm{Mum}}$.

Example 1. Consider the genus 2 hyperelliptic curve defined by $C : y^2 = (x^5 + 2x^3 - 7x^2 + 5x + 1)$ over $\mathbb{F}_{37}$. A general degree two divisor $D \in \hat{\mathrm{J}}\mathrm{ac}(C)$ takes the form $D = (x^2 + u_1 x + u_0, v_1 x + v_0)$. Substituting $y = v_1 x + v_0$ into C and reducing modulo $\langle x^2 + u_1 x + u_0\rangle$ gives

$$(v_1 x + v_0)^2 - (x^5 + 2x^3 - 7x^2 + 5x + 1) \equiv \Psi_1 x + \Psi_0 \equiv 0 \bmod \langle x^2 + u_1 x + u_0\rangle$$

where

$$\Psi_1(u_1, u_0, v_1, v_0) = 3\,u_0 {u_1}^2 - {u_1}^4 - {u_0}^2 + 2\,v_0 v_1 - {v_1}^2 u_1 + 2\,(u_0 - {u_1}^2) - 7u_1 - 5,$$
$$\Psi_0(u_1, u_0, v_1, v_0) = {v_0}^2 - {v_1}^2 u_0 + 2\,{u_0}^2 u_1 - {u_1}^3 u_0 - 2u_1 u_0 - 7u_0 - 1.$$

The number of tuples $(u_0, u_1, v_0, v_1) \in \mathbb{F}_{37}$ lying in the intersection of $\Psi_0 = \Psi_1 = 0$ is 1373, which is the number of degree 2 divisors on $\mathrm{Jac}(C)$, i.e. $\#\hat{\mathrm{J}}\mathrm{ac}(C) = 1373$. There are 39 other divisors on $\mathrm{Jac}(C)$ with degrees less than 2, each of which is isomorphic to a point on the curve, so that

$\#\text{Jac}(C) = \#\hat{\text{J}}\text{ac}(C) + \#C = 1373 + 39 = 1412$. Formulas for performing full degree divisor additions are derived inside the Mumford function field $K_{\text{ADD}}^{\text{Mum}} = \text{Quot}(K[u_0, u_1, v_0, v_1, u_0', u_1', v_0', v_1']/\langle \Psi_0, \Psi_1, \Psi_0', \Psi_1' \rangle)$, whilst formulas for full degree divisor doublings are derived inside the Mumford function field $K_{\text{DBL}}^{\text{Mum}} = \text{Quot}(K[u_0, u_1, v_0, v_1]/\langle \Psi_0, \Psi_1 \rangle)$.

Performing the efficient composition of two divisors amounts to finding the least degree polynomial function that interpolates the union of their (assumed disjoint) non-trivial supports. The following two propositions show that in the general addition and doubling of divisors, finding the interpolating functions in the Mumford function fields can be accomplished by solving linear systems.

Proposition 2 (General divisor addition). *Let D and D' be reduced divisors of degree g on* $\text{Jac}(C_g)$ *such that* $\text{supp}(D) = \{(x_1, y_1), ..., (x_g, y_g)\} \cup \{P_\infty\}$, $\text{supp}(D') = \{(x_1', y_1'), ..., (x_g', y_g')\} \cup \{P_\infty\}$ *and $x_i \neq x_j'$ for all $1 \leq i, j \leq g$. A function ℓ on C_g that interpolates the $2g$ non-trivial elements in* $\text{supp}(D) \cup \text{supp}(D')$ *can be determined by solving a linear system of dimension $2g$ inside the Mumford function field $K_{\text{ADD}}^{\text{Mum}}$.*

Proof. Let $D = \big(u(x), v(x)\big) = \big(x^g + \sum_{i=0}^{g-1} u_i x^i\,,\, \sum_{i=0}^{g-1} v_i x^i\big)$ and $D' = \big(u'(x), v'(x)\big) = \big(x^g + \sum_{i=0}^{g-1} u_i' x^i\,,\, \sum_{i=0}^{g-1} v_i' x^i\big)$. Let the polynomial $y = \ell(x) = \sum_{i=0}^{2g-1} \ell_i x^i$ be the desired function that interpolates the $2g$ non-trivial elements in $\text{supp}(D) \cup \text{supp}(D')$, i.e. $y_i = \ell(x_i)$ and $y_i' = \ell(x_i')$ for $1 \leq i \leq g$. Focussing firstly on D, it follows that $v(x) - \ell(x) = 0$ for $x \in \{x_i\}_{1 \leq i \leq g}$. As in the proof of Proposition 1, we reduce modulo the ideal generated by $u(x)$ giving $\Omega(x) = v(x) - \ell(x) \equiv \sum_{i=0}^{g-1} \Omega_i x^i \equiv 0 \mod \langle x^g + \sum_{i=0}^{g-1} u_i x^i \rangle$. Since $\deg(\Omega(x)) \leq g - 1$ and $\Omega(x_i) = 0$ for $1 \leq i \leq g$, it follows that the g coefficients $\Omega_i = \Omega_i(u_0, ..., u_{g-1}, v_0, ..., v_{g-1}, \ell_0, ..., \ell_{2g-1})$ must be all identically zero. Each gives rise to an equation that relates the $2g$ coefficients of $\ell(x)$ linearly inside $K_{\text{ADD}}^{\text{Mum}}$. Defining $\Omega'(x)$ from D' identically and reducing modulo $u'(x)$ gives another g linear equations in the $2g$ coefficients of $\ell(x)$. □

Example 2. Consider the genus 3 hyperelliptic curve defined by $C : y^2 = x^7 + 1$ over $\mathbb{F}_{71}$, and take $D = \big(u(x), v(x)\big), D' = \big(u'(x), v'(x)\big) \in \hat{\text{J}}\text{ac}(C)$ as

$$D = \big(x^3 + 6x^2 + 41x + 33, 29x^2 + 22x + 47\big),$$
$$D' = \big(x^3 + 18x^2 + 15x + 37, 49x^2 + 46x + 59\big).$$

We compute the polynomial $\ell(x) = \sum_{i=0}^{5} \ell_i x^i$ that interpolates the six non-trivial elements in $\text{supp}(D) \cup \text{supp}(D')$ using $\ell(x) - v(x) \equiv 0 \mod \langle u(x) \rangle$ and $\ell(x) - v'(x) \equiv 0 \mod \langle u'(x) \rangle$, to obtain Ω_i and Ω_i' for $0 \leq i \leq 2$. For D and D', we respectively have that

$$0 \equiv \ell(x) - (29x^2 + 22x + 47) \equiv \Omega_2 x^2 + \Omega_1 x + \Omega_0 \mod \langle x^3 + 6x^2 + 41x + 33 \rangle,$$
$$0 \equiv \ell(x) - (49x^2 + 46x + 59) \equiv \Omega_2' x^2 + \Omega_1' x + \Omega_0' \mod \langle x^3 + 18x^2 + 15x + 37 \rangle,$$

with

$$\Omega_2 = \ell_2 + 65\ell_3 + 66\ell_4 + 30\ell_5 - 29; \qquad \Omega_2' = \ell_2 + 53\ell_3 + 25\ell_4 + 67\ell_5 - 49;$$
$$\Omega_1 = \ell_1 + 30\ell_3 + 48\ell_5 - 22; \qquad \Omega_1' = \ell_1 + 56\ell_3 + 20\ell_4 + 7\ell_5 - 46;$$
$$\Omega_0 = \ell_0 + 38\ell_3 + 56\ell_4 + 23\ell_5 - 47; \qquad \Omega_0' = \ell_0 + 34\ell_3 + 27\ell_4 + 69\ell_5 - 59.$$

Solving $\Omega_{0\le i\le 2}, \Omega'_{0\le i\le 2} = 0$ simultaneously for $\ell_0, ..., \ell_5$ gives $\ell(x) = 21x^5 + x^4 + 36x^3 + 46x^2 + 64x + 57$.

Proposition 3 (General divisor doubling). *Let D be a divisor of degree g representing a class on* $\mathrm{Jac}(C_g)$ *with* $\mathrm{supp}(D) = \{P_1, ..., P_g\} \cup \{P_\infty\}$. *A function ℓ on C_g such that each non-trivial element in* $\mathrm{supp}(D)$ *occurs with multiplicity two in* $\mathrm{div}(\ell)$ *can be determined by a linear system of dimension $2g$ inside the Mumford function field $K_{\mathrm{DBL}}^{\mathrm{Mum}}$.*

Proof. Let $D = \big(u(x), v(x)\big) = \big(x^g + \sum_{i=0}^{g-1} u_i x^i\,,\, \sum_{i=0}^{g-1} v_i x^i\big)$ and write $P_i = (x_i, y_i)$ for $1 \le i \le g$. Let the polynomial $y = \ell(x) = \sum_{i=0}^{2g-1} \ell_i x^i$ be the desired function that interpolates the g non-trivial elements of $\mathrm{supp}(D)$, and also whose derivative $\ell'(x)$ is equal to dy/dx on $C_g(x,y)$ at each such element. Namely, $\ell(x) = \sum_{i=0}^{2g-1} \ell_i x^i$ is such that $\ell(x_i) = y_i$ and $\frac{d\ell}{dx}(x_i) = \frac{dy}{dx}(x_i)$ on C for $1 \le i \le g$. This time the first g equations come from the direct interpolation as before, whilst the second g equations come from the general expression for the equated derivates, taking $\frac{d\ell}{dx}(x_i) = \frac{dy}{dx}(x_i)$ on C_g as

$$\sum_{i=1}^{g-1} i\ell_i x^{i-1} = \frac{(2g+1)x^{2g} + \sum_{i=1}^{2g-1} i f_i x^{i-1} + (\sum_{i=0}^{g} i h_i x^{i-1}) \cdot y}{2y + \sum_{i=0}^{g} h_i x^i}$$

for each x_i with $1 \le i \le g$. Again, it is easy to see that substituting $y = v(x)$ and reducing modulo the ideal generated by $u(x)$ will produce a polynomial $\Omega'(x)$ with degree less than or equal to $g-1$. Since $\Omega'(x)$ has g roots, $\Omega_i' = 0$ for $0 \le i \le g-1$, giving rise to the second g equations which importantly relate the coefficients of $\ell(x)$ linearly inside $K_{\mathrm{DBL}}^{\mathrm{Mum}}$. □

Example 3. Consider the genus 3 hyperelliptic curve defined by $C : y^2 = x^7 + 5x + 1$ over $\mathbb{F}_{257}$, and take $D \in \hat{\mathrm{J}}\mathrm{ac}(C)$ as $D = (u(x), v(x)) = (x^3 + 57x^2 + 26x + 80, 176x^2 + 162x + 202)$. We compute the polynomial $\ell(x) = \sum_{i=0}^{5} \ell_i x^i$ that interpolates the three non-trivial points in $\mathrm{supp}(D)$, and also has the same derivative as C at these points. For the interpolation only, we obtain $\Omega_0, \Omega_1, \Omega_2$ (collected below) identically as in Example 2.

For $\Omega_0', \Omega_1', \Omega_2'$, equating dy/dx on C with $\ell'(x)$ gives

$$\frac{7x^6 + 5}{2y} \equiv 5\ell_5 x^4 + 4\ell_4 x^3 + 3\ell_3 x^2 + 2\ell_2 x + \ell_1 \mod \langle x^3 + 57x^2 + 26x + 80\rangle,$$

which, after substituting $y = 176x^2 + 162x + 202$, rearranges to give $0 \equiv \Omega_2' x^2 + \Omega_1' x + \Omega_0'$, where

$$\Omega_2 = 118\ell_4 + 256\ell_2 + 57\ell_3 + 96\ell_5; \qquad \Omega_2' = 76\ell_5 + 2541\ell_4 + 254\ell_3 + 166;$$
$$\Omega_1 = 140\ell_4 + 256\ell_1 + 26\ell_3 + 82\ell_5; \qquad \Omega_1' = 209 + 255\ell_2 + 104\ell_4 + 186\ell_5;$$
$$\Omega_0 = 256\ell_0 + 80\ell_3 + 69\ell_5 + 66\ell_4; \qquad \Omega_0' = 73\ell_5 + 63\ell_4 + 256\ell_1 + 31.$$

Solving $\Omega_{0\leq i\leq 2}, \Omega'_{0\leq i\leq 2} = 0$ simultaneously for $\ell_0, ..., \ell_5$ gives $\ell(x) = 84x^5 + 213x^3 + 78x^2 + 252x + 165$.

This section showed that divisor composition on hyperelliptic curves can be achieved via linear operations in the Mumford function fields.

4 Generating Explicit Formulas in Genus 2

This section applies the results of the previous section to develop explicit formulas for group law computations involving full degree divisors on Jacobians of genus 2 hyperelliptic curves. Assuming an underlying field of large prime characteristic, such genus 2 hyperelliptic curves $C'/\mathbb{F}_q$ can always be isomorphically transformed into $C_2/\mathbb{F}_q$ given by $C_2 : y^2 = x^5 + f_3x^3 + f_2x^2 + f_1x + f_0$, where $C_2 \cong C'$ (see §2). The Mumford representation of a general degree two divisor $D \in \hat{\text{J}}\text{ac}(C_2) \subset \text{Jac}(C_2)$ is given as $D = (x^2 + u_1x + u_0, v_1x + v_0)$. From Proposition 1, we compute the $g = 2$ hypersurfaces whose intersection is the set of all such divisors $\hat{\text{J}}\text{ac}(C_2)$ as follows. Substituting $y = v_1x + v_0$ into the equation for C_2 and reducing modulo the ideal $\langle x^2 + u_1x + u_0\rangle$ gives the polynomial $\Psi(x)$ as

$$\Psi(x) \equiv \Psi_1x + \Psi_0 \equiv (v_1x + v_0)^2 - (x^5 + f_3x^3 + f_2x^2 + f_1x + f_0) \mod \langle x^2 + u_1x + u_0\rangle,$$

where

$$\begin{aligned}\Psi_0 &= {v_0}^2 - f_0 + f_2u_0 - {v_1}^2u_0 + 2\,{u_0}^2u_1 - u_1f_3u_0 - {u_1}^3u_0,\\ \Psi_1 &= 2\,v_0v_1 - f_1 - {v_1}^2u_1 + f_2u_1 - f_3({u_1}^2 - u_0) + 3\,u_0{u_1}^2 - {u_1}^4 - {u_0}^2.\end{aligned} \quad (2)$$

We will derive doubling formulas inside $K^{\text{Mum}}_{\text{ADD}} = \text{Quot}(K[u_0, u_1, v_0, v_1]/\langle\Psi_0, \Psi_1\rangle)$ and addition formulas inside $K^{\text{Mum}}_{\text{ADD}} = \text{Quot}(K[u_0, u_1, v_0, v_1, u'_0, u'_1, v'_0, v'_1] /\langle\Psi_0, \Psi_1, \Psi'_0, \Psi'_1\rangle)$. In §4.2 particularly, we will see how the ideal $\langle\Psi_0, \Psi_1\rangle$ is useful in simplifying the formulas that arise.

4.1 General Divisor Addition in Genus 2

Let $D = (x^2 + u_1x + u_0, v_1x + v_0), D' = (x^2 + u'_1x + u'_0, v'_1x + v'_0) \in \hat{\text{J}}\text{ac}(C_2)$ be two divisors with $\text{supp}(D) = \{P_1, P_2\} \cup \{P_\infty\}$ and $\text{supp}(D') = \{P'_1, P'_2\} \cup \{P_\infty\}$, such that no P_i has the same x coordinate as P'_j for $1 \leq i, j \leq 2$. Let $D'' = (x^2 + u''_1x + u''_0, v''_1x + v''_0) = D \oplus D'$. The composition step in the addition of D and D' involves building the linear system inside $K^{\text{Mum}}_{\text{ADD}}$ that solves to give the coefficients ℓ_i of the cubic polynomial $y = \ell(x) = \sum_{i=0}^{3} \ell_ix^i$ which interpolates P_1, P_2, P'_1, P'_2. Following Proposition 2, we have

$$\begin{aligned}0 &\equiv \Omega_1x + \Omega_0 \equiv \ell_3x^3 + \ell_2x^2 + \ell_1x + \ell_0 - (v_1x + v_0)\\ &\equiv (\ell_3({u_1}^2 - u_0) - \ell_2u_1 + \ell_1 - v_1)x + (\ell_3u_1u_0 - \ell_2u_0 + \ell_0 - v_0)\\ &\qquad \mod \langle x^2 + u_1x + u_0\rangle \quad , \end{aligned} \quad (3)$$

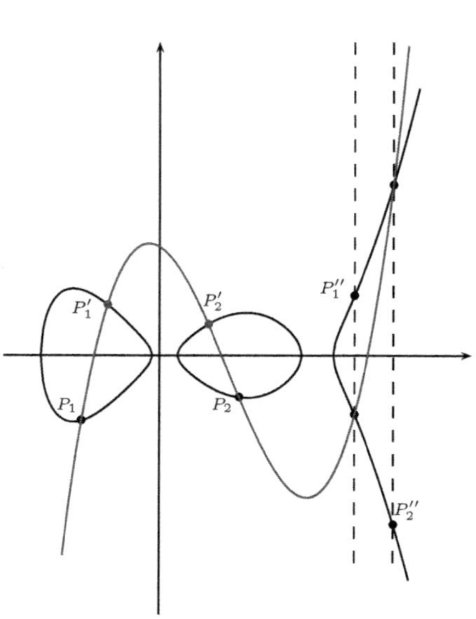

Fig. 3. The group law (general addition) on the Jacobian of the genus 2 curve C_2 over the reals $\mathbb{R}$, for $(P_1+P_2)\oplus(P_1'+P_2') = P_1''+P_2''$.

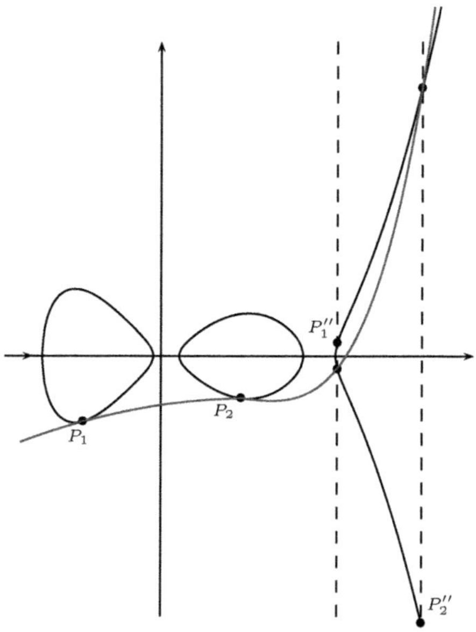

Fig. 4. A general point doubling on the Jacobian of a genus 2 curve C_2 over the reals $\mathbb{R}$, for $[2](P_1+P_2) = P_1''+P_2''$.

which provides two equations ($\Omega_1 = 0$ and $\Omega_0 = 0$) relating the four coefficients of the interpolating polynomial linearly inside $K_{\text{ADD}}^{\text{Mum}}$. Identically, interpolating the support of D' produces two more linear equations which allow us to solve for the four ℓ_i as

$$\begin{pmatrix} 1 & 0 & -u_0 & u_1u_0 \\ 0 & 1 & -u_1 & u_1^2-u_0 \\ 1 & 0 & -u_0' & u_1'u_0' \\ 0 & 1 & -u_1' & u_1'^2-u_0' \end{pmatrix} \cdot \begin{pmatrix} \ell_0 \\ \ell_1 \\ \ell_2 \\ \ell_3 \end{pmatrix} = \begin{pmatrix} v_0 \\ v_1 \\ v_0' \\ v_1' \end{pmatrix}.$$

Observe that the respective subtraction of rows 1 and 2 from rows 3 and 4 gives rise to a smaller system that can be solved for ℓ_2 and ℓ_3, as

$$\begin{pmatrix} u_0-u_0' & u_1'u_0'-u_1u_0 \\ u_1-u_1' & (u_1'^2-u_0')-(u_1^2-u_0) \end{pmatrix} \cdot \begin{pmatrix} \ell_2 \\ \ell_3 \end{pmatrix} = \begin{pmatrix} v_0'-v_0 \\ v_1'-v_1 \end{pmatrix}. \quad (4)$$

Remark 1. We will see in Section 5.1 that for all $g \geq 2$, the linear system that arises in the computation of $\ell(x)$ can always be trivially reduced to be of dimension g, but for now it is useful to observe that once we solve the dimension $g = 2$ matrix system for ℓ_i with $i \geq g$, calculating the remaining ℓ_i where $i < g$ is computationally straightforward.

The next step is to determine the remaining intersection points of $y = \ell(x)$ on C_2. Since $y = \ell(x)$ is cubic, its substitution into C_2 will give a degree six equation in x. Four of the roots will correspond to the four non-trivial points in $\text{supp}(D) \cup \text{supp}(D')$, whilst the remaining two will correspond to the two x coordinates of the non-trivial elements in $\text{supp}(\bar{D}'')$, which are the same as the x coordinates in $\text{supp}(D'')$ (see the intersection points in Figure 3). Let the Mumford representation of $\bar{D}''$ be $\bar{D}'' = (x^2 + u_1''x + u_0'', -v_1''x - v_0'')$; we then have

$$(x^2 + u_1x + u_0) \cdot (x^2 + u_1'x + u_0') \cdot (x^2 + u_1''x + u_0'') = \frac{(\sum_{i=0}^{3} \ell_i x^i)^2 - f(x)}{\ell_3^2}.$$

Equating coefficients is an efficient way to compute the exact division required above to solve for $u''(x)$. For example, equating coefficients of x^5 and x^4 above respectively gives

$$\begin{aligned} u_1'' &= -u_1 - u_1' - \frac{1 - 2\ell_2\ell_3}{\ell_3^2}; \\ u_0'' &= -(u_0 + u_0' + u_1u_1' + (u_1 + u_1')u_1'') + \frac{2\ell_1\ell_3 + \ell_2^2}{\ell_3^2}. \end{aligned} \tag{5}$$

It remains to compute v_1'' and v_0''. Namely, we wish to compute the linear function that interpolates the points in $\text{supp}(D'')$. Observe that reducing $\ell(x)$ modulo $\langle x^2 + u_1''x + u_0'' \rangle$ gives the linear polynomial $-v_1''x + -v_0''$ which interpolates the points in $\text{supp}(\bar{D}'')$, i.e. those points which are the involutions of the points in $\text{supp}(D'')$. Thus, the computation of v_1'' and v_0'' amounts to negating the result of $\ell(x) \bmod \langle x^2 + u_1''x + u_0'' \rangle$. From equation (3) then, it follows that

$$v_1'' = -(\ell_3(u_1''^2 - u_0'') - \ell_2u_1'' + \ell_1), \qquad v_0'' = -(\ell_3u_1''u_0'' - \ell_2u_0'' + \ell_0). \tag{6}$$

We summarize the process of computing a general addition $D'' = D \oplus D'$ on $\hat{\text{J}}\text{ac}(C_2)$, as follows. *Composition* involves constructing and solving the linear system in (4) for ℓ_2 and ℓ_3 before computing ℓ_0 and ℓ_1 via (3), whilst *reduction* involves computing u_1'' and u_0'' from (5) before computing v_1'' and v_0'' via (6). The explicit formulas for these computations are in Table 1, where **I**, **M** and **S** represent the costs of an $\mathbb{F}_q$ inversion, multiplication and squaring respectively. We postpone comparisons with other works until after the doubling discussion.

Remark 2. The formulas for computing v_0'' and v_1'' in (6) include operations involving $u_1''^2$ and $u_1''u_0''$. Since those quantities are also needed in the first step of the addition formulas (see the first line of Table 1) for any subsequent additions involving the divisor D'', it makes sense to carry those quantities along as extra coordinates to exploit these overlapping computations. It turns out that an analogous overlap arises in group operations for all $g \geq 2$, but for now we remark that both additions and doublings on genus 2 curves will benefit from extending the generic affine coordinate system to include two extra coordinates u_1^2 and u_1u_0.

Table 1. Explicit formulas for a divisor addition $D'' = D \oplus D'$ involving two distinct degree 2 divisors on $\mathrm{Jac}(C_2)$, and for divisor doubling $D'' = [2]D$ of a degree 2 divisor on $\mathrm{Jac}(C_2)$

	AFFINE ADDITION		
Input:	$D = (u_1, u_0, v_1, v_0, U_1 = u_1^2, U_0 = u_1u_0)$, $D' = (u_1', u_0', v_1', v_0', U_1' = u_1'^2, U_0' = u_1'u_0')$		Operations in $\mathbb{F}_q$
	$\sigma_1 \leftarrow u_1 + u_1'$, $\Delta_0 \leftarrow v_0 - v_0'$, $\Delta_1 \leftarrow v_1 - v_1'$, $M_1 \leftarrow U_1 - u_0 - U_1' + u_0'$, $M_2 \leftarrow U_0' - U_0$,		
	$M_3 \leftarrow u_1 - u_1'$, $M_4 \leftarrow u_0' - u_0$, $t_1 \leftarrow (M_2 - \Delta_0) \cdot (\Delta_1 - M_1)$, $t_2 \leftarrow (-\Delta_0 - M_2) \cdot (\Delta_1 + M_1)$,		2M
	$t_3 \leftarrow (-\Delta_0 + M_4) \cdot (\Delta_1 - M_3)$, $t_4 \leftarrow (-\Delta_0 - M_4) \cdot (\Delta_1 + M_3)$,		2M
	$\ell_2 \leftarrow t_1 - t_2$ $\ell_3 \leftarrow t_3 - t_4$, $d \leftarrow t_3 + t_4 - t_1 - t_2 - 2(M_2 - M_4) \cdot (M_1 + M_3)$,		1M
	$A \leftarrow 1/(d \cdot \ell_3)$, $B \leftarrow d \cdot A$, $C \leftarrow d \cdot B$, $D \leftarrow \ell_2 \cdot B$, $E \leftarrow \ell_3^2 \cdot A$, $CC \leftarrow C^2$,		I + 5M + 2S
	$u_1'' \leftarrow 2D - CC - \sigma_1$, $u_0'' \leftarrow D^2 + C \cdot (v_1 + v_1') - ((u_1'' - CC) \cdot \sigma_1 + (U_1 + U_1'))/2$,		2M + 1S
	$U_1'' \leftarrow u_1''^2$, $U_0'' \leftarrow u_1'' \cdot u_0''$, $v_1'' \leftarrow D \cdot (u_1 - u_1'') + U_1'' - u_0'' - U_1 + u_0$,		2M + 1S
	$v_0'' \leftarrow D \cdot (u_0 - u_0'') + U_0'' - U_0$, $v_1'' \leftarrow E \cdot v_1'' + v_1$ $v_0'' \leftarrow E \cdot v_0'' + v_0$.		3M
Output:	$D'' = \rho(D \oplus D') = (u_1'', u_0'', v_1'', v_0'', U_1'' = u_1''^2, U_0'' = u_1''u_0'')$.	**Total**	I + 17M + 4S
	PROJECTIVE ADDITION		
Input:	$D = (U_1, U_0, V_1, V_0, Z)$, $D' = (U_1', U_0', V_1', V_0', Z')$,		Operations
	$ZZ \leftarrow Z_1 \cdot Z_2$, $U1Z \leftarrow U_1 \cdot Z_2$, $U1Z' \leftarrow U_1' \cdot Z_1$, $U1ZS \leftarrow U1Z^2$, $U1ZS' \leftarrow U1Z'^2$,		3M + 2S
	$U0Z \leftarrow U_0 \cdot Z_2$, $U0Z' \leftarrow U_0' \cdot Z_1$, $V1Z \leftarrow V_1 \cdot Z_2$, $V1Z' \leftarrow V_1' \cdot Z_1$,		4M
	$M_1 \leftarrow U1ZS - U1ZS' + ZZ \cdot (U0dZ - U0Z)$, $M_2 \leftarrow U1Z' \cdot U0Z' - U1Z \cdot U0Z$;		3M
	$M_3 \leftarrow U1Z - U1Z'$, $M_4 \leftarrow U0Z' - U0Z$, $z_1 \leftarrow V0 \cdot Z_2 - V0' \cdot Z_1$, $z_2 \leftarrow V1Z - V1Z'$,		2M
	$t_1 \leftarrow (M_2 - z_1) \cdot (z_2 - M_1)$, $t_2 \leftarrow (-z_1 - M_2) \cdot (z_2 + M_1)$,		2M
	$t_3 \leftarrow (-z_1 + M_4) \cdot (z_2 - M_3)$, $t_4 \leftarrow (-z_1 - M_4) \cdot (z_2 + M_3)$,		2M
	$\ell_2 \leftarrow t_1 - t_2$, $\ell_3 \leftarrow t_3 - t_4$, $d \leftarrow t_3 + t_4 - t_1 - t_2 - 2 \cdot (M_2 - M_4) \cdot (M_1 + M_3)$,		1M
	$A \leftarrow d^2$, $B \leftarrow \ell_3 \cdot ZZ$, $C \leftarrow \ell_2 \cdot B$, $D \leftarrow d \cdot B$, $E \leftarrow \ell_3 \cdot B$, $F \leftarrow U1Z \cdot E$, $G \leftarrow ZZ \cdot E$,		6M + 1S
	$H \leftarrow U0Z \cdot G$, $J \leftarrow D \cdot G$, $K \leftarrow Z_2 \cdot J$, $U_1'' \leftarrow 2 \cdot C - A - E \cdot (U1Z + U1Z')$,		4M
	$U_0'' \leftarrow \ell_2^2 \cdot ZZ + D \cdot (V1Z + V1Z') - ((U_1'' - A) \cdot (U1Z + U1Z') + E \cdot (U1ZS + U1ZS'))/2$,		4M + 1S
	$V_1'' \leftarrow U_1'' \cdot (U_1'' - C) + F \cdot (C - F) + E \cdot (H - U_0'')$,		3M
	$V_0'' \leftarrow H \cdot (C - F) + U_0'' \cdot (U_1'' - C)$, $V_1'' \leftarrow V_1'' \cdot ZZ + K \cdot V_1$, $V_0'' \leftarrow V_0'' + K \cdot V_0$,		5M
	$U_1'' \leftarrow U_1'' \cdot D \cdot ZZ$, $U_0'' \leftarrow U_0'' \cdot D$, $Z'' \leftarrow ZZ \cdot J$.		4M
Output:	$D'' = \rho(D \oplus D') = (U_1'', U_0'', V_1'', V_0'', Z'')$.	**Total**	43M + 4S
	AFFINE DOUBLING		
Input:	$D = (u_1, u_0, v_1, v_0, U_1 = u_1^2, U_0 = u_1u_0)$, with constants f_2, f_3		Operations
	$vv \leftarrow v_1^2$, $vu \leftarrow (v_1 + u_1)^2 - vv - U_1$, $M_1 \leftarrow 2v_0 - 2vu$, $M_2 \leftarrow 2v_1 \cdot (u_0 + 2U_1)$,		1M + 2S
	$M_3 \leftarrow -2v_1$, $M_4 \leftarrow vu + 2v_0$, $z_1 \leftarrow f_2 + 2U_1 \cdot u_1 + 2U_0 - vv$, $z_2 \leftarrow f_3 - 2u_0 + 3U_1$,		1M
	$t_1 \leftarrow (M_2 - z_1) \cdot (z_2 - M_1)$, $t_2 \leftarrow (-z_1 - M_2) \cdot (z_2 + M_1)$,		2M
	$t_3 \leftarrow (M_4 - z_1) \cdot (z_2 - M_3)$, $t_4 \leftarrow (-z_1 - M_4) \cdot (z_2 + M_3)$,		2M
	$\ell_2 \leftarrow t_1 - t_2$, $\ell_3 \leftarrow t_3 - t_4$, $d \leftarrow t_3 + t_4 - t_1 - t_2 - 2(M_2 - M_4) \cdot (M_1 + M_3)$,		1M
	$A \leftarrow 1/(d \cdot \ell_3)$, $B \leftarrow d \cdot A$, $C \leftarrow d \cdot B$, $D \leftarrow \ell_2 \cdot B$, $E \leftarrow \ell_3^2 \cdot A$,		I + 5M + 1S
	$u_1'' \leftarrow 2D - C^2 - 2u_1$, $u_0'' \leftarrow (D - u_1)^2 + 2C \cdot (v_1 + C \cdot u_1)$, $U_1'' \leftarrow u_1''^2$, $U_0'' \leftarrow u_1'' \cdot u_0''$,		3M + 3S
	$v_1'' \leftarrow D \cdot (u_1 - u_1'') + U_1'' - U_1 - u_0'' + u_0$, $v_0'' \leftarrow D \cdot (u_0 - u_0'') + U_0'' - U_0$,		2M
	$v_1'' \leftarrow E \cdot v_1'' + v_1$, $v_0'' \leftarrow E \cdot v_0'' + v_0$.		2M
Output:	$D'' = \rho([2]D) = (u_1'', u_0'', v_1'', v_0'', U_1'' = u_1''^2, U_0'' = u_1''u_0'')$.	**Total**	I + 19M + 6S
	PROJECTIVE DOUBLING		
Input:	$D = (U_1, U_0, V_1, V_0, Z)$, curve constants f_2, f_3		Operations
	$UU \leftarrow U_1 \cdot U_0$, $U_{1S} \leftarrow U_1^2$, $Z_S \leftarrow Z^2$, $V0Z \leftarrow V0 \cdot Z$, $U0Z \leftarrow U0 \cdot Z$, $V_{1S} \leftarrow V1^2$,		3M + 3S
	$UV \leftarrow (V_1 + U_1)^2 - V_{1S} - U_{1S}$, $M_1 \leftarrow 2 \cdot V0Z - 2 \cdot UV$, $M_2 \leftarrow 2 \cdot V1 \cdot (U0Z + 2 \cdot U_{1S})$,		1M + 1S
	$M_3 \leftarrow -2 \cdot V_1$, $M_4 \leftarrow UV + 2 \cdot V0Z$, $z_1 \leftarrow Z \cdot (f_2 \cdot Z_S - V_{1S}) + 2 \cdot U_1 \cdot (U_{1S} + U0Z)$,		2M
	$z_2 \leftarrow f_3 \cdot Z_S - 2 \cdot U0Z + 3 \cdot U_{1S}$, $t_1 \leftarrow (M_2 - z1) \cdot (z_2 - M_1)$, $t_2 \leftarrow (-z_1 - M_2) \cdot (z_2 + M_1)$,		2M
	$t_3 \leftarrow (-z_1 + M_4) \cdot (z_2 - M_3)$, $t_4 \leftarrow (-z_1 - M_4) \cdot (z_2 + M_3)$,		2M
	$\ell_2 \leftarrow t_1 - t_2$, $\ell_3 \leftarrow t_3 - t_4$, $d \leftarrow t_3 + t_4 - t_1 - t_2 - 2 \cdot (M_2 - M_4) \cdot (M_1 + M_3)$,		1M
	$A \leftarrow \ell_2^2$, $B \leftarrow \ell_3^2$, $C \leftarrow ((\ell_2 + \ell_3)^2 - A - B)/2$, $D \leftarrow B \cdot Z$, $E \leftarrow B \cdot U_1$,		2M + 3S
	$F \leftarrow d^2$, $G \leftarrow F \cdot Z$, $H \leftarrow ((d + \ell_3)^2 - F - B)/2$, $J \leftarrow H \cdot Z$, $K \leftarrow V_1 \cdot J$, $L \leftarrow U0Z \cdot B$,		4M + 2S
	$U_1'' \leftarrow 2 \cdot C - 2 \cdot E - G$, $U_0'' \leftarrow A + U_1 \cdot (E - 2 \cdot C + 2 \cdot G) + 2 \cdot K$,		1M
	$V_1'' \leftarrow (C - E - U_1'') \cdot (E - U_1'') + B \cdot (L - U_0'')$, $V_0'' \leftarrow L \cdot (C - E) + (U_1'' - C) \cdot U_0''$.		4M
	$V_1'' \leftarrow V_1'' \cdot Z + K \cdot D$, $V_0'' \leftarrow V_0'' + V0Z \cdot H \cdot D$, $M \leftarrow J \cdot Z$, $U_1'' \leftarrow U_1'' \cdot M$, $U_0'' \leftarrow U_0'' \cdot J$,		7M
	$Z'' \leftarrow M \cdot D$.		1M
Output:	$D'' = \rho([2]D) = (U_1'', U_0'', V_1'', V_0'', Z'')$.	**Total**	30M + 9S

4.2 General Divisor Doubling in Genus 2

Let $D = (x^2 + u_1x + u_0, v_1x + v_0) \in \hat{\text{J}}\text{ac}(C_2)$ be a divisor with $\text{supp}(D) = \{P_1, P_2\} \cup \{P_\infty\}$. To compute $[2]D = D \oplus D$, we seek the cubic polynomial $\ell(x) = \sum_{i=0}^{3} \ell_i x^i$ that has zeroes of order two at both $P_1 = (x_1, y_1)$ and $P_2 = (x_2, y_2)$. We can immediately make use of the equations arising out of the interpolation of $\text{supp}(D)$ in (3) to obtain the first $g = 2$ equations.

There are two possible approaches to obtaining the second set of $g = 2$ equations. The first is the geometric flavored approach that was used in the proof of Proposition 3 and in Example 3, which involves matching the derivatives. The second involves reducing the substitution of $\ell(x)$ into C_g by $\langle u(x)^2 \rangle$ to ensure the prescribed zeros are of multiplicity two, and using the associated Mumford ideals to linearize the equations. For the purpose of presenting both approaches, we will illustrate the latter approach in this subsection, but it is important to highlight that the guaranteed existence of linear equations follows from the expression gained when matching derivatives in the geometric approach.

We start by setting $y = \ell(x)$ into C_2 and reducing modulo the ideal $\langle (x^2 + u_1x + u_0)^2 \rangle$, which gives

$$\Omega(x) = \Omega_0 + \Omega_1 x + \Omega_2 x^2 + \Omega_3 x^3 \equiv (\sum_{i=0}^{3} \ell_i x^i)^2 - f(x) \mod \langle (x^2 + u_1x + u_0)^2 \rangle$$

where

$$\begin{aligned}
\Omega_0 &= \ell_3^2(2u_0^3 - 3u_1^2u_0^2) + 4\ell_3\ell_2u_1u_0^2 - 2\ell_3\ell_1u_0^2 + \ell_0^2 - \ell_2^2u_0^2 - 2u_1u_0^2 - f_0, \\
\Omega_1 &= 6\ell_3^2(u_1u_0^2 - u_1^3u_0) + 2\ell_3\ell_2(4u_1^2u_0 - u_0^2) + 2\ell_1\ell_0 - 4\ell_3\ell_1u_0u_1 \\
&\quad - 2\ell_2^2u_0u_1 - 4u_1^2u_0 + u_0^2 - f_1, \\
\Omega_2 &= 3\ell_3^2(u_0^2 - u_1^4) + \ell_1^2 - \ell_2^2(u_1^2 + 2u_0) - 2u_0u_1 - 2u_1^3 + 4\ell_3\ell_2(u_1^3 + u_0u_1) \\
&\quad - 2\ell_3\ell_1(2u_0 + u_1^2) + 2\ell_2\ell_0 - f_2, \\
\Omega_3 &= 2\ell_3^2(3u_1u_0 - 2u_1^3) + 2\ell_2\ell_1 + 2\ell_3\ell_2(3u_1^2 - 2u_0) - 2\ell_2^2u_1 - 4\ell_3\ell_1u_1 + 2\ell_3\ell_0 \\
&\quad - 3u_1^2 + 2u_0 - f_3.
\end{aligned}$$

It follows that $\Omega_i = 0$ for $0 \leq i \leq 3$. Although we now have four more equations relating the unknown ℓ_i coefficients, these equations are currently nonlinear. We linearize by substituting the linear equations taken from (3) above, and reducing the results modulo the Mumford ideals given in (2). We use the two linear equations $\tilde{\Omega}_2, \tilde{\Omega}_3$ resulting from Ω_2, Ω_3, given as

$$\begin{aligned}
\tilde{\Omega}_2 &= 4\ell_1v_1 + 2\ell_2(v_0 - 2v_1u_1) - 6\ell_3u_0v_1 - 2u_0u_1 - 2u_1^3 - 3v_1^2 - f_2, \\
\tilde{\Omega}_3 &= 2v_1\ell_2 + \ell_3(2v_0 - 4u_1v_1) + 2u_0 - 3u_1^2 - f_3,
\end{aligned}$$

which combine with the linear interpolating equations (in (3)) to give rise to the linear system

$$\begin{pmatrix} -1 & 0 & u_0 & -u_1u_0 \\ 0 & -1 & u_1 & -u_1^2 + u_0 \\ 0 & 4v_1 & 2v_0 - 2v_1u_1 & -6u_0v_1 \\ 0 & 0 & 2v_1 & -4v_1u_1 + 2v_0 \end{pmatrix} \cdot \begin{pmatrix} \ell_0 \\ \ell_1 \\ \ell_2 \\ \ell_3 \end{pmatrix} = \begin{pmatrix} -v_0 \\ -v_1 \\ f_2 + 2u_1u_0 + 2u_1^3 + 3v_1^2 \\ f_3 - 2u_0 + 3u_1^2 \end{pmatrix}.$$

As was the case with the divisor addition in the previous section, we can first solve a smaller system for ℓ_2 and ℓ_3, by adding the appropriate multiple of the second row to the third row above, to give

$$\begin{pmatrix} 2v_1u_1 + 2v_0 & -2u_0v_1 - 4v_1u_1^2 \\ 2v_1 & -4v_1u_1 + 2v_0 \end{pmatrix} \cdot \begin{pmatrix} \ell_2 \\ \ell_3 \end{pmatrix} = \begin{pmatrix} f_2 + 2u_1u_0 + 2u_1^3 - v_1^2 \\ f_3 - 2u_0 + 3u_1^2 \end{pmatrix}.$$

After solving the above system for ℓ_2 and ℓ_3, the process of obtaining $D'' = [2]D = (x^2 + u_1''x + u_0'', v_1''x + v_0'')$ is identical to the case of addition in the previous section, giving rise to the analogous explicit formulas in Table 1.

4.3 Comparisons of Formulas in Genus 2

Table 2 draws comparisons between the explicit formulas obtained from the above approach and the explicit formulas presented in previous work. In implementations where inversions are expensive compared to multiplications (i.e. $\mathbf{I} > 20\mathbf{M}$), it can be advantageous to adopt projective formulas which avoid inversions altogether. Our projective formulas compute scalar multiples faster than all previous projective formulas for general genus 2 curves. We also note that our homogeneous projective formulas require only 5 coordinates in total, which is the heuristic minimum for projective implementations in genus 2.

In the case of the affine formulas, it is worth commenting that, unlike the case of elliptic curves where point doublings are generally much faster than additions, affine genus 2 operations reveal divisor additions to be the significantly cheaper operation. In cases where an addition would usually follow a doubling to compute $[2]D \oplus D'$, it is likely to be computationally favorable to instead compute $(D \oplus D') \oplus D$, provided temporary storage of the additional intermediate divisor is not problematic.

Lastly, the formulas in Table 1 all required the solution to a linear system of dimension 2. This would ordinarily require 6 $\mathbb{F}_q$ multiplications, but we applied Hisil's trick [26, eq. 3.8] to instead perform these computations using 5 $\mathbb{F}_q$ multiplications. In implementations where extremely optimized multiplication routines give rise to $\mathbb{F}_q$ addition costs that are relatively high compared to $\mathbb{F}_q$ multiplications, it may be advantageous to undo such tricks (including **M**-**S** trade-offs) in favor of a lower number of additions.

5 The General Description

This section presents the algorithm for divisor composition on hyperelliptic Jacobians of any genus g. The general method for reduction has essentially remained

Table 2. Comparisons between our explicit formulas for genus 2 curves over prime fields and previous formulas using CRT based composition

$\mathbb{F}_q$ inversions	Previous work	#	Doubling		Addition		Mixed	
I		coords	**M**	**S**	**M**	**S**	**M**	**S**
	Harley [24,20]	4	30	-	24	3	-	
2	Lange [34]	4	24	6	24	3	-	
	Matsuo *et al.* [43]	4	27	-	25	-	-	
	Takahashi [50]	4	29	-	25	-	-	
	Miyamoto *et al.* [45]	4	27	-	26	-	-	
1	Lange [38]	4	22	5	22	3	-	
	This work	**6**	**19**	**6**	**17**	**4**	-	
	Wollinger and Kovtun [52]	5	39	6	46	4	39	4
	Lange [36,38]	5	38	6	47	4	40	3
-	Fan *et al.* [12]	5	39	6	-	-	38	3
	Fan *et al.* [12]	8	35	7	-	-	36	5
	Lange [37,38]	8	34	7	47	7	36	5
	This work	**5**	**30**	**9**	**43**	**4**	**36**	**5**

the same in all related publications following Cantor's original paper (at least in the case of low genera), but we give a simple geometric interpretation of the number of reduction rounds required in Section 5.3 below.

5.1 Composition for $g \geq 2$

We extend the composition described for genus 2 in sections 4.1 and 4.2 to hyperelliptic curves of arbitrary genus. Importantly, there are two aspects of this general description to highlight.

(i) In contrast to Cantor's general description of composition which involves polynomial arithmetic, this general description is immediately explicit in terms of $\mathbb{F}_q$ arithmetic.
(ii) The required function $\ell(x)$ is of degree $2g-1$ and therefore has $2g$ unknown coefficients. Thus, we would usually expect to solve a linear system of dimension $2g$, but the linear system that requires solving in the Mumford function field is actually of dimension g.

Henceforth we use $\mathbf{M} \cdot \mathbf{x} = \mathbf{z}$ to denote the associated linear system of dimension g, and we focus our discussion on the structure of $\mathbf{M}$ and $\mathbf{z}$.

In the case of a general divisor addition, $\mathbf{M}$ is computed as $\mathbf{M} = \mathbf{U} - \mathbf{U}'$, where $\mathbf{U}$ and $\mathbf{U}'$ are described by D and D' respectively. In fact, as for the system derived from coordinates of points above, the matrix $\mathbf{M}$ is completely dependent on $u(x)$ and $u'(x)$, whilst the vector $\mathbf{z}$ depends entirely on $v(x)$ and $v'(x)$. Algorithm 1 details how to build $\mathbf{U}$ (resp. $\mathbf{U}'$), where the first column of $\mathbf{U}$ is initialized as the Mumford coordinates $\{u_i\}_{1 \leq i < g}$ of D, and the remaining $g^2 - g$ entries are computed by proceeding across the columns and taking

Algorithm 1. General composition (addition) of two distinct divisors.

Input: $D = \{u_i, v_i\}_{0 \leq i \leq g-1}$, $D' = \{u_i', v_i'\}_{0 \leq i \leq g-1}$.

Output: $\ell(x) = \sum_{i=0}^{2g-1} \ell_i x^i$ such that $\text{supp}(D) \cup \text{supp}(D') \subset \text{supp}(\text{div}(\ell))$.

$\mathbf{U}, \mathbf{U}', \mathbf{M} \leftarrow \{0\}^{g \times g} \in \mathbb{F}_q^{g \times g}$, $\mathbf{z} \leftarrow \{0\}^g \in \mathbb{F}_q^g$.
for i from 1 to g **do**
  $\mathbf{U}_{g+1-i,1} \leftarrow -u_{g-i}$; $\mathbf{U}'_{g+1-i,1} \leftarrow -u'_{g-i}$
end for
for j from 2 to g **do**
  $\mathbf{U}_{1,j} \leftarrow \mathbf{U}_{g,j-1} \cdot \mathbf{U}_{1,1}$; $\mathbf{U}'_{1,j} \leftarrow \mathbf{U}'_{g,j-1} \cdot \mathbf{U}'_{1,1}$.
  for i from 2 to g **do**
    $\mathbf{U}_{i,j} \leftarrow \mathbf{U}_{g,j-1} \cdot \mathbf{U}_{i,1} + \mathbf{U}_{i-1,j-1}$; $\mathbf{U}'_{i,j} \leftarrow \mathbf{U}'_{g,j-1} \cdot \mathbf{U}'_{i,1} + \mathbf{U}'_{i-1,j-1}$.
  end for
end for
$\mathbf{M} \leftarrow \mathbf{U} - \mathbf{U}'$.
for i from 1 to g **do**
  $\mathbf{z}_i \leftarrow v_{i-1} - v'_{i-1}$
end for
Solve $\mathbf{M} \cdot \mathbf{x} = \mathbf{z}$
Compute $\tilde{\mathbf{x}} = \mathbf{U} \cdot \mathbf{x}$
for i from 1 to g **do**
  $\tilde{\mathbf{x}}_i \leftarrow v_{g-i} - \tilde{\mathbf{x}}_i$
end for
return $\ell(x)$ (from $\tilde{\mathbf{x}} = \{\ell_0, ..., \ell_{g-1}\}$ and $\mathbf{x} = \{\ell_g, ..., \ell_{2g-1}\}$)

$\mathbf{U}_{i,j} = u_{i-1} \cdot \mathbf{U}_{g,j-1} + \mathbf{U}_{i-1,j-1}$. This relationship is obtained by a careful generalization of the process that computed (4) from (3) in the case of genus 2.

Depending on the genus, we remark that Algorithm 1 will most likely not be the fastest way to compute $\mathbf{M}$. Instead, we propose that a faster routine is likely to be achieved by using Algorithm 1 to determine the algebraic expression for each of the elements in $\mathbf{M}$, and tailor making optimized formulas to generate its entries, in the same way that the previous section did for genus 2.

In addition, there is alternative way to view the structure (and computation) of the matrix $\mathbf{M}$. This follows from observing that both $\mathbf{U}$ and $\mathbf{U}'$ can actually be written as a sum of g matrices that are computed as outer products; let $\mathbf{c} = (c_1, .., c_g), \tilde{\mathbf{c}} = (\tilde{c}_1, ..., \tilde{c}_g) \in \mathbb{F}_q^g$ be two vectors that are derived solely from the g Mumford coordinates belonging to D, then $\mathbf{U}$ is given by the sum

$$\begin{pmatrix} c_1\tilde{c}_1 & \cdots & c_1\tilde{c}_g \\ c_2\tilde{c}_1 & \cdots & c_2\tilde{c}_g \\ \vdots & \ddots & \vdots \\ c_{g-1}\tilde{c}_1 & \cdots & c_{g-1}\tilde{c}_g \\ c_g\tilde{c}_1 & \cdots & c_g\tilde{c}_g \end{pmatrix} + \begin{pmatrix} 0 & 0 & \cdots & 0 \\ 0 & c_1\tilde{c}_1 & \cdots & c_1\tilde{c}_{g-1} \\ \vdots & \cdots & \ddots & \vdots \\ 0 & c_{g-2}\tilde{c}_2 & \cdots & c_{g-2}\tilde{c}_{g-1} \\ 0 & c_{g-1}\tilde{c}_2 & \cdots & c_{g-1}\tilde{c}_{g-1} \end{pmatrix} + \ldots + \begin{pmatrix} 0 & \cdots & 0 & 0 \\ 0 & \cdots & 0 & 0 \\ \vdots & \cdots & \ddots & \vdots \\ 0 & \cdots & 0 & 0 \\ 0 & \cdots & 0 & c_1\tilde{c}_1 \end{pmatrix}.$$

Example 4. Assume a general genus 3 curve and let the Mumford representations of the divisors D and D' be as usual. The matrix $\mathbf{U}$ is given as

$$\mathbf{U} = \begin{pmatrix} -u_0 & u_2u_0 & (-u_2^2 + u_1)u_0 \\ -u_1 & u_2u_1 & (-u_2^2 + u_1)u_1 \\ -u_2 & u_2^2 & (-u_2^2 + u_1)u_2 \end{pmatrix} + \begin{pmatrix} 0 & 0 & 0 \\ 0 & -u_0 & u_2u_0 \\ 0 & -u_1 & u_2u_1 \end{pmatrix} + \begin{pmatrix} 0 & 0 & 0 \\ 0 & 0 & 0 \\ 0 & 0 & -u_0 \end{pmatrix},$$

and $\mathbf{U}'$ is given identically. In this case $\mathbf{c} = (u_0, u_1, u_2)^T$ and $\tilde{\mathbf{c}} = (-1, u_2, -u_2^2 + u_1)^T$. Setting $\mathbf{M} = \mathbf{U} - \mathbf{U}'$ and $\mathbf{z} = (v_0 - v_0', v_1 - v_1', v_2 - v_2')^T$, we find the $g = 3$ coefficients ℓ_3, ℓ_4 and ℓ_5 of the quintic $\ell(x) = \sum_{i=0}^{5} \ell_i x^i$ that interpolates the 6 non-trivial elements in $\mathrm{supp}(D) \cup \mathrm{supp}(D')$ by solving $\mathbf{M} \cdot \mathbf{x} = \mathbf{z}$ for $\mathbf{x} = (\ell_3, \ell_4, \ell_5)^T$. The remaining coefficients are found via a straightforward matrix multiplication as $\tilde{\mathbf{x}} = (\ell_0, \ell_1, \ell_2)^T = \mathbf{U} \cdot \mathbf{x}$.

The immediate observation in general is that $\mathbf{c}\tilde{\mathbf{c}}^T$ is the only outer product that requires computation in order to determine $\mathbf{U}$ entirely.

For general divisor doublings the description of the linear system is much longer; this is because the right hand side vector $\mathbf{z}$ is slightly more complicated than in the case of addition: as is the case with general Weierstrass elliptic curves, additions tend to be independent of the curve constants whilst doublings do not. We reiterate that, for low genus implementations at least, Algorithm 2 is intended to obtain the algebraic expressions for each element in $\mathbf{M}$; as was the case with genus 2, a faster computational route to determining the composition function will probably arise from genus specific attention that derives tailor-made explicit formulas. Besides, the general consequence of Remark 2 is that many (if not all) of the values constituting $\mathbf{U}$ will have already been computed in the previous point operation, and can therefore be temporarily stored and reused.

5.2 Handling Special Cases

The description of divisor composition herein naturally encompasses the special cases where either (or both) of the divisors have degree less than g. In fact, Proposition 1 trivially generalizes to describe the set of divisors on $\mathrm{Jac}(C_g)$ whose effective parts have degree $d \leq g$, and can therefore be used to obtain the Mumford ideals associated with special input divisors[2].

This will often result in fewer rounds of reduction and a simpler linear system. For example, whilst the general addition of two full degree divisors in genus 3 requires an additional round of reduction after the first points of intersection are found (see Figure 1 and Figure 2), it is easy to see that any group operation on a genus 3 curve involving a divisor of degree less than 3 will give rise to a reduced divisor immediately. Clearly, the linear systems in these cases are smaller, and therefore the explicit formulas arising in these special cases will always be much faster, in agreement with all prior expositions (cf. [3, §14]). In higher genus implementations that do not explicitly account for all special cases of inputs, Katagi *et al.* [28] noted that it can still be very advantageous to explicitly implement and optimize *one* of the special cases.

[2] Perhaps the most general consequence of Proposition 1 is using it to describe (or enumerate) the entire Jacobian by summing over all d, as $\#\mathrm{Jac}(C_g) = \#C_g + \sum_{d=2}^{g} n_d$, where n_d is the number of $2d$-tuples lying in the intersection of the d associated hypersurfaces.

Algorithm 2. General composition (doubling) of a unique divisor with itself

Input: $D = \{u_i, v_i\}_{0 \le i \le g-1}$ and curve coefficients $f_0, f_1, ..., f_{2g-1}$.

Output: $\ell(x) = \sum_{i=0}^{2g-1} \ell_i x^i$ such that each non-trivial element in supp(D) occurs with multiplicity two in div(ℓ) .

$\mathbf{U}, \mathbf{M} \leftarrow \{0\}^{g \times g} \in \mathbb{F}_q^{g \times g}$, $\mathbf{v} \leftarrow \{0\}^{g-1} \in \mathbb{F}_q^{g-1}$, $\mathbf{z} \leftarrow \{0\}^{g} \in \mathbb{F}_q^{g}$
for i from 1 to g **do**
    $\mathbf{U}_{g+1-i,1} \leftarrow -u_{g-i}$
end for
for j from 2 to g **do**
    $\mathbf{U}_{1,j} \leftarrow \mathbf{U}_{g,j-1} \cdot \mathbf{U}_{1,1}$.
    for i from 2 to g **do**
        $\mathbf{U}_{i,j} \leftarrow \mathbf{U}_{g,j-1} \cdot \mathbf{U}_{i,1} + \mathbf{U}_{i-1,j-1}$.
    end for
end for
$u_{\text{extra}} \leftarrow \mathbf{U}_{g,1} \cdot \mathbf{U}_{g,g} + \mathbf{U}_{g-1,g}$.
for i from 1 to g **do**
    $\mathbf{M}_{g+1-i,1} \leftarrow v_{g-i}$
end for
for j from 2 to g **do**
    $\mathbf{M}_{i,j} \leftarrow \mathbf{M}_{i,j} + \mathbf{U}_{g,j-1} \cdot \mathbf{M}_{i,1} + \mathbf{M}_{g,j-1} \cdot \mathbf{U}_{i,1} + \mathbf{M}_{i-1,j-1}$.
end for
for i from 1 to $g-1$ **do**
    $\mathbf{z}_{g+1-i} \leftarrow \mathbf{z}_{g+1-i} + 2 \cdot \mathbf{U}_{g,1} \cdot \mathbf{U}_{g+1-i,1} + \mathbf{U}_{g-i,1} + \mathbf{U}_{g,i+1} + f_{2g-i}$.
    for j from 1 to i **do**
        $\mathbf{z}_{g-i} \leftarrow \mathbf{z}_{g-i} + f_{2g-1-i+j} \cdot U_{g,j}$.
        $\mathbf{v}_i \leftarrow \mathbf{v}_i - \mathbf{M}_{g+1-j,1} \cdot \mathbf{M}_{g-i+j,1}$.
    end for
end for
$\mathbf{z}_1 \leftarrow \mathbf{z}_1 + 2 \cdot \mathbf{U}_{g,1} \cdot \mathbf{U}_{1,1} + f_g$.
$\mathbf{z}_{g-1} \leftarrow \mathbf{z}_{g-1} + \mathbf{v}_1$.
for i from 3 to g **do**
    for j from 2 to $i-1$ **do**
        $\mathbf{z}_{g+1-i} \leftarrow \mathbf{z}_{g+1-i} + \mathbf{v}_{i-j} \cdot \mathbf{U}_{g,j-1}$.
    end for
    $\mathbf{z}_{g+1-i} \leftarrow \mathbf{z}_{g+1-i} + \mathbf{v}_{i-1}$.
end for
$\mathbf{z}_{1,1} \leftarrow \mathbf{z}_{1,1} + u_{\text{extra}}$.
for i from 1 to g **do**
    $\mathbf{z}_i \leftarrow \mathbf{z}_i / 2$.
end for
Solve $\mathbf{M} \cdot \mathbf{x} = \mathbf{z}$
Compute $\tilde{\mathbf{x}} = -\mathbf{U} \cdot \mathbf{x}$
for i from 1 to g **do**
    $\tilde{\mathbf{x}}_i \leftarrow v_{g-i} + \tilde{\mathbf{x}}_i$
end for
return $\ell(x)$ (from $\tilde{\mathbf{x}} = \{\ell_0, ..., \ell_{g-1}\}$ and $\mathbf{x} = \{\ell_g, ..., \ell_{2g-1}\}$)

5.3 Reduction in Low Genera

Gaudry's chapter [18] gives an overview of different algorithms (and complexities) for the reduction phase. Our experiments lead us to believe that the usual method of reduction is still the most preferable for small g. In genus 2 we saw that point additions and doublings do not require more than one round of reduction, i.e. the initial interpolating function intersects C_2 in at most two more places (refer to Figure 3), immediately giving rise to the reduced divisor that is the sum. In genus $g \geq 3$ however, this is generally not the case. Namely, the initial interpolating function intersects C_g in more than g places, giving rise to an unreduced divisor that requires further reduction. We restate Cantor's complexity argument concerning the number of rounds of reduction ([6, §4]) in a geometric way in the following proposition.

Proposition 4. *In the addition of any two reduced divisor classes on the Jacobian of a genus g hyperelliptic curve, the number of rounds of further reduction required to form the reduced divisor is at most $\lfloor \frac{g-1}{2} \rfloor$, with equality occurring in the general case.*

Proof. For completeness note that addition on elliptic curves in Weierstrass form needs no reduction, so take $g \geq 2$. The composition polynomial $y = \ell(x)$ with the $2g$ prescribed zeros (including multiplicities) has degree $2g-1$. Substituting $y = \ell(x)$ into $C_g : y^2 + h(x)y = f(x)$ gives an equation of degree $\max\{2g+1, 3g-1, 2(2g-1)\} = 2(2g-1)$ in x, for which there are at most $2(2g-1)-2g = 2g-2$ new roots. Let n_t be the maximum number of new roots after t rounds of reduction, so that $n_0 = 2g-2$. While $n_t > g$, reduction is not complete, so continue by interpolating the n_t new points with a polynomial of degree $n_t - 1$, producing at most $2(n_t-1)-n_t = n_t-2$ new roots. It follows that $n_t = 2g-2t-2$, and since $t, g \in \mathbb{Z}$, the result follows. □

6 Further Implications and Potential

This section is intended to further illustrate the potential of coupling a geometric approach with linear algebra when performing arithmetic in Jacobians. It is our hope that the suggestions in this section encourage future investigations and improvements.

We start by commenting that our algorithm can naturally be generalized to much more than standard divisor additions and doublings. Namely, given any set of divisors $D_1, ..., D_n \in C_g$ and any corresponding set of scalars $r_1, ..., r_n \in \mathbb{Z}$, we can theoretically compute $D = \sum_{i=1}^{n}[r_i]D_i$ at once, by first prescribing a function that, for each $1 \leq i \leq n$, has a zero of order r_i at each of the non-trivial points in the support of D_i. Note that if $r_i \notin \mathbb{Z}^+$, then prescribing a zero of order r_i at some point P is equivalent to prescribing a pole of order $-r_i \in \mathbb{Z}^+$ at P instead. We first return to genus 1 to show that this technique can be used to recover several results that were previously obtained by alternatively merging or overlapping consecutive elliptic curve computations (cf. [10,7]).

Simultaneous Operations on Elliptic Curves. In the case of genus 1, the Mumford representation of reduced divisors is trivial, i.e. if $P = (x_1, y_1)$, the Mumford representation of the associated divisor is $D_P = (x - x_1, y_1)$, and the associated Mumford ideal is (isomorphic to) the curve itself. However, we can again explore using the Mumford representation as an alternative to derivatives in order to generate the required linear systems arising from prescribing multiplicities of greater than one. In addition, when unreduced divisors in genus 1 are encountered, the Mumford representation becomes non-trivial and very necessary for efficient computations.

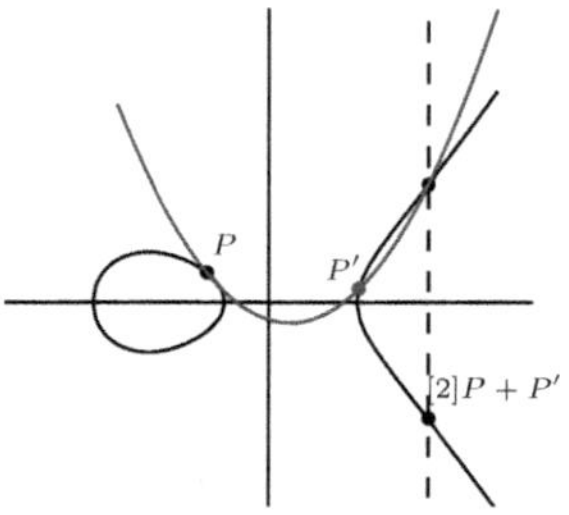

Fig. 5. Computing $[2]P + P'$ by prescribing a parabola which intersects E at P, P' with multiplicities two and one respectively.

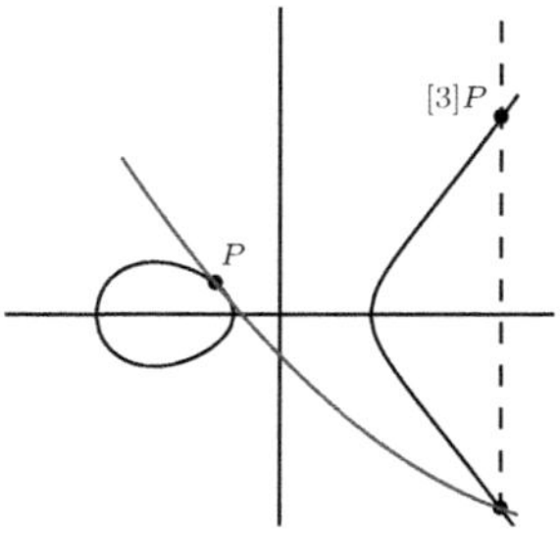

Fig. 6. Tripling the point $P \in E$ by prescribing a parabola which intersects E at P with multiplicity three.

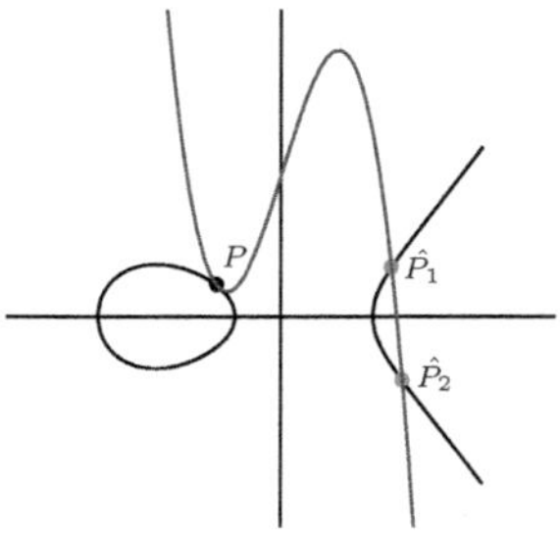

Fig. 7. Quadrupling the point $P \in E$ by prescribing a cubic which intersects E at P with multiplicity four.

To double-and-add or point triple on an elliptic curve, we can prescribe a parabola $\ell(x) = \ell_2 x^2 + \ell_1 x + \ell_0 \in \mathbb{F}_q(E)$ with appropriate multiplicities in advance, as an alternative to Eisenträger *et al.*'s technique of merging two consecutive chords into a parabola [10]. Depending on the specifics of an implementation, computing the parabola in this fashion offers the same potential advantage as that presented by Ciet *et al.* [7]; we avoid any intermediate computations and bypass computing $P + P'$ or $[2]P$ along the way. When tripling the point $P = (x_P, y_P) \in E$, the parabola is determined from the three equalities $\ell(x)^2 \equiv x^3 + f_1 x + f_0 \bmod \langle (x - u_0)^i \rangle$ for $1 \leq i \leq 3$, from which we take one of the coefficients that is identically zero in each of the three cases. As one example, we found projective formulas which compute triplings on curves of the form $y^2 = x^3 + f_0$ and cost $3\mathbf{M} + 10\mathbf{S}$. These are the second fastest tripling formulas reported across all curve models [5], being only slightly slower (unless $\mathbf{S} < 0.75\mathbf{M}$) than the formulas for tripling-oriented curves introduced by Doche *et al.* [9] which require $6\mathbf{M} + 6\mathbf{S}$.

We can quadruple the point P by prescribing a cubic function $\ell(x) = \ell_3 x^3 + \ell_2 x^2 + \ell_1 x + \ell_0$ which intersects E at P with multiplicity four (see Figure 7). This time however, the cubic is zero on E in two other places, resulting in an unreduced divisor $D_{\hat{P}} = \hat{P}_1 + \hat{P}_2$, which we can represent in Mumford coordinates as $D_{\hat{P}} = (\hat{u}(x), \hat{v}(x))$ (as if it were a reduced divisor in genus 2). Our experiments agree with prior evidence that it is unlikely that point quadruplings will outperform consecutive doublings in the preferred projective cases, although we believe that one application which could benefit from this description is pairing computations, where interpolating functions are necessary in the computations. To reduce $D_{\hat{P}}$, we need the line $y = \hat{\ell}(x)$ joining $\hat{P}_1$ with $\hat{P}_2$, which can be computed via $\hat{\ell}(x) \equiv \ell(x) \bmod \langle \hat{u}(x) \rangle$. The update to the pairing function requires both $\ell(x)$ and $\hat{\ell}(x)$, as $f_{\text{upd}} = \ell(x)/\hat{\ell}(x)$. We claim that it may be attractive to compute a quadrupling in this fashion and only update the pairing function once, rather than two doublings which update the pairing functions twice, particularly in implementations where inversions don't compare so badly against multiplications [41]. It is also worth pointing out that in a quadruple-and-add computation, the unreduced divisor $D_{\hat{P}}$ need not be reduced before adding an additional point P'. Rather, it could be advantageous to immediately interpolate $\hat{P}_1$, $\hat{P}_2$ and P' with a parabola instead.

Simultaneous Operations in Higher Genus Jacobians. Increasing the prescribed multiplicity of a divisor not only increases the degree of the associated interpolating function (and hence the linear system), but also generally increases the number of rounds of reduction required after composition. In the case of genus 1, we can get away with prescribing an extra zero (double-and-add or point tripling) without having to encounter any further reduction, but for genus $g \geq 2$, this will not be the case in general. For example, even when attempting to simultaneously compute $[2]D + D'$ for two general divisors $D, D' \in \text{Jac}(C_2)$, the degree of the interpolating polynomial becomes 5, instead of 3, and the dimension of the linear system that arises can only be trivially reduced from 6 to 4. Our preliminary experiments seem to suggest that unless the linear system can be reduced further, it is likely that computing $[2]D+D'$ simultaneously using our technique won't be as fast as computing two consecutive straightforward operations. However, as in the previous paragraph, we argue that such a trade-off may again become favorable in pairing computations where computing the higher-degree interpolating function would save a costly function update.

Explicit Formulas in Genus 3 and 4. Developing explicit formulas for hyperelliptic curves of genus 3 and 4 has also received some attention [51,53,22]. It will be interesting to see if the composition technique herein can further improve these results. In light of Remark 2 and the general description in Section 5, the new entries in the matrix $\mathbf{M}$ will often have been already computed in the previous point operation, suggesting an obvious extension of the coordinates if the storage space permits it. Therefore the complexity of our proposed composition essentially boils down to the complexity of solving the dimension g linear system in $\mathbb{F}_q$, and so it would also be interesting to determine for which (practically useful) genera one can find tailor-made methods of solving the special linear system that arises in Section 5.1.

Characteristic Two, Special Cases, and More Coordinates. Although the proofs in Section 3 were for arbitrary hyperelliptic curves over general fields, Section 4 simplified the exposition by focusing only on finite fields of large prime characteristic. Of course, it is possible that the description herein can be tweaked to also improve explicit formulas in the cases of special characteristic two curves (see [3, §14.5]). In addition, it is possible that the geometrically inspired derivation of explicit formulas for special cases of inputs will enhance implementations which make use of these (refer to Section 5.2). Finally, we only employed straightforward homogeneous coordinates to obtain the projective versions of our formulas. As was the case with the previous formulas based on Cantor's composition, it is possible that extending the projective coordinate system will give rise to even faster formulas.

7 Conclusion

This paper presents a new and explicit method of divisor composition for hyperelliptic curves. The method is based on using simple linear algebra to derive the required geometric functions directly from the Mumford coordinates of Jacobian elements. In contrast to Cantor's composition which operates in the polynomial ring $\mathbb{F}_q[x]$, the algorithm we propose is immediately explicit in terms of $\mathbb{F}_q$ operations. We showed that this achieves the current fastest general group law formulas in genus 2, and pointed out several other potential improvements that could arise from this exposition.

Acknowledgements. We wish to thank Huseyin Hisil and Michael Naehrig for many fixes and improvements to an earlier version of this paper.

References

1. Abu Salem, F.K., Khuri-Makdisi, K.: Fast Jacobian group operations for $C_{3,4}$ curves over a large finite field. CoRR, abs/math/0610121 (2006)
2. Avanzi, R., Thériault, N., Wang, Z.: Rethinking low genus hyperelliptic Jacobian arithmetic over binary fields: interplay of field arithmetic and explicit formulæ. J. Math. Crypt. 2(3), 227–255 (2008)
3. Avanzi, R.M., Cohen, H., Doche, C., Frey, G., Lange, T., Nguyen, K., Vercauteren, F.: The Handbook of Elliptic and Hyperelliptic Curve Cryptography. CRC (2005)
4. Bernstein, D.J.: Elliptic vs. hyperelliptic, part I. Talk at ECC (September 2006)
5. Bernstein, D.J., Lange, T.: Explicit-formulas database, `http://www.hyperelliptic.org/EFD`
6. Cantor, D.G.: Computing in the Jacobian of a hyperelliptic curve. Math. Comp. 48(177), 95–101 (1987)
7. Ciet, M., Joye, M., Lauter, K., Montgomery, P.L.: Trading inversions for multiplications in elliptic curve cryptography. Designs, Codes and Cryptography 39(2), 189–206 (2006)
8. Diem, C.: An Index Calculus Algorithm for Plane Curves of Small Degree. In: Hess, F., Pauli, S., Pohst, M. (eds.) ANTS 2006. LNCS, vol. 4076, pp. 543–557. Springer, Heidelberg (2006)

9. Doche, C., Icart, T., Kohel, D.R.: Efficient scalar multiplication by isogeny decompositions. In: PKC 2006 [54], pp. 191–206 (2006)
10. Eisenträger, K., Lauter, K., Montgomery, P.L.: Fast Elliptic Curve Arithmetic and Improved Weil Pairing Evaluation. In: Joye, M. (ed.) CT-RSA 2003. LNCS, vol. 2612, pp. 343–354. Springer, Heidelberg (2003)
11. Erickson, S., Jacobson Jr., M.J., Shang, N., Shen, S., Stein, A.: Explicit Formulas for Real Hyperelliptic Curves of Genus 2 in Affine Representation. In: Carlet, C., Sunar, B. (eds.) WAIFI 2007. LNCS, vol. 4547, pp. 202–218. Springer, Heidelberg (2007)
12. Fan, X., Gong, G., Jao, D.: Efficient Pairing Computation on Genus 2 Curves in Projective Coordinates. In: Avanzi, R.M., Keliher, L., Sica, F. (eds.) SAC 2008. LNCS, vol. 5381, pp. 18–34. Springer, Heidelberg (2009)
13. Flon, S., Oyono, R., Ritzenthaler, a.C.: Fast addition on non-hyperelliptic genus 3 curves. Algebraic geometry and its applications 5(3), 227–256 (2008)
14. Flon, S., Oyono, R.: Fast Arithmetic on Jacobians of Picard Curves. In: Bao, F., Deng, R., Zhou, J. (eds.) PKC 2004. LNCS, vol. 2947, pp. 55–68. Springer, Heidelberg (2004)
15. Galbraith, S.D.: Mathematics of Public Key Cryptography, 0.9 edition (February 11, 2011), `http://www.math.auckland.ac.nz/~sgal018/crypto-book/crypto-book.html`
16. Galbraith, S.D., Harrison, M., Mireles Morales, D.J.: Efficient Hyperelliptic Arithmetic using Balanced Representation for Divisors. In: van der Poorten, A.J., Stein, A. (eds.) ANTS-VIII 2008. LNCS, vol. 5011, pp. 342–356. Springer, Heidelberg (2008)
17. Gaudry, P.: An Algorithm for Solving the Discrete Log Problem on Hyperelliptic Curves. In: Preneel, B. (ed.) EUROCRYPT 2000. LNCS, vol. 1807, pp. 19–34. Springer, Heidelberg (2000)
18. Gaudry, P.: Hyperelliptic curves and the HCDLP. London Mathematical Society Lecture Notes, vol. 317, ch.VII, pp. 133–150. Cambridge University Press (2005)
19. Gaudry, P.: Fast genus 2 arithmetic based on Theta functions. J. Math. Crypt. 1(3), 243–265 (2007)
20. Gaudry, P., Harley, R.: Counting Points on Hyperelliptic Curves Over Finite Fields. In: Bosma, W. (ed.) ANTS 2000. LNCS, vol. 1838, pp. 313–332. Springer, Heidelberg (2000)
21. Gaudry, P., Thomé, E., Thériault, N., Diem, C.: A double large prime variation for small genus hyperelliptic index calculus. Math. Comp. 76(257), 475–492 (2007)
22. Gonda, M., Matsuo, K., Aoki, K., Chao, J., Tsujii, S.: Improvements of addition algorithm on genus 3 hyperelliptic curves and their implementation. IEICE Transactions on Fundamentals of Electronics Communications and Computer Sciences, 89–96 (2005)
23. Gurot, C., Kaveh, K., Patankar, V.M.: Explicit algorithm for the arithmetic on the hyperelliptic Jacobians of genus 3. Journal of the Ramanujan Mathematical Society 19, 75–115 (2004)
24. Harley, R.: Fast arithmetic on genus 2 curves, for C source code and further explanations, `http://cristal.inria.fr/~harley/hyper`
25. Hess, F.: Computing Riemann-Roch spaces in algebraic function fields and related topics. J. Symb. Comput. 33(4), 425–445 (2002)
26. Hisil, H.: Elliptic curves, group law, and efficient computation. PhD thesis, Queensland University of Technology (2010)
27. Huang, M.A., Ierardi, D.: Efficient algorithms for the Riemann-Roch problem and for addition in the Jacobian of a curve. J. Symb. Comput. 18(6), 519–539 (1994)

28. Katagi, M., Kitamura, I., Akishita, T., Takagi, T.: Novel Efficient Implementations of Hyperelliptic Curve Cryptosystems using Degenerate Divisors. In: Lim, C.H., Yung, M. (eds.) WISA 2004. LNCS, vol. 3325, pp. 345–359. Springer, Heidelberg (2005)
29. Khuri-Makdisi, K.: Linear algebra algorithms for divisors on an algebraic curve. Math. Comp. 73(245), 333–357 (2004)
30. Khuri-Makdisi, K.: Asymptotically fast group operations on jacobians of general curves. Math. Comp. 76(260), 2213–2239 (2007)
31. Koblitz, N.: Elliptic curve cryptosystems. Math. Comp. 48(177), 203–209 (1987)
32. Koblitz, N.: Hyperelliptic cryptosystems. J. Cryptology 1(3), 139–150 (1989)
33. Lang, S.: Introduction to algebraic geometry. Addison-Wesley (1972)
34. Lange, T.: Efficient arithmetic on hyperelliptic curves. PhD thesis, Universität-Gesamthochschule Essen (2001)
35. Lange, T.: Efficient arithmetic on genus 2 hyperelliptic curves over finite fields via explicit formulae. Cryptology ePrint Archive, Report 2002/121 (2002), `http://eprint.iacr.org/`
36. Lange, T.: Inversion-free arithmetic on genus 2 hyperelliptic curves. Cryptology ePrint Archive, Report 2002/147 (2002), `http://eprint.iacr.org/`
37. Lange, T.: Weighted coordinates on genus 2 hyperelliptic curves. Cryptology ePrint Archive, Report 2002/153 (2002), `http://eprint.iacr.org/`
38. Lange, T.: Formulae for arithmetic on genus 2 hyperelliptic curves. Appl. Algebra Eng. Commun. Comput. 15(5), 295–328 (2005)
39. Lange, T.: Elliptic vs. hyperelliptic, part II. Talk at ECC (September 2006)
40. Lauter, K.: The equivalence of the geometric and algebraic group laws for Jacobians of genus 2 curves. Topics in Algebraic and Noncommutative Geometry 324, 165–171 (2003)
41. Lauter, K., Montgomery, P.L., Naehrig, M.: An Analysis of Affine Coordinates for Pairing Computation. In: Joye, M., Miyaji, A., Otsuka, A. (eds.) Pairing 2010. LNCS, vol. 6487, pp. 1–20. Springer, Heidelberg (2010)
42. Leitenberger, F.: About the group law for the Jacobi variety of a hyperelliptic curve. Contributions to Algebra and Geometry 46(1), 125–130 (2005)
43. Matsuo, K., Chao, J., Tsujii, S.: Fast genus two hyperelliptic curve cryptosystems. Technical Report 214, IEIC (2001)
44. Miller, V.S.: Use of Elliptic Curves in Cryptography. In: Williams, H.C. (ed.) CRYPTO 1985. LNCS, vol. 218, pp. 417–426. Springer, Heidelberg (1986)
45. Miyamoto, Y., Doi, H., Matsuo, K., Chao, J., Tsujii, S.: A fast addition algorithm of genus two hyperelliptic curve. In: Symposium on Cryptography and Information Security - SCICS (2002) (in Japanese)
46. Mumford, D.: Tata lectures on theta II. In: Progress in Mathematics, vol. 43. Birkhiauser Boston Inc., Boston (1984)
47. Pollard, J.M.: Monte Carlo methods for index computation (mod p). Math. Comp. 32(143), 918–924 (1978)
48. Smith, B.: Isogenies and the discrete logarithm problem in Jacobians of genus 3 hyperelliptic curves. Journal of Cryptology 22(4), 505–529 (2009)
49. Sugizaki, H., Matsuo, K., Chao, J., Tsujii, S.: An extension of Harley addition algorithm for hyperelliptic curves over finite fields of characteristic two. Technical Report ISEC2002-9(2002-5), IEICE (2002)
50. Takahashi, M.: Improving Harley algorithms for Jacobians of genus 2 hyperelliptic curves. In: Symposium on Cryptography and Information Security - SCICS (2002) (in Japanese)

51. Wollinger, T.: Software and hardware implementation of hyperelliptic curve cryptosystems. PhD thesis, Ruhr-University of Bochum (2004)
52. Wollinger, T., Kovtun, V.: Fast explicit formulae for genus 2 hyperelliptic curves using projective coordinates. In: Fourth International Conference on Information Technology, pp. 893–897 (2007)
53. Wollinger, T., Pelzl, J., Paar, C.: Cantor versus Harley: optimization and analysis of explicit formulae for hyperelliptic curve cryptosystems. IEEE Transactions on Computers, 861–872 (2005)
54. Yung, M., Dodis, Y., Kiayias, A., Malkin, T. (eds.): PKC 2006. LNCS, vol. 3958. Springer, Heidelberg (2006)

Cryptographic Analysis of All 4×4-Bit S-Boxes

Markku-Juhani O. Saarinen

Revere Security
4500 Westgrove Drive, Suite 335, Addison, TX 75001, USA
mjos@reveresecurity.com

Abstract. We present cryptanalytic results of an exhaustive search of all 16! bijective 4-bit S-Boxes. Previously affine equivalence classes have been exhaustively analyzed in 2007 work by Leander and Poschmann. We extend on this work by giving further properties of the optimal S-Box linear equivalence classes. In our main analysis we consider two S-Boxes to be cryptanalytically equivalent if they are isomorphic up to the permutation of input and output bits and a XOR of a constant in the input and output. We have enumerated all such equivalence classes with respect to their differential and linear properties. These equivalence classes are equivalent not only in their differential and linear bounds but also have equivalent algebraic properties, branch number and circuit complexity. We describe a "golden" set of S-boxes that have ideal cryptographic properties. We also present a comparison table of S-Boxes from a dozen published cryptographic algorithms.

Keywords: S-Box, Differential cryptanalysis, Linear cryptanalysis, Exhaustive permutation search.

1 Introduction

Horst Feistel introduced the Lucifer cipher, which can be considered to be the first modern block cipher, some 40 years ago. Feistel followed closely the principles outlined by Claude Shannon in 1949 [36] when designing Lucifer. We quote from Feistel's 1971 patent text [20]:

> Shannon, in his paper, presents further developments in the art of cryptography by introducing the product cipher. That is, the successive application of two or more distinctly different kinds of message symbol transformations. One example of a product cipher consists of symbol substitution (nonlinear transformation) followed by a symbol transposition (linear transformation).

Cryptographic algorithms are still designed in 2011 according to these same principles. A key element of Lucifer's symbol substitution layer was a pair of 4×4-bit substitution boxes (S-Boxes).

Much research effort has been dedicated to the analysis of 4-bit S-Boxes in subsequent encryption algorithms during last the four decades. In this paper we present an analysis of all bijective 4-bit S-Boxes in the light of modern cryptanalytic techniques, together with comparison tables of 4-bit S-Boxes found in a dozen different published encryption algorithm proposals.

A. Miri and S. Vaudenay (Eds.): SAC 2011, LNCS 7118, pp. 118–133, 2012.

Overview of This Paper. In Section 2 we give definitions of differential probability, linear bias, algebraic degree, and branch number of an S-Box. Section 3 defines more key concepts such as linear (affine) equivalence (LE) and permutation equivalence (PE) classes, together with the concept of an ordering-based canonical representative identify LE, PE, and other equivalence classes uniquely. We also make new observations on the sixteen "optimal" LE classes first identified in [31]. Section 4 describes our exhaustive search of the 16! bijective 4 × 4-bit S-Boxes. We give a description of the search algorithm in Section 4.1 and the distribution of class sizes and Linear and Differential properties in Section 4.2. Section 5 discusses the "golden" S-Boxes discovered in our search. We conclude in 4.2. Appendix A tabulates the properties of 4 × 4-bit S-Boxes found in a dozen different cryptographic algorithms.

2 S-Box Properties

In the context of cryptographic operations, arithmetic is assumed to be performed on variables, vectors, or matrices whose individual elements belong to the finite field $\mathbb{F}_2$. Vectors are indexed from 0. We write $\mathrm{wt}(x) = \sum x_i$ to denote the Hamming weight of the bit vector (word) x.

We will first give definitions related to Differential Cryptanalysis [4,5], Linear Cryptanalysis (LC) [32], and various forms of Algebraic / Cube Cryptanalysis (AC) [16,17].

Definition 1. *Let S be an S-Box with $|S|$ input values. Let n be the number of elements x that satisfy $S(x \oplus \Delta_i) = S(x) \oplus \Delta_o$. Then $n/|S|$ is the differential probability p of the characteristic $S_D(\Delta_i \rightarrow \Delta_o)$.*

For 4×4 bijective S-Boxes the optimal differential bound (maximum of all differentials in an individual S-Box) is $p = 1/4$.

Definition 2. *Let S be an S-Box with $|S|$ input values. Let n be the number of elements x that satisfy $\mathrm{wt}(\beta_i \cdot x \oplus \beta_o \cdot S(x)) \bmod 2 = 1$ for two bit-mask vectors β_i and β_o. Then $\mathrm{abs}(\frac{n}{|S|} - \frac{1}{2})$ is the bias ϵ of the linear approximation $S_L(\beta_i \rightarrow \beta_o)$.*

It is well known that all 2^{2^n} functions f from n bits to a single bit can be uniquely expressed by a polynomial function with coefficients drawn from the Algebraic Normal Form $\hat{f}$, which has the same domain as f:

$$f(x) = \sum_{y \in \mathbb{F}_2^n} \hat{f}(y) x_0^{y_0} x_1^{y_1} \cdots x_{n-1}^{y_{n-1}}.$$

This transformation from f to $\hat{f}$ can also be seen to be equivalent to the Walsh transform [35].

Definition 3. *The algebraic degree* $\deg(f)$ *of a function* $f : \mathbb{F}_2^n \mapsto \mathbb{F}_2$ *is the maximal weight* $wt(x)$ *that satisfies* $\hat{f}(x) \neq 0$.

In other words, the degree of f is the number of variables in the biggest monomial in the polynomial representation of f. Naturally the maximum degree for a 4-bit function is 4. This monomial exists in the polynomial representation exactly when $f(0) \neq f(15)$.

We define S-Box branch number similarly to the way it is defined in [39].

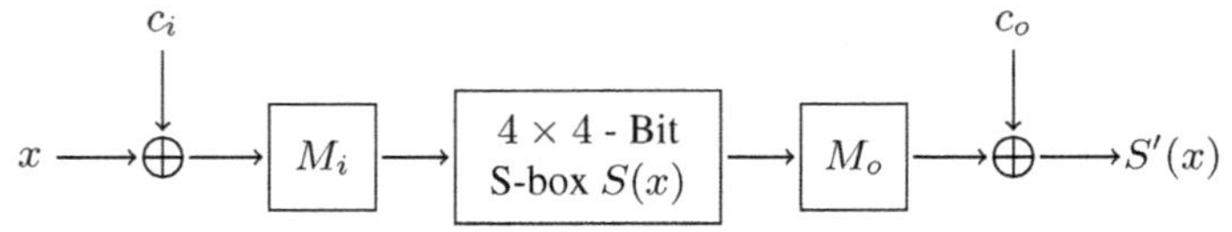

Fig. 1. Linear Equivalence (LE) and Permutation-XOR equivalence (PE). M_i and M_o boxes denote multiplication by an invertible matrix for LE and by a permutation matrix for PE.

Definition 4. *The branch number of an $n \times n$-bit S-Box is*

$$BN = \min_{a,b \neq a} \left(\mathrm{wt}(a \oplus b) + \mathrm{wt}(S(a) \oplus S(b))\right),$$

where $a, b \in \mathbb{F}_2^n$.

It is clear that for a bijective S-Box the branch number is at least 2.

3 Equivalence Classes and Canonical Representation

The classification of Boolean functions dates back to the fifties [22]. Previously 4-bit S-Boxes have been analyzed in relation to linear equivalence [6,31], defined as follows:

Definition 5. *Let M_i and M_o be two invertible matrices and c_i and c_o two vectors. The S-Box S' defined by two affine transformations*

$$S'(x) = M_o S(M_i(x \oplus c_i)) \oplus c_o$$

belongs to the linear equivalence set of S; $S' \in \mathrm{LE}(S)$.

We call $M_i(x \oplus c_i)$ the inner affine transform and $M_o x \oplus c_o$ the outer affine transform. There are 20,160 invertible 4×4 matrices defined over $\mathbb{F}_2$ and therefore $2^4 \times 20,160 = 322,560$ affine invertible transforms.

To be able to identify members of each equivalence class uniquely, we must define a canonical representation for it. Each member of the equivalence class can be reduced to this unique representative, which serves as an identifier for the entire class.

Definition 6. *The canonical representative of an equivalence class is the member that is first in lexicographic ordering.*

Table 1 gives the canonical members of all 16 "optimal" S-Box LE classes, together with references to their equivalents in [31].

It has been shown that the members of each LE class have the same differential and linear bounds [6,31]. However, these linear equivalence classes are not equivalent in many ways that have cryptographic significance.

Multiple Differential Characteristics and Linear Approximations. For cryptographic security, the differential and linear bounds are the most important factor. However, the methods of multiple differentials [8] and multiple linear approximations [7,21,29] raise the question of how many differentials and linear approximations there are at the respective boundaries. From Table 1 it can be observed that these numbers are not equivalent, making some S-Boxes "more optimal" than others in this respect.

Table 1. The canonical representatives of the 16 "optimal" linear equivalence classes. The G_i and G_i^{-1} identifier references are to Table 6 of [31]. We also give the DC and LC bounds, together with the number n_d of characteristics at the differential bound and the number n_l of approximations at the linear bound. The branch BN number given is the maximal branch number among all members of the given LE class.

Canonical representative	**Members**	**DC**		**LC**		**Max**
0123456789ABCDEF	**& Inverse**	p	n_d	ϵ	n_l	**BN**
0123468A5BCF79DE	$G_2\ G_0^{-1}$	$1/4$	24	$1/4$	36	3
0123468A5BCF7D9E	$G_{15}\ G_{14}^{-1}$	$1/4$	18	$1/4$	32	3
0123468A5BCF7E9D	$G_0\ G_2^{-1}$	$1/4$	24	$1/4$	36	3
0123468A5BCFDE79	$G_8\ G_8^{-1}$	$1/4$	24	$1/4$	36	2
0123468A5BCFED97	$G_1\ G_1^{-1}$	$1/4$	24	$1/4$	36	3
0123468B59CED7AF	$G_9\ G_9^{-1}$	$1/4$	18	$1/4$	32	3
0123468B59CEDA7F	$G_{13}\ G_{13}^{-1}$	$1/4$	15	$1/4$	30	2
0123468B59CF7DAE	$G_{14}\ G_{15}^{-1}$	$1/4$	18	$1/4$	32	3
0123468B5C9DE7AF	$G_{12}\ G_{12}^{-1}$	$1/4$	15	$1/4$	30	2
0123468B5C9DEA7F	$G_4\ G_4^{-1}$	$1/4$	15	$1/4$	30	2
0123468B5CD79FAE	$G_6\ G_6^{-1}$	$1/4$	15	$1/4$	30	2
0123468B5CD7AF9E	$G_5\ G_5^{-1}$	$1/4$	15	$1/4$	30	2
0123468B5CD7F9EA	$G_3\ G_3^{-1}$	$1/4$	15	$1/4$	30	2
0123468C59BDE7AF	$G_{10}\ G_{10}^{-1}$	$1/4$	18	$1/4$	32	3
0123468C59BDEA7F	$G_7\ G_7^{-1}$	$1/4$	15	$1/4$	30	2
0123468C59DFA7BE	$G_{11}\ G_{11}^{-1}$	$1/4$	15	$1/4$	30	2

Avalanche. For members of an LE class there is no guarantee that a single-bit difference in input will not result in single-bit output difference. If this happens, only a single S-Box is activated in the next round of a simple substitution-permutation network such as PRESENT [9]. This is equivalent to the case where the branch number is 2.

It is somewhat surprising that those optimal S-Boxes with most attractive n_d and n_l numbers cannot be affinely transformed so that differentials with $\mathrm{wt}(\Delta_i) = \mathrm{wt}(\Delta_o) = 1$ would all have $p = 0$. Only the seven of the sixteen optimal S-Box classes, G_0, G_1, G_2, G_9, G_{10}, G_{14}, and G_{15}, have members that do not have such single-bit differentials. This has been verified by exhaustive search by the authors.

We may illustrate the importance of this property by considering a variant of PRESENT where the S-Box has been replaced by a linearly equivalent one from $\mathrm{LE}(G_1)$ such as (0123468A5BCFED97) that has $p = 1/4$ for the single-bit differential $S_D(\Delta_i = 1 \rightarrow \Delta_o = 1)$. Due to the fact that the bit 0 is mapped to bit 0 in the PRESENT pLayer, this variant has an iterative differential in bit 0 that holds through all 31 rounds with probability 2^{-62}. We may utilize the average branch number in the last rounds to estimate that this variant would be breakable with less than 2^{56} effort.

This motivates us to define the PE class.

Definition 7. *Let P_i and P_o be two bit permutation matrices and c_i and c_o two vectors. The S-Box S' defined by*

$$S'(x) = P_o S(P_i(x \oplus c_i)) \oplus c_o$$

belongs to the permutation-xor equivalence set of S; $S' \in \mathrm{PE}(S)$.

Algebraic Properties. While the maximal algebraic degree of all output bits may be preserved in LE [31], some of the output bits may still be almost linear. It is noteworthy that despite belonging to LE(G_1), one of the PRESENT output bits only has one nonlinear monomial (of degree 2) and therefore this output bit depends only linearly on 2 of the input bits. This can be crucial when determining the number of secure rounds; final rounds can be peeled off using such properties.

Circuit Complexity. From an implementation viewpoint, the members of an LE class may vary very much but the members of a PE class are usually equivalent. This is important in bit-slicing implementations such as [3].

It can be shown that circuits that use all 2-input Boolean functions [35,40] can be transformed to equal-size circuits that use only the four commonly available instructions (AND, OR, XOR, AND NOT) but may require a constant XOR on input and output bit vectors. These XOR constants may be transferred to round key addition in most substitution-permutation networks and therefore there is no additional cost.

Note that the methods described in [39] utilize only five registers and two-operand instructions AND, OR, XOR, NOT and MOV. Most recent CPUs have sixteen 256-bit YMM registers, three-operand instructions (making MOV redundant) and the ANDNx instruction for AND NOT [28]. Therefore 2-input boolean circuit complexity is a more relevant measure for optimality of a circuit. However, for hardware implementation these gates have uneven implementation-dependent cost [34].

We may also consider the concept of feeble one-wayness [25,26,27]. This property is also shared between the members of a PE class.

Other Properties. Some researchers put emphasis on the cycle structure of an S-Box. Cycle structure properties are not usually shared between members of LE and PE classes. This may be relevant if the cipher design does not protect against the effects of fixed points or other similar special cases. However, such properties are difficult to analyze in the context of a single S-Box removed from its setting within an encryption algorithm. Care should be taken when choosing input and output bit ordering so that diffusion layers will achieve maximum effect.

Historical Developments. The original DES S-Box design principles are described in [10]. In hindsight it can be seen that the criteria given in that 1976 document already offer significantly better resistance against primitive DC and LC than what can be achieved with entirely random S-Boxes [11]. For a perspective on the development of DES and the evaluation of its S-Boxes between the years 1975 and 1990 we refer to [13]. We may compare our current view on the topic of "good" S-Boxes to that given by Adams and Tavares in 1990 [2]. Four evaluation criteria for S-Boxes were given in that work: bijectivity, nonlinearity, strict avalanche, and independence of output bits. In current terminology nonlinearity would map to the algebraic degree, strict avalanche to the branch number, and independence of output bits roughly to both DC and LC. Note that modern DC, LC, and AC were (re)discovered after 1990.

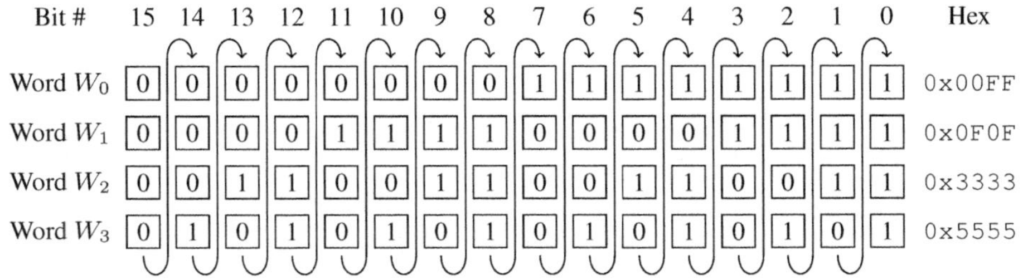

Fig. 2. Our internal 4×16-bit representation of the identity permutation $(0, 1, \ldots, 15)$. The words are always stored in increasing order and the highest bit is normalized to zero.

4 An Exhaustive Search Over All PE Classes

We have performed an exhaustive search over all PE classes. Since there are $16! \approx 2^{44.25}$ different bijective 4-bit S-Boxes, some shortcuts had to be used. We are currently unable to extend our methods to 5-bit S-Boxes or beyond.

Internally our program uses another (non-lexicographic) ordering to determine the unique canonical member of each PE class. The permutations are stored as four 16-bit words W_i that are always in ascending order.

Theorem 1. *Any 4×4-bit bijective S-Box can be uniquely expressed as*

$$S(x) = \Big(\sum_{i=0}^{3} 2^{P(i)} W_{i,(15-x)} \Big) \oplus c$$

for some bit permutation P of numbers $(0, 1, 2, 3)$, a vector $c \in \mathbb{F}_2^4$ and words $W_i = \sum_{j=0}^{15} 2^i W_{i,j}$ satisfying $0 < W_0 < W_1 < W_2 < W_3 < 2^{15}$.

Proof. Output bits can be permuted in $4! = 24$ different ways (as each W_i must be different from others) and each one of the $2^4 = 16$ masks c creates a different permutation due to the limit $W_i < 2^{15}$. P and c uniquely define the $4!2^4 = 384$ outer transformations while W_i uniquely defines the rest. □

This representation offers a natural and quick way to normalize a S-Box in respect to the outer permutation P_o and mask c_o by sorting the four words and inverting all bits of a word if the highest bit is set. Figure 2 illustrates this ordering.

From the fact that S is bijective it follows that $\mathrm{wt}(W_i) = 8$ for all W_i. There are $\binom{16}{8} = 12,870$ 16-bit words of weight 8, of which we may remove half due to the c_o normalization limit $W_i < 2^{15}$, yielding $6,535$ candidates. Furthermore, each word has a minimal equivalent up to permutation among all input permutations P_i and input constants c_i. We call this minimal word $\mathrm{mw}(x)$. At program start, a table is initialized that contains $\mathrm{mw}(x)$ for each 16-bit word by trying all 24 permutations of input bits and 16 values of c_i on the 4×1-bit Boolean function that the word x represents. If the resulting word is greater or equal to 2^{15} (indicating that the highest bit is set) all bits of the word are inverted, normalizing the constant. Each one of the $\mathrm{wt}(x) = 8$ candidates map to a set of just 58 different $\mathrm{mw}(x)$ values.

Algorithm 1. A bit-combinatorial permutation search algorithm.

1: **for** $i_0 = 0$ to 6534 **do**
2: $W_0 = \mathrm{wt8tab}[i_0]$
3: **if** $\mathrm{mw}(W_0) = W_0$ **then**
4: **for** $i_1 = i_0 + 1$ to 6534 **do**
5: $W_1 = \mathrm{wt8tab}[i_1]$
6: **if** $\mathrm{mw}(W_1) > W_0$ and
$\mathrm{wt}(t_2 = \neg W_0 \wedge W_1) = 4$ and $\mathrm{wt}(t_3 = W_0 \wedge W_1) = 4$ and
$\mathrm{wt}(t_1 = W_0 \wedge \neg W_1) = 4$ and $\mathrm{wt}(t_0 = \neg W_0 \wedge \neg W_1) = 4$ **then**
7: **for** $i_2 = i_1 + 1$ to 6534 **do**
8: $W_2 = \mathrm{wt8tab}[i_2]$
9: **if** $\mathrm{mw}(W_1) > W_0$ and
$\mathrm{wt}(u_0 = t_0 \wedge \neg W_2) = 2$ and $\mathrm{wt}(u_4 = t_0 \wedge W_2) = 2$ and
$\mathrm{wt}(u_1 = t_1 \wedge \neg W_2) = 2$ and $\mathrm{wt}(u_5 = t_1 \wedge W_2) = 2$ and
$\mathrm{wt}(u_2 = t_2 \wedge \neg W_2) = 2$ and $\mathrm{wt}(u_6 = t_2 \wedge W_2) = 2$ and
$\mathrm{wt}(u_3 = t_3 \wedge \neg W_2) = 2$ and $\mathrm{wt}(u_7 = t_3 \wedge W_2) = 2$ **then**
10: **for** $j = 0$ to 8 **do**
11: $v_j = \mathrm{lsb}(u_j)$
12: **end for**
13: **for** $b = 0$ to 255 **do**
14: $W_3 = \bigoplus_{j=0}^{7} (u_j \oplus b_j v_j)$
15: **if** $W_3 \geq 2^{15}$ **then**
16: $W_3 = \neg W_3$
17: **end if**
18: **if** $W_3 > W_2$ **then**
19: $\mathrm{test}(W_0, W_1, W_2, W_3)$
20: **end if**
21: **end for**
22: **end if**
23: **end for**
24: **end if**
25: **end for**
26: **end if**
27: **end for**

4.1 The Search Algorithm

We will now describe the bit-combinatorial equivalence class search method given in Algorithm 1. There are basically four nested loops. Various early exit strategies are used that are based on properties of the permutation (see Theorem 1 and Figure 2). Lines 1–3 select the smallest word W_0 from a table of weight-eight words and checks that it is indeed minimal w.r.t. permutation of the four input bits. In lines 4–6 we select W_1 such that it is larger than W_0 and these two words have each one of the four bit pairs $(0, 0)$, $(0, 1)$, $(1, 0)$, and $(1, 1)$ exactly four times at corresponding locations $(W_{0,i}, W_{1,i})$. This is a necessary condition for them to be a part of a permutation as described by Theorem 1. The corresponding masks are stored in four temporary variables t_i. In Lines 7–9 we choose W_2 such that the three words make up two permutations of numbers $0, 1, \ldots, 7$. The vector u_i containing the two bit positions of i simultaneously computed. We are

Table 2. Distribution of PE classes. The first column gives the number of elements in each class. The second column $|C_n|$ gives the number of such classes, followed by their product, which sums to $16! = 20,922,789,888,000$ as expected.

$\frac{n}{4!2^4}$	$\lvert C_n\rvert$	$n\,\lvert C_n\rvert$	**Representative**
1	2	768	0123456789ABCDEF
4	4	6144	01234567FEDCBA98
6	1	2304	01237654BA98CDEF
8	4	12288	0123456879ABCDEF
12	30	138240	0123456798BADCFE
16	18	110592	0123457689BADCFE
24	192	1769472	0123456789ABFEDC
32	104	1277952	0123456789ABCDFE
48	1736	31997952	0123456789ABCEDF
64	264	6488064	012345678ACD9EBF
96	13422	494788608	0123456789ABDEFC
128	324	15925248	0123456789ADCEBF
192	373192	27514699776	0123456789ABCEFD
384	141701407	20894722670592	0123456789ACBEFD
1–384	**142090700**	**20922789888000**	

Table 3. Distribution of the 16! permutations in relation to Differential Cryptanalysis (rows) and Linear Cryptanalysis (columns)

LC →	$\epsilon \leq 1/4$		$\epsilon \leq 3/8$		$\epsilon \leq 1/2$	
DC ↓	n	%	n	%	n	%
$p \leq 1/4$	749123665920	3.5804	326998425600	1.5629	0	0.0000
$p \leq 3/8$	1040449536000	4.9728	11448247910400	54.7166	118908518400	0.5683
$p \leq 1/2$	52022476800	0.2486	5812644741120	27.7814	330249830400	1.5784
$p \leq 5/8$	0	0.0000	728314675200	3.4810	193458585600	0.9246
$p \leq 3/4$	0	0.0000	52022476800	0.2486	68098867200	0.3255
$p \leq 1$	0	0.0000	309657600	0.0015	1940520960	0.0093

now left with exactly $2^8 = 256$ options for the last word W_3. In lines 10–12 we store in vector v_i the lesser bit from the two-bit mask u_i. In lines 13–20 we loop through the remaining W_3 possibilities. In line 14 we use the bit i of the loop index b to select which one of the two bits in u_i is used as part of W_3. Note that this part may be implemented a bit faster with a Gray-code sequence.

The unique permutation is then tested by the subroutine on line 19 to see if it is the least member of its class (here an early exit strategy will usually exit the exhaustive loop early). If (W_0, W_1, W_2, W_3) is indeed the canonical member in the special ordering that we're using, it is stored on on disk together with the size of the class. The entire process of creating the 1.4 GB file takes about half an hour with a 2011 consumer laptop.

4.2 Results of the Exhaustive Search

There are 142,090,700 different PE classes of various sizes. Table 2 gives the size distribution of these PE classes, which sum up to $20,922,789,888,000 = 16!$ examined

Table 4. Golden S-Boxes with ideal properties are all members of these four PE classes. Both the S-Boxes and their inverses satisfy the bounds $p \leq 1/4$, $\epsilon \leq 1/4$, have branch number 3, all output bits have algebraic degree 3 and are dependent on all input bits in nonlinear fashion. n gives the total size of the class and n' the number of members which additionally have a perfect cycle structure.

PE Representative	LE	n	n'
`035869C7DAE41FB2`	G_9	147456	19584
`03586CB79EADF214`	G_9	147456	19584
`03586AF4ED9217CB`	G_{10}	147456	22656
`03586CB7A49EF12D`	G_{10}	147456	22656

S-Boxes. Each class size is divisible by $4!2^4 = 384$ due to the fact that the output bits can be permuted $4! = 24$ ways and the output constant c_o can have $2^4 = 16$ different values. However, it is less obvious how the inner transform defined by P_i and c_i affect the size of the class together with S. For example, for the identity permutation (`0123456789ABCDEF`) the bit shuffles P_i and P_o and constant additions c_i and c_o may be presented with a single bit permutation and addition of constant and hence hence $n = 384$. It is interesting to note that that there is one other class with this size, the one with the largest canonical representative, (`07BCDA61E952348F`).

Table 3 gives the distribution of differential and linear properties among the 16! S-Boxes examined. It can be seen that a majority, 54.7155% of all S-Boxes have a differential bound $p \leq 3/4$ and linear bound $\epsilon \leq 3/4$. There are no bijective S-Boxes with differential bound $p = 7/8$. Appendix A gives results on some well-known 4-bit S-Boxes.

5 Golden S-Boxes

Based on our exhaustive search, we may describe *golden* S-Boxes that have ideal properties. From Table 1 we see that the most tempting candidates belong to the LE sets of G_9, G_{10}, G_{14}, and G_{15} as they have the smallest n_d and n_l numbers among those S-Boxes that have branch number 3. Note that $\text{LE}(G_{14}) = \text{LE}(G_{15}^{-1})$ and vice versa.

The only problem with G_{14} and G_{15} in comparison to G_9 and G_{10} is that if we want the branch number to be larger than 2, there are no S-Boxes in these classes that have the desired property that all output bits are nonlinearly dependent on all input bits and have degree 3. Either the permutation or its inverse will not satisfy this condition. This has been verified with exhaustive search. All golden S-Boxes belong to the four PE classes given in Table 4.

The Serpent [1] S-Box $S3$, Hummingbird-1 [18] S-Boxes $S1$, $S2$, and $S3$ and Hummingbird-2 [19] S-Boxes[1] $S0$ and $S1$ are the only known examples of "golden" S-Boxes in literature. Note that cipher designers may want to avoid re-using the same LE class in multiple S-Boxes and hence not all can be "golden". Please see Appendix A for a more detailed comparison.

[1] Hummingbird-2 was tweaked in May 2011 to use these S-Boxes, and they are also contained in [19]. Some early prototypes used S-Boxes from Serpent.

6 Conclusions

We have analyzed all 16! bijective 4×4-bit S-Boxes and classified them into linear equivalence (LE) and permutation equivalence (PE) classes. Members of a LE class have equivalent differential and linear bounds but not necessarily branch number, algebraic properties and circuit complexity. Members of PE classes share these properties. Each equivalence class can be uniquely identified with the use of a canonical representative, which we define to be the member which is first in lexicographic ordering of the class members.

There are 142,090,700 different PE classes, the vast majority (99.7260%) of which have $(4!2^4)^2 = 147456$ elements. We classify the S-Boxes according to their differential and linear properties. It turns out that that a majority (54.7155%) of S-Boxes have differential bound $p \leq 3/4$ and linear bound $\epsilon \leq 3/4$.

Furthermore, we have discovered that not all of the "optimal" S-Boxes described in [31] are equal if we take the branch number and multiple differential and linear cryptanalysis into account.

In an appendix we give comparison tables of the S-Boxes from Lucifer [37], Present [9], JH [41], ICEBERG [38], LUFFA [15] NOEKEON [12], HAMSI [30], Serpent [1], Hummingbird-1 [18], Hummingbird-2 [19], GOST [14,23,24] and DES [33].

Acknowledgements. The author wishes to thank Whitfield Diffie and numerous other commentators for their input. This work is still ongoing.

References

1. Anderson, R., Biham, E., Knudsen, L.: Serpent: A Proposal for the Advanced Encryption Standard (1999), `http://www.cl.cam.ac.uk/~rja14/Papers/serpent.pdf`
2. Adams, C., Tavares, S.: The Structured Design of Cryptographically Good S-Boxes. Journal of Cryptology 3(1), 27–41 (1990)
3. Biham, E.: A Fast New DES Implementation in Software. In: Biham, E. (ed.) FSE 1997. LNCS, vol. 1267, pp. 260–272. Springer, Heidelberg (1997)
4. Biham, E., Shamir, A.: Differential Cryptanalysis of DES-Like Cryptosystems. In: Menezes, A., Vanstone, S.A. (eds.) CRYPTO 1990. LNCS, vol. 537, pp. 2–21. Springer, Heidelberg (1991)
5. Biham, E., Shamir, A.: Differential Cryptanalysis of the Data Encryption Standard. Springer, Heidelberg (1993)
6. Biryukov, A., De Cannière, C., Braeken, A., Preneel, B.: A Toolbox for Cryptanalysis: Linear and Affine Equivalence Algorithms. In: Biham, E. (ed.) EUROCRYPT 2003. LNCS, vol. 2656, pp. 33–50. Springer, Heidelberg (2003)
7. Biryukov, A., De Cannière, C., Quisquater, M.: On Multiple Linear Approximations. In: Franklin, M. (ed.) CRYPTO 2004. LNCS, vol. 3152, pp. 1–22. Springer, Heidelberg (2004)
8. Blondeau, C., Gérard, B.: Multiple Differential Cryptanalysis: Theory and Practice. In: Joux, A. (ed.) FSE 2011. LNCS, vol. 6733, pp. 35–54. Springer, Heidelberg (2011)
9. Bogdanov, A.A., Knudsen, L.R., Leander, G., Paar, C., Poschmann, A., Robshaw, M.J.B., Seurin, Y., Vikkelsoe, C.: PRESENT: An Ultra-Lightweight Block Cipher. In: Paillier, P., Verbauwhede, I. (eds.) CHES 2007. LNCS, vol. 4727, pp. 450–466. Springer, Heidelberg (2007)

10. Branstad, D.K., Gait, J., Katzke, S.: Report of the Workshop on Cryptography in Support of Computer Security. Tech. Rep. NBSIR 77-1291, National Bureau of Standards (September 1976)
11. Coppersmith, D.: The Data Encryption Standard (DES) and its strength against attacks. IBM Journal of Research and Development Archive 38(3) (May 1994)
12. Daemen, J., Peeters, M., Van Assche, G., Rijmen, V.: Nessie Proposal: NOEKEON. NESSIE Proposal (October 27, 2000)
13. Denning, D.: The Data Encryption Standard – Fifteen Years of Public Scrutiny. In: Distinguished Lecture in Computer Security, Sixth Annual Computer Security Applications Conference, Tucson, December 3-7 (1990)
14. Dolmatov, V. (ed.): GOST 28147-89: Encryption, Decryption, and Message Authentication Code (MAC) Algorithms. Internet Engineering Task Force RFC 5830 (March 2010)
15. De Cannière, C., Sato, H., Watanabe, D.: Hash Function Luffa - Specification Ver. 2.0.1. NIST SHA-3 Submission, Round 2 document (October 2, 2009)
16. Courtois, N.T., Pieprzyk, J.: Cryptanalysis of Block Ciphers with Overdefined Systems of Equations. In: Zheng, Y. (ed.) ASIACRYPT 2002. LNCS, vol. 2501, pp. 267–287. Springer, Heidelberg (2002)
17. Dinur, I., Shamir, A.: Cube Attacks on Tweakable Black Box Polynomials. In: Joux, A. (ed.) EUROCRYPT 2009. LNCS, vol. 5479, pp. 278–299. Springer, Heidelberg (2009)
18. Engels, D., Fan, X., Gong, G., Hu, H., Smith, E.M.: Hummingbird: Ultra-Lightweight Cryptography for Resource-Constrained Devices. In: Sion, R., Curtmola, R., Dietrich, S., Kiayias, A., Miret, J.M., Sako, K., Sebé, F. (eds.) RLCPS, WECSR, and WLC 2010. LNCS, vol. 6054, pp. 3–18. Springer, Heidelberg (2010)
19. Engels, D., Saarinen, M.-J.O., Schweitzer, P., Smith, E.M.: The Hummingbird-2 Lightweight Authenticated Encryption Algorithm. In: RFIDSec 2011, The 7th Workshop on RFID Security and Privacy, Amherst, Massachusetts, USA, June 26-28 (2011)
20. Feistel, H.: Block Cipher Cryptographic System. U.S.Patent 3,798,359 (Filed June 30, 1971)
21. Hermelin, M., Nyberg, K.: Dependent Linear Approximations: The Algorithm of Biryukov and Others Revisited. In: Pieprzyk, J. (ed.) CT-RSA 2010. LNCS, vol. 5985, pp. 318–333. Springer, Heidelberg (2010)
22. Golomb, S.: On the classification of Boolean functions. IEEE Transactions on Information Theory 5(5), 176–186 (1959)
23. Government Committee of the USSR for Standards. Cryptographic Protection for Data Processing System. GOST 28147-89, Gosudarstvennyi Standard of USSR (1989) (in Russian)
24. Government Committee of the Russia for Standards. Information technology. Cryptographic Data Security. Hashing function. GOST R 34.11-94, Gosudarstvennyi Standard of Russian Federation (1994) (in Russian)
25. Hiltgen, A.P.: Constructions of Feebly-One-Way Families of Permutations. In: Zheng, Y., Seberry, J. (eds.) AUSCRYPT 1992. LNCS, vol. 718, pp. 422–434. Springer, Heidelberg (1993)
26. Hiltgen, A.P.: Towards a Better Understanding of One-Wayness: Facing Linear Permutations. In: Nyberg, K. (ed.) EUROCRYPT 1998. LNCS, vol. 1403, pp. 319–333. Springer, Heidelberg (1998)
27. Hirsch, E.A., Nikolenko, S.I.: A Feebly Secure Trapdoor Function. In: Frid, A., Morozov, A., Rybalchenko, A., Wagner, K.W. (eds.) CSR 2009. LNCS, vol. 5675, pp. 129–142. Springer, Heidelberg (2009)
28. Intel: Intel Advanced Vector Extensions Programming Reference. Publication 319433-010, Intel (April 2011)

29. Kaliski Jr., B.S., Robshaw, M.J.B.: Linear Cryptanalysis Using Multiple Approximations. In: Desmedt, Y.G. (ed.) CRYPTO 1994. LNCS, vol. 839, pp. 26–39. Springer, Heidelberg (1994)
30. Küçük, Ö.: The Hash Function Hamsi. NIST SHA-3 Submission, Round 2 document (September 14, 2009)
31. Leander, G., Poschmann, A.: On the Classification of 4 Bit S-Boxes. In: Carlet, C., Sunar, B. (eds.) WAIFI 2007. LNCS, vol. 4547, pp. 159–176. Springer, Heidelberg (2007)
32. Matsui, M.: Linear Cryptanalysis Method for DES Cipher. In: Helleseth, T. (ed.) EUROCRYPT 1993. LNCS, vol. 765, pp. 386–397. Springer, Heidelberg (1994)
33. National Bureau of Standards: Data Encryption Standard. FIPS PUB 46. National Bureau of Standards, U.S. Department of Commerce, Washington D.C. (January 15, 1977)
34. Poschmann, A.: Lightweight Cryptography - Cryptographic Engineering for a Pervasive World. Doktor-Ingenieur Thesis, Ruhr-University Bochum, Germany. Also available as Cryptology ePrint Report 2009/516 (2009)
35. Saarinen, M.-J.O.: Chosen-IV Statistical Attacks Against eSTREAM CIPHERS. In: Proc. SECRYPT 2006, International Conference on Security and Cryptography, Setubal, Portugal, August 7-10 (2006)
36. Shannon, C.E.: Communication Theory of Secrecy Systems. Bell System Technical Journal 28, 656–717 (1949)
37. Sorkin, A.: Lucifer: A cryptographic algorithm. Cryptologia 8(1), 22–42 (1984)
38. Standaert, F.-X., Piret, G., Rouvroy, G., Quisquater, J.-J., Legat, J.-D.: ICEBERG: An Involutional Cipher Efficient for Block Encryption in Reconfigurable Hardware. In: Roy, B., Meier, W. (eds.) FSE 2004. LNCS, vol. 3017, pp. 279–299. Springer, Heidelberg (2004)
39. Ullrich, M., De Cannière, C., Indesteege, S., Kü̧, Ö., Mouha, N., Preneel, B.: Finding Optimal Bitsliced Implementations of 4 × 4-bit S-Boxes. In: SKEW 2011 Symmetric Key Encryption Workshop, Copenhagen, Denmark, February 16-17 (2011)
40. Wegener, I.: The complexity of Boolean functions. WileyTeubner series in computer science. Wiley, Teubner (1987)
41. Wu, H.: The Hash Function JH. NIST SHA-3 Submission, Round 3 document (January 16, 2011)

A Cryptographic Analysis of Some Well-Known 4×4 - Bit S-Boxes

Algorithm & Source: A normative identifier for the S-Box in question, together with a literary reference.
S-Box: The S-Box permutation $S(x)$ in Hex.
Canonical PE: The lexicographically smallest member of the Permutation-XOR equivalence class $\mathrm{PE}(S)$.
Lin Eqv.: The linear equivalence class $\mathrm{LE}(s)$.
One Δ: number of instances where flipping a single input bit will cause single output bit to change (out of 64).
BN #: Branch number.
DC: Differential bound p and the number n_d of characteristics at that bound.
LC: Linear bias ϵ and the number n_l of linear approximations at that bound.
Bit n: The linear set LS of input bits that only have linear effect on this output bit, together with its degree.

Algorithm	S-Box	Canonical PE	Lin.	One	BN	DC		LC		Bit 0		Bit 1		Bit 2		Bit 3	
& Source	0123456789ABCDEF	0123456789ABCDEF	Eqv.	Δ	#	p	n_d	ϵ	n_l	LS	deg	LS	deg	LS	deg	LS	deg
Lucifer S0 [37]	CF7AEDB026319458	01254F9C6AB78D3E		12	2	$3/8$	5	$3/8$	3	{}	3	{}	3	{}	3	{}	3
Lucifer S1 [37]	72E93B04CD1A6F85	01245F3BC7DAE896		10	2	$3/8$	1	$1/4$	30	{}	3	{}	3	{}	3	{}	3
Present [9]	C56B90AD3EF84712	03567ABCD4E9812F	G_1	0	3	$1/4$	24	$1/4$	36	{0,3}	2	{}	3	{}	3	{}	3
Present^{-1} [9]	5EF8C12DB463079A	0358BC6FE9274AD1	G_1	0	3	$1/4$	24	$1/4$	36	{0,2}	2	{}	3	{}	3	{}	3
JH S0 [41]	904BDC3F1A26758E	01256BD79CF384AE	G_{13}	12	2	$1/4$	15	$1/4$	30	{}	3	{}	3	{}	3	{}	3
JH S1 [41]	3C6D5719F204BAE8	012485EADF3B697C	G_{13}	20	2	$1/4$	15	$1/4$	30	{}	3	{}	3	{}	3	{}	3
ICEBERG0 [38]	D7329AC1F45E60B8	012758E46DFA93BC	G_4	8	2	$1/4$	15	$1/4$	30	{}	3	{}	3	{}	3	{}	3
ICEBERG1 [38]	4AFC0D9BE6173582	0127568CA49EDB3F	G_4	8	2	$1/4$	15	$1/4$	30	{}	3	{}	3	{}	3	{}	3
LUFFA [15]	DE015A76B39CF824	012476AFC3E98B5D	G_1	18	2	$1/4$	24	$1/4$	36	{}	3	{}	3	{}	3	{}	3
NOEKEON [12]	7A2C48F0591E3DB6	01245EF3C786BAD9	G_8	12	2	$1/4$	24	$1/4$	36	{}	3	{}	3	{0}	2	{0,3}	2
HAMSI [30]	86793CAFD1E40B52	035869A7BCE21FD4	G_1	0	3	$1/4$	24	$1/4$	36	{1,3}	2	{}	3	{}	3	{}	3

Algorithm & Source	S-Box 0123456789ABCDEF	Canonical PE 0123456789ABCDEF	Lin. Eqv.	One Δ	BN #	DC p	DC n_d	LC ϵ	LC n_l	Bit 0 LS	Bit 0 deg	Bit 1 LS	Bit 1 deg	Bit 2 LS	Bit 2 deg	Bit 3 LS	Bit 3 deg
HB1 S0 [18]	865F1CA9EB2470D3	03586CF1A49EDB27	G_{15}	0	3	$^1/_4$	18	$^1/_4$	32	{}	3	{}	3	{}	3	{}	3
HB1 S1 [18]	07E15B823AD6FC49	035869C7DAE41FB2	G_9	0	3	$^1/_4$	18	$^1/_4$	32	{}	3	{}	3	{}	3	{}	3
HB1 S2 [18]	2EF5C19AB468073D	03586CB7A49EF12D	G_{10}	0	3	$^1/_4$	18	$^1/_4$	32	{}	3	{}	3	{}	3	{}	3
HB1 S3 [18]	0734C1AFDE6B2895	03586CB79EADF214	G_9	0	3	$^1/_4$	18	$^1/_4$	32	{}	3	{}	3	{}	3	{}	3
HB1^{-1} S0 [18]	D4AFB21C07695E83	035879BEADF4C261	G_{14}	0	3	$^1/_4$	18	$^1/_4$	32	{0}	2	{}	3	{}	3	{}	3
HB1^{-1} S1 [18]	0378E4B16F95DA2C	03586CB79EADF214	G_9	0	3	$^1/_4$	18	$^1/_4$	32	{}	3	{}	3	{}	3	{}	3
HB1^{-1} S2 [18]	C50E93ADB6784F12	03586AF4ED9217CB	G_{10}	0	3	$^1/_4$	18	$^1/_4$	32	{}	3	{}	3	{}	3	{}	3
HB1^{-1} S3 [18]	05C23FA1DE6B4897	035869C7DAE41FB2	G_9	0	3	$^1/_4$	18	$^1/_4$	32	{}	3	{}	3	{}	3	{}	3
HB2 S0 [19]	7CE9215FB6D048A3	035869C7DAE41FB2	G_9	0	3	$^1/_4$	18	$^1/_4$	32	{}	3	{}	3	{}	3	{}	3
HB2 S1 [19]	4A168F7C30ED59B2	03586AF4ED9217CB	G_{10}	0	3	$^1/_4$	18	$^1/_4$	32	{}	3	{}	3	{}	3	{}	3
HB2 S2 [19]	2FC156ADE8340B97	035879BEADF4C261	G_{14}	0	3	$^1/_4$	18	$^1/_4$	32	{}	3	{}	3	{}	3	{1}	2
HB2 S3 [19]	F4589721A30E6CDB	03586CF1A49EDB27	G_{15}	0	3	$^1/_4$	18	$^1/_4$	32	{}	3	{}	3	{}	3	{}	3
HB2^{-1} S0 [19]	B54FC690D3E81A27	03586CB79EADF214	G_9	0	3	$^1/_4$	18	$^1/_4$	32	{}	3	{}	3	{}	3	{}	3
HB2^{-1} S1 [19]	92F80C364D1E7BA5	03586CB7A49EF12D	G_{10}	0	3	$^1/_4$	18	$^1/_4$	32	{}	3	{}	3	{}	3	{}	3
HB2^{-1} S2 [19]	C30AB45F9E6D2781	03586CF1A49EDB27	G_{15}	0	3	$^1/_4$	18	$^1/_4$	32	{}	3	{}	3	{}	3	{}	3
HB2^{-1} S3 [19]	A76912C5348FDEB0	035879BEADF4C261	G_{14}	0	3	$^1/_4$	18	$^1/_4$	32	{0}	2	{}	3	{}	3	{}	3
DES S0-0 [33]	E4D12FB83A6C5907	035679CAED2B84F1		0	3	$^1/_2$	1	$^3/_8$	4	{}	3	{}	3	{}	3	{}	3
DES S0-1 [33]	0F74E2D1A6CB9538	035869B7CFA412DE		0	3	$^1/_2$	1	$^3/_8$	4	{}	3	{}	3	{}	3	{}	3
DES S0-2 [33]	41E8D62BFC973A50	035678BDCAF1942E		0	3	$^1/_2$	1	$^3/_8$	4	{}	3	{}	3	{}	3	{}	3
DES S0-3 [33]	FC8249175B3EA06D	035879AFBEC2D461		0	3	$^1/_2$	1	$^3/_8$	2	{2}	2	{}	3	{1}	2	{}	3
DES S1-0 [33]	F18E6B34972DC05A	035874BEF6ADC912		0	3	$^3/_8$	3	$^3/_8$	2	{}	3	{3}	3	{0}	2	{}	3
DES S1-1 [33]	3D47F28EC01A69B5	03586CF2ED971BA4		0	3	$^1/_2$	1	$^3/_8$	2	{3}	2	{}	3	{}	3	{2}	3
DES S1-2 [33]	0E7BA4D158C6932F	03567CEBADF84192		0	3	$^1/_2$	1	$^3/_8$	2	{}	3	{}	3	{}	3	{0,2}	2
DES S1-3 [33]	D8A13F42B67C05E9	0358BDC6E92F741A		0	3	$^3/_8$	6	$^3/_8$	4	{}	3	{}	3	{}	3	{}	3

Algorithm & Source	S-Box	Canonical PE	Lin. Eqv.	One	BN	DC		LC		Bit 0		Bit 1		Bit 2		Bit 3	
	0123456789ABCDEF	0123456789ABCDEF		Δ	#	p	n_d	ϵ	n_l	LS	deg	LS	deg	LS	deg	LS	deg
DES S2-0 [33]	A09E63F51DC7B428	03586DF47E92A1CB		0	3	$1/2$	1	$3/8$	3	{3}	2	{}	3	{}	3	{}	3
DES S2-1 [33]	D709346A285ECBF1	03586CB79EF2A14D		0	3	$1/2$	1	$3/8$	4	{3}	2	{2}	3	{}	3	{}	3
DES S2-2 [33]	D6498F30B12C5AE7	035879BED62FAC41		0	3	$1/2$	1	$3/8$	2	{1}	3	{}	3	{3}	2	{1}	3
DES S2-3 [33]	1AD069874FE3B52C	03589CF6DEA72B41		0	3	$1/2$	3	$3/8$	4	{}	3	{}	3	{}	3	{0,1}	2
DES S3-0 [33]	7DE3069A1285BC4F	035869BECFA412D7		0	3	$3/8$	6	$3/8$	4	{}	3	{}	3	{}	3	{}	3
DES S3-1 [33]	D8B56F03472C1AE9	035869BECFA412D7		0	3	$3/8$	6	$3/8$	4	{}	3	{}	3	{}	3	{}	3
DES S3-2 [33]	A690CB7DF13E5284	035869BECFA412D7		0	3	$3/8$	6	$3/8$	4	{}	3	{}	3	{}	3	{}	3
DES S3-3 [33]	3F06A1D8945BC72E	035869BECFA412D7		0	3	$3/8$	6	$3/8$	4	{}	3	{}	3	{}	3	{}	3
DES S4-0 [33]	2C417AB6853FD0E9	03586DF47EA1CB92		0	3	$1/2$	1	$3/8$	3	{}	3	{}	3	{0,2}	2	{}	3
DES S4-1 [33]	EB2C47D150FA3986	035869BECF241AD7		0	3	$3/8$	5	$3/8$	3	{}	3	{}	3	{}	3	{}	3
DES S4-2 [33]	421BAD78F9C5630E	03586DF2A49E1BC7		0	3	$3/8$	2	$3/8$	2	{}	3	{}	3	{}	3	{}	3
DES S4-3 [33]	B8C71E2D6F09A453	03586AB79CE2F14D		0	3	$3/8$	5	$3/8$	3	{}	3	{1}	3	{}	3	{}	3
DES S5-0 [33]	C1AF92680D34E75B	03586DF29EA4CB17		0	3	$1/4$	24	$3/8$	1	{}	3	{}	3	{}	3	{}	3
DES S5-1 [33]	AF427C9561DE0B38	0358749FDAB6E12C		0	3	$1/2$	1	$3/8$	3	{}	3	{}	3	{}	3	{}	3
DES S5-2 [33]	9EF528C3704A1DB6	035869BEA4CFD721		0	3	$3/8$	6	$3/8$	4	{}	3	{1}	3	{}	3	{}	3
DES S5-3 [33]	432C95FABE17608D	035874BEF6ADC912		0	3	$3/8$	3	$3/8$	2	{3}	2	{}	3	{0}	3	{}	3
DES S6-0 [33]	4B2EF08D3C975A61	03586CB79EF2A14D		0	3	$1/2$	1	$3/8$	4	{}	3	{2}	3	{0}	2	{}	3
DES S6-1 [33]	D0B7491AE35C2F86	03586DF47ECBA192		0	3	$1/2$	1	$3/8$	2	{}	3	{}	3	{}	3	{0,2}	2
DES S6-2 [33]	14BDC37EAF680592	035869BECFA412D7		0	3	$3/8$	6	$3/8$	4	{}	3	{}	3	{}	3	{}	3
DES S6-3 [33]	6BD814A7950FE23C	035869B7F4AD1EC2		0	3	$1/2$	2	$3/8$	5	{2}	3	{2}	3	{0}	3	{}	3
DES S7-0 [33]	D2846FB1A93E50C7	03589CE2F6AD4B71		0	3	$3/8$	4	$3/8$	1	{2}	3	{3}	2	{}	3	{}	3
DES S7-1 [33]	1FD8A374C56B0E92	03587ACF96EB4D21		0	3	$5/8$	1	$3/8$	5	{}	3	{}	3	{}	3	{2}	3
DES S7-2 [33]	7B419CE206ADF358	035869BEF4ADC217		0	3	$3/8$	5	$3/8$	3	{}	3	{1}	3	{0}	3	{}	3
DES S7-3 [33]	21E74A8DFC90356B	035678EB9F2CA4D1		0	3	$1/2$	1	$3/8$	4	{}	3	{}	3	{1,3}	2	{}	3

Algorithm	S-Box	Canonical PE	Lin.	One	BN	DC		LC		Bit 0		Bit 1		Bit 2		Bit 3	
& Source	0123456789ABCDEF	0123456789ABCDEF	Eqv.	Δ	#	p	n_d	ϵ	n_l	LS	deg	LS	deg	LS	deg	LS	deg
Serpent S0 [1]	38F1A65BED42709C	0358749EF62BADC1	G_2	0	3	$^1/_4$	24	$^1/_4$	36	{}	3	{}	3	{}	3	{1,2}	2
Serpent S1 [1]	FC27905A1BE86D34	035A7CB6D429E18F	G_0	0	3	$^1/_4$	24	$^1/_4$	36	{}	3	{}	3	{2,3}	2	{}	3
Serpent S2 [1]	86793CAFD1E40B52	035869A7BCE21FD4	G_1	0	3	$^1/_4$	24	$^1/_4$	36	{1,3}	2	{}	3	{}	3	{}	3
Serpent S3 [1]	0FB8C963D124A75E	03586CB79EADF214	G_9	0	3	$^1/_4$	18	$^1/_4$	32	{}	3	{}	3	{}	3	{}	3
Serpent S4 [1]	1F83C0B6254A9E7D	035879BEADF4C261	G_{14}	0	3	$^1/_4$	18	$^1/_4$	32	{2}	2	{}	3	{}	3	{}	3
Serpent S5 [1]	F52B4A9C03E8D671	035879BEADF4C261	G_{14}	0	3	$^1/_4$	18	$^1/_4$	32	{2}	2	{}	3	{}	3	{}	3
Serpent S6 [1]	72C5846BE91FD3A0	0358BC6FE9274AD1	G_1	0	3	$^1/_4$	24	$^1/_4$	36	{}	3	{1,2}	2	{}	3	{}	3
Serpent S7 [1]	1DF0E82B74CA9356	035869C7DAE41FB2	G_9	0	3	$^1/_4$	18	$^1/_4$	32	{}	3	{}	3	{}	3	{}	3
Serpent^{-1} S0 [1]	D3B0A65C1E47F982	035A7CB6D429E18F	G_0	0	3	$^1/_4$	24	$^1/_4$	36	{}	3	{}	3	{2,3}	2	{}	3
Serpent^{-1} S1 [1]	582EF6C3B4791DA0	0358749EF62BADC1	G_2	0	3	$^1/_4$	24	$^1/_4$	36	{}	3	{}	3	{}	3	{0,2}	2
Serpent^{-1} S2 [1]	C9F4BE12036D58A7	03586CB7AD9EF124	G_1	0	3	$^1/_4$	24	$^1/_4$	36	{0}	2	{}	3	{}	3	{}	3
Serpent^{-1} S3 [1]	09A7BE6D35C248F1	035869C7DAE41FB2	G_9	0	3	$^1/_4$	18	$^1/_4$	32	{}	3	{}	3	{}	3	{}	3
Serpent^{-1} S4 [1]	5083A97E2CB64FD1	03586CF1A49EDB27	G_{15}	0	3	$^1/_4$	18	$^1/_4$	32	{}	3	{}	3	{}	3	{}	3
Serpent^{-1} S5 [1]	8F2941DEB6537CA0	03586CF1A49EDB27	G_{15}	0	3	$^1/_4$	18	$^1/_4$	32	{}	3	{}	3	{}	3	{}	3
Serpent^{-1} S6 [1]	FA1D536049E72C8B	03567ABCD4E9812F	G_1	0	3	$^1/_4$	24	$^1/_4$	36	{}	3	{1,3}	2	{}	3	{}	3
Serpent^{-1} S7 [1]	306D9EF85CB7A142	03586CB79EADF214	G_9	0	3	$^1/_4$	18	$^1/_4$	32	{}	3	{}	3	{}	3	{}	3
GOST K1 [14]	4A92D80E6B1C7F53	01243DFA856B97EC		14	2	$^3/_8$	2	$^1/_4$	36	{}	3	{}	3	{}	3	{}	3
GOST K2 [14]	EB4C6DFA23810759	01254DC68BE3F79A		14	2	$^3/_8$	3	$^3/_8$	2	{}	3	{}	3	{}	3	{}	3
GOST K3 [14]	581DA342EFC7609B	01254EB97AF38D6C		14	2	$^3/_8$	5	$^3/_8$	3	{}	3	{}	3	{}	3	{}	3
GOST K4 [14]	7DA1089FE46CB253	0132586FC79DBEA4		8	2	$^3/_8$	5	$^3/_8$	3	{}	3	{}	3	{}	3	{3}	3
GOST K5 [14]	6C715FD84A9E03B2	0124B78EDF6CA359		12	2	$^1/_4$	21	$^3/_8$	1	{}	3	{}	3	{}	3	{}	3
GOST K6 [14]	4BA0721D36859CFE	01273CFAB85ED649		4	2	$^3/_8$	2	$^3/_8$	2	{}	3	{1}	3	{}	3	{}	3
GOST K7 [14]	DB413F590AE7682C	01256D8BCA47F3E9		12	2	$^1/_2$	1	$^3/_8$	2	{}	3	{}	3	{}	3	{}	3
GOST K8 [14]	1FD057A4923E6B8C	012546F8EB7A39CD		12	2	$^1/_2$	1	$^3/_8$	4	{}	3	{}	3	{}	3	{}	3

The Cryptographic Power of Random Selection

Matthias Krause and Matthias Hamann

Theoretical Computer Science
University of Mannheim
Mannheim, Germany

Abstract. The principle of random selection and the principle of adding biased noise are new paradigms used in several recent papers for constructing lightweight RFID authentication protocols. The cryptographic power of adding biased noise can be characterized by the hardness of the intensively studied Learning Parity with Noise (LPN) Problem. In analogy to this, we identify a corresponding learning problem for random selection and study its complexity. Given L secret linear functions $f_1, \ldots, f_L : \{0,1\}^n \longrightarrow \{0,1\}^a$, $RandomSelect(L, n, a)$ denotes the problem of learning $f_1, \ldots, f_L$ from values $(u, f_l(u))$, where the secret indices $l \in \{1, \ldots, L\}$ and the inputs $u \in \{0,1\}^n$ are randomly chosen by an oracle. We take an algebraic attack approach to design a nontrivial learning algorithm for this problem, where the running time is dominated by the time needed to solve full-rank systems of linear equations over $O(n^L)$ unknowns. In addition to the mathematical findings relating correctness and average running time of the suggested algorithm, we also provide an experimental assessment of our results.

Keywords: Lightweight Cryptography, Algebraic Attacks, Algorithmic Learning, Foundations and Complexity Theory.

1 Introduction

The very limited computational resources available in technical devices like RFID (radio frequency identification) tags implied an intensive search for lightweight authentication protocols in recent years. Standard block encryption functions like Triple-DES or AES seem to be not suited for such protocols largely because the amount of hardware to implement and the energy consumption to perform these operations is too high (see, e.g., [7] or [17] for more information on this topic).

This situation initiated two lines of research. The first resulted in proposals for new lightweight block encryption functions like PRESENT [4], KATAN and KTANTAN [10] by use of which standard block cipher-based authentication protocols can be made lightweight, too. A second line, and this line we follow in the paper, is to look for new cryptographic paradigms which allow for designing new symmetric lightweight authentication protocols. The two main suggestions discussed so far in the relevant literature are the principle of random selection and the principle of adding biased noise.

A. Miri and S. Vaudenay (Eds.): SAC 2011, LNCS 7118, pp. 134–150, 2012.

The principle of adding biased noise to the output of a linear basis function underlies the HB-protocol, originally proposed by Hopper and Blum [16] and later improved to HB^+ by Juels and Weis [17], as well as its variants $HB^\#$ and Trusted-HB (see [13] and [6], respectively). The protocols of the HB-family are provably secure against passive attacks with respect to the Learning Parity with Noise Conjecture but the problem to design HB-like protocols which are secure against active adversaries seems to be still unsolved (see, e.g., [14], [21], [12]).

The principle of random selection underlies, e.g., the CKK-protocols of Cichoń, Klonowski, and Kutyłowski [7] as well as the F_f-protocols in [3] and the Linear Protocols in [18]. It can be described as follows.

Suppose that the verifier Alice and the prover Bob run a challenge-response authentication protocol which uses a lightweight symmetric encryption operation $E : \{0,1\}^n \times \mathcal{K} \longrightarrow \{0,1\}^m$ of block length n, where $\mathcal{K}$ denotes an appropriate key space. Suppose further that E is weak in the sense that a passive adversary can efficiently compute the secret key $K \in \mathcal{K}$ from samples of the form $(u, E_K(u))$. This is obviously the case if E is linear.

Random selection denotes a method for compensating the weakness of E by using the following mode of operation. Instead of holding a single $K \in \mathcal{K}$, Alice and Bob share a collection $K_1, \ldots, K_L$ of keys from $\mathcal{K}$ as their common secret information, where $L > 1$ is a small constant. Upon receiving a challenge $u \in \{0,1\}^n$ from Alice, Bob chooses a random index $l \in \{1, \ldots, L\}$ and outputs the response $y = E(u, K_l)$. The verification of y with respect to u can be efficiently done by computing $E_{K_l}^{-1}(y)$ for all $l = 1, \ldots, L$.

The main problem this paper is devoted to is to determine the level of security which can be reached by applying this principle of random selection.

Note that the protocols introduced in [7], [3], and [18] are based on random selection of $GF(2)$-linear functions. The choice of linear basis functions is motivated by the fact that they can be implemented efficiently in hardware and have desirable pseudo-random properties with respect to a wide range of important statistical tests.

It is quite obvious that, with respect to passive adversaries, the security of protocols which use random selection of linear functions can be bounded from above by the complexity of the following learning problem referred to as *RandomSelect* (L, n, a): Learn $GF(2)$-linear functions $f_1, \ldots, f_L : \{0,1\}^n \longrightarrow \{0,1\}^a$ from values $(u, f_l(u))$, where the secret indices $l \in \{1, \ldots, L\}$ and the inputs $u \in \{0,1\}^n$ are randomly chosen by an oracle. In order to illustrate this notion, we sketch in appendix B how an efficient learning algorithm for *RandomSelect* (L, n, a) can be used for attacking the linear $(n, k, L)^+$-protocol described by Krause and Stegemann [18].

In this paper, we present an algebraic attack approach for solving the above learning problem *RandomSelect* (L, n, a). The running time of our algorithm is dominated by the effort necessary to solve a full-rank system of linear equations of $O(n^L)$ unknowns over the field $GF(2^a)$. Note that trivial approaches for solving *RandomSelect* (L, n, a) lead to a running time exponential in n.

In recent years, people from cryptography as well as from complexity and coding theory devoted much interest to the solution of learning problems around linear structures. Prominent examples in the context of lightweight cryptography are the works by Goldreich and Levin [15], Regev [22], and Arora and Ge [2]. But all these results are rather connected to the Learning Parity with Noise Problem. To the best of our knowledge, there are currently no nontrivial results with respect to the particular problem of learning randomly selected linear functions, which is studied in the present paper.

We are strongly convinced that the complexity of *RandomSelect* also defines a lower bound on the security achievable by protocols using random selection of linear functions, e.g., the improved $(n, k, L)^{++}$-protocol in [18]. Thus, the running time of our algorithm hints at how the parameters n, k, and L should be chosen in order to achieve an acceptable level of cryptographic security. Note that choosing $n = 128$ and $L = 8$ or $n = 256$ and $L = 4$, solving $RandomSelect\,(L, n, a)$ by means of our algorithm implies solving a system of around 2^{28} unknowns, which should be classified as sufficiently difficult in many practical situations.

The paper is organized as follows. In sections 2, 3, and 4, our learning algorithm, which conducts an algebraic attack in the spirit of [23], will be described in full detail. We represent the L linear basis functions as assignments A to a collection $X = \left(x_i^l\right)_{i=1,\ldots,n,l=1,\ldots,L}$ of variables taking values from the field $K = GF(2^a)$. We will then see that each example $(u, f_l\,(u))$ induces a degree-L equation of a certain type in the X-variables, which allows for reducing the learning problem $RandomSelect\,(L, n, a)$ to the problem of solving a system of degree-L equations over K. While, in general, the latter problem is known to be NP-hard, we can show an efficient way to solve this special kind of systems.

One specific problem of our approach is that, due to inherent symmetries of the degree-L equations, we can never reach a system which has full linear rank with respect to the corresponding monomials. In fact, this is the main difference between our learning algorithm and the well-known algebraic attack approaches for cryptanalyzing LFSR-based keystream generators (see, e.g., [20], [8], [9], [1]).

We circumvent this problem by identifying an appropriate set $T(n, L)$ of basis polynomials of degree at most L which allow to express the degree-L equations as linear equations over $T(n, L)$. The choice of $T(n, L)$ will be justified by Theorem 2 saying that if $|K| \geq L$, then the system of linear equations over $T(n, L)$ induced by all possible examples has full rank $|T(n, L)|$. (Note that according to Theorem 1, this is not true if $|K| < L$.) Our experiments, which are presented in section 5, indicate that if $|K| \geq L$, then with probability close to one, the number of examples needed to get a full rank system over $T(n, L)$ exceeds $|T(n, L)|$ only by a small constant factor. This implies that the effort to compute the unique *weak* solution $t\,(A) = (t_*\,(A))_{t_* \in T(n,L)}$ corresponding to the *strong* solution A equals the time needed to solve a system of $|T(n, L)|$ linear equations over K.

But in contrast to the algebraic attacks in [20], [8], [9], [1], we still have to solve another nontrivial problem, namely, to compute the *strong* solution A, which identifies the secret functions $f_1, \ldots, f_L$, from the unique weak solution. An efficient way to do this will complete our learning algorithm for

RandomSelect (L, n, a) in section 4. Finally, we also provide an experimental evaluation of our estimates using the computer algebra system Magma [5] in section 5 and conclude this paper with a discussion of the obtained results as well as an outlook on potentially fruitful future work in section 6.

2 The Approach

We fix positive integers n, a, L and secret $GF(2)$-linear functions $f_1, \dots, f_L : \{0,1\}^n \longrightarrow \{0,1\}^a$. The learner seeks to deduce specifications of $f_1, \dots, f_L$ from an oracle which outputs in each round an example $(u, w) \in \{0,1\}^n \times \{0,1\}^a$ in the following way. The oracle chooses independently and uniformly a random input $u \in_U \{0,1\}^n$, then chooses secretly a random index $l \in_U [L]$[1], computes $w = f_l(u)$ and outputs (u, w).

It is easy to see that *RandomSelect* can be efficiently solved in the case $L = 1$ by collecting examples $(u^1, w_1), \dots, (u^m, w_m)$ until $\{u^1, \dots, u^m\}$ contains a basis of $GF(2)^n$. The expected number of iterations until the above goal is reached can be approximated by $n + 1.61$ (see, e.g., the appendix in [11]).

We will now treat the case $L > 1$, which immediately yields a sharp rise in difficulty. First we need to introduce the notion of a *pure basis.*

Definition 1. *Let us call a set $\mathcal{V} = \{(u^1, w_1), \dots, (u^n, w_n)\}$ of n examples a pure basis, if $\{u^1, \dots, u^n\}$ is a basis of $GF(2)^n$ and there exists an index $l \in [L]$ such that $w_i = f_l(u^i)$ is satisfied for all $i = 1, \dots, n$.*

Recalling our preliminary findings, we can easily infer that for $m \in Ln + \Omega(1)$, a set of m random examples contains such a pure basis with high probability. Moreover, note that for a given set $\tilde{\mathcal{V}} = \{(\tilde{u}^1, \tilde{w}_1), \dots, (\tilde{u}^n, \tilde{w}_n)\}$ the pure basis property can be tested efficiently. The respective strategy makes use of the fact that in case of a random example (u, w), where $u = \bigoplus_{i \in I} \tilde{u}^i$ and $I \subseteq [n]$[2], the probability p that $w = \bigoplus_{i \in I} \tilde{w}_i$ holds is approximately L^{-1} if $\tilde{\mathcal{V}}$ is pure and at most $(2 \cdot L)^{-1}$ otherwise. The latter estimate is based on the trivial observation that if $\tilde{\mathcal{V}}$ is not a pure basis, it contains at least one tuple $(\tilde{u}^j, \tilde{w}_j)$, $j \in [n]$, which would have to be exchanged to make the set pure. As $j \in I$ holds true for half of all possible (but valid) examples, the probability that $w = \bigoplus_{i \in I} \tilde{w}_i$ is fulfilled although $\tilde{\mathcal{V}}$ is not pure can be bounded from above by $(2 \cdot L)^{-1}$.

However, it seems to be nontrivial to extract a pure basis from a set of $m \in Ln + \Omega(1)$ examples. Exhaustive search among all subsets of size n yields a running time exponential in n. This can be shown easily by applying Stirling's formula[3] to the corresponding binomial coefficient $\binom{m}{n}$.

---

[1] For a positive integer N, we denote by $[N]$ the set $\{1, \dots, N\}$.

[2] Let $B = \{v^1, \dots, v^n\}$ denote a basis spanning the vector space V. It is a simple algebraic fact that every vector $v \in V$ has a unique representation $I \subseteq [n]$ over B, i.e., $v = \bigoplus_{i \in I} v^i$.

[3] Stirling's formula is an approximation for large factorials and commonly written $n! \approx \sqrt{2\pi n} \left(\frac{n}{e}\right)^n$.

We exhibit the following alternative idea for solving *RandomSelect* (L, n, a) for $L > 1$. Let $e^1, \ldots, e^n$ denote the standard basis of the $GF(2)$-vector space $\{0,1\}^n$ and keep in mind that $\{0,1\}^n = GF(2)^n \subseteq K^n$, where K denotes the field $GF(2^a)$. For all $i = 1, \ldots, n$ and $l = 1, \ldots, L$ let us denote by x_i^l a variable over K representing $f_l\left(e^i\right)$. Analogously, let A denote the $(n \times L)$-matrix with coefficients in K completely defined by $A_{i,l} = f_l\left(e^i\right)$. Henceforth, we will refer to A as a *strong solution* of our learning problem, thereby indicating the fact that its coefficients fully characterize the underlying secret $GF(2)$-linear functions $f_1, \ldots, f_L$.

Observing an example (u, w), where $u = \bigoplus_{i \in I} e^i$, the only thing we know is that there is some index $l \in [L]$ such that $w = \bigoplus_{i \in I} A_{i,l}$. This is equivalent to the statement that A is a solution of the following degree-L equation in the x_i^l-variables.

$$\left(\bigoplus_{i \in I} x_i^1 \oplus w\right) \cdot \ldots \cdot \left(\bigoplus_{i \in I} x_i^L \oplus w\right) = 0. \tag{1}$$

Note that equation (1) can be rewritten as

$$\bigoplus_{J \subseteq I, 1 \leq |J| \leq L'} \bigoplus_{j=|J|}^{L} w^{L-j} t_{J,j} = w^L, \tag{2}$$

$L' = \min\{L, |I|\}$, where the basis polynomials $t_{J,j}$ are defined as

$$t_{J,j} = \bigoplus_{g, |dom(g)|=j, im(g)=J} m_g$$

for all $J \subseteq [n]$, $1 \leq |J| \leq L$, and all j, $|J| \leq j \leq L$. The corresponding monomials m_g are in turn defined as

$$m_g = \prod_{l \in dom(g)} x_{g(l)}^l$$

for all partial mappings g from $[L]$ to $[n]$, where $dom\,(g)$ denotes the domain of g and $im\,(g)$ denotes its image.

Let $T\,(n, L) = \{t_{J,j} \mid J \subseteq [n], 1 \leq |J| \leq L, |J| \leq j \leq L\}$ denote the set of all basis polynomials $t_{J,j}$ which may appear as part of equation (2). Moreover, we define

$$\Phi\,(a, b) = \sum_{i=0}^{b} \binom{a}{i}$$

for integers $0 \leq b \leq a$ and write

$$
\begin{aligned}
|T(n,L)| &= \sum_{j=1}^{L} \binom{n}{j} (L-j+1) \\
&= (L+1)(\Phi(n,L)-1) - \sum_{j=1}^{L} n \binom{n-1}{j-1} \\
&= (L+1)(\Phi(n,L)-1) - n\Phi(n-1,L-1).
\end{aligned} \tag{3}
$$

Consequently, each set of examples $\mathcal{V} = \{(u^1, w_1), \ldots, (u^m, w_m)\}$ yields a system of m degree-L equations in the x_i^l-variables, which can be written as m K-linear equations in the $t_{J,j}$-variables. In particular, the strong solution $A \in K^{n \times L}$ satisfies the relation

$$
M(\mathcal{V}) \circ t(A) = W(\mathcal{V}), \tag{4}
$$

where

- $K^{n \times L}$ denotes the set of all $(n \times L)$-matrices with coefficients from K,
- $M(\mathcal{V})$ is an $(m \times |T(n,L)|)$-matrix built by the m linear equations of type (2) corresponding to the examples in $\mathcal{V}$,
- $W(\mathcal{V}) \in K^m$ is defined by $W(\mathcal{V})_i = w_i^L$[4] for all $i = 1, \ldots, m$,
- $t(A) \in K^{T(n,L)}$ is defined by $t(A) = (t_{J,j}(A))_{J \subseteq [n], 1 \le |J| \le L, |J| \le j \le L}$.

Note that in section 3, we will treat the special structure of $M(\mathcal{V})$ in further detail. Independently, it is a basic fact from linear algebra that if $M(\mathcal{V})$ has full column rank, then the linear system (4) has the unique solution $t(A)$, which we will call the *weak solution*.

Our learning algorithm proceeds as follows:

(1) Grow a set of examples $\mathcal{V}$ until $M(\mathcal{V})$ has full column rank $|T(n,L)|$.
(2) Compute the unique solution $t(A)$ of system (4), i.e., the weak solution of our learning problem, by using an appropriate algorithm which solves systems of linear equations over K.
(3) Compute the strong solution A from $t(A)$.

We discuss the correctness and running time of steps (1) and (2) in section 3 and an approach for step (3) in section 4.

3 On Computing a Weak Solution

Let n and L be arbitrarily fixed such that $2 \le L \le n$ holds. Moreover, let $\mathcal{V} \subseteq \{0,1\}^n \times K$ denote a given set of examples obtained through linear functions

[4] Keep in mind that, unlike for the previously introduced K-variables $x_s^1, \ldots, x_s^L$, $s \in [n]$, the superscripted L in case of w_i^L is not an index but an exponent. See, e.g., equation (2).

$f_1, \ldots, f_L : \{0,1\}^n \longrightarrow K$, where $K = GF(2^a)$. By definition, for each tuple $(u, w) \in \mathcal{V}$, where $u = \bigoplus_{i \in I} e^i$ and $I \subseteq [n]$ denotes the unique representation of u over the standard basis $e^1, \ldots, e^n$ of $\{0,1\}^n$, the relation $w = f_{l'}(u) = \bigoplus_{i \in I} f_{l'}(e^i)$ is bound to hold for some $l' \in [L]$. We denote by $K^{\min} \subseteq K$ the subfield of K generated by all values $f_l(e^i)$, where $l \in [L]$ and $i \in [n]$. Note that $w \in K^{\min}$ for all examples (u, w) induced by $f_1, \ldots, f_l$.

In the following, we show that our learning algorithm is precluded from succeeding if the secret linear functions $f_1, \ldots, f_L$ happen to be of a certain type or if K itself lacks in size.

Theorem 1. *If $|K^{\min}| < L$, then the columns of $M(\mathcal{V})$ are linearly dependent for any set $\mathcal{V}$ of examples, i.e., a unique weak solution does not exist.*

Proof: Let n, K, L, and $f_1, \ldots, f_L$ be arbitrarily fixed such that $2 \leq |K^{\min}| < L \leq n$ holds and let $\mathcal{V}$ denote a corresponding set of examples. Obviously, for each tuple $(u, w) \in \mathcal{V}$, where $u = \bigoplus_{i \in I} e^i$ and $I \subseteq [n]$, the two cases $1 \in I$ and $1 \notin I$ can be differentiated.

If $1 \in I$ holds, then it follows straightforwardly from equation (2) that the coefficient with coordinates (u, w) and $t_{\{1\},(L-1)}$ in $M(\mathcal{V})$ equals $w^{L-(L-1)} = w^1$. Analogously, the coefficient with coordinates (u, w) and $t_{\{1\},(L-|K^{\min}|)}$ in $M(\mathcal{V})$ equals $w^{L-(L-|K^{\min}|)} = w^{|K^{\min}|}$. Note that $t_{\{1\},(L-|K^{\min}|)}$ is a valid (and different) basis polynomial as

$$|\{1\}| = 1 \leq (L - |K^{\min}|) \leq (L-2) < (L-1) < L$$

holds for $2 \leq |K^{\min}| < L$. As $K^{\min} \subseteq K$ is a finite field of characteristic 2, we can apply Lagrange's theorem and straightforwardly conclude that the relation $z^1 = z^{|K^{\min}|}$ holds for all $z \in K^{\min}$ (including $0 \in K^{\min}$). Hence, if $1 \in I$ holds for an example (u, w), then in the corresponding row of $M(\mathcal{V})$ the two coefficients indexed by $t_{\{1\},(L-1)}$ and $t_{\{1\},(L-|K^{\min}|)}$ are always equal.

If $1 \notin I$ holds for an example (u, w), then the coefficient with coordinates (u, w) and $t_{\{1\},(L-1)}$ in $M(\mathcal{V})$ as well as the coefficient with coordinates (u, w) and $t_{\{1\},(L-|K^{\min}|)}$ in $M(\mathcal{V})$ equals 0.

Consequently, if $|K^{\min}| < L$ holds, then the column of $M(\mathcal{V})$ indexed by $t_{\{1\},(L-1)}$ equals the column indexed by $t_{\{1\},(L-|K|)}$ for any set $\mathcal{V}$ of examples, i.e., $M(\mathcal{V})$ can never achieve full column rank. □

Corollary 1. *If K is chosen such that $|K| < L$, then the columns of $M(\mathcal{V})$ are linearly dependent for any set $\mathcal{V}$ of examples, i.e., a unique weak solution does not exist.* □

While we are now aware of a lower bound for the size of K, it yet remains to prove that step (1) of our learning algorithm is, in fact, correct. This will be achieved by introducing the $((2^n |K|) \times |T(n, L)|)$-matrix $M^* = M(\{0,1\}^n \times K)$, which clearly corresponds to the set of *all* possible examples, and showing that M^* has full column rank $|T(n, L)|$ if $L \leq |K|$ holds.

However, be careful not to misinterpret this finding, which is presented below in the form of Theorem 2. The fact that M^* has full column rank $|T(n, L)|$ by no means implies that, eventually, this will also hold for $M(\mathcal{V})$ if only the corresponding set of observations $\mathcal{V}$ is large enough. In particular, the experimental results summarized in section 5 (see, e.g., table 1) show that there are cases in which the rank of $M(\mathcal{V})$ is always smaller than $|T(n, L)|$, even if $L \leq |K|$ is satisfied and $\mathcal{V}$ equals the set $\{(u, f_l(u)) \mid u \in \{0,1\}^n, l \in [L]\} \subseteq \{0,1\}^n \times K$[5] of all possible *valid* examples.

Still, as a counterpart of Theorem 1, the following theorem proves the possibility of existence of a unique weak solution for arbitrary parameters n and L satisfying $2 \leq L \leq n$. In other words, choosing $T(n, L)$ to be the set of basis polynomials does not necessarily lead to systems of linear equations which cannot be solved uniquely.

Theorem 2. *Let n and L be arbitrarily fixed such that $2 \leq L \leq n$ holds. If K satisfies $L \leq |K|$, then M^* has full column rank $|T(n, L)|$.*

Proof: We denote by $\mathcal{Z}(n)$ the set of monomials $z_0^{d_0} \cdot \ldots \cdot z_n^{d_n}$, where $0 \leq d_i \leq |K| - 1$ for $i = 0, \ldots, n$. Obviously, the total number of such monomials is $|\mathcal{Z}(n)| = |K|^{n+1}$. Let us recall the aforementioned fact that the relation $z^1 = z^{|K|}$ holds for all $z \in K$ (including $0 \in K$). This straightforwardly implies that each monomial in the variables $z_0, \ldots, z_n$ is (as a function from K^{n+1} to K) equivalent to a monomial in $\mathcal{Z}(n)$. Let $\mu_{J,j}$ denote the monomial $\mu_{J,j} = z_0^{L-j} \prod_{r \in J} z_r$ for all $J \subseteq [n]$ and j, $0 \leq j \leq L$. The following lemma can be easily verified:

Lemma 2.1. *For all $J \subseteq [n]$, $1 \leq |J| \leq L$, and j, $|J| \leq j \leq L$, and examples $(u, w) \in \{0,1\}^n \times K$, it holds that $\mu_{J,j}(w, u)$ equals the coefficient in M^* which has the coordinates (u, w) and $t_{J,j}$.* □

For $i = 1, \ldots, |K|$, we denote by k_i the i-th element of the finite field K. Moreover, we suppose the convention that $0^0 = 1$ in K. Let (u, w) be an example defined as above and keep in mind that we are treating the case $L \leq |K|$. It should be observed that the coefficients in the corresponding equation of type (2) are given by w^{L-j}, where $1 \leq j \leq L$. Thus, the set of possible exponents $\{L - j \mid 1 \leq j \leq L\}$ is bounded from above by $(L-1) < L \leq |K|$. It follows straightforwardly from Lemma 2.1 that the (distinct) columns of M^* are columns of the matrix $W \otimes B^{\otimes n}$, where

$$W = \left(k_i^j\right)_{i=1,\ldots,|K|, j=0,\ldots,|K|-1} \quad \text{and} \quad B = \begin{bmatrix} 1 & 0 \\ 1 & 1 \end{bmatrix}.$$

As W and B are regular, $W \otimes B^{\otimes n}$ is regular, too. This, in turn, implies that the columns of M^* are linearly independent, thus proving Theorem 2. □

[5] It can be seen easily that for random linear functions $f_1, \ldots, f_L$, the relation $\{(u, f_l(u)) \mid u \in \{0,1\}^n, l \in [L]\} \neq \{0,1\}^n \times K$ will always hold if $L < |K|$ and is still very likely to hold if $L = |K|$.

We will see in section 4 that for $|K| \in O\left(dnL^4\right)$, the strong solution can be reconstructed from the weak solution in time $n^{O(L)}$ with error probability at most d^{-1}. Furthermore, section 5 will feature an experimental assessment of the number of random (valid) observations needed until $M\left(\mathcal{V}\right)$ achieves full column rank $|T\left(n, L\right)|$ for various combinations of n, L, and K (see table 2).

4 On Computing a Strong Solution from the Unique Weak Solution

Let n, K, L, and $f_1, \ldots, f_L$ be defined as before. Remember that the goal of our learning algorithm is to compute a strong solution fully characterized by the L sets $\left\{\left(e^i, f_l\left(e^i\right)\right) \mid i \in [n]\right\}$, $l = 1, \ldots, L$, where e^i denotes the i-th element of the standard basis of $GF(2)^n$ and $f_l\left(e^i\right) = x_i^l \in K$. Obviously, this information can equivalently be expressed as a matrix $A \in K^{n \times L}$ defined by $A_{i,\cdot} = \left(x_i^1, \ldots, x_i^L\right)$ for all $i = 1, \ldots, n$.

Hence, we have to solve the following problem: Compute the matrix $A \in K^{n \times L}$ from the information $t\left(A\right)$, where

$$t\left(A\right) = \left(t_{J,j}\left(A\right)\right)_{J \subseteq [n], 1 \leq |J| \leq L, |J| \leq j \leq L}$$

is the unique weak solution determined previously. But before we lay out how (and under which conditions) a strong solution A can be found, we need to introduce the following two definitions along with an important theorem linking them:

Definition 2. *Let for all vectors $x \in K^L$ the signature $sgt\left(x\right)$ of x be defined as $sgt\left(x\right) = \left(|x|_k\right)_{k \in K}$, where $|x|_k$ denotes the number of components of x which equal k.*

Furthermore, consider the following new family of polynomials:

Definition 3. *a) For all $L \geq 1$ and $j \geq 0$ let the simple symmetric polynomial s_j over the variables $x_1, \ldots, x_L$ be defined by $s_0 = 1$ and*

$$s_j = \bigoplus_{S \subseteq [L], |S| = j} m_S,$$

where $m_S = \prod_{i \in S} x_i$ for all $S \subseteq [L]$. Moreover, we denote

$$s\left(x\right) = \left(s_0\left(x\right), s_1\left(x\right), \ldots, s_L\left(x\right)\right)$$

for all $x \in K^L$.

b) Let n, L, $1 \leq L \leq n$, hold as well as j, $0 \leq j \leq L$, and $J \subseteq [n]$. The symmetric polynomial $s_{J,j} : K^{n \times L} \longrightarrow K$ is defined by

$$s_{J,j}\left(A\right) = s_j\left(\bigoplus_{i \in J} A_{i,\cdot}\right)$$

for all matrices $A \in K^{n \times L}$. *Moreover, we denote*

$$s_J(A) = (s_{J,0}(A), \dots, s_{J,L}(A)).$$

The concept of signatures introduced in Definition 2 and the family of simple symmetric polynomials described in Definition 3 will now be connected by the following theorem:

Theorem 3. *For all* $L \geq 1$ *and* $x, x' \in K^L$ *it holds that* $s(x) = s(x')$ *if and only if* $sgt(x) = sgt(x')$.

Proof: See appendix A.

Building on this result, we can then prove the following proposition, which is of vital importance for computing the strong solution A on the basis of the corresponding weak solution $t(A)$:

Theorem 4. *Let* $A \in K^{n \times L}$ *and* $t(A)$ *be defined as before. For each subset* $I \subseteq [n]$ *of rows of* A*, the signature of the sum of these rows, i.e.,* $sgt\left(\bigoplus_{i \in I} A_{i,\cdot}\right)$*, can be computed by solely using information derived from* $t(A)$*, in particular, without knowing the underlying matrix* A *itself.*

Proof: We first observe that the s-polynomials can be written as linear combinations of the t-polynomials. Trivially, the relation $t_{\{i\},j} = s_{\{i\},j}$ holds for all $i \in [n]$ and j, $1 \leq j \leq L$. Moreover, for all $I \subseteq [n]$, $|I| > 1$, it holds that

$$s_{I,j} = \bigoplus_{Q \subseteq I, 1 \leq |Q| \leq j} \left(\bigoplus_{g:[L] \longrightarrow [n], |dom(g)|=j, im(g)=Q} m_g \right) = \bigoplus_{Q \subseteq I, 1 \leq |Q| \leq j} t_{Q,j}. \quad (5)$$

Note that for all $J \subseteq [n]$ and j, $|J| \leq j \leq L$, relation (5) implies

$$t_{J,j} = s_{J,j} \oplus \bigoplus_{Q \subset J} t_{Q,j}. \quad (6)$$

By an inductive argument, we obtain from relation (6) that the converse is also true, i.e., the t-polynomials can be written as linear combinations of the s-polynomials.

We have seen so far that given $t(A)$, we are able to compute $s_{I,j}$ for all j, $1 \leq j \leq L$, and each subset $I \subseteq [n]$ of rows of A. Recall

$$s_{I,j}(A) = s_j\left(\bigoplus_{i \in I} A_{i,\cdot}\right) \quad \text{and} \quad s_I(A) = (s_{I,0}(A), \dots, s_{I,L}(A))$$

from Definition 3 and let $x \in K^L$ be defined by $x = \bigoplus_{i \in I} A_{i,\cdot}$. It can be easily seen that $s_I(A) = s(x)$ holds.

In conjunction with Theorem 3, this straightforwardly implies the validity of Theorem 4. □

Naturally, it remains to assess the degree of usefulness of this information when it comes to reconstructing the strong solution $A \in K^{n \times L}$. In the following, we will prove that if K is large enough, then with high probability, A can be completely (up to column permutations) and efficiently derived from the signatures of all single rows of A and the signatures of all sums of pairs of rows of A:

Theorem 5. *Let $K = GF(2^a)$ fulfill $|K| \geq \frac{1}{4} \cdot d \cdot n \cdot L^4$, i.e., $a \geq \log(n) + \log(d) + 4\log(L) - 2$. Then, for a random matrix $A \in_U K^{n \times L}$, the following is true with a probability of approximately at least $\left(1 - \frac{1}{d}\right)$: A can be completely reconstructed from the signatures $sgt(A_{i,\cdot})$, $1 \leq i \leq n$, and $sgt(A_{i,\cdot} \oplus A_{j,\cdot})$, $1 \leq i < j \leq n$.*

Proof: See appendix A.

As we have seen now that, under certain conditions, it is possible to fully reconstruct the strong solution A by solely resorting to information obtained from the weak solution $t(A)$, we can proceed to actually describe a conceivable approach for step (3) of the learning algorithm:

We choose a constant error parameter d and an exponent a, i.e., $K = GF(2^a)$, in such a way that Theorem 5 can be applied. Note that $L \leq n$ and $|K| \in n^{O(1)}$. In a pre-computation, we generate two databases DB_1 and DB_2 of size $n^{O(L)}$. While DB_1 acts as a lookup table with regard to the one-to-one relation between $s(x)$ and $sgt(x)$ for all $x \in K^L$, we use DB_2 to store all triples of signatures $S, S', \tilde{S}$ for which there is exactly one solution pair $x, y \in K^L$ fulfilling $sgt(x) = S$ and $sgt(y) = S'$ as well as $sgt(x \oplus y) = \tilde{S}$.

Given $t(A)$, i.e., the previously determined weak solution, we then compute $sgt(A_{i,\cdot})$ for all i, $1 \leq i \leq n$, and $sgt(A_{i,\cdot} \oplus A_{j,\cdot})$ for all i, j, $1 \leq i < j \leq n$, in time $n^{O(1)}$ by using DB_1 and relation (5), which can be found in the proof of Theorem 4. According to Theorem 5, it is now possible to reconstruct A by the help of database DB_2 with probability at least $1 - \frac{1}{d}$.

5 Experimental Results

To showcase the detailed workings of our learning algorithm as well as to evaluate its efficiency at a practical level, we created a complete implementation using the computer algebra system Magma. In case of success, it takes approximately 90 seconds on standard PC hardware (Intel i7, 2.66 GHz, with 6 GB RAM) to compute the unique strong solution on the basis of a set of 10,000 randomly generated examples for $n = 10$, $a = 3$ (i.e., $K = GF(2^a)$), and $L = 5$. Relating to this, we performed various simulations in order to assess the corresponding probabilities, which were already discussed in sections 3 and 4 from a theoretical point of view.

The experimental results summarized in table 1 clearly suggest that if $|K|$ is only slightly larger than the number L of secret linear functions, then in all likelihood, $M(\mathcal{V})$ will eventually reach full (column) rank $|T(n, L)|$, thus allowing for the computation of a unique weak solution. Moreover, in accordance with

Table 1. An estimate of the rank of $M(\mathcal{V})$ on the basis of all possible valid observations for up to 10,000 randomly generated instances of *RandomSelect* (L, n, a). For each choice of parameters, $|T(n,L)|$ denotes number of columns of $M(\mathcal{V})$ as defined in section 2 and listed in table 2.

Parameters			Performed Iterations				
			Rank of $M(\mathcal{V}) < \lvert T(n,L)\rvert$		Rank of $M(\mathcal{V}) = \lvert T(n,L)\rvert$		Total
n	K	L	Number	Ratio	Number	Ratio	Number
4	$GF(2^2)$	2	37	0.37 %	9,963	99.63 %	10,000
4	$GF(2^2)$	3	823	8.23 %	9,177	91.77 %	10,000
4	$GF(2^2)$	4	7,588	75.88 %	2,412	24.12 %	10,000
5	$GF(2^2)$	4	4,556	45.56 %	5,444	54.44 %	10,000
5	$GF(2^2)$	5	10,000	100.00 %	0	0.00 %	10,000
6	$GF(2^3)$	4	0	0.00 %	1,000	100.00 %	1,000
8	$GF(2^3)$	4	0	0.00 %	1,000	100.00 %	1,000
8	$GF(2^3)$	6	0	0.00 %	100	100.00 %	100
8	$GF(2^3)$	7	0	0.00 %	100	100.00 %	100
8	$GF(2^3)$	8	0	0.00 %	100	100.00 %	100
9	$GF(2^3)$	8	0	0.00 %	10	100.00 %	10
9	$GF(2^3)$	9	10	100.00 %	0	0.00 %	10

Corollary 1, the columns of $M(\mathcal{V})$ were always linearly dependent in the case of $n = 5$, $K = GF(2^2)$ and $L = 5$, i.e., $|K| = 4 < 5 = L$. A further analysis of the underlying data revealed in addition that, for arbitrary combinations of n, K, and L, the matrix $M(\mathcal{V})$ never reached full column rank if at least two of the corresponding L random linear functions $f_1, \ldots, f_L$ were identical during an iteration of our experiments. Note that, on the basis of the current implementation, it was not possible to continue table 1 for larger parameter sizes because, e.g., in the case of $n = 8$, $K = GF(2^3)$ and $L = 7$, performing as few as 100 iterations already took more than 85 minutes on the previously described computer system.

Table 2 features additional statistical data with respect to the number of examples needed (in case of success) until the matrix $M(\mathcal{V})$ reaches full column rank $|T(n,L)|$. Please note that, in contrast to the experiments underlying table 1, such examples $(u, f_l(u))$ are generated iteratively and independently choosing random pairs $u \in_U \{0,1\}^n$ and $l \in_U [L]$, i.e., they are not processed in their canonical order but observed randomly (and also repeatedly) to simulate a practical passive attack. While we have seen previously that for most choices of n, K and L, the matrix $M(\mathcal{V})$ is highly likely to eventually reach full column rank, the experimental results summarized in table 2, most notably the observed p-quantiles, strongly suggest that our learning algorithm for *RandomSelect* (L, n, a) will also be able to efficiently construct a corresponding LES which allows for computing a unique weak solution.

It remains to clear up the question, to what extent Theorem 5 reflects reality concerning the probability of a random $(n \times L)$-matrix over K being $sgt(2)$-identifiable (see Definitions 5.1 and 5.2 in the proof of Theorem 5), which is necessary and sufficient for the success of step (3) of our learning algorithm. Our

Table 2. An estimate of the number of randomly generated examples $(u, f_l(u))$ which have to be processed (in case of success) until the matrix $M(\mathcal{V})$ reaches full column rank $|T(n,L)|$. Given a probability p, we denote by Q_p the p-quantile of the respective sample.

Parameters				Number of Random Examples until $\text{Rank}(M(\mathcal{V})) = \lvert T(n,L) \rvert$							
n	K	L	$\lvert T(n,L) \rvert$	Avg.	Max.	Min.	$Q_{0.1}$	$Q_{0.25}$	$Q_{0.5}$	$Q_{0.75}$	$Q_{0.9}$
4	$GF(2^2)$	1	4	5.5	18	4	4	4	5	6	8
4	$GF(2^2)$	2	14	24.4	93	14	18	20	23	27	32
4	$GF(2^2)$	3	28	71.8	273	33	51	58	67	81	99
4	$GF(2^2)$	4	43	226.2	701	95	147	175	211	261	317
5	$GF(2^2)$	4	75	218.5	591	140	176	192	211	237	263
6	$GF(2^3)$	4	124	201.6	318	162	184	192	200	211	220
8	$GF(2^3)$	4	298	378.7	419	345	365	371	378	386	393
8	$GF(2^3)$	6	762	1401.6	1565	1302	1342	1364	1405	1427	1458
8	$GF(2^3)$	7	1016	2489.7	2731	2275	2369	2417	2477	2547	2645
8	$GF(2^3)$	8	1271	5255.3	7565	4302	4706	4931	5227	5557	5706
9	$GF(2^3)$	8	2295	6266.1	6553	6027	6078	6136	6199	6415	6504

Table 3. An estimate of the ratio of $sgt(2)$-identifiable $(n \times L)$-matrices over K

Parameters			Performed Iterations (i.e., randomly chosen $A \in_U K^{n \times L}$)				
			A **not** $sgt(2)$-identifiable		A **was** $sgt(2)$-identifiable		Total
n	K	L	Number	Ratio	Number	Ratio	Number
4	$GF(2^2)$	2	0	0.00 %	10,000	100.00 %	10,000
4	$GF(2^2)$	3	69	0.69 %	9,931	99.31 %	10,000
4	$GF(2^2)$	4	343	3.43 %	9,657	96.57 %	10,000
6	$GF(2^3)$	4	0	0.00 %	10,000	100.00 %	10,000
8	$GF(2^3)$	4	0	0.00 %	10,000	100.00 %	10,000
8	$GF(2^3)$	6	0	0.00 %	1,000	100.00 %	1,000
8	$GF(2^3)$	7	0	0.00 %	1,000	100.00 %	1,000
8	$GF(2^3)$	8	0	0.00 %	100	100.00 %	100
9	$GF(2^3)$	8	0	0.00 %	100	100.00 %	100

corresponding simulations yielded table 3, which immediately suggests that even for much smaller values of $|K|$ than those called for in Theorem 5, a strong solution $A \in_U K^{n \times L}$ can be completely reconstructed from the signatures $sgt(A_{i,\cdot})$, $1 \le i \le n$, and $sgt(A_{i,\cdot} \oplus A_{j,\cdot})$, $1 \le i < j \le n$. In conjunction with the experimental results concerning the rank of $M(\mathcal{V})$, this, in turn, implies that our learning algorithm will efficiently lead to success in the vast majority of cases.

6 Discussion

The running time of our learning algorithm for *RandomSelect* (L, n, a) is dominated by the complexity of solving a system of linear equations with $|T(n,L)|$ unknowns. Our hardness conjecture is that this complexity also constitutes a lower bound to the complexity of *RandomSelect* (L, n, a) itself, which would imply acceptable cryptographic security for parameter choices like $n = 128$ and $L = 8$ or $n = 256$ and $L = 6$. The experimental results summarized in the previous section clearly support this view. Consequently, employing the principle of random selection to design new symmetric lightweight authentication protocols might result in feasible alternatives to current HB-based cryptographic schemes.

A problem of independent interest is to determine the complexity of reconstructing an $sgt(r)$-identifiable matrix A from the signatures of all sums of at most r rows of A. Note that this problem is wedded to determining the complexity of *RandomSelect* (L, n, a) with respect to an *active* learner, who is able to receive examples (u, w) for inputs u of his choice, where $w = f_l(u)$ and $l \in_U [L]$ is randomly chosen by the oracle. It is easy to see that such learners can efficiently compute $sgt(f_1(u), \ldots, f_L(u))$ by repeatedly asking for u. As the approach for reconstructing A which was outlined in section 4 needs a data structure of size exponential in L, it would be interesting to know if there are corresponding algorithms of time and space costs polynomial in L.

From a theoretical point of view, another open problem is to determine the probability that a random $(n \times L)$-matrix over K is $sgt(r)$-identifiable for some r, $2 \leq r \leq L$. Based on the results of our computer experiments, it appears more than likely that the lower bound derived in Theorem 5 is far from being in line with reality and that identifiable matrices occur with much higher probability for fields K of significantly smaller size.

References

1. Armknecht, F., Krause, M.: Algebraic Attacks on Combiners with Memory. In: Boneh, D. (ed.) CRYPTO 2003. LNCS, vol. 2729, pp. 162–175. Springer, Heidelberg (2003)
2. Arora, S., Ge, R.: New algorithms for learning in presence of errors (submitted, 2010), `http://www.cs.princeton.edu/~rongge/LPSN.pdf`
3. Blass, E.-O., Kurmus, A., Molva, R., Noubir, G., Shikfa, A.: The F_f-family of protocols for RFID-privacy and authentication. In: 5th Workshop on RFID Security, RFIDSec 2009 (2009)
4. Bogdanov, A., Knudsen, L.R., Leander, G., Paar, C., Poschmann, A., Robshaw, M.J.B., Seurin, Y., Vikkelsoe, C.: PRESENT: An Ultra-Lightweight Block Cipher. In: Paillier, P., Verbauwhede, I. (eds.) CHES 2007. LNCS, vol. 4727, pp. 450–466. Springer, Heidelberg (2007)
5. Bosma, W., Cannon, J., Playoust, C.: The Magma algebra system. I. The user language. J. Symbolic Comput. 24(3-4), 235–265 (1997)
6. Bringer, J., Chabanne, H.: Trusted-HB: A low cost version of HB^+ secure against a man-in-the-middle attack. IEEE Trans. Inform. Theor. 54, 4339–4342 (2008)
7. Cichoń, J., Klonowski, M., Kutyłowski, M.: Privacy Protection for RFID with Hidden Subset Identifiers. In: Indulska, J., Patterson, D.J., Rodden, T., Ott, M. (eds.) PERVASIVE 2008. LNCS, vol. 5013, pp. 298–314. Springer, Heidelberg (2008)
8. Courtois, N.: Fast Algebraic Attacks on Stream Ciphers with Linear Feedback. In: Boneh, D. (ed.) CRYPTO 2003. LNCS, vol. 2729, pp. 176–194. Springer, Heidelberg (2003)

9. Courtois, N., Meier, W.: Algebraic Attacks on Stream Ciphers with Linear Feedback. In: Biham, E. (ed.) EUROCRYPT 2003. LNCS, vol. 2656, pp. 345–359. Springer, Heidelberg (2003)
10. De Cannière, C., Dunkelman, O., Knežević, M.: KATAN and KTANTAN — A Family of Small and Efficient Hardware-Oriented Block Ciphers. In: Clavier, C., Gaj, K. (eds.) CHES 2009. LNCS, vol. 5747, pp. 272–288. Springer, Heidelberg (2009)
11. Gołębiewski, Z., Majcher, K., Zagórski, F.: Attacks on CKK Family of RFID Authentication Protocols. In: Coudert, D., Simplot-Ryl, D., Stojmenovic, I. (eds.) ADHOC-NOW 2008. LNCS, vol. 5198, pp. 241–250. Springer, Heidelberg (2008)
12. Frumkin, D., Shamir, A.: Untrusted-HB: Security vulnerabilities of Trusted-HB. Cryptology ePrint Archive, Report 2009/044 (2009), `http://eprint.iacr.org`
13. Gilbert, H., Robshaw, M.J.B., Seurin, Y.: $HB^{\#}$: Increasing the security and efficiency of HB^{+}. In: Smart, N.P. (ed.) EUROCRYPT 2008. LNCS, vol. 4965, pp. 361–378. Springer, Heidelberg (2008)
14. Gilbert, H., Robshaw, M.J.B., Sibert, H.: Active attack against HB^{+}: A provable secure lightweight authentication protocol. Electronic Letters 41, 1169–1170 (2005)
15. Goldreich, O., Levin, L.A.: A hard-core predicate for all one-way functions. In: Proceedings of the Twenty-First Annual ACM Symposium on Theory of Computing (STOC), pp. 25–32. ACM Press (1989)
16. Hopper, N.J., Blum, M.: Secure Human Identification Protocols. In: Boyd, C. (ed.) ASIACRYPT 2001. LNCS, vol. 2248, pp. 52–66. Springer, Heidelberg (2001)
17. Juels, A., Weis, S.A.: Authenticating Pervasive Devices with Human Protocols. In: Shoup, V. (ed.) CRYPTO 2005. LNCS, vol. 3621, pp. 293–308. Springer, Heidelberg (2005)
18. Krause, M., Stegemann, D.: More on the Security of Linear RFID Authentication Protocols. In: Jacobson Jr., M.J., Rijmen, V., Safavi-Naini, R. (eds.) SAC 2009. LNCS, vol. 5867, pp. 182–196. Springer, Heidelberg (2009)
19. Krause, M., Hamann, M.: The cryptographic power of random selection. Cryptology ePrint Archive, Report 2011/511 (2011), `http://eprint.iacr.org/`
20. Meier, W., Pasalic, E., Carlet, C.: Algebraic Attacks and Decomposition of Boolean Functions. In: Cachin, C., Camenisch, J.L. (eds.) EUROCRYPT 2004. LNCS, vol. 3027, pp. 474–491. Springer, Heidelberg (2004)
21. Ouafi, K., Overbeck, R., Vaudenay, S.: On the Security of $HB^{\#}$ against a Man-in-the-Middle Attack. In: Pieprzyk, J. (ed.) ASIACRYPT 2008. LNCS, vol. 5350, pp. 108–124. Springer, Heidelberg (2008)
22. Regev, O.: On lattices, learning with errors, random linear codes, and cryptography. In: Proceedings of the Thirty-Seventh Annual ACM Symposium on Theory of Computing (STOC), pp. 84–93. ACM Press (2005)
23. Courtois, N.T., Klimov, A.B., Patarin, J., Shamir, A.: Efficient Algorithms for Solving Overdefined Systems of Multivariate Polynomial Equations. In: Preneel, B. (ed.) EUROCRYPT 2000. LNCS, vol. 1807, pp. 392–407. Springer, Heidelberg (2000)

A The Proofs of Theorems 3 and 5

Please refer to [19] for the full version of this paper including the proofs of Theorems 3 and 5.

B On Attacking the $(n, k, L)^+$-protocol by Solving *RandomSelect* (L, n, a)

The following outline of an attack on the $(n, k, L)^+$-protocol by Krause and Stegemann [18] is meant to exemplify the immediate connection between the previously introduced learning problem *RandomSelect* (L, n, a) and the security of this whole new class of lightweight authentication protocols. Similar to the basic communication mode described in the introduction, the $(n, k, L)^+$-protocol is based on L n-dimensional, injective linear functions $F_1, \ldots, F_L : GF(2)^n \longrightarrow GF(2)^{n+k}$ (i.e., the secret key) and works as follows.

Each instance is initiated by the verifier Alice, who chooses a random vector $a \in_U GF(2)^{n/2}$ and sends it to Bob, who then randomly (i.e., independently and uniformly) chooses $l \in_U [L]$ along with an additional value $b \in_U GF(2)^{n/2}$, in order to compute his response $w = F_l(a, b)$. Finally, Alice accepts $w \in GF(2)^{n+k}$ if there is some $l \in [L]$ with $w \in V_l$ and the prefix of length $n/2$ of $F_l^{-1}(w)$ equals a, where V_l denotes the n-dimensional linear subspace of $GF(2)^{n+k}$ corresponding to the image of F_l.

This leads straightforwardly to a problem called *Learning Unions of L Linear Subspaces* (LULS), where an oracle holds the specifications of L secret n-dimensional linear subspaces $V_1, \ldots, V_L$ of $GF(2)^{n+k}$, from which it randomly chooses examples $v \in_U V_l$ for $l \in_U [L]$ and sends them to the learner. Knowing only n and k, he seeks to deduce the specifications of $V_1, \ldots, V_L$ from a sufficiently large set $\{w_1, \ldots, w_s\} \subseteq \bigcup_{l=1}^{L} V_l$ of such observations. It is easy to see that this corresponds to a passive key recovery attack against (n, k, L)-type protocols. Note that there is a number of exhaustive search strategies to solve this problem, e.g., the generic exponential time algorithm called search-for-a-basis heuristic, which was presented in the appendix of [18].

It should be noted that an attacker who is able to solve the LULS problem needs to perform additional steps to fully break the $(n, k, L)^+$-protocol as impersonating the prover requires to send responses $w \in GF(2)^{n+k}$ which not only fulfill $w \in \bigcup_{l=1}^{L} V_l$ but also depend on some random nonce $a \in GF(2)^{n/2}$ provided by the verifier. However, having successfully obtained the specifications of the secret subspaces $V_1, \ldots, V_L$ allows in turn for generating a specification of the image of $F_l(a, \cdot)$ for each $l \in [L]$ by repeatedly sending an arbitrary but fixed (i.e., selected by the attacker) $a \in GF(2)^{n/2}$ to the prover. Remember that, although the prover chooses a random $l \in_U [L]$ each time he computes a response w based on some fixed a, an attacker who has determined $V_1, \ldots, V_L$ will know which subspace the vector w actually belongs to. Krause and Stegemann pointed out that this strategy allows for efficiently constructing specifications of linear functions $G_1, \ldots, G_L : GF(2)^n \longrightarrow GF(2)^{n+k}$ and bijective linear functions $g_1, \ldots, g_L : GF(2)^{n/2} \longrightarrow GF(2)^{n/2}$ such that

$$F_l(a,b) = G_l(a, g_l(b))$$

for all $l \in [L]$ and $a, b \in GF(2)^{n/2}$ [18]. Hence, the efficiently obtained specifications of the functions $((G_1, \ldots, G_L), (g_1, \ldots, g_L))$ are equivalent to the actual secret key $(F_1, \ldots, F_L)$. However, keep in mind that the running time of this attack is dominated by the effort needed to solve the LULS problem first and that *RandomSelect* (L, n, a) in fact refers to a special case of the LULS problem, which assumes that the secret subspaces have the form

$$V_l = \{(v, f_l(v)) \mid v \in GF(2)^n\} \subseteq GF(2)^{n+k}$$

for all $l \in [L]$ and secret $GF(2)$-linear functions $f_1, \ldots, f_L : GF(2)^n \longrightarrow GF(2)^k$. This is true with probability $p(n) \approx 0.2887$ as, given an arbitrary $((n+k) \times n)$-matrix A over $GF(2)$, the general case $V = \{A \circ v \mid v \in GF(2)^n\}$ can be written in the special form iff the first n rows of A are linearly independent (see, e.g., [11]).

In order to solve this special problem efficiently, we suggest the following approach, which makes use of our learning algorithm for *RandomSelect* (L, n, a) and works by

- determining an appropriate number $a \in O(\log(n))$ which, w.l.o.g., divides k (i.e., $k = \gamma \cdot a$ for some $\gamma \in \mathbb{N}$),
- identifying vectors $w \in \{0,1\}^k$ with vectors $w = (w_1, \ldots, w_\gamma) \in GF(2^a)^\gamma$ and functions $f : \{0,1\}^n \longrightarrow \{0,1\}^k$ with γ-tuples $(f^1, \ldots, f^\gamma)$ of component functions $f^1, \ldots, f^\gamma : \{0,1\}^n \longrightarrow GF(2^a)$ based on the following rule: $f^i(u) = w_i$ for all $i = 1, \ldots, \gamma$ if and only if $f(u) = (w_1, \ldots, w_\gamma)$,
- learning $f_1, \ldots, f_L : \{0,1\}^n \longrightarrow \{0,1\}^k$ by learning each of the corresponding sets of component functions $f_1^i, \ldots, f_L^i : \{0,1\}^n \longrightarrow GF(2^a)$ in time $n^{O(L)}$ for $i = 1, \ldots, \gamma$.

Clearly, for efficiency reasons, a should be as small as possible. However, in section 4 we show that a needs to exceed a certain threshold, which can be bounded from above by $O(\log(n))$, to enable our learning algorithm to find a unique solution with high probability.

Please note that, throughout this paper, a is assumed to be fixed as we develop a learning algorithm for sets of secret $GF(2)$-linear functions $f_1, \ldots, f_L : \{0,1\}^n \longrightarrow K$, where $K = GF(2^a)$. In particular, for the sake of simplicity, we write $f_1, \ldots, f_L$ while actually referring to a set of component functions as explained above.

Proof of Empirical RC4 Biases and New Key Correlations

Sourav Sen Gupta[1], Subhamoy Maitra[1], Goutam Paul[2], and Santanu Sarkar[1]

[1] Applied Statistics Unit, Indian Statistical Institute, Kolkata 700 108, India
[2] Dept. of Computer Science and Engg., Jadavpur University, Kolkata 700 032, India
{sg.sourav,sarkar.santanu.bir}@gmail.com, subho@isical.ac.in, goutam.paul@ieee.org,

Abstract. In SAC 2010, Sepehrdad, Vaudenay and Vuagnoux have reported some empirical biases between the secret key, the internal state variables and the keystream bytes of RC4, by searching over a space of all linear correlations between the quantities involved. In this paper, for the first time, we give theoretical proofs for all such significant empirical biases. Our analysis not only builds a framework to justify the origin of these biases, it also brings out several new conditional biases of high order. We establish that certain conditional biases reported earlier are correlated with a third event with much higher probability. This gives rise to the discovery of new keylength-dependent biases of RC4, some as high as $50/N$, where N is the size of the RC4 permutation. The new biases in turn result in successful *keylength prediction* from the initial keystream bytes of the cipher.

Keywords: Conditional Bias, Key Correlation, Keylength Prediction, RC4.

1 Introduction

RC4 is one of the most popular stream ciphers for software applications. Designed by Ron Rivest in 1987, the algorithm of RC4 has two parts; Key Scheduling (KSA) and Pseudo-Random Generation (PRGA), presented in Table 1.

Given a secret key k of length l bytes, an array K of size N bytes is created to hold the key such that $K[y] = k[y \bmod l]$ for all $y \in [0, N-1]$. Generally, N is chosen to be 256. The first part of the cipher, KSA, uses this K to scramble an initial identity permutation $\{0, 1, \ldots, N-1\}$ to obtain a 'secret' state S. Then the PRGA generates keystream bytes from this initial state S, which are used for encrypting the plaintext. Two indices i (deterministic) and j (pseudo-random) are used in KSA as well as PRGA to point to the locations of S. All additions in the RC4 algorithm are performed modulo N.

After r (≥ 1) rounds of RC4 PRGA, we denote the variables by S_r, i_r, j_r, z_r and the output index $S_r[i_r] + S_r[j_r]$ by t_r. After r rounds of KSA, we denote the same by adding a superscript K to each variable. By S_0^K and S_0, we denote the initial permutations before KSA and PRGA respectively. Note that S_0^K is the identity permutation and $S_0 = S_N^K$.

A. Miri and S. Vaudenay (Eds.): SAC 2011, LNCS 7118, pp. 151–168, 2012.

Table 1. The RC4 Algorithm: KSA and PRGA

Key Scheduling (KSA)	Pseudo-Random Generation (PRGA)
Input: Secret Key K. **Output**: S-Box S generated by K.	**Input**: S-Box S, output of KSA. **Output**: Random stream Z.
Initialize $S = \{0, 1, 2, \ldots, N-1\}$; Initialize counter: $j = 0$;	Initialize the counters: $i = j = 0$;

for $i = 0, \ldots, N-1$ **do**
  $j = j + S[i] + K[i]$;
  Swap $S[i] \leftrightarrow S[j]$;
end
	while *TRUE* **do**
	  $i = i + 1$, $j = j + S[i]$;
	  Swap $S[i] \leftrightarrow S[j]$;
	  Output $Z = S[S[i] + S[j]]$;
	end

Existing Results. In SAC 2010, Sepehrdad, Vaudenay and Vuagnoux [12] have reported experimental results of an exhaustive search for biases in all possible linear combinations of the state variables and the keystream bytes of RC4. In the process, they have discovered many new biases that are significantly high compared to random association. Some of these biases were further shown to be useful for key recovery in WEP [3] mode. In a recent work [13] at Eurocrypt 2011, the same authors have utilized the pool of all existing biases of RC4, including a few reported in [12], to mount a distinguishing attack on WPA [4].

In the above approach, RC4 is treated as a black box, where the secret key bytes are the *inputs*, the permutation and the index j are *internal state variables* and the keystream bytes are the *outputs*. The goal of [12] was to find out empirical correlations between the inputs, internal state and the outputs and no attempt was made to theoretically prove these biases. Finding empirical biases without any justification or proof may be useful from application point of view. However, cryptanalysis is a disciplined branch of science and a natural quest in RC4 cryptanalysis should be: *Where do all these biases come from?*

Motivation. We felt three primary reasons behind a theoretical investigation into the source and nature of these biases.

- We attempt to build a framework to analyze the biases and their origin.
- In the process of proving the existing biases, one may need to consider some additional events and thus may end up discovering new biases, leading to further insight into the cipher. We have observed some interesting events with strong biases, which have not yet been reported in the literature.
- When there is a conditional bias in the event 'A given B', there may be three reasons behind it: either some subset of A directly causes B or some subset of B directly causes A or another set C of different events cause both A and B. Just from empirical observation, it is impossible to infer what is the actual reason behind the bias. Only a theoretical study can shed light upon the interplay between the events. Our observations and analysis suggest that some conditional biases reported in [12] are possibly of the third kind discussed above and this provides us with some interesting new results depending on the length of the RC4 secret key.

Contribution. Our main contribution in this paper is summarized as follows.

1. In Section 2, we provide theoretical proofs for some significant empirical biases of RC4 reported in SAC 2010 [12]. In particular, we justify the reported biases of order approximately $2/N$, summarized in Table 2. Note that the authors of [12] denote the PRGA variables by primed indices. Moreover, the probabilities mentioned in the table are the ones observed in [12], and the values for 'biases at all rounds (round-dependent)' are the ones for $r = 3$. We provide general proofs and formulas for all of these biases.

Table 2. Significant biases observed in [12] and proved in this paper

Type of Bias	Label as in [12]	Event	Probability
Bias at Specific Initial Rounds	New_004	$j_2 + S_2[j_2] = S_2[i_2] + z_2$	$2/N$
	New_noz_007	$j_2 + S_2[j_2] = 6$	$2.37/N$
	New_noz_009	$j_2 + S_2[j_2] = S_2[i_2]$	$2/N$
	New_noz_014	$j_1 + S_1[i_1] = 2$	$1.94/N$
Bias at All Rounds (round-independent)	New_noz_001	$j_r + S_r[i_r] = i_r + S_r[j_r]$	$2/N$
	New_noz_002	$j_r + S_r[j_r] = i_r + S_r[i_r]$	$2/N$
Bias at All Rounds (round-dependent)	New_000	$S_r[t_r] = t_r$	$1.9/N$ at $r = 3$
	New_noz_004	$S_r[i_r] = j_r$	$1.9/N$ at $r = 3$
	New_noz_006	$S_r[j_r] = i_r$	$2.34/N$ at $r = 3$

2. In Section 3, we try to justify the bias $\Pr[S_{16}[j_{16}] = 0 \mid z_{16} = -16] = 0.038488$ observed in [12], for which the authors have commented:

   "So far, we have no explanation about this new bias." [12, Section 3]

   We have observed that the implied correlation arises because both the events depend on some other event based on the length of RC4 secret key. We also prove some related correlations in this direction, in full generality for any keylength l.
3. In Section 3, we also prove an array of *new keylength-dependent conditional biases* of RC4 that are of the same or even higher magnitude. To the best of our knowledge, these are not reported in the literature [1, 2, 6, 9–15].
4. In Section 3.3, we prove a strong correlation between the length l of the secret key and the l-th output byte (typically for $5 \leq l \leq 30$), and thus propose a method to predict the keylength of the cipher by observing the keystream. As far as we know, no such significant keylength related bias exists in the RC4 literature [1, 2, 6, 9–15].

2 Proofs of Recent Empirical Observations

In this section, we investigate some significant empirical biases discovered and reported in [12]. We provide theoretical justification only for the new biases which are of the approximate order of $2/N$ or more, summarized in Table 2. In this target list, general biases refer to the ones occurring in all initial rounds of PRGA ($1 \le r \le N-1$), whereas the specific ones have been reported only for rounds 1 and 2 of PRGA. *We do not consider the biases reported for rounds* 0 mod 16 *in this section, as they are of order* $1/N^2$ *or less.*

For the proofs and numeric probability calculations in this paper, we require [6, Theorem 6.3.1], restated as Proposition 1 below.

Proposition 1. *At the end of RC4 KSA, for* $0 \le u \le N-1$, $0 \le v \le N-1$,

$$\Pr(S_0[u] = v) = \begin{cases} \frac{1}{N}\left[\left(\frac{N-1}{N}\right)^v + \left(1 - \left(\frac{N-1}{N}\right)^v\right)\left(\frac{N-1}{N}\right)^{N-u-1}\right] & \text{if } v \le u; \\ \frac{1}{N}\left[\left(\frac{N-1}{N}\right)^{N-u-1} + \left(\frac{N-1}{N}\right)^v\right] & \text{if } v > u. \end{cases}$$

If a pseudorandom permutation is taken as the initial state S_0 of RC4 PRGA, then we would have $\Pr(S_0[u] = v) = \frac{1}{N}$ for all $0 \le u \le N-1$, $0 \le v \le N-1$.

2.1 Bias at Specific Initial Rounds of PRGA

In this part of the paper, we prove the biases labeled New_noz_014, New_noz_007, New_noz_009 and New_004, as in [12, Fig. 3 and Fig. 4] and Table 2.

Theorem 1. *After the first round* ($r = 1$) *of RC4 PRGA,*

$$\Pr(j_1 + S_1[i_1] = 2) = \Pr(S_0[1] = 1) + \sum_{X \neq 1} \Pr(S_0[X] = 2 - X) \cdot \Pr(S_0[1] = X)$$

Proof. Note that $j_1 = S_0[1]$ and $S_1[i_1] = S_0[j_1]$. So, in the case $j_1 = S_0[1] = 1$, we will have $j_1 + S_0[j_1] = S_0[1] + S_0[1] = 2$ with probability 1. Otherwise, the probability turns out to be $\Pr(j_1 + S_0[j_1] = 2 \;\&\; j_1 = S_0[1] \neq 1) = \sum_{X \neq 1} \Pr(X + S_0[X] = 2 \;\&\; S_0[1] = X)$. Thus, the probability $\Pr(j_1 + S_1[i_1] = 2)$ can be written as $\Pr(j_1 + S_1[i_1] = 2) = \Pr(S_0[1] = 1) + \sum_{X \neq 1} \Pr(S_0[X] = 2 - X) \cdot \Pr(S_0[1] = X)$, as desired. Hence the claimed result. □

Numerical Values. If we consider the practical RC4 scheme, the probabilities involving S_0 in the expression for $\Pr(j_1 + S_1[i_1] = 2)$ should be evaluated using Proposition 1, giving a total probability of approximately $1.937/N$ for $N = 256$. This closely matches the observed value $1.94/N$. If we assume that RC4 PRGA starts with a truly pseudorandom initial state S_0, the probability turns out to be approximately $2/N - 1/N^2 \approx 1.996/N$ for $N = 256$, i.e., almost twice that of a random occurrence.

Theorem 2. *After the second round* ($r = 2$) *of RC4 PRGA, the following probability relations hold between the index* j_2 *and the state variables* $S_2[i_2], S_2[j_2]$.

$$\Pr\left(j_2 + S_2[j_2] = 6\right) \approx \Pr(S_0[1] = 2) + \sum_{X \text{ even},\, X \neq 2} (2/N) \cdot \Pr(S_0[1] = X) \quad (1)$$

$$\Pr\left(j_2 + S_2[j_2] = S_2[i_2]\right) \approx 2/N - 1/N^2 \quad (2)$$

$$\Pr\left(j_2 + S_2[j_2] = S_2[i_2] + z_2\right) \approx 2/N - 1/N^2 \quad (3)$$

Proof. In Equation (1), we have $j_2+S_2[j_2] = (j_1+S_1[2])+S_1[i_2] = S_0[1]+2\cdot S_1[2]$. In this expression, note that if $S_0[1] = 2$, then one must have the positions 1 and 2 swapped in the first round of PRGA, and thus $S_1[2] = S_0[1] = 2$ as well. This provides one path for $j_2 + S_2[j_2] = S_0[1] + 2 \cdot S_1[2] = 2 + 2 \times 2 = 6$, with probability $\Pr(S_0[1] = 2) \cdot 1 \approx \frac{1}{N}$. If on the other hand, $S_0[1] = X \neq 2$, we have $\Pr(j_2 + S_2[j_2] = 6 \ \& \ S_0[1] \neq 2) = \sum_{X\neq 2} \Pr(X + 2 \cdot S_1[2] = 6 \ \& \ S_0[1] = X)$. Note that the value of X is bound to be even and for each such value of X, the variable $S_1[2]$ can take 2 different values to satisfy the equation $2\cdot S_1[2] = 6-X$. Thus, we have $\sum_{X\neq 2} \Pr(2 \cdot S_1[2] = 6 - X \ \& \ S_0[1] = X) \approx \sum_{X \text{ even}, \, X\neq 2} \frac{2}{N} \cdot \Pr(S_0[1] = X)$. Combining the two disjoint cases $S_0[1] = 2$ and $S_0[1] \neq 2$, we get Equation (1).

In case of Equation (2), we have a slightly different condition $S_0[1]+2\cdot S_1[2] = S_2[i_2] = S_1[j_2] = S_1[S_0[1] + S_1[2]]$. In this expression, if we have $S_1[2] = 0$, then the left hand side reduces to $S_0[1]$ and the right hand side becomes $S_1[S_0[1] + S_1[2]] = S_1[S_0[1]] = S_1[j_1] = S_0[i_1] = S_0[1]$ as well. This provides a probability $\frac{1}{N}$ path for the condition to be true. In all other cases with $S_1[2] \neq 0$, we can approximate the probability for the condition as $\frac{1}{N}$, and hence approximate the total probability $\Pr(j_2 + S_2[j_2] = S_2[i_2])$ as $\Pr(j_2 + S_2[j_2] = S_2[i_2] \ \& \ S_1[2] = 0) + \Pr(j_2 + S_2[j_2] = S_2[i_2] \ \& \ S_1[2] \neq 0) \approx \frac{1}{N} + \left(1 - \frac{1}{N}\right) \cdot \frac{1}{N} = \frac{2}{N} - \frac{1}{N^2}$.

Finally, for Equation (3), the main observation is that this is almost identical to the condition of Equation (2) apart from the inclusion of z_2. But our first path of $S_1[2] = 0$ in the previous case also provides us with $z_2 = 0$ with probability 1 (this path was first observed by Mantin and Shamir [7]). Thus, we have $\Pr(j_2 + S_2[j_2] = S_2[i_2] + z_2 \ \& \ S_1[2] = 1) \approx \frac{1}{N} \cdot 1$. In all other cases with $S_1[2] \neq 0$, we assume the conditions to match uniformly at random, and therefore have $\Pr(j_2 + S_2[j_2] = S_2[i_2] + z_2) \approx \frac{1}{N} \cdot 1 + \left(1 - \frac{1}{N}\right) \cdot \frac{1}{N} = \frac{2}{N} - \frac{1}{N^2}$. Hence the desired results of Equations (1), (2) and (3). □

Numerical Values. In case of Equation (1), if we assume S_0 to be the practical initial state for RC4 PRGA, and substitute all probabilities involving S_0 using Proposition 1, we get the total probability equal to $2.36/N$ for $N = 256$. This value closely match the observed probability $2.37/N$. If we suppose that S_0 is pseudorandom, we will get probability $2/N - 2/N^2 \approx 1.992/N$ for Equation (1). The theoretical results are summarized in Table 3 along with the experimentally observed probabilities of [12].

Table 3. Theoretical and observed biases at specific initial rounds of RC4 PRGA

Label [12]	Event	Observed Probability [12]	Theoretical Probability	
			S_0 of RC4	Random S_0
New_noz_014	$j_1 + S_1[i_1] = 2$	$1.94/N$	$1.937/N$	$1.996/N$
New_noz_007	$j_2 + S_2[j_2] = 6$	$2.37/N$	$2.363/N$	$1.992/N$
New_noz_009	$j_2 + S_2[j_2] = S_2[i_2]$	$2/N$	$1.996/N$	$1.996/N$
New_noz_004	$j_2 + S_2[j_2] = S_2[i_2] + z_2$	$2/N$	$1.996/N$	$1.996/N$

2.2 Biases at All Initial Rounds of PRGA (Round-Independent)

In this section, we turn our attention to the biases labeled New_noz_001 and New_noz_002 in [12], both of which continue to persist in all initial rounds ($1 \leq r \leq N-1$) of RC4 PRGA.

Theorem 3. *At any initial round $1 \leq r \leq N-1$ of RC4 PRGA, the following two relations hold between the indices i_r, j_r and the state variables $S_r[i_r], S_r[j_r]$.*

$$\Pr(j_r + S_r[j_r] = i_r + S_r[i_r]) \approx 2/N \tag{4}$$
$$\Pr(j_r + S_r[i_r] = i_r + S_r[j_r]) \approx 2/N \tag{5}$$

Proof. For both the events mentioned above, we shall take the path $i_r = j_r$. Notice that $i_r = j_r$ occurs with probability $\frac{1}{N}$ and in that case both the events mentioned above hold with probability 1. In the case where $i_r \neq j_r$, we rewrite the events as $S_r[j_r] = (i_r - j_r) + S_r[i_r]$ and $S_r[j_r] = (j_r - i_r) + S_r[i_r]$. Here we already know that $S_r[j_r] \neq S_r[i_r]$, as $j_r \neq i_r$ and S_r is a permutation. Thus in case $i_r \neq j_r$, the values of $S_r[i_r]$ and $S_r[j_r]$ can be chosen in $N(N-1)$ ways (drawing from a permutation without replacement) to satisfy the relations stated above. This gives the total probability for each event approximately as $\Pr(j_r = i_r) \cdot 1 + \sum_{j_r \neq i_r} \frac{1}{N(N-1)} = \frac{1}{N} + (N-1) \cdot \frac{1}{N(N-1)} = \frac{2}{N}$. Hence the claimed result for Equations (4) and (5). □

The probabilities for New_noz_001 and New_noz_002 proved in Theorem 3 do not vary with change in r (i.e., they continue to persist at the same order of $2/N$ at any arbitrary round of PRGA), and our theoretical results match the probabilities reported in [12, Fig. 2].

2.3 Biases at All Initial Rounds of PRGA (Round-Dependent)

Next, we consider the biases that are labeled as New_000, New_noz_004 and New_noz_006 in [12, Fig. 2]. We prove the biases for rounds 3 to 255 in RC4 PRGA, and we show that all of these decrease in magnitude with increase in r, as observed experimentally in the original paper.

Let us first prove observation New_noz_006 of [12]. This proof was also attempted in [5, Lemma 1], where the event was equivalently stated as $S_{r-1}[r] = r$. But that proof used a crude approximation which resulted in a slight mismatch of the theoretical and practical patterns in the main result of the paper [5, Fig. 2]. Our proof of Theorem 4, as follows, corrects the proof of [5, Lemma 1], and removes the mismatch in [5, Fig. 2].

Theorem 4. *For PRGA rounds $r \geq 3$, value of $\Pr(S_r[j_r] = i_r)$ is approximately*

$$\Pr(S_1[r] = r) \left[1 - \frac{1}{N}\right]^{r-2} + \sum_{t=2}^{r-1} \sum_{k=0}^{r-t} \frac{\Pr(S_1[t] = r)}{k! \cdot N} \left[\frac{r-t-1}{N}\right]^k \left[1 - \frac{1}{N}\right]^{r-3-k}$$

Before proving Theorem 4, let us first prove a necessary technical result.

Lemma 1. *After the first round of RC4 PRGA, the probability* $\Pr(S_1[t] = r)$ *is*

$$\Pr(S_1[t] = r) = \begin{cases} \sum_{X=0}^{N-1} \Pr(S_0[1] = X) \cdot \Pr(S_0[X] = r), & t = 1; \\ \Pr(S_0[1] = r) + (1 - \Pr(S_0[1] = r)) \cdot \Pr(S_0[r] = r), & t = r; \\ (1 - \Pr(S_0[1] = t)) \cdot \Pr(S_0[t] = r), & t \neq 1, r. \end{cases}$$

Proof. After the first round of RC4 PRGA, we obtain the state S_1 from the initial state S_0 through a single swap operation between the positions $i_1 = 1$ and $j_1 = S_0[i_1] = S_0[1]$. Thus, all other positions of S_0 remain the same apart from these two. This gives us the value of $S_1[t]$ as follows: $S_1[t] = S_0[S_0[1]]$ if $t = 1$, $S_1[t] = S_0[1]$ if $t = S_0[1]$, and $S_1[t] = S_0[t]$ in all other cases. Now, we can compute the probabilities $\Pr(S_1[t] = r)$ based on the probabilities for S_0, which are in turn derived from Proposition 1. We have three cases:

- Case $t = 1$. In this case, using the recurrence relation $S_1[1] = S_0[S_0[1]]$, we can write $\Pr(S_1[1] = r) = \sum_{X=0}^{N-1} \Pr(S_0[1] = X) \cdot \Pr(S_0[X] = r)$.
- Case $t = r$. In this situation, if $S_0[1] = r$, we will surely have $S_1[r] = r$ as these are the positions swapped in the first round, and if $S_0[1] \neq r$, the position $t = r$ remains untouched and $S_1[r] = r$ is only possible if $S_0[r] = r$. Thus, $\Pr(S_1[r] = r) = \Pr(S_0[1] = r) + (1 - \Pr(S_0[1] = r)) \cdot \Pr(S_0[r] = r)$.
- Case $t \neq 1, r$. In all other cases where $t \neq 1, r$, it can either take the value $S_0[1]$ with probability $\Pr(S_0[1] = t)$, or not. If $t = S_0[1]$, the value $S_0[t]$ will get swapped with $S_0[1] = t$ itself, i.e., we will get $S_1[t] = t \neq r$ for sure. Otherwise, the value $S_1[t]$ remains the same as $S_0[t]$. Hence, $\Pr(S_1[t] = r) = (1 - \Pr(S_0[1] = t)) \cdot \Pr(S_0[t] = r)$.

Combining all the above cases together, we obtain the desired result. □

Proof of Theorem 4. Let us start from the PRGA state S_1, that is, the state that has been updated once in the PRGA (we refer to the state after KSA by S_0). We know that the event $\Pr(S_1[r] = r)$ is positively biased for all r, and hence the natural path for investigation is the effect of the event $(S_1[r] = r)$ on $(S_{r-1}[r] = r)$, i.e, on $(S_r[j_r] = i_r)$. Notice that there can be two cases, as follows.

Case I. In the first case, suppose that $(S_1[r] = r)$ after the first round, and the r-th index is not disturbed for the next $r - 2$ state updates. Notice that index i varies from 2 to $r - 1$ during these period, and hence never touches the r-th index. Thus, the index r will retain its state value r if index j does not touch it. The probability of this event is $\left(1 - \frac{1}{N}\right)^{r-2}$ over all the intermediate rounds. Hence the first part of the probability is $\Pr(S_1[r] = r)\left(1 - \frac{1}{N}\right)^{r-2}$.

Case II. In the second case, suppose that $S_1[r] \neq r$ and $S_1[t] = r$ for some $t \neq r$. In such a case, only a swap between the positions r and t during rounds 2 to $r - 1$ of PRGA can make the event $(S_{r-1}[r] = r)$ possible. Notice that if t does not fall in the *path of* i, that is, if the index i does not touch the t-th location, then the value at $S_1[t]$ can only go to some position behind i, and this can never reach $S_{r-1}[r]$, as i can only go up to $(r - 1)$ during this period. Thus we must have $2 \leq t \leq r - 1$ for $S_1[t]$ to reach $S_{r-1}[r]$. Note that the way $S_1[t]$ can move to the r-th position may be either a one hop or a multi-hop route.

- In the easiest case of single hop, we require j not to touch t until i touches t, and $j = r$ when $i = t$, and j not to touch r for the next $r-t-1$ state updates. Total probability comes to be $\Pr(S_1[t] = r)\left(1 - \frac{1}{N}\right)^{t-2} \cdot \frac{1}{N} \cdot \left(1 - \frac{1}{N}\right)^{r-t-1} = \Pr(S_1[t] = r) \cdot \frac{1}{N}\left(1 - \frac{1}{N}\right)^{r-3}$.
- Suppose that it requires $(k+1)$ hops to reach from $S_1[t]$ to $S_{r-1}[r]$. Then the main issue to note is that the transfer will never happen if the position t swaps with any index which does not lie in the future *path of* i. Again, this path of i starts from $\frac{r-t-1}{N}$ for the first hop and decreases approximately to $\frac{r-t-1}{lN}$ at the l-th hop. We would also require j not to touch the position r for the remaining $(r-3-k)$ number of rounds. Combining all, we get the second part of the probability as $\Pr(S_1[t] = r)\left[\prod_{l=1}^{k} \frac{r-t-1}{lN}\right]\left[1 - \frac{1}{N}\right]^{r-3-k} = \frac{\Pr(S_1[t]=r)}{k! \cdot N}\left[\frac{r-t-1}{N}\right]^{k}\left[1 - \frac{1}{N}\right]^{r-3-k}$.

Finally, note that the number of hops $(k+1)$ is bounded from below by 1 and from above by $(r - t + 1)$, depending on the initial gap between t and r positions. Considering the sum over t and k with this consideration, we get the desired expression for $\Pr(S_{r-1}[r] = r)$. □

Remark 1. In proving Theorem 4, we use the initial condition $S_1[r] = r$ to branch out the probability paths, and not $S_0[r] = r$ as in [5, Lemma 1]. This is because the probability of $S[r] = r$ takes a leap from around $1/N$ in S_0 to about $2/N$ in S_1, and this turns out to be the actual cause behind the bias in $S_{r-1}[r] = r$.

Fig. 1 illustrates the experimental observations (averages taken over 100 million runs with 16-byte key) and the theoretical values for the distribution of $\Pr(S_r[j_r] = i_r)$ over the initial rounds $3 \le r \le 255$ of RC4 PRGA. It is evident that our theoretical formula matches the experimental observations in this case.

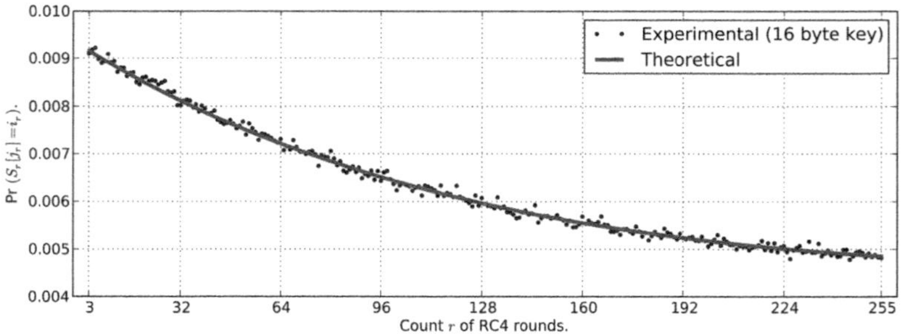

Fig. 1. Distribution of $\Pr(S_r[j_r] = i_r)$ for initial rounds $3 \le r \le 255$ of RC4 PRGA

Now let us take a look at the other two round-dependent biases of RC4, observed in [12]. We can state the related result in Theorem 5 (corresponding to observations New_noz_004 and New_000).

Theorem 5. *For PRGA rounds $r \geq 3$, the probabilities* $\Pr(S_r[i_r] = j_r)$ *and* $\Pr(S_r[t_r] = t_r)$ *are approximately*

$$\frac{r}{N^2} + \sum_{X=r}^{N-1} \frac{1}{N} \left[\Pr(S_1[X] = X) \left[1 - \frac{1}{N}\right]^{r-2} + \sum_{t=2}^{r-1} \sum_{k=0}^{r-t} \frac{\Pr(S_1[t] = r)}{k! \cdot N} \left[\frac{r-t-1}{N}\right]^k \left[1 - \frac{1}{N}\right]^{r-3-k} \right]$$

The proof of this result is omitted for brevity, as it follows the same logic as in the proof of Theorem 4. A brief proof sketch is presented as follows. For this proof sketch, we consider the variables j_r and t_r to be pseudorandom variables that can take any value between 0 to 255 with probability $1/N$. The reader may note that this is a crude approximation, especially for small values of r, and causes minor mismatch with the experimental observations in the final result.

Proof-sketch for $\Pr(S_r[i_r] = j_r)$. For this probability computation, we first rewrite the event as $(S_{r-1}[j_r] = j_r)$ to make it look similar to $S_{r-1}[r] = r$, as in Theorem 4. The only difference is that we were concentrating on a fixed index r in Theorem 4 instead of a variable index j_r. This produces two cases.

Case I. First, suppose that j_r assumes a value $X \geq r$. In this case, the probability calculation can be split in two paths, one in which $S_1[X] = X$ is assumed, and the other in which $S_1[X] \neq X$. If we assume $S_1[X] = X$, the probability of $(S_{r-1}[X] = X)$ becomes $\Pr(S_1[X] = X) \left[1 - \frac{1}{N}\right]^{r-2}$, similar to the logic in Theorem 4. If we suppose that $S_1[t] = X$ was the initial state, then one may notice the following two sub-cases:

- The probability for this path is identical to that in Theorem 4 if $2 \leq t \leq r-1$.
- The probability is 0 in case $t \geq r$, as in this case the value X will always be behind the position of $i_r = r$, whereas $X > r$ as per assumption. That is, the value X can never reach index X from t.

Assuming $\Pr(j_r = X) = 1/N$, this gives $\sum_{X=r}^{N-1} \frac{1}{N} \Big[\Pr(S_1[X] = X) \left[1 - \frac{1}{N}\right]^{r-2}$ $+ \sum_{t=2}^{r-1} \sum_{k=0}^{r-t} \frac{\Pr(S_1[t]=r)}{k! \cdot N} \left[\frac{r-t-1}{N}\right]^k \left[1 - \frac{1}{N}\right]^{r-3-k}\Big]$.

Case II. In the second case, we assume that j_r takes a value X between 0 to $r-1$. Approximately this complete range is touched by index i for sure, and may also be touched by index j. Thus, with probability approximately 1, the index $j_r = X$ is touched by either of the indices. Simplifying all complicated computations involving the initial position of value X and the exact location of index X in this case, we shall assume that the approximate value of $\Pr(S_{r-1}[X] = X)$ is $1/N$. Thus, the total contribution of Case II, assuming $\Pr(j_r = X) = 1/N$, is given by $\sum_{X=0}^{r-1} \Pr(j_r = X) \cdot \Pr(S_{r-1}[X] = X) \approx \sum_{X=0}^{r-1} \frac{1}{N} \cdot \frac{1}{N} = \frac{r}{N^2}$.

Adding the contributions of the two disjoint cases I and II, we obtain the total probability for $(S_r[i_r] = j_r)$ as desired. One may investigate Case II in more details to incorporate all intertwined sub-cases, and obtain a better closed form expression for the probability.

Proof-sketch for $\Pr(S_r[t_r] = t_r)$. In this case, notice that t_r is just another random variable like j_r, and may assume all values from 0 to 255 with approximately the same probability $1/N$. Thus we can approximate $\Pr(S_r[t_r] = t_r)$ by $\Pr(S_{r-1}[j_r] = j_r)$ with a high confidence margin to obtain the desired expression.

This approximation is particularly close for higher values of r because the effect of a single state change $S_{r-1} \to S_r$ is low in such a case. For smaller values of r, one may approximate $\Pr(S_{r-1}[t_r] = t_r)$ by $\Pr(S_{r-1}[j_r] = j_r)$ and critically analyze the effect of the r-th round of PRGA thereafter. However, in spite of the approximations we made, one may note that the theoretical values closely match the experimental observations (averages taken over 100 million runs of RC4 with 16-byte key), as shown in Fig. 2.

Fig. 2 illustrates the experimental observations (averages taken over 100 million runs with 16-byte key) and the theoretical values for the distributions of $\Pr(S_r[i_r] = j_r)$ and $\Pr(S_r[t_r] = t_r)$ over the initial rounds $3 \le r \le 255$ of RC4 PRGA. It is evident that our theoretical formulas approximately match the experimental observations in both the cases; the cause of the little deviation is explained in the proof sketch above.

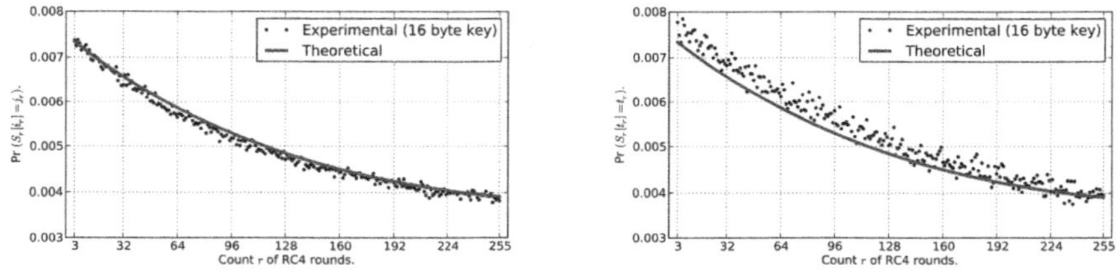

Fig. 2. Distributions of $\Pr(S_r[i_r] = j_r)$ and $\Pr(S_r[t_r] = t_r)$ for initial rounds $3 \le r \le 255$ of RC4 PRGA

Apart from the biases proved so far, all other unconditional biases reported in [12] are of order $1/N^2$ or less, and we omit their analysis in this paper. The next most significant bias reported in [12] was a new conditional bias arising from a set of correlations in RC4 PRGA. A careful study of this new bias gives rise to several related observations and results related to the KSA as well, as presented in the next section.

3 Biases Based on Keylength

In SAC 2010, Sepehrdad, Vaudenay and Vuagnoux [12] discovered several correlations in PRGA using DFT based approach. A list of such biases was presented in [12, Fig. 10], and the authors commented that:

> "After investigation, it seems that all the listed biases are artifact of a new conditional bias which is $\Pr[S'_{16}[j'_{16}] = 0 \mid z_{16} = -16] = 0.038488$."

However, the authors also admitted that

> *"So far, we have no explanation about this new bias."*

In our notation, the above event is denoted as $\Pr(S_{16}[j_{16}] = 0 \mid z_{16} = -16)$. While exploring this conditional bias and related parameters of RC4 PRGA, we could immediately observe two things:

1. The number 16 in the result comes from the keylength that is consistently chosen to be 16 in [12] for most of the experimentation. In its general form, the conditional bias should be stated as (crude approximation):
$$\Pr(S_l[j_l] = 0 \mid z_l = -l) \approx \frac{10}{N}. \tag{6}$$
It is surprising why this natural observation could not be identified earlier.
2. Along the same line of investigation, we could find a family of related conditional biases, stated in their general form as follows (crude approximations):
$$\Pr(z_l = -l \mid S_l[j_l] = 0) \approx 10/N \tag{7}$$
$$\Pr(S_l[l] = -l \mid S_l[j_l] = 0) \approx 30/N \tag{8}$$
$$\Pr(t_l = -l \mid S_l[j_l] = 0) \approx 30/N \tag{9}$$
$$\Pr(S_l[j_l] = 0 \mid t_l = -l) \approx 30/N \tag{10}$$

Note that bias (7) follows almost immediately from bias (6), and biases (10) and (9) are related in a similar fashion. Moreover, bias (8) implies bias (9) as $t_l = S_l[l] + S_l[j_l] = -l$ under the given condition. However, we investigate even further to study the bias caused in z_l due to the state variables.

3.1 Dependence of Conditional Biases on RC4 Secret Key

We found that all of the aforementioned conditional biases between the two events under consideration are related to the following third event that is dependent on the values and the length of the RC4 secret key.

$$\sum_{i=0}^{l-1} K[i] + \frac{l(l-1)}{2} \equiv -l \pmod N$$

We shall henceforth denote the above event by $(f_{l-1} = -l)$, following the notation of Paul and Maitra [9], and this event is going to constitute the base for most of the conditional probabilities we consider hereafter. We consider $\Pr(f_{l-1} = -l) \approx \frac{1}{N}$, assuming that f_{l-1} can take any value modulo N uniformly at random.

Extensive experimentation with different keylengths (100 million runs for each keylength $1 \le l \le 256$) revealed strong bias in all of the following events:

$$\Pr(S_l[j_l] = 0 \mid f_{l-1} = -l), \qquad \Pr(S_l[l] = -l \mid f_{l-1} = -l),$$
$$\Pr(t_l = -l \mid f_{l-1} = -l), \qquad \Pr(z_l = -l \mid f_{l-1} = -l).$$

Each of the correlations (6), (7), (8), (9), and (10) is an artifact of these common keylength-based correlations in RC4 PRGA. In this section, we discuss and justify all these conditional biases.

To prove our observations in this paper, we shall require the following existing results from the literature of key-correlation in RC4. These are the correlations observed by Roos [11] in 1995, which were later proved by Paul and Maitra [9].

Proposition 2. [9, Lemma 1] *If index j is pseudorandom at each KSA round, we have* $\Pr\left(j^K_{y+1} = f_y\right) \approx \left(1 - \frac{1}{N}\right)^{1+\frac{y(y+1)}{2}} + \frac{1}{N}$.

Proposition 3. [9, Corollary 1] *On completion of KSA in the RC4 algorithm,* $\Pr(S_0[y] = f_y) = \Pr(S^K_N[y] = f_y) \approx \left(1 - \frac{y}{N}\right) \cdot \left(1 - \frac{1}{N}\right)^{\frac{y(y+1)}{2}+N} + \frac{1}{N}$.

Proposition 4. [9, Corollary 1] *On completion of KSA,* $\Pr(S_0[S_0[y]] = f_y) \approx \left[\frac{y}{N} + \frac{1}{N}\left[1 - \frac{1}{N}\right]^{2-y} + \left[1 - \frac{y}{N}\right]^2 \left[1 - \frac{1}{N}\right]\right]\left[1 - \frac{1}{N}\right]^{\frac{y(y+1)}{2}+2N-4}$ *for* $0 \leq y \leq 31$.

Note that in each of the above statements,

$$f_y = S^K_0\left[\sum_{x=0}^{y} S^K_0[x] + \sum_{x=0}^{y} K[x]\right] = \sum_{x=0}^{y} x + \sum_{x=0}^{y} K[x] = \sum_{x=0}^{y} K[x] + \frac{y(y+1)}{2}.$$

3.2 Proof of Keylength-Dependent Conditional Biases

In this section, we will prove the four main conditional biases that we have observed. Each depends on the event $(f_{l-1} = -l)$, and can be justified as follows. In each of the following theorems, the notation '$x : A \xrightarrow{\alpha} B$' denotes that the value x transits from position A to position B with probability α.

Theorem 6. *Suppose that l is the length of the secret key used in the RC4 algorithm. Given* $f_{l-1} = \sum_{i=0}^{l-1} K[i] + l(l-1)/2 = -l$, *we have*

$$\Pr(S_l[j_l] = 0) \approx \frac{1}{N} + \left[1 - \frac{l}{N}\right]\left[1 - \frac{1}{N}\right]^{N+l-2}\left[\left[1 - \frac{1}{N}\right]^{1+\frac{l(l+1)}{2}} + \frac{1}{N}\right]$$

$$\Pr(S_{l-2}[l-1] = -l) \approx \frac{1}{N} + \left[1 - \frac{1}{N}\right]^{l-1}\left[\left[1 - \frac{l-1}{N}\right]\left[1 - \frac{1}{N}\right]^{N+\frac{l(l-1)}{2}} + \frac{1}{N}\right]$$

Proof. For proving the first conditional bias, we need to trace the value 0 over KSA and the first l rounds of PRGA. We start from $S^K_0[0] = 0$, as the initial state S^K_0 of KSA is the identity permutation in RC4. The following gives the trace pattern for 0 through the complete KSA and l initial rounds of PRGA. We shall discuss some of the transitions in details.

$$0 : S^K_0[0] \xrightarrow{1} S^K_1[K[0]] \xrightarrow{p_1} S^K_l[K[0]] \xrightarrow{p_2} S^K_{l+1}[l] \xrightarrow{p_3} S_{l-1}[l] \xrightarrow{1} S_l[j_l]$$

Here $p_1 = \left(1 - \frac{l}{N}\right)\left(1 - \frac{1}{N}\right)^{l-1}$ denotes the probability that index $K[0]$ is not touched by i^K and j^K in the first l rounds of KSA, $p_2 = \left(1 - \frac{1}{N}\right)^{1+\frac{l(l+1)}{2}} + \frac{1}{N}$

denotes the probability $\Pr(j_{l+1}^K = f_l = K[0])$ (using Proposition 2) such that 0 is swapped from $S_l^K[K[0]]$ to $S_{l+1}^K[l]$, and $p_3 = \left(1 - \frac{1}{N}\right)^{N-2}$ denotes the probability that the location $S_{l+1}^K[l]$ containing 0 is not touched by i^K, j^K in the remaining $N - l - 1$ rounds of KSA or by i, j in the first $l - 1$ rounds of PRGA. So, this path gives a total probability of $p_1p_2p_3$. If this path does not hold, we assume that the event $(S_l[j_l] = 0)$ still holds at random, with probability $1/N$. Thus, the total probability is obtained as

$$\Pr(S_l[j_l] = 0) = p_1p_2p_3 + (1 - p_1p_2p_3) \cdot \frac{1}{N} = \frac{1}{N} + \left(1 - \frac{1}{N}\right) p_1p_2p_3.$$

We do a similar propagation tracking for the value $f_{l-1} = -l$ to prove the second result, and the main path for this tracking looks as follows.

$$-l : S_0^K[-l] \xrightarrow{p_4} S_0[l-1] \xrightarrow{p_5} S_{l-2}[l-1]$$

Here we get $p_4 = \Pr(S_0[l-1] = f_{l-1}) = \left(1 - \frac{l-1}{N}\right)\left(1 - \frac{1}{N}\right)^{N + \frac{l(l-1)}{2}} + \frac{1}{N}$ using Proposition 3 directly, and $p_5 = \left(1 - \frac{1}{N}\right)^{l-2}$ denotes the probability that the index $(l-1)$, containing $-l$, is not touched by i, j in the first $l - 2$ rounds of PRGA. Similar to the previous proof, the total probability can be calculated as

$$\Pr(S_{l-2}[l-1] = -l) = p_4p_5 + (1 - p_4p_5) \cdot \frac{1}{N} = \frac{1}{N} + \left(1 - \frac{1}{N}\right) p_4p_5.$$

We get the claimed results by substituting p_1, p_2, p_3 and p_4, p_5 appropriately. □

Numerical Values. If we substitute $l = 16$, the most common keylength for RC4, and $N = 256$, we get the probabilities of Theorem 6 of magnitude

$$\Pr(S_l[j_l] = 0 \mid f_{l-1} = -l) \approx \Pr(S_{l-2}[l-1] = -l \mid f_{l-1} = -l) \approx 50/N.$$

These are, to the best of our knowledge, *the best known key-dependent conditional biases in RC4 PRGA till date.* The estimates closely match the experiments we performed over 100 million runs with 16-byte keys. In the next theorem, we look at a few natural consequences of these biases.

Theorem 7. *Suppose that l is the length of the RC4 secret key. Given that $f_{l-1} = \sum_{i=0}^{l-1} K[i] + l(l-1)/2 = -l$, the probabilities $\Pr(S_l[l] = -l \mid f_{l-1} = -l)$ and $\Pr(t_l = -l \mid f_{l-1} = -l)$ are approximately*

$$\frac{1}{N} + \left(1 - \frac{1}{N}\right) \cdot \left[\frac{1}{N} + \left[1 - \frac{l}{N}\right]\left[1 - \frac{1}{N}\right]^{N+l-2} \left[\left[1 - \frac{1}{N}\right]^{1+\frac{l(l+1)}{2}} + \frac{1}{N}\right]\right] \cdot \left[\frac{1}{N} + \left[1 - \frac{1}{N}\right]^{l-1} \left[\left[1 - \frac{1}{N}\right]^{N-l} + \frac{1}{N}\right]\right]$$

Proof. Before proving the path for the target events, let us take a look at rounds $l-1$ and l of RC4 PRGA when $S_{l-2}[l-1] = -l$ and $S_{l-1}[l] = 0$. In this situation, we have the following propagation for the value $-l$.

$$-l : S_{l-2}[l-1] \xrightarrow{1} S_{l-1}[j_{l-1}] = S_{l-1}[j_l] \xrightarrow{1} S_l[l]$$

In the above path, the equality holds because $j_l = j_{l-1} + S_{l-1}[l] = j_{l-1} + 0$ as per the conditions. Again, we have $S_l[j_l] = S_{l-1}[l] = 0$, implying $t_l = S_l[l] + S_l[j_l] = -l + 0 = -l$ as well. This explains the same expression for the probabilities of the two events in the statement.

Note that we require both the events $(S_l[j_l] = 0 \mid f_{l-1} = -l)$ and $(S_{l-2}[l-1] = -l \mid f_{l-1} = -l)$ to occur simultaneously, and need to calculate the joint probability. Also note that there is a significant overlap between the tracking paths of these two events, as they both assume that the first l positions of the state S_0^K are not touched by j^K in the first l rounds of KSA (refer to the proof of Theorem 6 of this paper and proofs of [9, Theorem 1, Corollary 1] for details). In other words, if we assume the occurrence of event $(S_l[j_l] = 0 \mid f_{l-1} = -l)$ (with probability p_6, as derived in Theorem 6, say), then the precondition for $(S_{l-2}[l-1] = -l \mid f_{l-1} = -l)$ will be satisfied, and thus the modified conditional probability is $\Pr(S_{l-2}[l-1] = -l \mid S_l[j_l] = 0 \ \& \ f_{l-1} = -l) = \frac{1}{N} + \left[1 - \frac{1}{N}\right]^{l-1} \left[\left[1 - \frac{1}{N}\right]^{N-l} + \frac{1}{N}\right] = p_7$, say. Now, we can compute the joint probability of the two events as

$$\Pr(S_l[l] = -l \mid f_{l-1} = -l) = p_6 p_7 + (1 - p_6 p_7) \cdot \frac{1}{N} = \frac{1}{N} + \left(1 - \frac{1}{N}\right) \cdot p_6 p_7.$$

Substituting the values of p_6 and p_7, we obtain the desired result. Event $(t_l = -l)$ follows immediately from $(S_l[l] = -l)$, with the same conditional probability. □

Numerical Values. Substituting $l = 16$ and $N = 256$, we get the probabilities of Theorem 7 of the magnitude $\Pr(S_l[l] = -l \mid f_{l-1} = -l) = \Pr(t_l = -l \mid f_{l-1} = -l) \approx 20/N$. These estimates closely match our experimental results taken over 100 million runs of RC4 with 16-byte keys.

Conditional Bias in Output. We could also find that the bias in $(z_l = -l)$ is caused due to the event $f_{l-1}[l]$, but in a different path than the one we have discussed so far. We prove the formal statement next as Theorem 8.

Theorem 8. *Suppose that l is the length of the secret key of RC4. Given that $f_{l-1} = \sum_{i=0}^{l-1} K[i] + l(l-1)/2 = -l$, the probability $\Pr(z_l = -l)$ is approximately*

$$\frac{1}{N} + \left[1 - \frac{1}{N}\right] \cdot \left[\frac{1}{N} + \left[1 - \frac{l}{N}\right]\left[1 - \frac{1}{N}\right]^{N+l-2} \left[\left[1 - \frac{1}{N}\right]^{1+l} + \frac{1}{N}\right]\right.$$
$$\left. \cdot \left[\frac{1}{N} + \left[1 - \frac{1}{N}\right]^{l+1} \Pr(S_0[S_0[l-1]] = f_{l-1})\right]\right]$$

Proof. The proof is similar to that of Theorem 7 as both require $S_l[j_l] = S_{l-1}[l] = 0$ to occur first. Note that if $S_l[j_l] = S_{l-1}[l] = 0$, we will always have

$$z_l = S_l[S_l[l] + S_l[j_l]] = S_l[S_{l-2}[l-1] + 0] = S_l[S_{l-2}[l-1]].$$

Thus the basic intuition is to use the path $S_0[S_0[l-1]] = f_{l-1} = -l$ to get

$$-l : S_0[S_0[l-1]] \xrightarrow{p_8} S_{l-2}[S_{l-2}[l-1]] \xrightarrow{p_9} S_l[S_{l-2}[l-1]]$$

In the above expression, $p_8 = \left(1 - \frac{1}{N}\right)^{l-2}$ and $p_9 = \left(1 - \frac{1}{N}\right)^2$ denote the probabilities of j not touching the state index that stores the value $-l$. This introduces a probability $\left(1 - \frac{1}{N}\right)^l$. Thus $\Pr(S_l[S_{l-2}[l-1]] = -l \mid f_{l-1} = -l)$ is cumulatively given by $\frac{1}{N} + \left[1 - \frac{1}{N}\right]^{l+1} \Pr(S_0[S_0[l-1]] = f_{l-1}) = p_{10}$, say. Note that one of the preconditions to prove [9, Theorem 4] is that the first $(l-1)$ places of state S_0^K remain untouched by j^K for the first $l-1$ rounds of KSA. This partially matches with the precondition to prove $\Pr(S_l[j_l] = 0 \mid f_{l-1} = -l)$ (see Theorem 6), where we require the same for first l places over the first l rounds of KSA. Thus we derive the formula for $\Pr(S_l[j_l] = 0 \mid S_0[S_0[l-1]] = -l \;\&\; f_{l-1} = -l)$ by modifying the result of Theorem 6 as $\frac{1}{N} + \left[1 - \frac{l}{N}\right]\left[1 - \frac{1}{N}\right]^{N+l-2}\left[\left[1 - \frac{1}{N}\right]^{1+l} + \frac{1}{N}\right] = p_{11}$, say. The final probability for $(z_l = -l \mid f_{l-1} = -l)$ can now be computed as

$$\Pr(z_l = -l \mid f_{l-1} = -l) = p_{10}p_{11} + (1 - p_{10}p_{11}) \cdot \frac{1}{N} = \frac{1}{N} + \left(1 - \frac{1}{N}\right) \cdot p_{10}p_{11}.$$

Substituting appropriate values for p_{10} and p_{11}, we get the desired result. □

Let us consider $\Pr(z_l = -l \mid S_l[j_l] = 0) = \Pr(S_l[S_{l-2}[l-1]] = -l \mid S_l[j_l] = 0)$. From the proof of Theorem 8, it is evident that the events $(S_l[S_{l-2}[l-1]] = -l)$ and $(S_l[j_l] = 0)$ have no obvious connection. Yet, there exists a strong correlation between them, possibly due to some hidden events that cause them to co-occur with a high probability. We found that one of these hidden events is $(f_{l-1} = -l)$.

From the proofs of Theorems 6 and 8, we know that both the aforementioned events depend strongly on $(f_{l-1} = -l)$, but along two different paths, as follows.

$$\begin{aligned} 0 &: S_0^K[0] \xrightarrow{1} S_1^K[K[0]] \xrightarrow{p_1} S_l^K[K[0]] \xrightarrow{p_2} S_{l+1}^K[l] \xrightarrow{p_3} S_{l-1}[l] \xrightarrow{1} S_l[j_l] \\ -l &: S_0^K[S_0^K[l-1]] \xrightarrow{p_{12}} S_0[S_0[l-1]] \xrightarrow{p_8} S_{l-2}[S_{l-2}[l-1]] \xrightarrow{p_9} S_l[S_{l-2}[l-1]] \end{aligned}$$

Here p_{12} depends on the probability $\Pr(S_0[S_0[l-1]] = f_{l-1})$ from Proposition 4. Using these two paths, one may obtain the value of $\Pr(z_l = -l \;\&\; S_l[j_l] = 0)$ as

$$\begin{aligned} &\Pr(z_l = -l \;\&\; S_l[j_l] = 0) \\ &\quad = \Pr(f_{l-1} = -l) \cdot \Pr(S_l[S_{l-2}[l-1]] = -l \;\&\; S_l[j_l] = 0 \mid f_{l-1} = -l) \\ &\quad\quad + \Pr(f_{l-1} \neq -l) \cdot \Pr(S_l[S_{l-2}[l-1]] = -l \;\&\; S_l[j_l] = 0 \mid f_{l-1} \neq -l). \end{aligned}$$

As before, $\Pr(f_{l-1} = -l)$ can be taken as $1/N$. If one assumes that the aforementioned two paths are independent, the probabilities from Theorems 6 and 8 can be substituted in the above expression. If one further assumes that the events occur uniformly at random if $f_{l-1} \neq -l$, the values of $\Pr(S_l[j_l] = 0 \mid z_l = -l)$ and $\Pr(z_l = -l \mid S_l[j_l] = 0)$ turn out to be approximately $5/N$ each (for $l = 16$).

However, our experiments show that the two paths mentioned earlier are *not entirely independent*, and we obtain $\Pr(z_l = -l \ \& \ S_l[j_l] = 0 \mid f_{l-1} = -l) \approx 5/N$. Moreover, the events are *not uniformly random* if $f_{l-1} \neq -l$; rather they are considerably biased for a range of values of f_{l-1} around $-l$ (e.g., for values like $-l+1$, $-l+2$ etc.). These hidden paths contribute towards the probability $\Pr(f_{l-1} \neq -l) \Pr(z_l = -l \ \& \ S_l[j_l] = 0 \mid f_{l-1} \neq -l) \approx 5/N^2$. Through a careful treatment of the dependences and all the hidden paths, one would be able to justify the above observations, and obtain

$$\Pr(S_l[j_l] = 0 \mid z_l = -l) \approx \Pr(z_l = -l \mid S_l[j_l] = 0) \approx 10/N.$$

Similar techniques for analyzing dependences and hidden paths would work for all correlations reported in Equations 6, 7, 8, 9 and, 10.

We now shift our focus to $\Pr(z_l = -l \mid f_{l-1} = -l)$ and its implications.

Numerical Values. First of all, notice that the value of $\Pr(z_l = -l \mid f_{l-1} = -l)$ depends on the value of $\Pr(S_0[S_0[l-1]] = f_{l-1})$. Proposition 4 gives an explicit formula for $\Pr(z_l = -l \mid f_{l-1} = -l)$ for l up to 32. As l increases beyond 32, one may check by experimentation that this probability converges approximately to $1/N$. Thus, for $1 \leq l \leq 32$, one can use the formula from Proposition 4, and for $l > 32$, one may replace $\Pr(S_0[S_0[l-1]] = f_{l-1})$ by $1/N$ to approximately compute the distribution of $(z_l = -l \mid f_{l-1} = -l)$ completely. In fact, after the state recovery attack by Maximov and Khovratovich [8], that is of time complexity around 2^{241}, choosing a secret key of length $l > 30$ is not meaningful. The value of $\Pr(z_l = -l \mid f_{l-1} = -l)$ for some typical values of l are

$$12/N \ \text{ for } \ l = 5 \qquad 11/N \ \text{ for } \ l = 8 \qquad 7/N \ \text{ for } \ l = 16 \qquad 2/N \ \text{ for } \ l = 30.$$

In the list above, each conditional probability is quite high in magnitude compared to the natural probability of random occurrence. We try to exploit this bias in the next section to predict the length of RC4 secret key.

3.3 Keylength Prediction from Keystream

The huge conditional bias proved in Theorem 8 hints that there may be a related unconditional bias present in the event $z_l = -l$ as well. In fact, New_007 in [12, Fig. 5] reports a bias in $(z_i = -i)$ for $i = 0 \bmod 16$. The reported bias for $i = 16$ is $1.0411/N$. Notice that almost all experiments of [12] used the keylength $l = 16$, which encourages our speculation for an unconditional bias in $(z_l = -l)$ for any general keylength l of RC4 secret key. Systematic investigation in this direction reveals the following result.

Theorem 9. *Suppose that l is the length of the secret key of RC4. The probability $\Pr(z_l = -l)$ is given by*

$$\Pr(z_l = -l) \approx \frac{1}{N} + [N \cdot \Pr(z_l = -l \mid f_{l-1} = -l) - 1] \cdot \frac{1}{N^2}.$$

Proof. We provide a quick sketch of the proof to obtain a crude approximation of this bias in z_l. Notice that we already have a path $(z_l = -l \mid f_{l-1} = -l)$ with probability calculated in Theorem 8. If we assume that for all other values of $f_{l-1} \neq -l$, the output z_l can take the value $-l$ uniformly at random, we have

$$\begin{aligned}\Pr(z_l = -l) &\approx \Pr(f_{l-1} = -l) \cdot \Pr(z_l = -l \mid f_{l-1} = -l)\\ &\quad + \Pr(f_{l-1} \neq -l) \cdot \Pr(z_l = -l \mid f_{l-1} \neq -l)\\ &= \frac{1}{N} \cdot \Pr(z_l = -l \mid f_{l-1} = -l) + \left(1 - \frac{1}{N}\right) \cdot \frac{1}{N}\\ &= \frac{1}{N} + [N \cdot \Pr(z_l = -l \mid f_{l-1} = -l) - 1] \cdot \frac{1}{N^2}.\end{aligned}$$

Thus we obtain the desired result. □

Numerical Values. We have a closed form expression for $\Pr(z_l = -l \mid f_{l-1} = -l)$ from Theorem 8 in cases where $1 \leq l \leq 32$ (using Proposition 4). We have also calculated some numerical values of this probability for $l = 5, 8, 16, 30$ and $N = 256$. Using those numeric approximations, the value of $\Pr(z_l = -l)$ is

$$1/N + 11/N^2 \text{ for } l = 5 \qquad 1/N + 10/N^2 \text{ for } l = 8$$

$$1/N + 6/N^2 \text{ for } l = 16 \qquad 1/N + 2/N^2 \text{ for } l = 30$$

Predicting the Keylength. The lower bound for $\Pr(z_l = -l)$ within the typical range of keylength ($5 \leq l \leq 30$) is approximately $1/N + 1/N^2$, which is quite high and easily detectable. In experiments with 100 million runs and different keylengths, we have found that the probabilities are even higher than those mentioned above. This helps us in predicting the length of the secret key from the output, as follows.

1. Find the output byte z_x biased towards $-x$. This requires $O(N^3)$ many samples as the bias is $O(1/N^2)$. A 'sample' in this case means the observation of keystream bytes z_x for all $5 \leq x \leq 30$ for a specific key. The bias is computed by examining these keystream bytes with different keys, which are all of the same length l, say.
2. Check if the probability $\Pr(z_x = -x)$ is equal or greater than the value proved in Theorem 9.
3. If the above statements hold for some $5 \leq x \leq 30$, the keylength can be accurately predicted as $l = x$.

Although the bias in $z_l = -l$ has been noticed earlier in the literature for specific keylengths, no attempts have been made for its generalization. Moreover, to the best of our knowledge, the prediction of keylength from the keystream has never been attempted. We have performed extensive experiments with varying keylengths to verify the practical feasibility of the prediction technique. This prediction technique proves to be successful for all keylengths within the typical usage range $5 \leq l \leq 30$. As already pointed out in Section 3.2, choosing a secret key of length $l > 30$ is not recommended. So, our *keylength prediction* effectively works for all practical values of the keylength.

4 Conclusion

In the paper [12] of SAC 2010, several empirical observations relating a few RC4 variables have been reported, and here we prove all the significant ones. In the process, we provide a framework for justifying such non-random events in their full generality. Our study identifies and proves a family of new key correlations beyond those observed in [12]. These, in turn, result in keylength dependent biases in initial keystream bytes of RC4, enabling effective keylength prediction.

Acknowledgments. The authors would like to thank the anonymous reviewers for their feedback that helped in improving the presentation of this paper.

References

1. Fluhrer, S.R., Mantin, I., Shamir, A.: Weaknesses in the Key Scheduling Algorithm of RC4. In: Vaudenay, S., Youssef, A.M. (eds.) SAC 2001. LNCS, vol. 2259, pp. 1–24. Springer, Heidelberg (2001)
2. Klein, A.: Attacks on the RC4 stream cipher. Designs, Codes and Cryptography 48(3), 269–286 (2008)
3. LAN/MAN Standard Committee. ANSI/IEEE standard 802.11b: Wireless LAN Medium Access Control (MAC) and Physical Layer (phy) Specifications (1999)
4. LAN/MAN Standard Committee. ANSI/IEEE standard 802.11i: Amendment 6: Wireless LAN Medium Access Control (MAC) and Physical Layer (phy) Specifications. Draft 3 (2003)
5. Maitra, S., Paul, G., Sen Gupta, S.: Attack on Broadcast RC4 Revisited. In: Joux, A. (ed.) FSE 2011. LNCS, vol. 6733, pp. 199–217. Springer, Heidelberg (2011)
6. Mantin, I.: Analysis of the stream cipher RC4. Master's Thesis, The Weizmann Institute of Science, Israel (2001), `http://www.wisdom.weizmann.ac.il/~itsik/RC4/Papers/Mantin1.zip`
7. Mantin, I., Shamir, A.: A Practical Attack on Broadcast RC4. In: Matsui, M. (ed.) FSE 2001. LNCS, vol. 2355, pp. 152–164. Springer, Heidelberg (2002)
8. Maximov, A., Khovratovich, D.: New State Recovery Attack on RC4. In: Wagner, D. (ed.) CRYPTO 2008. LNCS, vol. 5157, pp. 297–316. Springer, Heidelberg (2008)
9. Paul, G., Maitra, S.: On biases of permutation and keystream bytes of RC4 towards the secret key. Cryptography Communications 1, 225–268 (2009)
10. Paul, G., Rathi, S., Maitra, S.: On Non-negligible bias of the first output byte of RC4 towards the first three bytes of the secret key. Designs, Codes and Cryptography 49(1-3), 123–134 (2008)
11. Roos, A.: A class of weak keys in the RC4 stream cipher. Two posts in sci.crypt, message-id `43u1eh$1j3@hermes.is.co.za`, `44ebge$llf@hermes.is.co.za` (1995), `http://marcel.wanda.ch/Archive/WeakKeys`
12. Sepehrdad, P., Vaudenay, S., Vuagnoux, M.: Discovery and Exploitation of New Biases in RC4. In: Biryukov, A., Gong, G., Stinson, D.R. (eds.) SAC 2010. LNCS, vol. 6544, pp. 74–91. Springer, Heidelberg (2011)
13. Sepehrdad, P., Vaudenay, S., Vuagnoux, M.: Statistical Attack on RC4. In: Paterson, K.G. (ed.) EUROCRYPT 2011. LNCS, vol. 6632, pp. 343–363. Springer, Heidelberg (2011)
14. Vaudenay, S., Vuagnoux, M.: Passive–Only Key Recovery Attacks on RC4. In: Adams, C., Miri, A., Wiener, M. (eds.) SAC 2007. LNCS, vol. 4876, pp. 344–359. Springer, Heidelberg (2007)
15. Wagner, D.: My RC4 weak keys. Post in sci.crypt, message-id `447o1l$cbj@cnn.Princeton.EDU`. (September 26, 1995), `http://www.cs.berkeley.edu/~daw/my-posts/my-rc4-weak-keys`

Combined Differential and Linear Cryptanalysis of Reduced-Round PRINTCIPHER

Ferhat Karakoç[1,2], Hüseyin Demirci[1], and A. Emre Harmancı[2]

[1] Tübitak BILGEM UEKAE, 41470, Gebze, Kocaeli, Turkey
{ferhatk,huseyind}@uekae.tubitak.gov.tr
[2] Istanbul Technical University, Computer Engineering Department, 34469, Maslak, Istanbul, Turkey
harmanci@itu.edu.tr

Abstract. In this paper we analyze the security of PRINTCIPHER using a technique that combines differential and linear cryptanalysis. This technique is different from differential-linear cryptanalysis. We use linear approximations to increase the probability of differential characteristics. We show that specific choices of some of the key bits give rise to a certain differential characteristic probability, which is far higher than the best characteristic probability claimed by the designers. We give the underlying mechanism of this probability increase. We have developed attacks on 29 and 31 rounds of PRINTCIPHER-48 for 4.54% and 0.036% of the keys, respectively. Moreover, we have implemented the proposed attack algorithm on 20 rounds of the cipher.

Keywords: PRINTCIPHER, differential cryptanalysis, linear cryptanalysis, differential-linear cryptanalysis.

1 Introduction

The security and privacy in constrained environments such as RFID tags and sensor networks is a challenging subject in cryptography. Lightweight cryptographic algorithms and protocols are required for this reason. Some block and stream ciphers and hash functions are proposed to meet this requirement [2, 3, 8, 10–12, 17, 18, 22, 27, 28]. The encryption algorithm PRINTCIPHER was introduced in CHES 2010 as a lightweight block cipher by Knudsen et al. [19]. The authors aim to build an algorithm especially suitable for integrated circuit printing.

At FSE 2011, Abdelraheem et al. [1] applied a differential attack on reduced rounds of PRINTCIPHER. Their attack can break half of the rounds of the cipher. The authors have observed that the differential distribution has a key dependent structure. They have exploited this fact to get information about the key bits. Their attack uses the whole codebook and has a complexity about 2^{48} computational steps for the 48-bit version of the algorithm. The authors use the roots of permutations to deduce the key bits which affect the key-dependent permutations. There are also algebraic cryptanalysis and side channel analyses of PRINTCIPHER [9, 31]. But, the designers noticed that side channel and related key attacks were not their major concern in the design of PRINTCIPHER.

A. Miri and S. Vaudenay (Eds.): SAC 2011, LNCS 7118, pp. 169–184, 2012.

Recently, Leander et al. [21] have announced an attack on the full round PRINTCIPHER-48 for a class of 2^{52} keys. Also Ågren et al. [15] have applied a linear attack on 28-round PRINTCIPHER-48 which works for half of the keys.

Differential [7] and linear cryptanalysis [25] are the most used cryptanalysis techniques for block ciphers. Also there are some attacks which uses combinations of classical techniques such as impossible-differential [4], boomerang [30], and differential-linear attack [20]. In the differential-linear method, the attacker divides the cipher into two parts where a differential and a linear approximation are constructed for the first and second parts respectively. This combined attack method was enhanced by some other works [5, 23, 32] and applied on some ciphers such as IDEA and Serpent [6, 14, 16]. Also, there are some key-dependent attacks [13, 16, 26, 29] where [16] uses a differential-linear technique.

In this work, we combine differential and linear cryptanalysis in a different technique on PRINTCIPHER. We construct linear approximations to increase the probability of differential characteristics. Using this method we have found that for some of the keys, the probability of an r-round differential characteristic is significantly higher than the maximum probability of r-round characteristic claimed by the designers. We point out the special key values which induce to this weakness and explain the mechanism behind this observation. We show that 4.54% and 0.036% of the keys are weak for 29 and 31 rounds, respectively.

This paper proceeds as follows. In Section 2, we briefly introduce the notation we use and the PRINTCIPHER. In Section 3, we explain the weak key mechanism of the cipher. Section 4 is on the cryptanalytic attacks using the observations of the previous section. Finally, we conclude the paper in Section 5.

2 The PRINTCIPHER Encryption Algorithm

2.1 Notation

Throughout this paper, we use sk_1 for the key used in the xor part and sk_2 for the key which is used to determine the key dependent permutation. The letters x^i, y^i, z^i, t^i denote the inputs of the round, the permutation, the key dependent permutation and the S-box layers in the i-th round, respectively. $x[i]$ represents the i-th bit of the variable x where $x[0]$ is the rightmost bit of x. Also $x[i-j]$ is the bit string $x[i]x[i-1]...x[j]$, where $i > j$. We denote the number of 1's of a bit vector by $hw(x_i, ..., x_1, x_0)$. We write the bit values between parentheses. Also we use Δ to indicate the difference between two bit strings.

2.2 PRINTCIPHER

The PRINTCIPHER encryption algorithm has two versions, PRINTCIPHER-48 has block size of 48 bits, consists of 48 rounds and uses 80-bit key whereas PRINTCIPHER-96 has block size of 96 bits, consists of 96 rounds and admits 160-bit key.

PRINTCIPHER has an SP-network structure where the S-box is chosen to have the best differential and linear distributions among 3-bit functions. Each round function consists of a key xoring, a bitwise permutation over 48 (resp 96) bits, a round-constant xoring to the least significant bits, a bitwise permutation on 3 bits and an S-box layer.

Note that the round key $k = sk_1||sk_2$ is identical at each round. The first b bits of the key, sk_1, is xored to the state at the beginning of each round. After that the following bit permutation is applied:

$$P(i) = \begin{cases} 3i \bmod b-1 & \text{for } 0 \leq i \leq b-2, \\ b-1 & \text{for } i = b-1, \end{cases}$$

where $b \in \{48, 96\}$ is the block size. Then, a 6-bit or a 7-bit round constant is added to the least significant bits of the state according to the block size. We would like to point out that most significant bits are not affected from this addition. This is followed by a key dependent permutation. In this layer, sk_2 is divided into 2-bits and each 2-bit is used to determine the permutation on each 3-bit of the state. This permutation is defined as follows where $a_1||a_0$ are the bits of sk_2 and $c_2||c_1||c_0$ are the state bits:

$a_1\|\|a_0$	
00	$c_2\|\|c_1\|\|c_0$
01	$c_1\|\|c_2\|\|c_0$
10	$c_2\|\|c_0\|\|c_1$
11	$c_0\|\|c_1\|\|c_2$

Finally, the same S-box is applied in parallel to every 3-bit of the state. The unique S-box used in PRINTCIPHER is the following:

x	0	1	2	3	4	5	6	7
$S[x]$	0	1	3	6	7	4	5	2

The round function of PRINTCIPHER-48 is shown in Figure 1. For a more detailed description of PRINTCIPHER we refer to [19].

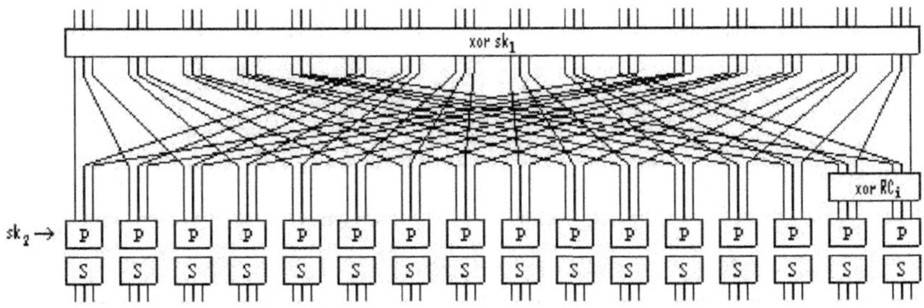

Fig. 1. One round of PRINTCIPHER-48

3 Key Dependent Differential and Linear Characteristics

According to the designers of PRINTCIPHER, maximum probability of an r-round differential characteristic for both versions of the cipher is $2^{-2\times r}$. However, we have found that an r-round differential characteristic for PRINTCIPHER-48 can have a probability of about $2^{-(6+1.68\times(r-3))}$ for 4.54% of the keys and a probability of $2^{-(7.68+1.51\times(r-4))}$ for 0.036% of the keys. To clarify the significance of the probabilities note that for 24-round differential characteristic we have a probability of $2^{-41.28}$ for the first and $2^{-37.88}$ for the second key subset. But according the designers of the algorithm the maximum probability of 24-round differential characteristic is 2^{-48}. Also for PRINTCIPHER-96 one can find similar subsets of the keys resulting higher probabilities than the probability expressed by the designers. We will focus on the analysis of PRINTCIPHER-48 in this paper.

The reason of this probability increase is the correlation of the input and output bits of active S-boxes in the differential paths in consecutive rounds. To express the reason in detail first we give differential and linear properties of the S-box.

3.1 Differential and Linear Properties of the S-Box

The S-box conserves one bit input difference in the same position in the output with probability 2^{-2}, see Table 1.

Table 1. Difference distribution table of the S-box

		Output Difference							
		000	001	010	011	100	101	110	111
	000	8	0	0	0	0	0	0	0
	001	0	2	0	2	0	2	0	2
	010	0	0	2	2	0	0	2	2
Input	011	0	2	2	0	0	2	2	0
Difference	100	0	0	0	0	2	2	2	2
	101	0	2	0	2	2	0	2	0
	110	0	0	2	2	2	2	0	0
	111	0	2	2	0	2	0	0	2

Similarly, it can be seen in Table 2 that i-th bit of the input of the S-box equals to i-th bit of the output with a bias 2^{-2} or -2^{-2}.

3.2 Characteristics for 4.54% of the Keys of PRINTCIPHER-48

Using the properties of the S-box mentioned in the previous section and putting some conditions on the key bits we are able to combine a differential and a linear characteristic resulting a differential characteristic with higher probability than

Table 2. Linear approximation table of the S-box

	Output Mask							
Input Mask	000	001	010	011	100	101	110	111
000	4	0	0	0	0	0	0	0
001	0	−2	0	2	0	2	0	2
010	0	0	2	2	0	0	2	−2
011	0	2	−2	0	0	2	2	0
100	0	0	0	0	2	−2	2	2
101	0	2	0	2	2	0	−2	0
110	0	0	2	−2	2	2	0	0
111	0	2	2	0	−2	0	0	2

2^{-2} for one round. We have found 3 different combined characteristics each of which puts 6-bit conditions on the key bits of PRINTCIPHER-48. One of the characteristics is shown in Figure 2 and the other characteristics are given in Figure 6 and Figure 7 in Appendix A. To express the reason of the probability increase we focus on the characteristic shown in Figure 2. The probability increase for the other characteristics depends on a similar reason.

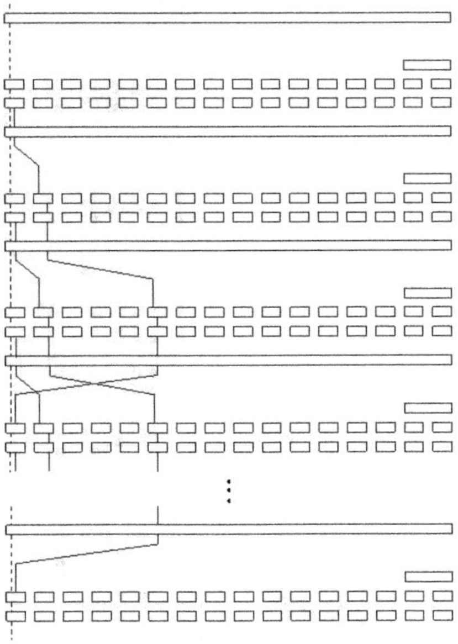

Fig. 2. Characteristic 1: A combined differential and linear characteristic which has probability $2^{-(6+1.68\times(r-3))}$ for r rounds

In Figure 2, the dotted line and the solid line shows the differential path and the linear path respectively. We give the following lemma to show the correlation of the input-output bits of the active S-boxes in the differential path in consecutive rounds using the linear path in Figure 2.

Lemma 1. *Let the key bits of* PRINTCIPHER-48 *satisfy the following equations*

$$sk_2[29] = 1, sk_2[28] = 1, sk_2[21] = 0, sk_2[20] = 1.$$

Then, the bias of the equation $x^i[46] \oplus sk_1[46] \oplus sk_1[42] \oplus sk_1[31] = z^{i+2}[46]$ is -2^{-3} where x^i is the input of the i-th round and z^{i+2} is the input of the key dependent permutation in the $(i+2)$-th round.

Proof. Let the three input bits of the S-box be $i_2i_1i_0$ and three output bits be $o_2o_1o_0$. From the linear approximation table of the S-box, the biases of equations $i_0 \oplus o_0 = 0$ and $i_1 \oplus o_1 = 0$ are -2^{-2} and 2^{-2} respectively. Using this information we can write the following equations with the corresponding biases:

$$t^i[42] = x^{i+1}[42] \quad , \epsilon = -2^{-2}$$
$$t^{i+1}[31] = x^{i+2}[31] \ , \epsilon = 2^{-2}.$$

Also using the following equations

$$x^i[46] \oplus sk_1[46] = t^i[42] \text{ (since } sk_2[29] = 1 \text{ and } sk_2[28] = 1)$$
$$x^{i+1}[42] \oplus sk_1[42] = t^{i+1}[31] \text{ (since } sk_2[21] = 0 \text{ and } sk_2[20] = 1)$$
$$x^{i+2}[31] \oplus sk_1[31] = z^{i+2}[46]$$

we can reach the equation $x^i[46] \oplus sk_1[46] \oplus sk_1[42] \oplus sk_1[31] = z^{i+2}[46]$ with bias $2 \times (-2^{-2}) \times 2^{-2} = -2^{-3}$ using the Piling-up Lemma [25].

The correlation of the input and output bits of the active S-boxes in consecutive rounds helps us to give one of our main statements for the probability of the differential characteristic shown in Figure 2.

Theorem 1. *Let the key bits of* PRINTCIPHER-48 *satisfy the following equations*

$$sk_2[30] = 0, sk_2[29] = 1, sk_2[28] = 1, sk_2[21] = 0, sk_2[20] = 1,$$
$$sk_1[46] \oplus sk_1[42] \oplus sk_1[31] = 1.$$

Then, the probability of the differential characteristic $(100...00) \rightarrow (100...00) \rightarrow ... \rightarrow (100...00)$ *for r rounds is* $2^{-(6+1.68\times(r-3))}$.

Proof. Since $sk_2[30] = 0$, the key dependent permutation layer keeps the difference in the leftmost bit. In the first three rounds, the probability of the differential characteristic is 2^{-6} because there is no linear relation between the input-output bits of the active S-boxes. In the fourth round, while $z^4[45]$ is distributed uniformly, $z^4[46]$ equals to $x^2[46] \oplus sk_1[46] \oplus sk_1[42] \oplus sk_1[31]$ with bias -2^{-3} putting $i = 2$ in Lemma 1. We know that $x^2[46] = 1$ because only the pair $(011, 111)$ conserves the difference in the leftmost bit for the S-box and the corresponding output pair is (110,010). Since $sk_1[46] \oplus sk_1[42] \oplus sk_1[31] = 1$, we have $z^4[46] = 1$ with bias 2^{-3}, that is with probability 10/16. Thus, for the fourth round the input pair of the S-box is $(011, 111)$ with probability $2^{-1} \times 10/16 = 2^{-1.68}$. That means the difference in the leftmost bit of the inputs of the S-box stays in the same position in the output of the S-box with probability $2^{-1.68}$. For the later rounds $z^i[46]$ equals to $x^{i-2}[46] \oplus sk_1[46] \oplus sk_1[42] \oplus sk_1[31] = 1$

with probability 10/16 and we may assume that $z^i[45]$ has a uniform distribution. That is, the probability for the rounds greater than four is $2^{-1.68}$. Thus the probability of the r-round differential characteristic is $2^{-(6+1.68\times(r-3))}$.

In Table 3, the key constraints for the combined characteristics are shown. We use the notation KS^i to show the key subsets which satisfy the i-th combined characteristic.

Table 3. Key constraints for the combined characteristics 1, 2, and 3

Combined Characteristic	Key Conditions	Key Subset
Characteristic 1	$sk_2[30]=0,\ sk_2[29]=1,\ sk_2[28]=1,\ sk_2[21]=0,$ $sk_2[20]=1,\ sk_1[46]\oplus sk_1[42]\oplus sk_1[31]=1$	KS^1
Characteristic 2	$sk_2[17]=1,\ sk_2[16]=0,\ sk_2[19]=0,\ sk_2[18]=1,$ $sk_2[27]\oplus sk_2[26]=0,\ sk_1[40]\oplus sk_1[29]\oplus sk_1[25]=0$	KS^2
Characteristic 3	$sk_2[15]=0,\ sk_2[14]=1,\ sk_2[13]=1,\ sk_2[12]=0,$ $sk_2[5]\oplus sk_2[4]=0,\ sk_1[22]\oplus sk_1[18]\oplus sk_1[7]=1$	KS^3

Analyzing the above conditions we have observed that the size of the key space which satisfies at least one of the constraints in Table 3 is 4.54% of the key space of the PRINTCIPHER-48.

3.3 Characteristics for 0.036% of the Keys of PRINTCIPHER-48

We increase the probability of r-round differential characteristic to $2^{-(7.68+1.51\times(r-4))}$ for 0.036% of the keys putting extra conditions on the key bits of PRINTCIPHER-48.

In Section 3.2, we use only one linear characteristic to increase the probability of the differential characteristic. To proceed the increase of the probability of the differential characteristic we use an extra linear characteristic in this section. We have found two different combined characteristics which puts 12 and 13-bit conditions on the key bits of PRINTCIPHER-48 with the probability $2^{-(7.68+1.51\times(r-4))}$ for r-round differential characteristic. One of the characteristics is shown in Figure 3 and the other characteristic is given in Figure 8 in Appendix B. We give the reason of the probability increase for the first characteristic. The second can be derived by similar techniques.

The correlation of the bits in one of the linear paths is stated in Lemma 1. The following lemma states the correlation of the bits in the new linear path.

Lemma 2. *Let the key bits of* PRINTCIPHER-48 *satisfy the following equations*

$$sk_2[10]=0, sk_2[27]=sk_2[26]=sk_2[15]=sk_2[14]=sk_2[11]=1.$$

Then, the bias of the equation $x^i[45]\oplus sk_1[45]\oplus sk_1[39]\oplus sk_1[21]\oplus sk_1[15]=z^{i+3}[45]$ *is* -2^{-4}.

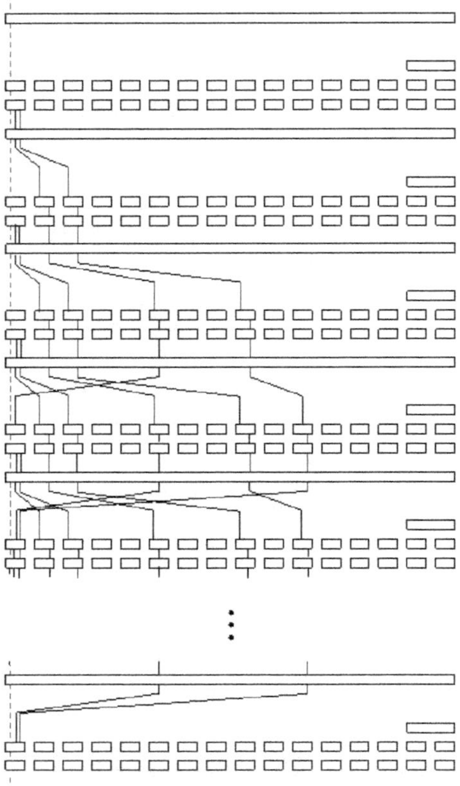

Fig. 3. Characteristic 4: A combined differential and linear characteristic which has probability $2^{-(7.68+1.51\times(r-4))}$ for r rounds

Proof. We can write the following equations with corresponding biases using linear approximation table of the S-box:

$$t^i[39] = x^{i+1}[39] \ , \ \epsilon = -2^{-2}$$
$$t^{i+1}[21] = x^{i+2}[21] \ , \ \epsilon = -2^{-2}$$
$$t^{i+2}[15] = x^{i+3}[15] \ , \ \epsilon = -2^{-2}.$$

Also using the following equations

$$x^i[45] \oplus sk_1[45] = t^i[39] \text{ (since } sk_2[27] = 1 \text{ and } sk_2[26] = 1),$$
$$x^{i+1}[39] \oplus sk_1[39] = t^{i+1}[21] \text{ (since } sk_2[15] = 1 \text{ and } sk_2[14] = 1) \ ,$$
$$x^{i+2}[21] \oplus sk_1[21] = t^{i+2}[15] \text{ (since } sk_2[11] = 1 \text{ and } sk_2[10] = 0),$$
$$x^{i+3}[15] \oplus sk_1[15] = z^{i+3}[45]$$

we can get the equation $x^i[45] \oplus sk_1[45] \oplus sk_1[39] \oplus sk_1[21] \oplus sk_1[15] = z^{i+3}[45]$ with bias $2^2 \times (-2^{-2}) \times (-2^{-2}) \times (-2^{-2}) = -2^{-4}$.

Using the correlation of the input and output bits of the active S-boxes in consecutive rounds we give our other main statement for the probability of the differential characteristic shown in Figure 3.

Theorem 2. *Let the key bits of* PRINTcipher-48 *satisfy the following constraints*

$$sk_2[30] = 0, sk_2[29] = 1, sk_2[28] = 1, sk_2[21] = 0, sk_2[20] = 1,$$
$$sk_1[46] \oplus sk_1[42] \oplus sk_1[31] = 1,$$
$$sk_2[10] = 0, sk_2[27] = 1, sk_2[26] = 1, sk_2[15] = 1, sk_2[14] = 1, sk_2[11] = 1,$$
$$sk_1[45] \oplus sk_1[39] \oplus sk_1[21] \oplus sk_1[15] = 0.$$

Then, the probability of the differential characteristic (100...00) → (100...00) → ... → (100...00) *for* r *rounds is* $2^{-(7.68+1.51\times(r-4))}$.

Proof. The probability of the first four rounds characteristic is derived as $2^{-7.68}$ in the proof of Theorem 1. For the fifth and later rounds as stated in Lemma 2 $z^i[45]$ equals to $x^{i-3}[45] \oplus sk_1[45] \oplus sk_1[39] \oplus sk_1[21] \oplus sk_1[15]$ with bias -2^{-4}. We know that $x^{i-3}[45] = 0$ because the S-box conserves the difference in the leftmost bit for only the input pair (011,111) where the corresponding output pair is (110,010). Since $sk_1[45] \oplus sk_1[39] \oplus sk_1[21] \oplus sk_1[15] = 0$, $z^i[45] = 1$ with bias 2^{-4} that is with probability 9/16. Also we know that the probability of being $z^i[46] = 1$ is 10/16 from the proof of Theorem 1. Thus, for the fifth and later rounds the input pair of the S-box is (011,111) with probability $10/16 \times 9/16 \approx 2^{-1.51}$. As a result, the probability of r-round differential characteristic shown in Figure 3 is $2^{-(7.68+1.51\times(r-4))}$.

In Table 4, the key constraints for the combined characteristics are shown.

Table 4. Key constraints for the combined characteristics 4 and 5

Combined Characteristic	Key Conditions	Key Subset
Characteristic 4	$sk_2[30] = 0$, $sk_2[29] = 1$, $sk_2[28] = 1$, $sk_2[27] = 1$, $sk_2[26] = 1$, $sk_2[21] = 0$, $sk_2[20] = 1$, $sk_2[15] = 1$, $sk_2[14] = 1$, $sk_2[11] = 1$, $sk_2[10] = 0$, $sk_1[46] \oplus sk_1[42] \oplus sk_1[31] = 1$, $sk_1[45] \oplus sk_1[39] \oplus sk_1[21] \oplus sk_1[15] = 0$	KS^4
Characteristic 5	$sk_2[15] = 0$, $sk_2[14] = 1$, $sk_2[13] = 1$, $sk_2[12] = 0$, $sk_2[11] = 1$, $sk_2[10] = 0$, $sk_2[31] = 0$, $sk_2[5] \oplus sk_2[4] = 0$, $sk_2[27] = 1$, $sk_2[26] = 1$, $sk_1[22] \oplus sk_1[18] \oplus sk_1[7] = 1$, $sk_1[45] \oplus sk_1[39] \oplus sk_1[21] \oplus sk_1[15] = 0$	KS^5

Counting the keys in the key space of PRINTcipher-48 which satisfies at least one of the conditions in Table 4 we find out that 0.036% of the key space of the PRINTcipher-48 is vulnerable to at least one of the combined characteristics.

4 Key Recovery

4.1 An Attack on 31-Round PRINTcipher-48 for KS^4

Assume that PRINTcipher-48 uses a key from KS^4. Therefore the key bits satisfy the conditions: $sk_2[30] = 0$, $sk_2[29] = 1$, $sk_2[28] = 1$, $sk_2[27] = 1$, $sk_2[26] = 1$,

$sk_2[21] = 0$, $sk_2[20] = 1$, $sk_2[15] = 1$, $sk_2[14] = 1$, $sk_2[11] = 1$, $sk_2[10] = 0$, $sk_1[46] \oplus sk_1[42] \oplus sk_1[31] = 1$, and $sk_1[45] \oplus sk_1[39] \oplus sk_1[21] \oplus sk_1[15] = 0$. Using the differential characteristic powered by linear characteristics for 28 rounds in Section 3.3 we have been able to attack on 31-round version of the cipher and recover the key bits $sk_2[25-22]$, $sk_2[19-16]$, $sk_1[47-39]$. For 28 rounds the probability of the differential characteristic is $2^{-43.92}$. The propagation of the active bit in the output of the 28-th round through 3 rounds is shown in Figure 4. In the figure, the difference in the bits in the dotted line is 0 or 1. We apply the attack using Algorithm 1.

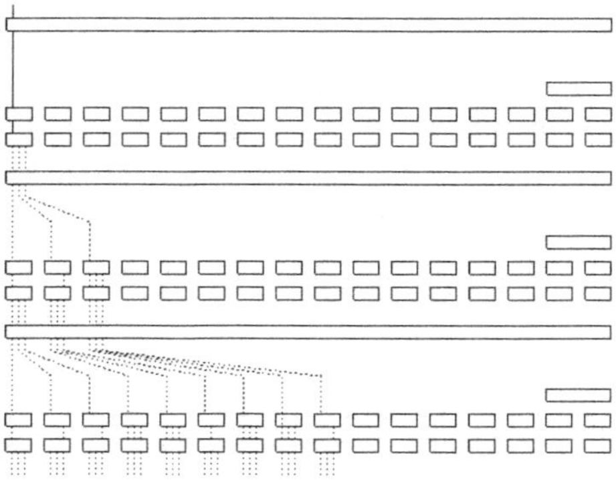

Fig. 4. 3-R attack for the key subset KS^4

We have calculated the signal to noise ratio as $2^{4.08}$ for the attack on the reduced 31-round PRINTcipher-48 using the formula

$$S/N = \frac{2^k \times p}{\alpha \times \beta} = \frac{2^{17} \times 2^{-43.92}}{2^4 \times 2^{-35}} = 2^{4.08}$$

where k denotes the number of guessed key bits, p is the probability of the characteristic, α is the average count of the subkeys per counted plaintext pairs and β is the ratio of the counted pairs to all pairs. Since S/N is bigger than 2, according to [7], about 4 right pairs are enough to determine the key bits. Thus we need about $4 \times 2^{43.92} = 2^{45.92}$ pairs.

The complexity of the attack is as follows. We use $2^{46.92}$ chosen plaintext-ciphertext data. The number of pairs used in the attack is $2^{45.92} \times 2^{-35} = 2^{10.92}$ because of the elimination in step 3 and 5 in the algorithm. Note that in step 4 we make $2^{25,92}$ inverse S-box operations. For the counted pairs we make $2^{19.92}$ key dependent permutations guessing the 8 bits ($sk_2[25-22]$ and $sk_2[19-16]$) of the key. We decrease the search space to $2^{15.92}$ using the elimination in step 9. Then we make $2^{24.92}$ two round decryptions guessing the 9 bits ($sk_1[47-39]$) of the key. In total, the number of operations in the attack approximately equivalent to $2^{24.92} \times 2 = 2^{25.92}$ one-round encryptions of PRINTcipher-48.

Algorithm 1. 3-R attack on r-round PRINTcipher-48 for KS^4.

1: N plaintext pairs which have the difference (100...000) in the plaintexts and the corresponding ciphertexts for reduced r-round cipher are given.
2: **for all** pairs **do**
3:   **if** $\Delta x^{r+1}[20-0] = (00...00)$ **then**
4:     Apply inverse of the S-box to the remaining ciphertexts.
5:     **if** $\Delta t^r[46-45] = (0,0)$, $\Delta t^r[44-43] = (0,0)$, $\Delta t^r[41-40] = (0,0)$, $hw(\Delta t^r[38-36]) \leq 1$, $hw(\Delta t^r[35-33]) \leq 1$, $\Delta t^r[32] = (0)$, $\Delta t^r[30] = (0)$, $hw(\Delta t^r[29-27]) \leq 1$, $hw(\Delta t^r[26-24]) \leq 1$, $\Delta t^r[23-22] = (0,0)$ **then**
6:       Guess the key bits $sk_2[25-22]$ and $sk_2[19-16]$.
7:       **for all** Guessed key in step 6 **do**
8:         Using the guessed key calculate $z^r[47-21]$ values of the pairs.
9:         **if** $\Delta z^r[37-36] = (0,0)$, $\Delta z^r[34-33] = (0,0)$, $\Delta z^r[28-27] = (0,0)$, $\Delta z^r[25-24] = (0,0)$ **then**
10:           Guess the key bits $sk_1[47-39]$.
11:           **for all** Guessed key in step 10 **do**
12:             Using the guessed key calculate $z^{r-1}[47-39]$ and $z^{r-2}[47-45]$ values of the pairs.
13:             **if** $\Delta z^{r-1}[46-45] = (0,0)$, $\Delta z^{r-1}[43-42] = (0,0)$, $\Delta z^{r-1}[40-39] = (0,0)$ and $\Delta z^{r-2}[47-45] = (100)$ **then**
14:               Increment the counter of the guessed key.
15:             **end if**
16:           **end for**
17:         **end if**
18:       **end for**
19:     **end if**
20:   **end if**
21: **end for**
22: The right key is the key that has the highest counter.

To verify the attack algorithm and the effect of the linear approximations we have implemented the attack for 20-round PRINTcipher-48 where the 17-round characteristic probability is $2^{-27.31}$ by Theorem 2. We have run Algorithm 1 using 2^{31} plaintext-ciphertext data 8 different times. In each of these experiments the correct key is found among the highest counted candidates. If there were no effect of linear approximations on the probability of the differential characteristic, then the probability would be 2^{-34} for 17 rounds and 2^{31} data would not be sufficient to recover the key bits.

4.2 An Attack on 29-Round PRINTcipher-48 for KS^1

We attack on 29-round PRINTcipher-48 for the assumption that the key used in the algorithm is in the key subset KS^1 using 26-round differential characteristic given in Section 3.2. We can recover the key bits $sk_2[27-22]$, $sk_2[19-14]$, $sk_1[47-39]$ applying the attack.

The propagation of the active bit in the output of the 26-th round through 3 rounds is shown in Figure 5. We use a similar algorithm as Algorithm 1 to recover the key bits. The differences between the attack algorithms for KS^1 and KS^4 are the followings:

- The condition in step 5 will be $\Delta t^r[46-45]=(0,0)$, $\Delta t^r[44-43]=(0,0)$, $hw(\Delta t^r[41-39])\leq 1$, $hw(\Delta t^r[38-36])\leq 1$, $hw(\Delta t^r[35-33])\leq 1$, $\Delta t^r[32]=(0)$, $\Delta t^r[30]=(0)$, $hw(\Delta t^r[29-27])\leq 1$, $hw(\Delta t^r[26-24])\leq 1$, $hw(\Delta t^r[23-21])\leq 1$,
- The guessed key bits will be $sk_2[27-22]$ and $sk_2[19-14]$ in step 6,
- The condition in step 9 will be $\Delta z^r[40-39]=(0,0)$, $\Delta z^r[37-36]=(0,0)$, $\Delta z^r[34-33]=(0,0)$, $\Delta z^r[28-27]=(0,0)$, $\Delta z^r[25-24]=(0,0)$, $\Delta z^r[22-21]=(0,0)$.

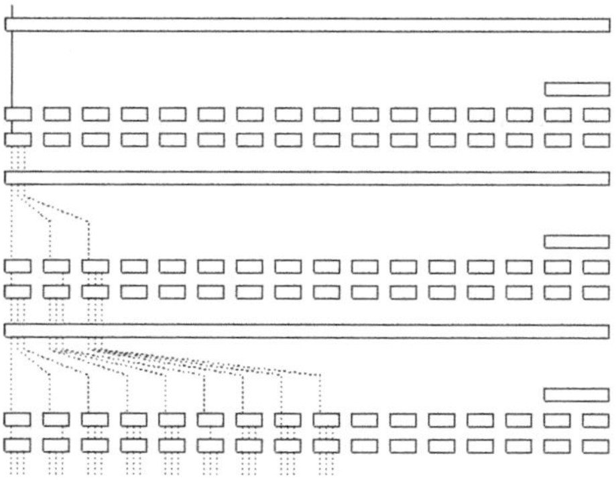

Fig. 5. 3-R attack for the key subset KS^1

We have calculated the signal to noise ratio as

$$S/N=\frac{2^k\times p}{\alpha\times\beta}=\frac{2^{21}\times 2^{-44.64}}{2^6\times 2^{-33}}=2^{3.59}.$$

About $4\times 2^{44.64}=2^{46.64}$ pairs are enough to get 4 right pairs.

The complexity of the attack is as follows. We use $2^{47.64}$ chosen plaintext-ciphertext data. The number of pairs used in the attack is $2^{46.64}\times 2^{-33}=2^{13.64}$ because of the elimination in step 3 and 5 in the algorithm. For the counted pairs we make $2^{26.64}$ key dependent permutations guessing the 12 bits ($sk_2[27-22]$ and $sk_2[19-14]$) of the key. We decrease the search space to $2^{20.64}$ using the elimination in step 9. Then we make $2^{29.64}$ two round decryptions guessing the 9 bits ($sk_1[47-39]$) of the key. In total, the number of operations in the attack is approximately equivalent to $2^{30.64}$ one-round encryptions of PRINTcipher-48.

5 Conclusion

In this paper, we have used differential and linear cryptanalysis techniques together to analyze the security of PRINTcipher. This combined usage is different from differential-linear cryptanalysis [20]. In differential-linear cryptanalysis, a cipher is divided into two parts where differentials and linear approximations are constructed for the first and second parts respectively. In this work, we have used linear approximations to increase the probability of the differentials. Using this method, we have found out that for some of the keys, the probability of an r-round differential characteristic is significantly higher than the designers' expected values. With the help of linear approximations we have constructed r-round differential characteristics with probability $2^{-(6+1.68\times(r-3))}$ for 4.54% of the keys and with probability $2^{-(7.68+1.51\times(r-4))}$ for 0.036% of the keys of PRINTcipher-48. These observations enable us to develop cryptanalytic attacks on 29 and 31 rounds of PRINTcipher-48 for these key subsets.

Acknowledgments. The authors would like to thank to anonymous reviewers for their valuable comments which helped to improve the quality of this paper.

References

1. Abdelraheem, M.A., Leander, G., Zenner, E.: Differential Cryptanalysis of Round-Reduced PRINTcipher: Computing Roots of Permutations. In: Joux, A. (ed.) FSE 2011. LNCS, vol. 6733, pp. 1–17. Springer, Heidelberg (2011)
2. Aumasson, J.-P., Henzen, L., Meier, W., Naya-Plasencia, M.: QUARK: A lightweight hash. In: Mangard and Standaert [24], pp. 1–15 (2010)
3. Badel, S., Dagtekin, N., Nakahara, J., Ouafi, K., Reffé, N., Sepehrdad, P., Susil, P., Vaudenay, S.: ARMADILLO: A Multi-Purpose Cryptographic Primitive Dedicated to Hardware. In: Mangard and Standaert [24], pp. 398–412 (2010)
4. Biham, E., Biryukov, A., Shamir, A.: Cryptanalysis of Skipjack Reduced to 31 Rounds using Impossible Differentials. In: Stern, J. (ed.) EUROCRYPT 1999. LNCS, vol. 1592, pp. 12–23. Springer, Heidelberg (1999)
5. Biham, E., Dunkelman, O., Keller, N.: Enhancing Differential-Linear Cryptanalysis. In: Zheng, Y. (ed.) ASIACRYPT 2002. LNCS, vol. 2501, pp. 254–266. Springer, Heidelberg (2002)
6. Biham, E., Dunkelman, O., Keller, N.: Differential-Linear Cryptanalysis of Serpent. In: Johansson, T. (ed.) FSE 2003. LNCS, vol. 2887, pp. 9–21. Springer, Heidelberg (2003)
7. Biham, E., Shamir, A.: Differential Cryptanalysis of DES-Like Cryptosystems. In: Menezes, A., Vanstone, S.A. (eds.) CRYPTO 1990. LNCS, vol. 537, pp. 2–21. Springer, Heidelberg (1991)
8. Bogdanov, A., Knudsen, L.R., Leander, G., Paar, C., Poschmann, A., Robshaw, M.J.B., Seurin, Y., Vikkelsoe, C.: Present: An Ultra-Lightweight Block Cipher. In: Paillier, P., Verbauwhede, I. (eds.) CHES 2007. LNCS, vol. 4727, pp. 450–466. Springer, Heidelberg (2007)
9. Bulygin, S.: Algebraic Cryptanalysis of the Round-Reduced and Side Channel Analysis of the Full PRINTcipher-48. Cryptology ePrint Archive, Report 2011/287 (2011), `http://eprint.iacr.org/`

10. De Cannière, C.: TRIVIUM: A Stream Cipher Construction Inspired by Block Cipher Design Principles. In: Katsikas, S.K., López, J., Backes, M., Gritzalis, S., Preneel, B. (eds.) ISC 2006. LNCS, vol. 4176, pp. 171–186. Springer, Heidelberg (2006)
11. De Cannière, C., Dunkelman, O., Knežević, M.: KATAN and KTANTAN — A Family of Small and Efficient Hardware-Oriented Block Ciphers. In: Clavier, C., Gaj, K. (eds.) CHES 2009. LNCS, vol. 5747, pp. 272–288. Springer, Heidelberg (2009)
12. Cheng, H., Heys, H.M., Wang, C.: PUFFIN: A Novel Compact Block Cipher Targeted to Embedded Digital Systems. In: Fanucci, L. (ed.) DSD, pp. 383–390. IEEE (2008)
13. Daemen, J., Govaerts, R., Vandewalle, J.: Weak Keys for IDEA. In: Stinson, D.R. (ed.) CRYPTO 1993. LNCS, vol. 773, pp. 224–231. Springer, Heidelberg (1994)
14. Dunkelman, O., Indesteege, S., Keller, N.: A Differential-Linear Attack on 12-Round Serpent. In: Chowdhury, D.R., Rijmen, V., Das, A. (eds.) INDOCRYPT 2008. LNCS, vol. 5365, pp. 308–321. Springer, Heidelberg (2008)
15. Ågren, M., Johansson, T.: Linear Cryptanalysis of PRINTcipher — Trails and Samples Everywhere. Cryptology ePrint Archive, Report 2011/423 (2011), http://eprint.iacr.org/
16. Hawkes, P.: Differential-Linear Weak Key Classes of IDEA. In: Nyberg, K. (ed.) EUROCRYPT 1998. LNCS, vol. 1403, pp. 112–126. Springer, Heidelberg (1998)
17. Hong, D., Sung, J., Hong, S., Lim, J., Lee, S., Koo, B., Lee, C., Chang, D., Lee, J., Jeong, K., Kim, H., Kim, J., Chee, S.: HIGHT: A New Block Cipher Suitable for Low-Resource Device. In: Goubin, L., Matsui, M. (eds.) CHES 2006. LNCS, vol. 4249, pp. 46–59. Springer, Heidelberg (2006)
18. Izadi, M., Sadeghiyan, B., Sadeghian, S.S., Khanooki, H.A.: MIBS: A New Lightweight Block Cipher. In: Garay, J.A., Miyaji, A., Otsuka, A. (eds.) CANS 2009. LNCS, vol. 5888, pp. 334–348. Springer, Heidelberg (2009)
19. Knudsen, L.R., Leander, G., Poschmann, A., Robshaw, M.J.B.: PRINTcipher: A Block Cipher for IC-Printing. In: Mangard and Standaert [24], pp. 16–32
20. Langford, S.K., Hellman, M.E.: Differential-Linear Cryptanalysis. In: Desmedt, Y.G. (ed.) CRYPTO 1994. LNCS, vol. 839, pp. 17–25. Springer, Heidelberg (1994)
21. Leander, G., Abdelraheem, M.A., AlKhzaimi, H., Zenner, E.: A cryptanalysis of PRINTcipher: The Invariant Subspace Attack. In: Rogaway, P. (ed.) CRYPTO 2011. LNCS, vol. 6841, pp. 206–221. Springer, Heidelberg (2011)
22. Lim, C.H., Korkishko, T.: mCrypton – A Lightweight Block Cipher for Security of Low-Cost RFID Tags and Sensors. In: Song, J.-S., Kwon, T., Yung, M. (eds.) WISA 2005. LNCS, vol. 3786, pp. 243–258. Springer, Heidelberg (2006)
23. Liu, Z., Gu, D., Zhang, J., Li, W.: Differential-Multiple Linear Cryptanalysis. In: Bao, F., Yung, M., Lin, D., Jing, J. (eds.) Inscrypt 2009. LNCS, vol. 6151, pp. 35–49. Springer, Heidelberg (2010)
24. Mangard, S., Standaert, F.-X. (eds.): CHES 2010. LNCS, vol. 6225. Springer, Heidelberg (2010)
25. Matsui, M.: Linear Cryptanalysis Method for DES Cipher. In: Helleseth, T. (ed.) EUROCRYPT 1993. LNCS, vol. 765, pp. 386–397. Springer, Heidelberg (1994)
26. Ohkuma, K.: Weak Keys of Reduced-Round Present for Linear Cryptanalysis. In: Jacobson Jr., M.J., Rijmen, V., Safavi-Naini, R. (eds.) SAC 2009. LNCS, vol. 5867, pp. 249–265. Springer, Heidelberg (2009)
27. Ojha, S.K., Kumar, N., Jain, K., Sangeeta, L.: TWIS – A Lightweight Block Cipher. In: Prakash, A., Sen Gupta, I. (eds.) ICISS 2009. LNCS, vol. 5905, pp. 280–291. Springer, Heidelberg (2009)

28. Standaert, F.-X., Piret, G., Gershenfeld, N., Quisquater, J.-J.: SEA: A Scalable Encryption Algorithm for Small Embedded Applications. In: Domingo-Ferrer, J., Posegga, J., Schreckling, D. (eds.) CARDIS 2006. LNCS, vol. 3928, pp. 222–236. Springer, Heidelberg (2006)
29. Sun, X., Lai, X.: The Key-Dependent Attack on Block Ciphers. In: Matsui, M. (ed.) ASIACRYPT 2009. LNCS, vol. 5912, pp. 19–36. Springer, Heidelberg (2009)
30. Wagner, D.: The Boomerang Attack. In: Knudsen, L.R. (ed.) FSE 1999. LNCS, vol. 1636, pp. 156–170. Springer, Heidelberg (1999)
31. Guo, S.-Z., Zhao, X.-J., Wang, T.: Fault-Propagation Pattern Based Dfa on Spn Structure Block Ciphers using Bitwise Permutation, with Application to Present and PRINTcipher. Cryptology ePrint Archive, Report 2011/086 (2011), http://eprint.iacr.org/
32. Zhang, W., Zhang, L., Wu, W., Feng, D.: Related-Key Differential-Linear Attacks on Reduced AES-192. In: Srinathan, K., Rangan, C.P., Yung, M. (eds.) INDOCRYPT 2007. LNCS, vol. 4859, pp. 73–85. Springer, Heidelberg (2007)

A Characteristics for 4.54% of the Keys of PRINTcipher-48

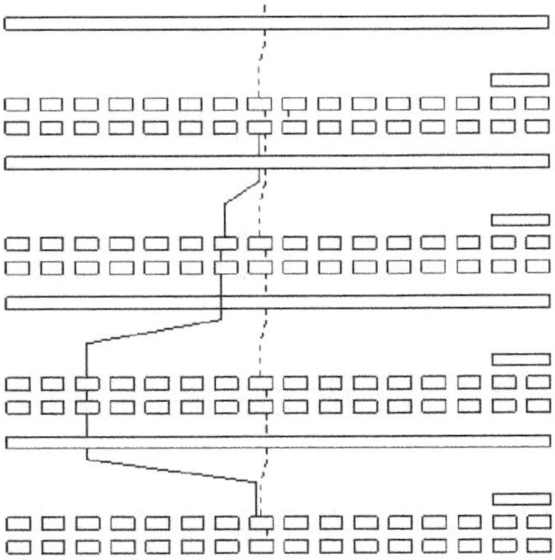

Fig. 6. Combined characteristic 2

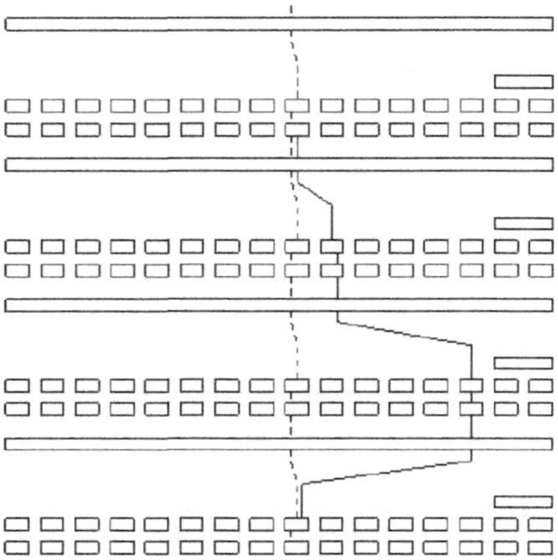

Fig. 7. Combined characteristic 3

B Characteristic for 0.036% of the Keys of PRINTcipher-48

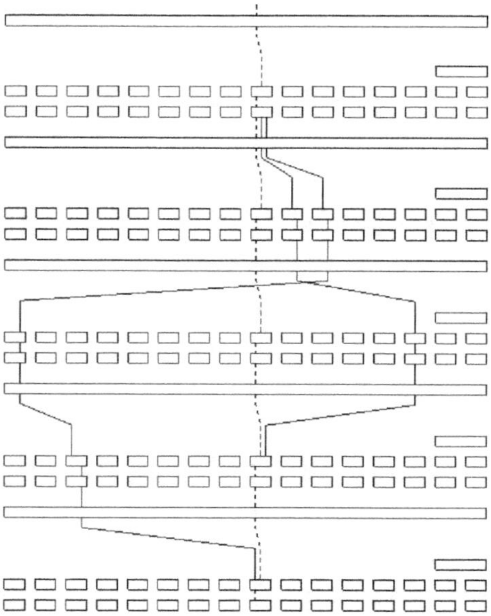

Fig. 8. Combined characteristic 5

Practical Attack on the Full MMB Block Cipher*

Keting Jia[1], Jiazhe Chen[2,3], Meiqin Wang[2,3], and Xiaoyun Wang[1,2,3,**]

[1] Institute for Advanced Study, Tsinghua University, Beijing 100084, China
{ktjia,xiaoyunwang}@mail.tsinghua.edu.cn

[2] Key Laboratory of Cryptologic Technology and Information Security, Ministry of Education, Shandong University, Jinan 250100, China
jiazhechen@mail.sdu.edu.cn, mqwang@sdu.edu.cn

[3] School of Mathematics, Shandong University, Jinan 250100, China

Abstract. Modular Multiplication based Block Cipher (MMB) is a block cipher designed by Daemen *et al.* as an alternative to the IDEA block cipher. In this paper, we give a practical sandwich attack on MMB with adaptively chosen plaintexts and ciphertexts. By constructing a 5-round sandwich distinguisher of the full 6-round MMB with probability 1, we recover the main key of MMB with text complexity 2^{40} and time complexity 2^{40} MMB encryptions. We also present a chosen plaintexts attack on the full MMB by employing the rectangle-like sandwich attack, which the complexity is $2^{66.5}$ texts, $2^{66.5}$ MMB encryptions and $2^{70.5}$ bytes of memory. In addition, we introduce an improved differential attack on MMB with 2^{96} chosen plaintexts, 2^{96} encryptions and 2^{66} bytes of memory. Especially, even if MMB is extended to 7 rounds, the improved differential attack is applicable with the same complexity as that of the full MMB.

Keywords: MMB block cipher, sandwich distinguisher, practical attack, differential attack.

1 Introduction

Modular Multiplication based Block Cipher (MMB) [7] was designed as an alternative to the IDEA block cipher [9] by Daemen, Govaerts and Vandewalle in 1993. It has 6 rounds, and both of the block size and key size are 128 bits. In [13], Wang *et al.* proposed a differential attack on the full 6-round MMB with 2^{118} chosen plaintexts, $2^{95.61}$ encryptions and 2^{66} bytes of memory. They also presented linear and square attacks on the reduced-round MMB.

Our main contribution to this paper is to introduce a fast sandwich attack on MMB. Sandwich attack was recently formalized by Dunkelman *et al.* [11], is

* Supported by 973 Project (No.2007CB807902), the National Natural Science Foundation of China (Grant No.60931160442), Tsinghua University Initiative Scientific Research Program (2009THZ01002) and China Postdoctoral Science Foundation(20110490442).

** Corresponding author.

A. Miri and S. Vaudenay (Eds.): SAC 2011, LNCS 7118, pp. 185–199, 2012.

aimed to improve the former theoretic related-key rectangle attack on the full KASUMI block cipher [3] into a fast attack. Sandwich attack is an extension of the boomerang attack, which was introduced by Wagner [14]. Similar cryptanalysis techniques with sandwich attack were also used in [4,5,14]. Usually, boomerang attack is an adaptively chosen plaintexts and ciphertexts attack. It was further developed by Kelsey *et al.* [6] into a chosen plaintexts attack called the amplified boomerang attack, which was independently introduced by Biham *et al.* with the name of the rectangle attack [2]. In [10], sandwich attack is also converted into a chosen plaintexts attack, called rectangle-like sandwich attack.

In this paper, we construct an interesting sandwich distinguisher of 5-round MMB with probability 1. Using the distinguisher, we present an adaptively chosen texts attack on MMB, which the complexity is 2^{40} texts and 2^{40} MMB encryptions. We also give a rectangle-like sandwich attack on MMB with $2^{66.5}$ chosen plaintexts, $2^{66.5}$ encryptions and $2^{70.5}$ bytes of memory.

Furthermore, we introduce a 6-round differential with probability 2^{-94}. Utilizing a 5-round differential by truncating the given 6-round differential, we show an improved differential attack on MMB with 2^{96} chosen plaintexts, 2^{96} MMB encryptions and 2^{66} bytes of memory. It is interesting that, even if MMB block cipher is increased to 7 rounds, it is still vulnerable to the differential attack with the same complexity.

The rest of this paper is organized as follows. A brief description of MMB is given in Sect. 2. We recall the sandwich attack in Sect. 3. The fast sandwich attack on MMB is introduced in Sect. 4. Section 5 describes the rectangle-like attack on MMB. And Section 6 shows the improved differential attack. Finally, we conclude the paper in Sect. 7.

2 Description of the Block Cipher MMB

MMB is a block cipher with 128-bit block and 128-bit key. It has a Substitution-Permutation Network (SPN) structure and 6-round iterations. It has two versions, called MMB 1.0 and MMB 2.0. Compared to MMB 1.0, the key schedule of MMB 2.0 is tweaked against the related-key attack [8]. In this paper, we only focus on MMB 2.0 which is simplified as MMB.

We give a brief description of MMB in the following.

Key Schedule. Let the 128-bit key of MMB be $K = (k_0, k_1, k_2, k_3)$, the subkey can be computed as:

$$k_i^j = k_{(i+j) \mod 4} \oplus (B \lll j),$$

where $B = 0x0dae$, k^j is the $(j+1)$-th round subkey, $k^j = (k_0^j, k_1^j, k_2^j, k_3^j)$, $k_i^j (i = 0, \ldots, 3)$ are 32-bit words, and $j = 0, \ldots, 6$.

MMB Encryption. MMB includes the following 6 round-transformations:

$$X_{j+1} = \rho[k^j](X_j) = \theta \circ \eta \circ \gamma \circ \sigma[k^j](X_j)$$

where X_j is the 128-bit input to the $(j+1)$-th round, and X_0 is the plaintext. The ciphertext is denoted as $C = \sigma[k^6](X_6)$.

The details of the four functions $\sigma, \gamma, \eta, \theta$ are given as follows.

1. $\sigma[k^j]$ is a bitwise XOR operation with the round subkey.

$$\sigma[k^j](a_0, a_1, a_2, a_3) = (a_0 \oplus k_0^j, a_1 \oplus k_1^j, a_2 \oplus k_2^j, a_3 \oplus k_3^j),$$

   where (a_0, a_1, a_2, a_3) is the 128-bit intermediate value, and $a_i (i = 0, 1, 2, 3)$ are 32-bit words.
2. The nonlinear transformation γ is a cyclic multiplication of the four 32-bit words respectively by factors G_0, G_1, G_2 and G_3.

$$\gamma(a_0, a_1, a_2, a_3) = (a_0 \otimes G_0, a_1 \otimes G_1, a_2 \otimes G_2, a_3 \otimes G_3).$$

   The cyclic multiplication $\otimes$ is defined as:

$$x \otimes y = \begin{cases} x \times y \mod 2^{32} - 1 & \text{if } x < 2^{32} - 1, \\ 2^{32} - 1 & \text{if } x = 2^{32} - 1. \end{cases}$$

   $G_i, G_i^{-1} = (G_i)^{-1} \ mod\ 2^{32} - 1,\ i = 0, 1, 2, 3$ are listed.

$$\begin{array}{ll} G_0 = 0x025f1cdb, & G_0^{-1} = 0x0dad4694, \\ G_1 = 2 \otimes G_0 = 0x04be39b6, & G_1^{-1} = 0x06d6a34a, \\ G_2 = 2^3 \otimes G_0 = 0x12f8e6d8, & G_2^{-1} = 0x81b5a8d2, \\ G_3 = 2^7 \otimes G_0 = 0x2f8e6d81, & G_3^{-1} = 0x281b5a8d. \end{array}$$

   There are two differential characteristics with probability 1 for G_i $(i = 0, 1, 2, 3)$ [7],

$$0 \xrightarrow[1]{G_i} 0, \quad \bar{0} \xrightarrow[1]{G_i} \bar{0}.$$

   The two differential characteristics result in a 2-round differential with probability 1.
3. The asymmetrical transformation η is defined as:

$$\eta(a_0, a_1, a_2, a_3) = (a_0 \oplus (lsb(a_0) \times \delta), a_1, a_2, a_3 \oplus ((1 \oplus lsb(a_3)) \times \delta)),$$

   where 'lsb' means the least significant bit and $\delta = 0x2aaaaaaa$.
4. The linear transformation θ is a diffusion operation:

$$\theta(a_0, a_1, a_2, a_3) = (a_3 \oplus a_0 \oplus a_1, a_0 \oplus a_1 \oplus a_2, a_1 \oplus a_2 \oplus a_3, a_2 \oplus a_3 \oplus a_0).$$

3 Sandwich Attack

Sandwich attack dates from boomerang attack, and was utilized to break efficiently the block cipher KASUMI in the related-key setting [10]. We give a brief description of the boomerang attack and the sandwich attack.

3.1 Boomerang Attack

The boomerang attack belongs to differential attack [1]. The purpose is to construct a quartet structure to achieve a distinguisher with more rounds by utilizing and connecting two short differential. Let E be a block cipher with block size n, that is considered as a cascade of two sub-ciphers: $E = E_1 \circ E_0$. For the sub-cipher E_0, there is a differential $\alpha \xrightarrow{E_0} \beta$ with high probability p, and for E_1, there is a differential $\gamma \xrightarrow{E_1} \zeta$ with high probability q. $E^{-1}, {E_0}^{-1}$ and ${E_1}^{-1}$ stand for the inverse of E, E_0, E_1 respectively. The boomerang distinguisher (see Fig.1) can be constructed as follows:

- Randomly choose a pair of plaintexts (P, P') such that $P' \oplus P = \alpha$.
- Ask for the encryption, and get the corresponding ciphertexts $C = E(P)$, $C' = E(P')$.
- Compute $\widetilde{C} = C \oplus \zeta$, $\widetilde{C}' = C' \oplus \zeta$.
- Ask for the decryption, and obtain $\widetilde{P} = E^{-1}(\widetilde{C})$, $\widetilde{P}' = E^{-1}(\widetilde{C}')$.
- Check whether $\widetilde{P}' \oplus \widetilde{P} = \alpha$.

For the distinguisher (see Fig. 1), $\widetilde{P}' \oplus \widetilde{P} = \alpha$ holds with probability p^2q^2. That is to say, a quarter satisfies the following conditions besides $P' \oplus P = \alpha$ and $\widetilde{P}' \oplus \widetilde{P} = \alpha$,

$$E_0(P') \oplus E_0(P) = \beta,$$
$${E_1}^{-1}(\widetilde{C}) \oplus {E_1}^{-1}(C) = E_1^{-1}(\widetilde{C}') \oplus {E_1}^{-1}(C') = \gamma.$$

It is clear that, the boomerang distinguisher is available to cryptanalyze a cipher if $pq > 2^{-n/2}$.

The rectangle (amplified boomerang) attack is a chosen plaintext attack instead of adaptive chosen plaintext and ciphertext attack by involving a birthday attack to guarantee the collision of two middle values $E_0(P)$ and $E_0(\widetilde{P}) \oplus \gamma$. A right quarter $(P, P', \widetilde{P}, \widetilde{P}')$ can be distinguished with probability $p^2q^22^{-n}$, which should satisfy the following conditions besides $P \oplus P' = \alpha$, $\widetilde{P} \oplus \widetilde{P}' = \alpha$, $C \oplus \widetilde{C} = \zeta$, $C' \oplus \widetilde{C}' = \zeta$,

$$E_0(P') \oplus E_0(P) = \beta \ , \ E_0(\widetilde{P}') \oplus E_0(\widetilde{P}) = \beta,$$
$$E_0(P) \oplus E_0(\widetilde{P}) = \gamma \ .$$

3.2 Sandwich Attack

The sandwich attack is obtained by pushing a middle layer in the quartet structure of the boomerang attack. So, in the sandwich attack, the block cipher should be divided into three sub-ciphers: $E = E_1 \circ E_M \circ E_0$, see Fig. 2. We denote $X = E_0(P), Y = E_M(X), C = E_1(Y)$. Let $\alpha \overset{E_0}{\to} \beta$ be a differential with probability p on the top layer, and $\gamma \overset{E_1}{\to} \zeta$ be a differential with probability q on the bottom layer, where

$$\alpha = P \oplus P' = \widetilde{P} \oplus \widetilde{P}' \ , \beta = X \oplus X' = \widetilde{X} \oplus \widetilde{X}'$$
$$\gamma = Y \oplus \widetilde{Y} = Y' \oplus \widetilde{Y}' \ , \zeta = C \oplus \widetilde{C} = C' \oplus \widetilde{C}'.$$

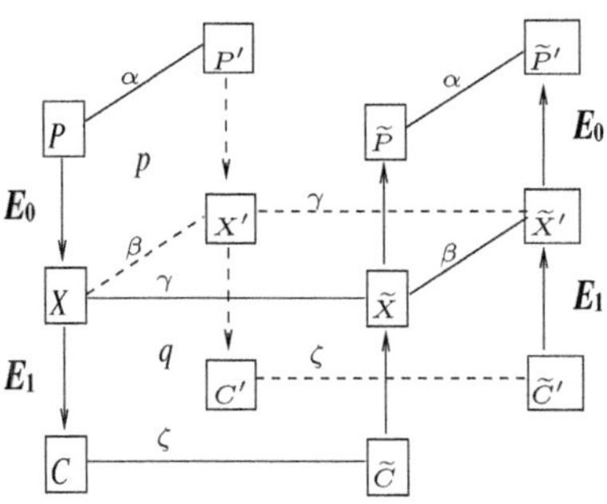

Fig. 1. Boomerange distinguisher

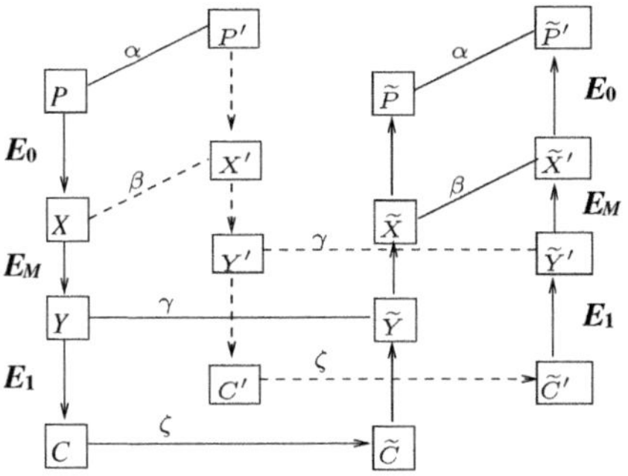

Fig. 2. Sandwich distinguisher

The middle layer is a transition differential connecting the top and bottom differentials. The probability of the transition differential is computed as follows.

$$r = Pr((\widetilde{X} \oplus \widetilde{X}' = \beta)|(Y \oplus \widetilde{Y} = \gamma) \wedge (Y' \oplus \widetilde{Y}' = \gamma) \wedge (X \oplus X' = \beta)).$$

Thus the sandwich distinguisher holds with probability p^2q^2r.

The rectangle-like sandwich attack is the combination of sandwich attack and rectangle attack, and it is a chosen plaintexts attack (see Fig. 4). The probability of the rectangle-like sandwich distinguisher is $p^2q^2r'2^{-n}$,

$$r' = Pr((Y' \oplus \widetilde{Y}' = \gamma)|(\widetilde{X} \oplus \widetilde{X}' = \beta) \wedge (X \oplus X' = \beta) \wedge (Y \oplus \widetilde{Y} = \gamma)).$$

4 Practical Sandwich Attack on the Full MMB

In this section, we first construct a sandwich distinguisher for 5-round MMB with probability 1 without related key, then give a practical key recovery attack on MMB.

4.1 5-Round Sandwich Distinguisher with Probability 1

We decompose 5-round MMB into $E = E_1 \circ E_M \circ E_0$. E_0 contains the first 2 rounds, E_M consists of the third round, and E_1 includes the last 2 rounds. See Fig. 2.

We use the following 2-round differential characteristic with probability 1 in E_0 and E_1 [13].

$$\begin{aligned}(0,\bar{0},\bar{0},0) &\xrightarrow{\sigma[k^i]} (0,\bar{0},\bar{0},0) \xrightarrow{\gamma} (0,\bar{0},\bar{0},0) \xrightarrow{\eta} (0,\bar{0},\bar{0},0) \xrightarrow{\theta} (\bar{0},0,0,\bar{0}) \\ &\xrightarrow{\sigma[k^{i+1}]} (\bar{0},0,0,\bar{0}) \xrightarrow{\gamma} (\bar{0},0,0,\bar{0}) \xrightarrow{\eta} (\bar{0} \oplus \delta,0,0,\bar{0} \oplus \delta) \xrightarrow{\theta} (0,\bar{0} \oplus \delta,\bar{0} \oplus \delta,0),\end{aligned}$$

where '0' denotes a 32-bit zero difference word, and $\bar{0} = 2^{32} - 1 = 0xffffffff$. So $\alpha = \gamma = (0, \bar{0}, \bar{0}, 0)$, $\beta = \zeta = (0, \bar{0} \oplus \delta, \bar{0} \oplus \delta, 0)$, and $Pr(\alpha \xrightarrow{E_0} \beta) = 1$, $Pr(\gamma \xrightarrow{E_1} \zeta) = 1$.

The remaining is to prove that the probability of the transition differential keeps 1, i.e.,

$$Pr((\widetilde{X} \oplus \widetilde{X}' = \beta) | (Y \oplus \widetilde{Y} = \gamma) \wedge (Y' \oplus \widetilde{Y}' = \gamma) \wedge (X \oplus X' = \beta)) = 1.$$

X_i', $\widetilde{X}_i$, $\widetilde{X}_i'$ and X_i denote the i-th words of $X, X', \widetilde{X}, \widetilde{X}'$, $i = 0, 1, 2, 3$. The subkey of the third round is denoted as $\bar{k} = (\bar{k}_0, \bar{k}_1, \bar{k}_2, \bar{k}_3)$.

Since θ and η are linear, by

$$\begin{aligned} Y \oplus \widetilde{Y} &= (0, \bar{0}, \bar{0}, 0), \\ Y' \oplus \widetilde{Y}' &= (0, \bar{0}, \bar{0}, 0), \\ X \oplus X' &= (0, \bar{0} \oplus \delta, \bar{0} \oplus \delta, 0), \end{aligned} \tag{1}$$

we get

$$(\eta^{-1} \circ \theta^{-1}(Y)) \oplus (\eta^{-1} \circ \theta^{-1}(\widetilde{Y})) = (\bar{0} \oplus \delta, 0, 0, \bar{0} \oplus \delta), \tag{2}$$

$$(\eta^{-1} \circ \theta^{-1}(Y')) \oplus (\eta^{-1} \circ \theta^{-1}(\widetilde{Y}')) = (\bar{0} \oplus \delta, 0, 0, \bar{0} \oplus \delta). \tag{3}$$

From the round transformation, we know that,

$$\begin{aligned} Y &= \theta \circ \eta \circ \gamma \circ \sigma[k](X), \\ Y' &= \theta \circ \eta \circ \gamma \circ \sigma[k](X'), \\ \widetilde{Y} &= \theta \circ \eta \circ \gamma \circ \sigma[k](\widetilde{X}), \\ \widetilde{Y}' &= \theta \circ \eta \circ \gamma \circ \sigma[k](\widetilde{X}'). \end{aligned} \tag{4}$$

Using (2), (3) and (4), we deduce the equations

$$((X_1 \oplus \bar{k}_1) \otimes G_1) \oplus ((\widetilde{X}_1 \oplus \bar{k}_1) \otimes G_1) = 0, \tag{5}$$

$$((X_2 \oplus \bar{k}_2) \otimes G_2) \oplus ((\widetilde{X}_2 \oplus \bar{k}_2) \otimes G_2) = 0, \tag{6}$$

$$((X_1' \oplus \bar{k}_1) \otimes G_1) \oplus ((\widetilde{X}_1' \oplus \bar{k}_1) \otimes G_1) = 0, \tag{7}$$

$$((X_2' \oplus \bar{k}_2) \otimes G_2) \oplus ((\widetilde{X}_2' \oplus \bar{k}_2) \otimes G_2) = 0. \tag{8}$$

$$((X_0 \oplus \bar{k}_0) \otimes G_0) \oplus ((\widetilde{X}_0 \oplus \bar{k}_0) \otimes G_0) = \bar{0} \oplus \delta, \tag{9}$$

$$((X_3 \oplus \bar{k}_3) \otimes G_3) \oplus ((\widetilde{X}_3 \oplus \bar{k}_3) \otimes G_3) = \bar{0} \oplus \delta, \tag{10}$$

$$((X_0' \oplus \bar{k}_0) \otimes G_0) \oplus ((\widetilde{X}_0' \oplus \bar{k}_0) \otimes G_0) = \bar{0} \oplus \delta, \tag{11}$$

$$((X_3' \oplus \bar{k}_3) \otimes G_3) \oplus ((\widetilde{X}_3' \oplus \bar{k}_3) \otimes G_3) = \bar{0} \oplus \delta. \tag{12}$$

From (5), (6), (7) and (8), it is clear that,

$$X_1 = \widetilde{X}_1, \; X_2 = \widetilde{X}_2, \; X_1' = \widetilde{X}_1', \; X_2' = \widetilde{X}_2'.$$

Therefore, we deduce the conditions

$$\widetilde{X}_1 \oplus \widetilde{X}_1' = X_1 \oplus X_1' = \bar{0} \oplus \delta,$$
$$\widetilde{X}_2 \oplus \widetilde{X}_2' = X_2 \oplus X_2' = \bar{0} \oplus \delta. \tag{13}$$

From (9), (10), (11) and (12), we obtain

$$((X_0 \oplus \bar{k}_0) \otimes G_0) \oplus ((\widetilde{X}_0 \oplus \bar{k}_0) \otimes G_0) = ((X_0' \oplus \bar{k}_0) \otimes G_0) \oplus ((\widetilde{X}_0' \oplus \bar{k}_0) \otimes G_0), \tag{14}$$
$$((X_3 \oplus \bar{k}_3) \otimes G_3) \oplus ((\widetilde{X}_3 \oplus \bar{k}_3) \otimes G_3) = ((X_3' \oplus \bar{k}_3) \otimes G_3) \oplus ((\widetilde{X}_3' \oplus \bar{k}_3) \otimes G_3). \tag{15}$$

Combining with (1), the following two equations hold.

$$((\widetilde{X}_0 \oplus \bar{k}_0) \otimes G_0) = ((\widetilde{X}_0' \oplus \bar{k}_0) \otimes G_0),$$
$$((\widetilde{X}_3 \oplus \bar{k}_3) \otimes G_3) = ((\widetilde{X}_3' \oplus \bar{k}_3) \otimes G_3).$$

Then,

$$\widetilde{X}_0 \oplus \widetilde{X}_0' = 0,$$
$$\widetilde{X}_3 \oplus \widetilde{X}_3' = 0. \tag{16}$$

Combining (13) and (16), we have

$$\widetilde{X} \oplus \widetilde{X}' = (0, \bar{0} \oplus \delta, \bar{0} \oplus \delta, 0) = \beta.$$

Therefore,

$$r = Pr((\widetilde{X} \oplus \widetilde{X}' = \beta) | (Y \oplus \widetilde{Y} = \gamma) \wedge (Y' \oplus \widetilde{Y}' = \gamma) \wedge (X \oplus X' = \beta)) = 1.$$

This proves that we get a 5-round sandwich distinguisher with probability 1.

4.2 The Key Recovery Attack

In this subsection, if we apply the 5-round sandwich distinguisher described in Subsect. 4.1 to rounds 2-6, we can recover 64 bits of the subkey in the first round. When we locate the distinguisher at rounds 1-5, 64 bits of the equivalent subkey in the final can be easily captured. The total key can be deduced from the recovered subkey bits by the key schedule.

Recovering 64 Bits of the First Round Subkey

Collecting Right Quartets. The sandwich distinguisher is from round 2 to round 6. In order to easily produce the sandwich distinguisher, we select the 1-st round differential as:

$$(0xfdff77ef, 0, 0, 0xdffbfeef) \xrightarrow{\sigma[k^i]} (0xfdff77ef, 0, 0, 0xdffbfeef) \xrightarrow{\gamma}$$
$$(\bar{0} \oplus \delta, 0, 0, \bar{0} \oplus \delta) \xrightarrow{\eta} (\bar{0}, 0, 0, \bar{0}) \xrightarrow{\theta} (0, \bar{0}, \bar{0}, 0).$$

By computer searching, both $0xfdff77ef \xrightarrow{G_0} \bar{0} \oplus \delta$ and $0xdffbfeef \xrightarrow{G_3} \bar{0} \oplus \delta$ occur with probability about 2^{-18}, so the probability of the differential is about 2^{-36}.

We collect 2^{38} plaintext pairs (P, P') and their corresponding ciphertext pairs (C, C'), where P and P' satisfy

$$P' = P \oplus (0xfdff77ef, 0, 0, 0xdffbfeef).$$

For each pair, we construct the quartet, and detect whether the quartet satisfies the differentials. The details are as follows.

- For the collected plaintext-ciphertext pair $((P, C), (P', C'))$, calculate

$$\widetilde{C} = C \oplus (0, \bar{0} \oplus \delta, \bar{0} \oplus \delta, 0),$$

$$\widetilde{C}' = C' \oplus (0, \bar{0} \oplus \delta, \bar{0} \oplus \delta, 0).$$

- Query the decryption to obtain $\widetilde{P} = E^{-1}(\widetilde{C})$, $\widetilde{P}' = E^{-1}(\widetilde{C}')$, and get the quartet $(P, P', \widetilde{P}, \widetilde{P}')$.
- For the constructed quartet $(P, P', \widetilde{P}, \widetilde{P}')$, check whether $\widetilde{P} \oplus \widetilde{P}' = (*, 0, 0, *)$ holds, where '*' stands for any non-zero 32-bit value. If $\widetilde{P} \oplus \widetilde{P}$ equals to $(*, 0, 0, *)$, output the quartet.

It is clear that, if the 1-st round differential holds, $\widetilde{P} \oplus \widetilde{P}'$ always equals to $(*, 0, 0, *)$, so among 2^{38} plaintext-ciphertext pairs $((P, C), (P', C'))$, there are about 4 quartets $(P, P', \widetilde{P}, \widetilde{P}')$ are left, and each sieved quartet is right with probability $1 - 2^{38-64} = 1 - 2^{-26}$.

Partial Key Recovery. For the right quartet $(P, P', \widetilde{P}, \widetilde{P}')$, we search the right subkey k_0^0 among 2^{32} candidates by the following equations:

$$((P_0 \oplus k_0^0) \otimes G_0) \oplus ((P_0' \oplus k_0^0) \otimes G_0) = \bar{0} \oplus \delta,$$
$$((\widetilde{P}_0 \oplus k_0^0) \otimes G_0) \oplus ((\widetilde{P}_0' \oplus k_0^0) \otimes G_0) = \bar{0} \oplus \delta.$$

Similarly, the subkey k_3^0 is derived from the equations

$$((P_3 \oplus k_3^0) \otimes G_3) \oplus ((P_3' \oplus k_3^0) \otimes G_3) = \bar{0} \oplus \delta,$$
$$((\widetilde{P}_3 \oplus k_3^0) \otimes G_3) \oplus ((\widetilde{P}_3' \oplus k_3^0) \otimes G_3) = \bar{0} \oplus \delta.$$

Because $\bar{0} \xrightarrow[1]{G_i} \bar{0}$, there are two k_0^0 can be obtained, i.e. the right subkey k_0^0 and its complement $k_0^0 \oplus \bar{0}$. It is the same for k_3^0.

Recovering 64 Bits of the Last Subkey

Collecting Right Quartets. We apply the distinguisher to rounds 1-5, and calculate 64 bits of the last subkey.

Select the final round differential

$$(0,\bar{0}\oplus\delta,\bar{0}\oplus\delta,0) \overset{\sigma^{-1}[k^5]}{\longleftarrow} (0,\bar{0}\oplus\delta,\bar{0}\oplus\delta,0) \overset{\gamma^{-1}}{\longleftarrow}$$
$$(0,0xfcfbdfff,0xf3ef7fff,0) \overset{\eta^{-1}}{\longleftarrow} (0,0xfcfbdfff,0xf3ef7fff,0) \overset{\theta^{-1}}{\longleftarrow}$$
$$(0xfcfbdfff,0x0f14a000,0x0f14a000,0xf3ef7fff).$$

The probability of $0xfcfbdfff \xrightarrow{G_1^{-1}} \bar{0}\oplus\delta$ and $0xf3ef7fff \xrightarrow{G_2^{-1}} \bar{0}\oplus\delta$ are both 2^{-18}, so the total probability of the final round differential is 2^{-36}.

We collect 2^{38} ciphertext pairs $(C,\widetilde{C})$ and their corresponding plaintext pairs $(P,\widetilde{P})$ such that,

$$\widetilde{C} = C \oplus (0xfcfbdfff,0x0f14a000,0x0f14a000,0xf3ef7fff).$$

For each pair, we build the framework of the quartet, and test whether the quartet satisfies the differential.

- For the collected plaintext-ciphertext pair $((P,C),(\widetilde{P},\widetilde{C}))$, calculate

$$P' = P \oplus (0,\bar{0},\bar{0},0),$$
$$\widetilde{P}' = P' \oplus (0,\bar{0},\bar{0},0).$$

- Ask for the ciphertexts C', $\widetilde{C}'$ of P', $\widetilde{P}'$ respectively. We obtain the quartet $(C,C',\widetilde{C},\widetilde{C}')$.
- For the collected quartet $(C,C',\widetilde{C},\widetilde{C}')$, check whether C' and $\widetilde{C}'$ satisfy the following equation.

$$C' \oplus \widetilde{C}' = (V_1, V_1\oplus V_2, V_1\oplus V_2, V_2),$$

  where V_1, V_2 are non-zero 32-bit words. If the equation holds, output the quartet.

Partial Key Recovery. We firstly recover 64 bits of the equivalent key $k^{6'}$ of k^6, i.e.,

$$k_1^{6'} = k_0^6 \oplus k_1^6 \oplus k_2^6,$$
$$k_2^{6'} = k_1^6 \oplus k_2^6 \oplus k_3^6.$$

We find the right subkey $k_1^{6'}$ by searching 2^{32} candidates with the verification of the equations

$$(G_1^{-1} \otimes (C_0\oplus C_1\oplus C_2\oplus k_1^{6'})) \oplus (G_1^{-1} \otimes (C_0'\oplus C_1'\oplus C_2'\oplus k_1^{6'})) = \bar{0}\oplus\delta,$$
$$(G_1^{-1} \otimes (\widetilde{C}_0\oplus \widetilde{C}_1\oplus \widetilde{C}_2\oplus k_1^{6'})) \oplus (G_1^{-1} \otimes (\widetilde{C}_0'\oplus \widetilde{C}_1'\oplus \widetilde{C}_2'\oplus k_1^{6'})) = \bar{0}\oplus\delta.$$

In the similar way, we search the right subkey $k_2^{6'}$ among 2^{32} candidates by the following equations.

$$(G_2^{-1} \otimes (C_1\oplus C_2\oplus C_3\oplus k_2^{6'})) \oplus (G_2^{-1} \otimes (C_1'\oplus C_2'\oplus C_3'\oplus k_2^{6'})) = \bar{0}\oplus\delta,$$
$$(G_2^{-1} \otimes (\widetilde{C}_1\oplus \widetilde{C}_2\oplus \widetilde{C}_3\oplus k_2^{6'})) \oplus (G_2^{-1} \otimes (\widetilde{C}_1'\oplus \widetilde{C}_2'\oplus \widetilde{C}_3'\oplus k_2^{6'})) = \bar{0}\oplus\delta.$$

From the key schedule algorithm, we know that, $k_0^0 = k_0 \oplus B$, $k_3^0 = k_3 \oplus B$, $k_1^{6'} = k_0 \oplus k_2 \oplus k_3 \oplus (B \lll 6)$, and $k_2^{6'} = k_0 \oplus k_1 \oplus k_3 \oplus (B \lll 6)$. As a result, we compute the whole 128 bits of the key. $2^4 = 16$ key can be computed, for there are 2 values for a subkey. Filter the right key by a known plaintext and corresponding ciphertexts.

Complexity. The data complexity is 2^{39} adaptive chosen plaintexts and ciphertexts. The collection of the pairs is dominant the time complexity, which is 2^{40} MMB encryptions. Once a right quarter is obtained, the right subkey can be computed. So the success rate is $(0.98)^2 = 0.96$.

4.3 Experimental Results

We performed an experiment on the number of right quartets. We implement the quartet framework in Sect. 4.2, check the right quartets, and we repeated the procedure for 1320 times. The number of right quartet are given in Tab. 1, and we can see from Fig. 3 that the experimental data approximates well to the theoretic data.

Table 1. The Number of Right Quartets

#Right Quartets	0	1	2	3	4	5	6	7	8	9	10	11	12
Experiment	23	106	202	252	273	185	137	86	30	17	5	4	0
Theory	24.1	96.7	193.4	257.8	257.8	206.3	137.5	78.5	39.2	17.4	6.9	2.5	0.8

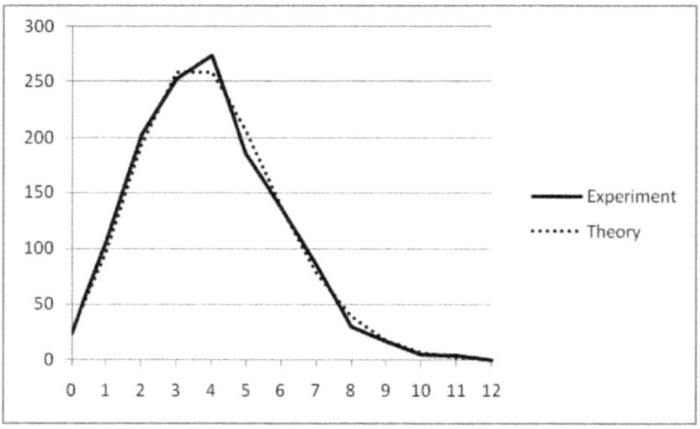

Fig. 3. The Number of Right Quartets in Our Experiment and the Theory

Our experiment was carried out on a IBM X3950 M2 server, with 64 Intel Xeon E7330 2.4GHz cores inside. The operation system is Red Hat 4.1.2-46, Linux 2.6.18. The compiler is gcc 4.1.2, and we use the standard optimization flags, one thread in each core. It takes about 1 hour to identify a right quartet, and recovery the main key of MMB.

5 Rectangle-Like Sandwich Attack on MMB

The sandwich attack is an adaptive chosen plaintexts and ciphertexts attack. So we have to query the decryptions of the adapted ciphertexts. This section is to fulfill the rectangle-like sandwich attack, which can result in a chosen-plaintext attack.

5.1 5-Round Rectangle-Like Sandwich Distinguisher

Firstly, we give a 5-round rectangle-like sandwich distinguisher which can be detected with the birthday attack complexity. We transform the above 5-round sandwich distinguisher into a rectangle-like sandwich distinguisher directly.

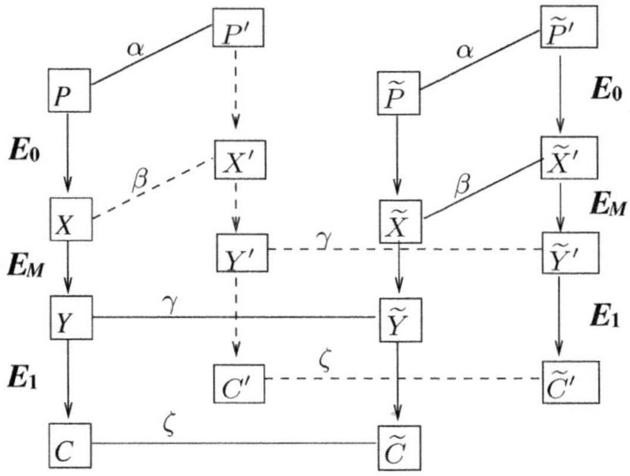

Fig. 4. Rectangle-like sandwich distinguisher

We decompose 5-round MMB into $E = E_1 \circ E_M \circ E_0$ the same as Subsect. 4.1. Let $\alpha = \gamma = (0, \bar{0}, \bar{0}, 0)$, $\beta = \zeta = (0, \bar{0} \oplus \delta, \bar{0} \oplus \delta, 0)$. In the rectangle-like sandwich distinguisher (see Fig. 4), we choose $P \oplus P' = \alpha$, $\widetilde{P} \oplus \widetilde{P}' = \alpha$. Query the corresponding ciphertexts of the 5-round MMB (C, C', $\widetilde{C}$, $\widetilde{C}'$). If the equations $C \oplus \widetilde{C} = \zeta$ and $C' \oplus \widetilde{C}' = \zeta$ hold, the quartet is right.

Since the probability of the 2-round differential is 1, similar with Subsect. 4.1, we know that

$$Pr((Y' \oplus \widetilde{Y}' = \gamma)|(Y \oplus \widetilde{Y} = \gamma) \wedge (\widetilde{X} \oplus \widetilde{X}' = \beta) \wedge (X \oplus X' = \beta)) = 1,$$
$$Pr((Y \oplus \widetilde{Y} = \gamma)|(Y' \oplus \widetilde{Y}' = \gamma) \wedge (\widetilde{X} \oplus \widetilde{X}' = \beta) \wedge (X \oplus X' = \beta)) = 1.$$

It is easy to know that, $C \oplus \widetilde{C} = \zeta$ holds if and only if $C' \oplus \widetilde{C}' = \zeta$ holds.

Using the birthday searching algorithm, we get a pair $(C, \widetilde{C})$ corresponding to the collision $C = \widetilde{C} \oplus \zeta$ by searching two sets with 2^{64} chosen pairs (P, P') and $(\widetilde{P}, \widetilde{P}')$ respectively. $(C, \widetilde{C})$ and the corresponding $(C', \widetilde{C}')$ consists of a right quartet. So, the 5-round rectangle-like sandwich distinguisher can be distinguished with 2^{64} chosen plaintexts and 2^{64} table lookups.

5.2 The Key Recovery Attack

We set the 5-round rectangle-like sandwich distinguisher from round 1 to round 5. If a right quartet occurs, the ciphertext differences should satisfy the following two equations:

$$C \oplus \widetilde{C} = (V_1, V_1 \oplus V_2, V_1 \oplus V_2, V_2) \tag{17}$$

$$C' \oplus \widetilde{C}' = (W_1, W_1 \oplus W_2, W_1 \oplus W_2, W_2) \tag{18}$$

where V_1 and W_1 are output diffrences of G_1 corresponding to input difference $(\bar{0} \oplus \delta)$, V_2 and W_2 are output differences of G_2 corresponding to input difference $(\bar{0} \oplus \delta)$.

In order to be available to search the right quartet by fulfilling the birthday attack, we convert (17) and (18) into the following equivalent four equations.

$$(C_0 \oplus C_1 \oplus C_3) \oplus (\widetilde{C}_0 \oplus \widetilde{C}_1 \oplus \widetilde{C}_3) = 0,$$
$$(C_0 \oplus C_2 \oplus C_3) \oplus (\widetilde{C}_0 \oplus \widetilde{C}_2 \oplus \widetilde{C}_3) = 0,$$
$$(C'_0 \oplus C'_1 \oplus C'_3) \oplus (\widetilde{C}'_0 \oplus \widetilde{C}'_1 \oplus \widetilde{C}'_3) = 0,$$
$$(C'_0 \oplus C'_2 \oplus C'_3) \oplus (\widetilde{C}'_0 \oplus \widetilde{C}'_2 \oplus \widetilde{C}'_3) = 0.$$

We choose $2^{65.5}$ plaintext pairs (P, P') at random with the difference $(0, \bar{0}, \bar{0}, 0)$. Encrypt the corresponding ciphertext pairs (C, C'). Compute $2^{65.5}$ 128-bit values which consist of set A.

$$A = \{Z |\ Z = (C_0 \oplus C_1 \oplus C_3, C_0 \oplus C_2 \oplus C_3, C'_0 \oplus C'_1 \oplus C'_3, C'_0 \oplus C'_2 \oplus C'_3)\}.$$

Search all the collisions of set A by birthday attack. The expected number of collisions is 8. This is because, for each 2^{64} pairs of A, there is a right quartet according to Subsect. 5.1. So, there are about 4 collisions in A which implies 4 right quartets. According to birthday attack, there are another $2^{65.5} \cdot 2^{65.5} \cdot 2^{-1} \cdot 2^{-128} = 4$ collisions $(Z, \widetilde{Z})$ occur. So, we have totally 8 corresponding quartets $(C, C', \widetilde{C}, \widetilde{C}')$, and there are 4 right quartets.

For each sieved quartet, we get the equivalent key $k_1^{6'}$ and $k_2^{6'}$ respectively as in Subsect. 4.2 with 2^{30} MMB encryptions. Then we find the rest 64-bit keys by exhaustively searching. The data complexity of the attack is $2 \cdot 2^{65.5} = 2^{66.5}$ chosen plaintexts, the memory complexity is $2^{65.5}$ 128-bit block pairs, i.e., $2^{70.5}$ bytes.

6 The Improved Differential Cryptanalysis of MMB

A 6-round differential with high probability is given in this section, which can be used to 7-round extended MMB. The differential path is given as,

$$(0, \bar{0}, \bar{0}, 0) \xrightarrow[1]{\rho[k^0]} (\bar{0}, 0, 0, \bar{0}) \xrightarrow[1]{\rho[k^1]} (0, \bar{0} \oplus \delta, \bar{0} \oplus \delta, 0) \xrightarrow[p_1]{\rho[k^2]} (\tau, 0, 0, \tau) \xrightarrow[p_2]{\rho[k^3]} (0, \bar{0}, \bar{0}, 0) \xrightarrow{\rho[k^4]}$$
$$(\bar{0}, 0, 0, \bar{0}) \xrightarrow[1]{\rho[k^5]} (0, \bar{0} \oplus \delta, \bar{0} \oplus \delta, 0),$$

where τ satisfies the following two differtials.

$$\bar{0} \oplus \delta \xrightarrow{G_1} \tau \xrightarrow{G_0} \bar{0}, \tag{19}$$

$$\bar{0} \oplus \delta \xrightarrow{G_2} \tau \xrightarrow{G_3} \bar{0}. \tag{20}$$

By search all the τ, the 5-round differential holds with probability $p_1.p_2 = 2^{-94}$. Because there are 16862718720 pairs make the differential characteristics (19) and (20) hold together, the probability is $16862718720/(2^{128}) \doteq 2^{-94}$.

6.1 Improved Differential Attack on the Full MMB

We use the last five rounds of the differential path to attack the full round MMB. The 5-round differential is as follows.

$$(\bar{0},0,0,\bar{0}) \xrightarrow[1]{\rho[k^0]} (0,\bar{0}\oplus\delta,\bar{0}\oplus\delta,0) \xrightarrow[p_1]{\rho[k^1]} (\tau,0,0,\tau) \xrightarrow[p_2]{\rho[k^2]} (0,\bar{0},\bar{0},0) \xrightarrow[1]{\rho[k^3]}$$
$$(\bar{0},0,0,\bar{0}) \xrightarrow[1]{\rho[k^4]} (0,\bar{0}\oplus\delta,\bar{0}\oplus\delta,0),$$

We mount the 5-round differential path to rounds 1-5 of the 6 rounds. In the rest of the section, we give the attack algorithm.

The Key Recovery Attack. We choose 2^{96} pairs of plaintext with difference $(\bar{0},0,0,\bar{0})$, then there are 4 right pairs. The output difference of the 5-th round for a right pair is $(0,\bar{0}\oplus\delta,\bar{0}\oplus\delta,0)$, so the difference of the ciphertext should be $(V_1, V_1\oplus V_2, V_1\oplus V_2, V_2)$, where V_1, V_2 are non-zero 32-bit words. We use this to sieve the ciphertext pairs, and there will be $2^{96}\cdot 2^{-64} = 2^{32}$ pairs left. Furthermore, the input difference of the 6-th round is $(0,\bar{0}\oplus\delta,\bar{0}\oplus\delta,0)$, the number of possible output difference values given the input difference $\bar{0}\oplus\delta$ for G_1 or G_2 is about $2^{28.56}$. So there are $2^{32}\cdot 2^{(28.56-32)\times 2} = 2^{25.12}$ pairs satisfying the output difference.

For each of $2^{25.12}$ pairs, we recover the key as Subsect. 4.2. Calculate the 32-bit words $k_1^{6'}$, $k_2^{6'}$ respectively, and increase the counter corresponding to $(k_1^{6'}, k_2^{6'})$ by 1. For G_1 and G_2, the number of pairs with input difference $\bar{0}\oplus\delta$ and any given output difference is at most $2^{14.28}$, so the maximum count per counted pair of the wrong subkey words will be $2^{14.28}\cdot 2^{14.28} = 2^{28.56}$. The signal-to-noise ratio is :

$$S/N = \frac{p\cdot 2^k}{\alpha\cdot\beta} = \frac{2^{-94}\times 2^{64}}{2^{-64-6.88}\times 2^{28.56}} = 2^{10.32}.$$

According to [12], the success probability is

$$Ps = \int_{-\frac{\sqrt{\mu S/N}-\Phi^{-1}(1-2^{-a})}{\sqrt{S/N+1}}}^{\infty} \Phi(x)dx = 0.9686,$$

where $a = 64$ is the number of subkey bits guessed, μ is the number of right pairs and $\mu = 4$.

The data complexity of the attack is 2^{96} chosen plaintexts, which is dominant the time complexity. We need $2\cdot 2^{14.28}\cdot 2^{25.12} = 2^{40.40}$ XOR operations and $2^{14.28}$.

Table 2. Summary of the Attacks on MMB

#Rounds	Type	Time	Data	Memory	Source
3	LC	2^{126} EN	$2^{114.56}$ KP	-	[13]
4	SQ	$2^{126.32}$ EN	2^{34} CP	2^{66}	[13]
6	DC	2^{118} EN	2^{118} CP	2^{66}	[13]
6	SW	2^{40}EN	2^{39} ACP	2^{18}	this paper
6	SR	$2^{66.5}$ EN	$2^{66.5}$ CP	$2^{70.5}$	this paper
6	DC	2^{96} EN	2^{96} CP	2^{66}	this paper
7	DC	2^{96} EN	2^{96} CP	2^{66}	this paper

LC: Linear Cryptanalysis; DC: Differential Cryptanalysis.
SQ: Square Attack; SW: Sandwich Attack; SR: Rectangle-like Sandwich Attack.
EN: MMB Encryption.
KP: Known Plaintexts; CP: Chosen Plaintexts; ACP: adaptive chosen Texts.

$2^{14.28} \cdot 2^{25.12} = 2^{53.68}$ counts, equivalent to 2^{43} MMB encryptions to recovery the 64-bit subkey. The memory complexity is 2^{64} 64-bit counters, equivalent to 2^{66} bytes. There are 4 values for 64 bits of the key, and the rest 64 bits can be recovered by exhaustive search.

6.2 Differential Attack of MMB$^+$

If we call the 7-round version of MMB as MMB$^+$, we show that MMB$^+$ can also be broken with the same complexity of the 6-round differential attack. Note that in the above subsection, we only use 5 rounds out of the 6-round differential path, and the probability of the 5-round path is the same as the 6-round path. So if we use the 6-round differential path, we can also attack MMB$^+$ by the same manner described in the above subsection. It means that even if MMB has 7 rounds it is still vulnerable to the differential attack.

7 Conclusion

In this paper, we construct a 5-round sandwich distinguisher for MMB with high probability 1. With the distinguisher, we recover the 128-bit key of MMB with 2^{39} adaptive chosen plaintexts and ciphertexts, 2^{40} MMB encryptions. On this bases, we present a rectangle-like sandwich attack to MMB, with $2^{66.5}$ chosen plaintexts, $2^{66.5}$ MMB encryptions and $2^{70.5}$ bytes memory. Besides, we improve the differential attack on MMB in [13]. The data complexity is 2^{96} chosen plaintexts, the time complexity is 2^{96} MMB encryptions and the memory complexity is 2^{66} bytes. We summarize the results on MMB in Table 2.

Acknowledgements. We would like to thank anonymous reviewers for their very helpful comments on the paper. We also hope to thank Yuliang Zheng for the discussion on the cryptanalysis of 7-round MMB during his stay in Tsinghua University.

References

1. Biham, E., Shamir, A.: Differential Cryptanalysis of The Data Encryption Standard. Springer, London (1993)
2. Biham, E., Dunkelman, O., Keller, N.: The Rectangle Attack - Rectangling the Serpent. In: Pfitzmann, B. (ed.) EUROCRYPT 2001. LNCS, vol. 2045, pp. 340–357. Springer, Heidelberg (2001)
3. Biham, E., Dunkelman, O., Keller, N.: A Related-Key Rectangle Attack on the Full KASUMI. In: Roy, B. (ed.) ASIACRYPT 2005. LNCS, vol. 3788, pp. 443–461. Springer, Heidelberg (2005)
4. Biryukov, A., De Cannière, C., Dellkrantz, G.: Cryptanalysis of SAFER++. In: Boneh, D. (ed.) CRYPTO 2003. LNCS, vol. 2729, pp. 195–211. Springer, Heidelberg (2003)
5. Biryukov, A., Khovratovich, D.: Related-Key Cryptanalysis of the Full AES-192 and AES-256. In: Matsui, M. (ed.) ASIACRYPT 2009. LNCS, vol. 5912, pp. 1–18. Springer, Heidelberg (2009)
6. Kelsey, J., Kohno, T., Schneier, B.: Amplified Boomerang Attacks Against Reduced-Round MARS and Serpent. In: Schneier, B. (ed.) FSE 2000. LNCS, vol. 1978, pp. 75–93. Springer, Heidelberg (2001)
7. Daemen, J., Govaerts, R., Vandewalle, J.: Block Ciphers Based on Modular Multiplication. In: Wolfowicz, W. (ed.) Proceedings of 3rd Symposium on State and Progress of Research in Cryptography, Fondazione Ugo Bordoni, pp. 80–89 (1993)
8. Daemen, J.: Cipher and Hash Function Design Strategies based on Linear and Differential Cryptanalysis. PhD Thesis, Dept. Elektrotechniek, Katholieke Universiteit Leuven, Belgium (1995)
9. Lai, X., Massey, J.: A Proposal for a New Block Encryption Standard. In: Damgård, I.B. (ed.) EUROCRYPT 1990. LNCS, vol. 473, pp. 389–404. Springer, Heidelberg (1991)
10. Dunkelman, O., Keller, N., Shamir, A.: A Practical-Time Attack on the A5/3 Cryptosystem Used in Third Generation GSM Telephony, `http://eprint.iacr.org/2010/013`
11. Dunkelman, O., Keller, N., Shamir, A.: A Practical-Time Related-Key Attack on the KASUMI Cryptosystem Used in GSM and 3G Telephony. In: Rabin, T. (ed.) CRYPTO 2010. LNCS, vol. 6223, pp. 393–410. Springer, Heidelberg (2010)
12. Selçuk, A.A., Biçak, A.: On Probability of Success in Linear and Differential Cryptanalysis. In: Cimato, S., Galdi, C., Persiano, G. (eds.) SCN 2002. LNCS, vol. 2576, pp. 174–185. Springer, Heidelberg (2003)
13. Wang, M., Nakahara Jr., J., Sun, Y.: Cryptanalysis of the Full MMB Block Cipher. In: Jacobson Jr., M.J., Rijmen, V., Safavi-Naini, R. (eds.) SAC 2009. LNCS, vol. 5867, pp. 231–248. Springer, Heidelberg (2009)
14. Wagner, D.: The Boomerang Attack. In: Knudsen, L.R. (ed.) FSE 1999. LNCS, vol. 1636, pp. 156–170. Springer, Heidelberg (1999)

Conditional Differential Cryptanalysis of Trivium and KATAN

Simon Knellwolf*, Willi Meier, and María Naya-Plasencia**

FHNW, Switzerland

Abstract. The concept of conditional differential cryptanalysis has been applied to NLFSR-based cryptosystems at ASIACRYPT 2010. We improve the technique by using automatic tools to find and analyze the involved conditions. Using these improvements we cryptanalyze the stream cipher Trivium and the KATAN family of lightweight block ciphers. For both ciphers we obtain new cryptanalytic results. For reduced variants of Trivium we obtain a class of weak keys that can be practically distinguished up to 961 of 1152 rounds. For the KATAN family we focus on its security in the related-key scenario and obtain practical key-recovery attacks for 120, 103 and 90 of 254 rounds of KATAN32, KATAN48 and KATAN64, respectively.

Keywords: Trivium, KATAN, conditional differential cryptanalysis.

1 Introduction

The stream cipher Trivium and the KATAN family of block ciphers are lightweight cryptographic primitives dedicated to hardware implementation. They share a very similar structure based on non-linear feedback shift registers (NLFSR). In [12], conditional differential cryptanalysis, first introduced in [3], has been applied to such constructions. The idea is to control the propagation of differences by imposing conditions on the public variables of the cipher. Depending whether these conditions involve secret variables or not, key-recovery or distinguishing attacks can be mounted. The technique extends to higher order differential cryptanalysis. A similar concept is the dynamic cube attack presented in [9]. Deriving the conditions by hand is a time consuming and error prone task. In this paper we use automatic tools to find and simplify these conditions. The method is applied to KATAN and Trivium. In both cases we obtain new cryptanalytic results.

In the single-key scenario, the KATAN family was already analyzed with respect to conditional differential cryptanalysis in [12]. Table 1 summarizes the

* Supported by the Hasler Foundation `www.haslerfoundation.ch` under project number 08065.

** Supported by the National Competence Center in Research on Mobile Information and Communication Systems (NCCR-MICS), a center of the Swiss National Science Foundation under grant number 5005-67322.

A. Miri and S. Vaudenay (Eds.): SAC 2011, LNCS 7118, pp. 200–212, 2012.

Table 1. Cryptanalytic results for KATAN. All attacks have practical complexity and recover parts of the key. The results in the single-key scenario also apply to KTANTAN.

block size	scenario	rounds	reference
32	single-key	78	[12]
	related-key	120	this paper
48	single-key	70	[12]
	related-key	103	this paper
64	single-key	68	[12]
	related-key	90	this paper

results and compares them to the results in the related-key scenario presented in this paper. The question about the related-key security of KATAN was raised by very efficient such attacks on KTANTAN [1]. The KTANTAN family of block ciphers differs from KATAN only by its key scheduling. The latter has shown some vulnerability which was also exploited for a meet-in-the-middle attack [4].

The most relevant cryptanalytic results on Trivium are obtained by cube attacks [8] and cube testers [2,15]. Our analysis can be seen as a refinement of cube testers. Exploiting these refinements for Trivium is the subject of the second part of this paper. Table 2 summarizes the results and compares them to existing analysis.

Table 2. Cryptanalytic results for Trivium

rounds	complexity	# keys	type of attack	reference
767	2^{45}	all	key recovery	[8]
790	2^{31}	all	distinguisher	[2]
798	2^{25}	all	distinguisher	this paper
806	2^{44}	all	distinguisher	[15]
868	2^{25}	2^{31}	distinguisher	this paper
961	2^{25}	2^{26}	distinguisher	this paper

The paper is organized as follows. Section 2 reviews conditional differential cryptanalysis and describes an approach to analyze the conditions more automatically. In Sections 3 and 4 we apply the technique to KATAN and Trivium.

2 Review of Conditional Differential Cryptanalysis

The idea of conditional differential cryptanalysis has been introduced in [3]. In [12] it has been extended to higher order cryptanalysis and applied to NLFSR-based constructions. We briefly review the concept and then sketch our strategies to analyze the conditions more automatically.

2.1 Conditional Differential Cryptanalysis

Suppose a prototypical NLFSR-based cipher with an internal state of length ℓ which is initialized with a key k and an initial value x. Let $s_0, s_1, \ldots$ be the consecutive state bits generated by the cipher, such that $(s_i, \ldots, s_{i+\ell})$ is the state after i rounds, and let h be the output function of the cipher such that $h(s_i, \ldots, s_{i+\ell})$ is the output after i rounds. Every state bit is a function of (k, x) and the same is true for the output of h. For some fixed i, let $f = h(s_i, \ldots, s_{i+\ell})$.

In differential cryptanalysis one computes derivatives of f. Following [13], the derivative of f with respect to a is defined as

$$\Delta_a f(k, x) = f(k, x) + f(k, x \oplus a).$$

A biased output distribution distinguishes the cipher from an ideal primitive and may reveals information on the key. The idea of conditional differential cryptanalysis is to derive conditions on x that control the propagation of the difference up to some round r. This results in a system of equations

$$\Delta_a s_i(k, x) = \gamma_i, \quad 0 \leq i < r. \tag{1}$$

The γ_i are either 0 or 1 and describe the differential characteristic. Values x that satisfy all conditions are called *valid*. The goal is to find a large sample of valid inputs $\mathcal{X}$, such that a bias can be detected in the output of $\Delta_a f$ on $\mathcal{X}$. The conditions may also involve variables of the key. This allows for key recovery or classification of weak keys.

The technique extends to higher order derivatives (corresponding to higher order differential cryptanalysis). The d-th derivative of f with respect to $a_1, \ldots, a_d$ is defined as

$$\Delta^{(d)}_{a_1,\ldots,a_d} f(k, x) = \sum_{c \in L(a_1,\ldots,a_d)} f(k, x \oplus c),$$

where $L(a_1, \ldots, a_d)$ is the set of all 2^d linear combinations of $a_1, \ldots, a_d$. In [12] it was proposed to analyze the first order propagation of each difference a_i and to merge the obtained conditions. This technique was successfully applied to Grain-128 in and we will apply it to Trivium in this paper.

2.2 Automatic Strategies for Analyzing the Conditions

Analyzing the conditions is a crucial part of conditional differential cryptanalysis. There is a trade-off between the number of controlled rounds and the size of the sample $\mathcal{X}$. Controlling more rounds means to impose more conditions, which reduces the number of valid inputs that can be derived. In general, the conditions are not independent of each other and may be simplified during the process. This makes the analysis complicated and prone to error when done by hand. In the case of higher order derivatives this tends to be even more intricate.

In order to do a more automatic analysis, we represent the system of conditions as an ideal J in the ring of Boolean polynomials $\mathbb{F}_2[K, X]$. All (k, x) in the algebraic variety of J satisfy the imposed conditions[1]. We then use the PolyPoRi library [5] to perform computations in Boolean polynomial rings. Specifically, we use modular reductions to analyze new conditions with respect to already imposed conditions, and to obtain a simple representation of J.

We distinguish two strategies for computing J. The strategies differ in whether the differential characteristic is fixed in advance (for example by linearization) or if it is derived in parallel with the conditions.

Differential Characteristic Fixed in Advance. This is the simple strategy and we will use it in our analysis of KATAN. Consider the system of equations given by (1) and assume that $\gamma_0, \ldots, \gamma_{r-1}$ are given. Algorithm 1 either returns the ideal describing the exact conditions on k and x for following the characteristic, or it returns with a message that the characteristic is impossible.

Algorithm 1. Deriving conditions for a given characteristic.

```
Input: a, γ_0, ..., γ_{r-1}
Output: Ideal of conditions
J ← ∅
for i ← 0 to r − 1 do
    f ← Δ_a s_i(k, x) ⊕ γ_i  mod J
    if f = 1 then
        return impossible characteristic
    else
        add f to J
return J
```

Differential Characteristic Derived in Parallel. In some cases it can be difficult to choose a characteristic in advance. This is particularly true for higher order derivatives where several characteristics have to be chosen such that their respective conditions do not contradict each other. A straightforward extension of Algorithm 1 would fail in most cases. Algorithm 2 provides more flexibility. It takes as input only the initial difference, and at each step develops the characteristic based on the conditions imposed so far. At those steps where γ_i can take both values (0 or 1), the algorithm chooses $\gamma_i = 0$ (it prevents the propagation of the difference). Other strategies are possible, but we found this strategy the most successful in our applications.

Algorithm 3 is an extension to the higher order case and we will use it in our analysis of Trivium. Note that this algorithm does not explicitly compute the characteristics. They are not used for the attack, and in Algorithm 2 the characteristic is computed only for illustration.

[1] The algebraic variety of J is the set $\{(k, x) \mid f(k, x) = 0 \text{ for all } f \in J\}$.

Algorithm 2. Deriving characteristic in parallel to conditions.

```
Input: a, r
Output: Differential characteristic and ideal of conditions
J ← ∅
for i ← 0 to r − 1 do
    f ← Δ_a s_i(k, x)  mod J
    if f = 1 then
        γ_i ← 1
    else
        γ_i ← 0
        add f to J
return (γ_0, ..., γ_{r−1}), J
```

Algorithm 3. Extension of Algorithm 2 to higher order derivatives.

```
Input: a_1, ..., a_d, r
Output: Ideal of conditions
J ← ∅
foreach a ∈ {a_1, ..., a_d} do
    for i ← 0 to r − 1 do
        f ← Δ_a s_i(k, x)  mod J
        if f ≠ 1 then
            add f to J
return J
```

The algorithms usually produce a very simple representation of J which directly allows to analyze the dependence on bits of the key, and to derive the respective sample(s) $\mathcal{X}$. If necessary, more advanced techniques can be applied, for example Gröbner basis algorithms.

3 Related-Key Attacks for Reduced KATAN

We now evaluate the security of KATAN against conditional differential cryptanalysis in a related-key attack scenario. More specifically, an attacker is assumed to obtain two ciphertexts for each chosen plaintext: one encrypted under a secret key k and the other encrypted under $k \oplus b$ for a chosen difference b.

3.1 Description of KATAN

KATAN [7] is a family of lightweight block ciphers proposed De Cannière, Dunkelman and Knezevic. The family consists of three ciphers denoted by KATANn for $n = 32, 48, 64$ indicating the block size. All instances accept an 80-bit key. KATANn has a state of n bits which are aligned as two non-linear feedback shift registers. For $n = 32$, the registers have lengths 13 and 19, respectively. They are initialized with the plaintext:

$$(s_1, \ldots, s_{19}) \leftarrow (x_0, \ldots, x_{18})$$
$$(s_{20}, \ldots, s_{32}) \leftarrow (x_{19}, \ldots, x_{31}).$$

The key is expanded to 508 bits according to the linear recursion

$$k_{j+80} = k_j + k_{j+19} + k_{j+30} + k_{j+67}, \quad 0 \leq j < 428,$$

where $k_0, \ldots, k_{79}$ are the bits of k. At each round of the encryption process two consecutive bits of the expanded key are used. The round updates further depend on a bit c_i. The sequence of c_i is produced by an 8-bit linear feedback shift register which is used as a counter. It is initialized by $(c_0, \ldots, c_7) = (1, \ldots, 1, 0)$ and expanded according to $c_{i+8} = c_i + c_{i+1} + c_{i+3} + c_{i+8}$. Round i, for $0 \leq i < 254$, corresponds to the following transformation of the state:

$$t_1 \leftarrow s_{32} + s_{26} + s_{28}s_{25} + s_{23}c_i + k_{2i}$$
$$t_2 \leftarrow s_{19} + s_7 + s_{12}s_{10} + s_8s_3 + k_{2i+1}$$
$$(s_1, \ldots, s_{19}) \leftarrow (t_2, s_1, \ldots, s_{18})$$
$$(s_{19}, \ldots, s_{32}) \leftarrow (t_1, s_{19}, \ldots, s_{31})$$

After 254 rounds, the state is output as the ciphertext. All three members of the KATAN family use the same key expansion and the same sequence of c_i. The algebraic structure of the non-linear update functions is the same. They differ in the length of the non-linear registers and the tap positions for the non-linear update functions. All members perform 254 rounds, but for KATAN48 the non-linear registers are updated twice per round and for KATAN64 even thrice (using the same c_i and k_i for all updates at the same round).

3.2 Basic Analysis Strategy

As in the analysis of KATAN in [12] we use first order differentials. The basic strategy is as follows:

1. Find a key difference b whose expansion does not introduce differences for many rounds after some round r. The idea is to cancel all differences introduced by b up to round r and to maximize the number of rounds, where no differences are introduced again.
2. Compute backwards from round r in order to find a plaintext difference a that cancels the differences introduced by b. This fixes a differential characteristic.
3. Use Algorithm 1 to compute the ideal J, describing the conditions for the characteristic to be followed.
4. Derive a sample of valid plaintexts and empirically find the maximal number of rounds for which a bias can be detected in the ciphertext differences.

The automated techniques for condition analysis allow to test many configurations for a and b. The maximal number of consecutive rounds b does not introduce differences is 39 (the key expansion is a 80-bit linear feedback shift register with maximum period and two bits are used per round). It is easy to compute differences which have this maximal run of zeros at any desired round r, and the choice of b essentially reduces to a choice of r. We try to find the largest r that can be controlled by conditions. If key bits are involved in the conditions, several samples will be derived and tested for the correct guess.

3.3 Analysis of KATAN32

We now describe the details to attack 120 rounds of KATAN32. We use the key difference $b = [6, 14, 25, 44]$ which means differences at positions 6,14,25 and 44 of the key. The expanded key difference is given in Table 3. Note that no differences are introduced after round $r = 22$ for the subsequent 39 rounds. By backward computation we find that the plaintext difference $a = [6, 9, 19]$ cancels all differences up to round 22. The corresponding characteristic is given in Table 4.

Table 3. Expanded key difference $b = [6, 14, 25, 44]$

Rnds	Round key differences
0-19	00 00 00 10 00 00 00 10 00 00 00 00 01 00 00 00 00 00 00 00
20-39	00 00 10 00 00 00 00 00 00 00 00 00 00 00 00 00 00 00 00 00
40-59	00 00 00 00 00 00 00 00 00 00 00 00 00 00 00 00 00 00 00 00
60-79	00 00 10 00 00 00 00 00 01 00 00 00 00 00 00 10 00 00 00 00
80-99	00 01 00 00 00 00 00 10 10 00 00 00 01 00 01 00 00 00 00 00
100-119	10 10 10 00 00 01 00 01 00 00 00 00 10 10 10 10 00 00 00 00
...	...
240-253	01 01 00 10 11 10 11 10 11 10 00 01 10 11

Using Algorithm 1 we compute the following ideal J given by

$$
\begin{aligned}
J = \langle & x_{11} + 1, x_1, x_7, x_8 + 1, x_{22}, x_4, x_5 + x_{10} + x_{16} + k_5, x_6 + x_9 + x_{17} + k_3, \\
& x_0 + x_3x_{10} + x_3x_{16} + x_3k_5 + k_{15}, x_2x_{20} + x_2x_{24} + x_2x_{29} + x_2k_4 + x_{12} + k_{13}, \\
& x_3x_{10}x_{21} + x_3x_{10}x_{23}x_{26} + x_3x_{10}x_{25} + x_3x_{10}x_{30} + x_3x_{10}k_2 + x_3x_{16}x_{21} \\
& + x_3x_{16}x_{23}x_{26} + x_3x_{16}x_{25} + x_3x_{16}x_{30} + x_3x_{16}k_2 + x_3x_{19} + x_3x_{21}x_{24} \\
& + x_3x_{21}k_5 + x_3x_{23}x_{26}k_5 + x_3x_{23} + x_3x_{25}k_5 + x_3x_{28} + x_3x_{30}k_5 + x_3k_2k_5 \\
& + x_3k_6 + x_3 + x_9 + x_{10}x_{12}x_{19} + x_{10}x_{12}x_{21}x_{24} + x_{10}x_{12}x_{23} + x_{10}x_{12}x_{28} \\
& + x_{10}x_{12}k_6 + x_{10}x_{12} + x_{17} + x_{18}x_{19} + x_{18}x_{21}x_{24} + x_{18}x_{23} + x_{18}x_{28} + x_{18}k_6 \\
& + x_{18} + x_{19}x_{23} + x_{19}k_1 + x_{19}k_{16} + x_{20}x_{23} + x_{21}x_{23}x_{24} + x_{21}x_{24}k_1 + x_{21}x_{24}k_{16} \\
& + x_{21}k_{15} + x_{23}x_{26}k_{15} + x_{23}x_{28} + x_{23}k_1 + x_{23}k_6 + x_{23}k_{16} + x_{23} + x_{25}k_{15} + x_{27} \\
& + x_{28}k_1 + x_{28}k_{16} + x_{30}k_{15} + k_1k_6 + k_1 + k_2k_{15} + k_3 + k_6k_{16} + k_8 + k_{25} \rangle .
\end{aligned}
$$

Table 4. Differential characteristic for $a = [6, 9, 19]$ and $b = [6, 14, 25, 44]$

Round	Difference in state
0	00000010010000000001000000000000
1	00000001001000000000100000000000
2	00000000100100000000010000000000
3	00000000010010000000001000000000
4	00000000001001000000000100000000
5	00000000000100100001000010000000
6	00000000000010010000100001000000
7	00000000000001001000010000100000
8	00000000000000100100001000010000
9	00000000000000010010000100001000
10	00000000000000001001000010000100
11	00000000000000000100100001000010
12	00000000000000000010010000100001
13	00000000000000000000001000010000
14	00000000000000000000000100001000
15	00000000000000000000000010000100
16	00000000000000000000000001000010
17	00000000000000000000000000100001
18	00000000000000000000000000010000
19	00000000000000000000000000001000
20	00000000000000000000000000000100
21	00000000000000000000000000000010
22	00000000000000000000000000000001
23	00000000000000000000000000000000
	...
62	00000000000000000000000000000000
63	10000000000000000000000000000000
64	01000000000000000000000000000000

All pairs (k, x) in the algebraic variety of J will follow the characteristic given in Table 4. The conditions involve 10 bits of the key which can not be chosen. However, we can guess them and adjust x accordingly. It is not difficult to derive a sample of 2^{20} valid inputs for each guess. One adjusts a linear variable of each condition in order to nullify the expression. The remaining variables can be freely chosen. The correct guess is detected by a significant bias in the difference of state bit 18 after 120 rounds. Testing one sample costs 2^{21} queries and at most 2^{10} samples have to tested. Hence, the attack needs not more than 2^{31} queries to the cipher. The number of different queries can be even smaller, since the samples for the different guesses may overlap. The attack recovers 10 bits of the key, and we note that the recovered bits are essentially those of the first few rounds. This enables us to mount the same procedure starting at a later round, and finally to recover the full key at essentially the same cost.

3.4 Summary of Results

Table 5 presents the best configurations we found for the different members of the KATAN family. It contains the differences a and b, the number of rounds for which a bias can be detected and the cost of the attack. The latter is computed as $2^{|\mathcal{X}|+\kappa+1}$, where $|\mathcal{X}|$ is the sample size and κ is the number of key bits that must be guessed.

Table 5. Summary of the results for KATANn

n	plaintext difference	key difference	# rounds	cost
32	[6, 9, 19]	[6, 14, 25, 44]	120	2^{31}
48	[1, 2, 10, 11, 19, 20, 28, 38, 39, 44, 45]	[8, 27]	103	2^{25}
64	[6, 7, 8, 19, 20, 21, 34, 58, 59, 60]	[2, 21]	90	2^{27}

4 Weak Keys for Reduced Trivium

We now apply conditional differential cryptanalysis to the stream cipher Trivium. Our analysis leads to a classification of weak keys for reduced variants.

4.1 Description of Trivium

Trivium [6] was designed by De Cannière and Preneel and was selected for the final eSTREAM portfolio [10]. It takes a 80-bit key k and a 80-bit initial value x as input. The internal state consists of 288 bits which are aligned in three non-linear feedback shift registers of lengths 93, 84 and 111, respectively. They are initialized as follows:

$$
\begin{aligned}
(s_1, \ldots, s_{93}) &\leftarrow (k_0, \ldots, k_{79}, 0, \ldots, 0) \\
(s_{94}, \ldots, s_{177}) &\leftarrow (x_0, \ldots, x_{79}, 0, 0, 0, 0) \\
(s_{178}, \ldots, s_{288}) &\leftarrow (0, \ldots, 0, 1, 1, 1).
\end{aligned}
$$

The state is then updated iteratively by the following round transformation:

$$
\begin{aligned}
t_1 &\leftarrow s_{66} + s_{93} \\
t_2 &\leftarrow s_{162} + s_{177} \\
t_3 &\leftarrow s_{243} + s_{288} \\
z &\leftarrow t_1 + t_2 + t_3 \\
t_1 &\leftarrow t_1 + s_{91}s_{92} + s_{171} \\
t_2 &\leftarrow t_2 + s_{175}s_{176} + s_{264} \\
t_3 &\leftarrow t_3 + s_{286}s_{287} + s_{69} \\
(s_1, \ldots, s_{93}) &\leftarrow (t_3, s_1, \ldots, s_{92}) \\
(s_{94}, \ldots, s_{177}) &\leftarrow (t_1, s_{94}, \ldots, s_{176}) \\
(s_{178}, \ldots, s_{288}) &\leftarrow (t_2, s_{178}, \ldots, s_{287}).
\end{aligned}
$$

No output is produced during the first 1152 rounds. After this initialization phase the value of z is output as the key stream at each round.

4.2 Basic Strategy of Analysis

We will use a derivative of order $d = 24$ in our analysis. For the 24 differences, we derive conditions using Algorithm 3. Instead of deriving a set of valid inputs we will derive neutral variables for the derivative. Neutral variables have been used in a similar context in [2,11], for example. Let $\Delta f(k, x)$ be the derivative under consideration, and let e_i be the 1-bit difference at bit position i of x. By the *neutrality* of x_i in Δf we mean the probability that $\Delta f(k, x) = \Delta f(k, x \oplus e_i)$ for a random key k. Using a single neutral variable as a distinguisher needs at least two evaluations of Δf. In the case of a d-th derivative this reveals to 2^{d+1} queries to f. If the neutrality of x_i is p, the resulting distinguishing advantage is $|1/2 - p|$.

4.3 Choosing the Differences

It turns out that differences of hamming weight one give the best results. That is, the $a_1, \ldots, a_d$ are unit vectors in $\mathbb{F}_2^n$. We note that this special case of a higher order derivative is called a superpoly in [2]. Some heuristic techniques for choosing the differences have been proposed. We use none of them, but briefly explain our choice. The propagation of the single differences should be as independent as possible. This excludes for example, choosing two differences at a distance one. Such neighboring differences influence each other in the very early rounds due to the quadratic monomials in the update functions. Further, the regular structure of Trivium suggests a regular choice of the differences. Motivated by an observation in [14] we chose the differences at a distance of three. Empirical tests confirmed that this choice indeed outperforms all other choices. Specifically, we choose $a_i = e_{3(i-1)}$ for $1 \le i \le 24$, where $(e_0, \ldots, e_{n-1})$ is the standard basis of $\mathbb{F}_2^n$. In the following we use the shorthand $\Delta z_j = \Delta^{(24)}_{a_1,\ldots,a_{24}} z_j$, where z_j is the keystream produced in round j. (In the terminology of [2], Δz_j corresponds to the superpoly of $\{x_0, x_3, \ldots, x_{69}\}$.)

4.4 Analysis of Conditions

For the condition analysis we use Algorithm 3 with $r = 200$, that is, each difference is controlled for the first 200 rounds. After processing the first difference (the difference in x_0) we obtain

$$\begin{gathered} J = \langle x_1, x_{12}x_{13} + x_{14}, x_{14}x_{15} + x_{16}, x_{77} + k_{65}, \\ x_{62} + x_{75}x_{76} + x_{75}k_{64} + x_{76}k_{63} + k_{50} + k_{63}k_{64} + k_{75}k_{76} + k_{77}, \\ x_{64} + k_{52} + k_{77}k_{78} + k_{79}, k_{12}k_{13} + k_{14} + k_{56}, \\ k_{14}k_{15} + k_{16} + k_{58}\rangle. \end{gathered}$$

At this stage, J has the following interpretation: all pairs (k, x) in the algebraic variety of J follow the same differential characteristic up to round $r = 200$ with respect to a_1. We already note that two conditions can not be satisfied by the attacker, since they only involve bits of the key. After processing the remaining differences we have

$$J = \langle x_1, x_2, x_4, x_5, x_7, x_8, x_{10}, x_{11}, x_{13}, x_{14}, x_{16}, x_{17}, x_{19}, x_{20},$$
$$x_{22}, x_{23}, x_{25}, x_{26}, x_{28}, x_{29}, x_{31}, x_{32}, x_{34}, x_{35}, x_{37}, x_{38}, x_{40}, x_{41},$$
$$x_{43}, x_{44}, x_{46}, x_{47}, x_{49}, x_{50}, x_{52}, x_{53}, x_{55}, x_{56}, x_{58}, x_{59}, x_{61}, x_{62},$$
$$x_{64}, x_{65}, x_{67}, x_{68}, x_{70}, x_{71}, x_{73}, x_{74}, x_{76}, x_{77}, x_{79}, k_1, k_2, k_4,$$
$$k_5, k_7, k_8, k_{10}, k_{11}, k_{13}, k_{14}, k_{16}, k_{17}, k_{19}, k_{20}, k_{22}, k_{23}, k_{25},$$
$$k_{26}, k_{28}, k_{29}, k_{31}, k_{32}, k_{34}, k_{35}, k_{37}, k_{38}, k_{40}, k_{41}, k_{43}, k_{44}, k_{46},$$
$$k_{47}, k_{49}, k_{50}, k_{52}, k_{53}, k_{55}, k_{56}, k_{58}, k_{59}, k_{61}, k_{62}, k_{64}, k_{65}, k_{66},$$
$$k_{67} + 1, k_{68}, k_{70}, k_{71}, k_{73}, k_{74}, k_{76}, k_{77}, k_{79}\rangle.$$

All conditions collapse to conditions on single bits. From x, only the bits x_{72}, x_{75} and x_{78} are not fixed by conditions and not touched by the differences. This makes them candidate neutral bits for Δz_j, when all other variables x_i are set to zero. Empirical results confirm that they are probabilistically neutral up to round 798. Table 6 shows the neutrality which we obtained in an experiment with 100 random keys. Note that a neutrality of zero means that Δz_j is linear in the corresponding variable (which can be exploited as a distinguishing property in the same way as neutrality).

Table 6. Neutrality of the bits x_{72}, x_{75} and x_{78}

j	72	75	78
772	1.00	1.00	1.00
782	0.05	0.10	0.05
789	0.30	0.20	0.25
798	0.40	0.40	0.30

4.5 Classes of Weak Keys

From the above representation of J we can directly read a class of weak keys, namely the keys satisfying the given 54 conditions on the k_i. This class contains 2^{26} keys. Analogous to Table 6, Table 7 shows the neutrality of the bits x_{72}, x_{75} and x_{78} for a random weak key. We note that x_{75} can not be used anymore as a distinguisher at round $j = 961$, but x_{72} and x_{78} still can.

In order to reduce the number of conditions on the key we processed only a part of the differences by Algorithm 3. For example, for the first 17 differences we obtain only 49 conditions, and for the corresponding class of 2^{31} keys, the bits x_{72}, x_{75} and x_{78} are neutral up to round 868.

Table 7. Neutrality of the bits x_{72}, x_{75} and x_{78} for weak keys

j	72	75	78
953	1.00	1.00	1.00
961	0.00	0.50	1.00

5 Conclusion

We evaluated the security of Trivium and KATAN with respect to conditional differential cryptanalysis. We used an automatic approach to find and analyze the conditions in terms of polynomial ideals. For reduced Trivium we identified a class of 2^{26} keys that can be distinguished for 961 of 1152 rounds. For reduced KATAN we presented a key recovery attack up to 120 of 254 rounds in a related key scenario. KATAN seems to have a comfortable security margin with respect to the approach described in this paper.

Acknowledgements. We thank the reviewers of SAC 2011 for their helpful comments encouraging us to describe our analysis in more detail. This work was partially supported by the European Commission through the ICT programme under contract ICT-2007-216676 ECRYPT II.

References

1. Ågren, M.: Some Instant- and Practical-Time Related-Key Attacks on KTANTAN32/48/64. In: Miri, A., Vaudenay, S. (eds.) SAC 2011. LNCS, vol. 7118, pp. 217–233. Springer, Heidelberg (2011)
2. Aumasson, J.-P., Dinur, I., Meier, W., Shamir, A.: Cube Testers and Key Recovery Attacks on Reduced-Round MD6 and Trivium. In: Dunkelman, O. (ed.) FSE 2009. LNCS, vol. 5665, pp. 1–22. Springer, Heidelberg (2009)
3. Ben-Aroya, I., Biham, E.: Differential Cryptanalysis of Lucifer. In: Stinson, D.R. (ed.) CRYPTO 1993. LNCS, vol. 773, pp. 187–199. Springer, Heidelberg (1994)
4. Bogdanov, A., Rechberger, C.: A 3-Subset Meet-in-the-Middle Attack: Cryptanalysis of the Lightweight Block Cipher KTANTAN. In: Biryukov, A., Gong, G., Stinson, D.R. (eds.) SAC 2010. LNCS, vol. 6544, pp. 229–240. Springer, Heidelberg (2011)
5. Brickenstein, M., Dreyer, A.: PolyBoRi: A framework for Groebner-basis computations with Boolean polynomials. Journal of Symbolic Computation 44(9), 1326–1345 (2009)
6. De Cannière, C.: TRIVIUM: A Stream Cipher Construction Inspired by Block Cipher Design Principles. In: Katsikas, S.K., López, J., Backes, M., Gritzalis, S., Preneel, B. (eds.) ISC 2006. LNCS, vol. 4176, pp. 171–186. Springer, Heidelberg (2006)
7. De Cannière, C., Dunkelman, O., Knežević, M.: KATAN and KTANTAN — A Family of Small and Efficient Hardware-Oriented Block Ciphers. In: Clavier, C., Gaj, K. (eds.) CHES 2009. LNCS, vol. 5747, pp. 272–288. Springer, Heidelberg (2009)
8. Dinur, I., Shamir, A.: Cube Attacks on Tweakable Black Box Polynomials. In: Joux, A. (ed.) EUROCRYPT 2009. LNCS, vol. 5479, pp. 278–299. Springer, Heidelberg (2009)

9. Dinur, I., Shamir, A.: Breaking Grain-128 with Dynamic Cube Attacks. In: Joux, A. (ed.) FSE 2011. LNCS, vol. 6733, pp. 167–187. Springer, Heidelberg (2011)
10. ECRYPT: The eSTREAM project, http://www.ecrypt.eu.org/stream/
11. Fischer, S., Khazaei, S., Meier, W.: Chosen IV Statistical Analysis for Key Recovery Attacks on Stream Ciphers. In: Vaudenay, S. (ed.) AFRICACRYPT 2008. LNCS, vol. 5023, pp. 236–245. Springer, Heidelberg (2008)
12. Knellwolf, S., Meier, W., Naya-Plasencia, M.: Conditional Differential Cryptanalysis of NLFSR-Based Cryptosystems. In: Abe, M. (ed.) ASIACRYPT 2010. LNCS, vol. 6477, pp. 130–145. Springer, Heidelberg (2010)
13. Lai, X.: Higher order derivatives and differential cryptanalysis. In: Blahut, R.E., Costello, D.J., Maurer, U., Mittelholzer, T. (eds.) Communicationis and Cryptography: Two Sides of one Tapestry, pp. 227–233. Kluwer Academic Publishers (1994)
14. Maximov, A., Biryukov, A.: Two Trivial Attacks on Trivium. In: Adams, C., Miri, A., Wiener, M. (eds.) SAC 2007. LNCS, vol. 4876, pp. 36–55. Springer, Heidelberg (2007)
15. Stankovski, P.: Greedy Distinguishers and Nonrandomness Detectors. In: Gong, G., Gupta, K.C. (eds.) INDOCRYPT 2010. LNCS, vol. 6498, pp. 210–226. Springer, Heidelberg (2010)

Some Instant- and Practical-Time Related-Key Attacks on KTANTAN32/48/64

Martin Ågren

Dept. of Electrical and Information Technology, Lund University,
P.O. Box 118, 221 00 Lund, Sweden
martin.agren@eit.lth.se

Abstract. The hardware-attractive block cipher family KTANTAN was studied by Bogdanov and Rechberger who identified flaws in the key schedule and gave a meet-in-the-middle attack. We revisit their result before investigating how to exploit the weakest key bits. We then develop several related-key attacks, e.g., one on KTANTAN32 which finds 28 key bits in time equivalent to $2^{3.0}$ calls to the full KTANTAN32 encryption. The main result is a related-key attack requiring $2^{28.44}$ time (half a minute on a current CPU) to recover the full 80-bit key. For KTANTAN48, we find three key bits in the time of one encryption, and give several other attacks, including full key recovery. For KTANTAN64, the attacks are only slightly more expensive, requiring $2^{10.71}$ time to find 38 key bits, and $2^{32.28}$ for the entire key. For all attacks, the requirements on related-key material are modest as in the forward and backward directions, we only need to flip a single key bit. All attacks succeed with probability one. Our attacks directly contradict the designers' claims. We discuss why this is, and what can be learnt from this.

Keywords: cryptanalysis, related key, block cipher, key schedule, lightweight cipher, key-recovery.

1 Introduction

KTANTAN is a hardware-oriented block cipher designed by De Cannière, Dunkelman and Knežević. It is part of the KATAN family [4] of six block ciphers. There are three variants KTANTANn where $n \in \{32, 48, 64\}$. All ciphers consist of 254 very simple, hardware-efficient rounds.

The only difference between KATAN and KTANTAN is the key schedule. The goal with KTANTAN is to allow an implementation to use a burnt-in key, which rules out loading the key into a register and applying some state updates to it in order to produce subkeys. Instead, subkeys are chosen as original key bits, selected according to a fixed schedule. This schedule is the same for all three variants.

Aiming for a lightweight cipher, the designers of KTANTAN did not provide the key schedule as a large table of how to select the key bits. Rather, a small state machine generates numbers between 0 and 79. In this way, key bits can hopefully be picked in an irregular fashion. As shown by Bogdanov and

A. Miri and S. Vaudenay (Eds.): SAC 2011, LNCS 7118, pp. 213–229, 2012.

Rechberger [3], the sequence in which the key bits are used has some unwanted properties.

We will revisit the result of Bogdanov and Rechberger. We adjust the presentation slightly, before using their observation to launch a related-key attack. Bogdanov and Rechberger noted this as a possible direction of research, but did not look into it further.

Related-key attacks have been known for almost twenty years [5,1]. Like most other related-key attacks, the ones presented in this paper are quite academic in their nature. They are still a good measurement of the security of the cipher, which should appear as an ideal permutation, and several notable properties make the attacks in this paper very interesting:

1. They are minimal: they only require flipping one bit in the key and in several cases, it is enough for the attacker to use only one triplet: one plaintext and two ciphertexts.
2. They are extreme: we find a large number of key bits in time equivalent to just a few encryptions. For KTANTAN32, the entire key can be found in half a minute on a current CPU.
3. They never fail: All the properties exploited in this paper have probability one, meaning the correct (partial) key *always* shows the property we look for.
4. They directly contradict the designers' claims. We will discuss why this is, and what can be learnt from this.

The remainder of this paper is organized as follows: In Section 2 we describe the cipher KTANTAN, and Section 3 introduces (truncated) differentials. Section 4 discusses the result by Bogdanov and Rechberger [3]. Section 5 develops our attacks on KTANTAN32, while we summarize our results on KTANTAN48 and KTANTAN64 in Section 6. In Section 7 we compare our results to the designers' original claims on related-key security before concluding the paper in Section 8.

2 KTANTAN

The n-bit plaintext $P = p_{n-1} \dots p_0$ is loaded into the state of the cipher, which consists of two shift registers, L_1 and L_2, see Fig. 1. For KTANTAN32, these are of lengths $|L_1| = 13$ and $|L_2| = 19$. The other variants use longer registers.

The 254 rounds are denoted as round $0, 1, \dots, 253$. Each round uses two key bits, k_a^r and k_b^r, which are picked straight from the 80-bit master key. The key schedule is provided in Appendix A.

The contents of the registers are shifted, and the new bit in each register (L_1/L_2) is created from five or six bits from the other register (L_2/L_1), through some simple functions of degree two. For all versions of KTANTAN, the update is specified by

$$f_a(L_1) = L_1[x_1] \oplus L_1[x_2] \oplus (L_1[x_3] \cdot L_1[x_4]) \oplus (L_1[x_5] \cdot IR^r) \oplus k_a^r$$
$$f_b(L_2) = L_2[y_1] \oplus L_2[y_2] \oplus (L_2[y_3] \cdot L_2[y_4]) \oplus (L_2[y_5] \cdot L_2[y_6]) \oplus k_b^r.$$

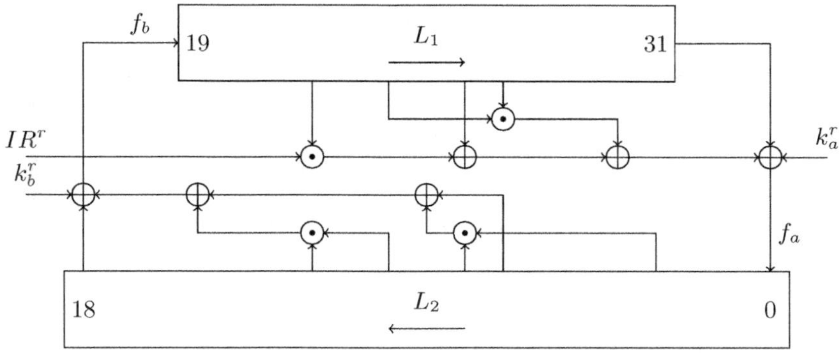

Fig. 1. An overview of KTANTAN32. In each clocking, one shift is made and two key bits, k_a^r and k_b^r, are added to the state. IR^r is a round constant which decides whether or not $L_1[3]$ is used in the state update or not. Indices denote how bits in the plaintext/ciphertext are identified. L_1 is shifted to the right and L_2 to the left.

Table 1. The parameters defining KTANTANn, where $n \in \{32, 48, 64\}$

n	$\lvert L_1\rvert$	$\lvert L_2\rvert$	x_1	x_2	x_3	x_4	x_5	y_1	y_2	y_3	y_4	y_5	y_6
32	13	19	12	7	8	5	3	18	7	12	10	8	3
48	19	29	18	12	15	7	6	28	19	21	13	15	6
64	25	39	24	15	20	11	9	38	25	33	21	14	9

The indices are given by Table 1.

There is a round constant IR^r, 0 or 1, which decides whether a certain bit from L_1 is included in the feedback to L_2 or not, and is taken from a sequence with long period in order to rule out sliding attacks and similar.

For KTANTAN32, one state update is performed per round. In KTANTAN48 and KTANTAN64, there are two resp. three updates per round using the same key bits and round constant. This larger amount of state updates means the state mixing is faster, making our attacks slightly more expensive on the larger versions of KTANTAN. We use KTANTAN32 to describe our attacks but also give the characteristics for the attacks on KTANTAN48/64.

Note how the key bits are added linearly to the state. Only after three clockings will they start to propagate nonlinearly. This gives a very slow diffusion, which we will be able to use in our attacks.

We adopt and refine the notation from [3]: define $\phi_{r_1,r_2}(S,K)$ as the partial encryption that applies rounds $r_1, r_1+1, \ldots, r_2-1$ to the state S using key K. Similarly, $\phi^{-1}_{r_1,r_2}(S,K)$ applies the decryption rounds $r_2-1, \ldots, r_1+1, r_1$ to the state S using key K. This allows us to decompose the full KTANTAN as e.g., $C = \phi_{127,254}(\phi_{0,127}(P,K),K)$.

The final encryption is denoted $C = c_{n-1} \cdots c_0$.

2.1 On Bit Ordering and Test Vectors

We denote the key $K = k_{79} \dots k_0$ as in [3]. Test vectors for KTANTAN can be produced by the reference code. As an example, the all-ones key and the all-zeros plaintext produce the ciphertext `0x22ea3988`. Unfortunately, this does not highlight the bit order in the plaintext and, more importantly, the key. For completeness and using the reference code given by the designers, we thus provide the key `0xfffffffffffffffffffe`, plaintext `0x00000001`, and ciphertext `0x8b4f0824` to indicate the bit orders involved.

3 (Truncated) Differentials

Differential cryptanalysis was publicly introduced by Biham and Shamir [2] in 1990. The idea is to study how a difference in the plaintext propagates through the state of the encryption. If a partial key is correctly guessed, this property should show up with some probability — ideally one but often very close to one half — while a bad guess should lead to a more random behaviour.

Knudsen [6] extended the technique to truncated differentials, where similar properties are studied only in some part of the state.

In [3], a differential is denoted by $(\Delta P, \Delta K) \rightarrow \Delta S$, where a difference in the plaintext and key gives a difference in the state some number of rounds into the encryption. We adopt and extend this notation. To denote truncated differentials, i.e., differentials where we only know the differences in certain bit positions, we will use a mask and a value denoted [mask : value]. As an example, [00010a00:00010800] denotes a known difference in bits 16, 11, and 9. In bits 16 and 11, there is a difference, while there is a bit-equality in bit 9. For the other bits, we do not know or care about the difference. In pseudo-C code, such a mask-value pair could be used to identify a match by

```
if ( ((s1^s2)&mask) == value ) { ... }.
```

In this paper, ΔK always involves only a single bit, so we will name this bit specifically, e.g., as in $(0, k_{32}) \rightarrow$ [08075080 : 00000080].

With each (truncated) differential, there is also a probability that it holds. In this paper, we only use differentials with probability one, which means there are only false positives, which can be ruled out by repeated filtering, and no false negatives. As a result, all attacks given in this paper have probability one of succeeding. When we give data complexities, these will be the expected number of samples needed to obtain a unique solution. Similarly, time complexities will account for the work needed to rule out false alarms. We assume that an alarm is raised with probability 2^{-b} for a differential that involves b bits.

Due to the unicity distance, we will always need some extra material in order to find a unique key. This is a fundamental property of KTANTAN as we can only access plaintexts and ciphertexts of 32 to 64 bits, but want to find a key consisting of 80 bits.

Table 2. The nine most extreme key bits in both directions during encryption. Six bits do not appear before round 111, while six others are not used after round 131.

Key bit	Used first in round	Key bit	Used last in round
k_{13}	109	k_{38}	164
k_{27}	110	k_{46}	158
k_{59}	110	k_{15}	157
k_{39}	111	k_{20}	131
k_{66}	123	k_{74}	130
k_{75}	127	k_{41}	122
k_{44}	136	k_3	106
k_{61}	140	k_{47}	80
k_{32}	218	k_{63}	79

4 A Previous Result on KTANTAN

Bogdanov and Rechberger [3] note that some key bits are not used until very late in the cipher, while some others are never used after some surprisingly small number of rounds, see Table 2. Given a plaintext–ciphertext pair, this results in a guess-and-determine attack, where the "determine" part is a meet-in-the-middle: Guess 68 key bits. Of the twelve remaining key bits, six are not used in the first part of the cipher, meaning there are only $2^{12-6} = 2^6$ different states after calculating $\phi_{0,111}$ from the plaintext. Similarly, there are 2^6 possible states after calculating $\phi^{-1}_{132,254}$ from the ciphertext. By checking the 2^{12} combinations for matches, one can find the key. In KTANTAN32, one can use eight bits in the mid-cipher state to judge equality, so false positives should appear with rate 2^{-8}. Some additional plaintext–ciphertext pairs will help rule out the false positives, but they are needed anyway due to the unicity distance.

Bogdanov and Rechberger dub this a 3-subset meet-in-the-middle attack and give similar attacks for KTANTAN48 and KTANTAN64.

4.1 Reformulating the Attack

We note that the last step is not trivial, as the computations that need to be carried out in order to check for matches are similar to calculating the round functions themselves. Further, while the original authors choose to only use eight bits for matching, we have found that one can even use twelve bits, given by the mask `2a03cd44`. This slightly lowers the complexity of the attack as one can expect fewer false positives.

Summing up, we prefer to view the attack as follows:

1. Define $A_f = \{k_{63}, k_{47}, k_3, k_{41}, k_{74}, k_{20}\}$ and $A_b = \{k_{32}, k_{61}, k_{44}, k_{75}, k_{66}, k_{39}\}$.
2. Guess key bits $K \backslash (A_f \cup A_b)$.
3. Compute 2^6 partial encryptions $m_0, \ldots, m_{63}$ using $\phi_{0,127}$ for each choice of bit assignments for A_f.
4. Compute 2^6 partial decryptions $m'_0, \ldots, m'_{63}$ using $\phi^{-1}_{127,254}$ for each choice of bit assignments for A_b.

Table 3. Probabilistic truncated differentials on the full KTANTAN32

Differential	Probability
$(0, k_{32}) \to$ [00020000 : 00020000]	$.687 = .5 + .187$
$(0, k_{32}) \to$ [40000000 : 00000000]	$.640 = .5 + .140$
$(0, k_{32}) \to$ [40020000 : 00020000]	$.453 = .25 + .203$

5. For the 2^{12} combinations, check twelve specific bits for equality:
```
if ( ((mi^m'j)&0x2a03cd44) == 0 ) { ... }.
```
Alarms will be raised with probability 2^{-12}, so we expect one alarm.
6. Use some additional plaintext–ciphertext pairs to rule out false alarms.

An implementation improvement is to only calculate those 12 bits that we actually need. We have then reached something similar to the original formulation of the attack, with the notable difference that we only perform the computations involved in matching $(\phi_{111,127}, \phi^{-1}_{127,132})$ once, during the 2^6-parts. (We can split at any round between and including 123 and 127, and still get twelve known (but different) bit positions to look at, but opted for 127 as it makes both halves equally expensive to calculate.)

5 Related-Key Attacks on KTANTAN32

We first study further how k_{32} enters the key schedule very late. We then formulate our attack idea and derive various attacks that find some parts of the key.

5.1 On the Bad Mixing of k_{32}

Key bit 32 is especially weak as it appears for the first time in round 218 of 254. We have thus studied this bit closer. It is worth noting that if the cipher had used 253 rounds rather than 254, there would have been one ciphertext bit that is linear in k_{32}. That is, there is a 253-round differential $(0, k_{32}) \to$ [00040000 : 00040000] with probability one. The single bit involved is state bit 18 in Figure 1, i.e., the leftmost bit in L_2. This bit is shifted out of the state in the very last round, so such a probability-one differential is not available on the full KTANTAN. However, there are some high-probability truncated differentials on the full KTANTAN as given in Table 3. We do not exploit these differentials in this paper, but note that they give a very non-random behaviour to the cipher.

5.2 The General Attack Idea

We will present several related-key attacks that recover some or all key bits. The general outline of our attacks can be formulated as follows: We group key bits into disjoint subsets $A_0, \ldots, A_{l-1}$ of sizes $s_i = |A_i|$, $i = 0, \ldots, l-1$. These subsets do not necessarily need to collectively contain all 80 key bits. Define $s = \sum_i s_i$.

We attack these subsets one after another, i.e., when attempting to find the correct bit assignments for A_j, we assume that we already know the correct bit assignments for A_i, $i = 0, \ldots, j-1$. We then follow this simple outline:

1. Guess the bit assignments for A_j.
2. If the (truncated) differential matches, we have a candidate subkey.
3. If the (truncated) differential does not match, we discard the candidate subkey.

In the first step, we can make 2^{s_j} guesses for the subkey. Note that the last step can be performed without risk, since all our differentials have probability one. Due to this, we can immediately discard large numbers of guesses.

The second step of the attack can however give false positives. As already noted, we assume that an alarm is raised with probability 2^{-b} for a differential that involves b bits. To discard the false alarms, we can recheck the differential on more material.

After finding the key bits specified by $\cup_i A_i$, we can conclude by a brute force for the remaining $80-s$ key bits. The total complexity would be $2^{s_0}+\ldots+2^{s_{l-1}}+2^{80-s}$. However, the different operations in these terms have different costs. All time complexities in this paper will be normalized to KTANTAN calls, and also incorporate the expected increase of calculations due to false positives. We will denote this time measurement t and it will, depending on context, refer to the time required to recover either the full key or only some part of it.

5.3 A First Approach: Finding 28 Bits of the Key

Assume that we have a known plaintext P, and two ciphertexts C_0, C_1, where the difference is that k_{32} has been flipped in the unknown key between the calculations of the two ciphertexts. During the calculations of these two ciphertexts, the first 218 states followed the same development. Only after k_{32} entered could the calculations diverge to produce different ciphertexts.

Bogdanov and Rechberger give the probability-1 differential $(0, k_{32}) \to 0$ for 218 rounds. We note that this differential can be easily extended into 222 rounds, still with probability 1: $(0, k_{32}) \to 00000008$. The flipped bit in ΔS is the linear appearance of k_{32}.

We will use "triplets" consisting of one plaintext and *two* ciphertexts to exploit these differentials. A first attempt to use such a plaintext–ciphertexts triplet in an attack could look like this: We note that there are 42 key bits used when decrypting into round 222, see Appendix B. We guess these bits and denote them by K. Denote by K' the same partial key but with k_{32} flipped. Calculate $S_0 = \phi^{-1}_{222,254}(C_0, K)$ and $S_1 = \phi^{-1}_{222,254}(C_1, K')$. For a correct guess, both ciphertexts will decrypt into the same state $S_0 = S_1$.

However, we will have problems with false positives. The first key bits to enter the decryptions, k_{71} and k_7, will enter into a lot of nonlinearity meaning that a wrong guess here should give different partial encryptions S_0, S_1 with high

Table 4. Key bits recovered in Sections 5.3 and 5.5. In the second set, the 11 reappearing key bits have been underlined.

The 28 key bits guessed and found in Section 5.3, exploiting k_{32}.
$\{k_0, k_1, k_2, k_4, k_5, k_7, k_8, k_{11}, k_{12}, k_{14}, k_{16}, k_{17}, k_{22}, k_{27}, k_{29},$ $k_{32}, k_{34}, k_{55}, k_{56}, k_{60}, k_{62}, k_{64}, k_{66}, k_{68}, k_{69}, k_{71}, k_{73}, k_{75}\}$
The 40 key bits guessed and found in Section 5.5, exploiting k_{63}.
$\{\underline{k_7}, k_{10}, \underline{k_{11}}, \underline{k_{14}}, k_{15}, \underline{k_{17}}, k_{19}, k_{21}, \underline{k_{22}}, k_{25}, k_{26}, k_{28}, k_{30}, k_{31},$ $\underline{k_{34}}, k_{35}, k_{37}, k_{38}, k_{40}, k_{41}, k_{43}, k_{45}, k_{47}, k_{49}, k_{52}, k_{53}, k_{54},$ $k_{58}, \underline{k_{60}}, \underline{k_{62}}, k_{63}, k_{67}, \underline{k_{68}}, \underline{k_{69}}, k_{70}, \underline{k_{71}}, k_{74}, k_{76}, k_{77}, k_{79}\}$

probability. However, the very last bit we guess, k_{37}, will only enter linearly, and if the other 41 key bits are correct, we will have $S_0 = S_1$ no matter how we guess k_{37}.

Generalizing, we realize that the bits which enter the partial decryption "late" will not affect the comparison of S_0 and S_1 at all as they enter only linearly. We have found that there are only 28 key bits that affect the equality between S_0 and S_1. These bits are listed in Table 4.

We thus need to guess 28 bits and for each guess perform two partial decryptions of 32 out of 254 rounds. The total number of round function calls is expected to be $2^{28} \cdot 2 \cdot 32 = 2^{34}$, which corresponds to $2^{34}/254 \approx 2^{26.01}$ full KTANTAN evaluations. Thus the total time complexity of finding 28 bits is $t \approx 2^{26}$. All time complexities in the remainder of the paper will be calculated in this way.

By using brute-force for the remaining key bits, the entire key can be found in time $t \approx 2^{26} + 2^{62} \approx 2^{62}$.

5.4 Making It Faster

Rather than guessing 28 bits at once, we note that we can apply a divide-and-conquer approach to these bits, determining a few bits at a time. This will significantly improve the complexity of the attack. Due to the slow diffusion, we cannot find any truncated differential on 247 rounds or more for our purposes, but for 246 rounds, there is $(0, k_{32}) \rightarrow$ [80050800 : 00000800]. This differential can be used to find three bits, $A_0 = \{k_{11}, k_{66}, k_{71}\}$, in time $t \approx 2^{-0.9}$. (That this work is performed in time less than one unit results from the fact that we only perform a small number of round calculations, compared to the full 254 rounds that are calculated in one time unit.)

We now know these three bits specified by A_0 and attempt to find more bits. There is no useful 245-round differential, but the 244-round truncated differential $(0, k_{32}) \rightarrow$ [20054200 : 00000200] can be used to obtain one additional key bit, specified by $A_1 = \{k_2\}$, with $t \approx 2^{-0.5}$.

Continuing with such small chunks, we can find the 28 bits with $t \approx 2^{-0.9} + 2^{-0.5} + \ldots \approx 2^{3.0}$. All differentials involved are listed in Table 5.

5.5 Using One Ciphertext and Two Plaintexts

k_{32} appeared very late in the encryption, and we exploited this above. Similarly, k_{63} is only used in the first 80 rounds, meaning that during *de*cryption it shows similar properties. With one ciphertext and two plaintexts, corresponding to a secret key with a flipped k_{63}, we can launch an attack similar to that above, with a truncated differential involving a single bit. With A_0 and using $\phi_{0,43}$, we guess and obtain 40 bits, listed in Table 4, using 40 data and $t \approx 2^{39.44}$. We can then exploit k_{63} for more subsets $A_1, \ldots, A_{15}$ and partial encryptions $\phi_{0,45}, \ldots, \phi_{0,71}$, finding in total 65 bits of the key still with $t \approx 2^{39.44}$. Concluding with a brute force for the remaining bits, we can find the entire key in $t \approx 2^{39.44}+2^{15} \approx 2^{39.44}$. All subsets, truncated differentials, etc. can be found in Table 6.

5.6 Going in Both Directions for a Practical-Time Key-Recovery

We first go backwards in time $t \approx 2^{3.0}$ to find 28 bits as outlines above. We then go forwards using k_{63}. However, of the 40 bits we needed to guess above, we have learnt 11 while using k_{32}, so we only need to guess 29 bits. We have $t \approx 2^{28.44}$. Finally, we brute force the remaining $80 - 28 - 29 = 23$ bits. The total cost for finding the entire 80-bit key is $t \approx 2^{3.0} + 2^{28.44} + 2^{23} \approx 2^{28.47}$.

A similar attack has been implemented, and requires less than five minutes to recover the complete key using a single processor of a 2 Xeon E5520 (2.26 Ghz, quadcore). Utilizing all eight processors in parallel, the attack runs in 35 seconds. The implementation uses the more naive approaches for finding the first 28 bits, as this is easier to implement and leads to a total time complexity of about $t \approx 2^{28.71}$, which represents a negligible change from the attack described in this section.

We can use k_{63} for finding more key bits, and also exploit several different key bits. This attack does not require a concluding brute force, and recovers the entire key in $t \approx 2^{28.44}$. The truncated differentials involved can be found in Table 5.

In Table 5, note especially the differential on a single state bit involving 29 unknown key bits. This gives a large data requirement in order to rule out false positives, and gives a time complexity which dominates all other parts of the full key recovery attack. Any time improvements we make in other partial key recoveries will only be minor compared to this dominating term.

This leads to the interesting observation that if k_{32} had been *stronger*, i.e., appeared *earlier* in the key schedule, we might have been able to find more key bits at a higher cost ($> 2^3$) using it. This would then have lowered the data and time requirements for utilizing k_{63} which would have made the entire cipher *less* secure. Of course, had both key bits been stronger, the attack would again have become more expensive.

Table 5. The differentials used on KTANTAN32 in this paper. PCC means that the differential is of type $(\Delta P, \Delta K) \rightarrow \Delta S$, where S is the state some rounds into the encryption. Similarly, CPP means a differential $(\Delta C, \Delta K) \rightarrow \Delta S$, extending some rounds into the decryption. (The 'Rounds' column then denote the round into which we decrypt, not the number of decryption rounds.) The '#Key bits' column counts how many key bits need to be guessed. We also give the reduced number of guessed key bits in A_j when we have already acquired a part of the key, $\cup_{i<j} A_i$, by using the differentials found earlier in the table.

Type	Rounds	#Key bits	A_j	Differential
PCC	246	3	$\{k_{11}, k_{66}, k_{71}\}$	$(0, k_{32}) \rightarrow$ [80050800 : 00000800]
PCC	244	4/1	$\{k_2\}$	$(0, k_{32}) \rightarrow$ [20054200 : 00000200]
PCC	243	7/3	$\{k_5, k_7, k_{73}\}$	$(0, k_{32}) \rightarrow$ [1006a100 : 00000100]
PCC	242	8/1	$\{k_4\}$	$(0, k_{32}) \rightarrow$ [08075080 : 00000080]
PCC	241	11/3	$\{k_{32}, k_{68}, k_{75}\}$	$(0, k_{32}) \rightarrow$ [8407a840 : 00000040]
PCC	239	14/3	$\{k_1, k_{34}, k_{69}\}$	$(0, k_{32}) \rightarrow$ [a107ea10 : 80000010]
PCC	238	15/1	$\{k_0\}$	$(0, k_{32}) \rightarrow$ [d087f508 : 40000008]
PCC	237	17/2	$\{k_8, k_{16}\}$	$(0, k_{32}) \rightarrow$ [e847fa84 : 20040004]
PCC	236	19/2	$\{k_{12}, k_{17}\}$	$(0, k_{32}) \rightarrow$ [f427fd42 : 10020002]
PCC	234	20/1	$\{k_{64}\}$	$(0, k_{32}) \rightarrow$ [bd0fff50 : 04008000]
PCC	233	21/1	$\{k_{27}\}$	$(0, k_{32}) \rightarrow$ [de87ffa8 : 02004000]
PCC	232	22/1	$\{k_{29}\}$	$(0, k_{32}) \rightarrow$ [ef47ffd4 : 01002000]
PCC	231	24/2	$\{k_{14}, k_{62}\}$	$(0, k_{32}) \rightarrow$ [f7a7ffea : 00801000]
PCC	230	25/1	$\{k_{60}\}$	$(0, k_{32}) \rightarrow$ [fbd7fff5 : 00400800]
PCC	229	27/2	$\{k_{22}, k_{56}\}$	$(0, k_{32}) \rightarrow$ [fdeffffa : 00200400]
PCC	222	28/1	$\{k_{55}\}$	$(0, k_{32}) \rightarrow$ [ffffffff : 00000008]
CPP	43	40/29	A_{16} (see below)	$(0, k_{63}) \rightarrow$ [00000001 : 00000001]
CPP	45	45/4	$\{k_3, k_9, k_{18}, k_{33}\}$	$(0, k_{63}) \rightarrow$ [00000005 : 00000004]
CPP	46	49/2	$\{k_{20}, k_{24}\}$	$(0, k_{63}) \rightarrow$ [0000000b : 00000008]
CPP	51	52/1	$\{k_6\}$	$(0, k_{63}) \rightarrow$ [0000017f : 00000108]
CPP	55	54/1	$\{k_{51}\}$	$(0, k_{63}) \rightarrow$ [000017ff : 00001080]
CPP	57	57/1	$\{k_{72}\}$	$(0, k_{63}) \rightarrow$ [00085fff : 00084200]
CPP	58	58/1	$\{k_{46}\}$	$(0, k_{63}) \rightarrow$ [0010bfff : 00108400]
CPP	60	59/1	$\{k_{23}\}$	$(0, k_{63}) \rightarrow$ [0042ffff : 00421000]
CPP	61	60/1	$\{k_{48}\}$	$(0, k_{63}) \rightarrow$ [008dffff : 00842000]
CPP	67	62/1	$\{k_{65}\}$	$(0, k_{63}) \rightarrow$ [237fffff : 21080000]
CPP	68	64/1	$\{k_{50}\}$	$(0, k_{63}) \rightarrow$ [46ffffff : 42100000]
CPP	71	65/1	$\{k_{36}\}$	$(0, k_{63}) \rightarrow$ [37ffffff : 10800000]
CPP	83	68/1	$\{k_{78}\}$	$(0, k_3) \rightarrow$ [00000155 : 00000040]
CPP	98	70/1	$\{k_{42}\}$	$(0, k_{41}) \rightarrow$ [000017ff : 00001080]
CPP	102	71/1	$\{k_{57}\}$	$(0, k_{41}) \rightarrow$ [00217fff : 00210800]
CPP	115	72/1	$\{k_{59}\}$	$(0, k_{74}) \rightarrow$ [046955ff : 04214008]
CPP	116	73/1	$\{k_{13}\}$	$(0, k_{74}) \rightarrow$ [08daabff : 08428010]
CPP	118	75/1	$\{k_{39}\}$	$(0, k_{74}) \rightarrow$ [237aafff : 210a0040]
PCC	172	70/2	$\{k_{44}, k_{61}\}$	$(0, k_{61}) \rightarrow$ [00050000 : 00040000]

$A_{16} = \{k_{10}, k_{15}, k_{19}, k_{21}, k_{25}, k_{26}, k_{28}, k_{30}, k_{31}, k_{35}, k_{37}, k_{38}, k_{40}, k_{41}, k_{43}, k_{45}, k_{47}, k_{49}, k_{52}, k_{53}, k_{54}, k_{58}, k_{63}, k_{67}, k_{70}, k_{74}, k_{76}, k_{77}, k_{79}\}$

Table 6. The attack parameters for finding 65 key bits with $t \approx 2^{39.44}$, exploiting k_{63}

Type	Rounds	#Key bits	A_j	Differential
CPP	43	40	A_0 (see below)	$(0, k_{63}) \to$ [00000001 : 00000001]
CPP	45	45/5	$\{k_3, k_5, k_9, k_{18}, k_{33}\}$	$(0, k_{63}) \to$ [00000005 : 00000004]
CPP	46	49/4	$\{k_2, k_{20}, k_{24}, k_{73}\}$	$(0, k_{63}) \to$ [0000000b : 00000008]
CPP	47	51/2	$\{k_1, k_{56}\}$	$(0, k_{63}) \to$ [00000017 : 00000010]
CPP	51	52/1	$\{k_6\}$	$(0, k_{63}) \to$ [0000017f : 00000108]
CPP	53	53/1	$\{k_8\}$	$(0, k_{63}) \to$ [000005ff : 00000420]
CPP	55	54/1	$\{k_{51}\}$	$(0, k_{63}) \to$ [000017ff : 00001080]
CPP	56	55/1	$\{k_{55}\}$	$(0, k_{63}) \to$ [00002fff : 00002100]
CPP	57	57/2	$\{k_{12}, k_{72}\}$	$(0, k_{63}) \to$ [00085fff : 00084200]
CPP	58	58/1	$\{k_{46}\}$	$(0, k_{63}) \to$ [0010bfff : 00108400]
CPP	60	59/1	$\{k_{23}\}$	$(0, k_{63}) \to$ [0042ffff : 00421000]
CPP	61	60/1	$\{k_{48}\}$	$(0, k_{63}) \to$ [008dffff : 00842000]
CPP	65	61/1	$\{k_{16}\}$	$(0, k_{63}) \to$ [08dfffff : 08420000]
CPP	67	62/1	$\{k_{65}\}$	$(0, k_{63}) \to$ [237fffff : 21080000]
CPP	68	64/2	$\{k_4, k_{50}\}$	$(0, k_{63}) \to$ [46ffffff : 42100000]
CPP	71	65/1	$\{k_{36}\}$	$(0, k_{63}) \to$ [37ffffff : 10800000]

$$A_0 = \{k_7, k_{10}, k_{11}, k_{14}, k_{15}, k_{17}, k_{19}, k_{21}, k_{22}, k_{25}, k_{26}, k_{28}, k_{30}, k_{31}, k_{34}, k_{35}, k_{37}, k_{38}, k_{40}, k_{41}, k_{43}, k_{45}, k_{47}, k_{49}, k_{52}, k_{53}, k_{54}, k_{58}, k_{60}, k_{62}, k_{63}, k_{67}, k_{68}, k_{69}, k_{70}, k_{71}, k_{74}, k_{76}, k_{77}, k_{79}\}$$

Table 7. Characteristics for some attacks on KTANTAN32. We typically first go backwards, exploiting k_{32}, then forwards using k_{63}, then perhaps forwards exploiting several other key bits before reverting to backwards, using k_{61}. Slashes indicate shift of direction, commas separate needed triplets for different flipped key bits. Differentials and other details are found in Tables 5 and 6.

KTANTAN32		80 bits	80 bits	28 bits	3 bits
Low time	Time	$2^{28.44}$	$2^{28.47}$	$2^{3.02}$	$2^{-0.90}$
	Data	1/29, 1, 1, 1/1	1/29	1	1
Low data	Time	$2^{39.44}$	$2^{39.97}$	as above	as above
	Data	−/1	1/2	as above	as above

5.7 Minimizing the Data Complexities

When using truncated differentials involving only a few bits, the probabilities of getting false positives are high, which leads to large data requirements. For the forward direction, we can use the 62-round differential $(0, k_{63}) \to$ [011bffff : 01084000]. It requires guessing 41 bits and the false-alarm probability is 2^{-21}. The total time complexity for obtaining the full key then becomes $t \approx 2^{39.97}$. The data requirement is one and two triplets, respectively, in the backward and forward directions.

Table 8. Characteristics for some attacks on KTANTAN48

KTANTAN48		80 bits	36 bits	3 bits
Low time	Time	$2^{31.77}$	$2^{4.73}$	$2^{0.01}$
	Data	3/32	3	3
Low data	Time	$2^{37.34}$	$2^{31.66}$	as above
	Data	1/1	1	as above

Table 9. Characteristics for some attacks on KTANTAN64

KTANTAN64		80 bits	38 bits	13 bits
Low time	Time	$2^{32.28}$	$2^{10.75}$	$2^{10.71}$
	Data	13/17	13	13
Low data	Time	$2^{36.54}$	$2^{30.53}$	as above
	Data	1/1	1	as above

6 Attacking KTANTAN48 and KTANTAN64

We summarize our results on KTANTAN32 in Table 7. Similar attacks can be realized on the two other members of the KTANTAN family, i.e., KTANTAN48 and KTANTAN64. The corresponding complexities are found in Table 8 and Table 9, respectively, and the differentials in Appendices C and D.

Complexities have been optimized in both dimensions: using a small amount of related-key data, and using low time complexities.

We give full key-recovery attacks, but also some partial-key recoveries with extremely low time complexities, similar to the $2^{3.0}$ attack on KTANTAN32 for 28 bits. We also give costs on finding the smallest possible set of key bits.

Generally, the first step is done in the backwards direction, exploiting k_{32}. Following this, we switch to the forward direction and k_{63}. For more advanced attacks, we can use more key bits in the forward direction: k_3, k_{41}, k_{74}. We may then end using more backward calculations on k_{61}. Attacks that require less data are completed through a brute force.

Note that the benefit of using more data quickly becomes very marginal. Thus, the implementation overhead may consume any theoretic advantage of the extremely data-consuming attacks.

6.1 Possible Improvements

We have used a greedy approach for finding the differentials used in this paper. As an example, on $\phi_{0,248}$, there is the truncated differential $(0, k_{32}) \rightarrow$ [00021000 : 00001000], but due to the slow diffusion we cannot find any key bits using it with probability one. This forces us to use the differential $(0, k_{32}) \rightarrow$ [80050800 : 00000800] on $\phi_{0,247}$, where three key bits affect the differential so all three bits need to be guessed. We could truncate this truncated differential further to only involve a single bit, possibly allowing us to only guess a single key bit. In this way, we could perhaps partition the 28 bits that can be recovered using k_{32} into 28 subsets $A_0, \ldots, A_{27}$, and reach a very small time complexity for the attack. We have not investigated this optimization as the time complexities are already impressive enough.

Note that for the key recovery attack on KTANTAN32 the time complexity is dominated by exploiting k_{63} to find the 29-bit subkey defined by A_{16} (see Table 5). For this, we already use a one-bit truncated differential so this cannot be improved by the technique outlined above.

7 Comparison to Specification Claims

In the specification of KTANTAN, the authors state the design goal that "no related-key key-recovery or slide attack with time complexity smaller than 2^{80} exists on the entire cipher" [4]. They also claim to have searched for related-key differentials on KTANTAN. However, it appears the approach has been randomized over the huge space of differences in plaintext and key. With hindsight, the authors should have made sure to try differentials where we flip only some small number of plaintext or key bits. This strategy would have been a good choice due to the bitwise and irregular nature of the key schedule coupled with the slow diffusion of the state. If all key bits had been investigated individually, it would have become apparent e.g., that k_{32} could not affect encryptions before round 218, that one state bit in KTANTAN32 only contained this key bit linearly until the very last round, and that there are some high-probability truncated differentials on the full KTANTAN32.

Note that the first reference implementation of KTANTAN provided by the designers used an incorrect key schedule. The pre-proceedings version of [3] only improved the exhaustive search slightly, while with the correct key schedule, i.e., the one described in the design document, the attack eventually published in [3] gave a more significant speedup. As the incorrect key schedule was in a sense better than the intended one, the original search for related-key differentials might have indicated a better behaviour of the cipher than one carried out with the correct key schedule. Still, even on the incorrect key schedule, using low-weight differentials would have alerted the designers to the unwanted behaviour of some key bits.

8 Conclusion

We have presented several weaknesses related to the key schedule of KTANTAN. We first noted how the exceptionally weak key bit k_{32} allowed for a nonrandomness result on KTANTAN32.

As the main result, we then derived several related-key attacks allowing for (partial-)key recovery: With a single triplet, 3 bits can be found in time $2^{-0.90}$ and 28 bits can be obtained in time $2^{3.0}$. Using one triplet in the backward and 29 in the forward direction, the full 80-bit key is recovered in time $2^{28.47}$. Requiring only three triplets, the full key is instead recovered in time $2^{39.97}$. Our implementation of one of the attacks verifies the general attack idea and the specific results.

Finally, note that none of these attacks are directly applicable to KATAN. The slow diffusion, which allowed for e.g., the $2^{3.0}$-attack on 28 bits, is present also in KATAN, but one needs a weak key bit in order to exploit this.

For the design of future primitives with a bitwise key schedule such as the one in KTANTAN, we encourage designers to carefully study how individual key bits are used, either by specifically ensuring that they are used both early and late in the key schedule, or by investigating all differentials of modest weight.

Acknowledgment. This work was supported by the Swedish Foundation for Strategic Research (SSF) through its Strategic Center for High Speed Wireless Communication at Lund. The author wishes to thank Andrey Bogdanov and Christian Rechberger for their valuable comments, and the anonymous reviewers for their insightful remarks.

References

1. Biham, E.: New Types of Cryptanalytic Attacks using Related Keys. Journal of Cryptology 7(4), 229–246 (1994)
2. Biham, E., Shamir, A.: Differential Cryptanalysis of the Data Encryption Standard. Springer, Heidelberg (1993)
3. Bogdanov, A., Rechberger, C.: A 3-Subset Meet-in-the-Middle Attack: Cryptanalysis of the Lightweight Block Cipher KTANTAN. In: Biryukov, A., Gong, G., Stinson, D.R. (eds.) SAC 2010. LNCS, vol. 6544, pp. 229–240. Springer, Heidelberg (2011)
4. De Cannière, C., Dunkelman, O., Knežević, M.: KATAN and KTANTAN — A Family of Small and Efficient Hardware-Oriented Block Ciphers. In: Clavier, C., Gaj, K. (eds.) CHES 2009. LNCS, vol. 5747, pp. 272–288. Springer, Heidelberg (2009)
5. Knudsen, L.R.: Cryptanalysis of LOKI 91. In: Zheng, Y., Seberry, J. (eds.) AUSCRYPT 1992. LNCS, vol. 718, pp. 196–208. Springer, Heidelberg (1993)
6. Knudsen, L.R.: Truncated and Higher Order Differentials. In: Preneel, B. (ed.) FSE 1994. LNCS, vol. 1008, pp. 196–211. Springer, Heidelberg (1995)

A The Key Schedule of KTANTAN

r	k_a^r	k_b^r	r	k_a^r	k_b^r	r	k_a^r	k_b^r	r	k_a^r	k_b^r	r	k_a^r	k_b^r	r	k_a^r	k_b^r	r	k_a^r	k_b^r	r	k_a^r	k_b^r
0	63	31	1	31	63	2	31	63	3	15	47	4	14	14	5	60	76	6	40	40	7	49	17
8	35	67	9	54	22	10	45	77	11	58	26	12	37	69	13	74	10	14	69	69	15	74	10
16	53	21	17	43	43	18	71	7	19	63	79	20	30	62	21	45	45	22	11	11	23	54	70
24	28	60	25	41	41	26	3	19	27	38	70	28	60	28	29	25	73	30	34	34	31	5	21
32	26	74	33	20	52	34	9	41	35	2	18	36	20	68	37	24	56	38	1	33	39	2	2
40	52	68	41	24	56	42	17	49	43	3	35	44	6	6	45	76	76	46	72	8	47	49	17
48	19	51	49	23	55	50	15	63	51	14	46	52	12	28	53	24	72	54	16	48	55	1	49
56	2	34	57	4	20	58	40	72	59	48	16	60	17	65	61	18	50	62	5	53	63	10	58
64	4	36	65	8	8	66	64	64	67	64	0	68	65	1	69	51	19	70	23	55	71	47	47
72	15	15	73	78	78	74	76	12	75	73	9	76	67	3	77	55	23	78	47	47	79	63	31
80	47	79	81	62	30	82	29	77	83	26	58	84	5	37	85	10	26	86	36	68	87	56	24
88	33	65	89	50	18	90	21	69	91	42	42	92	5	5	93	58	74	94	20	52	95	25	57
96	3	51	97	6	38	98	12	12	99	56	72	100	16	48	101	33	33	102	3	3	103	70	70
104	60	28	105	41	41	106	67	3	107	71	71	108	78	14	109	77	13	110	59	27	111	39	39
112	79	15	113	79	79	114	62	30	115	45	45	116	59	27	117	23	71	118	46	46	119	13	29
120	42	74	121	52	20	122	41	73	123	66	2	124	53	69	125	42	42	126	53	21	127	27	75
128	38	38	129	13	13	130	74	74	131	52	20	132	25	57	133	35	35	134	7	7	135	62	78
136	44	44	137	73	9	138	51	67	139	22	54	140	29	61	141	11	43	142	6	22	143	44	76
144	72	8	145	65	65	146	50	18	147	37	37	148	75	11	149	55	71	150	46	46	151	77	13
152	75	75	153	70	6	154	61	29	155	27	59	156	39	39	157	15	31	158	46	78	159	76	12
160	57	73	161	34	34	162	69	5	163	59	75	164	38	38	165	61	29	166	43	75	167	70	6
168	77	77	169	58	26	170	21	53	171	43	43	172	7	23	173	30	78	174	44	44	175	9	25
176	18	66	177	36	36	178	9	9	179	50	66	180	36	36	181	57	25	182	19	67	183	22	54
184	13	45	185	10	10	186	68	68	187	56	24	188	17	49	189	19	51	190	7	39	191	14	30
192	28	76	193	40	40	194	1	1	195	66	66	196	68	4	197	57	25	198	35	35	199	55	23
200	31	79	201	30	62	202	13	61	203	10	42	204	4	4	205	72	72	206	48	16	207	33	33
208	51	19	209	39	71	210	78	14	211	61	77	212	26	58	213	21	53	214	11	59	215	6	54
216	12	44	217	8	24	218	32	64	219	64	0	220	49	65	221	18	50	222	37	37	223	11	27
224	22	70	225	28	60	226	9	57	227	2	50	228	4	52	229	8	40	230	0	0	231	48	64
232	32	32	233	65	1	234	67	67	235	54	22	236	29	61	237	27	59	238	7	55	239	14	62
240	12	60	241	8	56	242	0	32	243	0	16	244	16	64	245	32	32	246	1	17	247	34	66
248	68	4	249	73	73	250	66	2	251	69	5	252	75	11	253	71	7						

B Key Bits Used in Round 222 and Forward

0	1	2	4	5	7	8	9	11	12	14	16	17	22	27	28	29	32	34	37	40
48	50	52	54	55	56	57	59	60	61	62	64	65	66	67	68	69	70	71	73	75

C Differentials for KTANTAN48

The differentials used on KTANTAN48 are given in Table 10.

Table 10. Similar to Table 5, this table gives the truncated differentials used on KTANTAN48

Type	Rounds	#Key bits	A_j	Differential
PCC	246	3/3	$\{k_7, k_{11}, k_{73}\}$	$(0, k_{32}) \rightarrow$ [000000010000 : 000000000000]
PCC	242	7/4	$\{k_2, k_4k_{32}, k_{71}\}$	$(0, k_{32}) \rightarrow$ [000000010100 : 000000000000]
PCC	241	11/4	$\{k_5, k_{64}, k_{66}, k_{75}\}$	$(0, k_{32}) \rightarrow$ [00000001c040 : 000000000000]
PCC	240	18/7	A_3 (see below)	$(0, k_{32}) \rightarrow$ [000c00007010 : 000000000000]
PCC	239	19/1	$\{k_{17}\}$	$(0, k_{32}) \rightarrow$ [700011c04000 : 000000000000]
PCC	238	20/1	$\{k_{56}\}$	$(0, k_{32}) \rightarrow$ [1c001c701000 : 000000000000]
PCC	237	23/3	$\{k_{12}, k_{14}, k_{60}\}$	$(0, k_{32}) \rightarrow$ [0c7001f1c400 : 000400000000]
PCC	236	24/1	$\{k_{62}\}$	$(0, k_{32}) \rightarrow$ [071c01fc7100 : 000100000000]
PCC	235	25/1	$\{k_{55}\}$	$(0, k_{32}) \rightarrow$ [1c701ff1c040 : 000040000000]
PCC	234	26/1	$\{k_{27}\}$	$(0, k_{32}) \rightarrow$ [871c1ffc7010 : 000010000000]
PCC	233	30/4	$\{k_{29}, k_{54}, k_{61}, k_{67}\}$	$(0, k_{32}) \rightarrow$ [e1c71fff1c04 : 000004010000]
PCC	232	32/2	$\{k_{22}, k_{65}\}$	$(0, k_{32}) \rightarrow$ [f871dfffc701 : 00000100c000]
PCC	230	33/1	$\{k_{48}\}$	$(0, k_{32}) \rightarrow$ [cf871ffffc70 : 000000100c00]
PCC	229	34/1	$\{k_{59}\}$	$(0, k_{32}) \rightarrow$ [f3e1dfffff1c : 000000040300]
PCC	225	36/2	$\{k_{40}, k_{52}\}$	$(0, k_{32}) \rightarrow$ [fff3ffffffff : 000000003000]
CPP	54	53/32	A_{15} (see below)	$(0, k_{63}) \rightarrow$ [000000000002 : 000000000000]
CPP	55	54/1	$\{k_6\}$	$(0, k_{63}) \rightarrow$ [000000000009 : 000000000000]
CPP	57	57/3	$\{k_{23}, k_{46}, k_{51}\}$	$(0, k_{63}) \rightarrow$ [00000000009f : 00000000000c]

$$A_3 = \{k_0, k_1, k_8, k_{16}, k_{34}, k_{68}, k_{69}\}$$

$$A_{15} = \{k_3, k_9, k_{10}, k_{15}, k_{18}, k_{19}, k_{20}, k_{21}, k_{24}, k_{25}, k_{26}, k_{28}, k_{30}, k_{31}, k_{33}, k_{35}, k_{37}, k_{38}, k_{41}, k_{43}, k_{45}, k_{47}, k_{49}, k_{53}, k_{58}, k_{63}, k_{70}, k_{72}, k_{74}, k_{76}, k_{77}, k_{79}\}$$

D Differentials for KTANTAN64

The differentials used on KTANTAN64 are given in Table 11.

Table 11. Similar to Table 5, this table gives the truncated differentials used on KTANTAN64

Type	Rounds	#Key bits	A_j	Differential
PCC	241	13/13	A_0 (see below)	$(0, k_{32}) \rightarrow$ [0000000000000400 : 0000000000000000]
PCC	237	21/8	A_1 (see below)	$(0, k_{32}) \rightarrow$ [0000000704000000 : 0000000000000000]
PCC	236	27/6	A_2 (see below)	$(0, k_{32}) \rightarrow$ [00c000007e800000 : 0000000000000000]
PCC	235	29/2	$\{k_{29}, k_{61}\}$	$(0, k_{32}) \rightarrow$ [f800007fc0100000 : 0000000e00000000]
PCC	234	30/1	$\{k_{22}\}$	$(0, k_{32}) \rightarrow$ [3f00007ff8020000 : 00000001c0000000]
PCC	233	32/2	$\{k_{54}, k_{67}\}$	$(0, k_{32}) \rightarrow$ [c7e0007fff004000 : 0000000038000000]
PCC	232	33/1	$\{k_{65}\}$	$(0, k_{32}) \rightarrow$ [78fc007fffe00800 : 0000000007000000]
PCC	228	34/1	$\{k_{48}\}$	$(0, k_{32}) \rightarrow$ [f8c78fffffffe00 : 0000070038000000]
PCC	226	36/2	$\{k_{40}, k_{50}\}$	$(0, k_{32}) \rightarrow$ [ffe31e7ffffffff8 : 0000000000e00000]
PCC	225	38/2	$\{k_9, k_{52}\}$	$(0, k_{32}) \rightarrow$ [fffc63ffffffffff : 00000000001c0000]
CPP	58	55/33	A_{10} (see below)	$(0, k_{63}) \rightarrow$ [0000000000000003 : 0000000000000001]
CPP	59	59/2	$\{k_{46}, k_{51}\}$	$(0, k_{63}) \rightarrow$ [000000000000001f : 000000000000000e]
CPP	69	65/1	$\{k_{36}\}$	$(0, k_{63}) \rightarrow$ [00000407ffffffff : 0000040380000000]

$$A_0 = \{k_2, k_4, k_5, k_7, k_{11}, k_{17}, k_{32}, k_{64}, k_{66}, k_{69}, k_{71}, k_{73}, k_{75}\}$$

$$A_1 = \{k_1, k_{16}, k_{34}, k_{55}, k_{56}, k_{60}, k_{62}, k_{68}\}$$

$$A_2 = \{k_0, k_8, k_{12}, k_{14}, k_{27}, k_{59}\}$$

$$A_{10} = \{k_3, k_6, k_{10}, k_{15}, k_{18}, k_{19}, k_{20}, k_{21}, k_{23}, k_{24}, k_{25}, k_{26}, k_{28}, k_{30}, k_{31}, k_{33}, k_{35}, k_{37}, k_{38}, k_{41}, k_{43}, k_{45}, k_{47}, k_{49}, k_{53}, k_{58}, k_{63}, k_{70}, k_{72}, k_{74}, k_{76}, k_{77}, k_{79}\}$$

Analysis of the Initial and Modified Versions of the Candidate 3GPP Integrity Algorithm 128-EIA3

Thomas Fuhr, Henri Gilbert, Jean-René Reinhard, and Marion Videau*

ANSSI, France
{thomas.fuhr,henri.gilbert,jean-rene.reinhard,
marion.videau}@ssi.gouv.fr

Abstract. In this paper we investigate the security of the two most recent versions of the message authentication code 128-EIA3, which is considered for adoption as a third integrity algorithm in the emerging 3GPP standard LTE. We first present an efficient existential forgery attack against the June 2010 version of the algorithm. This attack allows, given any message and the associated MAC value under an unknown integrity key and an initial vector, to predict the MAC value of a related message under the same key and the same initial vector with a success probability 1/2. We then briefly analyse the tweaked version of the algorithm that was introduced in January 2011 to circumvent this attack. We give some evidence that while this new version offers a provable resistance against similar forgery attacks under the assumption that (key, IV) pairs are never reused by any legitimate sender or receiver, some of its design features limit its resilience against IV reuse.

Keywords: cryptanalysis, message authentication codes, existential forgery attacks, universal hashing.

1 Introduction

A set of two cryptographic algorithms is currently considered for inclusion in the emerging mobile communications standard LTE of the 3rd Generation Partnership Project 3GPP. It consists of an encryption algorithm named 128-EEA3 and an integrity algorithm named 128-EIA3[1] — that are both derived from a core stream cipher named ZUC. The algorithms ZUC, 128-EEA3, and 128-EIA3 were designed by the Data Assurance and Communication Security Research Center (DACAS) of the Chinese Academy of Sciences.

An initial version of the specifications of 128-EEA3/EIA3 and ZUC, that is referred to in the sequel as v1.4, was produced in June 2010 and published on the

* also with Université Henri Poincaré-Nancy 1 / LORIA, France.

[1] EEA stands for "EPS Encryption Algorithm" and EIA stands for "EPS Integrity Algorithm". EPS (Evolved Packet System) is an evolution of the third generation system UMTS that consists of new radio access system named LTE (Long Term Evolution) and a new core network named SAE (System Architecture Evolution).

A. Miri and S. Vaudenay (Eds.): SAC 2011, LNCS 7118, pp. 230–242, 2012.

GSMA web site for an initial public evaluation [5,6]. Following the discovery of some cryptographic weaknesses in the ZUC v1.4 initialisation [20,18] and of the forgery attack on 128-EIA3 v1.4 reported in this paper, tweaks to the specifications of ZUC and EIA3 were introduced by the designers and a modified version of the specifications referred to in the sequel as v1.5 was published in January 2011 for a second public evaluation period [8,9]. After its adoption by 3GPP, 128-EEA3/EIA3 will represent the third LTE encryption and integrity algorithm set, in addition to the already adopted sets 128-EEA1/EIA1 [4] based on the stream cipher SNOW 3G and 128-EEA2/EIA2 [1, Annex B] based on AES.

The integrity algorithm 128-EIA3 is an IV-dependent MAC that takes as input (1) a 128-bit key, (2) various public parameters that together determine a 128-bit initial vector, (3) an input message of length between 1 and 20000 bits, and produces a 32-bit MAC value. It uses an universal hash function-based construction and has therefore many features in common with the algorithms of the well known Wegman-Carter family of message authentication codes [3,19].

As already mentioned, we denote by 128-EIA3 v1.4 (resp. 128-EIA3 v1.5) the initial version specified in [5] (resp.the modified version specified in [8]). In this paper we analyse the security of both versions. We first show that 128-EIA3 v1.4 is vulnerable to a simple existential forgery attack. Given any known message M, any known or unknown initial vector, and the associated MAC under an unknown key, it is possible to predict the MAC value associated with a new message $M' \neq M$ derived from M under the same initial vector and the same unknown key, with a success probability 1/2. This attack is generic, it does not rely on any specific feature of ZUC and works with any underlying stream cipher. It exploits a subtle deviation of 128-EIA3 v1.4 from the requirements of the Wegman-Carter paradigm. The latter requirements can be informally summarized by saying that mask values must behave as one-time masks, which is not the case for 128-EIA3 v1.4. As will be shown in the sequel, distinct 128-EIA3 v1.4 mask values are not necessarily independent. Indeed, in 128-EIA3 v1.4, the mechanism used to generate the masking values applied to the output of the universal hash function does not match the model used in the proof. Consequently, the arguments from [12] and [16] that are invoked in the design and evaluation report [7] to infer bounds on the success probability of forgery attacks on 128-EIA3 v1.4 are not applicable.

In [8], a tweak leading to 128-EIA3 v1.5 has been proposed to circumvent this attack. Through an improved generation procedure, masking values are either equal or independent. However, it can be observed that for distinct messages, no separation between the ZUC keystream bits involved in the universal hash function computation and those involved in the generation of the masking values is ensured.

While this represents a deviation from the requirements on masking values used in the Wegman-Carter paradigm, the security consequences are much less dramatic than for the initial MAC (v1.4) since an ad hoc proof given in [10] allows to show that the modified MAC offers a provable resistance against existential forgery attacks under the assumption that the same (key, IV) pair can never be re-used, neither by the MAC issuer nor by the MAC verifier. We show that this property however affects the resilience of 128-EIA3 v1.5 against forgery attacks if IV repetitions occur. We further observe that independently of this property, the universal hash function structure also results in some limitations of this resilience. This leads us to investigate the resistance of 128-EIA3 v1.5 and one natural variant of this MAC against forgery attacks involving three pairwise distinct messages and the same IV value. We make no claims regarding the practical applicability of the identified nonce repetition attacks to the LTE system.

In Section 3, we give a short description of the 128-EIA3 algorithms. We then describe the attack on v1.4 in Section 4 and discuss the reasons why the security proofs for related constructions by Krawczyk [12] and Shoup [16] do not guarantee the security of 128-EIA3 v1.4. In Section 5, we state a property which, although it may not be considered as an attack in standard security models, underscores the lack of robustness of 128-EIA3 v1.5 against nonce repetition. We also explain why a simple modification of 128-EIA3 fails to completely suppress such properties because of the universal hashing underlying structure.

2 Notation

Throughout the paper, we use the following notation.

- $\mathcal{S}$ is a stream cipher.
- For two finite bitstrings $A = (a^0, \dots, a^{\ell-1})$ and $B = (b^0, \dots, b^{m-1})$, $A \| B$ denotes the concatenation of A and B, i.e. the bitstring $(a^0, \dots, a^{\ell-1}, b^0, \dots, b^{m-1})$.
- For a bitstring $A = (a^0, \dots)$ of length $\geq j+1$, $A|_j^i, 0 \leq i \leq j$, denotes the $(j-i+1)$-bit string obtained from the consecutive bits of A between indices i and j, i.e. $A|_j^i = (a^i, \dots, a^j)$.
- 0^ℓ denotes the bitstring of length ℓ whose bits are all zero.
- $W^{(i)}$ denotes the i-th bit of a 32-bit word W.
- Let consider a 32-bit word $W = (W^{(0)}, \dots, W^{(31)})$ and an integer a between 1 and 31. Then $W \ll a$ denotes the $(32-a)$-bit word resulting from a left shift of W by a positions and a truncation of the a rightmost bits. More precisely, $W \ll a = (W^{(a)}, \dots, W^{(31)})$. The $(32-b)$-bit word, $W \gg b$, resulting from the right shift of W by b positions and a truncation of the b leftmost bits is defined in the same way. We have $W \gg b = (W^{(0)}, \dots, W^{(31-b)})$.[2]

3 Description of the 128-EIA3 Integrity Algorithms

The integrity algorithms 128-EIA3 make a black box use of a stream cipher to generate a keystream from a key and an initial value. A stream cipher $\mathcal{S}$

[2] We are thus using the same somewhat unusual convention as in [6] for defining the symbols "$\gg$" and "$\ll$" as a "shift and truncate" rather than mere shifts. This is motivated by the fact that this convention is more convenient for presenting the attack of Section 4.

is an algorithm that takes as input a k-bit key IK and an n-bit initialisation value IV and outputs a binary sequence $z_0, \ldots, z_i, \ldots$ named the keystream. The keystream is used to compute a 32-bit MAC value Tag according to the procedure described in Algorithm 1 which includes versions v1.4 and v1.5 for conciseness.

Stated differently, the MAC value T associated with IK, IV, and an ℓ-bit message $M = (m_0, \ldots, m_{\ell-1})$ is derived by accumulating (for a set of positions i determined by the message bits and the message length) 32-bit words $W_i = (z_i, \ldots, z_{i+31})$ extracted from the keystream by applying it a 32-bit "sliding window":

$$T = (\bigoplus_{i=0}^{\ell-1} m_i W_i) \oplus W_\ell \oplus W_{mask},$$

where $W_{mask} = W_{L-32}$ with the value L being different between v1.4 and v1.5, i.e. $W_{mask} = W_{\ell+32}$ for v1.4 and $W_{mask} = W_{\lceil \frac{\ell}{32} \rceil \times 32+32}$ for v1.5. The parameter lengths used in 128-EIA3 are: $k = n = 128$ and $1 \leq \ell \leq 20000$.

In fact, the MAC of a message M is computed as

$$MAC(M) = H_{(z_0,\ldots,z_{\ell+31})}(M) \oplus W_{mask},$$

Algorithm 1. The 128-EIA3 MAC algorithms

Input: $IK \in \{0,1\}^k$, $IV \in \{0,1\}^n$, $1 \leq \ell \leq 20000$
Input: $M = (m_0, \ldots, m_{\ell-1}) \in \{0,1\}^\ell$
  if v1.4 **then**
    $L = \ell + 64$
  else if v1.5 **then**
    $L = \left\lceil \frac{\ell}{32} \right\rceil \times 32 + 64$ {**This is the only difference between v1.4 and v1.5**}
  end if
  $(z_0, \ldots, z_{L-1}) \leftarrow \mathcal{S}(IK, IV)|_{L-1}^{0}$
  $\mathsf{Tag} = 0$
  for $i = 0$ to $\ell - 1$ **do**
    $W_i \leftarrow (z_i, \ldots, z_{i+31})$
    if $m_i = 1$ **then**
      $\mathsf{Tag} \leftarrow \mathsf{Tag} \oplus W_i$
    end if
  end for
  $W_\ell \leftarrow (z_\ell, \ldots, z_{\ell+31})$
  $\mathsf{Tag} \leftarrow \mathsf{Tag} \oplus W_\ell$
  $W_{mask} \leftarrow (z_{L-32}, \ldots, z_{L-1})$
  $\mathsf{Tag} \leftarrow \mathsf{Tag} \oplus W_{mask}$
  return Tag

where $(H_{(.)})$ is a family of universal hash functions based on Toeplitz matrices with pseudorandom coefficients taken from a stream cipher output. We have:

$$H_{(z_0,\dots,z_{\ell+31})}(m_0,\dots,m_{\ell-1}) = [m_0, m_1, \dots, m_{\ell-1}, 1] \cdot \begin{bmatrix} z_0 & z_1 & \cdots & z_{31} \\ z_1 & z_2 & \cdots & z_{32} \\ z_2 & z_3 & \cdots & z_{33} \\ \vdots & \vdots & \ddots & \vdots \\ z_\ell & z_{\ell+1} & \cdots & z_{\ell+31} \end{bmatrix}.$$

4 An Existential Forgery Attack against 128-EIA3 v1.4

In this section we describe an attack on the first version of 128-EIA3, that we call 128-EIA3 v1.4. This algorithm has some specific properties that we will now exploit to transform a valid MAC for a message M into a valid MAC for a message M' related to M.

4.1 Description of the Substitution Attack

We can notice that the words W_i derived from the keystream and corresponding to message bits m_i are not independent from each other. More precisely, we have: $W_{i+1} = ((W_i \ll 1), z_{i+32})$.

Moreover the "one-time masks" W_{mask} associated with identical values of IV but different message lengths are related. We have:

$$W_{mask} = (z_{\ell(M)+32}, \dots, z_{\ell(M)+63}),$$

where $\ell(M)$ denotes the length of the message M. Let us suppose that W_{mask} is the one-time mask generated for the input (IK, IV, M) and W'_{mask} is the one-time mask generated for the input (IK, IV, M'). If $\ell(M') - \ell(M) = \Delta\ell$ with $0 < \Delta\ell < 32$, we have:

$$W'_{mask} = (W_{mask} \ll \Delta\ell, \beta_0, \dots, \beta_{\Delta\ell-1}),$$

for some bit values β_i. We can use these relations in a substitution attack.

Let us suppose that the adversary knows a valid MAC value T for a given message $M = (m_0, \dots, m_{\ell-1})$ of length ℓ bits under a given IV value IV and a key IK. This MAC can be transformed with probability 1/2 into a valid MAC, T', for the $(\ell+1)$-bit message $M' = (0, m_0, \dots, m_{\ell-1})$ under the same IV value IV and the same key IK.

Let us analyse what happens during the computation of the MAC for M' (under the same IV value IV and the same key IK). The generated keystream $z_0, \dots, z_{\ell+64}$ is the same as the keystream that was used to compute T, with one extra bit: $z_{\ell+64}$. As a consequence, the words $W_i, 0 \le i \le \ell$ are identical. The one-time mask used is $W'_{mask} = (z_{\ell+33}, \dots, z_{\ell+64}) = ((W_{mask} \ll 1), z_{\ell+64})$. Then, the MAC value T' is given by the following formula:

$$
\begin{aligned}
T' &= \left(\bigoplus_{i=0}^{\ell} m'_i W_i\right) \oplus W_{\ell+1} \oplus W'_{mask} \\
&= \left(\bigoplus_{i=0}^{\ell-1} m_i W_{i+1}\right) \oplus W_{\ell+1} \oplus W'_{mask} \\
&= \left(\bigoplus_{i=0}^{\ell-1} m_i \left((W_i \ll 1), z_{i+32}\right)\right) \oplus (W_\ell \ll 1, z_{\ell+32}) \oplus ((W_{mask} \ll 1), z_{\ell+64}) \\
&= \left(\left(\left(\bigoplus_{i=0}^{\ell-1} m_i W_i\right) \oplus W_\ell \oplus W_{mask}\right) \ll 1, \beta\right) \\
&= (T \ll 1, \beta)\,, \text{ with } \beta = \bigoplus_{i=0}^{\ell-1} m_i z_{i+32} \oplus z_{\ell+32} \oplus z_{\ell+64}.
\end{aligned}
$$

The value $(T \ll 1, \beta)$ is thus a valid MAC for M'. Knowing T, the adversary only needs to guess the value of bit β, which happens with probability 1/2. This attack can naturally be generalized by recurrence to generate a valid MAC for $(0^r||M)$, with probability 2^{-r}, when $r < 32$: the corresponding tag is then $T_r = ((T \ll r), \beta_0, \ldots, \beta_{r-1})$ for some value of the bits $(\beta_0, \ldots, \beta_{r-1})$.

Equivalently, we have that $T = (\alpha_0, \ldots, \alpha_{r-1}, T_r \gg r)$. This equation enables an adversary to transform a valid MAC IV, T_r for $(0^r||M)$ into a valid MAC for M with probability 2^{-r}.

The attack was checked for $r = 1$ and larger values of r on a few examples, using the implementation programs provided in the annexes of the specification documents [5,6].

4.2 Partial Flaw in 128-EIA3 v1.4 Security Arguments

The Design and Evaluation Report [7] that accompanied version 1.4 erroneously invokes the security proofs of [16] to infer that in the case of 128-EIA3 v1.4, no forgery of a new message can succeed with probability higher than 2^{-32}. The argument comes from the fact that the algorithm makes use of an ε-almost XOR universal (ε-AXU) family of hash functions with $\varepsilon = 2^{-32}$.

Definition 1. *[3,19,17,12,14] A family of hash functions $\{H_K\}_{K\in\{0,1\}^k}$ of range $\{0,1\}^t$ is ε-AXU if for any two distinct messages M, M' in $\{0,1\}^*$ and any $c \in \{0,1\}^t$*

$$Pr_{K\in\{0,1\}^k}[H_K(M) \oplus H_K(M') = c] \leq \varepsilon.$$

In [7], a proof is given that for any value of IV, the family of hash functions used in 128-EIA3, i.e. the intermediate value obtained in the MAC computation associated with key K just before before the exclusive or with W_{mask} is ε-AXU with $\varepsilon = 2^{-32}$.

As far as we know, the first construction of a secure MAC using ε-AXU hash functions has been issued by Krawczyk [12], who proved that given $H_K(M) \oplus r$

for secret uniformly drawn values of K and r, an adversary cannot determine $H_K(M') \oplus r$ with probability higher than ε. The one-time mask generation issue is briefly addressed by noticing that in most practical applications, the mask generation will rely on a stream cipher.

In [14, Appendix B], the security notions related to a Wegman-Carter MAC scheme using a pseudorandom function producing the one-time mask from a counter cnt is stated. In [15, Proposition 14], the probability of a forgery success is computed. The scheme is defined by: a finite PRF $F : \{0,1\}^\kappa \times \{0,1\}^n \rightarrow \{0,1\}^t$, a counter $\mathsf{cnt} \in \{0,1\}^n$, and a family of universal hash functions $\{H_K\}_{K \in \{0,1\}^k}$. The computation and the verification of MACs require to share an integrity key that consists of a random $a \in \{0,1\}^\kappa$ and a random $K \in \{0,1\}^k$. At most 2^n messages may be MACed with the same key a, and

$$MAC(M) = (\mathsf{cnt}, F_a(\mathsf{cnt}) \oplus H_K(M)).$$

All the models used for the proofs assume that the hash function and the pseudorandom function are randomly chosen and in particular that they are *independent* from each other. In the case of 128-EIA3 v1.4, the construction does not fit the model as the two are related. Moreover, what makes our attack work is that the one-time masks used for messages M and M' of distinct lengths are different but related. In fact, we have:

$$MAC(M) = (\mathsf{cnt}, \mathcal{S}(IK, \mathsf{cnt})|_{\ell(M)+63}^{\ell(M)+32} \oplus H_{\mathcal{S}(IK,\mathsf{cnt})|_{\ell(M)+31}^{0}}(M)).$$

We see that the mask computation also involves the message length and leads to distinct, but related mask values, for identical IVs and different message lengths. Therefore no existing proof applies and we manage to derive an attack against v1.4.

5 Sensitivity of 128-EIA3 v1.5 to Nonce Reuse

In order to resist to our forgery attack, 128-EIA3 has been tweaked [8], leading to the specification of 128-EIA3 v1.5. This new version corresponds to the condition v1.5 in Algorithm 1. The tweak ensures that mask values generated by the algorithm for a given (key, IV) pair for different messages are either equal or independent through an improved selection of the location in the keystream from which the mask value is extracted:

$$W_{mask} = (z_{L-32}, \ldots, z_{L-1}), \text{ with } L = \left\lceil \frac{\ell(M)}{32} \right\rceil \times 32 + 64.$$

This comes at the cost of using a slightly longer part of the keystream. Although this ensures resistance against forgery attacks under the assumptions that (1) neither the MAC issuer nor the MAC verifier reuse any IV value under the same key and the (2) the keystream bits generated by ZUC are indistiguishable from random, as proven in [10, Section 11], we remark that this scheme remains fragile towards IV reuse.

In [15,16], the question of a stateful MAC (implying a counter) against a stateless MAC (with a randomly chosen IV) is briefly discussed. It is underlined in [16] that reliably maintaining a state may be difficult. Practical experience shows that the correct handling of IVs is not a trivial task. Indeed, there is far from a theoretical security requirement to a practical implementation of a scheme and former IV critical modes like CBC have already been subjected to attacks against practical implementations (see e.g. [13]). Therefore we think that it is also important to assess the level of robustness of a scheme in the case of an improper handling of the IV.

In this section we expose two specific properties of 128-EIA3 v1.5, which do not affect a generic Wegman-Carter authentication scheme. These properties involve the MACs of three distinct messages under the same key/IV pair. Therefore, they might threaten the security of 128-EIA3 v1.5 if an adversary can get the MAC of two distinct messages under the same (key, IV) pair. Such an event can happen if IVs are mistakenly repeated by the MAC generating party. It can also happen without deviating from the expected behaviour of the message authentication through substitution attacks: the attacker may use verification queries to gain knowledge on the system [2,11]. More in detail, two valid 128-EIA3 tag values can be obtained by an adversary for the same (key, IV) pair and two distinct messages with a non-negligible probability due to the short MAC size (32 bits): one from the MAC generating party and (with probability 2^{-32}) an extra one from the verifying party. This may allow the adversary to predict with certainty the MAC value of a third message with the same (key, IV) pair.[3]

5.1 On the Independance of Universal Hashing Keys and Masking Values

In the following we consider tags generated using the same key/IV pair. We remark that in the case of 128-EIA3 v1.5, even though masking values for two distinct messages are either equal or independent, the independence of the universal hash function keys (i.e. the keystream bits used in the computation of the hash value) and the masking values is not guaranteed. Parts of the keystream (z_i) used as masking values for a message can be used during the universal hash function computation for a longer message, and conversely. This represents a deviation of the mask value generation of 128-EIA3 v1.5 from the Wegman-Carter paradigm. We show that consequently, while the proof of [10] guarantees that the MACs associated with two distinct messages and the same IV value are independent and uniformly distributed, the knowledge of the tags of two related messages under the same (key, IV) pair may allow to compute the tag of a third message under the same key and IV. Consider any message M_1 of arbitrary length ℓ_1, any message M_2 of length $\ell_2 \geq 1 + 32(\lceil \frac{\ell_1}{32} \rceil + 1)$, and the message $M_3 = M_2 \oplus \delta$ of length $\ell_3 = \ell_2$, where δ is the bitstring of length ℓ_2 whose prefix of length ℓ_1

[3] Whether this third message and the associated tag can be successfully submitted to the verifying entity depends on wheter the IV repetition detection of this entity is effective or not.

is M_1 and whose other bits are zero except for the two bits at positions ℓ_1 and $32(\lceil \frac{\ell_1}{32} \rceil + 1)$. Then we have $MAC(M_1) \oplus MAC(M_2) \oplus MAC(M_3) = 0$. Indeed,

$$\begin{aligned}
MAC(M_1) &= \oplus_{i=0}^{\ell_1 - 1}(m_i^1 W_i) \oplus W_{\ell_1} \oplus W_{32(\lceil \frac{\ell_1}{32} \rceil + 1)}, \\
MAC(M_2) &= \oplus_{i=0}^{\ell_2 - 1}(m_i^2 W_i) \oplus W_{\ell_2} \oplus W_{32(\lceil \frac{\ell_2}{32} \rceil + 1)}, \\
MAC(M_3) &= \oplus_{i=0}^{\ell_1 - 1}(m_i^1 W_i) \oplus \oplus_{i=0}^{\ell_2 - 1}(m_i^2 W_i) \oplus W_{\ell_1} \oplus W_{32(\lceil \frac{\ell_1}{32} \rceil + 1)} \oplus W_{\ell_2} \oplus W_{32(\lceil \frac{\ell_2}{32} \rceil + 1)}.
\end{aligned}$$

Consequently, for any such triplet of pairwise distinct messages the authentication codes of two messages gives a forgery for the third one.

The above 3-message forgery can be avoided by making the masking values and the universal hashing keys independent, for example by following the slightly modified MAC described in Algorithm 2.

Algorithm 2. A modified version of 128-EIA3

```
Input: IK ∈ {0,1}^k, IV ∈ {0,1}^n, ℓ ∈ ℕ*
Input: M = (m_0, ..., m_{ℓ-1}) ∈ {0,1}^ℓ
  (z_0, ..., z_{ℓ+63}) ← S(IK, IV)|_{ℓ+63}^0
  Tag = 0
  W_mask ← (z_0, ..., z_31)
  for i = 0 to ℓ − 1 do
    W_i ← (z_{i+32}, ..., z_{i+63})
    if m_i = 1 then
      Tag ← Tag ⊕ W_i
    end if
  end for
  W_ℓ ← (z_{ℓ+32}, ..., z_{ℓ+63})
  Tag ← Tag ⊕ W_ℓ
  Tag ← Tag ⊕ W_mask
  return Tag
```

This algorithm is quite similar to 128-EIA3 and requires the same number of keystream bits and the same amount of computation as 128-EIA3 v1.4 — the single difference being that the mask value consists of the first keystream bits and the universal hash function output value is derived from the subsequent keystream bits. This scheme ensures the equality or independence of keystream bits used as masking values or universal hashing key when tagging two different messages. It is also closer to the Wegman-Carter paradigm in that the masking value computation does not depend on the message being tagged — which is not the case in 128-EIA3 v1.4 and v1.5, where the length of the tagged message impacts the masking value. Unfortunately some non-generic properties remain, that are related to the Toeplitz matrix structure underlying the universal hash function construction rather than to the masking values generation method and hold for both 128-EIA3 v1.5 and Algorithm 2.

5.2 On the Sliding Property of the Universal Hash Function of 128-EIA3

In Section 4 we exploited a sliding property of the universal hash function used by 128-EIA3. Let z be the keystream sequence used in the computation of the universal hash function (i.e. without the final encrypting mask value). We denote by H_z the universal hash function. Using the "sliding-window" property of the construction based on Toeplitz matrices, we can derive the following property. For $r < 32$, we have

$$H_z(0^r \| M) \gg r = H_z(M) \ll r.$$

Let us now consider two messages M and $M' = 0\|M$ and assume that we got their tags T and T' under the same key/IV pair. Assume furthermore that these tag computations involve the same masking value W_{mask}. This is always the case in Algorithm 2 and is true in 128-EIA3 v1.5 under some mild assumption on the length of M (namely that $\ell \pmod{32} \neq 0$). Thus we get

$$\begin{aligned} H_z(M') \oplus W_{mask} &= T', \\ H_z(M) \oplus H_z(M') &= T \oplus T'. \end{aligned}$$

Let us now consider $M'' = 0^2\|M$. We have

$$\begin{aligned} (H_z(M') \oplus H_z(M'')) \gg 1 &= (H_z(0\|M) \oplus H_z(0\|M')) \gg 1 \\ &= (H_z(0\|M) \gg 1) \oplus (H_z(0\|M') \gg 1) \\ &= (H_z(M) \ll 1) \oplus (H_z(M') \ll 1) \\ &= (H_z(M) \oplus H_z(M'))) \ll 1 \\ &= (T \oplus T') \ll 1. \end{aligned}$$

By guessing a single bit, we thus get the value of $H_z(M') \oplus H_z(M'')$. Provided that the computation of the tag of M'' involves the same masking value W_{mask} (i.e. $\ell \pmod{32} \neq 31$ in the case of 128-EIA3 v1.5), by adding $H_z(M') \oplus H_z(M'')$ to T' we get a tag value for M''.

In other words, one can find a triplet (M, M', M'') of pairwise distinct messages such that given the tags T and T' of the first two messages under the same IV, the tag T'' of the third one under the same IV can be guessed with a probability as large as $1/2$. This results from the lack of 2-independence of the universal hash function H_z used in 128-EIA3. While H_z is uniformly distributed and 2^{-32}-AXU — this implies the independence of the MACs of any two distinct messages under the same key and the same IV as shown in [10] — H_z is far from being 2-universal, i.e. the hashes of two distinct messages can be strongly correlated and this results in the lack of independence of the MACs of three pairwise distinct messages illustrated here.[4]

[4] While another choice of H_z might have led to a much lower maximum success probability for a 3-message forgery, the existence of 4-message forgeries of success probability 1 seems difficult to avoid for any $GF(2)$-linear universal function family.

5.3 The IV Construction in 128-EIA-3 and Prevention of Nonce Reuse

The input to the IV construction for 128-EIAx are [1]:

- a 32-bit counter COUNT,
- a 5-bit bearer identity BEARER,
- a 1-bit direction of transmission DIRECTION.

This differs notably from the UMTS Integrity Algorithm (UIA) where the inputs for the IV construction are [4]:

- a 32-bit counter COUNT-I,
- a 32-bit random value FRESH,
- a 1-bit direction of transmission DIRECTION.

In the case of 128-EIA3, the IV is 128 bits and defined by 4 32-bit words, $IV_0 \| IV_1 \| IV_2 \| IV_3$ where:

$$\begin{aligned} IV_0 &= \mathsf{COUNT} \\ IV_1 &= \mathsf{BEARER} \| 0^{27} \\ IV_2 &= IV_0 \oplus (\mathsf{DIRECTION} \| 0^{31}) \\ IV_3 &= IV_1 \oplus (0^{16} \| \mathsf{DIRECTION} \| 0^{15}) \end{aligned}$$

We notice that while in UMTS two distinct values managed by the sending and receiving parties ensure the non-repetition of IVs, one single 32-bit counter is used for this purpose in LTE. Enforcing the use of fresh IVs by both the MAC issuer and the MAC verifier might therefore be more complex and we may express some concerns about the assurance that in LTE implementations the strong security requirement of (key, IV) pair never being reused at either side will always be verified.

6 Conclusion

The existential forgery attack presented in Section 4 was forwarded to the designers of 128-EIA3 v1.4, who produced the modified version 128-EIA3 v1.5 to address the issue. While our analysis of 128-EIA3 v1.5 did not reveal any security issue of similar significance and the new MAC offers a provable resistance (under some assumptions) against a large class of forgery attacks, we have highlighted some structural properties of the mask values computation and the universal family of hash functions underlying 128-EIA3 v1.5, and shown that these may lead to limitations of its resilience against nonce reuse. None of the security properties we have investigated here relates to the specific features of the underlying IV-dependent stream cipher ZUC.

Acknowledgements. The authors would like to thank Steve Babbage for insightful comments on an early version of this paper.

References

1. 3GPP Technical Specification Group Services and System Aspects: 3GPP System Architecture Evolution (SAE); Security architecture (Release 9). Tech. Rep. 3G TS 33.401 V 9.3.1, 3rd Generation Partnership Project (2010-04)
2. Bellare, M., Goldreich, O., Mityagin, A.: The Power of Verification Queries in Message Authentication and Authenticated Encryption. Tech. Rep. 2004/309, Cryptology ePrint Archive (2004)
3. Carter, J., Wegman, M.: Universal Classes of Hash Functions. Journal of Computer and System Science 18, 143–154 (1979)
4. ETSI/SAGE: Specification of the 3GPP Confidentiality and Integrity Algorithms UEA2 & UIA2. Document 1: UEA2 and UIA2 Specification. Version 2.1. Tech. rep., ETSI (March 16, 2009), `http://www.gsmworld.com/documents/uea2_uia2_d1_v2_1.pdf`
5. ETSI/SAGE: Specification of the 3GPP Confidentiality and Integrity Algorithms 128-EEA3 & 128-EIA3. Document 1: 128-EEA3 and 128-EIA3 Specification. Version 1.4. Tech. rep., ETSI (July 30, 2010)
6. ETSI/SAGE: Specification of the 3GPP Confidentiality and Integrity Algorithms 128-EEA3 & 128-EIA3. Document 2: ZUC Specification. Version 1.4. Tech. rep., ETSI (July 30, 2010)
7. ETSI/SAGE: Specification of the 3GPP Confidentiality and Integrity Algorithms 128-EEA3 & 128-EIA3. Document 4: Design and Evaluation Report. Version 1.1. Tech. rep., ETSI (August 11, 2010)
8. ETSI/SAGE: Specification of the 3GPP Confidentiality and Integrity Algorithms 128-EEA3 & 128-EIA3. Document 1: 128-EEA3 and 128-EIA3 Specification. Version 1.5. Tech. rep., ETSI (January 4, 2011), `http://www.gsmworld.com/documents/EEA3_EIA3_specification_v1_5.pdf`
9. ETSI/SAGE: Specification of the 3GPP Confidentiality and Integrity Algorithms 128-EEA3 & 128-EIA3. Document 2: ZUC Specification. Version 1.5. Tech. rep., ETSI (January 4, 2011), `http://www.gsmworld.com/documents/EEA3_EIA3_ZUC_v1_5.pdf`
10. ETSI/SAGE: Specification of the 3GPP Confidentiality and Integrity Algorithms 128-EEA3 & 128-EIA3. Document 4: Design and Evaluation Report. Version 1.3, Tech. rep., ETSI (January 18, 2011), `http://www.gsmworld.com/documents/EEA3_EIA3_Design_Evaluation_v1_3.pdf`
11. Handschuh, H., Preneel, B.: Key-Recovery Attacks on Universal Hash Function Based MAC Algorithms. In: Wagner, D. (ed.) CRYPTO 2008. LNCS, vol. 5157, pp. 144–161. Springer, Heidelberg (2008)
12. Krawczyk, H.: LFSR-Based Hashing and Authentication. In: Desmedt, Y.G. (ed.) CRYPTO 1994. LNCS, vol. 839, pp. 129–139. Springer, Heidelberg (1994)
13. Martin Albrecht, K.P., Watson, G.: Plaintext Recovery Attacks Against SSH. In: Proceedings of IEEE Symposium on Security and Privacy 2009, pp. 16–26. IEEE Computer Society (2009)
14. Rogaway, P.: Bucket Hashing and Its Application to Fast Message Authentication. In: Coppersmith, D. (ed.) CRYPTO 1995. LNCS, vol. 963, pp. 29–42. Springer, Heidelberg (1995)
15. Rogaway, P.: Bucket Hashing and its Application to Fast Message Authentication. Journal of Cryptology 12(2), 91–115 (1999)
16. Shoup, V.: On Fast and Provably Secure Message Authentication Based on Universal Hashing. In: Koblitz, N. (ed.) CRYPTO 1996. LNCS, vol. 1109, pp. 313–328. Springer, Heidelberg (1996)

17. Stinson, D.: Universal Hashing and Authentication Codes. Design, Codes and Cryptography 4, 369–380 (1994)
18. Sun, B., Tang, X., Li, C.: Preliminary Cryptanalysis Results of ZUC. Presented at the First International Workshop on ZUC Algorithm, vol. 12 (2010)
19. Wegman, M., Carter, J.: New Hash Functions and Their Use in Authentication and Set Equality. Journal of Computer and System Science 22, 265–279 (1981)
20. Wu, H.: Cryptanalysis of the Stream Cipher ZUC in the 3GPP Confidentiality & Integrity Algorithms 128-EEA3 & 128-EIA3. Presented at the ASIACRYPT 2010 rump session (2010), http://www.spms.ntu.edu.sg/Asiacrypt2010/Rump%20Session-%207%20Dec%202010/wu_rump_zuc.pdf

New Insights on Impossible Differential Cryptanalysis

Charles Bouillaguet[1], Orr Dunkelman[2,3], Pierre-Alain Fouque[1], and Gaëtan Leurent[4]

[1] Département d'Informatique
École normale supérieure
45 Rue d'Ulm
75320 Paris, France
{charles.bouillaguet,pierre-alain.fouque}@ens.fr

[2] Computer Science Department
University of Haifa
Haifa 31905, Israel
orrd@cs.haifa.ac.il

[3] Faculty of Mathematics and Computer Science
Weizmann Institute of Science
P.O. Box 26, Rehovot 76100, Israel

[4] Faculty of Science, Technology and Communications
University of Luxembourg
6 Rue Richard Coudenhove-Kalergi
L-1359 Luxembourg
gaetan.leurent@uni.lu

Abstract. Since its introduction, impossible differential cryptanalysis has been applied to many ciphers. Besides the specific application of the technique in various instances, there are some very basic results which apply to generic structures of ciphers, e.g., the well known 5-round impossible differential of Feistel ciphers with bijective round functions.

In this paper we present a new approach for the construction and the usage of impossible differentials for Generalized Feistel structures. The results allow to extend some of the previous impossible differentials by one round (or more), answer an open problem about the ability to perform this kind of analysis, and tackle, for the first time the case of non-bijective round functions.

Keywords: Impossible differential cryptanalysis, Miss in the middle, Generalized Feistel, Matrix method.

1 Introduction

Impossible differential attack [3] is a method of using differential concepts in cryptanalytic attacks. While regular differential cryptanalysis [5] exploits differentials with as high probability as possible, impossible differential cryptanalysis exploits differentials that cannot happen, i.e., have probability of zero. The actual

A. Miri and S. Vaudenay (Eds.): SAC 2011, LNCS 7118, pp. 243–259, 2012.

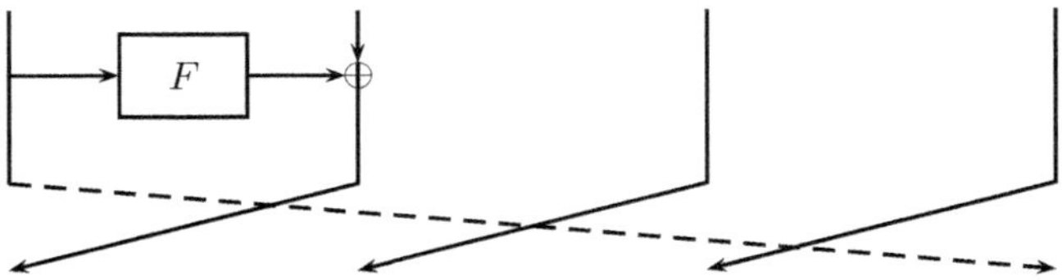

Fig. 1. CAST-like Structure with Four Threads

use of the impossible differential resembles the one of a high probability differentials: given a pair that may "satisfy" the differential, the adversary obtains the subkey(s) suggested by the pair. Unlike differential cryptanalysis, where such a subkey is more likely to be the right subkey, in impossible differential cryptanalysis, once a subkey is suggested by a candidate pair, it is necessarily a wrong one (and thus discarded).

To start an impossible differential attack, the adversary has to identify such impossible differentials. Most of these differentials are constructed in a miss-in-the-middle approach [4]. The approach is based on combining two probability 1 truncated differentials that cannot coexist. For example, there is a generic 5-round impossible differential for Feistel constructions with a bijective round function (first identified in [12]) of the form $(0, \alpha) \not\rightarrow (0, \alpha)$ (depicted in Figure 2).

A method for finding such impossible differentials is presented in [11] under the name *$\mathcal{U}$-method*. In this method, one can construct probability 1 truncated differentials, which in turn leads to finding contradictions. An automated version of the method is presented in [10]. The tool (called *the matrix method*). The automated analysis shows several results for generalizations of the Feistel cipher (the Generalized Feistel Network of [14], MARS-like constructions [6], and CAST-like constructions [1]).

As an example, consider a CAST-like construction (depicted in Figure 1). The matrix method suggests an impossible differential of $n^2 - 1$ rounds for $n \geq 3$ threads assuming that the round function is bijective. The impossible differential has the form of $(0, 0, \ldots, 0, \alpha) \not\rightarrow (0, 0, \ldots, 0, \omega)$ for any non-zero α and ω, and is based on the fact that the $(n-1)$-round truncated differential starting at $(0, 0, \ldots, 0, \alpha)$ predicts a zero difference in the one before last word, while the $n(n-1)$-round truncated differential ending at $(0, 0, \ldots, 0, \omega)$ predicts that the same word has a non-zero difference.

The $\mathcal{U}$-method was later improved in [13] to incorporate a much larger set of contradictions. Such new set of contradictions may include the use of specific differences in the input and the output (rather than truncated differences) or conditions on XORing a few words together.

In this paper we take a deeper look into the construction of impossible differentials. We start the analysis by considering a slightly different approach for the analysis, a one which does not classify the state of the word as part of a small

Table 1. Comparison of Impossible Differentials for Feistel Networks

Structure	Number of		Round	Source
	Words	Rounds	Function	
Feistel	2	5	bijective	[12]
Generalized Feistel Network	2	7	bijective	[10]
Generalized Feistel Network	$2n$	$3n+2$	bijective	[10]
CAST-like	n	n^2-1	bijective	[11]
CAST-like	n	n^2+3	bijective	[7,13]
MARS-like	n	$2n-1$	bijective	[10]
MARS-like	n	$2n+3$	bijective	[13]
RC6-like	$2n$	$4n+1$	bijective	[10]
CAST-like	n	n^2	any	Sect. 4
MARS-like	n	$2n$	any	Sect. 4

set of values.[1] Instead, we try to look at the specific differences that may form a contradiction, taking the structure of the round function into account. The main property we use is the existence of impossible differentials in the round function.

This allows us to extend the impossible differentials by an additional round, leading to improved attacks on some structures of block ciphers. Moreover, following the new point of view, one can even reduce the requirements from the round function. For example, as part of our analysis, we can offer n^2-round impossible differentials for CAST-like ciphers, even if their round function is not bijective. We note that our results contradict a claim made in [16], which claims that "generic" impossible differentials for this structure exist only up to n^2-1 rounds. We compare the previously known results with our new results in Table 1.

We continue and define the *differential expansion rate* of a round function for a (set of) input difference(s). The rate tries to measure the speed in which the set of possible differences evolves through invocations of the round function. To some extent, it is the equivalent of the expanding rate of a graph.

We then study how to use our new impossible differential in an actual attack, and how useful is the new impossible differential. We describe attacks using our new extended impossible differentials, with the same time complexity as previous attacks (under some natural conditions on the round function), and covering more rounds.

The structure of this paper is as follows: In Section 2 we cover the basics of differential cryptanalysis and impossible differential cryptanalysis. Section 3 discusses the previous results and the matrix method. In Section 4 we suggest a new approach for constructing impossible differentials, and in Section 5 we show that impossible differential attacks that use the previous impossible differentials can be extended to more rounds when instantiated with our newly found impossible differentials (almost with no additional complexity). Finally, Section 6 concludes this paper.

[1] The matrix method classifies the state of a word as one of five states: zero difference, fixed difference, unknown non-zero difference, the XOR of a fixed difference with an unknown non-zero difference, or unknown.

2 Preliminaries

Differential cryptanalysis [5] is one of the corner stones of modern cryptanalytic techniques. It was used to successfully attack block ciphers, hash functions, and even stream ciphers. The core idea behind differential cryptanalysis is to look at the development of differences through the encryption function rather than at the actual values directly. This approach leads to a much stronger knowledge of the adversary concerning the encryption process, as it allows "replacing" the key addition with probabilistic behavior in the nonlinear parts of the cipher.

For sake of simplicity we shall concentrate on differential cryptanalysis used for the cryptanalysis of block ciphers. In such a case, the adversary first finds a differential (or a differential characteristic) of high probability p, e.g., $\Delta_{IN} \rightarrow \Delta_{OUT}$ with probability p. The differential can be for the full cipher, but in many cases, a slightly shorter differential is used. After identifying the differential (characteristic), the adversary asks for the encryption of $O(1/p)$ pairs of plaintexts with input difference Δ_{IN} and collects the corresponding ciphertexts. Then, the adversary tries to identify the subkey used in the last rounds of the cipher, by partially decrypting the ciphertext pairs, or by analyzing the last rounds of the differential characteristics. For the right subkey, it is expected that a few pairs with difference Δ_{OUT} appear, while the number of pairs with difference Δ_{OUT} is expected to be significantly lower for wrong guesses.

As the data complexity (and consequently, the time complexity) of differential attacks are proportional to $1/p$, the existence of high probability differentials is considered a weakness of the block cipher. Hence, many block cipher designers suggest methodologies to ensure that there are no differentials with high probability for (almost) the entire cipher. For example, in the case of AES [19], it can be shown that any 4-round differential characteristic has probability not higher than 2^{-150} [8] and that no 4-round differential with probability higher than 2^{-113} exists [9].

At that point, it was observed that differential cryptanalysis, as a statistical attack, uses the fact that the number of pairs counted for the right subkey guess and the wrong subkey guesses differs. The standard differential attack assumes that the number of pairs suggested by right subkey is higher than for a wrong subkey, but it is also possible to mount an attack when the number of pairs suggested by the right subkey is lower. This led to the introduction of impossible differential attacks (first at [12] as a dedicated attack on the DEAL cipher, and then as a general cryptanalytic tool at [3,4]). These attacks are based on finding differentials whose probability is 0. Namely, for the right subkey guess *no pairs* with output difference Δ_{OUT} exist, while for wrong subkey guesses, such pairs may be "discovered".

Hence, the impossible differential attack is based on taking a set of plaintext pairs, asking for their encryption, and then partially decrypting these pairs under the subkey candidates. Once a subkey candidate suggests that a specific ciphertext pair "satisfies" the differential, i.e., that $\Delta_{IN} \rightarrow \Delta_{OUT}$ has occurred, we can be assured that this subkey is wrong and discard it.

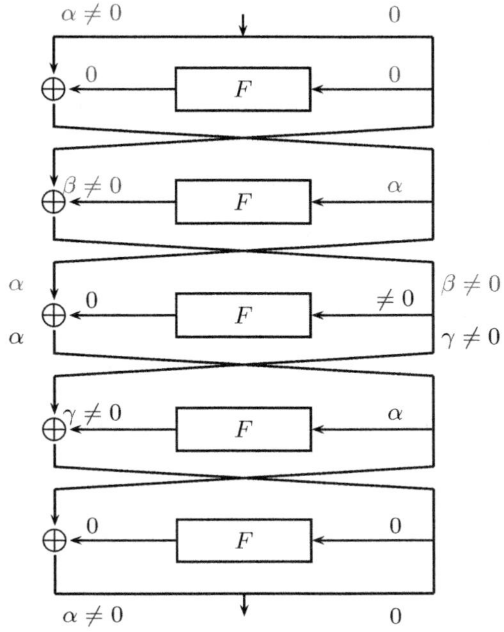

The miss-in-the-middle follows the fact that the input and output differences force the output difference of the third round to be 0. At the same time, due to the bijectiveness of the round function the input difference of the third round is necessarily non-zero. The two cannot coexist, as the round function is bijective.

Fig. 2. A Generic 5-Round Impossible Differential for Feistel Ciphers with a Bijective Round Function

The most successful method for constructing impossible differentials is the *miss in the middle* method. In this method, a probability one truncated differential $\Delta_{IN} \rightarrow \Delta_A$ and a probability one truncated differential in the backward direction $\Delta_B \leftarrow \Delta_{OUT}$ are identified, such that Δ_A and Δ_B cannot coexist simultaneously. For example, Figure 2 describes a 5-round Feistel construction with a bijective round function, for which $(\alpha, 0) \not\rightarrow (\alpha, 0)$ is an impossible differential.

2.1 Notations

In this paper we use the following notations:

- n — denotes the number of threads in a given structure.
- w — denotes the size (in bits) of a given thread.
- $\alpha, \beta, \ldots$ — denotes a non-zero difference.
- 0 — denotes a zero difference (in a thread).
- ? — denotes an unknown difference.
- $\rightarrow_i$, $\leftarrow_i$ — denotes the propagation of a (truncated) difference for i rounds in the encryption/decryption direction.
- $\alpha \rightsquigarrow \beta$ — denotes the event that an input difference α to a round function F may result in an output difference β, i.e., $Pr_x[F(x) \oplus F(x \oplus \alpha) = \beta] > 0$.

3 Previous Results and the Matrix Method

Similarly to looking for good differentials, the search for impossible differentials is not an easy task. While good impossible differentials were found by hand (e.g., the one of Figure 2 or the 24-round impossible differential of SKIPJACK from [3]), it was suggested to try and automate the process of finding these impossible differentials [10,11,13].

One tool, based on the $\mathcal{U}$-method (of [11]), is the matrix method [10], a mechanism to identify truncated differentials of probability 1. The intermediate encryption value is divided into words (or threads), where each such word can be in one of five states, each associated with a number: a zero difference (denoted by 0), a fixed non-zero difference (denoted by 1), a non-fixed non-zero difference (denoted by 1^*), the XOR of a fixed non-zero difference with a non-fixed one (denoted by 2), and an unknown difference (denoted by 2^* or any other number larger than 3, with or without *).

The tool targets mostly ciphers whose round function contains one nonlinear function, which is in itself a bijective function. The round function is represented as a matrix composed of 0's, 1's, and at most one special entry denoted by 1_F. The automated search starts with a vector $\{0,1\}^n$, which is multiplied by the special matrix, repeatedly, to reveal the properties of the truncated difference after each round.

The main idea behind the matrix multiplication, is to represent the possible transitions in a way that conveys the actual difference in the state. The matrix has size of $n \times n$ (for an n-thread construction). If thread i does not affect thread j, then entry (i, j) of the matrix is 0. If thread i affects thread j, then the entry is 1 (if thread i is XORed/copied into thread j) or 1_F (if thread i is sent through the nonlinear function F and the output is XORed or copied to thread j).

Now, one can define the arithmetics. For example, if the thread has state 0, then it has no affect on other threads (independent of the operation). A thread i whose state is 1, contributes 0, 1, or 1^*, to thread j when the corresponding entry in the matrix is 0,1, or 1_F, respectively. A thread i whose state is 1^*, contributes 0, 1^*, or 1^*, when the corresponding entry in the matrix is 0,1, or 1_F, respectively. Other states, α (or x^*), contribute 0, α (respectively, x^*), and $x+1$, when the matrix is 0,1, or 1_F, respectively.

Then, each new thread is summed under the following addition rules: $0+x = x$, $1+1 = 1$, $1+1^* = 2$, $1+x = 2^*$ (for $x > 1$ or $x^* > 1^*$), and any other addition just sums the actual numbers (and maintains the *). This gives the new state after the round function, and one can compute as many rounds as possible, until the entire intermediate encryption value is composed of only 2^* and $x > 2$ (with or without *), which denote the longest truncated differential of probability 1 that can be found and that conveys some "useful" characteristics.

It is also possible to run the same algorithm in the backward direction (with the corresponding matrix), to obtain the longest truncated differential or probability 1 of that direction.

Given two truncated differentials $\Delta_{IN} \rightarrow \Delta_A$ and $\Delta_B \leftarrow \Delta_{OUT}$, one can scan Δ_A and Δ_B to find inconsistencies. For example, if a word has a a non-zero

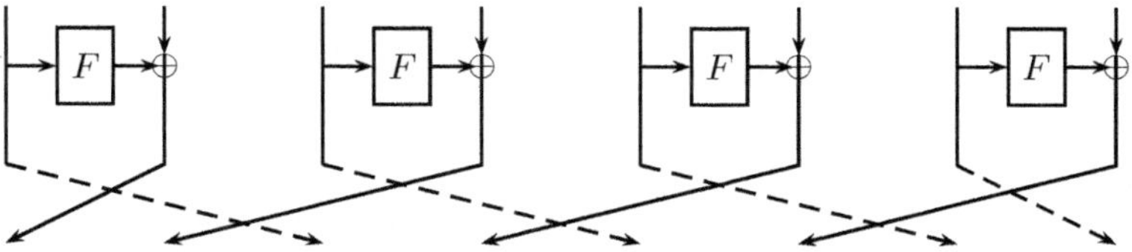

Fig. 3. A Generalized Feistel Network (GFN_4) with 8 Threads

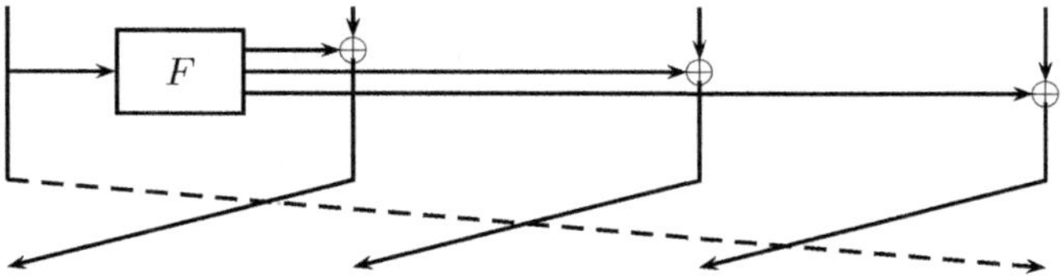

Fig. 4. A MARS-like Cipher

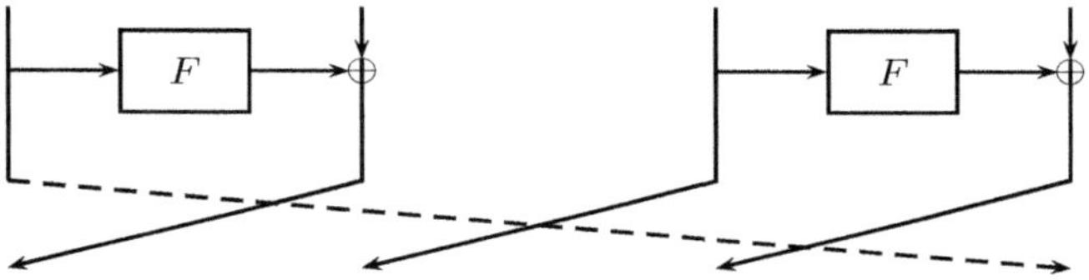

Fig. 5. An RC6-like Cipher

difference (fixed or not) in Δ_A but a zero difference in Δ_B, both Δ_A and Δ_B cannot coexist, which leads to the miss in the middle differential $\Delta_{IN} \not\rightarrow \Delta_{OUT}$. This fact is described by the matrix method as pairs of contradicting states, e.g., 0 and 1 (or 0 and 1^*) or 1 and 2.

The method was applied for several constructions: Generalized Feistel Networks (introduced in [14]), CAST-like ciphers (based on the CAST-256 block cipher [1]), MARS-like ciphers (based on MARS [6]), RC6-like ciphers (based on RC6 [17]), and various variants of SKIPJACK-like ciphers [18]. We outline the structure of the first four structures in Figures 3, 1, 4, and 5, respectively.

For GFN with 4 threads (called GFN_2), there exist several 7-round impossible differentials assuming that the round function is bijective. For example, the input difference $(0, 0, 0, \alpha)$ becomes after 6 rounds $(?, ?, ?, \delta)$, while the output difference $(\beta_1, 0, \beta_2, 0)$ is decrypted by one round to the difference $(\beta_2, ?, 0, 0)$ which cannot coexist. For sake of simplicity we use the notation $(0, 0, 0, \alpha) \rightarrow_6 (?, ?, ?, \delta)$ and $(\beta_2, ?, 0, 0) \leftarrow_1 (\beta_1, 0, \beta_2, 0)$ to denote these truncated differentials. Combining these two truncated differentials we obtain that $(0, 0, 0, \alpha) \not\rightarrow_7 (\beta_1, 0, \beta_2, 0)$.

Similarly, for GFN_n (with $2n$ threads) there exists a $(3n + 2)$-round impossible differential of the form $(0, 0, \ldots, 0, \alpha) \not\rightarrow_{3n+2} (\beta_1, 0, \beta_2, 0, 0, \ldots, 0)$ following the truncated differentials $(0, 0, \ldots, 0, \alpha) \rightarrow_{2n} (?, ?, \ldots, ?, \delta, ?, ?, ?, ?)$ and $(?, ?, \ldots, ?, 0, ?, ?, ?, ?) \leftarrow_{n+2} (\beta_1, 0, \beta_2, 0, 0, \ldots, 0)$.[2]

[2] We note that in [10], a small typo suggests that the word which causes the contradiction is the fourth from the right while it is actually the fifth.

For an n-thread CAST-like construction (for $n \geq 3$), there exists an (n^2-1)-round impossible differential $(0,0,\ldots,0,\alpha) \not\to_{n^2-1} (\beta,0,0,\ldots,0)$ following the truncated differentials $(0,0,\ldots,0,\alpha) \to_{3n-3} (?,?,\ldots,?,\delta)$ and $(?,?,\ldots,?,0) \leftarrow_{n^2-3n+2} (\beta,0,0,\ldots,0)$.

For an n-thread MARS-like construction (again, for $n \geq 3$), the two truncated differentials $(0,0,\ldots,0,\alpha) \to_{n+1} (?,?,\ldots,?,\delta)$ and $(?,?,\ldots,?,0) \leftarrow_{n-2} (\beta,0,0,\ldots,0)$ are combined into an $2n-1$-round impossible differential of the form $(0,0,\ldots,0,\alpha) \not\to_{2n-1} (\beta,0,0,\ldots,0)$.

In the case of RC6-like structure with n-threads, the impossible differential is $(0,0,\ldots,0,\alpha_i,0,\ldots,0) \not\to_{4n+1} (0,0,\ldots,0,\beta_{i+1},0,\ldots,0)$, where $\alpha_i = \beta_{i+1}$ and α_i is positioned in the ith thread (and β_{i+1} in the $(i+1)$'th thread) for some odd i.

For details concerning the SKIPJACK-like variants, we refer the interested reader to [10].

The UID-method of [13] is a generalization of the $\mathcal{U}$-method. In this variant, each word is not associated with a mere state, but its history (of the actual difference) is tracked. Using this history, it is possible to compose longer impossible differentials, as one may look at the XOR of a few words at some point (which may still contain non-trivial state information even after all words of the state become "?"). We note that this method still relies on the fact that the round function is bijective.

4 New Impossible Differentials

Our new impossible differentials on CAST-like and MARS-like ciphers follow a more subtle analysis.

4.1 CAST-Like Ciphers

We first consider a 4-thread CAST-like cipher. In such a cipher, there is a 4-round truncated differential with probability 1 of the form $(0,0,0,\alpha) \to_4 (\beta,0,0,\alpha)$ for non-zero α and some β (which may be zero if F is not bijective). At the same time, there exists a 12-round truncated differential in the decryption direction of the form $(\omega,?,?,\phi) \leftarrow_{12} (\omega,0,0,0)$ for non-zero ω and some ϕ (which may be zero if the round function is not bijective). We outline the differentials in Table 2.

Observation 1 *We note that the above two truncated differentials can coexist if and only if $\beta = \omega$. Hence, if an input difference α to the round function may not cause an ω difference at the output, i.e., if $\alpha \not\rightsquigarrow \omega$ is an impossible differential for F, then these two differentials cannot coexist, and we obtain a 16-round impossible differential of the form $(0,0,0,\alpha) \not\to_{16} (\omega,0,0,0)$ for the cipher.*

Given the structure of the round function F, it is possible to determine whether $\alpha \rightsquigarrow \omega$ through F. Consider for example the round function of DES, for which determining whether $\alpha \rightsquigarrow \omega$ can be easily done by checking each of

Table 2. The Two Truncated Differentials Used in Our New 16-Round Impossible Differential on 4-Thread CAST-like Ciphers

Round	Difference	Round	Difference
Input (0)	$(0,0,0,\alpha)$	Output (16)	$(\omega,0,0,0)$
1	$(0,0,\alpha,0)$	15	$(0,\omega,0,0)$
2	$(0,\alpha,0,0)$	14	$(0,0,\omega,0)$
3	$(\alpha,0,0,0)$	13	$(0,0,0,\omega)$
4	$(\beta,0,0,\alpha)$	12	$(\omega,\psi,0,0)$
		11	$(0,\omega,\psi,0)$
		10	$(0,0,\omega,\psi)$
		9	$(\psi,\chi,0,\omega)$
		8	$(\omega,?,\chi,0)$
		7	$(0,\omega,?,\chi)$
		6	$(\chi,\phi,\omega,?)$
		5	$(?,?,\phi,\omega)$
		4	$(\omega,?,?,\phi)$

Differences are given after the round.

the 8 S-boxes separately. We note that in DES' round function, given a pair of random input/output differences from an S-box, there is an 80% chance of the transition being possible. Hence, for a random α and ω, the probability of $x \rightsquigarrow a$ is only $0.8^8 \approx 0.17$.[3]

In the more general case, where the form of the round function is $F_k(x) = G(x \oplus k)$, one can exhaustively try all possible pairs with input difference α, and see if any of them leads to ω output difference. For a w-bit $G(\cdot)$ this takes 2^w invocations of $G(\cdot)$, even if we only have a black box access to $G(\cdot)$ (but not to $F_k(\cdot)$). Of course, when the description of $G(\cdot)$ is known, this verification is expected to be significantly faster. As we show in Section 5, even under the worst case assumption, i.e., when $G(\cdot)$ is unknown, this has no real effect on the actual attack that uses this impossible differential.

Moreover, we note that for a function $G(\cdot)$ of this form, the probability that $\alpha \rightsquigarrow \omega$ is at most 0.5 for a random[4] α and ω (following the fact that the row corresponding to α in the difference distribution table has at most half of its entries as non-zero). If we assume that $G(\cdot)$ is a random function, then according to [15] we can determine that about 60.6% of the possible (α, ω) pairs yield an impossible differential.

An interesting point concerning the truncated differentials suggested above is the fact that their existence is independent of the actual differential properties of the round functions. Namely, in the case $F_k(\cdot)$ is not bijective, the above truncated differentials still hold, and thus, also the impossible differential. More

[3] Even though the actual inputs to the different S-boxes are independent of each other, assuming the key is chosen randomly, the differences are not. Hence, the actual value of the full round function may be slightly different.

[4] Most impossible differential attacks face a large amount of (α, ω) pairs which are generated in a random manner.

precisely, even if different round functions are used, the only one of interest is the one of round 4.

Now, one can easily generalize the above impossible differential, and can easily see that for an n-thread CAST-like block cipher, the following is an impossible differential: $(0,0,0,\ldots,\alpha) \to_{n^2} (\omega,0,\ldots,0)$ if $\alpha \not\rightsquigarrow \omega$ following the n-round truncated differential $(0,0,0,\ldots,0,\alpha) \to_n (\beta,0,0,\ldots,0,\alpha)$ and the $n(n-1)$-round truncated differential $(\omega,?,\ldots,?,\phi) \leftarrow_{n(n-1)} (\phi,0,\ldots,0)$.

4.2 MARS-Like ciphers

The same approach can also be used to extend the impossible differential suggested for a MARS-like structure. As before, we start with a 4-thread example, and then generalize it. In such a cipher, there is a 5-round truncated differential $(0,0,0,\alpha) \to_5 (?,?,?,\beta)$ and a 3-round truncated differential $(\omega,0,0,0) \leftarrow_3 (0,0,0,\omega)$. As β is the output difference caused by an α input difference, the two can coexist if and only if $\alpha \rightsquigarrow \omega$ through the corresponding $F(\cdot)$. We outline the differentials in Table 3.[5]

Table 3. The Two Truncated Differentials Used in Our New 8-Round Impossible Differential on 4-Thread MARS-like Ciphers

Round	Difference	Round	Difference
Input (0)	$(0,0,0,\alpha)$	Output (8)	$(\omega,0,0,0)$
1	$(0,0,\alpha,0)$	7	$(0,\omega,0,0)$
2	$(0,\alpha,0,0)$	6	$(0,0,\omega,0)$
3	$(\alpha,0,0,0)$	5	$(0,0,0,\omega)$
4	$(\beta,\gamma,\delta,\alpha)$		
5	$(?,?,?,\beta)$		

Differences are given after the round.

We can of course generalize the above truncated differentials for the case of an n-thread MARS-like cipher. The backwards differential is the same, i.e.,

[5] We note that the differentials presented in Table 3 assume that the differences that are XORed into each of the three threads is different (as in the real MARS there are three different functions). When the same output is XORed into all the three threads (in the real MARS, additions and subtractions are also used) then one can construct a longer impossible differential for 9 rounds. In the forward direction we use the following 5-round differential:

$$(0,0,0,\alpha) \to_4 (\beta,\beta,\beta,\alpha) \to (\gamma,\gamma,\delta,\beta)$$

where $\delta = \alpha \oplus \beta \oplus \gamma \neq \gamma$ (whenever $\alpha \not\rightsquigarrow \alpha$ through $F(\cdot)$), and in the backward direction we use the following 4-round differential:

$$(\omega,\psi,\psi,\psi) \leftarrow (0,0,0,\omega) \leftarrow_3 (\omega,0,0,0)$$

and it is easy to see that the two cannot coexist, as the XOR of the two intermediate words cannot be the same.

an $(n-1)$-round differential of the form $(0,0,\ldots,0,\omega) \leftarrow_{n-1} (\omega,0,\ldots,0)$ and the forward differential is of the form $(0,0,\ldots,0,\alpha) \rightarrow_{n+1} (?,?,\ldots,?,\beta)$ which cannot coexist if $\alpha \not\rightarrow \omega$ through the corresponding $F(\cdot)$.

4.3 A Larger Class of Impossible Differentials

We can extend the above impossible differentials by taking an even closer look into the round function. Instead of looking for impossible differential in the round function, we now look for impossible differentials in the iterated round function. We can do this more delicate analysis based on the following definition of the output difference set of an unkeyed function $F(\cdot)$ and a set S of input difference:

Definition 1. *For a function $F(\cdot)$ and a set ΔS of input differences, we define the output difference set $\Delta F(\Delta S)$ to be the set containing all the output differences that are feasible by an input difference in ΔS.*

Now, we can define the differential expansion rate of an unkeyed function $f(\cdot)$:

Definition 2. *The* differential expansion rate *of a function $F(\cdot)$ is*

$$\max_{|\Delta S|>0} \frac{|\Delta F(\Delta S)|}{|\Delta S|},$$

i.e., the maximal increase in the size of a difference set through the round function.

We first note that the above definitions are set for unkeyed functions. However, for round functions of the form $F_k(x) = G(x \oplus k)$, one can disregard the key addition, and use the same results. Moreover, once the key is fixed, this is the case for any round function. For the following discussion, we shall assume that indeed $F(\cdot)$ is of that form.

Now, if the differential expansion rate of a function is small, then $\Delta F(\Delta F(\{\alpha\}))$ for a fixed input difference α may not be large enough to cover all possible differences. Assume that this is indeed the case for a round function $F(\cdot)$ (we later describe an example of such a round function), then one can easily extend the 16-round impossible differential for CAST-like structure with 4 threads by one round by using the following truncated differentials: $(0,0,0,\alpha) \rightarrow_5 (\gamma,0,\alpha,\beta)$ and $(\omega,?,?,\phi) \leftarrow_{12} (\omega,0,0,0)$. If $\omega \notin \Delta F(\Delta F(\{\alpha\}))$, one can easily see that $(0,0,0,\alpha) \not\rightarrow_{17} (\omega,0,0,0)$.

More generally, if the differential expansion rate is $c < 2^{w/2}$ then $|\Delta F(\Delta F(\{x\}))| < 2^w$, which means that there are many ω values for which $\omega \notin \Delta F(\Delta F(\{\alpha\}))$. The smaller the value of c is, there is a larger set of differences which are not in $|\Delta F(\Delta F(\{\alpha\}))|$, and thus, allow for longer impossible differentials.

These results can be generalized. If $c < 2^{w/3}$, then the above arguments can be repeated and the forward differential can be extended to a 6-round differential $(0,0,0,\alpha) \rightarrow_6 (\delta,\alpha,\beta,\gamma)$ where $\delta \in \Delta F(\Delta F(\Delta F(\{\alpha\})))$, and if $\omega \notin \Delta F(\Delta F(\Delta F(\{\alpha\})))$, then obviously both differentials cannot coexist. Extending this analysis to more rounds is feasible, by taking into consideration that the next set of differences is XORed with a difference α (which affects the difference set, but not its size).

We note that even when the differential expansion rate is large, there are still cases where we can extend the 16-round impossible differential. This follows the fact that the differential expansion rate may be determined by a special set of differences that are not relevant for the impossible differential.

Consider for example a CAST-like structure with 4 threads, whose round function is from 64 bits to 64 bits, and is based on applying eight 8-bit to 8-bit S-boxes in parallel, accompanied by a linear transformation L (e.g., the round function of Camellia [2]). We can even assume that this linear transformation has a branch number of 9, which ensures that a difference in one S-box affects all output bytes. Following the properties of differential cryptanalysis, consider an input difference α with one active byte, where all other bytes have a zero difference. $\Delta F(\{\alpha\})$, thus, contains at most 128 possible differences, each with all the bytes active. For each such difference, applying F again, can yield at most $128^8 = 2^{56}$ possible differences. This implies that the size of $\Delta F(\Delta F(\{\alpha\}))$ is upper bounded by 2^{63}, which allows the extension of the impossible differential to 17 rounds.

If the linear transformation L does not have a maximal branch number b (e.g., the actual round function of Camellia uses a linear transformation with branch number of 4), then we can extend the attack to 18 rounds. Indeed, given values ω and θ with a single active S-box and $\omega = L\theta$, we have $\omega \notin \Delta F(\Delta F(\Delta F(\{\alpha\})))$ for most choices of ω and u. This comes from the fact that $\alpha \not\rightarrow \omega$ is an impossible differential for $F \circ F \circ F$, following the miss in the middle principle. The differences in $\Delta F(\{\omega\})$ all have the same pattern of b active S-boxes with some inactive S-boxes. On the other hand, the differences in $\Delta F^{-1}(\{\omega\})$ have a single S-box (the same as in θ), therefore the differences in $\Delta F^{-1}(\Delta F^{-1}(\{\omega\}))$ all have the same pattern of at least b active S-boxes, with some inactive ones. If ω and α are chosen so that the pattern are incompatible, we have $\alpha \not\rightarrow \omega$ for $F \circ F \circ F$.

There are two issues that need to be addressed using this new extension. The first is what is the ratio of impossible combinations. In the first example given above, the probability that for a random ω, and a random α of the form suggested, the probability that $\omega \notin \Delta F(\Delta F(\{\alpha\}))$ is indeed at least 0.5, which still offers a high probability of contradiction (which is needed to form the impossible event).

The second concern is the ability to check whether a given ω is in $\Delta F(\Delta F(\{\alpha\}))$. Unfortunately, at the moment, even if $F(\cdot)$ is of the form $F_k(x) = G(x \oplus k)$, for an unknown $G(\cdot)$, we are not aware of any algorithm, besides enumerating all possible differences. At the same time, if the structure of the round function is known, it can be used to offer an easy way to check whether $\omega \in \Delta F(\Delta F(\{\alpha\}))$

For example, in the above example (with a Camellia round function), it is possible to use a meet-in-the-middle approach. First, apply the inverse linear transformation on ω, and obtain the required output differences in every S-box of the second $F(\cdot)$. Then, by trying all 128 values of $\Delta F(\{\alpha\})$ one can check whether the difference distribution table of the S-box offers this transition.

4.4 Changes to the Matrix Method

We note that it is possible to extend the matrix method of [10] such that it would suggest impossible differentials of the above structure. The main idea behind the change is to know for each non-fixed input difference the size of the set of possible differences.

The simplest change would be to store for each initial state the size of possible differences (which is 1 for each word, either active or not). Then, when an active word passes through the round function, the size of the set is increased by a factor of c, the differential expansion rate of the round function. Finally, when XORing two active thread, one with t_1 options, and one with t_2 options, the number of possible differences in the output is at most $t_1 \cdot t_2$.

In the step when we look for contradictions, we first search for the previous class of contradictions. Then, we also look for pairs of words, one in Δ_A (with t_1 options) and one in Δ_B (with t_2 options), such that $t_1 \cdot t_2 < 2^w$, as for such words, it is probable that the differences cannot coexist (the probability for contradiction is $1 - t_1 \cdot t_2/2^w$).

4.5 A 7-Round Impossible Differentials for Feistel Block Ciphers with Small Differential Expansion Rate

For some block ciphers with small differential expansion rate (or whose round function allows selecting such differences), it is possible to suggest a 7-round impossible differential. The impossible differential is based on two truncated differentials of three rounds each $(\alpha, 0) \rightarrow_3 (\{X\}, ?)$ and $(\{Y\}, ?) \leftarrow_3 (\omega, 0)$, where

$$\{X\} = \{\alpha \oplus \beta | \beta \in \Delta F(\Delta F(\{\alpha\}))\}$$

and

$$\{Y\} = \{\omega \oplus \psi | \psi \in \Delta F(\Delta F(\{\omega\}))\}.$$

If the differential expansion rate of the round function is smaller than $2^{w/4}$, then it is expected that $|\{X\}| \cdot |\{Y\}| < 2^n$, which means that there are combinations of X and Y which cannot coexist. We note that this impossible differential does not assume that the round function is bijective. We note that the 7-round impossible differential of DES mentioned in [4] can be found using this approach (when starting with α and ω for which there is only one active S-box).

5 New Attacks Using the New Impossible Differentials

Given the new impossible differentials, we need to show that they can be used for the analysis of block ciphers. As mentioned before, our impossible differentials are more restricted than the previous ones, and thus they may be of a lesser usage in attacks.

To show the contrary, we consider an attack which uses the 16-round impossible differential on 4-thread CAST-like structure and compare it to a similar attack the uses the original 15-round impossible differential. As before, for simplicity, we shall consider round functions of the form $F_k(x) = G(x \oplus k)$, which are very common in block ciphers.

We first note that both the 16-round impossible differential and the 15-round impossible differential share the same structure, i.e., $(0, 0, 0, \alpha) \not\rightarrow (\omega, 0, 0, 0)$. Hence, the use of structures and early abort in the attacks is (almost) the same.

In Figure 6 we compare the 16-round attacks using the 15-round impossible differential (there are two variants, in one the additional round is before the impossible differential, and in the second it is after the impossible differential) with the 17-round attacks using the 16-round impossible differential. As can be seen, the attack algorithms are very similar, and the analysis of them is also very similar. For example, the data complexity of the 16-round attack with an additional round after the impossible differential is $2w \cdot 2^{2w}$ chosen plaintexts, while for the equivalent 17-round attack, the data complexity is $4w \cdot 2^{2w}$ chosen plaintexts.[6] We compare the complexities of these attacks in Table 4.

Table 4. Comparison of the complexities of the $(n + 1)$-round attacks

Rounds in Imp. Diff.	Attacked Round	Size of Structures	Complexity Data	Time	Memory
15	After	2^w	$2w \cdot 2^{2w}$	$2w \cdot 2^{2w}$	2^w
	Before	2^{2w}	$w \cdot 2^{2w}$	$w \cdot 2^{2w}$	2^{2w}
16	After	2^w	$4w \cdot 2^{2w}$	$4w \cdot 2^{2w}$	2^w
	Before	2^{2w}	$2w \cdot 2^{2w}$	$2w \cdot 2^{2w}$	2^{2w}

We note that the attack, requires the identification whether $\omega \in \Delta G(\{\alpha\})$. We note that in the worst case, this requires calling $G(\cdot)$ about 2^w times (with all 2^{w-1} pairs of distinct pairs with input difference α). However, the number of candidate α and ω's is about $O(w \cdot 2^w)$ (depending on the attack), whose evaluation is faster than evaluating the full block cipher. Moreover, by collecting the pairs of α, ω, one can check several pairs using the same invocations of $G(\cdot)$, thus incurring very little overhead to the attack.

In cases where α and ω are known, one can discard the pairs for which $\alpha \rightsquigarrow \omega$ beforehand, and repeat the same steps as in the original attack. This allows extending previous attacks by one more round, in exchange for at most twice the data and time. In other cases, where there are more candidate pairs, and when α and ω cannot be determined directly from the plaintext/ciphertext pairs, one can postpone the verification whether $\omega \notin \Delta G(\{\alpha\})$, to the step just before discarding the full subkey. If such an attack uses an early abort approach (i.e., stops the analysis of a pair immediately as it found to be useless), it is possible

[6] This assumption is made under the worst case assumption, where the function $G(\cdot)$ is an almost perfect nonlinear permutation (for which half of the input/output differences α and ω satisfy that $\omega \in \Delta G(\{\alpha\})$).

16-Round Attacks	17-Round Attacks
– Pick structures of the form $(A_i, B_i, C_i, \star)$ (where A_i, B_i, C_i are fixed in the structure), and ask for their encryption.	– Pick structures of the form $(A, B, C, \star)$ (where A_i, B_i, C_i are fixed in the structure), and ask for their encryption.
– Locate in each structure (independently) ciphertext pairs whose difference is $(\psi, 0, 0, \omega)$.	– Locate in each structure (independently) ciphertext pairs whose difference is $(\psi, 0, 0, \omega)$, and denote their plaintext difference by $(0, 0, 0, \alpha)$.
	– If $\omega \in \Delta F(\{\alpha\})$, discard the pair.
– For each remaining pair, discard any subkey K_{16} that suggest that the difference before the last round is $(\omega, 0, 0, 0)$.	– For each remaining pair, discard any subkey K_{17} that suggest that the difference before the last round is $(\omega, 0, 0, 0)$.
– Pick structures of the form $(\star, \star, C_i, D_i)$ (where C_i, D_i are fixed in the structure), and ask for their encryption.	– Pick structures of the form $(\star, \star, C_i, D_i)$ (where C_i, D_i are fixed in the structure), and ask for their encryption.
– Locate in each structure (independently) ciphertext pairs whose difference is $(\omega, 0, 0, 0)$, and their plaintext difference is $(\alpha, \beta, 0, 0)$.	– Locate in each structure (independently) ciphertext pairs whose difference is $(\omega, 0, 0, 0)$, and their plaintext difference is $(\alpha, \beta, 0, 0)$.
	– If $\omega \in \Delta F(\{\alpha\})$, discard the pair.
– For each remaining pair, discard any subkey K_1 that suggest that the difference after the first round is $(0, 0, 0, \alpha)$.	– For each remaining pair, discard any subkey K_1 that suggest that the difference after the first round is $(0, 0, 0, \alpha)$.

Fig. 6. Attacks of $(n + 1)$ rounds using an n-round impossible differentials

to show that performing this check only when ω and α are both known, again increases the data and time by a factor of two at most.

We conclude that the new attacks are indeed one round longer (when the impossible differential is one round longer), and can be made longer, depending on the exact impossible differential. At the same time, the data and time complexities of the attacks increase by at most factor of two (the accurate increase is the $1/p$ where p is the ratio of non-zero entries in the difference distribution of $G(\cdot)$).

Finally, we note that when more complex impossible differentials are used, the same results apply, as long as the differential expansion rate of $G(\cdot)$ is small enough, or in the cases where the structure of $G(\cdot)$ allows quick verification of the existence of contradiction.

6 Summary and Conclusions

In this paper we show how to extend several impossible differentials for generalized Feistel schemes by one or more round, using a more subtle analysis of the round function. We follow and show that attacks which are based on these new impossible differentials require almost the same data and time complexity as the previous attacks, which proves that these impossible differentials are not only of theoretical interest, but can also be used in the analysis of block ciphers.

The new measure we introduced, the differential expansion rate of a round function, is expected to motivate block ciphers designers to re-think some of the basic approaches in block cipher design. For example, it is commonly believed that even if only a small amount of nonlinearity is used in the round function, then the cipher can still be secure. While this belief is not necessarily contradicted by our findings, we do show that it is possible to exploit this small nonlinearity in more complex attacks, such as impossible differential attacks, a combination that was not suggested before.

Additionally, our results may suggest that constructions which take the opposite approach than MARS, i.e., strong outer rounds with weaker inner rounds, may be susceptible to impossible differential attacks. This follows the fact that the development of difference sets that interest us, happen not in the outer rounds, but instead in the inner rounds.

Acknowledgements. We are grateful to the *Lesamnta* team, and especially to Hirotaka Yoshida, for helping us with this research. We would also like to thank Nathan Keller and Adi Shamir for the fruitful discussions and comments.

References

1. Adams, C., Heys, H., Tavares, S., Wiener, M.: The CAST-256 Encryption Algorithm (1998); AES Submission
2. Aoki, K., Ichikawa, T., Kanda, M., Matsui, M., Moriai, S., Nakajima, J., Tokita, T.: *Camellia*: A 128-Bit Block Cipher Suitable for Multiple Platforms - Design and Analysis. In: Stinson, D.R., Tavares, S. (eds.) SAC 2000. LNCS, vol. 2012, pp. 39–56. Springer, Heidelberg (2001)
3. Biham, E., Biryukov, A., Shamir, A.: Cryptanalysis of Skipjack Reduced to 31 Rounds Using Impossible Differentials. In: Stern, J. (ed.) EUROCRYPT 1999. LNCS, vol. 1592, pp. 12–23. Springer, Heidelberg (1999)
4. Biham, E., Biryukov, A., Shamir, A.: Miss in the Middle Attacks on IDEA and Khufu. In: Knudsen, L.R. (ed.) FSE 1999. LNCS, vol. 1636, pp. 124–138. Springer, Heidelberg (1999)
5. Biham, E., Shamir, A.: Differential Cryptanalysis of the Data Encryption Standard. Springer, Heidelberg (1993)

6. Burwick, C., Coppersmith, D., D'Avignon, E., Gennaro, R., Halevi, S., Jutla, C., Matyas Jr., S.M., O'Connor, L., Peyravian, M., Safford, D., Zunic, N.: MARS - a candidate cipher for AES (1998); AES submission
7. Choy, J., Yap, H.: Impossible Boomerang Attack for Block Cipher Structures. In: Takagi, T., Mambo, M. (eds.) IWSEC 2009. LNCS, vol. 5824, pp. 22–37. Springer, Heidelberg (2009)
8. Daemen, J., Rijmen, V.: AES Proposal: Rijndael (1998); NIST AES proposal
9. Keliher, L., Sui, J.: Exact Maximum Expected Differential and Linear Probability for 2-Round Advanced Encryption Standard (AES) (2005); IACR ePrint report 2005/321
10. Kim, J., Hong, S., Lim, J.: Impossible differential cryptanalysis using matrix method. Discrete Mathematics 310(5), 988–1002 (2010)
11. Kim, J., Hong, S., Sung, J., Lee, S., Lim, J., Sung, S.: Impossible Differential Cryptanalysis for Block Cipher Structures. In: Johansson, T., Maitra, S. (eds.) INDOCRYPT 2003. LNCS, vol. 2904, pp. 82–96. Springer, Heidelberg (2003)
12. Knudsen, L.R.: Deal — A 128-bit Block Cipher (1998); AES submission
13. Luo, Y., Wu, Z., Lai, X., Gong, G.: A Unified Method for Finding Impossible Differentials of Block Cipher Structures (2009); IACR ePrint report 2009/627
14. Nyberg, K.: Generalized Feistel Networks. In: Kim, K., Matsumoto, T. (eds.) ASIACRYPT 1996. LNCS, vol. 1163, pp. 91–104. Springer, Heidelberg (1996)
15. O'Connor, L.: On the Distribution of Characteristics in Bijective Mappings. In: Helleseth, T. (ed.) EUROCRYPT 1993. LNCS, vol. 765, pp. 360–370. Springer, Heidelberg (1994)
16. Pudovkina, M.: On Impossible Truncated Differentials of Generalized Feistel and Skipjack Ciphers. Presented at the Rump Session of the FSE 2009 Workshop (2009), `http://fse2009rump.cr.yp.to/e31bba5d1227eac5ef0daa6bcbf66f27.pdf`
17. Rivest, R.L., Robshaw, M.J., Sidney, R., Yin, Y.L.: The RC6 Block Cipher (1998); AES submission
18. US Government: SKIPJACK and KEA Algorithm Specification (1998)
19. US National Institute of Standards and Technology: Advanced Encryption Standard (2001); Federal Information Processing Standards Publications No. 197

A Unified Framework for Small Secret Exponent Attack on RSA

Noboru Kunihiro[1], Naoyuki Shinohara[2], and Tetsuya Izu[3]

[1] The University of Tokyo, Japan
kunihiro@k.u-tokyo.ac.jp
[2] NICT, Japan
[3] Fujitsu Labs, Japan

Abstract. We address a lattice based method on small secret exponent attack on RSA scheme. Boneh and Durfee reduced the attack into finding small roots of a bivariate modular equation: $x(N+1+y)+1 \equiv 0(\mod\ e)$, where N is an RSA moduli and e is the RSA public key. Boneh and Durfee proposed a lattice based algorithm for solving the problem. When the secret exponent d is less than $N^{0.292}$, their method breaks RSA scheme. Since the lattice used in the analysis is not full-rank, the analysis is not easy. Blömer and May gave an alternative algorithm. Although their bound $d \leq N^{0.290}$ is worse than Boneh–Durfee result, their method used a full rank lattice. However, the proof for their bound is still complicated. Herrmann and May gave an elementary proof for the Boneh–Durfee's bound: $d \leq N^{0.292}$. In this paper, we first give an elementary proof for achieving the bound of Blömer–May: $d \leq N^{0.290}$. Our proof employs unravelled linearization technique introduced by Herrmann and May and is rather simpler than Blömer–May's proof. Then, we provide a unified framework to construct a lattice that are used for solving the problem, which includes two previous method: Herrmann–May and Blömer–May methods as a special case. Furthermore, we prove that the bound of Boneh–Durfee: $d \leq N^{0.292}$ is still optimal in our unified framework.

Keywords: LLL algorithm, small inverse problem, RSA, lattice-based cryptanalysis.

1 Introduction

RSA cryptosystem is the widely used cryptosystem [12]. Let N be an RSA moduli and d be an RSA secret key. The small secret exponent d is often used to speed up the decryption or signature generation in some cryptographic applications. However, it is well known that RSA scheme is easily broken if secret exponent d is small.

In 1990, Wiener [14] showed that RSA scheme is broken by using continued fraction expansion when $d < \frac{1}{3}N^{1/4}$. In 1999, Boneh and Durfee reduced the small secret exponent attack into finding small roots of a bivariate modular equation: $x(A + y) \equiv 1(\mod e)$ and then proposed two algorithms for solving the problem [2]. They referred to the problem as the small inverse problem. Their

A. Miri and S. Vaudenay (Eds.): SAC 2011, LNCS 7118, pp. 260–277, 2012.

algorithms are based on Coppersmith's approach [3,4,5]. Their first algorithm breaks RSA scheme when $d \leq N^{0.284}$. Then, they presented another algorithm for solving the small inverse problem and improved the bound to $d \leq N^{0.292}$. It employed a non-full rank lattice for improving the bound. Evaluation of a volume of non-full rank lattice was needed in evaluating the bound, which is not so easy task in general. To overcome this difficulty, they introduced a concept of "Geometrically Progressive Matrix" and succeeded to evaluate an upper bound of its volume [2]. However, its proof is rather complicated.

In 2001, Blömer and May proposed another algorithm for solving the small inverse problem [1]. When $d \leq N^{0.290}$, their method solves the small inverse problem. One of good properties is that the lattice used in their method is full rank. However, the analysis for bound is still complicated. In 2010, Herrmann and May [7] presented another algorithm which achieves Boneh–Durfee's improved bound: $d \leq N^{0.292}$. In their proof, they employed unravelled linearization technique introduced in Asiacrypt2009 [6]. As opposed to the Boneh–Durfee's method, their method used a full rank lattice.

1.1 Our Contributions

In this paper, we first give a novel method for achieving the bound of Blömer–May by using unravelled linearization technique, which is also used in the proof of Herrmann–May. We use the same set of shift-polynomials as Blömer–May's and show that our method achieves the same bound as that of Blömer–May: $d \leq N^{0.290}$. Nevertheless, our proof is rather simpler than Blömer–May's original proof. Next, we provide a unified framework which includes two previous methods: Herrmann–May's and Blömer–May's as a special case. Our framework captures well the lattice structure in the previous methods. Then, we derive a condition such that the small inverse problem can be solved in polynomial time and make an optimization in our framework. Since our framework includes Herrmann–May's method, we have a chance to go beyond the Boneh–Durfee's bound: $d \leq N^{0.292}$. Unfortunately, that does not happen. We prove that the bound $d \leq N^{0.292}$ is still optimal in our framework (Theorem 3). Then, we present a hybrid method which enjoys the both advantages of Herrmann–May's and Blömer–May's methods. Finally, we generalize to the case when the upper bound of solution y is much smaller than $e^{1/2}$. We show that Blömer–May's method can be superior to Boneh–Durfee's method and is optimal in our framework (Theorem 4).

2 Preliminaries

First, we briefly recall the LLL algorithm and Howgrave-Graham's lemma. Then, we review the small secret exponent attack on RSA cryptosystem [2] and introduce the "small inverse problem." Then, we explain previous algorithms for solving the small inverse problem.

2.1 The LLL Algorithm and Howgrave-Graham's Lemma

For a vector $\boldsymbol{b}$, $||\boldsymbol{b}||$ denotes the Euclidean norm of $\boldsymbol{b}$. For an n-variate polynomial $h(x_1,\ldots,x_n) = \sum h_{j_1,\ldots,j_n} x_1^{j_1} \cdots x_n^{j_n}$, define the norm of a polynomial as $||h(x_1,\ldots,x_n)|| = \sqrt{\sum h_{j_1,\ldots,j_n}^2}$. That is, $||h(x_1,\ldots,x_n)||$ denotes the Euclidean norm of the vector which consists of coefficients of $h(x_1,\ldots,x_n)$.

Let $B = \{a_{ij}\}$ be a non-singular $w \times w$ square matrix of integers. The rows of B generate a lattice L, a collection of vectors closed under addition and subtraction; in fact the rows forms a basis of L. The lattice L is also represented as follows. Letting $\boldsymbol{a_i} = (a_{i1}, a_{i2}, \ldots, a_{iw})$, the lattice L spanned by $\langle \boldsymbol{a_1}, \ldots, \boldsymbol{a_w} \rangle$ consists of all integral linear combinations of $\boldsymbol{a_1}, \ldots, \boldsymbol{a_w}$, that is:

$$L = \left\{ \sum_{i=1}^{w} n_i \boldsymbol{a_i} | n_i \in \mathbb{Z} \right\}.$$

The volume of full-rank lattice is defined by $\mathrm{vol}(L) = |\det(B)|$.

The LLL algorithm outputs short vectors in a lattice L:

Proposition 1 (LLL [10]). *Let $B = \{a_{ij}\}$ be a non-singular $w \times w$ matrix of integers. The rows of B generate a lattice L. Given B, the LLL algorithm finds vectors $\boldsymbol{b_1}, \boldsymbol{b_2} \in L$ such that*

$$||\boldsymbol{b_1}|| \leq 2^{(w-1)/4} (\mathrm{vol}(L))^{1/w}, ||\boldsymbol{b_2}|| \leq 2^{w/4} (\mathrm{vol}(L))^{1/(w-1)}$$

in time polynomial in $(w, \max \log_2 |a_{ij}|)$.

To convert the modular equation into an equation over the integers, we use the following lemma.

Lemma 1 (Howgrave-Graham [8]). *Let $\hat{h}(x,y,z) \in \mathbb{Z}[x,y,z]$ be a polynomial, which is a sum of at most w monomials. Let m be a positive integer and X, Y, Z and ϕ be some positive integers. Suppose that*

1. *$\hat{h}(\bar{x}, \bar{y}, \bar{z}) = 0 \bmod \phi^m$, where $\bar{x}, \bar{y}$ and $\bar{z}$ are integers such that $|\bar{x}| < X, |\bar{y}| < Y, |\bar{z}| < Z$.*
2. *$||\hat{h}(xX, yY, zZ)|| < \phi^m / \sqrt{w}$.*

Then $\hat{h}(\bar{x}, \bar{y}, \bar{z}) = 0$ holds over integers.

2.2 Small Inverse Problem [2]

Let (N, e) be a public key in RSA cryptosystem, where $N = pq$ is the product of two distinct primes. For simplicity, we assume that $\gcd(p-1, q-1) = 2$. A secret key d satisfies that $ed = 1 \bmod (p-1)(q-1)/2$. Hence, there exists an integer k such that $ed + k((N+1)/2 - (p+q)/2) = 1$. Writing $s = -(p+q)/2$ and $A = (N+1)/2$, we have $k(A+s) = 1 \pmod{e}$.

We set $f(x,y) = x(A+y) + 1$. Note that the solution of $f(x,y) \equiv 0 (\bmod\ e)$ is $(x,y) = (-k, s)$. If one can solve a bivariate modular equation: $f(x,y) = x(A+y) + 1 = 0 \pmod{e}$, one has k and s and knows the prime factors p and

q of N by solving an equation: $v^2 + 2sv + N = 0$. Suppose that the secret key satisfies $d \leq N^{\delta}$. Further assume that $e \approx N$. To summarize, the secret key will be recovered by finding the solution $(x, y) = (\bar{x}, \bar{y})$ of the equation:

$$f(x, y) = x(A + y) + 1 \equiv 0 \pmod{e},$$

where $|\bar{x}| < e^{\delta}$ and $|\bar{y}| < e^{1/2}$. They referred to this as the *small inverse problem.*

2.3 Known Algorithms for Solving Small Inverse Problem

Boneh and Durfee proposed a lattice-based algorithm for solving the small inverse problem [2]. First, we briefly recall the algorithm though we use different symbols from the original description.

They define the polynomials $g_{[i,j]}(x, y) := x^i f(x, y)^j e^{m-j}$ and $h_{[i,u]}(x, y) := y^i f(x, y)^u e^{m-u}$. The $g_{[i,j]}$ polynomials are referred as x-shifts and the $h_{[i,u]}$ polynomials are referred as y-shifts. Let $\mathcal{F}_{\mathrm{BD}}(m; \tau)$ be a set of shift-polynomials. The set $\mathcal{F}_{\mathrm{BD}}(m; \tau)$ is given by $\mathcal{F}_{\mathrm{BD}}(m; \tau) := \mathcal{G}_{\mathrm{BD}}(m) \cup \mathcal{H}_{\mathrm{BD}}(m; \tau)$, where

$$\mathcal{G}_{\mathrm{BD}}(m) := \{g_{[u-i,i]} | u = 0, \ldots, m; i = 0, \ldots, u\} \text{ and}$$
$$\mathcal{H}_{\mathrm{BD}}(m; \tau) := \{h_{[i,u]} | u = 0, \ldots, m; i = 1, \ldots, \tau m\}.$$

They achieved a bound: $d \leq N^{0.284}$ using $\mathcal{F}_{\mathrm{BD}}(m; \tau)$. We refer to this method as Boneh–Durfee's weaker method. Then, Boneh and Durfee improved the bound to $d \leq N^{0.292}$ by removing y-shift polynomials whose coefficient of leading term exceeds e^m. The resulting lattice is not full rank and computing its volume is not easy. To overcome this difficulty, they introduced a concept of "Geometrically Progressive Matrix" and succeeded to obtain an upper bound of the volume. The analysis for its bound, especially its volume evaluation, is rather complicated.

Blömer and May [1] presented another algorithm. Although the bound: $d \leq N^{0.290}$ is worse than Boneh–Durfee's bound, their method has several interesting features. The first is that it requires a smaller lattice dimension for solving the problem. The second is that the involved lattice is full rank and the analysis for the bound is simpler than Boneh–Durfee's. However, the evaluation of bound is still complicated.

Herrmann and May [7] proposed a novel method which achieves the bound: $d \leq N^{0.292}$ by employing unravelled linearization technique. We briefly recall Herrmann–May's method. Note that we use different notation from the original description of [7]. First, $f(x, y)$ is transformed into $f(x, y) = x(A+y)+1 = (xy+1)+Ax$. The first step of their method is to perform a linearization of $f(x, y)$ into $\bar{f}(x, z) := z + Ax$ by setting $xy + 1 = z$. In a second step of analysis, xy is back-substituted by $xy = z - 1$ for each occurrence of xy. They define the polynomials as $\bar{g}_{[i,j]}(x, z) := x^i \bar{f}(x, z)^j e^{m-j}$ and $\bar{h}_{[i,u]}(x, y, z) := y^i \bar{f}(x, z)^u e^{m-u}$. Let τ be an optimization parameter with $0 < \tau \leq 1$. Let $\mathcal{F}_{\mathrm{HM}}(m; \tau)$ be a set of shift-polynomials. The $\mathcal{F}_{\mathrm{HM}}(m; \tau)$ is given by $\mathcal{F}_{\mathrm{HM}}(m; \tau) := \mathcal{G}_{\mathrm{HM}}(m) \cup \mathcal{H}_{\mathrm{HM}}(m; \tau)$, where

$$\mathcal{G}_{\mathrm{HM}}(m) := \{\bar{g}_{[u-i,i]} | u = 0, \ldots, m; i = 0, \ldots, u\} \text{ and}$$
$$\mathcal{H}_{\mathrm{HM}}(m;\tau) := \{\bar{h}_{[i,u]} | u = 0, \ldots, m; i = 1, \ldots, \tau u\}.$$

They achieved the bound: $d \leq N^{0.292}$ using $\mathcal{F}_{\mathrm{HM}}(m;\tau)$. Note that its lattice is also full rank.

3 A New Proof for Bound of Blömer–May: $d \leq N^{0.290}$

Blömer and May [1] presented the algorithm which achieves the bound: $d \leq N^{0.290}$. Although this bound is worse than the result of Boneh–Durfee, it has a desirable property. Since it uses full-rank lattice, the analysis for bound is rather easy. On the other hand, Herrmann and May [7] presented the algorithm which achieves $d \leq N^{0.292}$ by using unravelled linearization technique. In this section, we provide a new proof for the bound of Blömer–May: $d \leq N^{0.290}$ by using unravelled linearization technique as like as the proof of Herrmann–May.

3.1 A Set of Shift-Polynomials

First, we transform $f(x,y) = x(A+y)+1$ into $f(x,y) = (xy+1)+Ax$. We define $z = xy+1$ and

$$\bar{f}(x,z) := z + Ax$$

as well as Herrmann and May method [7]. Note that the term xy will be replaced by $xy = z-1$ for each occurrence of xy in the consequent analysis.

We define shift-polynomials as follows. For x-shifts, we define

$$\bar{g}_{[i,k]}(x,z) := x^i \bar{f}(x,z)^k e^{m-k}.$$

Let $\bar{z} = \bar{x}\bar{y}+1$. It is easy to see that $\bar{g}_{[i,k]}(\bar{x},\bar{z}) = 0(\bmod\ e^m)$ for any non-negative integers i and k. The upper bound of $|\bar{z}|$ is given by $XY+1$ and then we define $Z = XY+1$.

For y-shifts, we set

$$\bar{h}_{[i,k]}(x,y,z) := y^i \bar{f}(x,z)^k e^{m-k}.$$

It is easy to see that $\bar{h}_{[i,k]}(\bar{x},\bar{y},\bar{z}) = 0(\bmod\ e^m)$ for any non-negative integers i and k.

Remark 1. From the definition, it holds that $\bar{g}_{[0,u]}(x,z) = \bar{h}_{[0,u]}(x,y,z)$.

Next, we fix a set of indexes for shift-polynomials. Let t be a parameter which is optimized later with $0 \leq t \leq m$. Let $\mathcal{F}_{\mathrm{BM}}(m;t)$ be a set of shift-polynomials. The set $\mathcal{F}_{\mathrm{BM}}(m;t)$ is given by $\mathcal{F}_{\mathrm{BM}}(m;t) := \mathcal{G}_{\mathrm{BM}}(m;t) \cup \mathcal{H}_{\mathrm{BM}}(m;t)$, where

$$\mathcal{G}_{\mathrm{BM}}(m;t) := \{\bar{g}_{[u-i,i]} | u = m-t, \ldots, m; i = 0, \ldots, u\} \text{ and}$$
$$\mathcal{H}_{\mathrm{BM}}(m;t) := \{\bar{h}_{[i,u]} | u = m-t, \ldots, m; i = 1, \ldots, t-(m-u)\}.$$

Then, we define a polynomial order $\preceq$ in $\mathcal{F}_{\rm BM}(m;t)$ as follows:

- $\bar{g}_{[i,j]} \preceq \bar{h}_{[i',u]}$ for any i, j, i', u
- $\bar{g}_{[i,j]} \preceq \bar{g}_{[i',j']}$ if $(i+j < i'+j')$ or $(i+j = i'+j'$ and $j \leq j')$
- $\bar{h}_{[i,u]} \preceq \bar{h}_{[i',u']}$ if $(u < u')$ or $(u = u'$ and $i \leq i')$

We write $a \prec b$ if $a \preceq b$ and $a \neq b$.

Regarding the set $\mathcal{F}_{\rm BM}(m;t)$ for shift-polynomials and the above polynomial order, we have the following two lemmas.

Lemma 2. *If* $\bar{g}_{[u-j,j]} \in \mathcal{F}_{\rm BM}(m;t)$ *for* $j \geq 1$*, then* $\bar{g}_{[u-j+1,j-1]} \in \mathcal{F}_{\rm BM}(m;t)$ *and* $\bar{g}_{[u-j+1,j-1]} \prec \bar{g}_{[u-j,j]}$.

Lemma 3. *If* $\bar{h}_{[j,u]} \in \mathcal{F}_{\rm BM}(m;t)$*, then* $\bar{h}_{[j-1,u]}$ *and* $\bar{h}_{[j-1,u-1]} \in \mathcal{F}_{\rm BM}(m;t)$*. Furthermore, it holds that* $\bar{h}_{[j-1,u]} \prec \bar{h}_{[j,u]}$ *and* $\bar{h}_{[j-1,u-1]} \prec \bar{h}_{[j,u]}$.

Proof of Lemma 3. It is clear that $\bar{h}_{[j-1,u]} \in \mathcal{F}_{\rm BM}(m;t)$. Note that we can $\bar{g}_{[0,u]}$ instead of $\bar{h}_{[0,u]}$ since $\bar{h}_{[0,u]}$ and $\bar{g}_{[0,u]}$ are identical from Remark 1. Since $\bar{h}_{[j,u]} \in \mathcal{F}_{\rm BM}(m;t)$, it holds that $1 \leq j \leq u+t-m$. Then, $0 \leq j-1 \leq (u-1)+t-m$. Hence, it holds that $\bar{h}_{[j-1,u-1]} \in \mathcal{F}_{\rm BM}(m;t)$. □

3.2 Expansions of Shift-Polynomials

First, we introduce some definitions.

Definition 1. *We denote by* $\mathcal{S}(f)$ *a set of monomials appearing in expansion of* f.

Note that a monomial $x^i y^j z^k$ with $i, j \geq 1$ never appears in $\mathcal{S}(h_{[i,j]}(x,y,z))$ since we replace xy by $xy = z-1$. Hence, only the terms $x^i z^k$ and $y^j z^k$ appear in the expansion of shift-polynomials.

Definition 2. *We say* $f(x,y,z) \cong g(x,y,z)$ *if* $\mathcal{S}(f) = \mathcal{S}(g)$.

A lattice basis is constructed by using the coefficient vectors of shift-polynomials in $\mathcal{F}_{\rm BM}(m;t)$ as basis vectors. Note that the coefficient vectors of the shift-polynomials $g_{[u-i,i]}(xX, zZ)$ and $h_{[i,u]}(xX, yY, zZ)$ are written as row vectors. Let $B_{\rm BM}(m;t)$ be a matrix, where all rows of $B_{\rm BM}(m;t)$ are the coefficient vectors of shift-polynomials according to the ordering of $\mathcal{F}_{\rm BM}(m;t)$.

Theorem 1. *Let* m *and* t *be integers with* $t \leq m$*. A lattice basis matrix* $B_{\rm BM}(m;t)$ *is triangular for any* m *and* t.

Before giving a proof, we give three lemmas, whose proofs are given in Appendix A.1.

Lemma 4. *If* $0 \leq u \leq m$, $\mathcal{S}(\bar{g}_{[u,0]} - e^m x^u) = \emptyset$.

Lemma 5. *If* $0 \leq u \leq m$ *and* $1 \leq j \leq u$, $\mathcal{S}(\bar{g}_{[u-j,j]} - e^{m-j} x^{u-j} z^j) = \mathcal{S}(\bar{g}_{[u-j+1,j-1]})$.

Lemma 6. *If* $1 \le u \le m$ *and* $i \ge 1$, $\mathcal{S}(\bar{h}_{[i,u]} - e^{m-u}y^i z^u) \subseteq \mathcal{S}(\bar{h}_{[i-1,u-1]}) \cup \mathcal{S}(\bar{h}_{[i-1,u]})$.

Proof of Theorem 1. We show that the number of monomials newly appearing in expansion of shift-polynomial is one for any shift-polynomials in $\mathcal{F}_{\mathrm{BM}}(m;t)$. In this proof, we abbreviate $\mathcal{F}_{\mathrm{BM}}(m;t)$ as $\mathcal{F}$. We define $\mathcal{F}^f := \{g \in \mathcal{F} | g \prec f\}$ and $\mathcal{S}(\mathcal{F}^f) := \bigcup_{g \in \mathcal{F}^f} \mathcal{S}(g)$. It is enough for proving Theorem 1 to show that for any polynomial $f \in \mathcal{F}$ there exist a monomial m_f such that

- $\mathcal{S}(f - m_f) \subseteq \mathcal{S}(\mathcal{F}^f)$ and
- $m_f \notin \mathcal{S}(\mathcal{F}^f)$.

From Lemmas 2–3 and 4–6, for any $f \in \mathcal{F}$, there exists m_f such that $\mathcal{S}(f - m_f) \subseteq \mathcal{S}(\mathcal{F}^f)$. We can easily verify that $m_f \notin \mathcal{S}(\mathcal{F}^f)$. Then, the lattice basis matrix is triangular. □

We show an example for $m = 2$. We consider $\bar{g}_{[1,2]}(x,z)$. The expansion of $\bar{g}_{[1,2]}(x,z)$ is given by $x^1(z+Ax)^2 = xz^2 + 2Ax^2z + A^2x^3$. Since $\bar{g}_{[1,2]}(x,z) - xz^2 = 2Ax^2z + A^2x^3$, it holds that $\mathcal{S}(\bar{g}_{[1,2]} - xz^2) = \{x^2z, x^3\}$. On the other hand, since $\bar{g}_{[2,1]} = ex^2(z + Ax) = ex^2z + eAx^3$, it holds that $\mathcal{S}(\bar{g}_{[2,1]}) = \{x^2z, x^3\}$. Then, $\mathcal{S}(\bar{g}_{[1,2]} - xz^2) = \mathcal{S}(\bar{g}_{[2,1]})$ and Lemma 5 holds. We'll show another example. We consider $\bar{h}_{[2,2]}(x,y,z)$. The expansion of $\bar{h}_{[2,2]}(x,y,z)$ is given by $y^2(z + Ax)^2 = y^2z^2 + 2Axy^2z + A^2(xy)^2 = y^2z^2 + 2Ay(z-1)z + A^2(z-1)^2 = y^2z^2 + 2Ayz^2 - 2Ayz + A^2z^2 - 2A^2z + A^2$. Then, we have $\mathcal{S}(\bar{h}_{[2,2]} - y^2z^2) = \{yz^2, yz, z^2, z, 1\}$. On the other hand, since $\bar{h}_{[1,1]} = ey(z + Ax) = eyz + Aexy = eyz + Ae(z-1) = eyz + Aez - Ae$, we have $\mathcal{S}(\bar{h}_{[1,1]}) = \{yz, z, 1\}$. Furthermore, we have $\bar{h}_{[1,2]} = y(z + Ax)^2 = y(z^2 + 2Axz + A^2x^2) = yz^2 + 2Axyz + A^2x^2y = yz^2 + 2A(z-1)z + A^2x(z-1) = yz^2 + 2Az^2 - 2Az + A^2xz - A^2x$. Hence, we have $\mathcal{S}(\bar{h}_{[1,2]}) = \{yz^2, z^2, z, xz, x\}$. Then, it holds that $\mathcal{S}(\bar{h}_{[2,2]} - y^2z^2) = \{yz^2, yz, z^2, z, 1\} \subseteq \mathcal{S}(\bar{h}_{[1,1]}) \cup \mathcal{S}(\bar{h}_{[1,2]}) = \{yz^2, yz, z^2, z, xz, x, 1\}$ and Lemma 6 holds.

3.3 Deriving the Bound of Blömer–May: $d \le N^{0.290}$

A lattice basis is constructed by using coefficient vectors of x-shifts $\bar{g}_{[i,k]}(xX, zZ)$ in $\mathcal{G}_{\mathrm{BM}}(m;t)$ and y-shifts $\bar{h}_{[j,u]}(xX, yY, zZ)$ in $\mathcal{H}_{\mathrm{BM}}(m;t)$. We denote the number of shift-polynomials used in x-shifts and y-shifts by w_x and w_y, respectively. We also denote contributions in x-shifts and y-shifts to lattice volume by $\mathrm{vol}(L_X)$ and $\mathrm{vol}(L_Y)$, respectively. The total number of shift-polynomials w is given by $w = w_x + w_y$ and a lattice volume $\mathrm{vol}(L)$ is given by $\mathrm{vol}(L) = \mathrm{vol}(L_X)\mathrm{vol}(L_Y)$.

First, we derive w_x and $\mathrm{vol}(L_X)$. The lattice dimension w_x is given by $w_x = \sum_{l=m-t}^{m} \sum_{k=0}^{l} 1$. The volume $\mathrm{vol}(L_X)$ is given by

$$\mathrm{vol}(L_X) = \prod_{l=m-t}^{m} \prod_{k=0}^{l} X^{l-k} Z^k e^{m-k} = e^{mw_x} \prod_{l=m-t}^{m} \prod_{k=0}^{l} X^{l-k} (Z/e)^k.$$

Let $\mathrm{vol}(L_X) = e^{mw_x} X^{s_{XX}} (Z/e)^{s_{XZ}}$. Each s_{XX} and s_{XZ} is explicitly given as follows:

$$s_{XX} = \sum_{l=m-t}^{m} \sum_{k=0}^{l} l - k = \frac{m^3 - (m-t)^3}{6} + o(m^3) = \frac{1-(1-\eta)^3}{6} m^3 + o(m^3)$$

$$s_{XZ} = \sum_{l=m-t}^{m} \sum_{k=0}^{l} k = \frac{m^3 - (m-t)^3}{6} + o(m^3) = \frac{1-(1-\eta)^3}{6} m^3 + o(m^3),$$

where $\eta := t/m$. Then, we have $\mathrm{vol}(L_X) = e^{mw_x} X^{(1-(1-\eta)^3)m^3/6} (Z/e)^{(1-(1-\eta)^3)m^3/6}$.

Second, we derive w_y and $\mathrm{vol}(L_Y)$. The lattice dimension w_y is given by $w_y = \sum_{l=0}^{t} \sum_{j=1}^{l} 1$. The volume $\mathrm{vol}(L_Y)$ is given by

$$\mathrm{vol}(L_Y) = \prod_{l=0}^{t} \prod_{j=1}^{l} Y^j Z^{l+m-t} e^{m-l-m+t} = e^{mw_y} \prod_{l=0}^{t} \prod_{j=1}^{l} Y^j (Z/e)^{l+m-t}.$$

Let $\mathrm{vol}(L_Y) = e^{mw_y} Y^{s_{YY}} (Z/e)^{s_{YZ}}$. Each s_{YY} and s_{YZ} is explicitly given as follows:

$$s_{YY} = \sum_{l=0}^{t} \sum_{j=1}^{l} j = \sum_{l=0}^{t} \frac{l(l+1)}{2} = \frac{t^3}{6} + o(m^3) = \eta^3 \frac{m^3}{6} + o(m^3)$$

$$s_{YZ} = \sum_{l=0}^{t} \sum_{j=1}^{l} l + (m-t) = \frac{t^3}{3} + (m-t)\frac{t^2}{2} + o(m^3) = \eta^2(3-\eta)\frac{m^3}{6} + o(m^3).$$

Then, we have $\mathrm{vol}(L_Y) = e^{mw_y} Y^{\eta^3 m^3/6} (Z/e)^{\eta^2(3-\eta)m^3/6}$.

Summing up the above discussion, we have

$$\mathrm{vol}(L) = \mathrm{vol}(L_X)\mathrm{vol}(L_Y) = e^{mw} X^{(1-(1-\eta)^3)m^3/6} Y^{\eta^3 m^3/6} (Z/e)^{\eta m^3/2}. \quad (1)$$

By combining Proposition 1 and Lemma 1, the condition that the problem can be solved in polynomial time is given by $2^{w/4}\mathrm{vol}(L)^{1/(w-1)} \leq e^m/\sqrt{w}$. By ignoring small terms, we have the condition: $\mathrm{vol}(L) \leq e^{mw}$. From Eq. (1), we have the condition:

$$X^{3-3\eta+\eta^2} Y^{\eta^2} Z^3 \leq e^3. \quad (2)$$

By substituting $Z = XY + 1 \leq 2XY$ and $Y = e^{1/2}$ into Eq. (2) and neglecting small terms which don't depend on e, we have the following inequality about X:

$$X < e^{\frac{3-\eta^2}{2(6-3\eta+\eta^2)}}.$$

The maximum value of the exponent part in the right hand side is given by $(\sqrt{6}-1)/5 \approx 0.290$ when $\eta = 3 - \sqrt{6} \approx 0.55$. This is exactly the same as the bound of Blömer–May [1].

4 A Unified Framework for Solving Small Inverse Problem

As we showed in previous section, the Blömer–May method [1] can be explained by unravelled linearization technique. It is natural to think that Herrmann–May method [7] and Blömer–May method [1] have some kinds of relation. In this section, we will present an explicit relation and an interpolation between two methods. First, we present a unified framework for solving small inverse problem, which includes Herrmann–May method and Blömer–May method as a special case by adequately setting parameters. Then, we show that Boneh–Durfee's improved bound: $d \leq N^{0.292}$ is still optimal in our framework. Finally, we propose a hybrid method by interpolating two methods, which enjoys the both advantages of two methods.

4.1 A Set of Shift-Polynomials

We define $\bar{g}_{[i,k]}(x, z) := x^i \bar{f}(x, z)^k e^{m-k}$ for x-shifts and $\bar{h}_{[i,u]}(x, y, z) := y^i \bar{f}(x, z)^u e^{m-u}$ for y-shifts, respectively. The above are the same shift-polynomials described in Section 3. However, we use a different set of index for shift-polynomials. Let τ and η be parameters which are optimized later with $0 < \tau \leq 1$ and $0 < \eta \leq 1$.

We define sets $\mathcal{G}(m; \eta), \mathcal{H}(m; \tau, \eta)$ and $\mathcal{F}(m; \tau, \eta)$ of shift-polynomials as follows:

$$\mathcal{G}(m; \eta) := \{\bar{g}_{[u-i,i]} | u = \lceil m(1-\eta) \rceil, \ldots, m; i = 0, \ldots, u\}$$
$$\mathcal{H}(m; \tau, \eta) := \{\bar{h}_{[i,u]} | u = \lceil m(1-\eta) \rceil, \ldots, m; i = 1, \ldots, \lceil \tau(u - m(1-\eta)) \rceil\} \text{ and}$$
$$\mathcal{F}(m; \tau, \eta) := \mathcal{G}(m; \eta) \cup \mathcal{H}(m; \tau, \eta)$$

We define a polynomial order $\preceq$ in $\mathcal{F}(m; \tau, \eta)$ as follows:

- $\bar{g}_{[i,j]} \preceq \bar{h}_{[i',u]}$ for any i, j, i', u
- $\bar{g}_{[i,j]} \preceq \bar{g}_{[i',j']}$ if $(i + j < i' + j')$ or $(i + j = i' + j'$ and $j \leq j')$
- $\bar{h}_{[i,u]} \preceq \bar{h}_{[i',u']}$ if $(u < u')$ or $(u = u'$ and $i \leq i')$

Regarding the set $\mathcal{F}(m; \tau, \eta)$ for shift-polynomials and the above polynomial order, we have the following two lemmas.

Lemma 7. *Suppose that* $0 < \tau \leq 1$. *If* $\bar{g}_{[u-j,j]} \in \mathcal{F}(m; \tau, \eta)$ *for* $j \geq 1$, *then* $\bar{g}_{[u-j+1,j-1]} \in \mathcal{F}(m; \tau, \eta)$ *and* $\bar{g}_{[u-j+1,j-1]} \prec \bar{g}_{[u-j,j]}$.

Lemma 8. *Suppose that* $0 < \tau \leq 1$. *If* $\bar{h}_{[j,u]} \in \mathcal{F}(m; \tau, \eta)$, *then* $\bar{h}_{[j-1,u]}$ *and* $\bar{h}_{[j-1,u-1]} \in \mathcal{F}(m; \tau, \eta)$. *Furthermore, it holds that* $\bar{h}_{[j-1,u]} \prec \bar{h}_{[j,u]}$ *and* $\bar{h}_{[j-1,u-1]} \prec \bar{h}_{[j,u]}$.

Proof of Lemma 8. It is clear that $\bar{h}_{[j-1,u]} \in \mathcal{F}(m; \tau, \eta)$. Since $\bar{h}_{[j,u]} \in \mathcal{F}(m; \tau, \eta)$, it holds that $1 \leq j \leq \tau(u - m(1-\eta))$. Then, $0 \leq j - 1 \leq \tau(u - m(1-\eta)) - 1$. Since $\tau \leq 1$ from the setting, it holds that $\tau(u - m(1-\eta)) - 1 \leq \tau(u - m(1-\eta)) - \tau = \tau((u-1) - m(1-\eta))$. Then, $\bar{h}_{[j-1,u-1]} \in \mathcal{F}(m; \tau, \eta)$. □

Remark 2. If $\tau > 1$, Lemma 8 does not always hold.

We show that our framework includes previous works as special cases. First, we show that our Framework includes Herrmann–May's work [7] as a special case. We gave the set of shift-polynomials $\mathcal{F}_{\mathrm{HM}}(m;\tau)$ for Herrmann–May's method in Section 2.3. From the definition, it holds that

$$\mathcal{F}_{\mathrm{HM}}(m;\tau) = \mathcal{F}(m;\tau,1).$$

Then, Herrmann–May's method is obtained by setting $\eta = 1$ in our unified framework. Next, we show that our Framework includes Blömer–May's work [1] as a special case. We gave the set of shift-polynomials $\mathcal{F}_{\mathrm{BM}}(m;t)$ for Blömer–May's method in Section 3.1. From the definition, it holds that

$$\mathcal{F}_{\mathrm{BM}}(m;t) = \mathcal{F}(m;1,t/m).$$

Note that $t/m \leq 1$ from the definition. Then, Blömer–May's method is obtained by setting $\tau = 1$ in our unified framework.

4.2 Deriving a Condition for Solving Small Inverse Problem in Our Framework

A lattice basis is constructed by using the coefficient vectors of shift-polynomials in $\mathcal{F}(m;\tau,\eta)$ as basis vectors. Note that the coefficient vectors of the shift-polynomials $\bar{g}_{[u-i,i]}(xX,zZ)$ and $\bar{h}_{[i,u]}(xX,yY,zZ)$ are written as row vectors. Let $B(m;\tau,\eta)$ be a matrix, where all rows of $B(m;\tau,\eta)$ are the coefficient vectors of shift-polynomials according to the ordering of $\mathcal{F}(m;\tau,\eta)$.

Theorem 2. *Let m be an integer. Let τ and η be parameters with $0 < \tau \leq 1$ and $0 \leq \eta \leq 1$. A lattice basis matrix $B(m;\tau,\eta)$ is triangular for any m, τ and η.*

Proof of Theorem 2. We show that the number of monomials newly appearing in expansion of shift-polynomial is one for any shift-polynomials in $\mathcal{F}(m;\tau,\eta)$. In this proof, we abbreviate $\mathcal{F}(m;\tau,\eta)$ as $\mathcal{F}$. We define $\mathcal{F}^f := \{g \in \mathcal{F} | g \prec f\}$ and $\mathcal{S}(\mathcal{F}^f) := \bigcup_{g\in\mathcal{F}^f} \mathcal{S}(g)$. It is enough for proving Theorem 2 to show that for any polynomial $f \in \mathcal{F}$ there exist a monomial m_f such that

- $\mathcal{S}(f - m_f) \subseteq \mathcal{S}(\mathcal{F}^f)$ and
- $m_f \notin \mathcal{S}(\mathcal{F}^f)$.

From Lemmas 4–6 and 7–8, for any $f \in \mathcal{F}$, there exists m_f such that $\mathcal{S}(f - m_f) \subseteq \mathcal{S}(\mathcal{F}^f)$. We can easily verify that $m_f \notin \mathcal{S}(\mathcal{F}^f)$. Then, the lattice basis matrix is triangular. □

We show a small example for $m = 3, \tau = 1/2$ and $\eta = 1/3$. We have

$$\mathcal{G}(3;1/3) = \{g_{[u-i,i]} | u = 2,3; i = 0,\ldots,u\} \text{ and}$$
$$\mathcal{H}(3;1/2,1/3) = \{h_{[i,u]} | u = 2,3; i = 1,\ldots,u/2-1\}.$$

or we explicitly have

$$\mathcal{G}(3;1/3)=\{\bar{g}_{[2,0]},\bar{g}_{[1,1]},\bar{g}_{[0,2]},\bar{g}_{[3,0]},\bar{g}_{[2,1]},\bar{g}_{[1,2]},\bar{g}_{[0,3]}\} \text{ and } \mathcal{H}(3;1/2,1/3)=\{\bar{h}_{[1,3]}\}.$$

A lattice basis is constructed by using the coefficients vectors x-shifts $\bar{g}_{[i,j]}(xX,zZ)$ in $\mathcal{G}(3;1/3)$ and y-shifts $\bar{h}_{[i,u]}(xX,yY,zZ)$ in $\mathcal{H}(3;1/2,1/3)$.

$$\begin{array}{c} \\ \hline \bar{g}_{[2,0]} \\ \bar{g}_{[1,1]} \\ \bar{g}_{[0,2]} \\ \bar{g}_{[3,0]} \\ \bar{g}_{[2,1]} \\ \bar{g}_{[1,2]} \\ \bar{g}_{[0,3]} \\ \hline \bar{h}_{[1,3]} \end{array}
\left(\begin{array}{cccccccc}
x^2 & xz & z^2 & x^3 & x^2z & xz^2 & z^3 & yz^3 \\
X^2e^3 & & & & & & & \\
Ae^2X^2 & e^2XZ & & & & & & \\
A^2eX^2 & 2eAXZ & eZ^2 & & & & & \\
 & & & X^3e^3 & & & & \\
 & & & AX^3e^2 & e^2X^2Z & & & \\
 & & & eA^2X^3 & e2AX^2Z & eXZ^2 & & \\
 & & & A^3X^3 & 3A^2X^2Z & 3AXZ^2 & Z^3 & \\
-A^3X^2 & -3A^2XZ & -3AZ^2 & 0 & A^3X^2Z & 3A^2XZ^2 & 3AZ^3 & YZ^3
\end{array}\right)$$

Note that if we expand $\bar{h}_{[1,3]}$ by x and y instead of x and z, many monomials appears. The determinant of the above matrix is given by the product of diagonal elements: $e^{12}X^9Y^1Z^{12}$.

For the following asymptotic analysis, we omit roundings in setting of $\mathcal{F}(m;\tau,\eta)$ as their contribution is negligible for sufficiently large m. We denote by w_x and w_y the number of shift-polynomials used in x-shifts and y-shifts, respectively. And we denote by $\mathrm{vol}(L_X)$ and $\mathrm{vol}(L_Y)$ contributions in x-shifts and y-shifts to a lattice volume, respectively. The total number of shift-polynomials w is given by $w = w_x + w_y$ and a lattice volume $\mathrm{vol}(L)$ is given by $\mathrm{vol}(L) = \mathrm{vol}(L_X)\mathrm{vol}(L_Y)$.

First, we derive w_x and $\mathrm{vol}(L_X)$. The lattice dimension w_x is given by $w_x = \sum_{l=m(1-\eta)}^{m} \sum_{k=0}^{l} 1$. The volume $\mathrm{vol}(L_X)$ is given by

$$\mathrm{vol}(L_X) = \prod_{l=m(1-\eta)}^{m} \prod_{k=0}^{l} X^{l-k}Z^k e^{m-k} = e^{mw_x} \prod_{l=m(1-\eta)}^{m} \prod_{k=0}^{l} X^{l-k}\left(\frac{Z}{e}\right)^k.$$

Let $\mathrm{vol}(L_X) = e^{mw_x}X^{s_{XX}}(Z/e)^{s_{XZ}}$. Each s_{XX} and s_{XZ} is explicitly given as follows:

$$s_{XX} = \sum_{l=m(1-\eta)}^{m} \sum_{k=0}^{l} l-k = \frac{1-(1-\eta)^3}{6}m^3 + o(m^3) \text{ and}$$

$$s_{XZ} = \sum_{l=m(1-\eta)}^{m} \sum_{k=0}^{l} k = \frac{1-(1-\eta)^3}{6}m^3 + o(m^3).$$

Then, we have

$$\mathrm{vol}(L_X) = e^{mw_x}X^{(1-(1-\eta)^3)m^3/6}\left(\frac{Z}{e}\right)^{(1-(1-\eta)^3)m^3/6}.$$

Second, we derive w_y and $\mathrm{vol}(L_Y)$. The lattice dimension w_y is given by $w_y = \sum_{l=0}^{\eta m} \sum_{j=1}^{\tau l} 1$. The volume $\mathrm{vol}(L_Y)$ is given by

$$\mathrm{vol}(L_Y) = \prod_{l=0}^{\eta m} \prod_{j=1}^{\tau l} Y^j Z^{l+m(1-\eta)} e^{m-l-m(1-\eta)} = e^{mw_y} \prod_{l=0}^{\eta m} \prod_{j=1}^{\tau l} Y^j \left(\frac{Z}{e}\right)^{l+m(1-\eta)}.$$

Let $\mathrm{vol}(L_Y) = e^{mw_y} Y^{s_{YY}} (Z/e)^{s_{YZ}}$ Each s_{YY} and s_{YZ} is explicitly given as follows:

$$s_{YY} = \sum_{l=0}^{\eta m} \sum_{j=1}^{\tau l} j = \eta^3 \tau^2 \frac{m^3}{6} + o(m^3) \text{ and}$$

$$s_{YZ} = \sum_{l=0}^{\eta m} \sum_{j=1}^{\tau l} l + (1-\eta)m = \tau\eta^3 \frac{m^3}{3} + \tau(1-\eta)m \frac{\eta^2 m^2}{2} = \tau\eta^2 (3-\eta) \frac{m^3}{6} + o(m^3).$$

Then, we have

$$\mathrm{vol}(L_Y) = e^{mw_y} Y^{\eta^3 \tau^2 m^3/6} \left(\frac{Z}{e}\right)^{\tau\eta^2(3-\eta)m^3/6}.$$

Summing up the above discussion, we have

$$\begin{aligned} \mathrm{vol}(L) &= \mathrm{vol}(L_X)\mathrm{vol}(L_Y) \\ &= e^{mw} X^{\eta(3-3\eta+\eta^2)m^3/6} Y^{\eta^3\tau^2 m^3/6} \left(\frac{Z}{e}\right)^{(\eta(3-3\eta+\eta^2)+\tau\eta^2(3-\eta))m^3/6}. \end{aligned} \quad (3)$$

Remember that the condition that the problem can be solved in polynomial time is given by $\mathrm{vol}(L) \leq e^{mw}$ by ignoring small terms. From Eq. (3), we have the condition:

$$X^{3-3\eta+\eta^2} Y^{\tau^2\eta^2} \left(\frac{Z}{e}\right)^{(3-3\eta+\eta^2)+\tau(3\eta-\eta^2)} \leq 1. \quad (4)$$

As described in previous subsection, we obtain the same set as those of Herrmann–May or Blömer–May if we set $\eta = 1$ or $\tau=1$. Deriving bounds for each case are described in full version [9].

4.3 Optimal Bound in Our Framework

We have seen that the optimal bound of X is $e^{1-\sqrt{1/2}}$ if $\eta = 1$ or $\tau = 1$. Hence, we have a chance to go beyond the Boneh–Durfee's bound. Unfortunately, the following theorem shows that $d \leq N^{0.292}$ is still optimal in our framework.

Theorem 3. *Suppose that* $Y = e^{1/2}$. *The maximal bound of* X *in our framework is* $e^{1-\sqrt{1/2}}$.

Proof of Theorem 3. By substituting $Z = XY + 1$ and $Y = e^{1/2}$ into Eq. (4) and ignoring small terms, Eq. (4) is transformed into

$$X \le e^{\frac{1}{2}\frac{(3-3\eta+\eta^2)+(3\eta-\eta^2)\tau-\eta^2\tau^2}{2(3-3\eta+\eta^2)+\tau(3\eta-\eta^2)}}. \quad (5)$$

Let $\mathcal{P}$ and $\bar{\mathcal{P}}$ be sets such that $\mathcal{P} = \{(\tau,\eta) \mid 0 < \tau < 1,\ 0 < \eta < 1\}$ and $\bar{\mathcal{P}} = \{(\tau,\eta) \mid 0 < \tau \le 1,\ 0 < \eta \le 1\}$. In order to obtain the maximal value of the right side of Eq. (5) in $\bar{\mathcal{P}}$, we firstly consider the extremal values of the following function $\Psi(\tau,\eta)$ in $\mathcal{P}$:

$$\Psi(\tau,\eta) := \frac{(3-3\eta+\eta^2)+(3\eta-\eta^2)\tau-\eta^2\tau^2}{2(3-3\eta+\eta^2)+(3\eta-\eta^2)\tau}.$$

Let $Num(\tau,\eta)$ and $Den(\tau,\eta)$ be the numerator and denominator of $\Psi(\tau,\eta)$ respectively. Here, we show that $Den(\tau,\eta) \neq 0$ in $\mathcal{P}$. If $Den(\tau,\eta) = 0$, then we have

$$0 < \tau = \frac{2(3-3\eta+\eta^2)}{\eta^2-3\eta} = 2\frac{(\eta-3/2)^2+\frac{3}{4}}{(\eta-3)\eta}.$$

However, this contradicts the condition $0 < \eta < 1$. Therefore, the rational function $\Psi(\tau,\eta) \in \mathbb{Q}(\tau,\eta)$ is obviously differentiable in $\mathcal{P}$. By solving the algebraic equation $\frac{\partial\Psi}{\partial\tau} = \frac{\partial\Psi}{\partial\eta} = 0$, we show that there are no extremal values of $\Psi(\tau,\eta)$ in $\mathcal{P}$. Let $\Phi_\tau(\tau,\eta), \Phi_\eta(\tau,\eta)$ be polynomials such that

$$\Phi_\tau(\tau,\eta) := \frac{\partial\Psi}{\partial\tau}\cdot Den(\tau,\eta)^2,\ \Phi_\eta(\tau,\eta) := \frac{\partial\Psi}{\partial\eta}\cdot Den(\tau,\eta)^2.$$

Note that both Φ_τ and Φ_η are in $\mathbb{Z}[\tau,\eta]$, and we solve the algebraic equation $\Phi_\tau = \Phi_\eta = 0$ by introducing Gröbner basis. Let G be the Gröbner basis for the ideal generated by Φ_τ, Φ_η with respect to the lexicographic order $\prec_{\mathrm{LEX}}$ such that $\eta \prec_{\mathrm{LEX}} \tau$. Then G contains three polynomials in $\mathbb{Z}[\tau,\eta]$, and one of them is $m(\eta)$ such that

$$m(\eta) = \eta(\eta-1)(\eta-3)(\eta^2-3\eta+3)\{3(\eta-1)^2+2(\eta-3)^2\}.$$

This fact implies that, for every extremal value $\Psi(\tau_0,\eta_0)$ where $(\tau_0,\eta_0) \in \mathbb{R}^2$, η_0 is a root of $m(\eta)$ over $\mathbb{R}$. Since $m(\eta)$ does not have its root in the real interval $(0,1)$, there are no extremal values of $\Psi(\tau,\eta)$ in $\mathcal{P}$.

Hence, we only have to check the maximal values of $\Psi(0,\eta), \Psi(1,\eta)$ for $0 \le \eta \le 1$ and $\Psi(\tau,0), \Psi(\tau,1)$ for $0 \le \tau \le 1$, and furthermore the two cases $\tau = 1$ and $\eta = 1$ are discussed above. The maximal value of the right side of Eq. (5) for $\tau = 0$ or $\eta = 0$ is $e^{1/4}$ since $\Psi(0,\eta) = \Psi(\tau,0) = 1/2$, and thus the maximal value of the right side of Eq. (5) in $\bar{\mathcal{P}}$ is $e^{1-\sqrt{1/2}}$. □

4.4 A Hybrid Method

It has been known that Blömer–May method: $(\tau,\eta) = (1, 3-\sqrt{6})$ has an advantage because their method requires a smaller lattice dimension. On the other hands, Herrmann–May method: $(\tau, \eta) = (\sqrt{2} - 1, 1)$ has an advantage because it achieves a higher bound. We present a simple hybrid method which enjoys both of advantages by interpolating two methods. Letting t be a parameter with $0 \leq t \leq 1$, we set $\tau(t)$ and $\eta(t)$ by

$$(\tau(t), \eta(t)) = (1 - (2 - \sqrt{2})t, (\sqrt{6} - 2)t + (3 - \sqrt{6}))$$

and use the parameter $(\tau(t), \eta(t))$ for our framework. The setting $t = 0$ corresponds to Blömer–May's method: $(\tau(0), \eta(0)) = (1, 3 - \sqrt{6})$ and the setting $t = 1$ corresponds to Herrmann–May's method: $(\tau(1), \eta(1)) = (\sqrt{2} - 1, 1))$. We define $\bar{\Psi}(t) := \Psi(\tau(t), \eta(t))$. We can easily see that $\bar{\Psi}(t)$is monotonically increasing function in the interval $0 \leq t \leq 1$. Then, there is a trade-off between a lattice dimension and an achievable bound. That is, the choice of a bigger t implies a higher bound but less efficiency and the choice of a smaller t implies more efficiency but a lower bound. Our hybrid method makes it possible to choose the best lattice construction for a practical attack.

5 Extension to Cryptanalysis of Arbitrary $Y = e^{\alpha}$

In previous section, we discussed only the case of $Y = e^{1/2}$. In this section, we extend our results to arbitrary $Y = e^{\alpha}$. Sarkar et al. presented the small secret exponent attack under the situation that a few MSBs of the prime p is known [13]. Suppose that some estimate p_0 of p is known such that $|p - p_0| < N^{\alpha}$. Let q_0 be an estimation of q. Letting $A = N + 1 - p_0 - q_0$, a solution of the modular equation $x(A + y) + 1 = 0(\bmod\ e)$ is given by $(x, y) = (k, p_0 + q_0 - p - q)$. Note that $k < e^{\delta}$ and $|p_0 + q_0 - p - q| < e^{\alpha}$. They showed that the barrier $d < N^{0.292}$ can be broken through if α is strictly less than $1/2$. In this section, we focus on the problem: $x(A+y)+1 = 0(\bmod\ e)$ with upper bound of solution: $X = e^{\delta}$ and $Y = e^{\alpha}$. They showed extensions of three algorithms: two algorithms from Boneh and Durfee's paper [2], and one algorithm from Blömer and May's paper [1] into arbitrary α [13]. Although α should be $1/4 < \alpha \leq 1/2$ in this attack scenario[1], we show an analysis for $0 < \alpha < 1$.

It is important to point out that the discussion in Sections 3 and 4 (except Sections 4.3 and 4.4) is valid for an arbitrary α, which implies that a set of indexes $\mathcal{F}(m; \tau, \eta)$ of shift-polynomials and the determinant calculation of the volume are also valid. From the same analysis, we have the same condition as Eq. (4). Letting $X = e^{\delta}$ and $Y = e^{\alpha}$, we have the following theorem. A proof is given in Appendix A.2.

Theorem 4. *Suppose that $Y = e^{\alpha}$ and $X = e^{\delta}$. The maximal bound of δ in our framework is given by*

$$\delta < \begin{cases} 1 - \sqrt{\alpha} & \text{if } \alpha \geq 1/4, \\ \frac{2}{5}(\sqrt{4\alpha^2 - \alpha + 1} - 3\alpha + 1) & \text{if } 0 < \alpha < 1/4. \end{cases}$$

[1] Suppose that α is less than or equal to $1/4$. The whole prime factor p can be found by Coppersmith's attack [4] since the upper half of p is known.

We will present a hybrid method for arbitrary α in full version [9]. Theorem 4 shows that Blömer–May like method ($\tau = 1$) is superior to Herrmann–May like method ($\eta = 1$) if $\alpha < 1/4$. Interestingly, if α is extremely small ($\alpha < 3/35$), Herrmann–May like and Blömer–May like methods are not best-known algorithms. We show the details in full version [9]. We also show another extension in Appendix B.

6 Concluding Remarks

We should point out the relationship between our results and the discussion in May's PhD thesis [11]. He presented the interpolation between the results of Blömer–May and Boneh–Durfee by using a concept called *strictly decreasing pattern* in Section 7 of [11]. He also argued that Boneh–Durfee's stronger bound is optimal over all decreasing patterns. However, no *formal proof* of its optimality has been given in [11]. On the contrary to [11], we give a *strict proof* of the optimality within our framework in Section 4. Furthermore, we extend our results to arbitrary $Y = e^{\alpha}$, which has not been discussed in [11] and is also an advantage over [11].

It has been known that Blömer–May method has an advantage because their method requires a smaller lattice dimension than the Boneh–Durfee's lattice. Theorem 4 gives another view of their algorithm. Theorem 4 shows Blömer–May method has another advantage because it achieves a better bound in addition to less lattice dimension; Blömer–May method achieves a higher bound than Herrmann–May method (and Boneh–Durfee's method) if $\alpha \le 1/4$.

For the usual small secret exponent attack on RSA, we *just* showed that $d \le N^{0.292}$ is an optimal bound in our framework. Hence, the bound might be improved if we develop the other method outside of our framework, which is an open problem.

Acknowledgement. The first author was supported by KAKENHI 22700006.

References

1. Blömer, J., May, A.: Low Secret Exponent RSA Revisited. In: Silverman, J.H. (ed.) CaLC 2001. LNCS, vol. 2146, pp. 4–19. Springer, Heidelberg (2001)
2. Boneh, D., Durfee, G.: Cryptanalysis of RSA with private key d less than $N^{0.292}$. IEEE Transactions on Information Theory 46(4), 1339–1349 (2000); (Firstly appeared in Eurocrypt 1999)
3. Coppersmith, D.: Finding a Small Root of a Univariate Modular Equation. In: Maurer, U.M. (ed.) EUROCRYPT 1996. LNCS, vol. 1070, pp. 155–165. Springer, Heidelberg (1996)
4. Coppersmith, D.: Finding a Small Root of a Bivariate Integer Equation; Factoring with High Bits Known. In: Maurer, U.M. (ed.) EUROCRYPT 1996. LNCS, vol. 1070, pp. 178–189. Springer, Heidelberg (1996)
5. Coppersmith, D.: Small Solutions to Polynomial Equations, and Low Exponent RSA Vulnerabilities. J. Cryptology 10(4), 233–260 (1997)

6. Herrmann, M., May, A.: Attacking Power Generators Using Unravelled Linearization: When Do We Output Too Much? In: Matsui, M. (ed.) ASIACRYPT 2009. LNCS, vol. 5912, pp. 487–504. Springer, Heidelberg (2009)
7. Herrmann, M., May, A.: Maximizing Small Root Bounds by Linearization and Applications to Small Secret Exponent RSA. In: Nguyen, P.Q., Pointcheval, D. (eds.) PKC 2010. LNCS, vol. 6056, pp. 53–69. Springer, Heidelberg (2010)
8. Howgrave-Graham, N.: Finding Small Roots of Univariate Modular Equations Revisited. In: IMA Int. Conf., pp.131–142 (1997)
9. Kunihiro, N., Shinohara, N., Izu, T.: A Unified Framework for Small Secret Exponent Attack on RSA. IACR ePrint Archive
10. Lenstra, A.K., Lenstra, H.W., Lovász, L.: Factoring polynomials with rational coefficients. Mathematische Annalen 261, 515–534 (1982)
11. May, A.: New RSA Vulnerabilities Using Lattice Reduction Methods. PhD thesis, University of Paderborn (2003)
12. Rivest, R., Shamir, A., Adleman, L.: A Method for Obtaining Digital Signatures and Public-Key Cryptosystems. Communications of the ACM 21(2), 120–126 (1978)
13. Sarkar, S., Maitra, S., Sarkar, S.: RSA Cryptanalysis with Increased Bounds on the Secret Exponent using Less Lattice Dimension. IACR ePrint Archive: Report 2008/315 (2008)
14. Wiener, M.: Cryptanalysis of Short RSA Secret Exponents. IEEE Transactions on Information Theory 36, 553–558 (1990)

A Proofs

A.1 Proofs of Lemma 4–6

Proof of Lemma 4. The polynomial $\bar{g}_{[u,0]}$ is given by $\bar{g}_{[u,0]}(x,z) = e^m x^u$. Then, we have the lemma. □

Proof of Lemma 5. The expansion of $\bar{g}_{[u-j,j]}$ for $j \geq 1$ is given by

$$\begin{aligned}\bar{g}_{[u-j,j]}(x,z) = e^{m-j}x^{u-j}(z+Ax)^j &= \sum_{i=0}^{j} e^{m-j}x^{u-j}\binom{j}{i} z^i x^{j-i} A^{j-i} \\ &= e^{m-j}x^{u-j}z^j + \sum_{i=0}^{j-1} e^{m-j}A^{j-i}\binom{j}{i} x^{u-i}z^i.\end{aligned}$$

Then, we have

$$\begin{aligned}\bar{g}_{[u-j,j]}(x,z) - e^{m-j}x^{u-j}z^j &\cong \sum_{i=0}^{j-1} x^{u-i}z^i = x^{u-j+1}\sum_{i=0}^{j-1} x^{(j-1)-i}z^i \\ &\cong x^{u-j+1}(z+Ax)^{j-1} \cong \bar{g}_{[u-j+1,j-1]}.\end{aligned}$$

Then, we have $\mathcal{S}(\bar{g}_{[u-j,j]} - e^{m-j}x^{u-j}z^j) = \mathcal{S}(\bar{g}_{[u-j+1,j-1]})$. □

Proof of Lemma 6. The expansion of $\bar{h}_{[j,u]}$ for $j \geq 1$ is given as follows:

$$\bar{h}_{[j,u]}(x,y,z) = y^j(z+Ax)^u e^{m-u} = e^{m-u}\sum_{i=0}^{u}\binom{u}{i} y^j z^i (Ax)^{u-i}$$
$$= e^{m-u}y^j z^u + e^{m-u}\sum_{i=0}^{u-1}\binom{u}{i} A^{u-i}x^{u-i}y^j z^i.$$

Then, we have

$$\bar{h}_{[j,u]}(x,y,z) - e^{m-u}y^j z^u \cong \sum_{i=0}^{u-1} x^{u-i}y^j z^i = y^{j-1}xy\sum_{i=0}^{u-1} x^{(u-1)-i}z^i$$
$$\cong y^{j-1}(z-1)(z+Ax)^{u-1} \cong y^{j-1}(z+Ax)^{u-1}z + y^{j-1}(z+Ax)^{u-1}$$
$$\cong \bar{h}_{[j-1,u-1]}z + \bar{h}_{[j-1,u-1]}.$$

Hence, we have

$$\mathcal{S}(\bar{h}_{[j,u]}(x,y,z) - e^{m-u}y^j z^u) = \mathcal{S}(\bar{h}_{[j-1,u-1]}z) \cup \mathcal{S}(\bar{h}_{[j-1,u-1]})$$
$$\subseteq \mathcal{S}(h_{[j-1,u-1]}(z+Ax)) \cup \mathcal{S}(\bar{h}_{[j-1,u-1]}) = \mathcal{S}(\bar{h}_{[j-1,u]}) \cup \mathcal{S}(\bar{h}_{[j-1,u-1]}).$$

Then, we have the lemma. □

A.2 Proof of Theorem 4

By substituting $Z = XY + 1$ and $Y = e^{\alpha}$ into Eq. (4) and ignoring small terms, Eq. (4) is transformed into

$$X \leq e^{\frac{(1-\alpha)((3-3\eta+\eta^2)+(3\eta-\eta^2)\tau)-\alpha\eta^2\tau^2}{2(3-3\eta+\eta^2)+(3\eta-\eta^2)\tau}}. \tag{6}$$

Let $\mathcal{P}$ and $\bar{\mathcal{P}}$ be the sets defined in the proof of Theorem 3. In order to obtain the maximal value of the right side of (6) in $\bar{\mathcal{P}}$, we firstly consider the extremal values of the following function $\Psi_\alpha(\tau,\eta)$ in $\mathcal{P}$:

$$\Psi_\alpha(\tau,\eta) = \frac{(1-\alpha)((3-3\eta+\eta^2)+(3\eta-\eta^2)\tau)-\alpha\eta^2\tau^2}{2(3-3\eta+\eta^2)+(3\eta-\eta^2)\tau}$$

Notice that the denominator of $\Psi_\alpha(\tau,\eta)$ is $Den(\tau,\eta)$ given in the proof of Theorem 3, and so $\Psi_\alpha(\tau,\eta)$ is also differentiable in $\mathcal{P}$.

In the same manner as the proof of Theorem 3, we show that there are no extremal values of $\Psi_\alpha(\tau,\eta)$ in $\mathcal{P}$ for any $\alpha \in (0,1)$. Let $\Phi_\tau^{(\alpha)}(\tau,\eta), \Phi_\eta^{(\alpha)}(\tau,\eta)$ be polynomials such that

$$\Phi_\tau^{(\alpha)}(\tau,\eta) = \frac{\partial\Psi_\alpha}{\partial\tau}\cdot Den(\tau,\eta)^2,\ \Phi_\eta^{(\alpha)}(\tau,\eta) = \frac{\partial\Psi_\alpha}{\partial\eta}\cdot Den(\tau,\eta)^2.$$

We solve the algebraic equation $\Phi_\tau^{(\alpha)} = \Phi_\eta^{(\alpha)} = 0$ by introducing Gröbner basis. Let G_α be the Gröbner basis under $0 < \alpha < 1$ for the ideal generated by

$\Phi_\tau^{(\alpha)}, \Phi_\eta^{(\alpha)}$ with respect to the lexicographic order $\prec_{\mathrm{LEX}}$ such that $\eta \prec_{\mathrm{LEX}} \tau$. One of polynomials in G_α is $m_\alpha(\eta)$ such that

$$m_\alpha(\eta) = \eta(\eta-1)(\eta-3)(\eta^2-3\eta+3)\{3\alpha(\eta-1)^2+(\eta-3)^2\}.$$

This fact implies that, for every extremal value $\Psi_\alpha(\tau_0,\eta_0)$ where $(\tau_0,\eta_0) \in \mathbb{R}^2$, η_0 is a root of $m_\alpha(\eta)$ over $\mathbb{R}$. Since $m_\alpha(\eta)$ does not have its root in the real interval $(0,1)$, there are no extremal values of $\Psi_\alpha(\tau,\eta)$ in $\mathcal{P}$.

Hence, we only have to check the maximal values of $\Psi_\alpha(0,\eta), \Psi_\alpha(1,\eta)$ for $0 \le \eta \le 1$ and $\Psi_\alpha(\tau,0), \Psi_\alpha(\tau,1)$ for $0 \le \tau \le 1$. If $\eta = 0$ or $\tau = 0$, then $\Psi_\alpha(\tau,0) = \Psi_\alpha(0,\eta) = (1-\alpha)/2$, and so the maximal value for $\eta = 0$ or $\tau = 0$ is $(1-\alpha)/2$.

For $\eta = 1$, we have that

$$\Psi_\alpha(\tau,1) = \frac{-\alpha\tau^2 + (1-\alpha)(1+2\tau)}{2(\tau+1)},$$

and so the maximal value for $\eta = 1$ is

$$\begin{cases} \frac{3}{4}-\alpha & (\tau = 1, 0 < \alpha < \frac{1}{4}) \\ 1-\sqrt{\alpha} & (\tau = \sqrt{1/\alpha}-1, \frac{1}{4} \le \alpha < 1). \end{cases} \tag{7}$$

For $\tau = 1$, we have that

$$\Psi_\alpha(1,\eta) = \frac{3-\alpha(\eta^2+3)}{6-3\eta+\eta^2},$$

and so the maximal value for $\tau = 1$ is

$$\frac{2}{5}(\sqrt{\alpha^2-\alpha+1}-3\alpha+1). \tag{8}$$

By comparing with the above values, we have the theorem. □

B Extension to $x(A+y)+C = 0 (\mathrm{mod}\ e)$ for an Arbitrary Integer C

In Section 4, we discussed only the case of $x(A+y)+1 = 0(\mathrm{mod}\ e)$. In this section, we extend to $x(A+y)+C = 0(\mathrm{mod}\ e)$ for an arbitrary integer C. For simplicity, we assume that $0 < |C| < e$. In the discussion of Section 4, we set Z as $Z = XY+1$. For general C, Z should be replaced into $Z = XY+|C|$. The value Z is upper bounded by $2\max(XY,|C|)$. We consider two typical cases.

Suppose that $|C|$ is small compared to XY for the first case. Concretely, suppose that $XY \ge |C|$. Since $Z \le 2XY$, the discussion of Section 4 is valid and the same bound is obtained.

Suppose that $|C|$ is uniformly chosen from integers within the interval $(0,e)$. It is clear that $|C| \approx e$ with high probability. In this case, $Z \le 2e$. By ignoring small terms, Eq. (4) is transformed into $X^{3-3\eta+\eta^2}Y^{\tau^2\eta^2} < 1$. Since X and Y are positive integers, there are no ranges for X and Y satisfying the above inequality. Then, we cannot solve the problem by using our framework[2] in this case.

[2] Boneh and Durfee's weaker method is valid even if $|C|$ is large.

Very Compact Hardware Implementations of the Blockcipher CLEFIA

Toru Akishita and Harunaga Hiwatari

Sony Corporation
5-1-12 Kitashinagawa Shinagawa-ku, Tokyo 141-0001, Japan
{Toru.Akishita,Harunaga.Hiwatari}@jp.sony.com

Abstract. The 128-bit blockcipher CLEFIA is known to be highly efficient in hardware implementations. This paper proposes very compact hardware implementations of CLEFIA-128. Our implementations are based on novel serialized architectures in the data processing block. Three types of hardware architectures are implemented and synthesized using a 0.13 μm standard cell library. In the smallest implementation, the area requirements are only 2,488 GE, which are about half of the previous smallest implementation as far as we know. Furthermore, only additional 116 GE enable to support decryption.

Keywords: blockcipher, CLEFIA, compact hardware implementation, ASIC.

1 Introduction

CLEFIA [9,11] is a 128-bit blockcipher supporting key lengths of 128, 192 and 256 bits, which is compatible with AES [2]. CLEFIA achieves enough immunity against known attacks and flexibility for efficient implementation in both hardware and software. It is reported that CLEFIA is highly efficient particularly in hardware implementations [12,10,13].

Compact hardware implementations are very significant for small embedded devices such as RFID tags and wireless sensor nodes because of their limited hardware resources. As for AES with 128-bit keys, low-area hardware implementations have been reported in [3] and [4]. The former uses a RAM based architecture supporting both encryption and decryption with the area requirements of 3,400 GE, while the latter uses a shift-register based architecture supporting encryption only with the area requirements of 3,100 GE. Both implementations use an 8-bit serialized data path and implement only a fraction of the *MixColumns* operation with additional three 8-bit registers, where it takes several clock cycles to calculate one column. Very recently, another low-area hardware implementation of AES was proposed in [5] requiring 2,400 GE for encryption only. Unlike the previous two implementations, it implements *MixColumns* not in a serialized way, where one column of *MixColumns* is processed in 1 clock cycle. Thus it requires 4 times more XOR gates for *MixColumns*, but requires no additional register and can reduce gate requirements for control logic.

A. Miri and S. Vaudenay (Eds.): SAC 2011, LNCS 7118, pp. 278–292, 2012.

In this paper, we present very compact hardware architectures of CLEFIA with 128-bit keys based on 8-bit shift registers. We show that the data processing part of CLEFIA-128 can be implemented in a serialized way without any additional registers. Three types of hardware architectures are proposed according to required cycles for one block process by adaptively applying clock gating technique. Those architectures are implemented and synthesized using a 0.13 μm standard cell library. In our smallest implementation, the area requirements are only 2,488 GE, which are to the best of our knowledge about half as small as the previous smallest implementation, 4,950 GE [10,12], and competitive to the smallest AES implementation. Furthermore, only additional 116 GE are required to support decryption by switching the processing order of F-functions at even-numbered rounds.

The rest of the paper is organized as follows. Sect. 2 gives brief description of CLEFIA and its previously proposed hardware implementations. In Sect. 3, we propose three types of hardware architectures. Sect. 4 describes additional hardware resources to support decryption. Sect. 5 gives evaluation results for our implementations, compared with the previous results of CLEFIA and AES. Finally, we conclude in Sect. 6.

2 128-bit Blockcipher CLEFIA

2.1 Algorithm

CLEFIA [9,11] is a 128-bit blockcipher with its key length being 128, 192, and 256 bits. For brevity, we consider 128-bit key CLEFIA, denoted as CLEFIA-128, though similar techniques are applicable to CLEFIA with 192-bit and 256-bit keys. CLEFIA-128 is divided into two parts: the data processing part and the key scheduling part.

The data processing part employs a 4-branch Type-2 generalized Feistel network [14] with two parallel F-functions F_0 and F_1 per round. The number of rounds r for CLEFIA-128 is 18. The encryption function ENC_r takes a 128-bit plaintext $P = P_0|P_1|P_2|P_3$, 32-bit whitening keys WK_i $(0 \leq i < 4)$, and 32-bit round keys RK_j $(0 \leq j < 2r)$ as inputs, and outputs a 128-bit ciphertext $C = C_0|C_1|C_2|C_3$ as shown in Fig. 1.

The two F-functions F_0 and F_1 consist of round key addition, 4 non-linear 8-bit S-boxes, and a diffusion matrix. The construction of F_0 and F_1 is shown in Fig. 2. Two kind of S-boxes S_0 and S_1 are employed, and the order of these S-boxes is different in F_0 and F_1. The diffusion matrices of F_0 and F_1 are also different; the matrices M_0 for F_0 and M_1 for F_1 are defined as

$$M_0 = \begin{pmatrix} \texttt{01} & \texttt{02} & \texttt{04} & \texttt{06} \\ \texttt{02} & \texttt{01} & \texttt{06} & \texttt{04} \\ \texttt{04} & \texttt{06} & \texttt{01} & \texttt{02} \\ \texttt{06} & \texttt{04} & \texttt{02} & \texttt{01} \end{pmatrix}, \quad M_1 = \begin{pmatrix} \texttt{01} & \texttt{08} & \texttt{02} & \texttt{0A} \\ \texttt{08} & \texttt{01} & \texttt{0A} & \texttt{02} \\ \texttt{02} & \texttt{0A} & \texttt{01} & \texttt{08} \\ \texttt{0A} & \texttt{02} & \texttt{08} & \texttt{01} \end{pmatrix}.$$

The multiplications between these matrices and vectors are performed in GF(2^8) defined by a primitive polynomial $z^8 + z^4 + z^3 + z^2 + 1$.

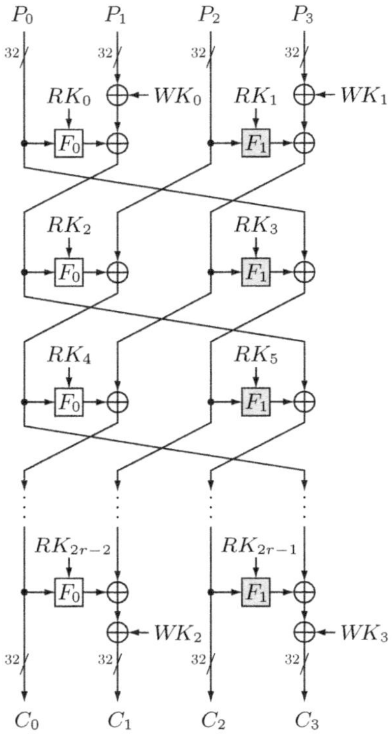

Fig. 1. Encryption function ENC_r

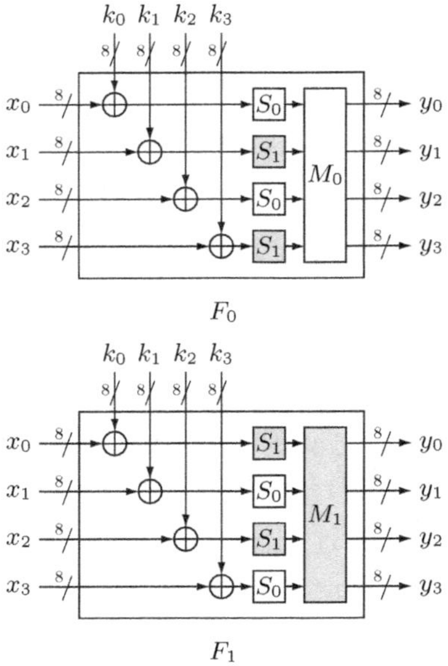

Fig. 2. F-functions F_0, F_1

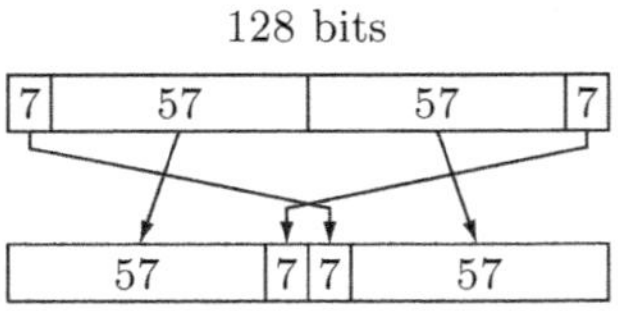

Fig. 3. *DoubleSwap* function Σ

The key scheduling part of CLEFIA-128 takes a secret key K as an input, and outputs 32-bit whitening keys WK_i $(0 \leq i < 4)$ and 32-bit round keys RK_j $(0 \leq j < 2r)$. It is divided into the following two steps: generating a 128-bit intermediate key L (step 1) and generating WK_i and RK_j from K and L (step 2). In step 1, the intermediate key L is generated by 12 rounds of encryption function which takes K as a plaintext and constant values CON_i $(0 \leq i < 24)$ as round keys. In step 2, the intermediate key L is updated by the *DoubleSwap* function Σ, which is illustrated in Fig. 3. Round keys RK_j $(0 \leq j < 36)$ is generated by mixing K, L, and constant values CON_i $(24 \leq i < 60)$. Whitening keys WK_i are equivalent to 32-bit chunks K_i of K as $K = K_0|K_1|K_2|K_3$.

2.2 Previous Hardware Implementations

Hardware implementations of CLEFIA-128 have been studied in [12,10,13]. In [12], optimization techniques in data processing part including S-boxes and diffusion matrices were proposed. The compact architecture, where F_0 is processed in one cycle and F_1 is processed in another cycle, was implemented, and its area requirements in area optimization are reported to be 4,950 GE.

In [10], two optimization techniques in key scheduling part were introduced. The first technique is related to implementation of the *DoubleSwap* function Σ. Σ is decomposed into the following *Swap* function Ω and *SubSwap* function Ψ as $\Sigma = \Psi \circ \Omega$.

$$\begin{aligned}\Omega &: X \mapsto Y \\ &\quad Y = X[64\text{-}127] \mid X[0\text{-}63] \\ \Psi &: X \mapsto Y \\ &\quad Y = X[71\text{-}127] \mid X[57\text{-}70] \mid X[0\text{-}56]\end{aligned}$$

$X[a\text{-}b]$ denotes a bit string cut from the a-th bit to the b-th bit of X. Please note that Ω and Ψ are both involutive. The 128-bit key register for the intermediate key L is updated by applying Ω and Ψ alternately. Round keys are always generated from the most significant 64-bit of the key register. After the final round of encryption, L is re-stored into the key register by applying the following *FinalSwap* function Φ.

$$\begin{aligned}\Phi &: X \mapsto Y \\ &\quad Y = X[49\text{-}55] \mid X[42\text{-}48] \mid X[35\text{-}41] \mid X[28\text{-}34] \mid X[21\text{-}27] \mid X[14\text{-}20] \mid \\ &\quad\quad X[7\text{-}13] \mid X[0\text{-}6] \mid X[64\text{-}71] \mid X[56\text{-}63] \mid X[121\text{-}127] \mid X[114\text{-}120] \mid \\ &\quad\quad X[107\text{-}113] \mid X[100\text{-}106] \mid X[93\text{-}99] \mid X[86\text{-}92] \mid X[79\text{-}85] \mid X[72\text{-}78]\end{aligned}$$

Please note that Φ is also involutive. In case of decryption, round keys are always generated from the most significant 64-bit of the key register by applying the inverse functions of Ω, Ψ and Φ in reverse order of encryption. Due to their involutive property, only three functions Ω, Ψ and Φ are required for encryption and decryption.

In the second technique, XOR operations with the parts of round keys related to a secret key K are moved by an equivalent transformation into the two data lines where key whitening operations are processed. Therefore, these XOR operations and key whitening operations can be shared.

In [13], five types of hardware architectures were designed and fairly compared to the ISO 18033-3 standard blockciphers under the same conditions. In their results, the highest efficiency of 400.96 Kbps/gates was achieved, which is at least 2.2 times higher than that of the ISO 18033-3 standard blockciphers.

3 Proposed Architectures

In this section we propose three types of hardware architectures. Firstly, we propose a compact matrix multiplier for CLEFIA-128. Next, in Type-I architecture, we propose a novel serialized architecture of the data processing block of CLEFIA-128. By adaptively applying clock gating logic to Type-I architecture,

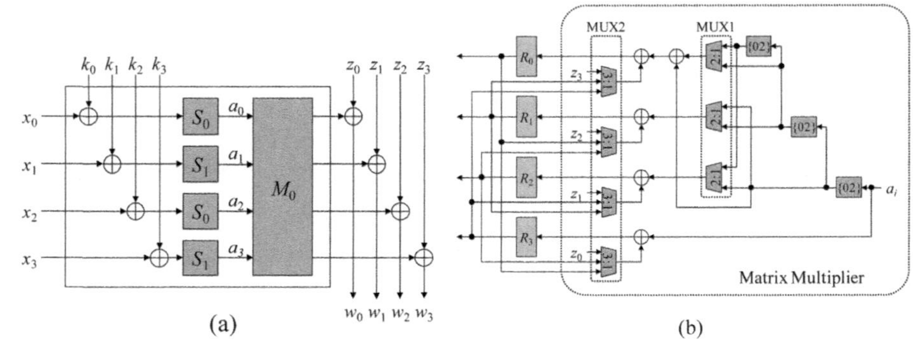

l	1	2	3	4
R_0	$z_3 \oplus \{06\}a_0$	$z_2 \oplus \{04\}a_0 \oplus \{06\}a_1$	$z_1 \oplus \{02\}a_0 \oplus a_1 \oplus \{06\}a_2$	$z_0 \oplus a_0 \oplus \{02\}a_1 \oplus \{04\}a_2 \oplus \{06\}a_3$
R_1	$z_2 \oplus \{04\}a_0$	$z_3 \oplus \{06\}a_0 \oplus \{04\}a_1$	$z_0 \oplus a_0 \oplus \{02\}a_1 \oplus \{04\}a_2$	$z_1 \oplus \{02\}a_0 \oplus a_1 \oplus \{06\}a_2 \oplus \{04\}a_3$
R_2	$z_1 \oplus \{02\}a_0$	$z_0 \oplus a_0 \oplus \{02\}a_1$	$z_3 \oplus \{06\}a_0 \oplus \{04\}a_1 \oplus \{02\}a_2$	$z_2 \oplus \{04\}a_0 \oplus \{06\}a_1 \oplus a_2 \oplus \{02\}a_3$
R_3	$z_0 \oplus a_0$	$z_1 \oplus \{02\}a_0 \oplus a_1$	$z_2 \oplus \{04\}a_0 \oplus \{06\}a_1 \oplus a_2$	$z_3 \oplus \{06\}a_0 \oplus \{04\}a_1 \oplus \{02\}a_2 \oplus a_3$

(c)

Fig. 4. Matrix multiplier: (a) F-function F_0, (b) Data path, (c) Contents of registers R_j $(0 \leq j < 4)$ at the l-th cycle

we can reduce the number of multiplexers (MUXes) in Type-II and Type-III architectures with increasing cycle counts.

Clock gating is a power-saving technique used in synchronous circuits. For hardware implementations of blockciphers, it was firstly introduced in [8] as a technique to reduce gate counts and power consumption, and have been applied to KATAN family [1] and AES [5]. Clock gating works by taking the enable conditions attached to registers. It can remove feedback MUXes to hold their present state and replace them with clock gating logic. In case that several bits of registers take the same enable conditions, their gate counts will be saved by applying clock gating.

3.1 Matrix Multiplier

Among low-area AES implementations, *MixColumns* matrix operations are computed row by row in [3], while they are computed column by column in [4]. In our architecture, matrix operations are computed column by column in the following way.

The 4-byte output of M_0 operation is XORed with the next 4-byte data as shown in Fig. 4 (a). The matrix multiplier in Fig. 4 (b) performs the matrix multiplication together with the above XOR operation in 4 clock cycles. Fig. 4 (c) presents the contents of the registers R_i at the l-th cycle $(1 \leq l \leq 4)$. At the 1st cycle, the output a_0 of S_0 are fed to the multiplier and multiplied by $\{01\}$, $\{02\}$, $\{04\}$, and $\{06\}$. The products are XORed with the data z_i $(0 \leq i < 4)$, and then the intermediate results are stored in the four registers R_j $(0 \leq j < 4)$. As each column in M_0 consists of the same coefficients, the matrix multiplication can be

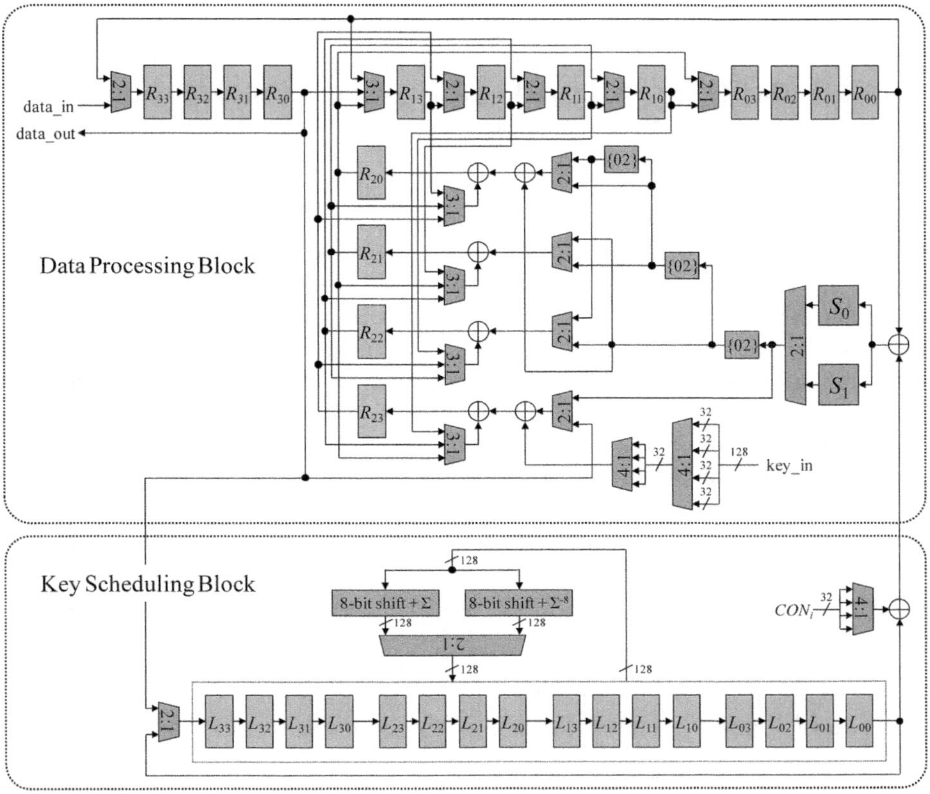

Fig. 5. Data path of Type-I architecture

performed by selecting the intermediate results through MUX2 and XORing the products of a_i $(i = 1, 2, 3)$ with them at the $(i+1)$-th cycle. After 4 clock cycles, w_i $(0 \leq i < 4)$ are stored in R_i. The multiplication by M_1 can be performed by switching MUX1.

In [4], three 8-bit registers are required for the construction of a parallel-to-serial converter due to avoiding register competition with the next calculation of a matrix. On the other hand, no competition occurs in our architecture because z_i is input at the 1st cycle of a matrix multiplication. w_i can be moved into the register where z_i for the newly processing F-function is stored.

3.2 Type-I Architecture

Fig. 5 shows the data path of Type-I architecture, where the width of data path is 8 bit except those written in the figure. It is divided into the following two blocks: the data processing block and the key scheduling block. Type-I architecture processes a round of the encryption function in 8 clock cycles. We show, in appendix, the detailed data flow of the data registers R_{ij} $(0 \leq i, j < 4)$ in Fig. 5

for a round of the encryption processing. As described in Sect. 3.1, at the 1st and the 5th cycle in the 8 cycles, the data stored in R_{20}–R_{23} are moved into R_{03}–R_{12}, and simultaneously the data stored in R_{10}–R_{13} are input to the matrix multiplier. Therefore, no additional register but the 128-bit data register exists in the data processing block. Please note that R_{30}–R_{33} hold the current state at the 5–8th cycle by clock gating.

In the start of encryption, a 128-bit plaintext is located to R_{ij} in 16 clock cycles by inputting it byte by byte from data_in. After 18 rounds of the encryption function which require 144 cycles, a 128-bit ciphertext is output byte by byte from data_out in 16 clock cycles. Therefore, it takes 176 cycles for encryption. The reason why data_out is connected to R_{30} is that no word rotation is necessary at the final round of encryption. In the start of key setup, a 128-bit secret key K input from key_in is located to R_{ij} in 16 clock. After 12 rounds of the encryption function which require 96 cycles, a 128-bit intermediate key L is stored into the key registers L_{ij} $(0 \leq i, j < 4)$ by shifting R_{ij} and L_{ij} in 16 clock cycles. Therefore, it takes 128 cycles for key setup.

The two S-box circuits S_0 and S_1 are located in the data processing block, and one of those outputs is selected by a 2-to-1 MUX (8-bit width) and input to the matrix multiplier. The encryption processing of CLEFIA-128 is modified by a equivalent transformation as shown in Fig. 7 (a). The 32-bit XOR operation with 32-bit chunks K_i is reduced to the 8-bit XOR operation by locating it in the matrix multiplier. The 32-bit chunk K_i selected by a 32-bit 4-to-1 MUX is divided into four 8-bit data, and then one of the data is selected by a 8-bit 4-to-1 MUX and fed into the matrix multiplier one by one in 4 clock cycles.

In the key scheduling block, the intermediate key L stored in L_{ij} is cyclically shifted by one byte, and the 8-bit chunk in L_{00} is fed into the data processing after being XORed with the 8-bit chunk of CON_i. At the end of even-numbered rounds, L_{ij} is updated by (8-bit shift+Σ) operation; at the end of encryption, L_{ij} is updated by (8-bit shift + Σ^{-8}) operation in order to recover the intermediate key L. After restoring the intermediate key L, L_{ij} holds it by clock gating until next start of encryption.

3.3 Type-II Architecture

In Type-II architecture, we aim the area optimization of the key scheduling block. Since *DoubleSwap* function Σ is decomposed as $\Sigma = \Psi \circ \Omega$, where Ψ and Ω are both involutive, as described in Sect. 2.2, Σ^{-8} satisfies the following equations.

$$\begin{aligned}
\Sigma^{-8} &= (\Psi \circ \Omega)^{-8} \\
&= (\Omega \circ \Psi)^{8} \\
&= (\Omega \circ \Psi)^{8} \circ (\Omega \circ \Omega) \\
&= (\Omega \circ \Psi) \circ \cdots \circ (\Omega \circ \Psi) \circ (\Omega \circ \Omega) \\
&= \Omega \circ (\Psi \circ \Omega)^{8} \circ \Omega \\
&= \Omega \circ \Sigma^{8} \circ \Omega
\end{aligned}$$

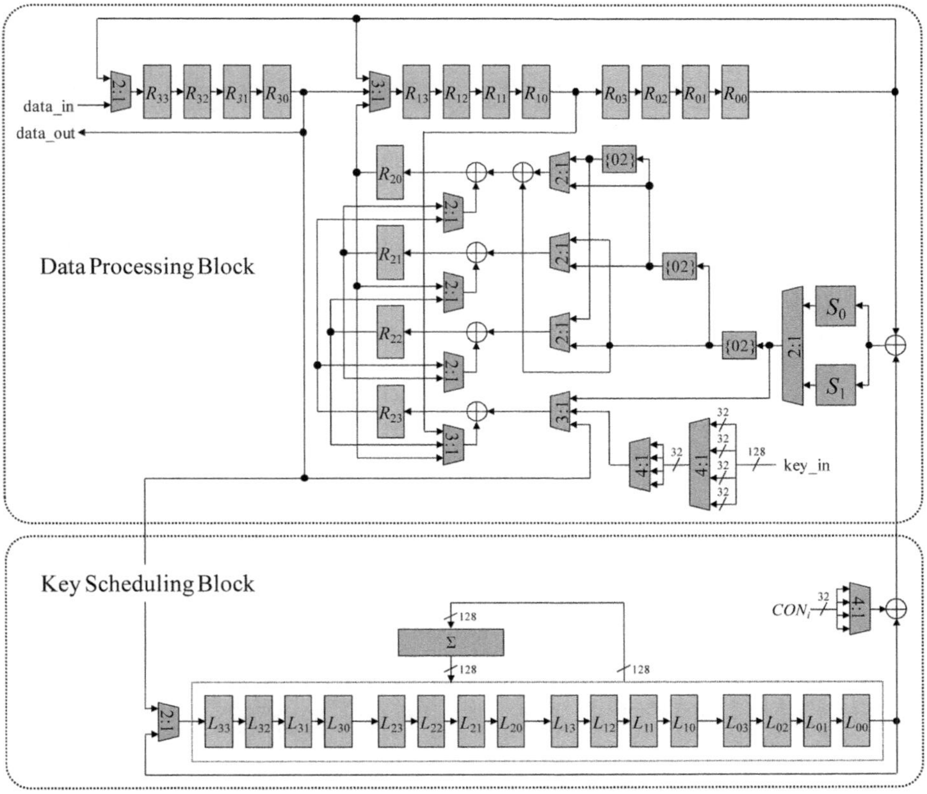

Fig. 6. Data path of Type-III architecture

Swap function Ω is realized by 8 iterations of cyclic shifting. Thus Σ^{-8} operation can be achieved by 8 iterations of cyclic shifting, 8 iterations of Σ operation, and 8 iterations of cyclic shifting again, which require 24 cycle counts.

During the encryption processing the intermediate key L is updated by Σ operation at the 17th cycle after 16 iterations of cyclic shifting every two rounds. At the 17th cycle, the data registers must hold the current data by clock gating. Accordingly, both 8 additional cycles for the encryption processing and 8 additional cycles to recover the intermediate key L after outputting a ciphertext are required, which results in 192 cycles for encryption. In compensation for the increase of 16 cycle counts, a 128-bit input of MUX in the key scheduling block can be discarded.

3.4 Type-III Architecture

In Type-III architecture, we achieve the area optimization of the data processing block by applying clock gating effectively. Fig. 6 shows the data path of Type-III architecture. Instead of using MUXes, the data stored in R_{10}–R_{13} and

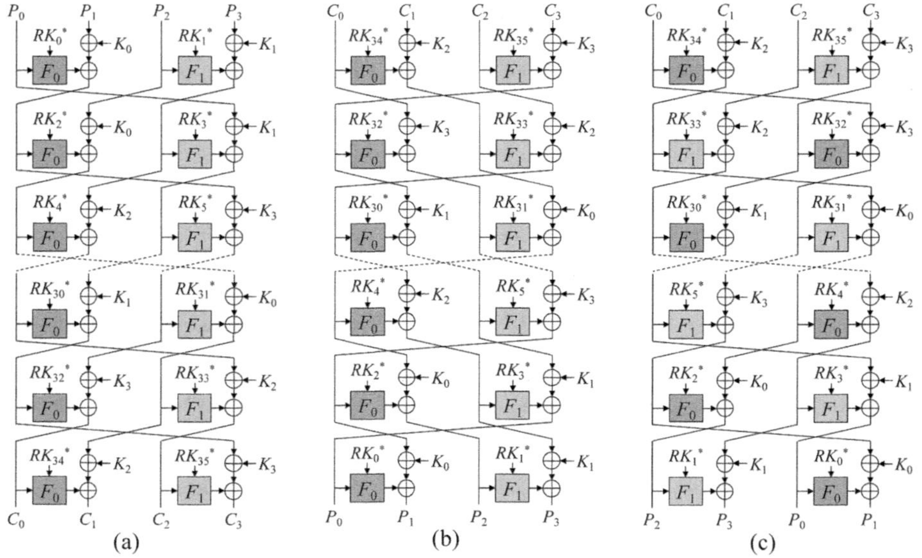

Fig. 7. (a) Encryption processing, (b) Decryption processing, (c) Optimized decryption processing. XOR operations with the part of round keys related to secret key K are moved by an equivalent transformation, and thus RK_j^* $(0 \leq j < 36)$ denote the remaining part of round keys.

those stored in R_{20}–R_{23} are swapped by cyclically shifting these registers in 4 clock cycles, while the other data register and the key registers hold the current state by clock gating. Simultaneously, the XOR operation with a 32-bit chunk K_i is done by XOR gates in the matrix multiplier, which leads the savings of 8 XOR gates. These data swaps are required twice for a round of the encryption processing. Therefore, it takes 16 cycles for a round of the encryption processing; in total 328 and 224 clock cycles are required for encryption and key setup, respectively. In compensation for the increase of many cycle counts, several 8-bit inputs of MUXes together with 8 XOR gates for secret key chunk can be discarded.

4 Supporting Decryption

Any encryption-only implementation can support decryption by using the CTR mode. Yet, if the implementation itself supports decryption, it can be used for more application, e.g., an application requiring the CBC mode. Accordingly, we consider the three types of hardware architectures supporting decryption.

Since the data processing part of CLEFIA employs a 4-branch Type-2 generalized Feistel network [14], the directions of word rotation are different between the encryption function and the decryption function. The encryption and

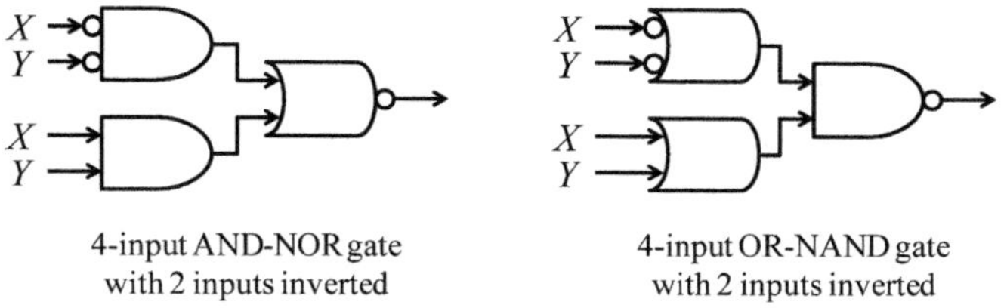

Fig. 8. 4-input AND-NOR and 4-input OR-NAND gate with 2 inputs inverted, which correspond to XOR and XNOR gate

decryption processing of CLEFIA-128 is shown in Fig. 7 (a) and (b), respectively. When the hardware architectures described in Sect. 3 support the decryption processing straightforwardly, many additional multiplexers are considered to be required due to these different directions of word rotation. For avoiding this, we switch the positions of F_0 and those of F_1 at even-numbered rounds as shown in Fig. 7 (c), and then the direction of word rotation becomes the same as the encryption processing shown in Fig. 7 (a). Thus we do not have to largely modify the data path of the above three architectures by processing F_1 ahead of F_0 at even-numbered rounds. However, as the order of round keys fed into the data processing block has been changed, the 8-bit round keys are fed from L_{10} when F_1 is processed at even-numbered rounds and from L_{30} when F_0 is processed at even-numbered rounds. Accordingly, a 8-bit 3-to-1 MUX is required for selecting the source registers of appropriate round keys including L_{00}. Since the leading byte of a ciphertext is stored in R_{10}, not R_{30} for encryption, at the end of decryption because of the optimized decryption processing, a 8-bit 2-to-1 MUX is required for selecting data_out.

5 Implementation Results

We designed and evaluated the three types of hardware architectures presented in Sect. 3 together with their versions supporting both encryption and decryption. The environment of our hardware design and evaluation is as follows:

Language	Verilog-HDL
Design library	0.13 μm CMOS ASIC library
Simulator	VCS version 2006.06
Logic synthesis	Design Compiler version 2007.03-SP3

One Gate Equivalent (GE) is equivalent to the area of a 2-way NAND with the lowest drive strength. For synthesis, we use a clock frequency of 100 KHz, which is widely used operating frequency for RFID applications.

Recently, scan flip-flops have been used in the low-area implementations of blockciphers instead of combinations of D flip-flops and 2-to-1 MUXes [8,1,5] to reduce area requirements. In our evaluation, a D flip-flop and a 2-to-1 MUX cost

Table 1. Detailed implementation figures

Components [GE]	Type-I	Type-II	Type-III
Data Processing Block	1392.5	1392.5	1314.5
Data Register (including MUX)	668	668	612
S-box (including MUX)	332.5	332.5	332.5
S0	117.25	117.25	117.25
S1	201.25	201.25	201.25
Matrix Multiplier	212	212	200
Secret Key MUX	136	136	136
Secret Key XOR	16	16	0*
Round Key XOR	16	16	16
Other MUX	12	12	18
Key Scheduling Block	952	824	824
Key Register (including MUX)	936	808	808
CON XOR	16	16	16
Controller	333	377.25	349.25
Total [GE]	2677.5	2593.75	2487.75
Cycles [clk]	176	192	328
Throughput @100KHz [Kbps]	73	67	39

∗: Secret key XOR is merged to XOR gates in matrix multiplier

4.5 and 2.0 GE, respectively, while a scan flip-flop costs 6.25 GE. Thus, we can save 0.25 GE per bit of storage. Moreover, the library we used has the 4-input AND-NOR and 4-input OR-NAND gates with 2 inputs inverted described in Fig. 8. The outputs of these cells are corresponding to those of XOR or XNOR gates when the inputs X, Y are set as shown in Fig. 8. Since these cells cost 2 GE instead of 2.25 GE required for XOR or XNOR cell, we can save 0.25 GE per XOR or XNOR gate. Clock gating logics are inserted into the design manually by instantiating Integrated Clock Gating (ICG) cells to gate the clocks of specific registers.

Table 1 shows the detailed implementations figures of the three types of hardware architectures presented in Sect. 3. CON generator and selector, ICG cells, and buffers are included in controller.

The area savings for the key scheduling block of Type-II/III implementation over Type-I implementation are 128 GE. In the library we used, a register with a 3-to-1 MUX costs 7.25 GE per bit; a register with a 4-to-1 MUX costs 8.25 GE per bit. The key register of Type-I implementation consists of 120 registers with a 3-to-1 MUX (870 GE) and 8 registers with a 4-to-1 MUX (66 GE), while the key register of Type-II/III implementation consists of 120 scan flip-flops (750 GE) and 8 registers with a 3-to-1 MUX (58 GE). Thus, the area savings of 128 GE are achieved.

The area savings for the data processing block of Type-III implementation over Type-I/II implementation are 78 GE. As for the data register of Type-III implementation 32 scan flips-flops (200 GE) is replaced with 32 D flip-flops (144 GE), which leads savings of 56 GE. 24 3-to-1 MUXes with output inverted (54 GE) can be replaced with 24 2-to-1 MUXes with output inverted (42 GE)

Table 2. Implementation results and comparison

Algorithm	Source	Mode	Cycles [clk]	Area [GE]	Throughput @100KHz [Kbps]	Technology [μm]
CLEFIA	Type-I	Enc	176	2,678	73	0.13
		Enc/Dec	176	2,781	73	
	Type-II	Enc	192	2,594	67	
		Enc/Dec	192/184	2,678	67/70	
	Type-III	Enc	328	2,488	39	
		Enc/Dec	328/320	2,604	39/40	
	[10,12]	Enc/Dec	36	4,950	356	0.09
AES	[3]	Enc/Dec	1,032/1,165	3,400	12/11	0.35
	[4]	Enc	177	3,100	72	0.13
	[5]	Enc	226	2,400	57	0.18

in the matrix multiplier, leading to savings of 12 GE. In addition, 8 XOR gates (16 GE) for secret key XOR is merged to XOR gates in the matrix multiplier. Therefore, the area savings of 78 GE are achieved despite the additional 6 GE for the other MUX.

Table 2 shows the implementation results of the proposed architectures together with their versions supporting both encryption and decryption. We also show, for comparison, the best known result of CLEFIA and low-area implementation results of AES. Our implementations supporting encryption only achieve 46–50% reduction of the area requirements compared to the smallest implementation [10,12] of CLEFIA. As for implementations supporting both encryption and decryption, our implementations are 44–47% smaller. Type-III implementation is 4% larger than the smallest encryption-only implementation [5] of AES, but its encryption/decryption version achieves 23% reduction of the area requirements compared to the smallest encryption/decryption implementation [3] of AES.

In order to investigate the components of 47% area reduction of Type-III implementation supporting both encryption and decryption over [10,12], we first optimized and synthesized the smallest design in [10,12] using the ASIC library in this paper. Next, we designed and evaluated Type-I architecture without using hardware implementation technique such as clock gating and the use of scan flip-flops. As a result, 10%, 29%, and 8% area reduction was shown to be achieved by the difference of ASIC libraries, data-path serialization, and hardware implementation techniques, respectively. 29% area reduction by data-path serialization in detail was divided into 8% by the S-box circuit, 5% by the matrix multiplier circuit, 6% by the reduction of XORs, and 10% by the reduction of MUXes. On the other hand, 8% area reduction by hardware implementation techniques was divided into 6% by clock gating, 1% by the use of scan flip-flops, and 1% by the other techniques.

6 Conclusion

In this paper, we have proposed very compact hardware architectures of CLEFIA with 128-bit keys based on 8-bit shift registers. We showed that the data processing part of CLEFIA-128 can be implemented in a serialized way without any additional registers. Three types of hardware architectures were proposed according to required cycles for one block process by adaptively applying clock gating technique. Those architectures were implemented and synthesized using a 0.13 μm standard cell library. In our smallest implementation, the area requirements are only 2,488 GE, which is 50% smaller than the smallest implementation of CLEFIA-128, and competitive to the smallest AES-128 implementation. Moreover, the area requirements for its version supporting both encryption and decryption are only 2,604 GE, which achieve 23% reduction of area requirement compared to the smallest encryption/decryption implementation of AES-128.

Future work will include the application of side-channel countermeasures such as threshold implementations [6,7] to the proposed architectures.

References

1. De Cannière, C., Dunkelman, O., Knežević, M.: KATAN and KTANTAN — A Family of Small and Efficient Hardware-Oriented Block Ciphers. In: Clavier, C., Gaj, K. (eds.) CHES 2009. LNCS, vol. 5747, pp. 272–288. Springer, Heidelberg (2009)
2. Daemen, J., Rijmen, V.: The Design of Rijndael: AES – The Advanced Encryption Standard (Information Security and Cryptography). Springer, Heidelberg (2002)
3. Feldhofer, M., Wolkerstorfer, J., Rijmen, V.: AES Implementation on a Grain of Sand. In: IEE Proceedings Information Security, vol. 152, pp. 13–20 (2005)
4. Hämäläinen, P., Alho, T., Hännikäinen, M., Hämäläinen, T.: Design and Implementation of Low-Area and Low-Power AES Encryption Hardware Core. In: DSD 2006, pp. 577–583. IEEE Computer Society (2006)
5. Moradi, A., Poschmann, A., Ling, S., Paar, C., Wang, H.: Pushing the Limits: A Very Compact and a Threshold Implementation of AES. In: Paterson, K.G. (ed.) EUROCRYPT 2011. LNCS, vol. 6632, pp. 69–88. Springer, Heidelberg (2011)
6. Nikova, S., Rechberger, C., Rijmen, V.: Threshold Implementations against Side-Channel Attacks and Glitches. In: Ning, P., Qing, S., Li, N. (eds.) ICICS 2006. LNCS, vol. 4307, pp. 529–545. Springer, Heidelberg (2006)
7. Nikova, S., Rijmen, V., Schläffer, M.: Secure Hardware Implementation of Nonlinear Functions in the Presence of Glitches. In: Lee, P.J., Cheon, J.H. (eds.) ICISC 2008. LNCS, vol. 5461, pp. 218–234. Springer, Heidelberg (2009)
8. Rolfes, C., Poschmann, A., Leander, G., Paar, C.: Ultra-Lightweight Implementations for Smart Devices – Security for 1000 Gate Equivalents. In: Grimaud, G., Standaert, F.-X. (eds.) CARDIS 2008. LNCS, vol. 5189, pp. 89–103. Springer, Heidelberg (2008)
9. Shirai, T., Shibutani, K., Akishita, T., Moriai, S., Iwata, T.: The 128-Bit Blockcipher CLEFIA (Extended Abstract). In: Biryukov, A. (ed.) FSE 2007. LNCS, vol. 4593, pp. 181–195. Springer, Heidelberg (2007)
10. Shirai, T., Shibutani, K., Akishita, T., Moriai, S., Iwata, T.: Hardware Implementations of the 128-bit Blockcipher CLEFIA, Technical Report of IEICE, 107(141), ISEC2007–49, 29–36 (2007) (in Japanese)

11. The 128-bit Blockcipher CLEFIA: Algorithm Specification, Revision 1.0 (2007), Sony Corporation,
`http://www.sony.net/Products/cryptography/clefia/download/data/clefia-spec-1.0.pdf`
12. The 128-bit Blockcipher CLEFIA: Security and Performance Evaluations, Revision 1.0 (2007), Sony Corporation,
`http://www.sony.net/Products/cryptography/clefia/download/download/data/clefia-eval-1.0.pdf`
13. Sugawara, T., Homma, N., Aoki, T., Satoh, A.: High-Performance ASIC Implementations of the 128-bit Block Cipher CLEFIA. In: ISCAS 2008, pp. 2925–2928 (2008)
14. Zheng, Y., Matsumoto, T., Imai, H.: On the Construction of Block Ciphers Provably Secure and not Relying on Any Unproved Hypotheses. In: Brassard, G. (ed.) CRYPTO 1989. LNCS, vol. 435, pp. 461–480. Springer, Heidelberg (1990)

Appendix

In this appendix, we show the detailed data flow of the registers R_{ij} in Fig. 5 during a round of the encryption processing for Type-I architecture. Fig. 9 defines the data structure of a round of the encryption processing. The contents of the registers R_{ij} $(0 \leq i < 4)$ are clarified in Table 3.

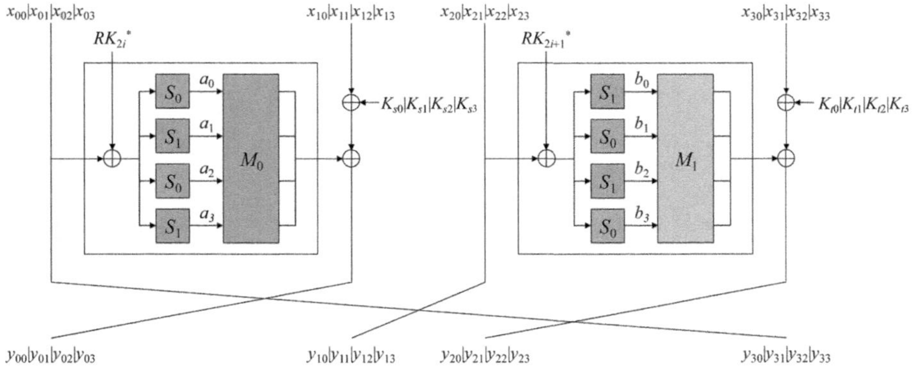

Fig. 9. A round of encryption processing

Table 3. Contents of registers R_{ij} $(0 \leq i, j < 4)$ at the l-th cycle

l	0	1	2	3	4
R_{00}	x_{00}	x_{01}	x_{02}	x_{03}	x_{20}
R_{01}	x_{01}	x_{02}	x_{03}	x_{20}	x_{21}
R_{02}	x_{02}	x_{03}	x_{20}	x_{21}	x_{22}
R_{03}	x_{03}	x_{20}	x_{21}	x_{22}	x_{23}
R_{10}	x_{10}	x_{21}	x_{22}	x_{23}	x_{30}
R_{11}	x_{11}	x_{22}	x_{23}	x_{30}	x_{31}
R_{12}	x_{12}	x_{23}	x_{30}	x_{31}	x_{32}
R_{13}	x_{13}	x_{30}	x_{31}	x_{32}	x_{33}
R_{20}	x_{20}	$x_{13} \oplus \{\texttt{06}\}a_0$	$x_{12} \oplus \{\texttt{04}\}a_0 \oplus \{\texttt{06}\}a_1$	$x_{11} \oplus \{\texttt{02}\}a_0 \oplus a_1 \oplus \{\texttt{06}\}a_2 \oplus K_{s1}$	y_{00}
R_{21}	x_{21}	$x_{12} \oplus \{\texttt{04}\}a_0$	$x_{13} \oplus \{\texttt{06}\}a_0 \oplus \{\texttt{04}\}a_1$	$x_{10} \oplus a_0 \oplus \{\texttt{02}\}a_1 \oplus \{\texttt{04}\}a_2 \oplus K_{s0}$	y_{01}
R_{22}	x_{22}	$x_{11} \oplus \{\texttt{02}\}a_0$	$x_{10} \oplus a_0 \oplus \{\texttt{02}\}a_1 \oplus K_{s0}$	$x_{13} \oplus \{\texttt{06}\}a_0 \oplus \{\texttt{04}\}a_1 \oplus \{\texttt{02}\}a_2$	y_{02}
R_{23}	x_{23}	$x_{10} \oplus a_0 \oplus K_{s0}$	$x_{11} \oplus \{\texttt{02}\}a_0 \oplus a_1 \oplus K_{s1}$	$x_{12} \oplus \{\texttt{04}\}a_0 \oplus \{\texttt{06}\}a_1 \oplus a_2 \oplus K_{s2}$	y_{03}
R_{30}	x_{30}	x_{31}	x_{32}	x_{33}	x_{00} $(= y_{30})$
R_{31}	x_{31}	x_{32}	x_{33}	x_{00}	x_{01} $(= y_{31})$
R_{32}	x_{32}	x_{33}	x_{00}	x_{01}	x_{02} $(= y_{32})$
R_{33}	x_{33}	x_{00}	x_{01}	x_{02}	x_{03} $(= y_{33})$
l	4	5	6	7	8
R_{00}	x_{20}	x_{21}	x_{22}	x_{23}	y_{00}
R_{01}	x_{21}	x_{22}	x_{23}	y_{00}	y_{01}
R_{02}	x_{22}	x_{23}	y_{00}	y_{01}	y_{02}
R_{03}	x_{23}	y_{00}	y_{01}	y_{02}	y_{03}
R_{10}	x_{30}	y_{01}	y_{02}	y_{03}	x_{20} $(= y_{10})$
R_{11}	x_{31}	y_{02}	y_{03}	x_{20}	x_{21} $(= y_{11})$
R_{12}	x_{32}	y_{03}	x_{20}	x_{21}	x_{22} $(= y_{12})$
R_{13}	x_{33}	x_{20}	x_{21}	x_{22}	x_{23} $(= y_{13})$
R_{20}	y_{00}	$x_{33} \oplus \{\texttt{0A}\}b_0$	$x_{32} \oplus \{\texttt{02}\}b_0 \oplus \{\texttt{0A}\}b_1$	$x_{31} \oplus \{\texttt{08}\}b_0 \oplus b_1 \oplus \{\texttt{0A}\}b_2 \oplus K_{t1}$	y_{20}
R_{21}	y_{01}	$x_{32} \oplus \{\texttt{02}\}b_0$	$x_{33} \oplus \{\texttt{0A}\}b_0 \oplus \{\texttt{02}\}b_1$	$x_{30} \oplus b_0 \oplus \{\texttt{08}\}b_1 \oplus \{\texttt{02}\}b_2 \oplus K_{t0}$	y_{21}
R_{22}	y_{02}	$x_{31} \oplus \{\texttt{08}\}b_0$	$x_{30} \oplus b_0 \oplus \{\texttt{08}\}b_1 \oplus K_{t0}$	$x_{33} \oplus \{\texttt{0A}\}b_0 \oplus \{\texttt{02}\}b_1 \oplus \{\texttt{08}\}b_2$	y_{22}
R_{23}	y_{03}	$x_{30} \oplus b_0 \oplus K_{t0}$	$x_{31} \oplus \{\texttt{08}\}b_0 \oplus b_1 \oplus K_{t1}$	$x_{32} \oplus \{\texttt{02}\}b_0 \oplus \{\texttt{0A}\}b_1 \oplus b_2 \oplus K_{t2}$	y_{23}
R_{30}	y_{30}	y_{30}	y_{30}	y_{30}	y_{30}
R_{31}	y_{31}	y_{31}	y_{31}	y_{31}	y_{31}
R_{32}	y_{32}	y_{32}	y_{32}	y_{32}	y_{32}
R_{33}	y_{33}	y_{33}	y_{33}	y_{33}	y_{33}

Another Look at Tightness

Sanjit Chatterjee[1], Alfred Menezes[2], and Palash Sarkar[3]

[1] Department of Computer Science and Automation, Indian Institute of Science
sanjit@csa.iisc.ernet.in
[2] Department of Combinatorics & Optimization, University of Waterloo
ajmeneze@uwaterloo.ca
[3] Applied Statistics Unit, Indian Statistical Institute
palash@isical.ac.in

Abstract. We examine a natural, but non-tight, reductionist security proof for deterministic message authentication code (MAC) schemes in the multi-user setting. If security parameters for the MAC scheme are selected without accounting for the non-tightness in the reduction, then the MAC scheme is shown to provide a level of security that is less than desirable in the multi-user setting. We find similar deficiencies in the security assurances provided by non-tight proofs when we analyze some protocols in the literature including ones for network authentication and aggregate MACs. Our observations call into question the practical value of non-tight reductionist security proofs. We also exhibit attacks on authenticated encryption schemes, disk encryption schemes, and stream ciphers in the multi-user setting.

1 Introduction

A reductionist security proof for a cryptographic protocol $\mathcal{P}$ with respect to a problem $\mathcal{S}$ is an algorithm $\mathcal{R}$ for solving $\mathcal{S}$, where $\mathcal{R}$ has access to a hypothetical subroutine $\mathcal{A}$ (called an oracle) that achieves the adversarial goal specified by the security definition for $\mathcal{P}$. Suppose that $\mathcal{A}$ takes time at most T and is successful with probability at least ϵ, where T and ϵ are functions of the security parameter. Suppose further that $\mathcal{R}$ solves $\mathcal{S}$ in time T' with probability at least ϵ'; again, T' and ϵ' are functions of the security parameter. Then the reductionist security proof $\mathcal{R}$ is said to be *tight* if $T' \approx T$ and $\epsilon' \approx \epsilon$. Roughly speaking, it is *non-tight* if $T' \gg T$ or if $\epsilon' \ll \epsilon$, in which case the *tightness gap* can be informally defined to be $(T'\epsilon)/(T\epsilon')$.

A tight proof for $\mathcal{P}$ with respect to $\mathcal{S}$ is desirable because one can then deploy $\mathcal{P}$ and be assured that breaking $\mathcal{P}$ (within the confines of the adversarial model specified by the security definition for $\mathcal{P}$) is at least as hard as solving $\mathcal{S}$. On the other hand, a non-tight proof for $\mathcal{P}$ with respect to $\mathcal{S}$ provides only the weaker assurance that breaking $\mathcal{P}$ requires at least as much work as a certain fraction of the work believed to be necessary for solving $\mathcal{S}$. In that case, the desired security assurance for $\mathcal{P}$ can be attained by using larger parameters — but at the expense of slower performance.

A. Miri and S. Vaudenay (Eds.): SAC 2011, LNCS 7118, pp. 293–319, 2012.

BBS Generator. As an example, consider the Blum-Blum-Shub (BBS) pseudorandom bit generator G [14]. For an n-bit integer N that is the product of two primes each of which is congruent to 3 modulo 4, the BBS generator takes a random integer $x \bmod N$ as the seed and produces $M = jk$ bits as follows: Let $x_0 = x$, and for $i = 1, \ldots, k$ let $x_i = \min\{x_{i-1}^2 \bmod N,\ N - (x_{i-1}^2 \bmod N)\}$. Then the output of G consists of the j least significant bits of x_i, $i = 1, \ldots, k$.

In [1] it was proven that $j = O(\log n)$ bits can be securely extracted in each iteration, under the assumption that factoring is intractable. More precisely, if one assumes that no algorithm can factor N in expected time less than $L(n)$, then the security proof in [1] (see [68]) shows that the BBS generator is (T, ϵ) secure if

$$T \leq \frac{L(n)(\epsilon/M)^8}{2^{4j+27}n^3}. \tag{1}$$

Here, (T, ϵ)-security means that there is no algorithm with running time bounded by T which can distinguish between the outputs of G and a purely random bit generator with advantage greater than ϵ.

The aforementioned security proof is an example of a polynomial-time reduction since, for $M = O(n^c)$ (where c is a constant), $j = O(\log n)$, and constant ϵ, the right-hand side of (1) is of the form $L(n)/f(n)$ where f is a polynomial in the security parameter n. Such polynomial-time security proofs provide security assurances in an asymptotic sense, i.e., as the security parameter n tends to infinity. However, for a fixed security parameter that might be used in practice, the proof might provide little or no security assurance. For example, suppose that one were to follow the recommendations in [29] and [72] and implement the BBS generator with $n = 768$ and $j = 9$. Then, as observed in [47], by using the number field sieve to estimate $L(n)$ and taking $M = 10^7$ and $\epsilon = 0.01$, one sees that the inequality (1) provides security assurances only against an adversary whose time is bounded by 2^{-264}. Thus, the security proof is completely meaningless for these parameters.

Does Tightness Matter? As discussed in [47], a non-tight reductionist security proof for a protocol $\mathcal{P}$ with respect to a problem $\mathcal{S}$ can be interpreted in several ways. An optimistic interpretation is that it is reasonable to expect that a tighter reduction will be found in the future, or perhaps that $\mathcal{P}$ is secure *in practice* in the sense that there is no attack on $\mathcal{P}$ that is faster than the best attack on $\mathcal{S}$ even though a tight reduction from $\mathcal{S}$ to $\mathcal{P}$ might not exist. However, strictly speaking, if one implements $\mathcal{P}$ using a security parameter for which the problem $\mathcal{S}$ is expected to take time T' to solve, then the security proof does not rule out the possibility that an attack on $\mathcal{P}$ which takes time considerably less than T' will be discovered in the future.

Researchers who work in theoretical cryptography are generally satisfied with polynomial-time reductions, although some of them caution about the validity of non-tight proofs in practice. For instance, Luby [52] writes "when we describe a reduction of one primitive to another we are careful to quantify how much of the security of the first instance is transferred to the second." Goldreich [36] cautions that a (non-tight) asymptotic proof offers only the "plausibility" of the protocol's security. On the other hand, Damgård [25] asserts that a non-tight polynomial-time reduction is useful because it rules out all polynomial-time attacks. However, such an assurance is not very comforting since proofs are meant to guarantee resistance to *all* attacks, and moreover there are many examples of practical cryptographic schemes that have succumbed to attacks that are deemed to be effective in practice even though in asymptotic terms they require super-polynomial time.

Considerable effort has been expended on devising tighter security proofs for existing protocols, and on designing new protocols with tighter security proofs. For example, the first security proof [5] for the traditional hash-then-sign RSA signature scheme (called RSA-FDH) was highly non-tight. Subsequently, Coron [23] found an alternate proof that is significantly tighter (although still considered non-tight), and proved that no tighter reduction exists [24]. Meanwhile, Katz and Wang [43] showed that a small modification of RSA-FDH yields a signature scheme that has a tight security proof, arguably increasing confidence in RSA-FDH itself. Nonetheless, another variant of RSA-FDH, called RSA-PSS, is commonly recommended in practice because it has a tight security proof [5]. As another example, Gentry and Halevi [35] designed a hierarchical identity-based encryption (HIBE) scheme that has a security proof whose tightness gap depends only linearly on the number of levels, in contrast to all previous HIBE schemes whose tightness gaps depend exponentially on the number of levels. Finally, we mention Bernstein's [7] tight proof in the random oracle model for the Rabin-Williams signature scheme, and Schäge's [65] tight proofs without the random oracle assumption for the Cramer-Shoup and Camenisch-Lysyanskaya signature schemes.

Despite ongoing efforts by some to tighten security proofs of existing protocols and to develop new protocols with tighter proofs, it is fair to say that, for the most part, the tightness gaps in security proofs are not viewed as a major concern in practice. Researchers who design protocols with non-tight proofs typically give arguments in favour of their protocol's efficiency by using parameters that would make sense if the proof had been tight. For example, the Schnorr signature scheme [66] is widely regarded as being secure, although its known security proofs are highly non-tight [58]. In fact, there are arguments which suggest that a tighter proof is not even possible [57]. Nevertheless, the Schnorr signature scheme is widely used in the cryptographic literature without any suggestion to use larger key sizes to account for the tightness gap in the proof.

Other examples of well-known protocols with highly non-tight proofs include the Boneh-Franklin (BF) [16,34], Sakai-Kasahara (SK) [22] and Boneh-Boyen (BB1) [15] identity-based encryption schemes, the Lu et al. aggregate signature scheme [51], and the HMQV key agreement protocol [48]. In [18], Boyen compares the tightness of the reductions for BB1, BF and SK. The reduction for BB1 is significantly tighter than the reduction for BF, which in turn is significantly tighter than that for SK. However, all three reductions are in fact highly non-tight, the tightness gap being (at least) linear, quadratic and cubic in the number of random oracle queries made by the adversary for BB1, BF and SK, respectively. Although all these proofs have large tightness gaps, Boyen recommends that SK should "generally be avoided as a rule of thumb", BF is "safe to use", and BB1 "appears to be the smartest choice" in part due to the "fairly efficient security reduction" of the latter. Despite the importance Boyen attaches to tightness as a reason for avoiding SK, a recent IETF standard co-authored by Boyen that describes BB1 and BF [19] does not recommend larger security parameters to account for tightness gaps in their security proofs.

Our Work. In §2, we examine a natural, but non-tight, reductionist security proof for MAC schemes in the multi-user setting. If parameters are selected without accounting for the tightness gap in the reduction, then the MAC scheme is shown to provide a level of security that is less than what one would desire in the multi-user setting. In particular, the attacks we describe are effective on HMAC as standardized in [33,26] and CMAC as standardized in [28,69]. In §3, we show that this deficiency in the security assurances provided by the non-tight proof appears in a network authentication protocol [20], and in §4 we obtain analogous results for aggregate MACs and aggregate designated verifier signatures. In §5, we exhibit attacks on some authenticated encryption schemes, disk encryption schemes, and stream ciphers in the multi-user setting. We draw our conclusions in §6.

2 MACs in the Multi-user Setting

Cryptographic protocols that provide basic confidentiality and authentication security services are typically examined in the *single-user setting*, where there is only one legitimate user (or a pair of legitimate users) and an adversary. However, these protocols are generally deployed in the *multi-user setting*, where there may be additional threats. Key establishment protocols were first analyzed in the multi-user setting in [4,13]. This was followed by a study of multi-user public-key encryption [2] and signatures [54]. In this section, we consider the security of MAC schemes in the multi-user setting.

2.1 Security Definition

A *MAC scheme* consists of a family of functions $\{H_k\}_{k \in \mathcal{K}}$, where $\mathcal{K} = \{0,1\}^r$ is the key space and $H_k : \mathcal{D} \to \{0,1\}^t$ for each $k \in \mathcal{K}$. Here, $\mathcal{D}$ is the set of all (non-empty) binary strings of some maximum length L. A pair of users A and B select a secret key $k \in \mathcal{K}$. To authenticate a message $m \in \mathcal{D}$, user A computes the tag $\tau = H_k(m)$ and sends (m, τ). The receiver B verifies that $\tau = H_k(m)$.

The traditional definition of MAC security (in the single-user setting) is the following. An adversary $\mathcal{B}$ has complete knowledge of the MAC scheme, i.e., it can select arbitrary $k \in \mathcal{K}$ and $m \in \mathcal{D}$ and compute $H_k(m)$. Now, a key k' is selected independently and uniformly at random from $\mathcal{K}$ and kept secret from $\mathcal{B}$. The adversary $\mathcal{B}$ has access to a MAC oracle indexed by k' in the following way: for any $m \in \mathcal{D}$ of $\mathcal{B}$'s choosing, $\mathcal{B}$ is given $H_{k'}(m)$. $\mathcal{B}$'s goal is to produce a *forgery*, i.e., a pair (m, τ) such that $m \in \mathcal{D}$ was not queried to the MAC oracle and $H_{k'}(m) = \tau$. We will henceforth denote $\mathcal{B}$'s task by *MAC1* (breaking a MAC scheme in the single-user setting). An adversary $\mathcal{B}$ is said to (T, ϵ)-break MAC1 if its running time is bounded by T and it produces a forgery with probability at least ϵ; the probability is assessed over the choice of k' and $\mathcal{B}$'s coin tosses. MAC1 is said to be (T, ϵ)-secure if there does not exist an adversary $\mathcal{B}$ that (T, ϵ)-breaks it.

Our definition of MAC security in the multi-user setting is the following. An adversary $\mathcal{A}$ has complete knowledge of the MAC scheme. First, n keys $k_1, k_2, \ldots, k_n$ corresponding to users[1] $1, 2, \ldots, n$ are chosen independently and uniformly at random from $\mathcal{K}$ and kept secret from $\mathcal{A}$; n is an upper bound on the total number of users in the system. The adversary $\mathcal{A}$ has access to MAC oracles indexed by $k_1, \ldots, k_n$ in the following way: for any (i, m) of $\mathcal{A}$'s choosing, where $i \in [1, n]$ and $m \in \mathcal{D}$, $\mathcal{A}$ is given $H_{k_i}(m)$. Furthermore, $\mathcal{A}$ is allowed to *corrupt* any oracle (or user); i.e., for any $i \in [1, n]$ of its choosing, $\mathcal{A}$ is given k_i. The adversary's goal is to produce a *forgery*, i.e., find a triple (i, m, τ) such that:

(i) $i \in [1, n]$ and $m \in \mathcal{D}$;
(ii) the adversary did not corrupt oracle i;
(iii) the adversary did not query H_{k_i} with m; and
(iv) $H_{k_i}(m) = \tau$.

Henceforth, $\mathcal{A}$'s task will be denoted by *MAC** (breaking a MAC scheme in the multi-user setting)[2]. $\mathcal{A}$ is said to (T, ϵ)-break MAC* if its running time is bounded by T and it produces a forgery with probability at least ϵ; the probability is assessed over the choices of $k_1, \ldots, k_n$ and $\mathcal{A}$'s coin tosses. MAC* is said to be (T, ϵ)-secure if there does not exist an adversary $\mathcal{A}$ that (T, ϵ)-breaks it.

2.2 Reductionist Security Proof

We present a natural reductionist security proof that a MAC scheme is secure in the multi-user setting, provided that it is secure in the single-user setting.

Suppose, by way of contradiction, that $\mathcal{A}$ is an adversary that (T, ϵ)-breaks MAC*. Suppose we are given access to a MAC oracle for H_k, where $k \in_R \mathcal{K}$; call the oracle MAC_k. We show how $\mathcal{A}$ can be used to design an adversary $\mathcal{B}$ that produces a forgery with respect to MAC_k.

$\mathcal{B}$ begins by selecting an index $j \in_R [1, n]$, guessing that if $\mathcal{A}$ succeeds then its forgery will be with respect to user j. For each $i \in [1, n]$ with $i \neq j$, $\mathcal{B}$ selects $k_i \in_R \mathcal{K}$ as i's secret key. User j's secret key is assigned to be k (which is unknown to $\mathcal{B}$). $\mathcal{B}$ now runs $\mathcal{A}$, answering $\mathcal{A}$'s MAC and corrupt queries to users $i \neq j$ using knowledge of k_i, and using the given oracle MAC_k to answer $\mathcal{A}$'s MAC queries to user j. If $\mathcal{A}$ corrupts user j, then $\mathcal{B}$ aborts with failure. If $\mathcal{A}$ outputs a forgery (j, m, τ), then $\mathcal{B}$ outputs (m, τ) as its forgery with respect to MAC_k; otherwise, $\mathcal{B}$'s experiment has failed.

---

[1] More precisely, a 'user' is a pair of entities who share a symmetric key.

[2] The MAC* problem without the corrupt capability was first formulated in [13].

Now, $\mathcal{A}$'s operation is independent of $\mathcal{B}$'s guess j, unless $\mathcal{A}$ corrupts user j in which case $\mathcal{B}$ is certain to fail. Hence, the probability that $\mathcal{A}$ succeeds and $\mathcal{B}$'s guess is correct is at least ϵ/n and so $\mathcal{B}$ $(T, \epsilon/n)$-breaks MAC1. We conclude that if a MAC scheme is (T, ϵ)-secure in the single-user setting, then it is $(T, n\epsilon)$-secure in the multi-user setting.

Remark 1. (*tightness gap in the security proof for MAC**) The security reduction is non-tight, having a tightness gap of n, the number of users of the MAC scheme. In §2.3, we present a generic attack on an ideal MAC scheme in the multi-user setting that, under the assumption that keys and tags are of the same bitlength r, produces a MAC forgery within time $2^r/n$. The attack is faster than the best possible attack — exhaustive key search with running time 2^r — on an ideal MAC scheme in the single-user setting. Note that the attack does not contradict the security proof for MAC* because of the tightness gap of n. The attack suggests that a reduction for MAC* that is tighter than the one given above does not exist.

Remark 2. (*tightness gap in the security proof for RSA-FDH*) The security proof for MAC* given above is somewhat similar to the Bellare-Rogaway security proof for RSA-FDH in the random oracle model [5]. Recall that the RSA-FDH signature on a message m is $s = H(m)^d \bmod N$, where (N, e) is an RSA public key and d is the corresponding private key, and where $H : \{0,1\}^* \to [0, N-1]$ is a hash function modeled as a public random oracle. In the Bellare-Rogaway proof, the simulator uses a signature forger $\mathcal{F}$ to solve a given instance (N, e, y) of the RSA problem, i.e., find $x \in [0, N-1]$ satisfying $y \equiv x^e \pmod N$. The forger $\mathcal{F}$ is executed with (N, e) as public key, and the simulator has to faithfully answer $\mathcal{F}$'s signature queries and queries to H. Assuming that $\mathcal{F}$ makes at most q H-queries, the simulator selects $j \in_R [1, q]$ and answers the jth H-query m with $H(m) = y$, hoping that $\mathcal{F}$ eventually produces a forger on m — since the signature on m must be x, the simulator thereby obtains the solution to its instance of the RSA problem. If $\mathcal{F}$ forges a signature on any of the other $q-1$ messages it presented to H, then the simulator fails. Consequently, the security reduction has a tightness gap of q.

Coron [23] gave an alternate security proof for RSA-FDH for which the tightness gap is q_S, the number of signature queries $\mathcal{F}$ is permitted to make. Since q_S can be expected to be significantly smaller than the number of hash queries a real-world forger can make, Coron's proof is significantly tighter. However, it is still non-tight, and in fact Coron [24] showed that no tighter proof is possible.

Unlike the non-tight proof for multi-user MAC schemes, the tightness gap in the RSA-FDH proof does not seem to be a concern because no one expects there to be a method for breaking RSA-FDH that is faster than solving the RSA problem (for which the fastest method known is to factor N). Indeed, it is shown in [46] that RSA-FDH is *tightly* equivalent to an interactive version of the RSA problem, called RSA1. Although Coron's separation result implies that the RSA1 problem cannot be proven to be tightly equivalent to the RSA problem, reasonable heuristic arguments suggest that the RSA1 and RSA problems are indeed equivalent in practice.

Remark 3. (*tightness gaps in security proofs for Diffie-Hellman key agreement protocols*) Numerous Diffie-Hellman key agreement protocols have been proposed in the literature, and many of them have been proven secure in the Canetti-Krawczyk (CK) [20] model (and its variants). In the CK model, there can be many users, any two of which can engage in several sessions of the key agreement protocol; suppose that there are at most n sessions in total. The security proofs are with respect to the computational Diffie-Hellman problem (CDH) or a variant of it: given g, g^x and g^y, where g is a generator of a cyclic group, compute g^{xy}. Typically, one part of the proof involves the simulator selecting a session j at random and then embedding g^x and g^y as the (ephemeral or static) public keys of each of the two communicating parties for that session. If the adversary of the key agreement protocol succeeds in compromising the security of the jth session, then the simulator is able to compute g^{xy}; otherwise the simulator fails. Consequently, the security reduction has a tightness gap of at least n.

To the best of our knowledge, all published security proofs for Diffie-Hellman protocols in the CK model (e.g., see [48,50,55,70]) have tightness gaps of at least n. However, no one has insisted that implementations of these protocols use larger security parameters in order to account for the possible existence of an attack that is better than the fastest known attack on the underlying Diffie-Hellman problem.

2.3 An Attack on MAC*

Select an arbitrary message m and obtain the tags $H_{k_i}(m)$ for $i = 1, 2, \ldots, n$. Next, select an arbitrary subset $\mathcal{W}$ of keys with $|\mathcal{W}| = w$. For each $\ell \in \mathcal{W}$, compute $H_\ell(m)$. If $H_\ell(m) = H_{k_i}(m)$ for some i (this event is called a *collision*), then conclude that $\ell = k_i$ and use ℓ to forge a message-tag pair for user i.

The expected running time of the attack is w, and there are n MAC queries. The attack is deemed successful if $\ell = k_i$ the first time a collision $H_\ell(m) = H_{k_i}(m)$ is detected. In §2.4, the attack's success probability is analyzed in the ideal MAC model. Recall that r is the key length and t is the tag length. Suppose that $n^2 \ll 2^{r+1}$ and $nw = c2^t$ for some constant c. One consequence of the analysis is that if $r = t$, then the success probability is approximately $\frac{1}{2}$. If $t \gg r$ then the success probability is essentially 1, whereas if $r \gg t$ then the attack is virtually certain to fail. These conclusions are not surprising, as the following informal argument shows. A collision can occur due to either a *key collision* (i.e., $k_i = k_j$) or a *tag collision* (i.e., $H_{k_i}(m) = H_{k_j}(m)$ but $k_i \neq k_j$). Given that a collision has occurred, if keys and tags are of the same size, then the probability that it is due to a key collision is about $\frac{1}{2}$; if keys are much longer than tags, the collision is most likely due to a tag collision; and if tags are much longer than the keys, then the collision is most likely due to a key collision.

In the remainder of the paper, the attack will be referred to as *Attack 1*.

Remark 4. (*a second attack on MAC**) Select an arbitrary message m and obtain the tags $H_{k_i}(m)$ for i=1, 2, ... until a *collision* is obtained: $H_{k_p}(m)$=$H_{k_q}(m)$ where $p < q$. Now corrupt user p and obtain k_p. Under the assumption that

$k_p = k_q$, use k_p to forge a message-tag pair with respect to user q. This attack is called *Attack 2*. One can show that if $r \leq t$ then the probability that the first collision is a key collision is significant only when the number of MAC queries is at least $2^{r/2}$. Since Attack 1 can succeed with fewer MAC queries, does not require corrupt queries, and is amenable to time-memory trade-offs (cf. Remark 7), it is always superior to Attack 2.

Remark 5. (*symmetric-key encryption*) Attack 1 shows that *existential key recovery* (i.e., finding the secret key of any one of a set of users) is easier than *universal key recovery* (i.e., finding the secret key of a specified user) for (deterministic) MAC schemes; these notions of key recovery were discussed in [47, Section 5] in the context of public-key cryptosystems. Gligor, Parno and Shin (see [67]) proved that existential key recovery is intractable for nonce-based symmetric-key encryption schemes that are indistinguishable against chosen-plaintext attacks; an example of such an encryption scheme is the counter mode of encryption (cf. §5). However, their proof is non-tight, the tightness gap being equal to the number of secret keys in the system. They then showed that this tightness gap allows an existential key recovery attack that is faster than the best attack known for universal key recovery for certain nonce-based encryption schemes including the counter mode of encryption. Attack 1 is analogous to their attack, which in turn was preceded by Biham's key collision attacks [9].

We next argue that Attack 1 is effective on HMAC as standardized in [33,26] and CMAC as standardized in [28,69].

HMAC. HMAC [3] is a hash function-based MAC scheme that is extensively standardized and has been widely deployed in practice. The MAC of a message m with secret key k is $\text{HMAC}_k(m) = \text{Trunc}_t\,(H(k \oplus \text{opad}, H(k \oplus \text{ipad}, m)))$, where $H : \{0,1\}^* \to \{0,1\}^d$ is an iterated hash function, opad and ipad are fixed strings, and Trunc_t is the truncation function that extracts the t most significant bits of its input. The HMAC parameters are r (the bitlength of the secret key k), t (the bitlength of MAC tags) and d (the output length of H, which is assumed to be an iterated hash function).

IETF RFC 4868 [44] specifies HMAC-SHA-256-128, i.e., HMAC with SHA-256 [32] as the underlying hash function and parameters r=d=256 and t=128, presumably intended to achieve a 128-bit security level. Since $r \gg t$, Attack 1 is certain to fail when HMAC-SHA-256-128 is used in the multi-user setting.

HMAC is also standardized in FIPS 198-1[33], with recommendations for parameter sizes given in SP 800-107 [26]. It is stated in [26] that the "security strength" of HMAC is the minimum of r and $2d$, and the only requirement on tag lengths is that $t \geq 8$. Hence, if one were to use HMAC with SHA-1 [32] (which has d=160) as the underlying hash function and select r=t=80, then the resulting MAC scheme would be compliant with SP 800-107 and be expected to achieve an 80-bit security level. However, this version of HMAC would succumb to Attack 1 in the multi-user setting. Namely, by selecting n=2^{20} and w=2^{60}, after querying 2^{20} users for the MAC of some fixed message m, the adversary would be able to determine the secret key of one of the 2^{20} users after performing about 2^{60} MAC operations. Since the work can be easily and effectively parallelized, the attack should be considered feasible today (cf. Remark 7).

The FIPS 198-1 standard allows 80-bit keys and 160-bit tags, i.e., r=80 and t=160. Attack 1 also applies to this choice of parameters. In fact, since $t \gg r$, a collision in the first phase of the attack will most likely be due to a key collision. In general, having tag length to be greater than the key length will not provide any additional resistance to Attack 1.

Remark 6. (*number of users*) The 2^{20} users in the attack described above need not be distinct pairs of entities. What is needed is 2^{20} keys. An entity might be engaged in multiple sessions with other entities, and might even have several active sessions with the same entity. Thus, the attacks could be mounted with far fewer than 2^{20} different entities.

CMAC. CMAC is a block cipher-based MAC scheme that has been standardized in [28] and [69]. Let E denote a block cipher with key length r bits and block length b bits. The r-bit key k is first used to generate two b-bit subkeys, k_1 and k_2. The message m is divided into blocks $m_1, m_2, \ldots, m_h$, where each m_i is b-bits in length with the possible exception of m_h, which might be less than b-bits long. Now, if m_h is b bits in length, then it is updated as follows: $m_h \leftarrow m_h \oplus k_1$. Otherwise, m_h is padded on its right with a single 1 bit followed by 0 bits until the length of the padded m_h is b bits; then m_h is updated as follows: $m_h \leftarrow m_h \oplus k_2$. Finally, one sets $c_0 = 0$ and computes $c_i = E_k(c_{i-1} \oplus m_i)$ for $1 \le i \le h$. The tag of m is defined to be $\text{CMAC}_k(m) = \text{Trunc}_t(c_h)$.

The standards [28] and [69] both use the AES block cipher (with r=b=128) and do not mandate truncation, so we can take t=128. With these parameters, CMAC in the multi-user setting is vulnerable to Attack 1. Indeed, after querying n=2^{32} users for the MAC of a fixed message m, the adversary is able to compute the secret key of one of the users after performing about 2^{96} MAC operations. Although this workload is considered infeasible today, the attack does demonstrate that CMAC-AES does not attain the 128-bit security level in the multi-user setting.

Remark 7. (*reducing the on-line running time*) Hellman [39] introduced the idea of time/memory trade-offs (TMTO) to search for a preimage of a target point in the range of a one-way function. The idea is to perform a one-time precomputation and store some of the results, subsequent to which the on-line search phase can be significantly sped up. Biryukov and Shamir [11] later applied TMTO to stream ciphers. They considered the problem of inverting any one out of D possible targets. Let N denote the size of the search space, M the amount of memory required, and T the on-line time, and suppose that $1 \le D \le T^2$. Then the Biryukov-Shamir TMTO can be implemented with these parameters provided that they satisfy the so-called multiple-data trade-off curve $TM^2D^2 = N^2$; the precomputation time P is N/D. The multiple-data trade-off curve has natural interpretations in other contexts. Biryukov et al. [10] considered the problem of finding any one of D keys for a block cipher. An extensive analysis of TMTO with multiple data in different cryptographic settings was carried out in [40].

The multiple-data trade-off curve can be applied in the current context to reduce the online search time. For HMAC with $r{=}t{=}80$ as considered above, consider the function $f : k \mapsto \text{HMAC}_k(m)$ where m is a fixed message. Treating f as a one-way function, the adversary's goal is to invert f on any one of the n tag values $f(k_1), \ldots, f(k_n)$. For $n = 2^{20}$, the precomputation time is $P = 2^{60}$ and T and M satisfy $TM^2 = 2^{120}$. Setting $T = M$ (as originally considered by Hellman), we have $T = M = 2^{40}$. Thus, the adversary can find any one of 2^{20} possible HMAC keys with an off-line computation of 2^{60} HMAC invocations, 2^{40} storage units, and an on-line search time of 2^{40}. Using presently available storage and computer technology, this attack should be considered feasible.

For the CMAC example considered above with $r{=}t{=}128$, if the adversary wishes to determine any one of $n = 2^{32}$ possible secret keys, the precomputation time would be $P = 2^{96}$. The parameters T and M are related by $TM^2 = 2^{192}$, so $T = M = 2^{64}$ is one solution. Hence, with 2^{64} storage units, an on-line search time of 2^{64} will find one of 2^{32} keys.

Remark 8. (*two-key and three-key variants of CMAC*) The predecessors of CMAC include a three-key variant called XCBC [12] and a two-key variant called TMAC [49]. Interestingly, these predecessors are not vulnerable to Attack 1 due to the use of multiple keys.

Remark 9. (*comparison with birthday attacks*) HMAC and CMAC are both vulnerable to the following birthday attack in the single-user setting. Suppose that keys and tags are each r bits in length. The adversary collects message-tag pairs (where the messages all have the same length) until two distinct messages m_1 and m_2 are found with the same tag τ. By the birthday paradox, the expected number of pairs needed is approximately $2^{r/2}$. Then, for any string x, (m_1, x) and (m_2, x) have the same tags (with high probability in the case of HMAC, and with certainty in the case of CMAC). The attacker can then request for the tag of (m_1, x), thereby also obtaining the tag of (m_2, x).

Note that Attack 1 can be successful by using signficantly fewer MAC queries, and additionally needs to issue only one MAC query per user. Moreover, the damage caused by Attack 1 is more severe than the birthday attack since the former is a key recovery attack.

2.4 Analysis of Attack 1

The *ideal MAC model* for a MAC scheme $\{H_k : \mathcal{D} \to \{0,1\}^t\}_{k \in \mathcal{K}}$ is the following. Let $\mathcal{F}$ be the set of all functions from $\mathcal{D}$ to $\{0,1\}^t$. The set $\mathcal{F}$ is finite and can be considered as the set of all strings of length $\#\mathcal{D}$ over the alphabet $\{0,1\}^t$. A total of 2^r independent and uniform random choices are made from $\mathcal{F}$, giving a family of 2^r independent random oracles. Each such oracle can be indexed by an r-bit string. The resulting indexed family is the idealized version of a MAC scheme. In what follows, $\{H_k\}_{k \in \mathcal{K}}$ will denote an idealized MAC family. In particular, the H_k's will be considered to be independent uniform random oracles.

Consider the following procedure. Suppose $k_1, \ldots, k_n$ are chosen independently and uniformly at random from $\mathcal{K} = \{0,1\}^r$. Let m (a message) be an arbitrary element of $\mathcal{D}$. Then, for $i \neq j$, we will need to consider the event that $H_{k_i}(m) = H_{k_j}(m)$. For the probability analysis, it will be useful to analyze this event in terms of the following three events, the last two of which are conditional events: (i) $k_i = k_j$; (ii) $H_{k_i} = H_{k_j}$ given that $k_i \neq k_j$; and (iii) $H_{k_i}(m) = H_{k_j}(m)$ given that $k_i \neq k_j$ and $H_{k_i} \neq H_{k_j}$. Clearly $\Pr[k_i = k_j] = 2^{-r}$ and $\Pr[H_{k_i} = H_{k_j} | k_i \neq k_j] = 1/\#\mathcal{F} = (2^{-t})^{\#\mathcal{D}}$. In practical applications, the maximum length L of messages can be expected to be at least around 2^{20} and so the probability that $H_{k_i} = H_{k_j}$ given $k_i \neq k_j$ is negligible. Furthermore, for $1 \leq s \leq 2^t$, the quantity $s/\#\mathcal{F}$ is also negligible. We will use these approximations in the remainder of the analysis.

The analysis of Attack 1 is done in two stages. In the first stage, we determine values for n and w for which there is a significant probability of detecting a collision. The second stage of the analysis considers the probability of the keys ℓ and k_i being equal once a collision $H_\ell(m) = H_{k_i}(m)$ is detected.

Let $\mathcal{W} = \{\ell_1, \ldots, \ell_w\}$ and consider the functions $H_{\ell_1}, \ldots, H_{\ell_w}$. Let A be the event that these functions are distinct. Then

$$\Pr[A] = \left(1 - \frac{1}{\#\mathcal{F}}\right)\left(1 - \frac{2}{\#\mathcal{F}}\right)\cdots\left(1 - \frac{w-1}{\#\mathcal{F}}\right) \approx 1.$$

The approximation is based on the fact that w^2 is negligible in comparison to $\#\mathcal{F} = (2^t)^{\#\mathcal{D}}$. Let C be the event that a collision occurs. Let $\mathsf{Lst}_1 = \{H_{k_1}(m), \ldots, H_{k_n}(m)\}$ and $\mathsf{Lst}_2 = \{H_{\ell_1}(m), \ldots, H_{\ell_w}(m)\}$. The event C is the event $\mathsf{Lst}_1 \cap \mathsf{Lst}_2 \neq \emptyset$. Now,

$$\Pr[C] = \Pr[C|A] \cdot \Pr[A] + \Pr[C|\overline{A}] \cdot \Pr[\overline{A}] \approx \Pr[C|A].$$

Let B_1 be the event that the keys $k_1, \ldots, k_n$ are pairwise distinct. Then

$$\Pr[B_1] = \left(1 - \frac{1}{2^r}\right)\cdots\left(1 - \frac{n-1}{2^r}\right) \approx \exp\left(-\frac{1}{2^r}(1 + 2 + \cdots + n - 1)\right)$$
$$\approx \exp\left(-\frac{n^2}{2^{r+1}}\right) \approx 1 - \frac{n^2}{2^{r+1}}.$$

As long as $n^2 \ll 2^{r+1}$, the probability of event B_1 occurring will be almost equal to 1. For the remainder of the analysis, we will assume that this condition holds.

Let B_2 be the event that the functions $H_{k_1}, \ldots, H_{k_n}$ are pairwise distinct. Conditioned on the event B_1, the probability of B_2 occurring is almost equal 1. This follows from an argument similar to the one which shows that $\Pr[A] \approx 1$. We introduce three more approximations:

$$\begin{aligned}
\Pr[C] \approx \Pr[C|A] &= \Pr[C|A, B_1] \cdot \Pr[B_1] + \Pr[C|A, \overline{B_1}] \cdot \Pr[\overline{B_1}] \\
&\approx \Pr[C|A, B_1] \qquad (\text{using } \Pr[B_1] \approx 1) \\
&= \Pr[C|A, B_1, B_2] \cdot \Pr[B_2] + \Pr[C|A, \overline{B_2}] \cdot \Pr[\overline{B_2}] \\
&\approx \Pr[C|A, B_1, B_2] \qquad (\text{using } \Pr[B_2] \approx 1).
\end{aligned}$$

Let $x_i = H_{k_i}(m)$ for $1 \leq i \leq n$ and $y_j = H_{\ell_j}(m)$ for $1 \leq j \leq w$. Conditioned on the conjunction of B_1 and B_2, the values $x_1, \ldots, x_n$ are independent and uniformly distributed. Conditioned on event A, the values $y_1, \ldots, y_w$ are independent and uniformly distributed. Hence, conditioned on the conjunction of A, B_1 and B_2, the event C is the event that a list of n independent and uniform values from $\{0,1\}^t$ has a non-empty intersection with another list of w independent and uniform values from $\{0,1\}^t$. By the birthday bound, this probability becomes significant when the product $n \cdot w$ is some constant times 2^t. As an example, one may choose $n = 2^{t/4}$ and w to be a constant times $2^{3t/4}$.

Suppose now that a collision is detected. The probability that the collision is due to a repetition of the keys can be estimated as follows. We have

$$\begin{aligned}\Pr[H_{k_i}(m) = H_{\ell_j}(m)] &= \Pr[k_i = \ell_j] + \Pr[H_{k_i}(m) = H_{\ell_j}(m) | k_i \neq \ell_j] \cdot \Pr[k_i \neq \ell_j] \\ &= \frac{1}{2^r} + \left(1 - \frac{1}{2^r}\right) \cdot \Big(\Pr[H_{k_i} = H_{\ell_j} | k_i \neq \ell_j] \\ &\quad + \Pr[H_{k_i}(m) = H_{\ell_j}(m) | k_i \neq \ell_j, H_{k_i} \neq H_{\ell_j}] \cdot \Pr[H_{k_i} \neq H_{\ell_j} | k_i \neq \ell_j] \Big) \\ &= \frac{1}{2^r} + \left(1 - \frac{1}{2^r}\right) \left(\frac{1}{\#\mathcal{F}} + \frac{1}{2^t} \left(1 - \frac{1}{\#\mathcal{F}}\right)\right) \approx \frac{1}{2^r} + \frac{1}{2^t} - \frac{1}{2^{t+r}} = \delta,\end{aligned}$$

and hence

$$\begin{aligned}\Pr[k_i = \ell_j | H_{k_i}(m) = H_{\ell_j}(m)] &= \frac{\Pr[k_i = \ell_j, H_{k_i}(m) = H_{\ell_j}(m)]}{\Pr[H_{k_i}(m) = H_{\ell_j}(m)]} \\ &= \frac{\Pr[k_i = \ell_j]}{\Pr[H_{k_i}(m) = H_{\ell_j}(m)]} \approx \frac{1}{2^r \delta} = \frac{2^{t+r}}{2^r(2^t + 2^r - 1)} = \frac{2^t}{2^t + 2^r - 1}.\end{aligned}$$

If $r = t$, then the last value is approximately $\frac{1}{2}$. However, if $r \gg t$, then the probability is essentially 0.

2.5 Fixes

We propose two generic countermeasures to Attack 1 on MAC schemes in the multi-user setting.

Remark 10. (preventing replay attacks) Some MAC standards make provisions for protecting against the replay of message-tag pairs. For example, NIST's SP 800-38B [28] suggests that replay can be prevented by "incorporating certain identifying information bits into the initial bits of every message. Examples of such information include a sequential message number, a timestamp, or a nonce." We note that sequential message numbers and timestamps do not necessarily circumvent Attack 1 because it is possible that each user selects the same sequential message number or timestamp when authenticating the chosen message m. Nonces can be an effective countermeasure provided that there is sufficient uncertainty in their selection.

rMAC. One countermeasure is to randomize the conventional MAC scheme $\{H_k\}_{k \in \mathcal{K}}$. That is, a user with secret key k now authenticates a message m by computing $\tau = H_k(s, m)$ where $s \in_R \{0,1\}^r$; the resulting tag is (s, τ). The verifier confirms that $\tau = H_k(s, m)$. This modified MAC scheme is called *rMAC* (randomized MAC).

Security of rMAC in the multi-user setting is defined analogously to security of MAC*: The adversary $\mathcal{A}$ is given access to n rMAC oracles with secret keys $k_1, k_2, \ldots, k_n \in_R \mathcal{K}$ and can corrupt any oracle (i.e., obtain its secret key). Its goal is to produce a triple $(i, m, (s, \tau))$ such that the ith oracle was not corrupted, $(m, (s, \tau))$ is a valid message-tag pair with respect to the ith oracle (i.e, $H_{k_i}(s, m) = \tau$), and m was not queried to the ith oracle. We denote $\mathcal{A}$'s task by *rMAC**. When $n = 1$, then rMAC* is called *rMAC1* (security of rMAC in the single-user setting).

It is easy to verify that rMAC* resists Attack 1. Let us denote by $\mathcal{P}_1 \leq_b \mathcal{P}_2$ a reduction from problem $\mathcal{P}_1$ to problem $\mathcal{P}_2$ that has a tightness gap of b; if $b = 1$ then the reduction is tight. In §2.2 we showed that MAC1 $\leq_n$ MAC*, i.e., the problem of breaking a MAC scheme in the single-user setting can be reduced to breaking the same MAC scheme in the multi-user setting, but the reduction has a tightness gap of n. Trivially, we have MAC* $\leq_1$ MAC1. The reductionist security proof in §2.2 can be adapted to show that rMAC1 $\leq_n$ rMAC*, and we trivially have rMAC* $\leq_1$ rMAC1. Moreover, it is easy to see that MAC1 $\leq_1$ rMAC1 and hence MAC1 $\leq_n$ rMAC*. However, it is unlikely that a generic reduction of rMAC1 to MAC1 exists because a MAC scheme $\{H_k\}_{k \in \mathcal{K}}$ having the property that there exists a (known) pair (s, τ) with $s \in \{0,1\}^r$, $\tau \in \{0,1\}^t$ and $H_k(s) = \tau$ for all $k \in \mathcal{K}$ would be considered insecure whereas the corresponding rMAC scheme could well be secure.

We do not know a tighter security reduction from MAC1 to rMAC*, nor do we know whether a tighter reduction is even possible (in general). However, we would expect that rMAC* and MAC1 are tightly related in practice. One approach to increasing confidence in rMAC* would be to derive tight lower bounds for MAC1 and rMAC* in the ideal MAC model, and hope that these lower bounds coincide.

fMAC. One drawback of rMAC is that tags are longer than before. An alternative countermeasure is to prepend all messages with a string that is fixed and unique to every pair of users (and every session between them). That is, a user with secret key k would authenticate a message m by computing the tag $\tau = H_k(f, m)$, where f is the fixed and unique string that the user shares with the intended recipient (for that session). All such strings are assumed to have the same length, and this length is at least r. The strings are assumed to be understood from context, so do not need to be transmitted. (For an example of such strings, see §3.3.) The verifier confirms that $\tau = H_k(f, m)$. This modified MAC scheme is called *fMAC* (fixed-string MAC).

Security of fMAC in the multi-user setting is defined analogously to security of MAC*: The adversary $\mathcal{A}$ is given access to n fMAC oracles with secret keys $k_1, \ldots, k_n \in_R \mathcal{K}$ and fixed strings $f_1, \ldots, f_n$, and can corrupt any oracle. Its goal is to produce a triple (i, m, τ) such that the ith oracle was not corrupted, (m, τ) is a valid message-tag pair with respect to the ith oracle (i.e, $H_{k_i}(f_i, m) = \tau$), and

m was not queried to the ith oracle. We denote $\mathcal{A}$'s task by *fMAC**. When $n = 1$, then fMAC* is called *fMAC1* (security of fMAC in the single-user setting).

As was the case with rMAC*, it is easy to verify that fMAC* resists Attack 1. Furthermore, one can show that fMAC* $\leq_1$ fMAC1 and MAC1 $\leq_1$ fMAC1 $\leq_n$ fMAC*, while we do not expect there to be a generic reduction from fMAC1 to MAC1. We do not know a tighter security reduction from MAC1 to fMAC*, nor do we know whether a tighter reduction is even possible (in general). However, we would expect that fMAC* and MAC1 are tightly related in practice. An intuitive reason for why fMAC* can be expected to be more secure than MAC* is that for fMAC* each of the n oracles available to the adversary can be viewed as having been chosen from an *independent* family of MAC functions, whereas in MAC* each of the n oracles available to the adversary is chosen from a *single* family of MAC functions.

Remark 11. (*use of MAC schemes*) Higher-level protocols that use MAC schemes for authentication generally include various data fields with the messages being MAC'ed, thus providing adequate defenses against Attack 1. For example, IPsec has an authentication-only mode [45] where a MAC scheme is used to authenticate the data in an IP packet. Among these data fields are the source and destination IP addresses, and a 32-bit "Security Parameter Index" (SPI) which identifies the "Security Association" (SA) of the sending party.

3 NetAut

NetAut is a network authentication protocol proposed by Canetti and Krawczyk [20] which combines a key establishment scheme with a conventional MAC scheme in a natural way. In [20], a security model and definition for key establishment are proposed. Then, NetAut is proved to be a secure network authentication protocol under the assumption that the underlying key establishment and MAC schemes are secure. We describe several shortcomings in the analysis of NetAut. The most serious of these shortcomings is the tightness gap in the security proof, which we exploit to formulate concrete attacks on plausible instantiations of NetAut.

3.1 Network Authentication

The NetAut protocol presented in [20] has two ingredients: a key establishment protocol π and a MAC scheme. NetAut utilizes a *session identifier* s, which is a string agreed upon by the parties before execution of the protocol commences. It is assumed that no two NetAut sessions in which a party $\hat{A}$ participates with another party $\hat{B}$ have the same session identifier.

In the initial stage of the NetAut protocol[3], a party $\hat{A}$ participates in a key establishment session with another party $\hat{B}$. Upon successful completion of the

[3] Our description of NetAut is informal and omits a lot of details; the reader can refer to [20] for a complete description.

session, $\hat{A}$ accepts a session key κ associated with the session identified by s and (presumably) shared with $\hat{B}$. Now, to send $\hat{B}$ an authenticated message m within session s, $\hat{A}$ computes $\tau = \text{MAC}_\kappa(m)$ and sends $(\hat{A}, s, m, \tau)$ to $\hat{B}$. Similarly, upon receipt of a message $(\hat{B}, s, m, \tau)$, $\hat{A}$ computes $\tau' = \text{MAC}_\kappa(m)$ and accepts if $\tau' = \tau$. At any point in time, $\hat{A}$ can have multiple active sessions, and can even have multiple active sessions with $\hat{B}$.

The security model for NetAut is developed in two stages. The first stage defines what it means for a key establishment protocol to be secure. The security model, which has come to be known as the 'CK model', allows for multiple parties and multiple sessions, and gives the adversary substantial powers including the ability to learn some session keys, corrupt parties (learn all their secret information), and learn some secret information that is specific to a particular session. Informally speaking, a key establishment protocol is said to be secure if no such adversary can distinguish the session key held by a fresh session from a randomly-generated session key, where a 'fresh' session is one for which the adversary cannot learn the corresponding session key through trivial means (such as corrupting the party that participates in that session or simply asking for the session key). A crucial feature of the definition is that any key establishment protocol that satisfies the security definition can be appropriately combined with secure MAC and symmetric-key encryption schemes to realize a 'secure channel'. In this paper, we will only consider NetAut — the combination of a key establishment protocol with a MAC scheme.

The second stage of the security model for NetAut starts with an idealized notion called a session-based message transmission (SMT) protocol in the authenticated links model. In the authenticated links model, the communications links between any two parties is perfectly authenticated — the SMT protocol is secure in this model by its very definition. A secure network authentication protocol is then defined as one that 'emulates' SMT in the unauthenticated links model in the sense that whatever an adversary can achieve against the protocol can also be accomplished by an adversary against SMT in the authenticated links model.

Canetti and Krawczyk prove that if π is a secure key establishment protocol and the MAC scheme is secure (in the single-user setting), then NetAut is a secure network authentication protocol. The proof and associated definitions are long and intricate. In §3.2 we describe some pitfalls that arise in interpreting the proof when NetAut is instantiated with the SIG-DH key establishment protocol.

3.2 A Concrete Analysis

For concreteness, we will consider the 80-bit security level. Let E be an elliptic curve defined over $\mathbb{F}_p$ where p is a 160-bit prime. Suppose that $N = \#E(\mathbb{F}_p)$ is prime, so that the group $E(\mathbb{F}_p)$ of $\mathbb{F}_p$-rational points offers an 80-bit security level against attacks on the discrete logarithm problem. Let G be a fixed generator of $E(\mathbb{F}_p)$. We consider CMAC at the 80-bit security level, i.e., with 80-bit keys and 80-bit tags; the block cipher SKIPJACK [56], which has 80-bit keys and 80-bit blocks, is a suitable ingredient.

In the SIG-DH key agreement scheme, $\text{sig}_{\hat{A}}$ and $\text{sig}_{\hat{B}}$ denote the signing algorithms of parties $\hat{A}$ and $\hat{B}$, respectively. It is assumed that each party has an authenticated copy of the other party's public verification key. The SIG-DH scheme proceeds as follows. The initiator $\hat{A}$ selects $x \in_R [0, N-1]$ and sends $(\hat{A}, s, X{=}xG)$ to party $\hat{B}$. In response, $\hat{B}$ selects $y \in_R [0, N-1]$ and sends $(\hat{B}, s, Y{=}yG, \text{sig}_{\hat{B}}(\hat{B}, s, Y, X, \hat{A}))$ to $\hat{A}$ and computes $\kappa = yX$. Upon receipt of $\hat{B}$'s message, $\hat{A}$ verifies the signature, sends the message $(\hat{A}, s, \text{sig}_{\hat{A}}(\hat{A}, s, X, Y, \hat{B}))$ to $\hat{B}$, and computes the session key $\kappa = xY$ associated with session s. Finally, upon receipt of $\hat{A}$'s message, $\hat{B}$ verifies the signature and accepts κ as the session key associated with session s.

Canetti and Krawzcyk proved that SIG-DH is secure in the CK model under the assumption that the decisional Diffie-Hellman problem[4] in $E(\mathbb{F}_p)$ is intractable (and the signature scheme is secure). The proof proceeds in two stages. In the first stage, the basic Diffie-Hellman protocol is proven secure in the authenticated links model under the assumption that DDH is intractable; this proof has a tightness gap of n, the total number of sessions. In the second stage, SIG-DH is proven secure (in the unauthenticated links model) under the assumption that the basic Diffie-Hellman protocol is secure in the authenticated links model; this proof has a tightness gap of $2n$. However, these tightness gaps do not seem to have any negative security consequences for SIG-DH.

Key Type Mismatch. The first problem encountered when using SIG-DH and CMAC as the ingredients of NetAut is that the SIG-DH session keys are points in $E(\mathbb{F}_p)$ whereas the CMAC secret keys are bit strings. This *key type mismatch* can be rectified by the commonly-used method of using a key derivation function KDF to derive a bit-string session key from the SIG-DH session key, i.e., the session key is now $\text{KDF}(xyG)$. We refer to the modified key agreement scheme as *hashed SIG-DH* (HSIG-DH).

The KDF is generally modeled as a random oracle in security proofs. HSIG-DH can then be proven secure under the assumption that the gap Diffie-Hellman (GDH) problem[5] is hard using standard techniques.

Keysize Mismatch. Security proofs for Diffie-Hellman key agreement protocols in the random oracle model sometimes make the assumption that the probability of a KDF collision during the adversary's operation is negligible (e.g., see [48,50,55]). If this probability were not negligible, then the adversary could conceivably force two non-related sessions (called 'non-matching' sessions in the literature) to compute the same session key — in that event, the adversary could learn the session key from one session by asking for it and thereby obtain the session key for the other session. Thus, because of the birthday paradox, at the 80-bit security level the assumption that the adversary has negligible probability

---

[4] The decisional Diffie-Hellman (DDH) problem in $E(\mathbb{F}_p)$ is the problem of determining whether $Z{=}xyG$ given G, $X{=}xG$, $Y{=}yG$ and $Z \in E(\mathbb{F}_p)$.

[5] The gap Diffie-Hellman (GDH) problem in $E(\mathbb{F}_p)$ is the problem of solving the computational Diffie-Hellman (CDH) problem in $E(\mathbb{F}_p)$ given an oracle for the DDH problem in $E(\mathbb{F}_p)$.

of obtaining a KDF collision requires that the KDF for HSIG-DH with our choice of elliptic curve parameters should have 160-bit outputs. However we then have a *keysize mismatch* since CMAC uses 80-bit keys. If the KDF is restricted to 80-bit outputs, then the aforementioned proofs have a logical gap since the probability of a KDF collision now becomes non-negligible.

One simple way to remove this gap is to include the identities of the communicating parties and the session identifier as input to the key derivation function (as is done in [70], for example), i.e., the HSIG-DH session key is now $\mathrm{KDF}(\hat{A}, \hat{B}, s, xyG)$. One can then argue that since the KDF is modelled as a random oracle, the adversary *must* know the inputs to the KDF for the two non-matching sessions (since the triples $(\hat{A}, \hat{B}, s)$ for the non-matching sessions must be distinct) in order to detect the collision. In particular, the adversary must know xyG — and such an adversary can be used to solve a CDH instance.

The Insecurity of NetAut. Attack 1 is applicable to our instantiation of NetAut with HSIG-DH (with 80-bit session keys) and CMAC at the 80-bit security level. Namely, the adversary monitors $n = 2^{20}$ NetAut sessions, each of which is induced to transmit some fixed message m. Then, as explained in §2.3, the adversary is able to deduce one of the 2^{20} session keys and thereafter use it to forge message-MAC pairs for that session.

We emphasize that the mechanisms of the attack are within the scope of the security model for NetAut considered in [20]. However, the attack does not contradict the security proof for NetAut given in [20, Theorem 12] for the following reason. At one point in the proof it is shown that the probability that an adversary succeeds in convincing a party $\hat{A}$ that a message m was sent by party $\hat{B}$ in a particular session s even though $\hat{B}$ did not send that message in that session is negligible provided that the underlying MAC scheme is secure. The reductionist proof for this claim (Lemma 13 of [20]) is analogous to the security proof for MAC* given in §2.2, and hence has a tightness gap equal to the total number n of sessions — this tightness gap is precisely what the attack exploits.

3.3 A Fix

One method for preventing the attack on NetAut described above is to use the fMAC variant of the MAC scheme. Here, a natural candidate for the unique fixed string f is the session identifier s and the identifiers of the communicating parties, i.e., after parties $\hat{A}$ and $\hat{B}$ complete session s of HSIG-DH and establish a session key κ, the authentication tag for a message m is computed as $\tau = \mathrm{MAC}_\kappa(s, \hat{A}, \hat{B}, m)$. This modification of NetAut resists Attack 1. However, even with this modification we do not know a tight security reduction, so the possibility of another attack that exploits the tightness gap cannot be ruled out.

4 Aggregate MAC Schemes

In the section, we show that some aggregate MAC schemes with non-tight security proofs and an aggregate designated verifier signature are vulnerable to Attack 1 for certain choices of the underlying MAC scheme, e.g., CMAC with 80-bit keys and 80-bit tags.

4.1 Aggregate MAC Schemes

Katz and Lindell [42] provided a formal security definition for the task of aggregating MACs, proposed an aggregate MAC scheme, and gave a security proof for their construction.

In the Katz-Lindell scheme, there are z parties, each of which randomly selects an r-bit key k_i for a deterministic MAC scheme; these keys are shared with a central authority. When parties[6] $i_1, i_2, \ldots, i_n$ wish to authenticate messages $m_1, m_2, \ldots, m_n$, respectively, for the authority, they each compute $\tau_i = \text{MAC}_{k_i}(m_i)$. The *aggregate tag* is $\tau = \tau_1 \oplus \tau_2 \oplus \cdots \oplus \tau_n$. The authority verifies the aggregate tag by computing the individual tags and checking that their xor is equal to τ.

In the security model of [42], the adversary can corrupt any party, and in addition can obtain the tag of any message from any party. The adversary's goal is to produce a set of party-message pairs $(i_1, m_1), (i_2, m_2), \ldots, (i_n, m_n)$ (for any $n \le z$) and an aggregate tag τ such that the tag passes the verification check and there is at least one party-message pair (i_j, m_j) for which party i_j has not been corrupted and was never queried for the MAC of m_j.

Katz and Lindell prove that their aggregate MAC scheme is secure provided that the underlying MAC scheme is secure in the single-user setting. Their proof is very similar to the one given for MAC* in §2.2, but is described asymptotically. The total number of parties is $z = p(r)$ for some unspecified polynomial p, and the adversary $\mathcal{A}$ of the aggregate MAC scheme is assumed to be polynomially bounded. The simulator $\mathcal{B}$ of $\mathcal{A}$'s environment makes a guess for the index j, and is successful in producing a forgery for the underlying MAC scheme provided that its guess is correct. Since $n \le z$, the proof has a tightness gap of $p(r)$.

It is easy to see that the Katz-Lindell aggregate MAC scheme succumbs to Attack 1. This security flaw in their scheme is a direct consequence of the tightness gap in their proof.

As with rMAC, randomizing the MACs will prevent the attack. However, since the randomizers would also have to be sent, this countermeasure defeats the primary objective of the aggregate MAC scheme — a small aggregate tag. A better solution would be to deploy fMAC as the underlying MAC scheme.

Hierarchical In-Network Data Aggregation. Chan, Perrig and Song [21] presented the first provably secure hierarchical in-network data aggregation algorithm. Such an algorithm can be used to securely perform queries on sensor network data. A crucial component of the algorithm is the (independently discovered) Katz-Lindell aggregate MAC scheme. In the data aggregation application, each sensor node shares a secret key k_i with the querier. At one stage of the application, each node computes the tag $\tau_i = \text{MAC}_{k_i}(N, OK)$, where MAC is a conventional MAC scheme, N is a nonce sent by the querier, and OK is a unique message identifier. The aggregate tag is $\tau = \tau_1 \oplus \tau_2 \oplus \cdots \oplus \tau_n$. We emphasize that the *same* nonce N and message identifier OK are used by each node. It follows that the MAC scheme is vulnerable to Attack 1. In fact, the attack is

[6] For simplicity, we assume the parties are distinct and hence $n \le z$.

easier to mount in this setting because the application itself requires each node to compute its tag on a fixed message. The security proof for the aggregate MAC scheme given in [21, Lemma 11] is very informal and assumes "that each of the distinct MACs are unforgeable (and not correlated with each other)", and then concludes that "the adversary has no information about this [aggregate tag]."

History-Free Aggregate MACs. Eikemeier et al. [31] presented and analyzed a MAC aggregation algorithm where the aggregation of individual tags must be carried out in a sequential manner, and where the aggregation algorithm depends only on the current message being MAC'ed and on the previous aggregate tag. They provided an elaborate security definition and a security proof for their scheme. We note that their security model allows the adversary to query individual parties for tags of messages of the adversary's choosing. Consequently, their history-free aggregate MAC scheme succumbs to Attack 1. Not surprisingly, the security reduction in [31] is non-tight, with a tightness gap of at least z (the total number of parties).

4.2 Aggregate Designated Verifier Signatures

An aggregate designated verifier signature (ADVS) scheme combines the ideas of aggregate signatures [17] and designated verifier signatures [41]. Bhaskar, Herranz and Laguillaumie [8] introduced the notion of ADVS and proposed two constructions in the public-key and identity-based settings. The constructions at their core use a MAC scheme and the identical idea of MAC aggregation as in Katz-Lindell (§4.1). The essential difference is that the common MAC key of a sender and the designated verifier is derived from the discrete-log static keys of the two parties through hashing.

It is easy to see that the Bhaskar et al. scheme is vulnerable to Attack 1. Such an attack, though realistic, is not captured in the security model of [8] which is essentially an adaptation of the aggregate signature security model of Boneh et al. [17]. In particular, both models fail to capture the scenario where multiple honest signers send individual as well as aggregated authenticated messages to a designated verifier, and an adversary is trying to forge a non-trivial (aggregate) signature involving at least one honest signer.

5 Symmetric-Key Encryption in the Multi-user Setting

Bellare, Boldyreva and Micali [2] proved that if a public-key encryption scheme is secure in the single-user setting, then it is also secure in the multi-user setting. Their security has a tightness gap equal to nq_e, where n is the number of users and q_e is the number of encryptions performed by each user. They mention that analogous results for symmetric-key encryption schemes can be easily proven. In this section, we examine the security of authenticated encryption (AE) schemes and stream ciphers in the multi-user setting.

5.1 Deterministic Authenticated Encryption

Rogaway and Shrimpton [62] proposed the notion of 'deterministic authenticated encryption' (DAE), presented a DAE scheme called Synthetic Initialization Vector (SIV), and proved the scheme secure. A primary motivation for their work was that prior protocols for the 'key-wrap problem' had "never received a provable-security treatment".

Let E be a block cipher with r-bit keys and r-bit blocks. The SIV mode of operation described in [62] uses CMAC and the counter (CTR) mode of operation for E [27]; recall that in CTR mode encryption, a one-time pad is generated by selecting a random IV which is repeatedly incremented and encrypted; the one-time pad is then xored with the blocks of the plaintext to obtain the ciphertext[7]. A plaintext message m is processed by first computing $IV = \mathrm{CMAC}_{k'}(m)$ and then $c = \mathrm{CTR}_{k''}(IV, m)$. Here, the secret key is $k = (k', k'')$, where k' is a key for CMAC and k'' is a key for the block cipher E. The ciphertext is (IV, c). To decrypt and verify, one computes $m = \mathrm{CTR}_{k''}(IV, c)$ and verifies that $IV = \mathrm{CMAC}_{k'}(m)$.

An Attack. For concreteness, suppose that SIV uses an 80-bit block cipher (such as SKIPJACK) as the underlying block cipher for CTR mode encryption as well as for CMAC. Our attack on SIV is a chosen-plaintext attack in the multi-user setting. The adversary selects an arbitrary message m and obtains the ciphertext (IV_i, c_i) from 2^{20} parties i with secret key pairs $k_i = (k'_i, k''_i)$. As in Attack 1, the adversary then finds k'_j for some user j in about 2^{60} steps. Next, the adversary finds two equal-length messages m_1 and m_2 with $m_1 \neq m_2$ and $\mathrm{CMAC}_{k'_j}(m_1) = \mathrm{CMAC}_{k'_j}(m_2)$; this can be accomplished in about 2^{40} steps using the van Oorschot-Wiener collision finding algorithm [71]. Finally, the adversary requests the encryption of m_1 from party j, receiving the ciphertext (IV_1, c_1). The adversary then computes the encryption of m_2 as $(IV_1, c_1 \oplus m_1 \oplus m_2)$ as its forgery. It can easily be checked that this ciphertext will decrypt to m_2 and pass the verification check.

Our attack shows that, despite the provable security guarantees of SIV in [62], this particular implementation of SIV does not achieve the desired 80-bit security level in the multi-user setting. Note, however, that the attack may not be relevant in the context of the key-wrap problem. Since "the plaintext carries a key", it will not be possible for the adversary to obtain 2^{20} (IV_i, c_i) pairs on the *same* message m.

A Fix. A possible countermeasure to the attack would be to encrypt IV under k'', i.e., the encryption of m would be $(E_{k''}(IV), \mathrm{CTR}_{k''}(IV, m))$ where $IV = \mathrm{CMAC}_{k'}(m)$.

---

[7] In the interest of simplicity, our description of SIV omits some details from [62]. In particular, we omit the header which in any case "may be absent", and use CMAC instead of CMAC*. These omissions do not have any bearing on our attack.

5.2 Authenticated Encryption

In many AE schemes, including OCB [61,59], GCM [53] and PAE [63], the encryption function uses a secret key k for a block cipher to map a nonce-message pair (IV, m) to a ciphertext of the form (c, τ). For these AE schemes, the only requirement on the IV is that it not be repeated with the same key. We consider the scenario where keys, tags and blocks all have the same length.

An Attack. Fix a nonce-message pair (IV, m) and consider the function $f : k \mapsto \tau$, where τ is the tag of the AE encryption of (IV, m) under key k. Attack 1 can then be mounted (cf. Remark 7). The attack requires many users to perform authenticated encryption of m with the fixed IV, but since the AE schemes only mandate that the IV not be repeated with the same key, the attack is legitimate in the multi-user setting.

Rogaway [60], on his web page that promotes OCB, states

> In the past, one had to wait years before using a new cryptographic scheme; one needed to give cryptanalysts a fair chance to attack the thing. Assurance in a scheme's correctness sprang from the *absence* of damaging attacks by smart people, so you needed to wait long enough that at least a few smart people would try, and fail, to find a damaging attack. But this entire approach has become largely outmoded, for schemes that are not true primitives, by the advent of provable security. With a provably-secure scheme assurance does not stem from a failure to find attacks; it comes from proofs, with their associated bounds and definitions.

In particular, he states that for OCB "the underlying definition is simple and rock solid". It is understandable that practitioners would be glad to hear the recommendation that they can have confidence in a newly proposed protocol solely based on the security proof, and need not wait for it to stand the test of time. However, our attack on OCB, which is a practical one under certain plausible assumptions, shows that it would be more prudent not to put all one's trust in a reductionist security proof and its associated definition, especially if the proof has a large tightness gap or the definition does not allow for the multi-user setting.

5.3 Disk Encryption

A disk encryption scheme is a special case of a tweakable enciphering scheme (TES) [37] where the message length is fixed. More concretely, a message is a disk sector and there is a 'tweak' which is the sector address. The tweak is not a nonce in the sense that it can be reused for encryptions with the same key. Formally, the encryption algorithm uses a secret key k to transform a tweak-message pair (IV, m) to a ciphertext c, where c and m have the same length.

For disk encryption schemes such as EME [38], k is a key of a block cipher. By treating c as a tag, one can apply Attack 1 to recover k. Note that since c

will typically be much longer than k, a collision encountered during the attack will most likely be due to a key collision. In the context of disk encryption, there is no notion of session keys — the different keys would correspond to different users. The encryption of a fixed tweak-message pair can be obtained by inducing the users to encrypt the chosen message for the chosen disk sector.

Fixes for AE and Disk Encryption Schemes. In the multi-user setting, one way to ensure that an r-bit security level is achieved against our attacks (without changing the underlying block cipher) is to use multiple keys that together are longer than r bits. Examples of such schemes are Poly1305-AES [6] and the disk encryption schemes in [64]. The use of multiple keys, however, does not immediately guarantee resistance to Attack 1 — as we have seen, SIV is vulnerable to the attack since the first ciphertext component depends only on the first SIV key – and hence the modification of a mode of operation to resist Attack 1 should be done with care.

5.4 Stream Ciphers

A stream cipher with IV takes as input an r-bit key k and a v-bit IV and produces a keystream which is then XORed with the message to obtain the ciphertext. The usual requirement on the IV is that it should not be repeated for the same key.

Fix a value IV_0 for the IV and define a map f that takes k to the first r bits of the keystream produced using k and IV_0. In the multi-user setting, Attack 1 can be mounted by inducing different users to encrypt known messages using IV_0 and their respective keys. Inverting f on any of the resulting keystreams yields one of the secret keys. For concreteness, consider 80-bit keys and suppose that the attacker is able to collect 2^{20} targets. A TMTO attack using a precomputation of 2^{60} and memory and on-line time of 2^{40} will (with high probability) find one of the 2^{20} keys. The attack parameters are feasible, thus bringing into question the adequacy of 80-bit keys for stream ciphers with IV. The importance of this issue can be seen in the context of the eSTREAM project [30] which recommends 80-bit stream ciphers such as Trivium.

Requiring that IVs be randomly generated does not circumvent the attack but instead makes it somewhat easier to mount. This is because random IVs must be communicated in the clear to a receiver. The attacker could then target the receiver and obtain the first 80 bits of the keystream produced by the receiver. Since a receiver expects IVs along with the ciphertext, an active attacker can legitimately use the same IV_0 for all the 2^{20} receivers. In contrast, if the IV is merely a nonce (such as a counter), then it may be more difficult to induce all senders to use IV_0. Note that the use of an authenticated encryption scheme together with random IVs foils the attack. The attack can also be foiled by using the technique employed in fMAC — prepending the IV with a string that is fixed and unique among all sessions.

6 Concluding Remarks

We showed that ignoring the tightness gaps in reductionist security proofs can have damaging consequences in practice. Our examples involve MAC schemes in the multi-user setting. In particular, the tightness gap in the natural reduction from MAC1 to MAC* indicates a real security weakness, whereas the tightness gap in the natural reductions from MAC1 to rMAC* and fMAC* do not seem to matter in practice. Our examples illustrate the difficulty of interpreting a non-tight security proof in practice. Although our examples all involve the multi-user setting, we feel that they call into question the practical value of *all* non-tight security proofs. We also demonstrated potential security weaknesses of provably-secure authenticated encryption schemes in the multi-user setting.

Practitioners who use security proofs as a tool to assess the security of a cryptographic system, but rely more heavily on extensive cryptanalysis and sound engineering principles, should not be alarmed by our observations. On the other hand, theoreticians who believe that a security proof is the essential, and perhaps the *only*, way to gain confidence in the security of a protocol should be much more skeptical of non-tight proofs (unless, of course, the proof is accompanied by a clearly-stated requirement that security parameters be increased to accommodate the tightness gap) and perhaps even reject these proofs as mere heuristic arguments for the protocol's security.

Acknowledgments. We wish to thank Greg Zaverucha for bringing reference [42] to our attention. We also thank Debrup Chakraborty, Koray Karabina, Ann Hibner Koblitz, Neal Koblitz, Berkant Ustaoglu and Greg Zaverucha for commenting on an earlier draft.

References

1. Alexi, W., Chor, B., Goldreich, O., Schnorr, C.P.: RSA and Rabin functions: Certain parts are as hard as the whole. SIAM J. Computing 17, 194–209 (1988)
2. Bellare, M., Boldyreva, A., Micali, S.: Public-Key Encryption in a Multi-User Setting: Security Proofs and Improvements. In: Preneel, B. (ed.) EUROCRYPT 2000. LNCS, vol. 1807, pp. 259–274. Springer, Heidelberg (2000)
3. Bellare, M., Canetti, R., Krawczyk, H.: Keying Hash Functions for Message Authentication. In: Koblitz, N. (ed.) CRYPTO 1996. LNCS, vol. 1109, pp. 1–15. Springer, Heidelberg (1996)
4. Bellare, M., Rogaway, P.: Entity Authentication and Key Distribution. In: Stinson, D.R. (ed.) CRYPTO 1993. LNCS, vol. 773, pp. 232–249. Springer, Heidelberg (1994)
5. Bellare, M., Rogaway, P.: The Exact Security of Digital Signatures - How to Sign with RSA and Rabin. In: Maurer, U.M. (ed.) EUROCRYPT 1996. LNCS, vol. 1070, pp. 399–416. Springer, Heidelberg (1996)
6. Bernstein, D.: The Poly1305-AES Message-Authentication Code. In: Gilbert, H., Handschuh, H. (eds.) FSE 2005. LNCS, vol. 3557, pp. 32–49. Springer, Heidelberg (2005)

7. Bernstein, D.: Proving Tight Security for Rabin-Williams Signatures. In: Smart, N.P. (ed.) EUROCRYPT 2008. LNCS, vol. 4965, pp. 70–87. Springer, Heidelberg (2008)
8. Bhaskar, R., Herranz, J., Laguillaumie, F.: Aggregate designated verifier signatures and application to secure routing. Int. J. Security and Networks 2, 192–201 (2007)
9. Biham, E.: How to decrypt or even substitute DES-encrypted messages in 2^{28} steps. Information Processing Letters 84, 117–124 (2002)
10. Biryukov, A., Mukhopadhyay, S., Sarkar, P.: Improved Time-Memory Trade-Offs with Multiple Data. In: Preneel, B., Tavares, S. (eds.) SAC 2005. LNCS, vol. 3897, pp. 110–127. Springer, Heidelberg (2006)
11. Biryukov, A., Shamir, A.: Cryptanalytic Time/Memory/Data Tradeoffs for Stream Ciphers. In: Okamoto, T. (ed.) ASIACRYPT 2000. LNCS, vol. 1976, pp. 1–13. Springer, Heidelberg (2000)
12. Black, J.A., Rogaway, P.: CBC MACs for Arbitrary-Length Messages: The Three-Key Constructions. In: Bellare, M. (ed.) CRYPTO 2000. LNCS, vol. 1880, pp. 197–215. Springer, Heidelberg (2000)
13. Blake-Wilson, S., Johnson, D., Menezes, A.: Key Agreement Protocols and Their Security Analysis. In: Darnell, M.J. (ed.) Cryptography and Coding 1997. LNCS, vol. 1355, pp. 30–45. Springer, Heidelberg (1997), `http://www.cacr.math.uwaterloo.ca/techreports/1997/corr97-17.ps`
14. Blum, L., Blum, M., Shub, M.: A simple unpredictable pseudo-random number generator. SIAM J. Computing 15, 364–383 (1986)
15. Boneh, D., Boyen, X.: Efficient Selective-ID Secure Identity-Based Encryption without Random Oracles. In: Cachin, C., Camenisch, J.L. (eds.) EUROCRYPT 2004. LNCS, vol. 3027, pp. 223–238. Springer, Heidelberg (2004)
16. Boneh, D., Franklin, M.: Identity-based encryption from the Weil pairing. SIAM J. Computing 32, 586–615 (2003)
17. Boneh, D., Gentry, C., Lynn, B., Shacham, H.: Aggregate and Verifiably Encrypted Signatures from Bilinear Maps. In: Biham, E. (ed.) EUROCRYPT 2003. LNCS, vol. 2656, pp. 416–432. Springer, Heidelberg (2003)
18. Boyen, X.: A tapestry of identity-based encryption: practical frameworks compared. Int. J. Applied Cryptography 1, 3–21 (2008)
19. Boyen, X., Martin, L.: Identity-based cryptography standard (IBCS) #1: Supersingular curve implementations of the BF and BB1 cryptosystems. IETF RFC 5091 (2007)
20. Canetti, R., Krawczyk, H.: Analysis of Key-Exchange Protocols and their Use for Building Secure Channels. In: Pfitzmann, B. (ed.) EUROCRYPT 2001. LNCS, vol. 2045, pp. 453–474. Springer, Heidelberg (2001), Full version at `http://eprint.iacr.org/2001/040`
21. Chan, H., Perrig, A., Song, D.: Secure hierarchical in-network aggregation in sensor networks. In: CCS 2006, pp. 278–287 (2006)
22. Chen, L., Cheng, Z.: Security Proof of Sakai-Kasahara's Identity-Based Encryption Scheme. In: Smart, N.P. (ed.) Cryptography and Coding 2005. LNCS, vol. 3796, pp. 442–459. Springer, Heidelberg (2005)
23. Coron, J.-S.: On the Exact Security of Full Domain Hash. In: Bellare, M. (ed.) CRYPTO 2000. LNCS, vol. 1880, pp. 229–235. Springer, Heidelberg (2000)
24. Coron, J.-S.: Optimal Security Proofs for PSS and Other Signature Schemes. In: Knudsen, L.R. (ed.) EUROCRYPT 2002. LNCS, vol. 2332, pp. 272–287. Springer, Heidelberg (2002)

25. Damgård, I.: A "Proof-Reading" of Some Issues in Cryptography. In: Arge, L., Cachin, C., Jurdziński, T., Tarlecki, A. (eds.) ICALP 2007. LNCS, vol. 4596, pp. 2–11. Springer, Heidelberg (2007)
26. Dang, Q.: Recommendation for applications using approved hash algorithms. NIST Special Publication 800-107 (2009)
27. Dworkin, M.: Recommendation for block cipher modes of operation: Methods and techniques. NIST Special Publication 800-38A (2001)
28. Dworkin, M.: Recommendation for block cipher modes of operation: The CMAC mode for authentication. NIST Special Publication 800-38B (2005)
29. Eastlake, D., Crocker, S., Schiller, J.: Randomness recommendations for security. IETF RFC 1750 (1994)
30. The eSTREAM project, `http://www.ecrypt.eu.org/stream/`
31. Eikemeier, O., Fischlin, M., Götzmann, J.-F., Lehmann, A., Schröder, D., Schröder, P., Wagner, D.: History-Free Aggregate Message Authentication Codes. In: Garay, J.A., De Prisco, R. (eds.) SCN 2010. LNCS, vol. 6280, pp. 309–328. Springer, Heidelberg (2010)
32. FIPS 180-3, Secure Hash Standard (SHS), Federal Information Processing Standards Publication 180-3, National Institute of Standards and Technology (2008)
33. FIPS 198-1, The Keyed-Hash Message Authentication Code (HMAC), Federal Information Processing Standards Publication 198, National Institute of Standards and Technology (2008)
34. Galindo, D.: Boneh-Franklin Identity Based Encryption Revisited. In: Caires, L., Italiano, G.F., Monteiro, L., Palamidessi, C., Yung, M. (eds.) ICALP 2005. LNCS, vol. 3580, pp. 791–802. Springer, Heidelberg (2005)
35. Gentry, C., Halevi, S.: Hierarchical Identity Based Encryption with Polynomially Many Levels. In: Reingold, O. (ed.) TCC 2009. LNCS, vol. 5444, pp. 437–456. Springer, Heidelberg (2009)
36. Goldreich, O.: On the Foundations of Modern Cryptography. In: Kaliski Jr., B.S. (ed.) CRYPTO 1997. LNCS, vol. 1294, pp. 46–74. Springer, Heidelberg (1997)
37. Halevi, S., Rogaway, P.: A Tweakable Enciphering Mode. In: Boneh, D. (ed.) CRYPTO 2003. LNCS, vol. 2729, pp. 482–499. Springer, Heidelberg (2003)
38. Halevi, S., Rogaway, P.: A Parallelizable Enciphering Mode. In: Okamoto, T. (ed.) CT-RSA 2004. LNCS, vol. 2964, pp. 292–304. Springer, Heidelberg (2004)
39. Hellman, M.: A cryptanalytic time-memory trade-off. IEEE Trans. Info. Th. 26, 401–406 (1980)
40. Hong, J., Sarkar, P.: New Applications of Time Memory Data Tradeoffs. In: Roy, B. (ed.) ASIACRYPT 2005. LNCS, vol. 3788, pp. 353–372. Springer, Heidelberg (2005)
41. Jakobsson, M., Sako, K., Impagliazzo, R.: Designated Verifier Proofs and their Applications. In: Maurer, U.M. (ed.) EUROCRYPT 1996. LNCS, vol. 1070, pp. 143–154. Springer, Heidelberg (1996)
42. Katz, J., Lindell, A.: Aggregate Message Authentication Codes. In: Malkin, T. (ed.) CT-RSA 2008. LNCS, vol. 4964, pp. 155–169. Springer, Heidelberg (2008)
43. Katz, J., Wang, N.: Efficiency improvements for signature schemes with tight security reductions. In: CCS 2003, pp. 155–164 (2003)
44. Kelly, S., Frankel, S.: Using HMAC-SHA-256, HMAC-SHA-384, and HMAC-SHA-512 with IPsec. IETF RFC 4868 (2007)
45. Kent, S., Atkinson, R.: IP authentication header. IETF RFC 4302 (2005)
46. Koblitz, N., Menezes, A.: Another look at "provable security". J. Cryptology 20, 3–37 (2007)

47. Koblitz, N., Menezes, A.: Another Look at "Provable Security". II. In: Barua, R., Lange, T. (eds.) INDOCRYPT 2006. LNCS, vol. 4329, pp. 148–175. Springer, Heidelberg (2006)
48. Krawczyk, H.: HMQV: A High-Performance Secure Diffie-Hellman Protocol. In: Shoup, V. (ed.) CRYPTO 2005. LNCS, vol. 3621, pp. 546–566. Springer, Heidelberg (2005), Full version at http://eprint.iacr.org/2005/176
49. Kurosawa, K., Iwata, T.: TMAC: Two-Key CBC MAC. In: Joye, M. (ed.) CT-RSA 2003. LNCS, vol. 2612, pp. 33–49. Springer, Heidelberg (2003)
50. LaMacchia, B., Lauter, K., Mityagin, A.: Stronger Security of Authenticated Key Exchange. In: Susilo, W., Liu, J.K., Mu, Y. (eds.) ProvSec 2007. LNCS, vol. 4784, pp. 1–16. Springer, Heidelberg (2007)
51. Lu, S., Ostrovsky, R., Sahai, A., Shacham, H., Waters, B.: Sequential Aggregate Signatures and Multisignatures without Random Oracles. In: Vaudenay, S. (ed.) EUROCRYPT 2006. LNCS, vol. 4004, pp. 465–485. Springer, Heidelberg (2006)
52. Luby, M.: Pseudorandomness and Cryptographic Applications. Princeton University Press (1996)
53. McGrew, D.A., Viega, J.: The Security and Performance of the Galois/Counter Mode (GCM) of Operation. In: Canteaut, A., Viswanathan, K. (eds.) INDOCRYPT 2004. LNCS, vol. 3348, pp. 343–355. Springer, Heidelberg (2004)
54. Menezes, A., Smart, N.: Security of signature schemes in the multi-user setting. Designs, Codes and Cryptography 33, 261–274 (2004)
55. Menezes, A., Ustaoglu, B.: Security arguments for the UM key agreement protocol in the NIST SP 800-56A standard. In: ASIACCS 2008, pp. 261–270 (2008)
56. National Security Agency, SKIPJACK and KEA algorithm specification, Version 2.0 (May 29, 1998)
57. Paillier, P., Vergnaud, D.: Discrete-Log-Based Signatures May Not Be Equivalent to Discrete Log. In: Roy, B. (ed.) ASIACRYPT 2005. LNCS, vol. 3788, pp. 1–20. Springer, Heidelberg (2005)
58. Pointcheval, D., Stern, J.: Security arguments for digital signatures and blind signatures. J. Cryptology 13, 361–396 (2000)
59. Rogaway, P.: Efficient Instantiations of Tweakable Blockciphers and Refinements to Modes OCB and PMAC. In: Lee, P.J. (ed.) ASIACRYPT 2004. LNCS, vol. 3329, pp. 16–31. Springer, Heidelberg (2004)
60. Rogaway, P.: OCB: Background, http://www.cs.ucdavis.edu/~rogaway/ocb/ocb-faq.htm
61. Rogaway, P., Bellare, M., Black, J.: OCB: A block-cipher mode of operation for efficient authenticated encryption. ACM Trans. Information and System Security 6, 365–403 (2003)
62. Rogaway, P., Shrimpton, T.: A Provable-Security Treatment of the Key-Wrap Problem. In: Vaudenay, S. (ed.) EUROCRYPT 2006. LNCS, vol. 4004, pp. 373–390. Springer, Heidelberg (2006), Full version at http://eprint.iacr.org/2006/221
63. Sarkar, P.: Pseudo-random functions and parallelizable modes of operations of a block cipher. IEEE Trans. Info. Th. 56, 4025–4037 (2010)
64. Sarkar, P.: Tweakable enciphering schemes using only the encryption function of a block cipher. Inf. Process. Lett. 111, 945–955 (2011)
65. Schäge, S.: Tight Proofs for Signature Schemes without Random Oracles. In: Paterson, K.G. (ed.) EUROCRYPT 2011. LNCS, vol. 6632, pp. 189–206. Springer, Heidelberg (2011)
66. Schnorr, C.: Efficient signature generation for smart cards. J. Cryptology 4, 161–174 (1991)

67. Shin, J.: Enhancing privacy in cryptographic protocols, Ph.D. thesis, University of Maryland (2009)
68. Sidorenko, A., Schoenmakers, B.: Concrete Security of the Blum-Blum-Shub Pseudorandom Generator. In: Smart, N.P. (ed.) Cryptography and Coding 2005. LNCS, vol. 3796, pp. 355–375. Springer, Heidelberg (2005)
69. Song, J.H., Poovendran, R., Lee, J., Iwata, T.: The AES-CMAC algorithm. IETF RFC 4493 (2006)
70. Ustaoglu, B.: Obtaining a secure and efficient key agreement protocol from (H)MQV and NAXOS. Designs, Codes and Cryptography 46, 329–342 (2008)
71. van Oorschot, P., Wiener, M.: Parallel collision search with cryptanalytic applications. J. Cryptology 12, 1–28 (1999)
72. Young, A., Yung, M.: Malicious Cryptography: Exposing Cryptovirology. Wiley (2004)

Duplexing the Sponge: Single-Pass Authenticated Encryption and Other Applications

Guido Bertoni[1], Joan Daemen[1], Michaël Peeters[2], and Gilles Van Assche[1]

[1] STMicroelectronics
[2] NXP Semiconductors

Abstract. This paper proposes a novel construction, called duplex, closely related to the sponge construction, that accepts message blocks to be hashed and—at no extra cost—provides digests on the input blocks received so far. It can be proven equivalent to a cascade of sponge functions and hence inherits its security against single-stage generic attacks. The main application proposed here is an authenticated encryption mode based on the duplex construction. This mode is efficient, namely, enciphering and authenticating together require only a single call to the underlying permutation per block, and is readily usable in, e.g., key wrapping. Furthermore, it is the first mode of this kind to be directly based on a permutation instead of a block cipher and to natively support intermediate tags. The duplex construction can be used to efficiently realize other modes, such as a reseedable pseudo-random bit sequence generators and a sponge variant that overwrites part of the state with the input block rather than to XOR it in.

Keywords: sponge functions, duplex construction, authenticated encryption, key wrapping, provable security, pseudo-random bit sequence generator, Keccak.

1 Introduction

While most symmetric-key modes of operations are based on a block cipher or a stream cipher, there exist modes using a fixed permutation as underlying primitive. Designing a cryptographically strong permutation suitable for such purposes is similar to designing a block cipher without a key schedule and this design approach was followed for several recent hash functions, see, e.g., [15].

The sponge construction is an example of such a mode. With its arbitrarily long input and output sizes, it allows building various primitives such as a stream cipher or a hash function [5]. In the former, the input is short (typically the key and a nonce) while the output is as long as the message to encrypt. In contrast, the latter takes a message of any length at input and produces a digest of small length.

Some applications can take advantage of both a long input and a long output size. For instance, authenticated encryption combines the encryption of a

A. Miri and S. Vaudenay (Eds.): SAC 2011, LNCS 7118, pp. 320–337, 2012.

message and the generation of a message authentication code (MAC) on it. It could be implemented with one sponge function call to generate a key stream (long output) for the encryption and another call to generate the MAC (long input). However, in this case, encryption and authentication are separate processes without any synergy.

The duplex construction is a novel way to use a fixed permutation (or transformation) to allow the alternation of input and output blocks at the same rate as the sponge construction, like a full-duplex communication. In fact, the duplex construction can be seen as a particular way to use the sponge construction, hence it inherits its security properties. By using the duplex construction, authenticated encryption requires only one call to the underlying permutation (or transformation) per message block. In a nutshell, the input blocks of the duplex are used to input the key and the message blocks, while the intermediate output blocks are used as key stream and the last one as a MAC.

Authenticated encryption (AE) has been extensively studied in the last ten years. Block cipher modes clearly are a popular way to provide simultaneously both integrity and confidentiality. Many block cipher modes have been proposed and most of these come with a security proof against generic attacks—see [8] for references. Interestingly, there have also been attempts at designing dedicated hybrid primitives offering efficient simultaneous stream encryption and MAC computation, e.g., Helix and Phelix [16,31]. However, these primitives were shown to be weak [22,24,32]. Another example of hybrid primitive is the Grain-128 stream cipher to which optional built-in authentication was recently added [33].

Our proposed mode shares with these hybrid primitives that it offers efficient simultaneous stream encryption and MAC computation. It shares with the block cipher modes that it has provable security against generic attacks. However, it is the first such construction that (directly) relies on a permutation rather than a block cipher and that proves its security based on this type of primitive. An important efficiency parameter of an AE mode is the number of calls to the block cipher or to the permutation per block. While encryption or authentication alone requires one call per block, some AE modes only require one call per block for both functions. The duplex construction naturally provides a good basis for building such an efficient AE mode. Also, the AE mode we propose natively supports intermediate tags and the authenticated encryption of a sequence of messages.

Authenticated encryption can also be used to transport secret keys in a confidential way and to ensure their integrity. This task, called key wrapping, is very important in key management and can be implemented with our construction if each key has a unique identifier.

Finally, the duplex construction can be used for other modes as well, such as a reseedable pseudo-random bit sequence generator (PRG) or to prove the security of an "overwrite" mode where the input block overwrites part of the state instead of XORing it in.

These modes can readily be used by the concrete sponge function KECCAK [10] and the members of a recent wave of lightweight hash functions that are in fact sponge functions: Quark [1], Photon [18] and Spongent [12]. For these, and for the small-width instances of KECCAK, our security bound against generic attacks beyond the birthday bound published in [9] allows constructing solutions that are at the same time compact, efficient and potentially secure.

The remainder of this paper is organized as follows. First, we propose a model for authenticated encryption in Section 2. Then in Section 3, we review the sponge construction. The core concept of this paper, namely the duplex construction, is defined in Section 4. Its use for authenticated encryption is given in Section 5 and for other applications in Section 6. Finally, Section 7 discusses the use of a flexible and compact padding. For compactness reasons, the proofs are omitted in this version and can be found in [8].

2 Modeling Authenticated Encryption

We consider authenticated encryption as a process that takes as input a key K, a data header A and a data body B and that returns a cryptogram C and a tag T. We denote this operation by the term *wrapping* and the operation of taking a data header A, a cryptogram C and a tag T and returning the data body B if the tag T is correct by the term *unwrapping*.

The cryptogram is the data body enciphered under the key K and the tag is a MAC computed under the same key K over both header A and body B. So here the header A can play the role of associated data as described in [26]. We assume the wrapping and unwrapping operations as such to be deterministic. Hence two equal inputs $(A, B) = (A', B')$ will give rise to the same output (C, T) under the same key K. If this is a problem, it can be tackled by expanding A with a nonce.

Formally, for a given key length k and tag length t, we consider a pair of algorithms W and U, with

$$W : \mathbb{Z}_2^k \times (\mathbb{Z}_2^*)^2 \to \mathbb{Z}_2^* \times \mathbb{Z}_2^t : (K, A, B) \to (C, T) = W(K, A, B), \text{ and}$$
$$U : \mathbb{Z}_2^k \times (\mathbb{Z}_2^*)^2 \times \mathbb{Z}_2^t \to \mathbb{Z}_2^* \cup \{\text{error}\} : (K, A, C, T) \to B \text{ or error.}$$

The algorithms are such that if $(C, T) = W(K, A, B)$ then $U(K, A, C, T) = B$. As we consider only the case of non-expanding encryption, we assume from now on that $|C| = |B|$.

2.1 Intermediate Tags and Authenticated Encryption of a Sequence

So far, we have only considered the case of the authentication and encryption of a single message, i.e., a header and body pair (A, B). It can also be interesting to authenticate and encrypt a sequence of messages in such a way that the authenticity is guaranteed not only on each (A, B) pair but also on the sequence received so far. Intermediate tags can also be useful in practice to be able to catch fraudulent transactions early.

Let $(\overline{A,B}) = (A^{(1)}, B^{(1)}, A^{(2)}, \ldots, A^{(n)}, B^{(n)})$ be a sequence of header-body pairs. We extend the function of wrapping and unwrapping as providing encryption over the last body $B^{(n)}$ and authentication over the whole sequence $(\overline{A,B})$. Formally, W and U are defined as:

$$W : \mathbb{Z}_2^k \times (\mathbb{Z}_2^*)^{2+} \rightarrow \mathbb{Z}_2^* \times \mathbb{Z}_2^t : (K, \overline{A,B}) \rightarrow (C^{(\text{last})}, T^{(\text{last})}) = W(K, \overline{A,B}), \text{ and}$$
$$U : \mathbb{Z}_2^k \times (\mathbb{Z}_2^*)^{2+} \times \mathbb{Z}_2^t \rightarrow \mathbb{Z}_2^* \cup \{\text{error}\} : (K, \overline{A,C}, T^{(\text{last})}) \rightarrow B^{(\text{last})} \text{ or error.}$$

Here, $(\mathbb{Z}_2^*)^{2+}$ means any sequence of binary strings, with an even number of such strings and at least two. To wrap a sequence of header-body pairs, the sender calls $W(K, A^{(1)}, B^{(1)})$ with the first header-body pair to get $(C^{(1)}, T^{(1)})$, then $W(K, A^{(1)}, B^{(1)}, A^{(2)}, B^{(2)})$ with the second one to get $(C^{(2)}, T^{(2)})$, and so on. To unwrap, the receiver first calls $U(K, A^{(1)}, C^{(1)}, T^{(1)})$ to retrieve the first body $B^{(1)}$, then $U(K, A^{(1)}, C^{(1)}, A^{(2)}, C^{(2)}, T^{(2)})$ to retrieve the second body, and so on. As we consider only the case of non-expanding encryption, we assume that $|C^{(i)}| = |B^{(i)}|$ for all i.

2.2 Security Requirements

We consider two security notions from [28] and works cited therein, called *privacy* and *authenticity*. Together, these notions are central to the security of authenticated encryption [2].

Privacy is defined in Eq. (1) below. Informally, it means that the output of the wrapping function looks like uniformly chosen random bits to an observer who does not know the key.

$$\mathrm{Adv}^{\mathrm{priv}}(\mathcal{A}) = \left| \Pr[K \stackrel{\$}{\leftarrow} \mathbb{Z}_2^k \;:\; \mathcal{A}[W(K,\cdot,\cdot)] = 1] - \Pr[\mathcal{A}[R(\cdot,\cdot)] = 1] \right|, \quad (1)$$

with $R(\overline{A,B}) = \lfloor \mathcal{RO}(\overline{A,B}) \rfloor_{|B^{(n)}|+t}$ where $B^{(n)}$ is the last body in $\overline{A,B}$, $|x|$ is the bitlength of string x, $\lfloor\cdot\rfloor_\ell$ indicates truncation to ℓ bits and $K \stackrel{\$}{\leftarrow} \mathbb{Z}_2^k$ means that K is chosen randomly and uniformly among the set $\mathbb{Z}_2^k$. In this definition, we use a random oracle $\mathcal{RO}$ as defined in [3], but allowing sequences of one or more binary strings as input (instead of a single binary string). Here, a random oracle is a map from $(\mathbb{Z}_2^*)^+$ to $\mathbb{Z}_2^\infty$, chosen by selecting each bit of $\mathcal{RO}(x)$ uniformly and independently, for every input. The original definition can still be used by defining an injective mapping from $(\mathbb{Z}_2^*)^+$ to $\mathbb{Z}_2^*$.

For privacy, we consider only adversaries who respect the nonce requirement. For a single header-body pair, it means that, for any two queries (A, B) and (A', B'), we have $A = A' \Rightarrow B = B'$. In general, the nonce requirement specifies that for any two queries $(\overline{A,B})$ and $(\overline{A',B'})$ of equal length n, we have

$$\mathrm{pre}(\overline{A,B}) = \mathrm{pre}(\overline{A',B'}) \Rightarrow B^{(n)} = B'^{(n)},$$

with $\text{pre}(\overline{A,B}) = (A^{(1)}, B^{(1)}, A^{(2)}, \ldots, B^{(n-1)}, A^{(n)})$ the sequence with the last body omitted. As for a stream cipher, not respecting the nonce requirement means that the adversary can learn the bitwise difference between two plaintext bodies.

Authenticity is defined in Eq. (2) below. Informally, it quantifies the probability of the adversary successfully generating a forged ciphertext-tag pair.

$$\text{Adv}^{\text{auth}}(\mathcal{A}) = \Pr[K \xleftarrow{\$} \mathbb{Z}_2^k \ : \ \mathcal{A}[W(K,\cdot,\cdot)] \text{ outputs a forgery}]. \tag{2}$$

Here a forgery is a sequence $(\overline{A,C},T)$ such that $U(K,\overline{A,C},T) \neq \text{error}$ and that the adversary made no query to W with input $(\overline{A,B})$ returning $(C^{(n)},T)$, with $C^{(n)}$ the last ciphertext body of $\overline{A,C}$. Note that authenticity does not need the nonce requirement.

2.3 An Ideal System

We can define an ideal system using a pair of independent random oracles $(\mathcal{RO}_\text{C}, \mathcal{RO}_\text{T})$. For a single header-body pair, encryption and tag computation are implemented as follows. The ciphertext C is produced by XORing B with a key stream. This key stream is the output of $\mathcal{RO}_\text{C}(K,A)$. If (K,A) is a nonce, key streams for different data inputs are the result of calls to $\mathcal{RO}_\text{C}$ with different inputs and hence one key stream gives no information on another. The tag T is the output of $\mathcal{RO}_\text{T}(K,A,B)$. Tags computed over different header-body pairs will be the result of calls to $\mathcal{RO}_\text{T}$ with different inputs. Key stream sequences give no information on tags and vice versa as they are obtained by calls to different random oracles.

Let us define the ideal system in the general case, which we call ROWRAP. Wrapping is defined as $W(K,\overline{A,B}) = (C^{(n)}, T^{(n)})$, if $\overline{A,B}$ contains n header-body pairs, with

$$C^{(n)} = \lfloor \mathcal{RO}_\text{C}(K, \text{pre}(\overline{A,B})) \rfloor_{|B^{(n)}|} \oplus B^{(n)},$$
$$T^{(n)} = \lfloor \mathcal{RO}_\text{T}(K, \overline{A,B}) \rfloor_t.$$

The unwrapping algorithm U first checks that $T^{(n)} = \lfloor \mathcal{RO}_\text{T}(K,\overline{A,B}) \rfloor_t$ and if so decrypts each body $B^{(i)} = \lfloor \mathcal{RO}_\text{C}(K, A^{(1)}, B^{(1)}, A^{(2)}, \ldots, A^{(i)}) \rfloor_{|C^{(i)}|} \oplus C^{(i)}$ from the first one to the last one and finally returns the last one $B^{(n)} = \lfloor \mathcal{RO}_\text{C}(K, \text{pre}(\overline{A,B})) \rfloor_{|C^{(n)}|} \oplus C^{(n)}$.

The security of ROWRAP is captured by Lemmas 1 and 2.

Lemma 1. *Let $\mathcal{A}[\mathcal{RO}_\text{C}, \mathcal{RO}_\text{T}]$ be an adversary having access to $\mathcal{RO}_\text{C}$ and $\mathcal{RO}_\text{T}$ and respecting the nonce requirement. Then,* $\text{Adv}^{\text{priv}}_{\text{ROWRAP}}(\mathcal{A}) \leq q2^{-k}$ *if the adversary makes no more than q queries to $\mathcal{RO}_\text{C}$ or $\mathcal{RO}_\text{T}$.*

Lemma 2. *Let $\mathcal{A}[\mathcal{RO}_\text{C}, \mathcal{RO}_\text{T}]$ be an adversary having access to $\mathcal{RO}_\text{C}$ and $\mathcal{RO}_\text{T}$. Then,* ROWRAP *satisfies* $\text{Adv}^{\text{auth}}_{\text{ROWRAP}}(\mathcal{A}) \leq q2^{-k} + 2^{-t}$ *if the adversary makes no more than q queries to $\mathcal{RO}_\text{C}$ or $\mathcal{RO}_\text{T}$.*

3 The Sponge Construction

The sponge construction [5] builds a function SPONGE$[f, \text{pad}, r]$ with variable-length input and arbitrary output length using a fixed-length permutation (or transformation) f, a padding rule "pad" and a parameter *bitrate* r.

For the padding rule we use the following notation: the padding of a message M to a sequence of x-bit blocks is denoted by $M||\text{pad}[x](|M|)$, where $|M|$ is the length of M. This notation highlights that we only consider padding rules that append a bitstring that is fully determined by the length of M and the block length x. We may omit $[x]$, $|M|$ or both if their value is clear from the context.

Definition 1. *A padding rule is* sponge-compliant *if it never results in the empty string and if it satisfies following criterion:*

$$\forall n \geq 0, \forall M, M' \in \mathbb{Z}_2^* : M \neq M' \Rightarrow M||\text{pad}[r](|M|) \neq M'||\text{pad}[r](|M'|)||0^{nr} \tag{3}$$

For the sponge construction to be secure (see Section 3.2), the padding rule pad must be sponge-compliant. As a sufficient condition, a padding rule that is reversible, non-empty and such that the last block must be non-zero, is sponge-compliant [5].

3.1 Definition

The permutation f operates on a fixed number of bits, the *width* b. The sponge construction has a state of b bits. First, all the bits of the state are initialized to zero. The input message is padded with the function pad$[r]$ and cut into r-bits blocks. Then it proceeds in two phases: the *absorbing phase* followed by the *squeezing phase*. In the absorbing phase, the r-bit input message blocks are XORed into the first r bits of the state, interleaved with applications of the function f. When all message blocks are processed, the sponge construction switches to the squeezing phase. In the squeezing phase, the first r bits of the state are returned as output blocks, interleaved with applications of the function f. The number of iterations is determined by the requested number of bits. Finally the output is truncated to the requested length. Algorithm 1 provides a formal definition.

The value $c = b - r$ is called the *capacity*. The last c bits of the state are never directly affected by the input blocks and are never output during the squeezing phase. The capacity c actually determines the attainable security level of the construction [6,9].

3.2 Security

Cryptographic functions are often designed in two steps. In the first step, one chooses a construction that uses a cryptographic primitive with fixed input and output size (e.g., a compression function or a permutation) and builds a function

Algorithm 1. The sponge construction SPONGE$[f, \text{pad}, r]$
Require: $r < b$

Interface: $Z = \text{sponge}(M, \ell)$ with $M \in \mathbb{Z}_2^*$, integer $\ell > 0$ and $Z \in \mathbb{Z}_2^\ell$
$P = M||\text{pad}[r](|M|)$
Let $P = P_0||P_1||\dots||P_w$ with $|P_i| = r$
$s = 0^b$
for $i = 0$ to w **do**
  $s = s \oplus (P_i||0^{b-r})$
  $s = f(s)$
end for
$Z = \lfloor s \rfloor_r$
while $|Z| < \ell$ **do**
  $s = f(s)$
  $Z = Z||\lfloor s \rfloor_r$
end while
return $\lfloor Z \rfloor_\ell$

that can take inputs and or generate outputs of arbitrary size. If the security of this construction can be proven, for instance as in this case using the indifferentiability framework, it reduces the scope of cryptanalysis to that of the underlying primitive and guarantees the absence of single-stage generic attacks (e.g., preimage, second preimage and collision attacks) [21]. However, generic security in the multi-stage setting using the indifferentiability framework is currently an open problem [25].

It is shown in [6] that the success probability of any single-stage generic attack for differentiating the sponge construction calling a random permutation or transformation from a random oracle is upper bounded by $2^{-(c+1)}N^2$. Here N is the number of calls to the underlying permutation or its inverse. This implies that any single-stage generic attack on a sponge function has success probability of at most $2^{-(c+1)}N^2$ plus the success probability of this attack on a random oracle.

In [9], we address the security of the sponge construction when the message is prefixed with a key, as it will be done in the mode of Section 5. In this specific case, the security proof goes beyond the $2^{c/2}$ complexity if the number of input or output blocks for which the key is used (data complexity) is upper bounded by $M < 2^{c/2-1}$. In that case, distinguishing the keyed sponge from a random oracle has time complexity of at least $2^{c-1}/M > 2^{c/2}$. Hence, for keyed modes, one can reduce the capacity c for the same targeted security level.

3.3 Implementing Authenticated Encryption

The simplest way to build an actual system that behaves as ROWRAP would be to replace the random oracles $\mathcal{RO}_\text{C}$ and $\mathcal{RO}_\text{T}$ by a sponge function with domain separation. However, such a solution requires two sponge function executions: one for the generation of the key stream and one for the generation of the tag, while we aim for a single-pass solution. To achieve this, we define a variant where the key stream blocks and tag are the responses of a sponge function to input sequences that are each other's prefix. This introduces a new construction that is closely related to the sponge construction: the duplex construction. Subsequently, we build an authenticated encryption mode on top of that.

4 The Duplex Construction

Like the sponge construction, the *duplex construction* DUPLEX$[f, \text{pad}, r]$ uses a fixed-length transformation (or permutation) f, a padding rule "pad" and a parameter bitrate r. Unlike a sponge function that is stateless in between calls, the duplex construction accepts calls that take an input string and return an output string depending on all inputs received so far. We call an instance of the duplex construction a *duplex object*, which we denote D in our descriptions. We prefix the calls made to a specific duplex object D by its name D and a dot.

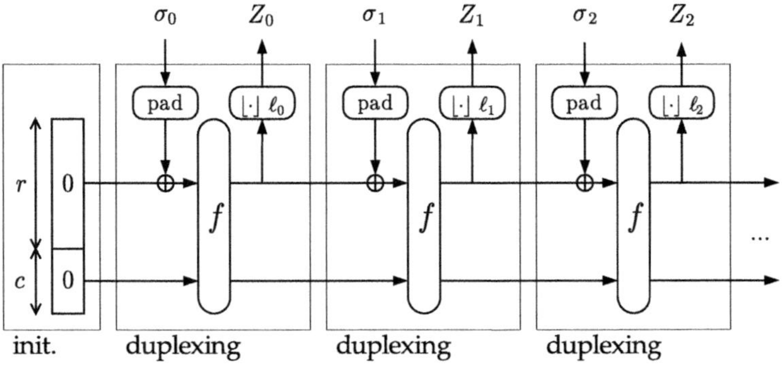

Fig. 1. The duplex construction

The duplex construction works as follows. A duplex object D has a state of b bits. Upon initialization all the bits of the state are set to zero. From then on one can send to it D.duplexing(σ, ℓ) calls, with σ an input string and ℓ the requested number of bits.

The maximum number of bits ℓ one can request is r and the input string σ shall be short enough such that after padding it results in a single r-bit block. We call the maximum length of σ the *maximum duplex rate* and denote it by $\rho_{\max}(\text{pad}, r)$. Formally:

$$\rho_{\max}(\text{pad}, r) = \min\{x : x + |\text{pad}[r](x)| > r\} - 1. \tag{4}$$

Upon receipt of a D.duplexing(σ, ℓ) call, the duplex object pads the input string σ and XORs it into the first r bits of the state. Then it applies f to the state

Algorithm 2. The duplex construction DUPLEX$[f, \text{pad}, r]$

Require: $r < b$
Require: $\rho_{\max}(\text{pad}, r) > 0$
Require: $s \in \mathbb{Z}_2^b$ (maintained across calls)

Interface: D.initialize()
$s = 0^b$

Interface: $Z = D.\text{duplexing}(\sigma, \ell)$ with $\ell \leq r$, $\sigma \in \bigcup_{n=0}^{\rho_{\max}(\text{pad},r)} \mathbb{Z}_2^n$, and $Z \in \mathbb{Z}_2^\ell$
$P = \sigma || \text{pad}[r](|\sigma|)$
$s = s \oplus (P || 0^{b-r})$
$s = f(s)$
return $\lfloor s \rfloor_\ell$

and returns the first ℓ bits of the state at the output. We call a *blank call* a call with σ the empty string, and a *mute call* a call without output, $\ell = 0$. The duplex construction is illustrated in Figure 1, and Algorithm 2 provides a formal definition.

The following lemma links the security of the duplex construction to that of the sponge construction with the same parameters, i.e., DUPLEX$[f, \text{pad}, r]$ and SPONGE$[f, \text{pad}, r]$. Generating the output of a D.duplexing() call using a sponge function is illustrated in Figure 2.

Lemma 3. [Duplexing-sponge lemma] *If we denote the input to the i-th call to a duplex object by* (σ_i, ℓ_i) *and the corresponding output by* Z_i *we have:*

$$Z_i = D.\text{duplexing}(\sigma_i, \ell_i) = \text{sponge}(\sigma_0 || \text{pad}_0 || \sigma_1 || \text{pad}_1 || \dots || \sigma_i, \ell_i)$$

with pad_i *a shortcut notation for* $\text{pad}[r](|\sigma_i|)$.

The output of a duplexing call is thus the output of a sponge function with an input $\sigma_0 || \text{pad}_0 \ || \sigma_1 || \text{pad}_1 || \dots || \sigma_i$ and from this input the exact sequence $\sigma_0, \sigma_1, \dots, \sigma_i$ can be recovered as shown in Lemma 4 below. As such, the duplex construction is as secure as the sponge construction with the same parameters. In particular, it inherits its resistance against (single-stage) generic attacks. The reference point in this case is a random oracle whose input is the sequence of inputs to the duplexing calls since the initialization.

Lemma 4. *Let* pad *and* r *be fixed. Then, the mapping from a sequence of binary strings* $(\sigma_0, \sigma_1, \dots, \sigma_n)$ *with* $|\sigma_i| \leq \rho_{\max}(\text{pad}, r)\ \forall i$ *to the binary string* $s = \sigma_0 || \text{pad}_0 || \sigma_1 || \text{pad}_1 || \dots || \text{pad}_{n-1} || \sigma_n$ *is injective.*

In the following sections we will show that the duplex construction is a powerful tool for building modes of use.

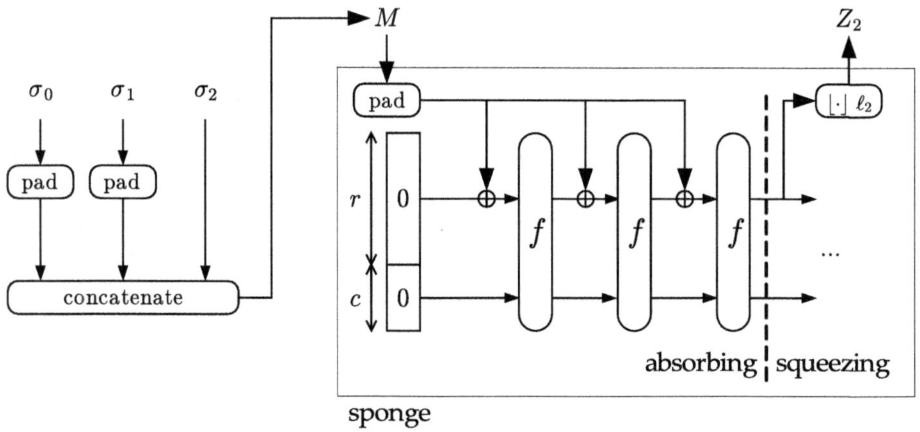

Fig. 2. Generating the output of a duplexing call with a sponge

5 The Authenticated Encryption Mode SpongeWrap

We propose an authenticated encryption mode SPONGEWRAP that realizes the authenticated encryption process defined in Section 2. Similarly to the duplex construction, we call an instance of the authenticated encryption mode a SPONGEWRAP object.

Upon initialization of a SPONGEWRAP object, it loads the key K. From then on one can send requests to it for wrapping and/or unwrapping data. The key stream blocks used for encryption and the tags depend on the key K and the data sent in all previous requests. The authenticated encryption of a sequence of header-body pairs, as described in Section 2.1, can be performed with a sequence of wrap or unwrap requests to a SPONGEWRAP object.

5.1 Definition

A SPONGEWRAP object W internally uses a duplex object D with parameters f, pad and r. Upon initialization of a SPONGEWRAP object, it initializes D and forwards the (padded) key blocks K to D using mute D.duplexing() calls.

When receiving a W.wrap(A, B, ℓ) request, it forwards the blocks of the (padded) header A and the (padded) body B to D. It generates the cryptogram C block by block $C_i = B_i \oplus Z_i$ with Z_i the response of D to the previous D.duplexing() call. The ℓ-bit tag T is the response of D to the last body block (possibly extended with the response to additional blank D.duplexing() calls in case $\ell > \rho$). Finally it returns the cryptogram C and the tag T.

When receiving a W.unwrap(A, C, T) request, it forwards the blocks of the (padded) header A to D. It decrypts the data body B block by block $B_i = C_i \oplus Z_i$ with Z_i the response of D to the previous D.duplexing() call. The response of D

to the last body block (possibly extended) is compared with the tag T received as input. If the tag is valid, it returns the data body B; otherwise, it returns an error. Note that in implementations one may impose additional constraints, such as SPONGEWRAP objects dedicated to either wrapping or unwrapping. Additionally, the SPONGEWRAP object should impose a minimum length t for the tag received before unwrapping and could break the entire session as soon as an incorrect tag is received.

Before being forwarded to D, every key, header, data or cryptogram block is extended with a so-called *frame bit*. The rate ρ of the SPONGEWRAP mode determines the size of the blocks and hence the maximum number of bits processed per call to f. Its upper bound is $\rho_{\max}(\text{pad}, r) - 1$ due to the inclusion of one frame bit per block. A formal definition of SPONGEWRAP is given in Algorithm 3.

5.2 Security

In this section, we show the security of SPONGEWRAP against generic attacks. To do so, we proceed in two steps. First, we define a variant of ROWRAP for which the key stream depends not only on A but also on previous blocks of B. Then, we quantify the increase in the adversary advantage when trading the random oracles $\mathcal{RO}_\text{C}$ and $\mathcal{RO}_\text{T}$ with a random sponge function and appropriate input mappings.

For a fixed block length ρ, let

$$\text{pre}_i(\overline{A, B}) = (A^{(1)}, B^{(1)}, A^{(2)}, \ldots, B^{(n-1)}, A^{(n)}, \lfloor B^{(n)} \rfloor_{i\rho}),$$

i.e., the last body $B^{(n)}$ is truncated to its first i blocks of ρ bits. We define ROWRAP[ρ] identically to ROWRAP, except that in the wrapping algorithm, we have

$$\begin{aligned} C^{(n)} = & \lfloor \mathcal{RO}_\text{C}(K, \text{pre}_0(\overline{A, B})) \rfloor_{|B_0^{(n)}|} \oplus B_0^{(n)} \\ & || \lfloor \mathcal{RO}_\text{C}(K, \text{pre}_1(\overline{A, B})) \rfloor_{|B_1^{(n)}|} \oplus B_1^{(n)} \\ & \ldots \\ & || \lfloor \mathcal{RO}_\text{C}(K, \text{pre}_w(\overline{A, B})) \rfloor_{|B_w^{(n)}|} \oplus B_w^{(n)} \end{aligned}$$

for $B^{(n)} = B_0^{(n)} || B_1^{(n)} || \ldots || B_w^{(n)}$ with $|B_i^{(n)}| = \rho$ for $i < w$, $|B_w^{(n)}| \leq \rho$ and $|B_w^{(n)}| > 0$ if $w > 0$. The unwrap algorithm U is defined accordingly.

The scheme ROWRAP[ρ] is as secure as ROWRAP, as expressed in the following two lemmas. We omit the proofs, as they are very similar to those of Lemma 1 and 2.

Lemma 5. *Let $\mathcal{A}[\mathcal{RO}_\text{C}, \mathcal{RO}_\text{T}]$ be an adversary having access to $\mathcal{RO}_\text{C}$ and $\mathcal{RO}_\text{T}$ and respecting the nonce requirement. Then,* $\text{Adv}^{\text{priv}}_{\text{ROWRAP}[\rho]}(\mathcal{A}) \leq q2^{-k}$ *if the adversary makes no more than q queries to $\mathcal{RO}_\text{C}$ or $\mathcal{RO}_\text{T}$.*

Algorithm 3. The authenticated encryption mode $\text{SpongeWrap}[f, \text{pad}, r, \rho]$

Require: $\rho \leq \rho_{\max}(\text{pad}, r) - 1$
Require: $D = \text{DUPLEX}[f, \text{pad}, r]$

Interface: W.initialize(K) with $K \in \mathbb{Z}_2^*$
Let $K = K_0||K_1||\ldots||K_u$ with $|K_i| = \rho$ for $i < u$, $|K_u| \leq \rho$ and $|K_u| > 0$ if $u > 0$
D.initialize()
for $i = 0$ to $u - 1$ **do**
    D.duplexing($K_i||1, 0$)
end for
D.duplexing($K_u||0, 0$)

Interface: $(C, T) = W$.wrap(A, B, ℓ) with $A, B \in \mathbb{Z}_2^*$, $\ell \geq 0$, $C \in \mathbb{Z}_2^{|B|}$ and $T \in \mathbb{Z}_2^{\ell}$
Let $A = A_0||A_1||\ldots||A_v$ with $|A_i| = \rho$ for $i < v$, $|A_v| \leq \rho$ and $|A_v| > 0$ if $v > 0$
Let $B = B_0||B_1||\ldots||B_w$ with $|B_i| = \rho$ for $i < w$, $|B_w| \leq \rho$ and $|B_w| > 0$ if $w > 0$
for $i = 0$ to $v - 1$ **do**
    D.duplexing($A_i||0, 0$)
end for
$Z = D$.duplexing($A_v||1, |B_0|$)
$C = B_0 \oplus Z$
for $i = 0$ to $w - 1$ **do**
    $Z = D$.duplexing($B_i||1, |B_{i+1}|$)
    $C = C||(B_{i+1} \oplus Z)$
end for
$Z = D$.duplexing($B_w||0, \rho$)
while $|Z| < \ell$ **do**
    $Z = Z||D$.duplexing($0, \rho$)
end while
$T = \lfloor Z \rfloor_\ell$
return (C, T)

Interface: $B = W$.unwrap(A, C, T) with $A, C, T \in \mathbb{Z}_2^*$, $B \in \mathbb{Z}_2^{|C|} \cup \{\text{error}\}$
Let $A = A_0||A_1||\ldots||A_v$ with $|A_i| = \rho$ for $i < v$, $|A_v| \leq \rho$ and $|A_v| > 0$ if $v > 0$
Let $C = C_0||C_1||\ldots||C_w$ with $|C_i| = \rho$ for $i < w$, $|C_w| \leq \rho$ and $|C_w| > 0$ if $w > 0$
Let $T = T_0||T_1||\ldots||T_x$ with $|T_i| = \rho$ for $i < x$, $|C_x| \leq \rho$ and $|C_x| > 0$ if $x > 0$
for $i = 0$ to $v - 1$ **do**
    D.duplexing($A_i||0, 0$)
end for
$Z = D$.duplexing($A_v||1, |C_0|$)
$B_0 = C_0 \oplus Z$
for $i = 0$ to $w - 1$ **do**
    $Z = D$.duplexing($B_i||1, |C_{i+1}|$)
    $B_{i+1} = C_{i+1} \oplus Z$
end for
$Z = D$.duplexing($B_w||0, \rho$)
while $|Z| < \ell$ **do**
    $Z = Z||D$.duplexing($0, \rho$)
end while
if $T = \lfloor Z \rfloor_\ell$ **return** $B_0||B_1||\ldots B_w$ **else return** Error

Lemma 6. *Let $\mathcal{A}[\mathcal{RO}_\mathrm{C}, \mathcal{RO}_\mathrm{T}]$ be an adversary having access to $\mathcal{RO}_\mathrm{C}$ and $\mathcal{RO}_\mathrm{T}$. Then,* ROWRAP *satisfies* $\mathrm{Adv}^{\mathrm{auth}}_{\mathrm{ROWRAP}[\rho]}(\mathcal{A}) \leq q2^{-k} + 2^{-t}$ *if the adversary makes no more than q queries to $\mathcal{RO}_\mathrm{C}$ or $\mathcal{RO}_\mathrm{T}$.*

Clearly, ROWRAP and ROWRAP[ρ] are equally secure if we implement $\mathcal{RO}_\mathrm{C}$ and $\mathcal{RO}_\mathrm{T}$ using a single random oracle with domain separation: $\mathcal{RO}_\mathrm{C}(x) = \mathcal{RO}(x||1)$ and $\mathcal{RO}_\mathrm{T}(x) = \mathcal{RO}(x||0)$. Notice that SPONGEWRAP uses the same domain separation technique: the last bit of the input of the last duplexing call is always a 1 (resp. 0) to produce key stream bits (resp. to produce the tag). With this change, SPONGEWRAP now works like ROWRAP[ρ], except that the input is formatted differently and that a sponge function replaces $\mathcal{RO}$. The next lemma focuses on the former aspect.

Lemma 7. *Let $(K, \overline{A, B})$ be a sequence of strings composed by a key followed by header-body pairs. Then, the mapping from $(K, \overline{A, B})$ to the corresponding sequence of inputs $(\sigma_0, \sigma_1, \ldots, \sigma_n)$ to the duplexing calls in Algorithm 3 is injective.*

We now have all the ingredients to prove the following theorem.

Theorem 1. *The authenticated encryption mode* SPONGEWRAP[f, pad, r, ρ] *defined in Algorithm 3 satisfies*

$$\mathrm{Adv}^{\mathrm{priv}}_{\mathrm{SPONGEWRAP}[f,\mathrm{pad},r,\rho]}(\mathcal{A}) < q2^{-k} + \frac{N(N+1)}{2^{c+1}} \quad \textit{and}$$

$$\mathrm{Adv}^{\mathrm{auth}}_{\mathrm{SPONGEWRAP}[f,\mathrm{pad},r,\rho]}(\mathcal{A}) < q2^{-k} + 2^{-t} + \frac{N(N+1)}{2^{c+1}},$$

against any single adversary $\mathcal{A}$ if $K \xleftarrow{\$} \mathbb{Z}_2^k$, tags of $\ell \geq t$ bits are used, f is a randomly chosen permutation, q is the number of queries and N is the number of times f is called.

Note that all the outputs of SPONGEWRAP are equivalent to calls to a sponge function with the secret key blocks as a prefix. So the results of [9] can also be applied to SPONGEWRAP as explained in Section 3.2.

5.3 Advantages and Limitations

The authenticated encryption mode SPONGEWRAP has the following unique combination of advantages:

- While most other authenticated encryption modes are described in terms of a block cipher, SPONGEWRAP only requires on a fixed-length permutation.
- It supports the alternation of strings that require authenticated encryption and strings that only require authentication.
- It can provide intermediate tags after each W.wrap(A, B, ℓ) request.
- It has a strong security bound against generic attacks with a simple proof.
- It is single-pass and requires only a single call to f per ρ-bit block.

- It is flexible as the bitrate can be freely chosen as long as the capacity is larger than some lower bound.
- The encryption is not expanding.

As compared to some block cipher based authenticated encryption modes, it has some limitations. First, the mode as such is serial and cannot be parallelized at algorithmic level. Some block cipher based modes do actually allow parallelization, for instance, the offset codebook (OCB) mode [27]. Yet, SPONGEWRAP variants could be defined to support parallel streams in a fashion similar to tree hashing, but with some overhead.

Second, if a system does not impose the nonce requirement on A, an attacker may send two requests (A, B) and (A, B') with $B \neq B'$. In this case, the first differing blocks of B and B', say B_i and B'_i, will be enciphered with the same key stream, making their bitwise XOR available to the attacker. Some block cipher based modes are *misuse resistant*, i.e., they are designed in such a way that in case the nonce requirement is not fulfilled, the only information an attacker can find out is whether B and B' are equal or not [29]. Yet, many applications already provide a nonce, such as a packet number or a key ID, and can put it in A.

5.4 An Application: Key Wrapping

Key wrapping is the process of ensuring the secrecy and integrity of cryptographic keys in transport or storage, e.g., [23,14]. A *payload key* is wrapped with a *key-encrypting key* (KEK). We can use the SPONGEWRAP mode with K equal to the KEK and let the data body be the payload key value. In a sound key management system every key has a unique identifier. It is sufficient to include the identifier of the payload key in the header A and two different payload keys will never be enciphered with the same key stream. When wrapping a private key, the corresponding public key or a digest computed from it can serve as identifier.

6 Other Applications of the Duplex Construction

Authenticated encryption is just one application of the duplex construction. In this section we illustrate it by providing two more examples: a pseudo-random bit sequence generator and a sponge-like construction that overwrites part of the state with the input block rather than to XOR it in.

6.1 A Reseedable Pseudo-random Bit Sequence Generator

In various cryptographic applications and protocols, random bits are used to generate keys or unpredictable challenges. While randomness can be extracted from a physical source, it is often necessary to provide many more bits than the entropy of the physical source. A pseudo-random bit sequence generator (PRG) is initialized with a seed, generated in a secret or truly random way, and it then expands the seed into a sequence of bits. For cryptographic purposes, it is required that the generated bits cannot be predicted, even if subsets of the sequence are revealed. In this context, a PRG is similar to a stream cipher. A PRG is also similar to a cryptographic hash function when gathering entropy coming from different sources. Finally, some applications require a pseudo-random bit sequence generator to support forward security: The compromise of the current state does not enable the attacker to determine the previously generated pseudo-random bits [4,13].

Conveniently, a pseudo-random bit sequence generator can be reseedable, i.e., one can bring an additional source of entropy after pseudo-random bits have been generated. Instead of throwing away the current state of the PRG, reseeding combines the current state of the generator with the new seed material. In [7] a reseedable PRG was defined based on the sponge construction that implements the required functionality. The ideas behind that PRG are very similar to the duplex construction. We however show that such a PRG can be defined on top of the duplex construction.

A duplex object can readily be used as a reseedable PRG. Seed material can be fed via the σ inputs in D.duplexing() call and the responses can be used as pseudo-random bits. If pseudo-random bits are required and there is no seed available, one can simply send blank D.duplexing() calls. The only limitation of this is that the user must split his seed material in strings of at most $\rho_{\max}$ bits and that at most r bits can be requested in a single call. This limitation is removed in a more elaborate generator called SpongePRG presented in [8]. This mode is similar to the one proposed in [7] in that it minimizes the number of calls to f, although explicitly based on the duplex construction.

6.2 The Mode Overwrite

In [17] sponge-like constructions were proposed and cryptanalyzed. In some of these constructions, absorbing is done by overwriting part of the state by the message block rather than XORing it in, e.g., as in the hash function Grindahl [19]. These overwrite functions have the advantage over sponge functions that between calls to f, only c bits must be kept instead of b. This may not be useful when hashing in a continuous fashion, as b bits must be processed by f anyway. However, when hashing a partial message, then putting it aside to continue later on, storing only c bits may be useful on some platforms.

Defined in [8], the mode Overwrite differs from the sponge construction in that it overwrites part of the state with an input block instead of XORing it in. Such a mode can be analyzed by building it on top of the duplex construction. If the first ρ bits of the state are known to be Z, overwriting them with a message block P_i is equivalent to XORing in $Z \oplus P_i$. In [8], we have proven that the security of Overwrite is equivalent to that of the sponge construction with the same parameter, but at a cost of 2 bits of bitrate (or equivalently, of capacity): one for the padding rule (assuming pad10* is used) and one for a frame bit.

7 A Flexible and Compact Padding Rule

Sponge functions and duplex objects feature the nice property of allowing a range of security-performance trade-offs, via capacity-rate pairs, using the same fixed permutation f. To be able to fully exploit this property in the scope of the duplex construction, and for performance reasons, the padding rule should be compact and should be suitable for a family of sponge functions with different rates.

For a given capacity and width, the padding reduces the maximum bitrate of the duplex construction, as in Eq. (4). To minimize this effect, especially when the width of the permutation is relatively small, one should look for the most compact padding rule. The sponge-compliant padding scheme (see Section 3) with the smallest overhead is the well-known *simple reversible padding*, which appends a single 1 and the smallest number of zeroes such that the length of the result is a multiple of the required block length. We denote it by $\text{pad10}^*[r](M)$. It satisfies $\rho_{\max}(\text{pad10}^*, r) = r - 1$ and hence has only one bit of overhead.

When considering the security of a set of sponge functions that make use of the same permutation f but with different bitrates, simple reversible padding is not sufficient. The indifferentiability proof of [6] actually only covers the indifferentiability of a single sponge function instance from a random oracle. As a solution, we propose the *multi-rate padding*, denoted $\text{pad10}^*1[r](|M|)$, which returns a bitstring 10^q1 with $q = (-|M| - 2) \bmod r$. This padding is sponge-compliant and has $\rho_{\max}(\text{pad10}^*1, r) = r - 2$. Hence, this padding scheme is compact as the duplex-level maximum rate differs from the sponge-level rate by only two bits. Furthermore, in Theorem 2 we will show it is sufficient for the indifferentiability of a set of sponge functions. The intuitive idea behind this is that, with the pad10*1 padding scheme, the last block absorbed has a bit with value 1 at position $r - 1$, while any other function of the family with $r' < r$ this bit has value 0.

Besides having a compact padding rule, it is also useful to allow the sponge function to have specific bitrate values. In many applications one prefers to have block lengths that are a multiple of 8 or even higher powers of two to avoid bit shifting or misalignment issues. With modes using the duplex construction, one has to distinguish between the mode-level block size and the bitrate of the underlying sponge function. For instance in the authenticated encryption mode SpongeWrap, the block size is at most $\rho_{\max}(\text{pad}, r) - 1$. To have a block size with the desired value, it suffices to take a slightly higher value as bitrate r; hence, the sponge-level bitrate may no longer be a multiple of 8 or of a higher power of two. Therefore it is meaningful to consider the security of a set of sponge functions with common f and different bitrates, including bitrates that are not multiples of 8 or of a higher power of two. For instance, the mode SpongeWrap could be based on Keccak$[r = 1027, c = 573]$ so as to process application-level blocks of $\rho_{\max}(\text{pad10}^*1, 1027) - 1 = 1024$ bits [10].

Regarding the indifferentiability of a set of sponge functions, it is clear that the best one can achieve is bounded by the strength of the sponge construction with the lowest capacity (or, equivalently, the highest bitrate), as an adversary can always just try to differentiate the weakest construction from a random oracle. The next theorem states that we achieve this bound by using the multi-rate padding.

Theorem 2. *Given a random permutation (or transformation) f, differentiating the array of sponge functions* SPONGE$[f, \text{pad}10^*1, r]$ *with* $0 < r \leq r_{\max}$ *from an array of independent random oracles* $(\mathcal{RO}_r)$ *has the same advantage as differentiating* SPONGE$[f, \text{pad}10^*, r_{\max}]$ *from a random oracle.*

References

1. Aumasson, J.-P., Henzen, L., Meier, W., Naya-Plasencia, M.: Quark: A lightweight hash. In: Mangard and Standaert [20], pp. 1–15
2. Bellare, M., Namprempre, C.: Authenticated Encryption: Relations among Notions and Analysis of the Generic Composition Paradigm. In: Okamoto, T. (ed.) ASIACRYPT 2000. LNCS, vol. 1976, pp. 531–545. Springer, Heidelberg (2000)
3. Bellare, M., Rogaway, P.: Random oracles are practical: A paradigm for designing efficient protocols. In: ACM (ed.) ACM Conference on Computer and Communications Security 1993, pp. 62–73 (1993)
4. Bellare, M., Yee, B.: Forward-security in private-key cryptography. Cryptology ePrint Archive, Report 2001/035 (2001), `http://eprint.iacr.org/`
5. Bertoni, G., Daemen, J., Peeters, M., Van Assche, G.: Sponge functions. In: Ecrypt Hash Workshop (May 2007), public comment to NIST, from `http://www.csrc.nist.gov/pki/HashWorkshop/Public_Comments/2007_May.html`
6. Bertoni, G., Daemen, J., Peeters, M., Van Assche, G.: On the Indifferentiability of the Sponge Construction. In: Smart, N.P. (ed.) EUROCRYPT 2008. LNCS, vol. 4965, pp. 181–197. Springer, Heidelberg (2008), `http://sponge.noekeon.org/`
7. Bertoni, G., Daemen, J., Peeters, M., Van Assche, G.: Sponge-based pseudo-random number generators. In: Mangard and Standaert [20], pp. 33–47
8. Bertoni, G., Daemen, J., Peeters, M., Van Assche, G.: Duplexing the sponge: single-pass authenticated encryption and other applications. Cryptology ePrint Archive, Report 2011/499 (2011), `http://eprint.iacr.org/`
9. Bertoni, G., Daemen, J., Peeters, M., Van Assche, G.: On the security of the keyed sponge construction. In: Symmetric Key Encryption Workshop (SKEW) (February 2011)
10. Bertoni, G., Daemen, J., Peeters, M., Van Assche, G.: The KECCAK reference (January 2011), `http://keccak.noekeon.org/`
11. Biryukov, A. (ed.): FSE 2007. LNCS, vol. 4593. Springer, Heidelberg (2007)
12. Bogdanov, A., Knežević, M., Leander, G., Toz, D., Varıcı, K., Verbauwhede, I.: SPONGENT: A Lightweight Hash Function. In: Preneel, B., Takagi, T. (eds.) CHES 2011. LNCS, vol. 6917, pp. 312–325. Springer, Heidelberg (2011)
13. Desai, A., Hevia, A., Yin, Y.L.: A Practice-Oriented Treatment of Pseudorandom Number Generators. In: Knudsen, L.R. (ed.) EUROCRYPT 2002. LNCS, vol. 2332, pp. 368–383. Springer, Heidelberg (2002)
14. Dworkin, M.: Request for review of key wrap algorithms. Cryptology ePrint Archive, Report 2004/340 (2004), `http://eprint.iacr.org/`

15. ECRYPT Network of excellence, The SHA-3 Zoo (2011), http://ehash.iaik.tugraz.at/index.php/The_SHA-3_Zoo
16. Ferguson, N., Whiting, D., Schneier, B., Kelsey, J., Lucks, S., Kohno, T.: Helix: Fast Encryption and Authentication in a Single Cryptographic Primitive. In: Johansson, T. (ed.) FSE 2003. LNCS, vol. 2887, pp. 330–346. Springer, Heidelberg (2003)
17. Gorski, M., Lucks, S., Peyrin, T.: Slide Attacks on a Class of Hash Functions. In: Pieprzyk, J. (ed.) ASIACRYPT 2008. LNCS, vol. 5350, pp. 143–160. Springer, Heidelberg (2008)
18. Guo, J., Peyrin, T., Poschmann, A.: The PHOTON Family of Lightweight Hash Functions. In: Rogaway, P. (ed.) CRYPTO 2011. LNCS, vol. 6841, pp. 222–239. Springer, Heidelberg (2011)
19. Knudsen, L., Rechberger, C., Thomsen, S.: The Grindahl hash functions. In: Biryukov [11], pp. 39–57
20. Mangard, S., Standaert, F.-X. (eds.): CHES 2010. LNCS, vol. 6225. Springer, Heidelberg (2010)
21. Maurer, U., Renner, R., Holenstein, C.: Indifferentiability, Impossibility Results on Reductions, and Applications to the Random Oracle Methodology. In: Naor, M. (ed.) TCC 2004. LNCS, vol. 2951, pp. 21–39. Springer, Heidelberg (2004)
22. Muller, F.: Differential attacks against the Helix stream cipher. In: Roy and Meier [30], pp. 94–108
23. NIST, AES key wrap specification (November 2001)
24. Paul, S., Preneel, B.: Solving Systems of Differential Equations of Addition. In: Boyd, C., González Nieto, J.M. (eds.) ACISP 2005. LNCS, vol. 3574, pp. 75–88. Springer, Heidelberg (2005)
25. Ristenpart, T., Shacham, H., Shrimpton, T.: Careful with Composition: Limitations of the Indifferentiability Framework. In: Paterson, K.G. (ed.) EUROCRYPT 2011. LNCS, vol. 6632, pp. 487–506. Springer, Heidelberg (2011)
26. Rogaway, P.: Authenticated-encryption with associated-data. In: ACM Conference on Computer and Communications Security 2002 (CCS 2002), pp. 98–107. ACM Press (2002)
27. Rogaway, P., Bellare, M., Black, J.: OCB: A block-cipher mode of operation for efficient authenticated encryption. ACM Trans. Inf. Syst. Secur. 6(3), 365–403 (2003)
28. Rogaway, P., Bellare, M., Black, J., Krovetz, T.: OCB: A block-cipher mode of operation for efficient authenticated encryption. In: CCS 2001: Proceedings of the 8th ACM Conference on Computer and Communications Security, pp. 196–205. ACM, New York (2001)
29. Rogaway, P., Shrimpton, T.: A Provable-Security Treatment of the Key-Wrap Problem. In: Vaudenay, S. (ed.) EUROCRYPT 2006. LNCS, vol. 4004, pp. 373–390. Springer, Heidelberg (2006)
30. Roy, B., Meier, W. (eds.): FSE 2004. LNCS, vol. 3017. Springer, Heidelberg (2004)
31. Whiting, D., Schneier, B., Lucks, S., Muller, F.: Fast encryption and authentication in a single cryptographic primitive, ECRYPT Stream Cipher Project Report 2005/027 (2005), http://www.ecrypt.eu.org/stream/phelixp2.html
32. Wu, H., Preneel, B.: Differential-linear attacks against the stream cipher Phelix. In: Biryukov [11], pp. 87–100
33. Ågren, M., Hell, M., Johansson, T., Meier, W.: A new version of Grain-128 with authentication. In: Symmetric Key Encryption Workshop, SKEW (February 2011)

Blockcipher-Based Double-Length Hash Functions for Pseudorandom Oracles

Yusuke Naito

Mitsubishi Electric Corporation

Abstract. PRO (Pseudorandom Oracle) is an important security of hash functions because it ensures that the PRO hash function inherits all properties of a random oracle in single stage games up to the PRO bound (e.g., collision resistant security, preimage resistant security and so on). In this paper, we propose new blockcipher-based double-length hash functions, which are PROs up to $\mathcal{O}(2^n)$ query complexity in the ideal cipher model. Our hash functions use a single blockcipher, which encrypts an n-bit string using a $2n$-bit key, and maps an input of arbitrary length to an n-bit output. Since many blockciphers supports a $2n$-bit key (e.g. AES supports a 256-bit key), the assumption to use the $2n$-bit key length blockcipher is acceptable. To our knowledge, this is the first time double-length hash functions based on a single (practical size) blockcipher with birthday PRO security.

1 Introduction

The blockcipher-based design (e.g. [19,26]) is the most popular method for constructing a cryptographic hash function. A hash function is designed by the following two steps: (1) designing a blockcipher and (2) designing a mode of operation. MD-family [28,29], SHA-family [23] and SHA-3 candidates follow the design method. Another design method is to utilize a practical blockcipher such as AES. Such hash functions are useful in size restricted devices such as RFID tags and smart cards: when implementing both a hash function and a blockcipher, one has only to implement a blockcipher. However, the output length of practical blockciphers is far too short for a collision resistant hash function, e.g., 128 bits for AES. Thus designing a collision resistant double length hash function (CR-DLHF) is an interesting topic. The core of the design of the CR-DLHF is to design a collision resistant double-length compression function (CR-DLCF) which maps an input of fixed length (more than $2n$-bits) to an output of $2n$-bit length when using an n-bit output length blockcipher. Then the hash function combined a domain extension (e.g. strengthened Merkle-Damgård (SMD) [5,21]), which preserves CR security, with the CR-DLCF yields a CR-DLHF. Many DLCFs, e,g,. [2,22,11,14,24,16,18], have been designed and the security is proven in the ideal cipher (IC) model [8,11,17,9,24,15,30].

The indifferentiability framework was introduced by Maurer *et al.* [20], which considers the reducibility of one system to another system. Roughly speaking,

A. Miri and S. Vaudenay (Eds.): SAC 2011, LNCS 7118, pp. 338–355, 2012.

if a system F is indifferentiable from another system G up to q query complexity, in single-stage games (e.g., IND-CCA, EUF-CMA, Collision game, Second Preimage game, Preimage game and many others), any cryptosystem is at least as secure under F as under G up to q query complexity. Recent proposed hash functions, e.g. SHA-3 candidates, considered the security of the indifferentiability from a random oracle (RO) (or Pseudorandom Oracle (PRO)). It ensures that in single stage games the hash function has no structural design flows in composition and has security against any generic attacks up to the PRO query complexity. So it is important to consider PRO security when a DLHF is designed.

Hereafter a blockcipher which encrypts an n-bit string using a k-bit key is denoted by (k,n)-BC. Gong *et al.* [10] proved that the prefix-free Merkle-Damgård using the PBGV compression function [25] is PRO up to $\mathcal{O}(2^{n/2})$ query complexity as long as the ($2n$,n)-BC is IC. The PRO security is not enough because the query complexity is 2^{64} when $n = 128$. Chang *et al.* [3] and Hirose *et al.* [12] proposed $2n$-bit output length DLHFs using a compression function $h : \{0,1\}^d \rightarrow \{0,1\}^n$ where $d > 2n$. Their proposals are PROs up to $\mathcal{O}(2^n)$ query complexity as long as h is a fixed input length RO (FILRO). Since IC where the plain text element is fixed by a constant is FILRO, these hash functions can be modified to blockcipher-based schemes which use a (d,n)-BC. However, practical blockciphers (such as AES) don't support d-bit key where $d > 2n$. Many other practical size[1] blockcipher-based DLHFs were proposed, e.g., [2,22,11,14,24,16,18], while none of them achieves PRO security.[2] There is no hash function with birthday PRO security, and thus, we rise the following question:

Can We Construct a DLHF from a "single practical size blockcipher" with "birthday PRO security"?

In this paper, we propose DLHFs using a single ($2n$,n)-BC, which are PROs up to $\mathcal{O}(2^n)$ query complexity in the IC model. Since many blockciphers support $2n$-bit key length, e.g., AES supports 256-bit key length, and the existing DLCFs (e.g., Hirose's compression function [11], Tandem-DM [14], Abreast-DM [14], and generalized DLCF [24]) use a ($2n$,n)-BC, the assumption to use a ($2n$,n)-BC is acceptable. To our knowledge, our hash functions are the first time DLHFs based on a practical size blockcipher with birthday PRO security.[3] When $n = 128$ which is supported by AES, our hash functions have 2^{128} security. Since our hash functions use only a *single* blockcipher, it is useful on size restricted devices when implementing both a hash function and a blockcipher. (the hybrid encryption

[1] "Practical size" is the size supported by practical blockciphers such as AES.

[2] Since PRO security is stronger security than CR security, CR security does not guarantee PRO security.

[3] Our hash functions don't satisfy the stronger notion called reset indifferentiability from RO, which ensure security in the multi-stage games [27]. Note that there is no hash function satisfying the notion. Thus to propose the hash function is an open problem.

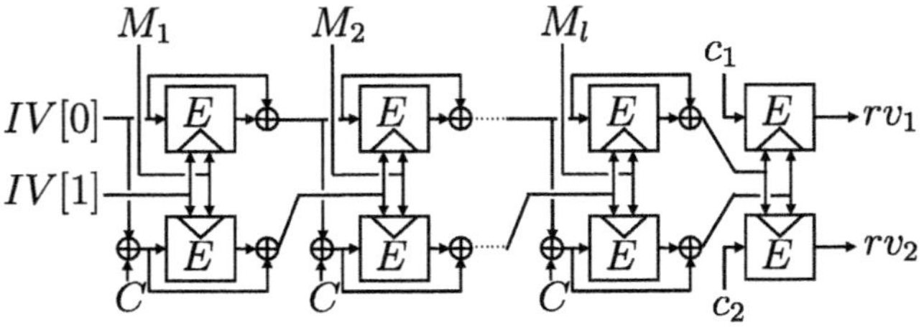

Fig. 1. Our DLHF using Hirose's compression function

schemes use both a blockcipher and a hash function used in a key derivation function, for example.)

Our DLHF. Our DLHFs, which use each of Hirose's compression function, Tandem-DM and Abreast-DM, iterate the compression function and use a new post-processing function f at the last iteration which calls a $(2n, n)$-BC twice. Our DLHFs are slightly lesser for speed than existing CR-DLHFs but have higher security (birthday PRO security).

Let $\mathsf{BC}_{2n,n} = (E, D)$ be a $(2n,n)$-BC where E is an encryption function and D is a decryption function. Let $\mathrm{DLCF}^{\mathsf{BC}_{2n,n}}$ be a DLCF: Hirose's compression function, Tandem-DM, or Abreast-DM. Let $\mathrm{SMD}^{\mathrm{DLCF}^{\mathsf{BC}_{2n,n}}} : \{0,1\}^* \to \{0,1\}^{2n}$ be the SMD hash function using the compression function $\mathrm{DLCF}^{\mathsf{BC}_{2n,n}}$. Our DLHF is defined as follows:

$$F^{\mathsf{BC}_{2n,n}}(M) = f^{\mathsf{BC}_{2n,n}}(\mathrm{SMD}^{\mathrm{DLCF}^{\mathsf{BC}_{2n,n}}}(M))$$

where $f^{\mathsf{BC}_{2n,n}}(x) = E(x, c_1)||E(x, c_2)$ and c_1 and c_2 are n-bit constant values. Note that the first element of the encryption function is the key element and the second element is the plain text element. The DLHF using Hirose's compression function is illustrated in Fig. 1 where each line is n bits and $IV[0], IV[1], C, c_1$ and c_2 are constant values. Note that in this figure we omit the suffix free padding function sfpad. So the hash function takes as its input a message M, $\mathsf{sfpad}(M) = M_1||M_2||\cdots||M_l$ with each block of n bits, and outputs the final value $rv_1||rv_2$. We use the DLHF $\mathrm{SMD}^{\mathrm{DLCF}^{\mathsf{BC}_{2n,n}}}$ to compress an arbitrary length input into an fixed input length value. Since SMD hash functions cannot be used as ROs [4], the post-processing function $f^{\mathsf{BC}_{2n,n}}$ is used to guarantee PRO security.

The use of the constant values c_1 and c_2 in the post-processing function is inspired by the design technique of EMD proposed by Bellare and Ristenpart [1]. This realizes the fact that we can treat our hash function as a NMAC-like hash function. Note that the security of EMD is proven when the compression function is FILRO, while the security of our hash functions is proven when the compression function is the DLCF in the IC model. So additional analyses are needed due to the invertible property of IC and the structures of DLCFs.We thus prove the PRO security of $F^{\mathsf{BC}_{2n,n}}$ by using three techniques: the PrA (Preimage Aware) design framework of Dodis *et al.* [6], PRO for a small function [4], and *indifferentiability from a hash function.* The first two techniques are existing techniques and the last technique is a new application of the indifferentiability framework [20].

First, we prove that the DLCFs are PrA up to $\mathcal{O}(2^n)$ query complexity. The PrA design framework offers the hash functions which are PROs up to $\mathcal{O}(2^n)$ query complexity where FILRO is used as the post-processing function. Second, we convert FILRO into the blockcipher-based post-processing function. We prove that the post-processing function is PRO up to $\mathcal{O}(2^n)$ query complexity in the IC model (PRO for a small function). Then, we prove that the PRO security of the post-processing function and the first PRO result ensure that the converted hash functions are PROs up to $\mathcal{O}(2^n)$ query complexity. We note that the hash functions use two blockciphers.[4] Finally, we consider the single-blockcipher-based hash functions $F^{\mathsf{BC}_{2n,n}}$. We prove that the single blockcipher-based hash functions are indifferentiable from the two-blockciphers-based hash functions in the IC model up to $\mathcal{O}(2^n)$ query complexity (indifferentiability from a hash function). Then we show that the indifferentiable security result and the second PRO result ensure that our hash functions are PROs up to $\mathcal{O}(2^n)$ query complexity in the IC model.

2 Preliminaries

Notation. For two values x, y, $x||y$ is the concatenated value of x and y. For some value y, $x \leftarrow y$ means assigning y to x. $\oplus$ is bitwise exclusive or. $|x|$ is the bit length of x. For a set (list) $\mathcal{T}$ and an element W, $\mathcal{T} \leftarrow W$ means to insert W into $\mathcal{T}$ and $\mathcal{T} \overset{\cup}{\leftarrow} W$ means $\mathcal{T} \leftarrow \mathcal{T} \cup \{W\}$. For some $2n$-bit value x, $x[0]$ is the first n bit value and $x[1]$ is the last n-bit value. $\mathsf{BC}_{d,n} = (E, D)$ be a blockcipher where $E : \{0,1\}^d \times \{0,1\}^n \rightarrow \{0,1\}^n$ is an encryption function, $D : \{0,1\}^d \times \{0,1\}^n \rightarrow \{0,1\}^n$ is a decryption function, the key size is d bits and the cipher text size is n bits. $\mathcal{C}_{d,n} = (E_I, D_I)$ be a ideal cipher (IC) where $E_I : \{0,1\}^d \times \{0,1\}^n \rightarrow \{0,1\}^n$ is an encryption oracle, $D_I : \{0,1\}^d \times \{0,1\}^n \rightarrow \{0,1\}^n$ is a decryption oracle, the key size is d bits and the cipher text size is n bits. $\mathcal{F}_{a,b} : \{0,1\}^a \rightarrow \{0,1\}^b$ is a random oracle (RO). An arbitrary input length random oracle is denoted by $\mathcal{F}_b : \{0,1\}^* \rightarrow \{0,1\}^b$. For any algorithm A, we write $\mathsf{Time}(A)$ to mean the sum of its description length and the worst-case number of steps.

Merkle-Damgård [5,21]. Let $h : \{0,1\}^{2n} \times \{0,1\}^d \rightarrow \{0,1\}^{2n}$ be a compression function using a primitive P (more strictly h^P) and $\mathsf{pad} : \{0,1\}^* \rightarrow (\{0,1\}^d)^*$ be a padding function. The Merkle-Damgård hash function MD^h is described as follows where IV is a $2n$-bit initial value.

[4] Two independent ideal cipher can be obtained from a single ideal cipher by victimizing one bit of the key space. So using a blockcipher with the $2n + 1$-bit key space and the n-bit key space, the hash functions which uses a single blockcipher can be realized. But the size of the blockcipher is not a practical size.

$\underline{\mathrm{MD}^h(M)}$
$z \leftarrow IV$;
Break $\mathsf{pad}(M)$ into d-bit blocks, $\mathsf{pad}(N) = M_1 || \cdots || M_l$;
for $i = 1, \ldots, l$ do $z \leftarrow h(z, M_i)$;
Ret z;

We denote MD^h, when padding pad is a suffix-free padding sfpad, by SMD^h, called strengthened Merkle-Damgård. We assume that it is easy to strip padding, namely that there exists an efficiently computable function $\mathsf{unpad} : (\{0,1\}^d)^* \rightarrow \{0,1\}^* \cup \{\perp\}$ such that $x = \mathsf{unpad}(\mathsf{pad}(x))$ for all $x \in \{0,1\}^*$. Inputs to unpad that are not valid outputs of pad are mapped to $\perp$ by unpad.

Pseudorandom Oracle [20]. Let $H^P : \{0,1\}^* \rightarrow \{0,1\}^n$ be a hash function that utilizes an ideal primitive P. We say that H^P is PRO if there exists an efficient simulator S that simulates P such that for any distinguisher A outputting a bit it is the case that

$$\mathsf{Adv}^{\mathsf{pro}}_{H^P,S}(A) = |\Pr[A^{H^P,P} \Rightarrow 1] - \Pr[A^{\mathcal{F}_n,S^{\mathcal{F}_n}} \Rightarrow 1]|$$

is small where the probabilities are taken over the coins used the experiments. S can make queries to $\mathcal{F}_n$. The S's task is to simulate P such that relations among responses of (H^P, P) hold in responses of $(\mathcal{F}_n, S)$ as well.

Preimage Awareness [6,7]. The notion of preimage awareness is useful for PRO security proofs of NMAC hash functions. We only explain the definition of preimage awareness. Please see Section 3 of [7] for the spirit of the notion. Let F^P be a hash function using an ideal primitive P. The preimage awareness of F^P is estimated by the following experiment.

$\mathsf{Exp}^{\mathsf{pra}}_{F^P,P,\mathcal{E},A}$	**oracle** $\mathsf{P}(m)$	**oracle** $\mathsf{Ex}(z)$
$x \xleftarrow{\$} A^{\mathsf{P},\mathsf{Ex}}$;	$c \leftarrow P(m)$;	$\mathsf{Q}[z] \leftarrow 1$;
$z \leftarrow F^P(x)$;	$\alpha \xleftarrow{\cup} (m, c)$;	$\mathsf{V}[z] \leftarrow \mathcal{E}(z, \alpha)$;
Ret $(x \neq \mathsf{V}[z] \wedge \mathsf{Q}[z] = 1)$;	Ret c;	Ret $\mathsf{V}[z]$;

Here an adversary A is provided two oracles P and Ex. The oracle P provides access to the ideal primitive P and records a query history α. The extraction oracle Ex provides an interface to an extractor $\mathcal{E}$, which is a deterministic algorithm that uses z and the query history α of P, and returns either $\perp$ or an element x' such that $F^P(x') = z$. If x' can be constructed from α, it returns x' and otherwise returns $\perp$. In this experiment, the (initially everywhere $\perp$) array Q and the (initially empty) array V are used. When z is queried to Ex, $\mathsf{Q}[z] \leftarrow 1$ and then the output of $\mathcal{E}(z, \alpha)$ is assigned to $\mathsf{V}[z]$. For the hash function F^P, the adversary A, and the extractor $\mathcal{E}$, we define the advantage relation

$$\mathsf{Adv}^{\mathsf{pra}}_{F^P,P,\mathcal{E}} = \Pr[\mathsf{Exp}^{\mathsf{pra}}_{F^P,P,\mathcal{E},A} \Rightarrow \mathsf{true}]$$

where the probabilities are over the coins used in running the experiments. When there exists an efficient extractor $\mathcal{E}$ such that for any adversary A the above advantage is small, we say that F^P is preimage aware (PrA).

The pra-advantage can be evaluated from the cr-advantage (collision resistance advantage) and the 1-wpra (1-weak PrA) advantage [7]. The 1-WPrA experiment is described as follows.

$\mathsf{Exp}^{\mathsf{1wpra}}_{F^P,P,\mathcal{E}^+,A}$	**oracle** $\mathsf{P}(m)$	**oracle** $\mathsf{Ex}^+(z)$
$x \xleftarrow{\$} A^{\mathsf{P},\mathsf{Ex}^+}$;	$c \leftarrow P(m)$;	$\mathsf{Q}[z] \leftarrow 1$;
$z \leftarrow F^P(x)$;	$\alpha \xleftarrow{\cup} (m,c)$;	$L \leftarrow \mathcal{E}^+(z,\alpha)$;
Ret $(x \notin L \wedge \mathsf{Q}[z] = 1)$;	Ret c;	Ret L;

The difference between the 1-WPrA experiment and the PrA experiment is the extraction oracle. In the 1-WPrA experiment, a multi-point extractor oracle Ex^+ is used. Ex^+ provides an interface to a multi-point extractor $\mathcal{E}^+$, which is a deterministic algorithm that uses z and α, and returns either $\perp$ or a set of an element in the domain of F^P. The output (set) of $\mathcal{E}^+$ is stored in list L. Thus, if $L \neq \{\perp\}$, for any $x' \in L$ $F^P(x') = z$. In this experiment, an adversary A can make only a single query to Ex^+. For a hash function F^P, an adversary A, and a multi-point extractor $\mathcal{E}^+$, we define the advantage relation

$$\mathsf{Adv}^{\mathsf{1wpra}}_{F^P,P,\mathcal{E}} = \Pr[\mathsf{Exp}^{\mathsf{1wpra}}_{F^P,P,\mathcal{E}^+,A} \Rightarrow \mathsf{true}]$$

where the probabilities are over the coins used in running the experiments. When there exists an efficient multi-point extractor $\mathcal{E}^+$ such that the above advantage is small for any adversary A, we say that F^P is 1-WPrA.

The definition of the cr-advantage as follows. Let A be an adversary that outputs a pair of values x and x'. To hash function F^P using primitive P and adversary A we associate the advantage relation

$$\mathsf{Adv}^{\mathsf{cr}}_{F^P,P}(A) = \Pr[(x,x') \xleftarrow{\$} A^P : F^P(x) = F^P(x') \wedge x \neq x']$$

where the probability is over the coins used by A and primitive P.

Then the pra-advantage can be evaluated as follows.

Lemma 1 (Lemmas 3.3 and 3.4 of [7]). *Let $\mathcal{E}^+$ be an arbitrary multi-point extractor. There exists an extractor $\mathcal{E}$ such that for any pra-advarsary A^{pra} making q_e extraction queries and q_P primitive queries there exists 1-wpra adversary A^{1wpra} and cr-adversary A^{cr} such that*

$$\mathsf{Adv}^{\mathsf{pra}}_{F^P,P,\mathcal{E}}(A^{\mathsf{pra}}) \leq q_e \cdot \mathsf{Adv}^{\mathsf{1wpra}}_{F^P,P,\mathcal{E}^+}(A^{\mathsf{1wpra}}) + \mathsf{Adv}^{\mathsf{cr}}_{F^P,P}(A^{\mathsf{cr}}).$$

A^{1wpra} runs in time at most $\mathcal{O}(q_e\mathsf{Time}(\mathcal{E}^+))$ and makes the same number of P queries as A^{pra}. A^{cr} asks q_P queries and run in time $\mathcal{O}(q_e \cdot \mathsf{Time}(\mathcal{E}^+))$. $\mathcal{E}$ runs in the same time as $\mathcal{E}^+$. ♦

NMAC Hash Function. Let $g : \{0,1\}^n \to \{0,1\}^n$ be a function and $H^P : \{0,1\}^* \to \{0,1\}^n$ be a hash function using primitive P such that g is not used in H^P. Dodis *et al.* [7] proved that the PRO security of the NMAC hash function $g \circ H^P$ can be reduced into the PrA security of H^P.

Lemma 2 (Theorem 4.1 of [7]). *Let P be an ideal primitive, g be a random oracle and $\mathcal{E}$ be any extractor for H^P. Then there exists a simulator $S = (S_P, S_g)$ such that for any PRO adversary A making at most q_F, q_P, q_g queries to its three oracles $(\mathcal{O}_F, \mathcal{O}_P, \mathcal{O}_g)$ where $(\mathcal{O}_F, \mathcal{O}_P, \mathcal{O}_g) = (g \circ H^P, P, g)$ or $(\mathcal{O}_F, \mathcal{O}_P, \mathcal{O}_g) = (\mathcal{F}_n, S_P, S_g)$, there exists a PrA adversary B such that*

$$\mathsf{Adv}^{\mathsf{pro}}_{g \circ H^P, S}(A) \le \mathsf{Adv}^{\mathsf{pra}}_{H^P, P, \mathcal{E}}(B).$$

S runs in time $\mathcal{O}(q_P + q_g \cdot \mathsf{Time}(\mathcal{E}))$. Let l be the length of the longest query made by A to $\mathcal{O}_H$. B runs in time $\mathcal{O}(\mathsf{Time}(A) + q_F t_H + q_P + q_g)$, makes $q_P + q_H q_F$ queries, q_g extraction queries, and outputs a preimage of length at most l where for any input M to H^P the output of $H^P(M)$ can be calculated within at most t_H times and q_H queries to P. ♦

Dodis *et al.* proved that the SMD construction preserves the PrA security as follows. Therefore, the PRO security of the NMAC hash function using the SMD hash function can be reduced into the PrA security of the compression function.

Lemma 3 (Theorem 4.2 of [7]). *Let h^P be a compression function using an ideal primitive P. Let $\mathcal{E}_h$ be an arbitrary extractor for h^P. There exists an extractor $\mathcal{E}_H$ for SMD^{h^P} such that for any adversary A_H making at most q_P primitive queries and q_e extraction queries and outputting a message at most l blocks there exists an adversary A_h such that*

$$\mathsf{Adv}^{\mathsf{pra}}_{\mathrm{SMD}^{h^P}, P, \mathcal{E}_H}(A_H) \le \mathsf{Adv}^{\mathsf{pra}}_{h^P, P, \mathcal{E}_h}(A_h)$$

$\mathcal{E}_H$ runs in time at most $l(\mathsf{Time}(\mathcal{E}_h) + \mathsf{Time}(\mathsf{unpad}))$. A_h runs in time at most $\mathcal{O}(\mathsf{Time}(A_H) + q_e l)$, makes at most $q_H + q_P$ ideal primitive queries, and makes at most $q_e l$ extraction queries where q_H is the maximum number of P queries to calculate SMD^{h^P}. ♦

3 Blockcipher-Based Double-Length Hash Functions for PROs

Let $\mathsf{BC}_{2n,n} = (E, D)$, $\mathsf{BC}^1_{2n,n} = (E1, D1)$, $\mathsf{BC}^2_{2n,n} = (E2, D2)$, and $\mathsf{BC}^3_{2n,n} = (E3, D3)$ be blockciphers. Let $g : \{0,1\}^{2n} \to \{0,1\}^{2n}$ be a function. In this section, we propose the following DLHFs using a single blockcipher and prove that our hash functions are PROs up to $\mathcal{O}(2^n)$ query complexity in the IC model.

$$F^{\mathsf{BC}_{2n,n}}(M) = f^{\mathsf{BC}_{2n,n}}(\mathrm{SMD}^{\mathrm{DLCF}^{\mathsf{BC}_{2n,n}}}(M))$$

where $f^{\mathsf{BC}_{2n,n}}(x) = E(x, c_1)||E(x, c_2)$ such that c_1 and c_2 are n-bit different constant values and are different from values which are defined by the compression function (see subsection 3.3). The hash functions use Hirose's compression function, Tandem-DM, and Abreast-DM as the underlying DLCF, respectively. We prove the PRO security by the three steps. Each step uses the PrA design framework, PRO for a small function and indifferentiability from a hash function, respectively.

- **Step 1.** We prove that Hirose's compression function, Tandem-DM, and Abreast-DM are PrA up to $\mathcal{O}(2^n)$ query complexity in the IC model. Lemma 2 and Lemma 3 then ensure that the following NMAC hash function is PRO up to $\mathcal{O}(2^n)$ query complexity as long as the blockcipher is IC and g is FILRO.

$$F_1^{g,\mathsf{BC}^1_{2n,n}}(M) = g(\mathrm{SMD}^{\mathrm{DLCF}^{\mathsf{BC}^1_{2n,n}}}(M))$$

- **Step 2.** We prove that $f^{\mathsf{BC}^3_{2n,n}}$ is PRO up to $\mathcal{O}(2^n)$ query complexity in the IC model where c_1 and c_2 are n-bit different values. Then, we prove that the PRO security of F_1 and the PRO security of f ensure that the following hash function is PRO up to $\mathcal{O}(2^n)$ query complexity in the IC model.

$$F_2^{\mathsf{BC}^2_{2n,n},\mathsf{BC}^3_{2n,n}}(M) = f^{\mathsf{BC}^3_{2n,n}}(\mathrm{SMD}^{\mathrm{DLCF}^{\mathsf{BC}^2_{2n,n}}}(M))$$

- **Step 3.** This is the final step. We use the indifferentiability from a hash function: we prove that $F^{\mathsf{BC}_{2n,n}}$ is indifferentiable from $F_2^{\mathsf{BC}^2_{2n,n},\mathsf{BC}^3_{2n,n}}$ up to $\mathcal{O}(2^n)$ query complexity in the IC model. Then, we prove that the indifferentiable result and the PRO security of F_2 ensure that $F^{\mathsf{BC}_{2n,n}}$ is PRO up to $\mathcal{O}(2^n)$ query complexity in the IC model.

3.1 Step 1

We prove that Hirose's compression function [11] is PrA up to $\mathcal{O}(2^n)$ query complexity as long as the blockcipher is an ideal cipher. Similarly, we can prove that Abreast-DM and Tandem-DM [14] are PrA. We prove the PrA security in the full version.

Definition 1 (Hirose's Compression Function). *Let* $\mathsf{BC}^1_{2n,n} = (E1, D1)$ *be a blockcipher. Let* $\mathsf{CF}^{\mathsf{Hirose}}[\mathsf{BC}^1_{2n,n}] : \{0,1\}^{2n} \times \{0,1\}^n \to \{0,1\}^{2n}$ *be a compression function such that* $(G_i, H_i) = \mathsf{CF}^{\mathsf{Hirose}}[\mathsf{BC}^1_{2n,n}](G_{i-1}||H_{i-1}, M_i)$ *where* $G_i, H_i, G_{i-1}, H_{i-1} \in \{0,1\}^n$ *and* $M_i \in \{0,1\}^n$. (G_i, H_i) *is calculated as follows:*

$$G_i = G_{i-1} \oplus E1(H_{i-1}||M_i, G_{i-1}) \quad (1)$$
$$H_i = C \oplus G_{i-1} \oplus E1(H_{i-1}||M_i, G_{i-1} \oplus C,) \quad (2)$$

We call the procedure 1 "first block" and the procedure 2 "second block". ♦

Lemma 4 (Hirose's Compression Function is PrA). *Let* $\mathcal{C}^1_{2n,n} = (E1_I, D1_I)$ *be an ideal cipher. There exists an extractor* $\mathcal{E}$ *such that for any adversary* A *making at most* q_P *queries to* $\mathcal{C}_{2n,n}$ *and* q_e *extraction queries we have*

$$\mathsf{Adv}^{\mathsf{pra}}_{\mathsf{CF}^{\mathsf{Hirose}}[\mathcal{C}^1_{2n,n}],\mathcal{C}^1_{2n,n},\mathcal{E}}(A) \leq \frac{2q_P^2}{(2^n - 2q_P)^2} + \frac{2q_P}{2^n - 2q_P} + \frac{2q_P q_e}{(2^n - q_P)^2}$$

where $\mathcal{E}$ *runs in time at most* $\mathcal{O}(q_e q_P)$. ♦

Proof. We prove that Hirose's compression function is 1-WPrA, and then Lemma 1 gives the final bound. We note that Theorem 3 of [9] upperbounds the cr-advantage of A by $2q_P^2/(2^n - 2q_P)^2 + 2q_P/(2^n - 2q_P)$, yielding the first two terms.

Intuitively, the 1-WPrA game for the compression function is that A declares a value z then an extractor outputs preimages, stored in L, of z which can be constructed from input-output values of A's queries to $\mathcal{C}^1_{2n,n}$. Then A outputs a new preimage of z which is not stored in L. Note that A can adaptively query to $\mathcal{C}^1_{2n,n}$. We define the multi-point extractor to utilize the preimage resistant bound, proven in [9], of Hirose's compression function as follows.

```
algorithm E+(z, α)
Let L be an empty list;
Parse (k_1, x_1, y_1), ..., (k_i, x_i, y_i) ← α; //E1(k_j, x_j) = y_j
For j = 1 to i do
   If z[0] = x_j ⊕ y_j then
      y ← E1_I(k_j, x_j ⊕ C);
      If z[1] = C ⊕ x_j ⊕ y then L ←∪ (x_j||k[0], k[1]);
   If z[1] = x_j ⊕ y_j then
      y ← E1_I(k_j, x_j ⊕ C);
      If z[0] = C ⊕ x_j ⊕ y then L ←∪ ((x_j ⊕ C)||k[0], k[1]);
If L is not an empty list then return L otherwise return ⊥;
```

If an input-output triple of the first block is defined, automatically the input of the second block is defined, and vice versa, from the definition of the compression function. For a query (z, α) to $\mathcal{E}^+$, when there is an input-output triple (k, x, y) such that $x \oplus y = z[0]$, $\mathcal{E}^+$ checks whether the output of the second block is equal to $z[1]$ or not and if this holds the multi-point extractor stores it in the return list L, and vice versa. Therefore, A must find a new preimage of z to win the 1-WPrA experiment. Thus one can straightforwardly adapt the preimage resistant advantage of the compression function (described in Theorem 5 of [9])[5] because the proof of Theorem 5 of [9] can be applied to the case that an adversary selects an image z of the compression function and then finds the preimage of z. The advantage is at most $2q_P/(2^n - q_P)^2$. □

[5] Note that while the 1-WPrA bound is equal to the preimage bound, this is not trivial because one needs to construct the extractor that converts the preimage bound into the 1-WPrA bound.

Lemma 4 ensures the following theorem via Lemma 2 and Lemma 3 where F_1 is PRO up to $\mathcal{O}(2^n)$ query complexity.

Theorem 1. *There exists a simulator $S_1 = (S1_g, S1_C)$ where $S1_C = (S1_E, S1_D)$ such that for any distinguisher A_1 making at most (q_H, q_g, q_E, q_D) queries to four oracles which are $(F_1, g, E1, D1)$ or $(\mathcal{F}_{2n}, S1_g, S1_E, S1_D)$, we have*

$$\mathsf{Adv}^{\mathsf{pro}}_{F_1^{g,C^1_{2n,n}},S1}(A_1) \leq \frac{2Q_1^2}{(2^n - 2Q_1)^2} + \frac{2Q_1}{2^n - 2Q_1} + \frac{2lq_gQ_1}{(2^n - Q_1)^2}$$

where S_1 works in time $\mathcal{O}(q_E + q_D + lq_gQ_1) + lq_g \times \mathsf{Time(unpad)}$ and $S1_g$ makes q_g queries to $\mathcal{F}_{2n}$ where l is the maximum number of n-bit blocks of a query to $F_1/\mathcal{F}_{2n}$, $Q_1 = 2l(q_H + 1) + q_E + q_D$. $S1_g$ simulates g, which makes one query to $\mathcal{F}_{2n}$ for one $S1_g$ query, and $S1_C$, which makes no query, simulates the ideal cipher. ♦

3.2 Step 2

Lemma 5 ($f^{C^3_{2n,n}}$ is PRO). *Let $C^3_{2n,n} = (E3_I, D3_I)$ be an ideal cipher. Let $g = \mathcal{F}_{2n,2n}$. There exists a simulator $\mathsf{S} = (\mathsf{S}_E, \mathsf{S}_D)$ such that for any distinguisher A_2 making at most q_f, q_E and q_D queries to oracles $(\mathcal{O}_f, \mathcal{O}_E, \mathcal{O}_D)$ where $(\mathcal{O}_f, \mathcal{O}_E, \mathcal{O}_D) = (f^{C^3_{2n,n}}, E3_I, D3_I)$ or $(\mathcal{O}_f, \mathcal{O}_E, \mathcal{O}_D) = (g, \mathsf{S}_E, \mathsf{S}_D)$, we have*

$$\mathsf{Adv}^{\mathsf{pro}}_{f^{C^3_{2n,n}},\mathsf{S}}(A_2) \leq \frac{q_f + q_E + q_D}{2^n}$$

where S works in time $\mathcal{O}(q_E + q_D)$ and makes at most queries $q_E + q_D$. S simulates the ideal cipher. ♦

We explain the intuition of the result of Lemma 5. The proof is given the full version. An ideal cipher where the plain text is fixed by a constant value is RO. So the first half value y_1 of an output of f is randomly chosen from $\{0,1\}^n$ and the last half value is chosen from $\{0,1\}^n \backslash \{y_1\}$, while an output of RO is randomly chosen from $\{0,1\}^{2n}$. The statistical distance appears in the PRO bound.

Theorem 1 and Lemma 5 ensure the following theorem where F_2 using Hirose's compression function is PRO up to $\mathcal{O}(2^n)$ query complexity in the IC model. We prove the theorem in the full version. Similarly, we can prove the PRO security of the hash functions using Tandem-DM and Abreast-DM, respectively.

Theorem 2 (F_2 is PRO). *There exists a simulator $S_2 = (S2, S3)$ where $S2 = (S2_E, S2_D)$ and $S3 = (S3_E, S3_D)$ such that for any distinguisher A_3 making at most $(q_H, q_{E2}, q_{D2}, q_{E3}, q_{D3})$ queries to five oracles which are $(F_2, E2, D2, E3, D3)$ or $(\mathcal{F}_{2n}, S2_E, S2_D, S3_E, S3_D)$, we have*

$$\mathsf{Adv}^{\mathsf{pro}}_{F_2^{C^2_{2n,n},C^3_{2n,n}},S_2}(A_3) \leq \frac{2Q_2^2}{(2^n - 2Q_2)^2} + \frac{2Q_2}{2^n - 2Q_2} + \frac{2lq_3Q_2}{(2^n - Q_2)^2} + \frac{q_H + q_3}{2^n}$$

where S_2 *works in time* $\mathcal{O}(q_2 + lq_3Q_2) + lq_3 \times \mathsf{Time}(\mathsf{unpad})$ *and* $S3$ *makes* q_3 *queries to* $\mathcal{F}_{2n}$ *where* l *is the maximum number of* n*-bit blocks of a query to* $F_2/\mathcal{F}_{2n}$*,* $Q_2 = 2l(q_H + 1) + q_{E2} + q_{D2}$*,* $q_2 = q_{E2} + q_{D2}$ *and* $q_3 = q_{E3} + q_{D3}$*.* ♦

3.3 Step 3

In this section, we consider the hash function using Hirose's compression function. The same discussion can be applied to the hash functions using Tandem-DM and Abreast-DM, respectively. The discussions are given in the full version.

When using Hirose's compression function, we use the constant values c_1 and c_2 of the post-processing function f such that c_1 and c_2 are not equal to $C \oplus IV[0]$ and $IV[0]$ where IV is the initial value of $\mathrm{SMD}^{\mathrm{DLCF}^{\mathsf{BC}_{2n,n}}}$ and C is the constant value used in Hirose's compression function. If c_1 and c_2 which are equal to $C \oplus IV[0]$ or $IV[0]$ are used, we cannot prove the security of the hash function. In this case, we fail to construct a simulator.

First, we define the indifferentiability from a hash function as follows.

Definition 2. *Let* $H_1^{P_1} : \{0,1\}^* \to \{0,1\}^{2n}$ *and* $H_2^{P_2} : \{0,1\}^* \to \{0,1\}^{2n}$ *be hash functions using ideal primitives* P_1 *and* P_2*, respectively.* $H_1^{P_1}$ *is indifferentiable from* $H_2^{P_2}$ *if there exists a simulator* $\mathcal{S}$ *such that for any distinguisher* A_4 *outputting a bit it is the case that*

$$\mathsf{Adv}^{\mathsf{indif}}_{H_1^{P_1}, H_2^{P_2}, \mathcal{S}}(A_4) \leq |\Pr[A_4^{H_1^{P_1}, P_1} \Rightarrow 1] - \Pr[A_4^{H_2^{P_2}, \mathcal{S}^{P_2}} \Rightarrow 1]|$$

is small where the probabilities are taken over the coins used the experiments. ♦

The following lemma is that F is indifferentiable from F_2 up to $\mathcal{O}(2^n)$ query complexity in the IC model.

Lemma 6. *Let* $\mathcal{C}_{2n,n} = (E_I, D_I)$ *be an ideal cipher. Let* $\mathcal{C}^2_{2n,n} = (E2_I, D2_I)$ *and* $\mathcal{C}^3_{2n,n} = (E3_I, D3_I)$ *be different ideal ciphers. There exists a simulator* $\mathcal{S} = (\mathcal{S}_E, \mathcal{S}_D)$ *such that for any distinguisher* A_4 *making at most* q_F*,* q_E *and* q_D *queries to its oracles* $(\mathcal{O}_F, \mathcal{O}_E, \mathcal{O}_D)$ *which are* $(F^{\mathcal{C}_{2n,n}}, E_I, D_I)$ *or* $(F_2^{\mathcal{C}^2_{2n,n}, \mathcal{C}^3_{2n,n}}, \mathcal{S}_E, \mathcal{S}_D)$*, we have*

$$\mathsf{Adv}^{\mathsf{indif}}_{F^{\mathcal{C}_{2n,n}}, F_2^{\mathcal{C}^2_{2n,n}, \mathcal{C}^3_{2n,n}}, \mathcal{S}}(A_4) \leq \frac{14 \times (2(lq_F + 1) + q_E + q_D)}{2^n - (2(lq_F + 1) + q_E + q_D)}$$

where $\mathcal{S}$ *works in time* $\mathcal{O}(3(q_E + q_D))$ *and makes at most ideal cipher queries* $q_E + q_D$*.* l *is the maximum number of* n*-bit blocks of a query to* $\mathcal{O}_F$*.* ♦

Proof. Without loss of generality, we omit the padding function of our hash function which is more general case than including the padding function. In Fig. 2, we define a simulator $\mathcal{S} = (\mathcal{S}_E, \mathcal{S}_D)$ such that it simulates the ideal cipher $\mathcal{C}_{2n,n} = (E_I, D_I)$ and the relation among responses of $(F^{\mathcal{C}_{2n,n}}, E_I, D_I)$ holds in responses of $(F_2^{\mathcal{C}^2_{2n,n}, \mathcal{C}^3_{2n,n}}, \mathcal{S}_E, \mathcal{S}_D)$ as well, namely, $F^{\mathcal{S}}(M) = F_2^{\mathcal{C}^2_{2n,n}, \mathcal{C}^3_{2n,n}}(M)$.

simulator $\mathcal{S}_E(k, x)$

```
E01 If E[k,x] ≠⊥ then ret E[k,x];
E02 If E[k,c1] =⊥,
E03     y ← E3_I(k,c1);
E04     E[k,c1] ← y; D[k,y] ← c1;
E05     y ← E3_I(k,c2);
E06     E[k,c2] ← y; D[k,y] ← c2;
E07 If x ≠ c1 and x ≠ c2,
E08     y ← E2_I(k,x);
E09     E[k,x] ← y; D[k,y] ← x;
E10 Ret E[k,x];
```

simulator $\mathcal{S}_D(k, y)$

```
D01 If D[k,y] ≠⊥ then ret D[k,y];
D02 If E[k,c1] =⊥,
D03     y ← E3_I(k,c1);
D04     E[k,c1] ← y; D[k,y] ← c1;
D05     y ← E3_I(k,c2);
D06     E[k,c2] ← y; D[k,y] ← c2;
D07 If D[k,y] =⊥,
D08     x ← D2_I(k,y);
D09     E[k,x] ← y; D[k,y] ← x;
D10 Ret x;
```

Fig. 2. Simulator

Since $E2_I$ is used in inner calculations and $E3_I$ is used in the post-processing calculations, if for a query (k, x) to $\mathcal{S}_E$ (k, x) is used in the post-processing calculations, it returns the output of $E3_I(k, x)$, and otherwise it returns the output of $E2_I(k, x)$. Since in post-processing calculation the second value x of a E query is c_1 or c_2, we define $\mathcal{S}$ such that $\mathcal{S}_E(k, x)$ is defined by $E3_I(k, x)$, if $x = c_1$ or $x = c_2$, and is defined by $E2_I(k, x)$ otherwise.[6] E and D are (initially everywhere $\perp$) arrays.

We give the proof via a game-playing argument on the game sequences Game 0, Game 1, and Game 2. Game 0 is the F scenario and Game 2 is the F_2 scenario. In each game, A_4 can make queries to three oracles $(\mathcal{O}_F, \mathcal{O}_E, \mathcal{O}_D)$. Let Gj be the event that in Game j the distinguisher A_4 outputs 1. Therefore, $\Pr[A_4^{F^{\mathcal{C}_{2n,n}}, E_I, D_I} \Rightarrow 1] = \Pr[G0]$ and $\Pr[A_4^{F_2^{\mathcal{C}^2_{2n,n}, \mathcal{C}^3_{2n,n}}, \mathcal{S}_E, \mathcal{S}_D} \Rightarrow 1] = \Pr[G2]$. Thus

$$\mathsf{Adv}^{\mathsf{indif}}_{F^{\mathcal{C}_{2n,n}}, F_2^{\mathcal{C}^2_{2n,n}, \mathcal{C}^3_{2n,n}}, \mathcal{S}}(A_4) \leq |\Pr[G1] - \Pr[G0]| + |\Pr[G2] - \Pr[G1]|$$

Game 0: Game 0 is the F scenario. So $(\mathcal{O}_F, \mathcal{O}_E, \mathcal{O}_D) = (F^{\mathcal{C}_{2n,n}}, E_I, D_I)$.

Game 1: We modify the underlying functions $(\mathcal{O}_E, \mathcal{O}_D)$ from (E_I, D_I) to $(\mathcal{S}_E, \mathcal{S}_D)$. So $(\mathcal{O}_F, \mathcal{O}_E, \mathcal{O}_D) = (F^{\mathcal{S}}, \mathcal{S}_E, \mathcal{S}_D)$ where only $\mathcal{S}$ has oracle access to $(\mathcal{C}^2_{2n,n}, \mathcal{C}^3_{2n,n})$.

We must show that the A_4's view has statistically close distribution in Game 0 and Game 1. Since the difference between the games is the underlying function, we show that the output of the functions is statistically close; this in turn shows that the A_4's view has statistically close distribution in Game 0 and Game 1. First we rewrite $\mathcal{S}$ in Fig. 3. $\mathcal{C}^3_{2n,n}$ is hard-coded in the steps e03-e05, e06-e08, d03-05 and d06-08 where $\mathsf{E2}$ and $\mathsf{D2}$ are (initially everywhere $\perp$) arrays to store the output of the ideal cipher and $\mathcal{T}_{E2}$ and $\mathcal{T}_{D2}$ are (initially everywhere empty) tables. Similarly, $\mathcal{C}^3_{2n,n}$ is hard-coded in Steps e10-e11 and d10-d11 where $\mathsf{E3}$ and $\mathsf{D3}$ are (initially everywhere $\perp$) arrays to store the output of the ideal cipher. For any k, if $\mathsf{E2}[k, x] \neq \perp$, $\mathsf{E2}[k, x] \in \mathcal{T}_{E2}[k]$, and if $\mathsf{D2}[k, y] \neq \perp$, $\mathsf{D2}[k, y] \in \mathcal{T}_{D2}[k]$.

[6] If c_1 and c_2 which are equal to $C \oplus IV[0]$ or $IV[0]$ are used, $\mathcal{S}$ cannot decide whether using $E2_I$ or $E3_I$.

simulator $\mathcal{S}_E(k,x)$

e01 If $\mathsf{E}[k,x] \neq \perp$ then ret $\mathsf{E}[k,x]$;
e02 If $\mathsf{E}[k,c_1] = \perp$,
e03 $\quad y_1 \xleftarrow{\$} \{0,1\}^n$;
e04 $\quad \mathsf{E3}[k,c_1] \leftarrow y_1$; $\mathsf{D3}[k,y_1] \leftarrow c_1$;
e05 $\quad \mathsf{E}[k,c_1] \leftarrow \mathsf{E3}[k,c_1]$; $\mathsf{D}[k,y_1] \leftarrow c_1$;
e06 $\quad y_2 \xleftarrow{\$} \{0,1\}^n \backslash \{y_1\}$;
e07 $\quad \mathsf{E3}[k,c_2] \xleftarrow{\$} y_2$; $\mathsf{D3}[k,y_2] \leftarrow c_2$;
e08 $\quad \mathsf{E}[k,c_1] \leftarrow \mathsf{E3}[k,c_1]$; $\mathsf{D}[k,y_2] \leftarrow c_1$;
e09 If $x \neq c_1$ and $x \neq c_2$,
e10 $\quad y \xleftarrow{\$} \{0,1\}^n \backslash \mathcal{T}_{E2}[k]$;
e11 $\quad \mathsf{E2}[k,x] \leftarrow y$; $\mathsf{D2}[k,y] \leftarrow x$;
e12 $\quad \mathsf{E}[k,x] \leftarrow y$; $\mathsf{D}[k,y] \leftarrow x$;
e13 Ret $\mathsf{E}[k,x]$;

simulator $\mathcal{S}_D(k,y)$

d01 If $\mathsf{D}[k,y] \neq \perp$ then ret $\mathsf{D}[k,y]$;
d02 If $\mathsf{E}[k,c_1] = \perp$,
d03 $\quad y_1 \xleftarrow{\$} \{0,1\}^n$;
d04 $\quad \mathsf{E3}[k,c_1] \leftarrow y_1$; $\mathsf{D3}[k,y_1] \leftarrow c_1$;
d05 $\quad \mathsf{E}[k,c_1] \leftarrow \mathsf{E3}[k,c_1]$; $\mathsf{D}[k,y_1] \leftarrow c_1$;
d06 $\quad y_2 \xleftarrow{\$} \{0,1\}^n \backslash \{y_1\}$;
d07 $\quad \mathsf{E3}[k,c_2] \xleftarrow{\$} y_2$; $\mathsf{D3}[k,y_2] \leftarrow c_2$;
d08 $\quad \mathsf{E}[k,c_1] \leftarrow \mathsf{E3}[k,c_1]$; $\mathsf{D}[k,y_2] \leftarrow c_1$;
d09 If $\mathsf{D}[k,y] = \perp$,
d10 $\quad x \xleftarrow{\$} \{0,1\}^n \backslash \mathcal{T}_{D2}[k]$;
d11 $\quad \mathsf{E2}[k,x] \leftarrow y$; $\mathsf{D2}[k,y] \leftarrow x$;
d12 $\quad \mathsf{E}[k,x] \leftarrow y$; $\mathsf{D}[k,y] \leftarrow x$;
d13 Ret x;

Fig. 3. Revised Simulator

Encryption Oracle $E_I(k,x)$

01 If $\mathsf{E}[k,x] \neq \perp$, ret $\mathsf{E}[k,x]$;
02 If $\mathsf{E}[k,c_1] = \perp$,
03 $\quad \mathsf{E}[k,c_1] \xleftarrow{\$} \{0,1\}^n$;
04 $\quad \mathsf{D}[k,\mathsf{E}[c_1,x]] \leftarrow c_1$;
05 $\quad \mathsf{E}[k,c_2] \xleftarrow{\$} \{0,1\}^n \backslash \{\mathsf{E}[k,c_1]\}$;
06 $\quad \mathsf{D}[k,\mathsf{E}[c_2,x]] \leftarrow c_2$;
07 If $x \neq c_1$ and $x \neq c_2$,
08 $\quad \mathsf{E}[k,x] \xleftarrow{\$} \{0,1\}^n \backslash \mathcal{T}_E[k]$;
09 $\quad \mathsf{D}[k,\mathsf{E}[k,x]] \leftarrow x$;
10 Ret $\mathsf{E}[k,x]$;

Decryption Oracle $D_I(k,y)$

11 If $\mathsf{D}[k,y] \neq \perp$, ret $\mathsf{D}[k,y]$;
12 If $\mathsf{E}[k,c_1] = \perp$,
13 $\quad \mathsf{E}[k,c_1] \xleftarrow{\$} \{0,1\}^n$;
14 $\quad \mathsf{D}[k,\mathsf{E}[c_1,x]] \leftarrow c_1$;
15 $\quad \mathsf{E}[k,c_2] \xleftarrow{\$} \{0,1\}^n \backslash \{\mathsf{E}[k,c_1]\}$;
16 $\quad \mathsf{D}[k,\mathsf{E}[c_2,x]] \leftarrow c_2$;
17 If $\mathsf{D}[k,y] \neq \perp$,
18 $\quad \mathsf{D}[k,y] \xleftarrow{\$} \{0,1\}^n \backslash \{\mathcal{T}_D[k]\}$;
19 $\quad \mathsf{E}[k,\mathsf{D}[k,y]] \leftarrow y$;
20 Ret $\mathsf{D}[k,y]$;

Fig. 4. Lazily-Sample Ideal Cipher

In the following, we use the lazily-sample ideal cipher in Fig. 4. E and D are (initially everywhere $\perp$) arrays and $\mathcal{T}_E$ and $\mathcal{T}_D$ (initially empty) tables. For any (k,x) such that $\mathsf{E}[k,x] \neq \perp$, $\mathsf{E}[k,x]$ is stored in $\mathcal{T}_E[k]$, and for any (k,y) such that $\mathsf{D}[k,y] \neq \perp$, $\mathsf{D}[k,y]$ is stored in $\mathcal{T}_D[k]$. On a query which the key element is k, first the output of $E_I(k,c_1)$ is determined (steps 03-04 or steps 13-14) and second the output of $E_I(k,c_2)$ is determined (Steps 05-06 or Steps 15-16). Then the outputs of $E_I(k,x)$ such that $x \neq c_1$ and $x \neq c_2$ are determined. Since no adversary (distinguisher) learns $E_I(k,c_1)$ and $E_I(k,c_2)$ until querying the corresponding value, the procedures of the steps 03-06 and 13-16 do not affect the lazily-sample ideal cipher simulation.

We compare the simulator with the lazily-sample ideal cipher. In the simulator and the ideal cipher, $\mathsf{E}[k,c_1]$ and $\mathsf{E}[k,c_2]$ (and also $\mathsf{D}[k,\mathsf{E}[k,c_1]]$ and $\mathsf{D}[k,\mathsf{E}[k,c_2]]$) are chosen from the same distribution, while $\mathsf{E}[k,x]$ (and $\mathsf{D}[k,\mathsf{E}[k,x]]$) where $x \neq c_1$ and $x \neq c_2$ is chosen different distribution. If in the step e10 y is randomly chosen from $\mathcal{T}_{E2}[k] \cup \{\mathsf{E}[k,c_1],\mathsf{E}[k,c_2]\}$ and in the step d10 x is randomly chosen from $\mathcal{T}_{D2}[k] \cup \{c_1, c_2\}$, then the output distribution of the simulator and the ideal cipher is the same. That is, if any value y randomly chosen from $\{0,1\}^n \backslash \mathcal{T}_{E2}[k]$ does not collide $\mathsf{E}[k, c_1]$ and $\mathsf{E}[k, c_2]$ and any value x randomly chosen from $\{0,1\}^n \backslash \mathcal{T}_{D2}[k]$ does not collide c_1 and c_2, then the output distribution between them is the same. Since for any k, the number of values in $\mathcal{T}_{E2}[k]$ and $\mathcal{T}_{D2}[k]$ is at most $2lq_F + q_E + q_D$, the statistical distance of $\mathsf{E}[k, x]$ (and $\mathsf{D}[k, \mathsf{E}[k, x]]$) where $x \neq c_1$ and $x \neq c_2$ is at most $2/(2^n - (2lq_F + q_E + q_D))$. So the statistical distance of the simulator and the ideal cipher is at most $(2lq_F + q_E + q_D) \times 2/(2^n - (2lq_F + q_E + q_D))$. We thus have that

$$|\Pr[G1] - \Pr[G0]| \leq \frac{2 \times (2lq_F + q_E + q_D)}{2^n - (2lq_F + q_E + q_D)}.$$

Game 2: We modify $\mathcal{O}_F$ from $F^{\mathcal{S}}$ to $F_2^{\mathcal{C}^2_{2n,n}, \mathcal{C}^3_{2n,n}}$. So $(\mathcal{O}_F, \mathcal{O}_E, \mathcal{O}_D) = (F_2^{\mathcal{C}^2_{2n,n}, \mathcal{C}^3_{2n,n}}, \mathcal{S}_E, \mathcal{S}_D)$ and this is the F_2 scenario.

We show that unless the following bad events occur, the A_4's view of Game 1 and Game 2 is the same.

- Event B1: On some query (k, x) to $\mathcal{S}_E$, the output y is such that $y \oplus x$ is equal to c_1 or c_2.
- Event B2: On some query (k, x) to $\mathcal{S}_E$, the output y is such that $y \oplus x \oplus C$ is equal to c_1 or c_2.
- Event B3: On some query (k, y) to $\mathcal{S}_D$, the output x is equal to c_1 or c_2 such that x is defined in the step D08.

To prove this, we use the proof method in [4,13]. Specifically, we prove the following two points.

1. In Game 1, unless the bad events occur, for any query M the output of $\mathcal{O}_F(M)$ is equal to that of $F_2^{\mathcal{C}^2_{2n,n}, \mathcal{C}^3_{2n,n}}(M)$. If this holds, the output distribution of $\mathcal{O}_F$ in Game 1 and Game 2 is equivalent.
2. In Game 2, unless the bad events occur, $\mathcal{O}_E$ and $\mathcal{O}_D$ are consistent with $\mathcal{O}_F$ as in Game 1. $\mathcal{O}_F$ uses $\mathcal{O}_E$ in Game 1 while does not in Game 2 (note that in both games $(\mathcal{O}_E, \mathcal{O}_D) = (\mathcal{S}_E, \mathcal{S}_D)$). So if this holds, the difference does not affect the output distribution of $\mathcal{O}_E$ and $\mathcal{O}_D$, namely, the output distribution of $\mathcal{O}_E$ and $\mathcal{O}_D$ in Game 1 and Game 2 is the same.

In the following, for input-output triple (k, x, y) of $\mathcal{S}$ we denote $x \oplus y$ by w, namely, $w = x \oplus y$. Before proving the above two points, we define chain triples and give a useful lemma.

Definition 3. $(k_1, x_1, y_1), \ldots, (k_i, x_i, y_i), (k'_1, x'_1, y'_1), \ldots, (k'_i, x'_i, y'_i), (k, x, y), (k', x', y')$ *stored in the simulator's tables* E, D *are chain triples if for some* M *the output of* $F^{\mathcal{S}}(M)$ *can be obtained from the triples. That is,* $x_1 = IV[0], k_1[0] = IV[1]$, $k_j = k'_j$ $(j = 1, \ldots, i)$, $w_j = x_{j+1}$ $(j = 1, \ldots, i-1)$, $w_j \oplus C = x'_{j+1}$ $(j = 1, \ldots, i-1)$, $w'_j = k_{j+1}[0]$ $(j = 1, \ldots, i-1)$, $x = c_1$, $x' = c_2$, $k = k'$, $k[0] = w_i$, $k[1] = w'_i$, $M = k_1[1] || \cdots || k_i[1]$, *and* $y || y' = F^{\mathcal{S}}(M)$.

Lemma 7. *For any chain triple* $(k_1, x_1, y_1), \ldots, (k_i, x_i, y_i), (k'_1, x'_1, y'_1), \ldots, (k'_i, x'_i, y'_i), (k, x, y), (k', x', y')$, *unless the bad events occur,* $F^{\mathcal{S}}(M) = F_2^{\mathcal{C}^2_{2n,n}, \mathcal{C}^3_{2n,n}}(M)$ *where* $M = k_1[1] || \cdots || k_i[1]$.

Proof. To contrary, assume that there exist chain triples $(k_1, x_1, y_1), \ldots, (k_i, x_i, y_i), (k'_1, x'_1, y'_1), \ldots, (k'_i, x'_i, y'_i), (k, x, y), (k', x', y')$ such that $F^{\mathcal{S}}(M) \neq F_2^{\mathcal{C}^2_{2n,n}, \mathcal{C}^3_{2n,n}}(M)$ where $M = k_1[1] || \cdots || k_i[1]$. Then, since the output of $\mathcal{S}$ is defined by $E2_I$ or $E3_I$, one of the following events occur.

- Event 1: In the inner calculation of $F^{\mathcal{S}}(M)$, some triple is defined by $E3_I$. That is, some of $(k_1, x_1, y_1), \ldots, (k_i, x_i, y_i), (k'_1, x'_1, y'_1), \ldots, (k'_i, x'_i, y'_i)$, is defined by $E3_I$.
- Event 2: In the post-processing function calculation of $F^{\mathcal{S}}(M)$, some triple is defined by $E2_I$. That is, (k, x, y) or (k', x', y') is defined by $E2_I$.

Consider Event 1. First consider the case that (k_j, x_j, y_j) is defined by $E3_I$. Since $x_1 = IV[0]$, $j \neq 1$. When the output of $\mathcal{S}_E(k_j, x_j)$ is defined by $E3_I$, $x_j = c_1$ or $x_j = c_2$. Which means that $w_{j-1} = c_1$ or $w_{j-1} = c_2$. So the bad event 1 occurs. Second consider the case that (k'_j, x'_j, y'_j) is defined by $E3_I$. Similarly, since $x_1 = IV[0] \oplus C$, $j \neq 1$. When the output of $\mathcal{S}_E(k_j, x_j)$ is defined by $E3_I$, $x_j = c_1$ or $x_j = c_2$. Which means that $w'_{j-1} \oplus C = c_1$ or $w'_{j-1} \oplus C = c_2$. So the bad event 2 occurs.

Next consider Event 2. First consider the case that (k, x, y) is defined by $E2_I$. Then the triple is defined in $\mathcal{S}_D$ because $x = c_1$ (if the triple is defined in $\mathcal{S}_E$, it is defined by $E2_I$ due to the condition of the step E07). So the triple is defined in the step D08. The bad event 3 occurs. Finally, consider the case that (k', x', y') is defined by $E2_I$. Then the triple is defined in $\mathcal{S}_D$ because $x = c_2$. So the triple is defined in the step D08. The bad event 3 occurs. □

Proof of Point 1. From the above lemma, unless the bad event occurs, the output of $\mathcal{O}_F(M) = F^{\mathcal{S}}(M) = F_2^{\mathcal{C}^2_{2n,n}, \mathcal{C}^3_{2n,n}}(M)$.

Proof of Point 2. Since in Game 1 for any M the output of $\mathcal{O}_F(M)$ is calculated by $F^{\mathcal{S}}(M)$, we must show that in Game 2 the relation also holds, that is, unless the bad events occur, for any chain triples $(k_1, x_1, y_1), \ldots, (k_i, x_i, y_i), (k'_1, x'_1, y'_1), \ldots, (k'_i, x'_i, y'_i), (k, x, y), (k', x', y')$ the output of $F^{\mathcal{S}}(M)$ is equal to $\mathcal{O}_F(M)$ $(= F_2^{\mathcal{C}^2_{2n,n}, \mathcal{C}^3_{2n,n}}(M))$ where $M = k_1[1] || \cdots || k_i[1]$. From the above lemma, unless the bad event occurs, this holds.

The Bound of $|\Pr[G2] - \Pr[G1]|$**.** The above two points imply that unless the bad events occur, the A_4's view of Game 1 and Game 2 is the same, and so we have that

$$\begin{aligned} &|\Pr[G2] - \Pr[G1]| \\ &\quad \leq 2 \times \max\{\Pr[B1_1] + \Pr[B2_1] + \Pr[B3_1], \Pr[B1_2] + \Pr[B2_2] + \Pr[B3_2]\} \end{aligned}$$

where Bi_j is the event Bi in Game j. Since the number of queries to $\mathcal{S}$ in Game 1 is more than that in Game 2,

$$|\Pr[G2] - \Pr[G1]| \leq 2 \times (\Pr[B1_1] + \Pr[B2_1] + \Pr[B3_1]).$$

First, we evaluate the probability $\Pr[B1_1]$. In Game 1, the number of queries to $\mathcal{S}$ is at most $2(lq_F + 1) + q_E + q_D$. So the output is randomly chosen from at least $2^n - (2(lq_F + 1) + q_E + q_D)$ values. We thus have that

$$\Pr[B1_1] \leq \frac{2 \times (2(lq_F + 1) + q_E + q_D)}{2^n - (2(lq_F + 1) + q_E + q_D)}.$$

Second, we evaluate the probability $\Pr[B2_1]$. From the same discussion as $\Pr[B1_1]$,

$$\Pr[B2_1] \leq \frac{2 \times (2(lq_F + 1) + q_E + q_D)}{2^n - (2(lq_F + 1) + q_E + q_D)}.$$

Finally, we evaluate the probability $\Pr[B3_1]$. A value in the step D08 is defined by $D2_I$. That is, in this case, the output of $D2_I$ is equal to c_1 or c_2. Since the number of queries to $\mathcal{C}^2_{2n,n}$ is at most $2(lq_F + 1) + q_E + q_D$, So the output of $D2_I$ is randomly chosen from at least $2^n - (2(lq_F + 1) + q_E + q_D)$ values. We thus have that

$$\Pr[B1_1] \leq (2(lq_F + 1) + q_E + q_D) \times \frac{2}{2^n - (2(lq_F + 1) + q_E + q_D)}.$$

We thus have that

$$|\Pr[G2] - \Pr[G1]| \leq 2 \times \frac{6 \times (2(lq_F + 1) + q_E + q_D)}{2^n - (2(lq_F + 1) + q_E + q_D)}$$

Consequently, we can obtain the following bound.

$$\mathsf{Adv}^{\mathsf{indif}}_{F^{\mathcal{C}_{2n,n}}, F_2^{\mathcal{C}^2_{2n,n}, \mathcal{C}^3_{2n,n}}, \mathcal{S}}(A_4) \leq \frac{14 \times (2(lq_F + 1) + q_E + q_D)}{2^n - (2(lq_F + 1) + q_E + q_D)}.$$

□

Theorem 2 and Lemma 6 ensure the following theorem where F is PRO up to $\mathcal{O}(2^n)$ query complexity in the IC model. We prove the theorem in the full version.

Theorem 3 (F is PRO). *There exists a simulator $S = (S_E, S_D)$ such that for any distinguisher A making at most (q_H, q_E, q_D) queries to three oracles which are (F, E_I, D_I) or $(\mathcal{F}_{2n}, S_E, S_D)$, we have*

$$\mathsf{Adv}^{\mathsf{pro}}_{F^{\mathcal{C}_{2n,n}}, S}(A) \leq \frac{2Q^2}{(2^n - 2Q)^2} + \frac{2Q}{2^n - 2Q} + \frac{2l(2q)Q}{(2^n - Q)^2} + \frac{q_H + 2q}{2^n} + \frac{14Q}{2^n - Q}$$

where S works in time $\mathcal{O}(q + 2lqQ) + 2lq \times \mathsf{Time}(\mathsf{unpad})$ and makes $2q$ queries to $\mathcal{F}_{2n}$ where $Q = 2l(q_H + 1) + q_E + q_D$ and $q = q_E + q_D$. ♦

4 Conclusion

We proposed new DLHFs constructed from a single practical size blockcipher, where the key size is twice of the plaintext size. The security was proven by that (1) the PRO security of F_1 is proven by the PrA framework, (2) the PRO security of F_2 is proven by PRO for a small function and the result (1), and (3) the PRO security of F is proven by indifferentiability from a hash function and the result (2). Our schemes are the first time DLHFs achieving birthday PRO security. This paper only considers PRO security, while the performance evaluation is not considered. So the evaluation is a future work.

References

1. Bellare, M., Ristenpart, T.: Multi-Property-Preserving Hash Domain Extension and the EMD Transform. In: Lai, X., Chen, K. (eds.) ASIACRYPT 2006. LNCS, vol. 4284, pp. 299–314. Springer, Heidelberg (2006)
2. Brachtl, B.O., Coppersmith, D., Hyden, M.M., Matyas Jr., S.M., Meyer, C.H.W., Oseas, J., Pilpel, S., Schilling, M.: Data authentication using modification detection codes based on a public one way encryption function. US Patent No. 4,908,861 (1990) (filed August 28, 1987)
3. Chang, D., Lee, S., Nandi, M., Yung, M.: Indifferentiable Security Analysis of Popular Hash Functions with Prefix-Free Padding. In: Lai, X., Chen, K. (eds.) ASIACRYPT 2006. LNCS, vol. 4284, pp. 283–298. Springer, Heidelberg (2006)
4. Coron, J.-S., Dodis, Y., Malinaud, C., Puniya, P.: Merkle-Damgård Revisited: How to Construct a Hash Function. In: Shoup, V. (ed.) CRYPTO 2005. LNCS, vol. 3621, pp. 430–448. Springer, Heidelberg (2005)
5. Damgård, I.B.: A Design Principle for Hash Functions. In: Brassard, G. (ed.) CRYPTO 1989. LNCS, vol. 435, pp. 416–427. Springer, Heidelberg (1990)
6. Dodis, Y., Ristenpart, T., Shrimpton, T.: Salvaging Merkle-Damgård for Practical Applications. In: Joux, A. (ed.) EUROCRYPT 2009. LNCS, vol. 5479, pp. 371–388. Springer, Heidelberg (2009)
7. Dodis, Y., Ristenpart, T., Shrimpton, T.: Salvaging Merkle-Damgård for Practical Applications. ePrint 2009/177 (2009)
8. Fleischmann, E., Forler, C., Gorski, M., Lucks, S.: Collision Resistant Double-Length Hashing. In: Heng, S.-H., Kurosawa, K. (eds.) ProvSec 2010. LNCS, vol. 6402, pp. 102–118. Springer, Heidelberg (2010)
9. Fleischmann, E., Gorski, M., Lucks, S.: Security of Cyclic Double Block Length Hash Functions. In: Parker, M.G. (ed.) Cryptography and Coding 2009. LNCS, vol. 5921, pp. 153–175. Springer, Heidelberg (2009)
10. Gong, Z., Lai, X., Chen, K.: A synthetic indifferentiability analysis of some block-cipher-based hash functions. In: Des. Codes Cryptography, vol. 48, pp. 293–305 (2008)
11. Hirose, S.: Some Plausible Constructions of Double-Block-Length Hash Functions. In: Robshaw, M.J.B. (ed.) FSE 2006. LNCS, vol. 4047, pp. 210–225. Springer, Heidelberg (2006)
12. Hirose, S., Park, J.H., Yun, A.: A Simple Variant of the Merkle-Damgård Scheme with a Permutation. In: Kurosawa, K. (ed.) ASIACRYPT 2007. LNCS, vol. 4833, pp. 113–129. Springer, Heidelberg (2007)

13. Hoch, J.J., Shamir, A.: On the Strength of the Concatenated Hash Combiner When All the Hash Functions Are Weak. In: Aceto, L., Damgård, I., Goldberg, L.A., Halldórsson, M.M., Ingólfsdóttir, A., Walukiewicz, I. (eds.) ICALP 2008, Part II. LNCS, vol. 5126, pp. 616–630. Springer, Heidelberg (2008)
14. Lai, X., Massey, J.L.: Hash Functions Based on Block Ciphers. In: Rueppel, R.A. (ed.) EUROCRYPT 1992. LNCS, vol. 658, pp. 55–70. Springer, Heidelberg (1993)
15. Lee, J., Kwon, D.: The Security of Abreast-DM in the Ideal Cipher Model. IEICE Transactions 94-A(1), 104–109 (2011)
16. Lee, J., Stam, M.: Mjh: A Faster Alternative to mdc-2. In: Kiayias, A. (ed.) CT-RSA 2011. LNCS, vol. 6558, pp. 213–236. Springer, Heidelberg (2011)
17. Lee, J., Stam, M., Steinberger, J.: The collision security of Tandem-DM in the ideal cipher model. ePrint 2010/409 (2010)
18. Lucks, S.: A collision-resistant rate-1 double-block-length hash function. In: Symmetric Cryptography, Symmetric Cryptography, Dagstuhl Seminar Proceedings 07021 (2007)
19. Matyas, S., Meyer, C., Oseas, J.: Generating strong one-way functions with cryptographic algorithms. IBM Technical Disclosure Bulletin 27(10a), 5658–5659 (1985)
20. Maurer, U.M., Renner, R.S., Holenstein, C.: Indifferentiability, Impossibility Results on Reductions, and Applications to the Random Oracle Methodology. In: Naor, M. (ed.) TCC 2004. LNCS, vol. 2951, pp. 21–39. Springer, Heidelberg (2004)
21. Merkle, R.C.: One Way Hash Functions and DES. In: Brassard, G. (ed.) CRYPTO 1989. LNCS, vol. 435, pp. 428–446. Springer, Heidelberg (1990)
22. Meyer, C.H.W., Schilling, M.: Chargement securise d'un programma avec code de detection (1987)
23. National Institute of Standards and Technoloty. FIPS PUB 180-3 Secure Hash Standard. In: FIPS PUB (2008)
24. Özen, O., Stam, M.: Another Glance at Double-Length Hashing. In: Parker, M.G. (ed.) Cryptography and Coding 2009. LNCS, vol. 5921, pp. 176–201. Springer, Heidelberg (2009)
25. Preneel, B., Bosselaers, A., Govaerts, R., Vandewalle, J.: Collision-free Hashfunctions Based on Blockcipher Algorithmsl. In: Proceedings of 1989 International Carnahan Conference on Security Technology, pp. 203–210 (1989)
26. Preneel, B., Govaerts, R., Vandewalle, J.: Hash Functions Based on Block Ciphers: A Synthetic Approach. In: Stinson, D.R. (ed.) CRYPTO 1993. LNCS, vol. 773, pp. 368–378. Springer, Heidelberg (1994)
27. Ristenpart, T., Shacham, H., Shrimpton, T.: Careful with Composition: Limitations of the Indifferentiability Framework. In: Paterson, K.G. (ed.) EUROCRYPT 2011. LNCS, vol. 6632, pp. 487–506. Springer, Heidelberg (2011)
28. Rivest, R.L.: The MD4 Message Digest Algorithm. In: Menezes, A., Vanstone, S.A. (eds.) CRYPTO 1990. LNCS, vol. 537, pp. 303–311. Springer, Heidelberg (1991)
29. Rivest, R.L.: The MD5 Message Digest Algorithm. In: RFC 1321 (1992)
30. Steinberger, J.P.: The Collision Intractability of MDC-2 in the Ideal-Cipher Model. In: Naor, M. (ed.) EUROCRYPT 2007. LNCS, vol. 4515, pp. 34–51. Springer, Heidelberg (2007)

ASC-1: An Authenticated Encryption Stream Cipher

Goce Jakimoski[1] and Samant Khajuria[2,⋆]

[1] Stevens Institute of Technology, USA
[2] Aalborg University, Denmark

Abstract. The goal of the modes of operation for authenticated encryption is to achieve faster encryption and message authentication by performing both the encryption and the message authentication in a single pass as opposed to the traditional encrypt-then-mac approach, which requires two passes. Unfortunately, the use of a block cipher as a building block limits the performance of the authenticated encryption schemes to at most one message block per block cipher evaluation.

In this paper, we propose the authenticated encryption scheme ASC-1 (Authenticating Stream Cipher One). Similarly to LEX, ASC-1 uses leak extraction from different AES rounds to compute the key material that is XOR-ed with the message to compute the ciphertext. Unlike LEX, the ASC-1 operates in a CFB fashion to compute an authentication tag over the encrypted message. We argue that ASC-1 is secure by reducing its (IND-CCA , INT-CTXT) security to the problem of distinguishing the case when the round keys are uniformly random from the case when the round keys are generated by a key scheduling algorithm.

Keywords: authenticated encryption, stream ciphers, message authentication, universal hash functions, block ciphers, maximum differential probability.

1 Introduction

Confidentiality and message authentication are two fundamental information security goals. Confidentiality addresses the issue of keeping the information secret from unauthorized users. Often, this is achieved by encrypting the data using a symmetric-key encryption scheme. Message authentication addresses the issues of source corroboration and improper or unauthorized modification of data. To protect the message authenticity, the sender usually appends an authentication tag that is generated by the signing (tagging) algorithm of some message authentication scheme.

Although symmetric-key encryption and message authentication have been mainly studied in a separate context, there are many applications where both are needed. The cryptographic schemes that provide both confidentiality and

⋆ The research was supported in part by the Center for Wireless Systems and Applications - CTIF Copenhagen.

A. Miri and S. Vaudenay (Eds.): SAC 2011, LNCS 7118, pp. 356–372, 2012.

authenticity are called authenticated encryption schemes. The authenticated encryption schemes consist of three algorithms: a key generation algorithm, an encryption algorithm, and a decryption algorithm. The encryption algorithm takes a key, a plaintext and an initialization vector and it returns a ciphertext. Given the ciphertext and the secret key, the decryption algorithm returns plaintext when the ciphertext is authentic, and invalid when the ciphertext is not authentic. The scheme is secure if it is both unforgeable and secure encryption scheme [1]. Two block cipher modes of operation for authenticated encryption, IACBC and IAPM, supported by a claim of provable security were proposed in [14]. Provably secure authenticated encryption schemes that use a block cipher as a building block were also presented in [9,10,24]. The previous authenticated encryption schemes use a block cipher as a building block. The duplex construction [2] iteratively applies a bijective transformation, and its main application is authenticated encryption. One can also incorporate some message authentication mechanisms in a stream cipher. The drawback of this approach is that one cannot reduce the security of the scheme to a well-known problem such as the indistinguishability of block ciphers from random permutations. However, this approach promises better efficiency. One such authenticated encryption scheme is Helix [7]. Another example of a heuristically designed authenticated encryption scheme is SOBER-128 [11].

We propose the authenticated encryption scheme ASC-1. The design of the scheme has roots in message authentication and encryption schemes that use four rounds of AES [8] as a building block such as the LEX [3] stream cipher, the ALRED [4,5] MAC scheme, and the MAC schemes proposed in [20,13]. However, unlike the previous constructions, we use a single cryptographic primitive to achieve both message secrecy and authenticity. To argue the security of the scheme, we show that the scheme is secure if one cannot tell apart the case when the scheme uses random round keys from the case when the round keys are derived by a key scheduling algorithm. Our information-theoretic security analysis uses the approach taken in [12,15,16,17,18,19,21,22] to provide differential probability bounds.

2 ASC-1 Specification

ASC-1 is an authenticated encryption scheme. Its key size can vary depending on the block cipher that is used. Our block cipher suggestion is AES with 128-bit key. The encryption and decryption algorithms for a message $M = m_1||m_2||m_3$ consisting of three 128-bit blocks are depicted in Figure 1.

The schemes uses a 56-bit representation of a counter that provides a unique initialization vector for each encrypted message. The encryption algorithm derives an initial state X_0 and three keys $K_{1,0}$, $K_{2,0}$ and $K_{3,0}$ by applying a block cipher to $0^{70}||00||Cntr$, $0^{70}||01||Cntr$, $0^{70}||10||Cntr$ and $l(M)||00000011||Cntr$ respectively, where $l(M)$ is a 64-bit representation of the bit length of the message M. The message is then processed in a CFB-like mode using the 4R-AES transformation. The 4R-AES transformation takes as input a 128-bit input state and outputs a 128-bit "random" leak r_i and a 128-bit output state. The first leak r_1 is used to encrypt the first message block m_1. The resulting ciphertext block c_1 is XOR-ed with the output state to give the input state for the second 4R-AES transformation. This process is repeated for all message blocks. The leak from the last 4R-AES application is ignored, and its output h is encrypted by $K_{3,0}$ to give the authentication tag. The ciphertext consists of the counter value, the ciphertext blocks and the authentication tag.

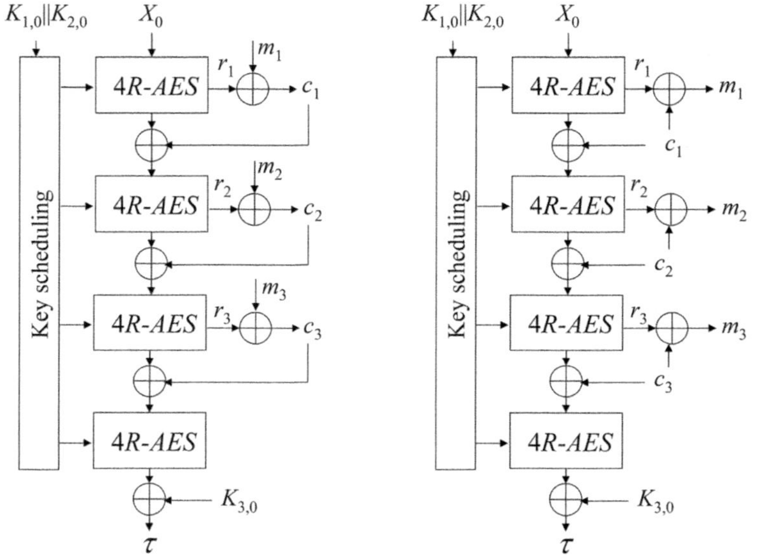

$X_0 = E_K(0^{70}||00||Cntr)$

$K_{1,0} = E_K(0^{70}||01||Cntr)$, $K_{2,0} = E_K(0^{70}||10||Cntr)$, $K_{3,0} = E_K(l(M)||0^6||11||Cntr)$

Fig. 1. The encryption and decryption algorithms of ASC-1. The message consists of three blocks. The ciphertext consists of the counter value, three ciphertext block and an authentication tag. The receiver recovers the original message and verifies its validity by checking whether the re-computed authentication tag is equal to the received one.

The decryption algorithm uses the same secret key and the received counter value to compute X_0, $K_{1,0}$, $K_{2,0}$ and $K_{3,0}$. The leak r_1 derived by applying 4R-AES to X_0 is used to decrypt c_1 into the original message block m_1. The output of the first 4R-AES is XOR-ed with the first ciphertext block to give the next input state, and the process is repeated until all message blocks are recovered and an authentication tag of the message is computed. If the computed tag is same as the one that was received, then the decrypted message is accepted as valid.

Although, we use 64-bit and 56-bit representations for the message length and the counter, we assume that both the maximum message length and the maximum number of messages to be encrypted is 2^{48}. The message length might not be a multiple of the block length. In this case, the last message block m_n with length $l_n < 128$ is padded with zeros to get a 128-bit block m'_n. A 128-bit ciphertext block c'_n is derived as $c'_n = m'_n \oplus r_n$, and it is XOR-ed with the n-th output state to give the $(n+1)$-st input state. However, the sender will not transmit c'_n, but c_n, which consists of the first l_n bits of c'_n. This will enable the receiver to recover the message length.

The 4R-AES transformation is depicted in Figure 2. Four AES rounds are applied to the initial state $x = (x_1, \ldots, x_{16})$ to give a 128-bit leak $r = l_{1..4}||l_{5..8}||l_{9..12}||l_{13..16}$ and an output state $y = (y_1, \ldots, y_{16})$. Here, we assume that the key addition is the first operation of the AES rounds. Four bytes are leaked after the MixColumns transformation in each round. The leak positions are same as in LEX. However, unlike LEX, we add a whitening key byte before each extracted byte.

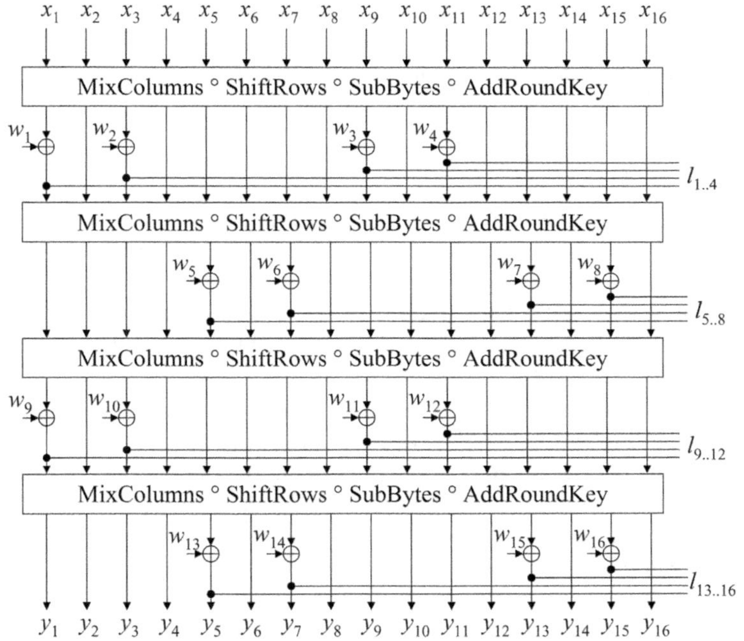

Fig. 2. The 4R-AES transfomration

The 4R-AES transformation uses five 128-bit keys: four round keys and one whitening key. These keys are derived from the 256-bit key $K_{1,0}||K_{2,0}$ as follows. The AES-256 key scheduling algorithm is applied to $K_{1,0}||K_{2,0}$ to derive 14 round keys $K_1, K_2, \ldots, K_{14}$. The keys K_2, K_3, K_4 and K_5 are used as round keys in the first 4R-AES transformation. The keys K_7, K_8, K_9 and K_{10} are used as round keys in the second 4R-AES transformation. The key K_1 is used as a whitening key in the second 4R-AES transformation, and the key K_{11} is used as a whitening key in the first 4R-AES transformation. The AES-256 key scheduling algorithm is again applied to $K_{13}||K_{14}$ to derive 14 keys that are used by the third and the fourth 4R-AES transformation, and the process is repeated as long as we need new keys.

3 Authenticated Encryption Based on Leak-Safe AXU (LAXU) Hash Functions

In this section, we introduce the concept of a leak-safe almost XOR universal (LAXU) hash function, which is an extension of the notion of an AXU hash function [23]. We also show how LAXU hash functions can be used to construct an unconditionally secure authenticated encryption scheme. This construction is used in the information-theoretic part of the security proof of ASC-1 in Section 4.

Definition 1 (LAXU). *A family of hash functions* $\mathcal{H} = \{h(m) = (l, h)|m \in M, l \in \{0,1\}^k, h \in \{0,1\}^n\}$ *is* leak-safe ϵ-almost XOR universal$_2$, *written* ϵ-LAXU$_2$, *if for all distinct messages* $m, m' \in M$, *for all leaks* $l \in \{0,1\}^k$ *and any constant* $c \in \{0,1\}^n$,

$$\Pr_{h\in\mathcal{H}}[\pi_h(h(m)) \oplus \pi_h(h(m')) = c|\pi_l(h(m)) = l] \leq \epsilon,$$

where $\pi_h(l, h) = h$ *and* $\pi_l(l, h) = l$ *are projection functions.*

One can use a LAXU hash function family as a building block to construct an unconditionally secure authenticated encryption scheme as shown in Figure 3. We assume that the message M consists of d n-bit blocks. Some techniques that deal with arbitrary length messages are discussed later on. The ciphertext blocks are computed as follows. A hash function h_{K_1} is selected randomly from $\mathcal{H}$ and it is applied to an initial value IV to get a leak l_1 and hash value h_1. The leak l_1 is used to encrypt the message block m_1 into a ciphertext block $c_1 = m_1 \oplus l_1$. A new hash function h_{K_2} is randomly drawn from $\mathcal{H}$. It is applied to $i_2 = h_1 \oplus c_1 \oplus k_1$, where k_1 is a random key, to get a leak l_2 and hash value h_2. The leak l_2 is used to encrypt the message block m_2 into a ciphertext block c_2, and the process is repeated until the encryption of the last message block m_d. The authentication tag τ is computed as $\tau = K_T \oplus h_{d+1}$, where K_T is a random n-bit key, and h_{d+1} is the hash value that is obtained by applying a randomly drawn hash function $h_{K_{d+1}}$ to $c_d \oplus h_d$. The ciphertext $C = IV||c_1||c_2||\ldots||c_d||\tau$ is a concatenation of the initial value, the ciphertext blocks, and the authentication tag.

We assume that the recipient has knowledge of the secret keys that were used to encrypt the message. The decryption and verification of the ciphertext proceeds as follows. First, h_{K_1} is applied to IV to get a leak l_1 and hash value h_1. The leak l_1 is used to decrypt the ciphertext block c_1 into a message block $m_1 = c_1 \oplus l_1$. Then, the hash function h_{K_2} is applied to $i_2 = h_1 \oplus c_1 \oplus k_1$ to get a leak l_2 and hash value h_2. The second message block is obtained as $m_2 = c_2 \oplus l_2$, and the process is repeated until all message blocks $m_1, m_2, \ldots, m_d$ are decrypted. To verify the authenticity of the received ciphertext, the recipient

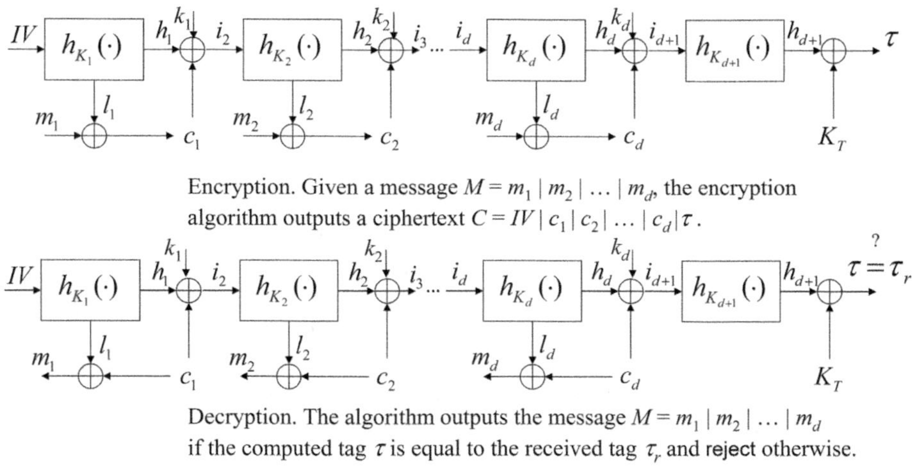

Fig. 3. An authenticated encryption scheme construction based on a LAXU hash function family in a CFB-like mode

recomputes the authentication tag τ as $\tau = h_{d+1} \oplus K_T$, where h_{d+1} is the hash value that is obtained when applying $h_{K_{d+1}}$ to $c_d \oplus h_d$. If the recomputed tag τ is equal to the received tag τ_r, then the decryption algorithm outputs the message $M = m_1||m_2||\ldots||m_d$. Otherwise, the decryption algorithm outputs reject.
The following theorem establishes the security of the previous construction.

Theorem 1. *Suppose that* $\mathcal{H} = \{h(m) = (l, h)|m \in \{0,1\}^n, l \in \{0,1\}^n, h \in \{0,1\}^n\}$ *is an* ϵ-LAXU$_2$ *family of hash functions such that (i)* $\pi_h(h(m))$ *is a bijection, and (ii)* $\Pr_{h \in_R \mathcal{H}}[\pi_l(h(m)) = l|m] = 2^{-n}$ *for any message* m *and any leak* l*. Then, the authenticated encryption scheme depicted in Figure 3 achieves:*

1. perfect secrecy. *The a posteriori probability that the message is* M *given a ciphertext* C *is equal to the a priori probability that the message is* M*.*
2. unconditionally secure ciphertext integrity. *The probability that a computationally unbounded adversary will successfully forge a ciphertext is at most* $q_v\epsilon$*, where* q_v *is the number of the verification queries that the adversary makes.*

Proof. The perfect secrecy of the scheme follows from the fact that the initial value IV is independent of the message, and all l_i and the key K_T have uniform probability distribution for any possible message. A more formal analysis is given below.

$$\Pr[\mathbf{M} = m_1||\ldots||m_d|\mathbf{C} = IV||c_1||\ldots||c_d||\tau] =$$

$$= \frac{\Pr[\mathbf{M} = m_1||\ldots||m_d] \times \Pr[\mathbf{C} = IV||c_1||\ldots||c_d||\tau|\mathbf{M} = m_1||\ldots||m_d]}{\sum_{\mathbf{M}'} \Pr[\mathbf{M}' = m'_1||\ldots||m'_d] \times \Pr[\mathbf{C} = IV||c_1||\ldots||c_d||\tau|\mathbf{M}' = m'_1||\ldots||m'_d]}$$

$$= \frac{\Pr[\mathbf{M} = m_1||\ldots||m_d] \times 2^{-(d+1)n} \times \Pr[IV]}{\sum_{\mathbf{M}'} \Pr[\mathbf{M}' = m'_1||\ldots||m'_d] \times 2^{-(d+1)n} \times \Pr[IV]}$$

$$= \Pr[\mathbf{M} = m_1||\ldots||m_d].$$

In the previous analysis, we used the fact that for any message $\mathbf{M}'$:

$$\begin{aligned}
&\Pr[\mathbf{C} = IV||c_1||\ldots||c_d||\tau|\mathbf{M}' = m'_1||\ldots||m'_d] = \\
&= \Pr[c_1||\ldots||c_d||\tau|IV, \mathbf{M}'] \times \Pr[IV|\mathbf{M}'] \\
&= \Pr[\mathbf{l} = m_1 \oplus c_1||\ldots||m_d \oplus c_d, K_T = h_{d+1} \oplus \tau|IV, \mathbf{M}'] \times \Pr[IV] \\
&= 2^{-(d+1)n} \times \Pr[IV].
\end{aligned}$$

There are two possible types of attacks when considering the authenticity of the ciphertext: an impersonation attack and a substitution attack.

In the case of an impersonation attack, the attacker constructs and sends a ciphertext to the receiver before he sees the encryption of the message. Due to the fact that the key K_T is uniformly random, the probability of success of an impersonation attack is at most 2^{-n}. If the adversary makes q_I impersonation attempts, then the probability that at least one of this attempts will be successful ia $1 - (1 - 2^{-n})^{q_I} \leq q_I \times 2^{-n}$.

In the case of substitution attack, the adversary has intercepted the ciphertext of a given message and tries to replace it with a different ciphertext that will be accepted as valid by the receiver. We will show that the probability of success in this case is at most $q_S \times \epsilon$, where q_S is the number of substitution attempts made by the adversary.

Suppose that $\mathbf{C} = IV||c_1||\ldots||c_d||\tau$ is the ciphertext of a chosen message $\mathbf{M}$ and $\mathbf{C}' = IV'||c'_1||\ldots||c'_d||\tau'$ is the substitution ciphertext. If the two ciphertexts $\mathbf{C}$ and $\mathbf{C}'$ differ only in their authentication tags (i.e., $\tau' \neq \tau$, $IV' = IV$ and $c_j = c'_j, 1 \leq j \leq d$), then the probability of successful substitution is zero. Therefore, the only interesting case is when the substitution ciphertext $\mathbf{C}'$ and the original ciphertext $\mathbf{C}$ differ in at least one block that is different from the tag block.

Let $0 \leq j \leq d$ be the index of the first block where $\mathbf{C}$ and $\mathbf{C}'$ differ, and let $\Delta i_{j+1} = c'_j \oplus c_j$ be the difference at the input of $h_{K_{j+1}}$, with $c_0 = IV$ and $c'_0 = IV'$. Then, due to the ϵ-LAXU and invertibility properties of $\mathcal{H}$, we have that $\Pr[\Delta h_{j+1} = 0|\mathbf{M}, \mathbf{C}, \mathbf{C}'] = 0$ and $\forall_{\Delta \in \{0,1\}^n, \Delta \neq 0} \Pr[\Delta h_{j+1} = \Delta|\mathbf{M}, \mathbf{C}, \mathbf{C}'] \leq \epsilon$, where Δh_{j+1} is the difference at the output of $h_{K_{j+1}}$. Hence, for the difference $\Delta i_{j+2} = \Delta h_{j+1} \oplus \Delta c_{j+1}$, we get that $\forall_{\Delta \in \{0,1\}^n} \Pr[\Delta i_{j+2} = \Delta|\mathbf{M}, \mathbf{C}, \mathbf{C}'] \leq \epsilon$. The probability $\Pr[\Delta h_{j+2} = 0|\mathbf{M}, \mathbf{C}, \mathbf{C}']$ is equal to the probability that $\Pr[\Delta i_{j+2} = 0|\mathbf{M}, \mathbf{C}, \mathbf{C}']$, and is at most ϵ. When the input difference Δi_{j+2} is nonzero, we get that $\forall_{\Delta \in \{0,1\}^n, \Delta \neq 0} \Pr[\Delta h_{j+2} = \Delta|\mathbf{M}, \mathbf{C}, \mathbf{C}'] \leq \epsilon$. If we continue in this manner, we get that $\forall_{\Delta \in \{0,1\}^n} \Pr[\Delta h_{d+1} = \Delta|\mathbf{M}, \mathbf{C}, \mathbf{C}'] \leq \epsilon$. The substitution ciphertext will be accepted as valid only if $h'_{d+1} \oplus K_T = \tau'$, i.e., only if $\Delta h_{d+1} = \Delta\tau$, where $\Delta\tau = \tau \oplus \tau'$. Given the previous analysis, this will happen with probability no larger than ϵ.

The probability that at least one out of q_S substitution queries will be successful is at most $q_S\epsilon$. The probability of success when making at most $q_v = q_I + q_S$ verification queries is at most $q_v\epsilon$ due to the fact that $\epsilon \leq 2^{-n}$. □

To deal with messages of arbitrary length, one can generate uniformly at random a key K_T for each possible message length. Now, if one substitutes a ciphertext with a different-length ciphertext, then the probability of success will be same as for the impersonation attack (i.e., 2^{-n}). In ASC-1, this is accomplished by having the message length as a part of the input when generating $K_{3,0}$.

4 Security of ASC-1

In this section, we show that if the block cipher used in ASC-1 is secure and one cannot tell apart the case when ASC-1 uses random round keys from the case when it uses round keys derived by a key scheduling algorithm, then ASC-1 is secure authenticated encryption scheme.

4.1 The Information-Theoretic Case

Here, we establish the unconditional security of ASC-1 with random keys. First, we consider the two round SPN structure of Figure 4. The input $\mathbf{x} = x_1||\ldots||x_n$ is an $n \times m$-bit string. The key addition operator is the bitwise XOR operator.

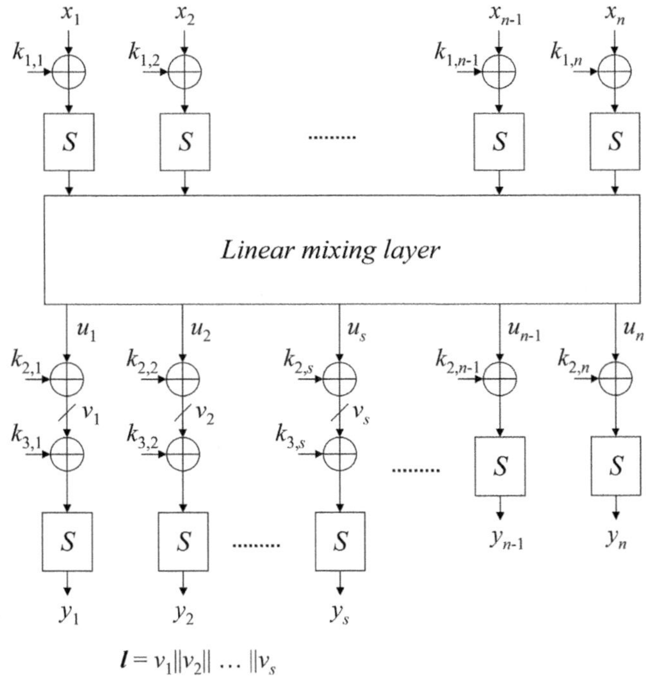

Fig. 4. A two round SPN structure with a leak. Each of the n S-boxes is a non-linear permutation on $\{0,1\}^m$, and the branch number of the linear mixing layer is $n+1$. Without loss of generality, we assume that the leak positions are the first s positions of $\mathbf{v}$ (i.e., $\mathbf{l} = v_1||v_2||\ldots||v_s$)

The non-linear substitution layer consists of n S-boxes. Each S-box is a non-linear permutation that transforms an m-bit string into an m-bit string. The mixing layer is defined by an $n \times n$ matrix. It is linear with respect to bitwise XOR and its branch number is $n+1$. We omit the mixing layer in the second round since it does not affect our analysis. The leak $\mathbf{l}$ consists of s values $v_1, \ldots, v_s$.

Each possible key $k_{1,1}, \ldots, k_{1,n}, k_{2,1}, \ldots k_{2,n}, k_{3,1}, \ldots, k_{3,s}$ defines a function that maps the input $\mathbf{x}$ into an output $\mathbf{y}$ and a leak $\mathbf{l}$. The collection of such functions $\mathcal{H}_{2R}$ forms a LAXU hash function family.

Lemma 1. *Suppose that the keys in the transformation depicted in Figure 4 are chosen uniformly at random. Then, we have that*

$$\Pr[\Delta\mathbf{y} = \Delta y | \mathbf{x} = x, \mathbf{x}' = x', \mathbf{l} = l] = \Pr[\Delta\mathbf{y} = \Delta y | \Delta\mathbf{x} = x \oplus x'].$$

Proof. Suppose that a function h (i.e., the key $k_{1,1}, \ldots, k_{1,n}$, $k_{2,1}, \ldots, k_{2,n}$, $k_{3,1}$, $\ldots, k_{3,s}$) is selected uniformly at random from $\mathcal{H}_{2R}$. Let $\mathbf{l}$ be the leak that is obtained when h is applied to an input $\mathbf{x}$, and let $\mathbf{x}'$ be an input bit string distinct from $\mathbf{x}$. The probability $\Pr[\Delta\mathbf{y} = \Delta y | \mathbf{x} = x, \mathbf{x}' = x', \mathbf{l} = l]$ is the probability that the output difference $\mathbf{y} \oplus \mathbf{y}'$ is Δy given $\mathbf{x} = x$, $\mathbf{x}' = x'$ and $\mathbf{l} = l$. Due to the initial key addition, this probability is equal to the probability $\Pr[\Delta\mathbf{y} = \Delta y | \Delta\mathbf{x} = x \oplus x', \mathbf{l} = l]$ that the output difference is Δy given the input difference is $\Delta x = x \oplus x'$ and the leak l. To prove the lemma, we use the following observations:

1. $\Pr[\Delta u | \Delta x, l] = \Pr[\Delta u | \Delta x]$, where $\Delta u = (\Delta u_1, \ldots, \Delta u_n)$, $\Delta u_i = u_i \oplus u_i'$. That is the difference Δu given input difference Δx is independent of the leak l. This is due to the second key addition, which makes the leak uniformly distributed for any possible value Δu.
2. $\Pr[\Delta y | \Delta u, l] = \prod_{i=1}^{s} \Pr[\Delta y_i | \Delta u_i, v_i] \times \prod_{i=s+1}^{n} \Pr[\Delta y_i | \Delta u_i]$. Given the difference Δu, the probability of having a difference $\Delta y_i = y_i \oplus y_i'$ at the output of the i-th S-box of the second round is independent of the probability of having a difference $\Delta y_j, j \neq i$ at the output of some other S-box in the second round.
3. $\Pr[\Delta y_i | \Delta u_i, v_i] = \Pr[\Delta y_i | \Delta u_i]$, $i = 1, \ldots, s$. After the third key addition, the input to the S-boxes is uniformly distributed and independent of the v_i values.

Using the previous observations, we can now prove the theorem.

$$\begin{aligned}
\Pr[\Delta y | \Delta x, l] &= \sum_{\Delta u} \Pr[\Delta y | \Delta u, \Delta x, l] \Pr[\Delta u | \Delta x, l] \\
&= \sum_{\Delta u} \Pr[\Delta y | \Delta u, l] \Pr[\Delta u | \Delta x] \\
&= \sum_{\Delta u} \Pr[\Delta u | \Delta x] \times \prod_{i=1}^{s} \Pr[\Delta y_i | \Delta u_i, v_i] \times \prod_{i=s+1}^{n} \Pr[\Delta y_i | \Delta u_i] \\
&= \sum_{\Delta u} \Pr[\Delta u | \Delta x] \times \prod_{i=1}^{s} \Pr[\Delta y_i | \Delta u_i] \times \prod_{i=s+1}^{n} \Pr[\Delta y_i | \Delta u_i]
\end{aligned}$$

$$= \sum_{\Delta u} \Pr[\Delta u|\Delta x] \times \prod_{i=1}^{n} \Pr[\Delta y_i|\Delta u_i]$$
$$= \sum_{\Delta u} \Pr[\Delta y|\Delta u] \times \Pr[\Delta u|\Delta x]$$
$$= \Pr[\Delta y|\Delta x]. \qquad \square$$

Corollary 1. *The family of functions $\mathcal{H}_{2R}$ defined by the 2-round transformation depicted in Figure 4 is ϵ-LAXU$_2$ with $\epsilon = \mathrm{DP}_{2R}$, where DP_{2R} is the maximum differential probability of the 2-round SPN structure when there is no leak.*

Proof. Due to the previous lemma, we get that $\Pr[\Delta\mathbf{y} = \Delta y|\mathbf{x} = x, \mathbf{x}' = x', \mathbf{l} = l] = \Pr[\Delta\mathbf{y} = \Delta y|\Delta\mathbf{x} = x \oplus x'] \leq \mathrm{DP}_{2R}$. $\square$

The previous results refer to two round SPN structures. In order to show that one can use four AES rounds to construct a LAXU hash function, we will first consider the composition of transformations depicted in Figure 5. The next lemma establishes independence of the differential probability of F_1 (resp., F_2) from the leak value l_2 (resp., l_1). This is due to the key addition operation that follows F_1 and precedes F_2.

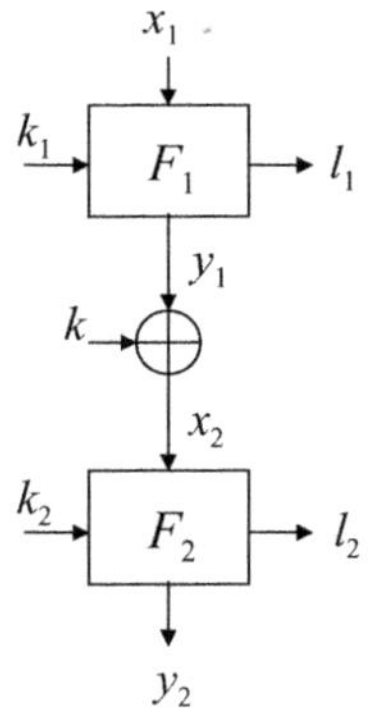

Fig. 5. A composition of a transformation F_1, key addition and transformation F_2. The length of the F_1's output y_1, the length of the F_2's input x_2 and the length of the key k are equal. Both F_1 and F_2 "leak" a value (l_1 and l_2 resp.).

Lemma 2. *The following holds for the differential probabilities of the transformations F_1 and F_2 depicted in Figure 5:*

$$\Pr[\Delta\mathbf{y_1} = \Delta y_1|\Delta\mathbf{x_1} = \Delta x_1, \mathbf{l_1} = l_1, \mathbf{l_2} = l_2] = \Pr[\Delta\mathbf{y_1} = \Delta y_1|\Delta\mathbf{x_1} = \Delta x_1, \mathbf{l_1} = l_1],$$

and

$$\Pr[\Delta\mathbf{y_2} = \Delta y_2|\Delta\mathbf{y_1} = \Delta y_1, \mathbf{l_1} = l_1, \mathbf{l_2} = l_2] = \Pr[\Delta\mathbf{y_2} = \Delta y_2|\Delta\mathbf{y_1} = \Delta y_1, \mathbf{l_2} = l_2].$$

Proof.

$$
\begin{aligned}
&\Pr[\Delta \mathbf{y_1} = \Delta y_1 | \Delta \mathbf{x_1} = \Delta x_1, \mathbf{l_1} = l_1, \mathbf{l_2} = l_2] \\
&= \sum_{y_1} \Pr[\Delta \mathbf{y_1} = \Delta y_1, \mathbf{y_1} = y_1 | \Delta \mathbf{x_1} = \Delta x_1, \mathbf{l_1} = l_1, \mathbf{l_2} = l_2] \\
&= \sum_{y_1} (\Pr[\Delta \mathbf{y_1} = \Delta y_1 | \mathbf{y_1} = y_1, \Delta \mathbf{x_1} = \Delta x_1, \mathbf{l_1} = l_1, \mathbf{l_2} = l_2] \times \\
&\quad \times \Pr[\mathbf{y_1} = y_1 | \Delta \mathbf{x_1} = \Delta x_1, \mathbf{l_1} = l_1, \mathbf{l_2} = l_2]) \\
&= \sum_{y_1} (\Pr[\Delta \mathbf{y_1} = \Delta y_1 | \mathbf{y_1} = y_1, \Delta \mathbf{x_1} = \Delta x_1, \mathbf{l_1} = l_1] \times \\
&\quad \times \Pr[\mathbf{y_1} = y_1 | \Delta \mathbf{x_1} = \Delta x_1, \mathbf{l_1} = l_1]) \\
&= \Pr[\Delta \mathbf{y_1} = \Delta y_1 | \Delta \mathbf{x_1} = \Delta x_1, \mathbf{l_1} = l_1].
\end{aligned}
$$

Here we used the fact that

$$
\begin{aligned}
&\Pr[\Delta \mathbf{y_1} = \Delta y_1 | \mathbf{y_1} = y_1, \Delta \mathbf{x_1} = \Delta x_1, \mathbf{l_1} = l_1, \mathbf{l_2} = l_2] \\
&= \frac{\Pr[\Delta \mathbf{y_1} = \Delta y_1, \mathbf{y_1} = y_1, \Delta \mathbf{x_1} = \Delta x_1, \mathbf{l_1} = l_1, \mathbf{l_2} = l_2]}{\Pr[\mathbf{y_1} = y_1, \Delta \mathbf{x_1} = \Delta x_1, \mathbf{l_1} = l_1, \mathbf{l_2} = l_2]} \\
&= \frac{\Pr[\mathbf{l_2} = l_2 | \Delta \mathbf{y_1} = \Delta y_1, \mathbf{y_1} = y_1, \Delta \mathbf{x_1} = \Delta x_1, \mathbf{l_1} = l_1]}{\Pr[\mathbf{l_2} = l_2 | \mathbf{y_1} = y_1, \Delta \mathbf{x_1} = \Delta x_1, \mathbf{l_1} = l_1]} \times \\
&\quad \times \frac{\Pr[\Delta \mathbf{y_1} = \Delta y_1, \mathbf{y_1} = y_1, \Delta \mathbf{x_1} = \Delta x_1, \mathbf{l_1} = l_1]}{\Pr[\mathbf{y_1} = y_1, \Delta \mathbf{x_1} = \Delta x_1, \mathbf{l_1} = l_1]} \\
&= \frac{\Pr[\mathbf{l_2} = l_2] \times \Pr[\Delta \mathbf{y_1} = \Delta y_1, \mathbf{y_1} = y_1, \Delta \mathbf{x_1} = \Delta x_1, \mathbf{l_1} = l_1]}{\Pr[\mathbf{l_2} = l_2] \times \Pr[\mathbf{y_1} = y_1, \Delta \mathbf{x_1} = \Delta x_1, \mathbf{l_1} = l_1]} \\
&= \Pr[\Delta \mathbf{y_1} = \Delta y_1 | \mathbf{y_1} = y_1, \Delta \mathbf{x_1} = \Delta x_1, \mathbf{l_1} = l_1].
\end{aligned}
$$

The equalities $\Pr[\mathbf{l_2} = l_2 | \mathbf{y_1} = y_1, \Delta \mathbf{x_1} = \Delta x_1, \mathbf{l_1} = l_1] = \Pr[\mathbf{l_2} = l_2]$ and $\Pr[\mathbf{l_2} = l_2 | \Delta \mathbf{y_1} = \Delta y_1, \mathbf{y_1} = y_1, \Delta \mathbf{x_1} = \Delta x_1, \mathbf{l_1} = l_1] = \Pr[\mathbf{l_2} = l_2]$ follow from the fact that the value of the second leak l_2 is independent of $\Delta x_1, y_1, \Delta y_1$ and l_1 since x_2 is uniformly distributed and independent of these values. Similarly, we can show that

$$\Pr[\mathbf{y_1} = y_1 | \Delta \mathbf{x_1} = \Delta x_1, \mathbf{l_1} = l_1, \mathbf{l_2} = l_2] = \Pr[\mathbf{y_1} = y_1 | \Delta \mathbf{x_1} = \Delta x_1, \mathbf{l_1} = l_1].$$

This concludes the first part of the proof. The second equation of the lemma can be proved in a similar fashion, and we omit its proof. □

Let us look now at the situation depicted in Figure 6. A keyed non-linear function F is applied to a vector $\mathbf{x}$ of n input values $(x_1, \ldots, x_n)$ to produce a vector $\mathbf{y} = (y_1, \ldots, y_n)$ of n output values. Without loss of generality, we assume that the first s output values are leaked after a uniformly random key is added to them. The knowledge of the leak $\mathbf{l}' = (l_1, \ldots, l_s)$ does not change the output differential probabilities of F.

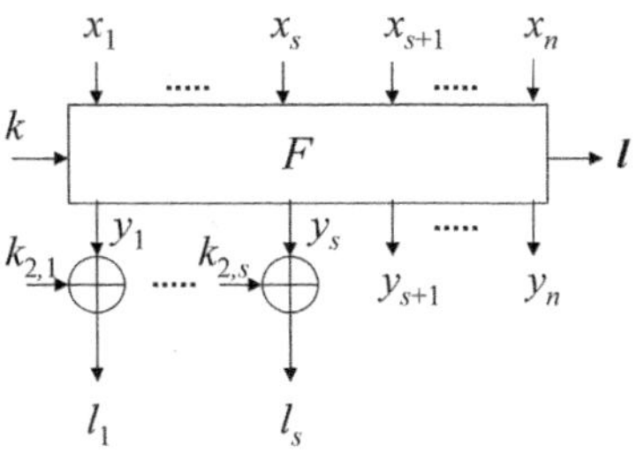

Fig. 6. The first s output values of a non-linear function F are "leaked" after a uniformly random key is added to them

Lemma 3. *Let* $\mathbf{o} = (l_1, \ldots, l_s, y_{s+1}, \ldots, y_n)$ *denote the output of the transformation depicted in Figure 6. The following holds for the output differential probability* $\Delta\mathbf{o}$*:*

$$\Pr[\Delta\mathbf{o}(\equiv \Delta\mathbf{y}) = \Delta o|\Delta\mathbf{x} = \Delta x, \mathbf{l} = l, \mathbf{l}' = l'] = \Pr[\Delta\mathbf{o} = \Delta o|\Delta\mathbf{x} = \Delta x, \mathbf{l} = l]$$

Proof. Since the output values are leaked after the random key is added, they tell nothing about the values $y_1, \ldots, y_s$ and do not affect the probability of having output difference Δy.

$$\begin{aligned}
&\Pr[\Delta\mathbf{o}(\equiv \Delta\mathbf{y}) = \Delta o|\Delta\mathbf{x} = \Delta x, \mathbf{l} = l, \mathbf{l}' = l'] \\
&= \sum_y \Pr[\Delta\mathbf{o} = \Delta o, \mathbf{y} = y|\Delta\mathbf{x} = \Delta x, \mathbf{l} = l, \mathbf{l}' = l'] \\
&= \sum_y (\Pr[\Delta\mathbf{o} = \Delta o|\mathbf{y} = y, \Delta\mathbf{x} = \Delta x, \mathbf{l} = l, \mathbf{l}' = l'] \times \\
&\quad \times Pr[\mathbf{y} = y|\Delta\mathbf{x} = \Delta x, \mathbf{l} = l, \mathbf{l}' = l']) \\
&= \sum_y \Pr[\Delta\mathbf{o} = \Delta o|\mathbf{y} = y, \Delta\mathbf{x} = \Delta x, \mathbf{l} = l] \times Pr[\mathbf{y} = y|\Delta\mathbf{x} = \Delta x, \mathbf{l} = l] \\
&= \Pr[\Delta\mathbf{o} = \Delta o|\Delta\mathbf{x} = \Delta x, \mathbf{l} = l].
\end{aligned}$$

□

The following theorem follows from the previous analysis.

Theorem 2. *Suppose that the initial state and all the keys in ASC-1 are uniformly random, then the scheme provides:*

- *perfect secrecy, and*
- *unconditional ciphertext integrity, where the probability of success of any adversary making* q_v *verifying queries is at most* $q_v \times 2^{-113}$.

Proof. We will show here that if the (round) keys are selected uniformly at random, then the family of functions defined by four rounds of AES with leak extraction is an ϵ-LAXU$_2$ hash function family with $\epsilon = 2^{-113}$. The first round key additions in the 4R-AES transformations play the role of the keys k_i of the construction depicted in Figure 3. Clearly, the transformation defined by four rounds of AES is a bijection, and the leak values are uniformly random and independent of the input due to the uniform probability distribution of the keys. Therefore, the sufficient conditions of Theorem 1 are satisfied, and the scheme provides perfect secrecy and unconditional ciphertext integrity.

In our analysis, we assume that the key addition is the first round operation instead of a last one as in the AES specification. Furthermore, all the keys are independent with uniform probability distribution. We use the following notation:

- $\mathbf{x_i}$, $i = 0, \ldots, 3$ is the input to the i-th round and consists of 16 bytes $x_{i,0}, \ldots, x_{i,15}$;
- $\mathbf{y_i}$, $i = 0, \ldots, 3$ is the output of the MixColumns layer of the i-th round and consists of 16 bytes $y_{i,0}, \ldots, y_{i,15}$;
- $\mathbf{z_i}$, $i = 0, \ldots, 3$ is the state after the leak extraction layer of the i-th round and consists of 16 bytes $z_{i,0}, \ldots, z_{i,15}$;
- $\mathbf{l_i}$, $i = 0, \ldots, 3$ is the leak extracted in the i-th round and consists of 4 bytes $l_{i,0}, \ldots, l_{i,15}$;

Suppose that x'_0 and x''_0 are two distinct input values, and let us consider the output difference $\mathbf{\Delta z_3}$ given the input difference $\Delta\mathbf{x_0} = \mathbf{x'_0} \oplus \mathbf{x''_0}$. By applying the previously presented lemmas, we get:

$$
\begin{aligned}
&\Pr[\Delta\mathbf{z_3} = \Delta z_3 | \mathbf{x'_0} = x'_0, \mathbf{x''_0} = x''_0, \mathbf{l_0} = l_0, \mathbf{l_1} = l_1, \mathbf{l_2} = l_2, \mathbf{l_3} = l_3] \\
&= \Pr[\Delta\mathbf{z_3} = \Delta z_3 | \Delta\mathbf{x_0} = x'_0 \oplus x''_0, \mathbf{l_0} = l_0, \mathbf{l_1} = l_1, \mathbf{l_2} = l_2, \mathbf{l_3} = l_3] \\
&= \sum_{\Delta z_1} (\Pr[\Delta\mathbf{z_1} = \Delta z_1 | \Delta\mathbf{x_0} = x'_0 \oplus x''_0, \mathbf{l_0} = l_0, \mathbf{l_1} = l_1, \mathbf{l_2} = l_2, \mathbf{l_3} = l_3] \times \qquad (1) \\
&\quad \times \Pr[\Delta\mathbf{z_3} = \Delta z_3 | \Delta\mathbf{z_1} = \Delta z_1, \Delta\mathbf{x_0} = x'_0 \oplus x''_0, \mathbf{l_0} = l_0, \mathbf{l_1} = l_1, \mathbf{l_2} = l_2, \mathbf{l_3} = l_3]) \\
&= \sum_{\Delta z_1} (\Pr[\Delta\mathbf{z_1} = \Delta z_1 | \Delta\mathbf{x_0} = x'_0 \oplus x''_0, \mathbf{l_0} = l_0, \mathbf{l_1} = l_1] \times \\
&\quad \times \Pr[\Delta\mathbf{z_3} = \Delta z_3 | \Delta\mathbf{z_1} = \Delta z_1, \mathbf{l_2} = l_2, \mathbf{l_3} = l_3]) \qquad (2) \\
&= \sum_{\Delta z_1} (\Pr[\Delta\mathbf{z_1} = \Delta z_1 | \Delta\mathbf{x_0} = x'_0 \oplus x''_0, \mathbf{l_0} = l_0] \times \\
&\quad \times \Pr[\Delta\mathbf{z_3} = \Delta z_3 | \Delta\mathbf{z_1} = \Delta z_1, \mathbf{l_2} = l_2]) \qquad (3) \\
&= \sum_{\Delta z_1} \Pr[\Delta\mathbf{z_1} = \Delta z_1 | \Delta\mathbf{x_0} = x'_0 \oplus x''_0] \times \Pr[\Delta\mathbf{z_3} = \Delta z_3 | \Delta\mathbf{z_1} = \Delta z_1] \qquad (4) \\
&= \Pr[\Delta\mathbf{z_3} = \Delta z_3 | \Delta\mathbf{x_0} = x'_0 \oplus x''_0] \\
&\leq \mathrm{DP}_{\mathrm{4rAES}},
\end{aligned}
$$

where $\mathrm{DP}_{\mathrm{4rAES}}$ is the differential probability of the transformation defined by four rounds (with no leak extraction) of AES when the round keys are random. The equation (2) follows from Lemma 2, the equation (3) follows from Lemma 3, and the equation (4) follows from Lemma 1.

Having the previous inequality in mind, we get that the family of functions defined by four rounds of AES with leak extraction is an ϵ-LAXU$_2$ hash function family with $\epsilon = \mathrm{DP}_{4\mathrm{rAES}} \leq 2^{-113}$ [18]. $\square$

4.2 Computational Security Analysis of ASC-1

In the previous subsection, we showed that if all the keys and the initial state are random, then ASC-1 is unconditionally secure authenticated encryption scheme. However, the keys and the initial state of ASC-1 are derived by combining a block cipher in a counter mode and a key scheduling algorithm. The security of the scheme in this case is based on two assumptions:

- the block cipher (e.g., AES) is indistinguishable from a random permutation, and
- one cannot tell apart the case when the initial state and the keys are random from the case when the initial state X_0 and the tag key $K_{3,0}$ are random, and the round keys are derived by applying a key scheduling algorithm to a random initial key $K_{1,0}||K_{2,0}$.

The first assumption is a standard assumption that is used in many security proofs such as the security proofs of the modes of operation for block ciphers. The second assumption is a novel one, and should be examined with more scrutiny. It asserts that an adversary cannot win in the following game. The adversary is given two oracles, an encryption oracle and a decryption oracle. A random coin b is flipped. If the outcome is zero, then a large table whose entries are random strings is generated. The number of entries in the table is equal to the maximum number of messages that can be encrypted. The length of each random string in the table is sufficient to encrypt a message of a maximum length. When the adversary submits an encryption query, the encryption oracle gets the next random string from the table, extracts the initial value and all the (round) keys from the random string, and encrypts the message. When the adversary submits a decryption query, the decryption oracle gets the random string corresponding to the counter value given in the ciphertext, and uses it to decrypt the ciphertext. If the outcome of the coin flipping is one, then the random strings in the table consist of four 128-bit random values: an initial state X_0 and three keys $K_{1,0}, K_{2,0}$ and $K_{3,0}$. When the adversary asks an encryption query, the encryption oracle uses the next available initial state and keys to encrypt the message following the ASC-1 algorithm. When the adversary asks a decryption query, the decryption oracle uses the initial state and keys corresponding to the counter value given in the ciphertext to decrypt the ciphertext. The goal of the adversary is to guess the outcome of the coin flipping. The adversary wins if it can guess the value of b with probability significantly greater than $\frac{1}{2}$.

It is not uncommon to make the assumption that the round keys are random when analyzing the security of cryptographic primitives. For instance, this assumption is always made when proving the resistance of a block cipher to linear and differential cryptanalysis (e.g., [22]). However, one can easily come up with a stream cipher that is secure when the random round keys assumption is made, but is trivial to break otherwise. Since the design of ASC-1 was inspired by the LEX stream cipher, we are going to address the known attacks on LEX:

- LEX applies iteratively a block cipher transformation to some initial state. During this process some bytes are leaked from different rounds (i.e., states), and then used as randomness to encrypt the message. The attack presented in [6] analyzes the state differences to find highly probable differentials and deduce the secret key. However, in our case, we do not use the same round keys repeatedly. So, in order for a differential cryptanalysis to work, one has to be able to guess the round key differences as well. Since these round keys are far apart in the key scheduling process, this does not appear to be an easy task.
- The attack presented in [25] looks for a repetition of a state, which can be easily detected due to the fact that same states will generate the same pseudo-random key material. The state in LEX is a 128-bit string since the round keys are reused, and it is possible to find collisions. In our case, the state is a 384-bit string, and finding collisions should not be a straightforward problem.
- Some modified variants of the previous attacks might work if the key scheduling algorithm generates short cycles. However, the probability of having a cycle of length less than 2^{64} when considering a random permutation on $\{0,1\}^{256}$ is at most $\approx 2^{-128}$, and we are not aware of the existence of short cycles.

It is not hard to show that given an adversary A_{ROR} that can distinguish the ciphertext generated by ASC-1 from a random string, one can construct two adversaries A_{PRP}, which can tell apart the block cipher from a PRP, and A_{KSOR}, which can distinguish the case when the round keys are random from the case when the round keys are derived by a key scheduling algorithm, such that at least one of these adversary wins with significant probability. Namely, the A_{PRP} and A_{KSOR} will use their oracles to simulate ASC-1 and answer A_{ROR}'s queries. The output of A_{PRP} and A_{KSOR} will be same as A_{ROR}'s output. If the advantage of A_{ROR} is non-negligible, then at least one of A_{PRP} and A_{KSOR} will have non-negligible advantage. A similar result will hold in the case of a forging adversary A_F. So, we have the following informal theorems.

Theorem 3. *If the block cipher used by ASC-1 is a pseudo-random permutation and one cannot tell apart the case when ASC-1 uses random keys from the case when ASC-1 uses a key scheduling algorithm to derive the round keys, then ASC-1 is a secure encryption scheme in the Real-Or-Random sense.*

Theorem 4. *If the block cipher used by ASC-1 is a pseudo-random permutation and one cannot tell apart the case when ASC-1 uses random keys from the case when ASC-1 uses a key scheduling algorithm to derive the round keys, then ASC-1 is a secure message authentication scheme in the ciphertext-integrity sense.*

The definition of Real-Or-Random security of a symmetric encryption scheme and the definition of a ciphertext integrity for an authenticated encryption scheme can be found in [1].

5 Conclusions

We have proposed ASC-1, which is an authenticated encryption scheme that is designed using a stream cipher approach instead of a block cipher mode approach. We argued the security of ASC-1 by showing that it is secure if one cannot distinguish the case when the round keys are uniformly random from the case when the round keys are derived by the key scheduling algorithm of ASC-1.

References

1. Bellare, M., Namprempre, C.: Authenticated Encryption: Relations among Notions and Analysis of the Generic Composition Paradigm. In: Okamoto, T. (ed.) ASIACRYPT 2000. LNCS, vol. 1976, pp. 531–545. Springer, Heidelberg (2000)
2. Bertoni, G., Daemen, J., Peeters, M., Van Assche, G.: Duplexing the Sponge: Authenticated Encryption and Other Applications. In: The Second SHA-3 Candidate Conference (2010)
3. Biryukov, A.: The Design of a Stream Cipher LEX. In: Biham, E., Youssef, A.M. (eds.) SAC 2006. LNCS, vol. 4356, pp. 67–75. Springer, Heidelberg (2007)
4. Daemen, J., Rijmen, V.: A New MAC Construction ALRED and a Specific Instance ALPHA-MAC. In: Gilbert, H., Handschuh, H. (eds.) FSE 2005. LNCS, vol. 3557, pp. 1–17. Springer, Heidelberg (2005)
5. Daemen, J., Rijmen, V.: The Pelican MAC Function, IACR ePrint Archive, 2005/088
6. Dunkelman, O., Keller, N.: A New Attack on the LEX Stream Cipher. In: Pieprzyk, J. (ed.) ASIACRYPT 2008. LNCS, vol. 5350, pp. 539–556. Springer, Heidelberg (2008)
7. Ferguson, N., Whiting, D., Schneier, B., Kelsey, J., Lucks, S., Kohno, T.: Helix: Fast Encryption and Authentication in a Single Cryptographic Primitive. In: Johansson, T. (ed.) FSE 2003. LNCS, vol. 2887, pp. 330–346. Springer, Heidelberg (2003)
8. Advanced Encryption Standard (AES), FIPS Publication 197 (November 26, 2001), `http://csrc.nist.gov/encryption/aes`
9. Gligor, V., Donescu, P.: Fast Encryption and Authentication: XCBC Encryption and XECB Authentication Modes. Presented at the 2nd NIST Workshop on AES Modes of Operation, Santa Barbara, CA (August 24, 2001)
10. Gligor, V.D., Donescu, P.: Fast Encryption and Authentication: XCBC Encryption and XECB Authentication Modes. In: Matsui, M. (ed.) FSE 2001. LNCS, vol. 2355, pp. 1–20. Springer, Heidelberg (2002)
11. Hawkes, P., Rose, G.: Primitive Specification for SOBER-128, `http://www.qualcomm.com.au/Sober128.html`
12. Hong, S., Lee, S., Lim, J., Sung, J., Cheon, D., Cho, I.: Provable Security against Differential and Linear Cryptanalysis for the SPN Structure. In: Schneier, B. (ed.) FSE 2000. LNCS, vol. 1978, pp. 273–283. Springer, Heidelberg (2001)

13. Jakimoski, G., Subbalakshmi, K.P.: On Efficient Message Authentication Via Block Cipher Design Techniques. In: Kurosawa, K. (ed.) ASIACRYPT 2007. LNCS, vol. 4833, pp. 232–248. Springer, Heidelberg (2007)
14. Jutla, C.S.: Encryption Modes with Almost Free Message Integrity. In: Pfitzmann, B. (ed.) EUROCRYPT 2001. LNCS, vol. 2045, pp. 529–544. Springer, Heidelberg (2001)
15. Kang, J.-S., Hong, S., Lee, S., Yi, O., Park, C., Lim, J.: Practical and Provable Security Against Differential and Linear Cryptanalysis for Ssubstitution-Permutation Networks. ETRI Journal 23(4), 158–167 (2001)
16. Keliher, L., Meijer, H., Tavares, S.: New Method for Upper Bounding the Maximum Average Linear Hull Probability for sPNs. In: Pfitzmann, B. (ed.) EUROCRYPT 2001. LNCS, vol. 2045, pp. 420–436. Springer, Heidelberg (2001)
17. Keliher, L., Meijer, H., Tavares, S.: Improving the Upper Bound on the Maximum Average Linear Hull Probability for Rijndael. In: Vaudenay, S., Youssef, A.M. (eds.) SAC 2001. LNCS, vol. 2259, pp. 112–128. Springer, Heidelberg (2001)
18. Keliher, L., Sui, J.: Exact Maximum Expected Differential and Linear Probability for 2-Round Advanced Encryption Standard (AES). IACR ePrint Archive, 2005/321
19. Matsui, M.: New Structure of Block Ciphers with Provable Security against Differential and Linear Cryptanalysis. In: Gollmann, D. (ed.) FSE 1996. LNCS, vol. 1039, pp. 205–218. Springer, Heidelberg (1996)
20. Minematsu, K., Tsunoo, Y.: Provably Secure MACs from Differentially-Uniform Permutations and AES-Based Implementations. In: Robshaw, M.J.B. (ed.) FSE 2006. LNCS, vol. 4047, pp. 226–241. Springer, Heidelberg (2006)
21. Park, S., Sung, S.H., Chee, S., Yoon, E.-J., Lim, J.: On the Security of Rijndael-Like Structures against Differential and Linear Cryptanalysis. In: Zheng, Y. (ed.) ASIACRYPT 2002. LNCS, vol. 2501, pp. 176–191. Springer, Heidelberg (2002)
22. Park, S., Sung, S.H., Lee, S., Lim, J.: Improving the Upper Bound on the Maximum Differential and the Maximum Linear Hull Probability for SPN Structures and AES. In: Johansson, T. (ed.) FSE 2003. LNCS, vol. 2887, pp. 247–260. Springer, Heidelberg (2003)
23. Rogaway, P.: Bucket Hashing and Its Application to Fast Message Authentication. In: Coppersmith, D. (ed.) CRYPTO 1995. LNCS, vol. 963, pp. 29–42. Springer, Heidelberg (1995)
24. Rogaway, P., Bellare, M., Black, J., Krovetz, T.: OCB: A block-cipher mode of operation for efficient authenticated encryption. In: Proc. 8th ACM Conf. Comp. and Comm. Security, CCS (2001)
25. Wu, H., Preneel, B.: Resynchronization Attacks on WG and LEX. In: Robshaw, M.J.B. (ed.) FSE 2006. LNCS, vol. 4047, pp. 422–432. Springer, Heidelberg (2006)

On Various Families of Twisted Jacobi Quartics*

Jérôme Plût

Université de Versailles–Saint-Quentin-en-Yvelines; Versailles, France
jerome.plut@prism.uvsq.fr

Abstract. We provide several results on some families of twisted Jacobi quartics. We give new addition formulæ for two models of twisted Jacobi quartic elliptic curves, which represent respectively 1/6 and 2/3 of all elliptic curves, with respective costs $7\mathbf{M} + 3\mathbf{S} + \mathbf{D}_a$ and $8\mathbf{M} + 3\mathbf{S} + \mathbf{D}_a$. These formulæ allow addition and doubling of points, except for points differing by a point of order two.

Furthermore, we give an intrinsic characterization of elliptic curves represented by the classical Jacobi quartic, by the action of the Frobenius endomorphism on the 4-torsion subgroup. This allows us to compute the exact proportion of elliptic curves representable by various models (the three families of Jacobi quartics, plus Edwards and Huff curves) from statistics on this Frobenius action.

1 Introduction

The interest for elliptic curves in cryptography arises from the fact that, given suitable parameter choices, they provide an efficient representation of the "generic group" model. However, the need for separate formulæ for point addition and doubling in Weierstraß coordinates critically exposes elliptic curve arithmetic to side-channel analysis.

One family of countermeasures protecting against these attacks is the use of a coordinate system that allows point additions and doublings to be performed with the same formulæ. Namely, addition formulæ are said to be *unified* if they also allow doubling of non-zero points, and *complete* if the allow addition of any pair of points, identical or not, zero or not.

Some curve models with such properties, over a field of odd characteristic, are:

- twisted Edwards curves [Edw07, BL07, BBJ+08, HWCD08], with equation $ax^2 + y^2 = 1 + dx^2y^2$, have a unified addition formula, that is complete in some cases, costing $9\mathbf{M} + \mathbf{D}_a + \mathbf{D}_d$ [HWCD08];
- Jacobi quartics, with equation $y^2 = x^4 + 2a\,x^2 + 1$, are unified [BJ03], and have an addition formula costing $7\mathbf{M} + 3\mathbf{S} + \mathbf{D}_a$ [HWCD09];
- Huff cubics [JTV10], with equation $ax(y^2 - 1) = by(x^2 - 1)$, have a unified addition formula costing $11\mathbf{M}$.

* This work was supported by the French *Agence Nationale de la Recherche* through the ECLIPSES project under Contract ANR-09-VERS-018.

A. Miri and S. Vaudenay (Eds.): SAC 2011, LNCS 7118, pp. 373–383, 2012.

Not all elliptic curves transform to the Edwards or Jacobi quartic forms: only the curves with a rational point of order four transform to Edwards curves [BBJ+08, Theorem 3.3][Mor09], whereas the condition for Jacobi quartics is examined in more detail in section 2.2 of this document. Since it is preferred that elliptic curves used in cryptography have a group of prime order (as is the case, for example, of NIST-recommended curves [Nat00]), they are not actually amenable to Edwards or Jacobi quartic form.

Recent research activity has focused on counting elliptic curves in various families using explicit computation of the j-invariant, for example in the families of Doche-Icart-Kohel [DIK06] and Edwards [RFS10], Legendre [FW10], and complete Edwards curves [AG11].

We count the Jacobi quartics using a direct method, relying on the action of the Frobenius on the 4-torsion points of elliptic curves. Throughout this document, k is a finite field of odd characteristic. Let E be an elliptic curve defined over k. The 4-torsion subgroup $E[4]$ of E has coordinates in the algebraic closure of k, and is thus equipped with an action of the Frobenius endomorphism φ of k. Since k has odd characteristic, by [Sil86, 6.4(b)], the group $E[4]$ is isomorphic to $(\mathbb{Z}/4\mathbb{Z})^2$, and the action $\varphi_E \pmod 4$ of φ is given by a matrix in $GL_2(\mathbb{Z}/4\mathbb{Z})$. Finally, a change of basis of $E[4]$ conjugates the matrix of $\varphi_E \pmod 4$. Therefore, to the curve E, one may canonically attach the conjugacy class of $\varphi_E \pmod 4$ in $GL_2(\mathbb{Z}/4\mathbb{Z})$.

This work gives an intrinsic characterization of representability of elliptic curves by the Jacobi quartic model (Theorem 5); this is given by a list of allowed conjugacy classes for $\varphi_E \pmod 4$. In particular, this does not depend on the representation chosen for the curve. Thus, it allows us to give an asymptotic count of the elliptic curves that can be represented as Jacobi quartics. This method generalizes to other quadrics intersection models such as Edwards, Jacobi, and Huff (Theorem 11).

Billet and Joye [BJ03, §3] also define a twist of the Jacobi model that represents all curves with at least one rational point of order two, and give unified addition formulæ for these curves with a cost of $10\mathbf{M} + 3\mathbf{S} + 2\mathbf{D}$. We give here improved addition formulæ for the two following variants of the twisted Jacobi model:

- A $7\mathbf{M}+3\mathbf{S}+\mathbf{D}_a$ multiplication for the *(2,2)-Jacobi quartic*, which represents all curves whose point group has $(\mathbb{Z}/2\mathbb{Z}) \times (\mathbb{Z}/2\mathbb{Z})$ as a subgroup (1/6 of all elliptic curves);
- A $8\mathbf{M} + 3\mathbf{S} + \mathbf{D}_a$ multiplication for the *(2)-Jacobi quartic*, which represents all curves whose point group has $(\mathbb{Z}/2\mathbb{Z})$ as a subgroup (2/3 of all elliptic curves).

These formulæ, as well as the Jacobi quartic formula from [HWCD09], are not unified. They are, however, "complete except at 2": any points P, Q such that the formulæ don't allow the computation of $P + Q$ differ by a point of order two (Propositions 6 and 8). Thus, these formulæ are usable for all computations in the subgroup of $E(k)$ of points of order coprime to 2, and in particular in the largest subgroup of $E(k)$ of prime order, which the subgroup of cryptographic significance.

2 Jacobi Quartics

2.1 Curve Equation

A *Jacobi quartic* is a projective curve with the quartic equation

$$y^2 = x^4 + 2ax^2 + 1, \tag{1}$$

where $a \in k$ is a parameter. The discriminant of the right-hand side polynomial is $2^8(a^2-1)^2$; therefore, if $a \notin \{-1, 1\}$, then the curve has the tacnode at the point at infinity $(0:1:0)$ as its only singular point. Resolution of this singularity yields the intersection of two quadrics

$$JQ_a: \quad y^2 = z^2 + 2ax^2 + t^2, \quad x^2 = z \cdot t, \tag{2}$$

where the tacnode $(0:1:0)$ has the two antecedents $(0:1:\pm 1:0)$.

The curve JQ_a contains the four points with coordinates $(x:y:z:t)$ equal to $(0:1:0:\pm 1)$ and $(0:1:\pm 1:0)$. We fix $\varepsilon = (0:1:0:1)$ as the neutral point; the three others are then the three points of order two.

As JQ_a is a smooth intersection of two quadrics in the projective space of dimension three, it is an elliptic curve, and the group law is defined by coplanarity [Ono94, LS01]. Namely, let ε be the neutral point; then any three points P_1, P_2, P_3 have zero sum if the four points $(\varepsilon, P_1, P_2, P_3)$ are coplanar. Of course, when two of the points, say P_1 and P_2, are identical, we replace P_2 by the direction of the tangent line at P_1 to JQ_a.

We may then check that the addition formulæ for $P_3 = P_1 + P_2$, where $P_i = (x_i : y_i : z_i : t_i)$, are

$$\begin{aligned} x_3 &= (x_1y_2 + y_1x_2) \cdot (t_1t_2 - z_1z_2); \\ y_3 &= (y_1y_2 + 2ax_1x_2)(z_1z_2 + t_1t_2) + 2x_1x_2(z_1t_2 + t_1z_2); \\ z_3 &= (x_1y_2 + y_1x_2)^2; \\ t_3 &= (t_1t_2 - z_1z_2)^2. \end{aligned} \tag{3}$$

The negative of the point $(x:y:z:t)$ is $(-x:y:z:t)$.

A speed-up of one multiplication is achieved [HWCD09] by observing that

$$z_3 = (z_1z_2 + t_1t_2)(z_1t_2 + t_1z_2) + 2x_1x_2(2ax_1x_2 + y_1y_2), \tag{4}$$

so that $y_3 + z_3$ factorizes as

$$y_3 + z_3 = (z_1z_2 + 2x_1x_2 + t_1t_2)(y_1y_2 + 2ax_1x_2 + z_1t_2 + t_1z_2). \tag{5}$$

The cost of a point addition using (5) is $7\mathbf{M} + 3\mathbf{S} + \mathbf{D}_a$.

Remark 1. The formulæ (3) are not unified. One checks that these formulæ yield

$$(x:y:z:t) + (-x:y:t:z) = (0:0:0:0). \tag{6}$$

This situation is examined in more detail in the proposition 6 below.

2.2 Representability

Proposition 2. *Let E be an elliptic curve over the field k of characteristic $\neq 2$. Then E is isomorphic to a Jacobi quartic if, and only if, it has an equation of the form*

$$\eta^2 = (\xi - r_1)(\xi - r_2)(\xi - r_3)$$

such that r_1, r_2 and $r_3 \in k$ and at least one of the $r_i - r_j$ for $i, j \in \{1, 2, 3\}$, $i \neq j$, is a square.

Proof. Let E be such an elliptic curve and assume for example that $r_2 - r_3$ is a square in k. We may then define parameters $a, c, d \in k$ by

$$a = \frac{r_2 + r_3 - 2r_1}{r_2 - r_3}, \qquad c = \frac{r_2 - r_3}{2}, \qquad 4d^2 = r_2 - r_3. \tag{7}$$

The equation of E may then be simplified to

$$2\left(\frac{\eta}{d}\right)^2 = \left(\frac{\xi - r_1}{c}\right)\left(\frac{\xi - r_1}{c} - a - 1\right)\left(\frac{\xi - r_1}{c} - a + 1\right). \tag{8}$$

We define coordinates (x, y, z, t) by the matrix relation

$$\begin{pmatrix} x \\ y \\ z \\ t \end{pmatrix} = \begin{pmatrix} 0 & 2 & 0 & 0 \\ 0 & 0 & 1 & 1 - a^2 \\ -2a & 0 & 1 & a^2 - 1 \\ 2 & 0 & 0 & 0 \end{pmatrix} \begin{pmatrix} \frac{\xi - r_1}{c} \\ \frac{\eta}{d} \\ \left(\frac{\xi - r_1}{c}\right)^2 \\ 1 \end{pmatrix}. \tag{9}$$

Then (x, y, z, t) satisfy the Jacobi quartic equations for JQ_a.

Conversely, the above computation shows that JQ_a is birationally equivalent to the elliptic curve with equation $2\eta^2 = \xi(\xi - a + 1)(\xi - a + 1)$, which amounts to the Weierstraß equation in $(\frac{\xi}{2}, \frac{\eta}{2})$:

$$\left(\frac{\eta}{2}\right)^2 = \frac{\xi}{2}\left(\frac{\xi}{2} - \frac{a-1}{2}\right)\left(\frac{\xi}{2} - \frac{a+1}{2}\right). \tag{10}$$

The right-hand side has the roots $\frac{a+1}{2}$ and $\frac{a-1}{2}$, the difference of which is 1, which is a square in k. □

Remark 3. If -1 is not a square in k, then exactly one of $r_1 - r_2$ and $r_2 - r_1$ is a square. Over such a field, an elliptic curve can be represented by a Jacobi quartic if, and only if, it has a rational 2-torsion subgroup.

Remark 4. If E has full rational 2-torsion subgroup, then so does its quadratic twist $\widetilde{E}$, and at least one of E or $\widetilde{E}$ can be represented by a Jacobi quartic.

Theorem 5. *Let k be a finite field of characteristic $\neq 2$, E be an elliptic curve over k. Let φ_E be the representation of the Frobenius automorphism of k on $E(\overline{k})$ and $\varphi_E \pmod 4$ be the action of φ_E on the 4-torsion group $E[4]$.*

Then E can be represented by a Jacobi quartic if, and only if, $\varphi_E \pmod 4$ belongs to one of the following conjugacy classes in $GL_2(\mathbb{Z}/4\mathbb{Z})$:

$$\begin{pmatrix} 1 & 0 \\ 0 & 1 \end{pmatrix} = \mathrm{id}, \begin{pmatrix} 1 & 2 \\ 0 & 1 \end{pmatrix}, \begin{pmatrix} -1 & 2 \\ 0 & -1 \end{pmatrix}, \begin{pmatrix} 1 & 0 \\ 0 & -1 \end{pmatrix}, \begin{pmatrix} 1 & 2 \\ 2 & -1 \end{pmatrix}. \tag{11}$$

Proof. The condition that E has a rational 2-torsion subgroup is equivalent to $\varphi_E \equiv \mathrm{id} \pmod 2$. It may be checked, for example by enumeration, that there are exactly six such conjugacy classes of matrices in $GL_2(\mathbb{Z}/4\mathbb{Z})$: namely, the five classes of (11) and the class of $-\mathrm{id}$.

Let q be the cardinality of k. Then, by the Hasse-Weil theorem [Sil86, Theorem 2.4], we have $\det(\varphi_E) = q$. Therefore, if $q \equiv -1 \pmod 4$, then $\det \varphi_E \equiv -1 \pmod 4$ and thus $\varphi_E \pmod 4$ is conjugate to one of the latter two matrices of (11). In this case, Remark 3 shows that E is representable by a Jacobi quartic.

It remains to prove the case when $q \equiv +1 \pmod 4$. In this case, there exists $i \in k$ such that $i^2 = -1$. Let $(r_n, 0)$, for $n = 1, 2, 3$, be the (rational) points of order two of E and (ξ_n, η_n) be (not necessarily rational) points of order four such that $2(\xi_n, \eta_n) = (r_n, 0)$. The condition on (ξ_1, η_1) is equivalent to

$$(\xi_1 - r_1)^2 = (r_1 - r_2)(r_1 - r_3), \qquad \eta_1^2 = (r_1 - r_2)(r_1 - r_3)(2\xi_1 - r_2 - r_3). \tag{12}$$

Define $d_1 = r_2 - r_3$, $d_2 = r_3 - r_1$, and $d_3 = r_1 - r_2$; by Proposition 2, representability by a Jacobi quartic is equivalent to at least one of the d_n being a square in k. Two cases may occur:

(i) all d_n reduce to the same class modulo squares in $k^\times$: then there exist $c_n \in k$ and $d \in k$ such that $d_n = c_n^2 d$. The equations (12) may be rewritten as:

$$(\xi_1 - r_1)^2 = -(c_2 c_3 d)^2, \qquad \eta_1^2 = -(c_2 c_3 d)^2 (c_3 \pm i c_2)^2 d. \tag{13}$$

We see that all ξ_n are rational, and therefore $\varphi_E(\xi_n, \eta_n) = (\xi_n, \pm\eta_n)$. Thus, $\varphi_E \pmod 4$ is diagonalizable, and thus belongs to $\{\mathrm{id}, -\mathrm{id}\}$. The case $\varphi_E \equiv +\mathrm{id} \pmod 4$ is equivalent to $\eta_1 \in k$ and thus to d being a square. Therefore, in the case (i), E is representable by a Jacobi quartic if, and only if, $\varphi_E \equiv \mathrm{id} \pmod 4$.

(ii) not all the d_n reduce to the same class modulo squares: then E can be represented by a Jacobi quartic. Moreover, if for example d_1 is a square and d_2 is not, then $(\xi_3 - r_3)^2 = -d_1 d_2$ is not a square, and therefore $\xi_3 \notin k$. Thus, $\varphi_E \pmod 4$ is not diagonalizable and belongs to one of the conjugacy classes $\begin{pmatrix} 1 & 2 \\ 0 & 1 \end{pmatrix}, \begin{pmatrix} -1 & 2 \\ 0 & -1 \end{pmatrix}$.

This shows that the cases where E transforms to a Jacobi quartic are exactly the cases where $\varphi_E \pmod 4$ is one of the five matrices listed above. □

3 (2, 2) Jacobi Quartics

3.1 Curve Equation

We expand the definition of the Jacobi quartics to allow representability of all curves with rational 2-torsion subgroup. To do this, we relax the condition that d, as defined in equation (7), belong to k. We then obtain the quadric intersection

$$JQ_{a,b}^{(2,2)}: \qquad b\,x^2 = zt, \qquad y^2 = z^2 + 2a\,x^2 + t^2. \tag{14}$$

It is smooth when $(a^2-1)b \neq 0$. We note that for all $\lambda \in k^\times$, the curve $JQ_{\lambda^2 a,\lambda^2 b}^{(2,2)}$ is isomorphic to $JQ_{a,b}^{(2,2)}$ by the coordinate change $(\lambda x : y : z : t)$. Therefore, we may choose b to be either one or a (small) preset quadratic non-residue in k.

This curve has the rational points of order two

$$\omega_1 = (0:1:0:-1), \quad \omega_2 = (0:1:1:0), \quad \omega_2' = \omega_2 + \omega_1 = (0:1:-1:0). \tag{15}$$

The point addition formulæ are deduced from (3):

$$\begin{aligned} x_3 &= (x_1y_2 + y_1x_2)\,(z_1z_2 - t_1t_2) \\ y_3 &= (y_1y_2 + 2a\,x_1x_2)\,(z_1z_2 + t_1t_2) + 2b\,x_1x_2\,(z_1t_2 + t_1z_2) \\ z_3 &= (z_1z_2 - t_1t_2)^2 \quad = (z_1z_2 + t_1t_2)^2 - (2b\,x_1x_2)^2 \\ t_3 &= b\,(x_1y_2 + y_1x_2)^2 \end{aligned} \tag{16}$$

$$y_3 + t_3 = (z_1z_2 + 2b\,x_1x_2 + t_1t_2)\,(y_1y_2 + 2a\,x_1x_2 + z_1t_2 + t_1z_2)$$

The full cost for a point addition is seen to be $7\mathbf{M}+3\mathbf{S}+\mathbf{D}_a+2\mathbf{D}_b$. The advantage of choosing a parameter b such that multiplication by b is fast is apparent. The probability that all $b < N$ are squares modulo p is asymptotically equivalent to e^{-N}, so that in practice we shall almost always be able to find such a b; moreover, whether this is the case is easy to check by quadratic reciprocity.

Proposition 6. *Let P_1, P_2 be two points of $JQ_{a,b}^{(2,2)}$ such that the addition formulæ (16) yield $P_3 = P_1 + P_2 = (0:0:0:0)$. Then we either have $P_2 = P_1 + \omega_2$ or $P_2 = P_1 + \omega_2'$, where ω_i are the points of order two defined in (15).*

Proof. Let $(x_i : y_i : z_i : t_i)$ be the coordinates of P_i. If $x_1 = x_2 = 0$, then both points belong to the 2-torsion group and the result follows by enumeration, so we may assume for example $x_1 \neq 0$. Since $bx_1^2 = z_1t_1$, this implies $z_1 \neq 0$ and $t_1 \neq 0$.

The relations $t_3 = 0$ and $z_3 = 0$ then imply that there exist $\alpha, \beta \in k$ such that $P_1 = (x_1 : \alpha x_1 : \beta t_1 : t_1)$ and $P_2 = (x_2 : -\alpha x_2 : z_2 : \beta z_2)$. Since $bx_1^2 = \beta t_1^2$, there exists $\xi \in k$ such that $\beta = b\xi^2$ and $x_1 = \xi t_1$. Let $\eta = \xi\alpha$; then

$$P_1 = (\xi : \eta : b\xi^2 : 1), \qquad P_2 = (\sigma\xi : -\sigma\eta : 1 : b\xi^2) \qquad \text{for } \sigma = \pm 1.$$

We then see that $\sigma = 1$ implies $P_2 = P_1 + \omega_2$ whereas $\sigma = -1$ implies $P_2 = P_1 + \omega_2'$. □

3.2 Representability

Proposition 7. *The* $(2,2)$*-Jacobi quartics represent exactly all elliptic curves* E *with rational* 2*-torsion subgroup.*

Proof. Let E be a curve with three rational points of order two and the equation $\eta^2 = (\xi - r_1)(\xi - r_2)(\xi - r_3)$ and define, for any $c \in k$,

$$a = c^{-2}(r_2 + r_3 - 2r_1), \quad b = c^{-2}(r_2 - r_3), \tag{17}$$

and coordinates $(x : y : z : t)$ by

$$\begin{pmatrix} x \\ y \\ z \\ t \end{pmatrix} = \begin{pmatrix} 0 & c & 0 & 0 \\ -2r_1 & 0 & 1 & r_1(r_2+r_3) - r_2 r_3 \\ -r_2 - r_3 & 0 & 1 & r_2 r_3 \\ r_2 - r_3 & 0 & 0 & -r_1(r_2 - r_3) \end{pmatrix} \begin{pmatrix} \xi \\ \eta \\ \xi^2 \\ 1 \end{pmatrix}. \tag{18}$$

Then we see that $(x : y : z : t)$ satisfy the quadric equations (14). □

4 (2)-Jacobi Quartics

4.1 Curve Equation

The (2)-*Jacobi quartic* is the intersection of the two quadrics

$$JQ^{(2)}_{a,b}: \qquad x^2 = zt, \qquad y^2 = z^2 + 2a\,x^2 + b\,t^2. \tag{19}$$

It is smooth (and thus an elliptic curve) whenever $(a^2 - 1)b \neq 0$. For all $\lambda \in k^\times$, $JQ^{(2)}_{\lambda^2 a, \lambda^4 b}$ is isomorphic to $JQ^{(2)}_{a,b}$ by the coordinate change $(\lambda x : y : z : \lambda^2 t)$.

The addition formulæ are given by

$$\begin{aligned} x_3 &= (x_1 y_2 + y_1 x_2)(z_1 z_2 - b t_1 t_2) \\ y_3 &= (y_1 y_2 + 2a x_1 x_2)(z_1 z_2 + b t_1 t_2) + 2b x_1 x_2 (z_1 t_2 + t_1 z_2) \\ z_3 &= (z_1 z_2 - b t_1 t_2)^2 \\ t_3 &= (x_1 y_2 + y_1 x_2)^2 \end{aligned} \tag{20}$$

The factorisation trick from [HWCD09] does not apply here, thus the total point addition cost is $8\mathbf{M} + 3\mathbf{S} + \mathbf{D}_a + 2\mathbf{D}_b$.

The point $\omega_1 = (0 : 1 : 0 : -1)$ is of order two.

Proposition 8. *Let* P_1, P_2 *be two points of* $JQ^{(2)}_{a,b}$ *such that the addition formulæ (20) yield* $P_3 = (0 : 0 : 0 : 0)$*. Then* $P_1 - P_2$ *is a point of order two, distinct from* ω_1*.*

Proof. After extending the scalars to $k(\sqrt{b})$, the curve $JQ^{(2)}_{a,b}$ becomes isomorphic to $JQ^{(2,2)}_{ab,\sqrt{b}}$. The result follows from Proposition 6 on that curve. □

4.2 Representability

Proposition 9. *The* (2)*-Jacobi quartics represent exactly all elliptic curves E with at least one rational point of order two.*

Proof. Let E be a curve with one rational point of order two; then there exist $r, s, p \in k$ such that E has the equation

$$E : \eta^2 = (\xi - r)(\xi^2 - s\xi + p). \tag{21}$$

We then define

$$a = s - 2r, \quad b = s^2 - 4p, \tag{22}$$

and coordinates $(x : y : z : t)$ by

$$\begin{pmatrix} x \\ y \\ z \\ t \end{pmatrix} = \begin{pmatrix} 0 & 1 & 0 & 0 \\ -2r & 0 & 1 & rs - p \\ -s & 0 & 1 & p \\ 1 & 0 & 0 & -r \end{pmatrix} \begin{pmatrix} \xi \\ \eta \\ \xi^2 \\ 1 \end{pmatrix}. \tag{23}$$

We then see that these coordinates satisfy equations (19). □

5 Asymptotic Count of Various Elliptic Curve Models

This section gives the asymptotic probability that a random elliptic curve is represented by one of the quadric intersection models presented above.

5.1 Statistics for the Frobenius Modulo 4

We use the fact that, given an elliptic curve E over a field k of characteristic $\neq 2$, the representability of E by the Jacobi, Edwards or Huff models is determined by the conjugacy class of $\varphi_E \pmod 4$.

For any real number x, let $\mathscr{E}(x)$ be the (finite) set of all isomorphism classes of elliptic curves over finite fields $\mathbb{F}_q$ with $q \leq x$ and q odd.

Proposition 10. *Let $S \subset GL_2(\mathbb{Z}/4\mathbb{Z})$ be a conjugacy class. For any elliptic curve E over a finite field k (of characteristic $\neq 2$), let $\varphi_E \pmod 4$ be the conjugacy class of the representation of the Frobenius endomorphism of k on the 4-torsion subgroup of E.*

Then we have the asymptotic probability

$$\lim_{x \to \infty} P(\varphi_E \equiv S \pmod 4 \mid E \in \mathscr{E}(x)) = \frac{\#S}{96}.$$

Proof. Let $X(n)$ be the moduli space of elliptic curves over $\mathbb{F}_q$ equipped with a basis for the n-torsion subgroup. Then the forgetful map $X(4) \to X(1)$ is a covering with Galois group $GL_2(\mathbb{Z}/4\mathbb{Z})$. According to the Artin-Čebotarev theorem [Ser65, Theorem 7][CH11, Theorem 2] applied to this covering map, the set of elliptic curves over $\mathbb{F}_q$ with Frobenius class equal to S has a Dirichlet density equal to $\#S/\#GL_2(\mathbb{Z}/4\mathbb{Z})$. Finally, the group $GL_2(\mathbb{Z}/4\mathbb{Z})$ is an extension of $GL_2(\mathbb{F}_2)$, which is isomorphic to the symmetric group $\mathfrak{S}_3$, by the group of matrices $\equiv 0 \pmod 2$, which is isomorphic to $(\mathbb{Z}/2\mathbb{Z})^4$; thus, it is a group of order 96. □

We note that the Huff cubic $ax(y^2-1) = by(x^2-1)$ is birationally equivalent to the homogenous quadric intersection form $uz = vt$, $zt = ab(u^2+v^2) - (a^2+b^2)uv$ by the variable change $t = (a^2-b^2)$, $z = (a^2-b^2)xy$, $u = ax - by$, $v = bx - ay$.

Theorem 11. *The asymptotic proportion of elliptic curves in odd characteristic representable by twisted Edwards, Jacobi quartics, or Huff models are listed in the table below.*

Curve	q odd	$q \equiv +1 \pmod 4$	$q \equiv -1 \pmod 4$
Twisted Edwards	17/48	1/3	3/8
Jacobi quartic	5/32	7/48	1/6
$(2,2)$-Jacobi quartic	1/6	1/6	1/6
(2)-Jacobi quartic	2/3	2/3	2/3
Huff	5/48	1/12	1/8

Proof. These elliptic curve models are all characterized by a set of conjugacy classes of the Frobenius in $GL_2(\mathbb{Z}/4\mathbb{Z})$; namely:

(i) the Jacobi quartics are characterized by the list of conjugacy classes of Theorem 5;
(ii) the $(2,2)$-Jacobi quartics are exactly the curves E satisfying $\varphi_E \equiv \mathrm{id} \pmod 2$ (by Proposition 7);
(iii) the (2)-Jacobi quartics are exactly the curves such that φ_E has a fixed point modulo 2 (by Proposition 9);
(iv) the twisted Edwards curves are exactly the curves with a rational 4-torsion point [BBJ+08, Theorem 3.3], which means that φ_E has a fixed point modulo 4;
(v) the Huff curves are the curves that contain $(\mathbb{Z}/2\mathbb{Z}) \times (\mathbb{Z}/4\mathbb{Z})$ as a subgroup [JTV10, Theorem 2] and are thus the intersection of $(2,2)$-Jacobi quartics and Edwards curves.

In each case, the results follow by counting the number of such matrices in $GL_2(\mathbb{Z}/4\mathbb{Z})$. By the Hasse-Weil theorem, $q = \det(\varphi_E)$; consequently, the conditional results on $q \pmod 4$ are derived by counting the number of such matrices with the suitable determinant.

For instance, the Jacobi quartics in the case where $q \equiv +1 \pmod 4$ correspond to the conjugacy classes of $\begin{pmatrix} 1 & 0 \\ 0 & 1 \end{pmatrix}$, $\begin{pmatrix} 1 & 2 \\ 0 & 1 \end{pmatrix}$ and $\begin{pmatrix} -1 & 2 \\ 0 & -1 \end{pmatrix}$, with respective cardinalities 1, 3 and 3. Therefore, asymptotically, 7/48 of all elliptic curves with $q \equiv +1$ are isomorphic to a Jacobi quartic. □

Remark 12. If the field k is a prime field then the results about some of these families of curves may also be derived, in a similar way, from statistics about the group structure of elliptic curves [Gek06, 2.18].

5.2 Summary of Quadrics Intersections

All coordinate systems in the following list may be represented as the smooth intersection of two three-dimensional quadrics. For each, we list the cost for a point addition according to literature, the condition for representability of a curve by such a model, and the asymptotic probability that this model represents a random curve, in the sense of Theorem 11.

Curve	Condition	Cost	Probability
Twisted Edwards	$(\mathbb{Z}/4\mathbb{Z})$	$9\mathbf{M} + \mathbf{D}_a + \mathbf{D}_d$	17/48
Jacobi quartic	$(\mathbb{Z}/2\mathbb{Z})^2, \sqrt{r_1 - r_2}$	$7\mathbf{M} + 3\mathbf{S} + \mathbf{D}_a$	9/32
$(2, 2)$-Jacobi	$(\mathbb{Z}/2\mathbb{Z})^2$	$7\mathbf{M} + 3\mathbf{S} + \mathbf{D}_a + 2\mathbf{D}_b$	1/6
(2)-Jacobi	$(\mathbb{Z}/2\mathbb{Z})$	$8\mathbf{M} + 3\mathbf{S} + \mathbf{D}_a + 2\mathbf{D}_b$	2/3
Huff	$(\mathbb{Z}/4\mathbb{Z}) \times (\mathbb{Z}/2\mathbb{Z})$	$11\mathbf{M}$	5/48

References

[AG11] Ahmadi, O., Granger, R.: On isogeny classes of edwards curves over finite fields. Arxiv preprint arXiv:1103.3381 (2011)

[BBJ+08] Bernstein, D.J., Birkner, P., Joye, M., Lange, T., Peters, C.: Twisted Edwards Curves. In: Vaudenay, S. (ed.) AFRICACRYPT 2008. LNCS, vol. 5023, pp. 389–405. Springer, Heidelberg (2008), doi:10.1007/978-3-540-68164-9_26

[BJ03] Billet, O., Joye, M.: The Jacobi Model of an Elliptic Curve and Side-Channel Analysis. In: Fossorier, M., Høholdt, T., Poli, A. (eds.) AAECC 2003. LNCS, vol. 2643, pp. 34–42. Springer, Heidelberg (2003), doi:10.1007/3-540-44828-4_5

[BL07] Bernstein, D.J., Lange, T.: Inverted Edwards Coordinates. In: Boztaş, S., Lu, H.-F. (eds.) AAECC 2007. LNCS, vol. 4851, pp. 20–27. Springer, Heidelberg (2007)

[CH11] Castryck, W., Hubrechts, H.: The distribution of the number of points modulo an integer on elliptic curves over finite fields (Preprint, 2011)

[DIK06] Doche, C., Icart, T., Kohel, D.R.: Efficient Scalar Multiplication by Isogeny Decompositions. In: Yung, M., Dodis, Y., Kiayias, A., Malkin, T. (eds.) PKC 2006. LNCS, vol. 3958, pp. 191–206. Springer, Heidelberg (2006)

[Edw07] Edwards, H.M.: A normal form for elliptic curves. Bulletin-American Mathematical Society 44(3), 393–422 (2007)

[FW10] Feng, R., Wu, H.: On the isomorphism classes of legendre elliptic curves over finite fields. Arxiv preprint arXiv:1001.2871 (2010)

[Gek06] Gekeler, E.-U.: The distribution of group structures on elliptic curves over finite prime fields. Documenta Mathematica 11, 119–142 (2006)

[HWCD08] Hisil, H., Wong, K.K.-H., Carter, G., Dawson, E.: Twisted Edwards Curves Revisited. In: Pieprzyk, J. (ed.) ASIACRYPT 2008. LNCS, vol. 5350, pp. 326–343. Springer, Heidelberg (2008)

[HWCD09] Hisil, H., Wong, K.K.-H., Carter, G., Dawson, E.: Faster group operations on elliptic curves. In: Proceedings of the Seventh Australasian Conference on Information Security, AISC 2009, vol. 98, pp. 7–20. Australian Computer Society, Inc., Darlinghurst (2009)

[JTV10] Joye, M., Tibouchi, M., Vergnaud, D.: Huff's Model for Elliptic Curves. In: Hanrot, G., Morain, F., Thomé, E. (eds.) ANTS-IX. LNCS, vol. 6197, pp. 234–250. Springer, Heidelberg (2010)

[LS01] Liardet, P.-Y., Smart, N.P.: Preventing SPA/DPA in ECC Systems using the Jacobi Form. In: Koç, Ç.K., Naccache, D., Paar, C. (eds.) CHES 2001. LNCS, vol. 2162, pp. 391–401. Springer, Heidelberg (2001), doi:10.1007/3-540-44709-1_32

[Mor09] Morain, F.: Edwards curves and cm curves. Arxiv preprint arXiv:0904.2243 (2009)

[Nat00] National Institute of Standards and Technology. FIPS PUB 186-2: Digital Signature Standard (DSS) (January 2000)

[Ono94] Ono, T.: Variations on a theme of Euler: quadratic forms, elliptic curves, and Hopf maps. Plenum. Pub. Corp. (1994)

[RFS10] Farashahi, R.R., Shparlinski, I.: On the number of distinct elliptic curves in some families. Designs, Codes and Cryptography 54, 83–99 (2010), doi:10.1007/s10623-009-9310-2

[Ser65] Serre, J.-P.: Zeta and L functions. In: Proc. Conf. on Arithmetical Algebraic Geometry, Purdue Univ., pp. 82–92. Harper & Row, New York (1965)

[Sil86] Silverman, J.H.: The arithmetic of elliptic curves. Springer, Heidelberg (1986)

Improved Three-Way Split Formulas for Binary Polynomial Multiplication

Murat Cenk[1], Christophe Negre[1,2,3], and M. Anwar Hasan[1]

[1] Department of Electrical and Computer Engineering, University of Waterloo, Canada
[2] LIRMM, Université Montpellier 2, France
[3] Team DALI, Université de Perpignan, France

Abstract. In this paper we deal with 3-way split formulas for binary field multiplication with five recursive multiplications of smaller sizes. We first recall the formula proposed by Bernstein at CRYPTO 2009 and derive the complexity of a parallel multiplier based on this formula. We then propose a new set of 3-way split formulas with five recursive multiplications based on field extension. We evaluate their complexities and provide a comparison.

1 Introduction

Several cryptographic applications like those relying on elliptic curve cryptography [7,9] or Galois Counter Mode [8] require efficient finite field arithmetic. For example, ciphering a message using the ElGamal [3] scheme over an elliptic curve requires several hundreds of multiplications and additions in the finite field.

In this paper we will consider only binary fields. A binary field $\mathbb{F}_{2^n}$ can be viewed as the set of binary polynomials of degree $< n$. An addition of two elements in $\mathbb{F}_{2^n}$ consists of a bitwise XOR of the n coefficients and it can be easily implemented either in software or hardware. The multiplication is more complicated: it consists of a polynomial multiplication and a reduction modulo an irreducible polynomial. The reduction is generally quite simple since the irreducible polynomial can be chosen as a trinomial or pentanomial. The most challenging operation is thus the polynomial multiplication.

The degree n of the field $\mathbb{F}_{2^n}$ used in today's elliptic curve cryptography (ECC) is in the range of $[160, 600]$. For this size of polynomials, recursive methods like Karatsuba [6] or Toom-Cook [11,12] are considered to be most appropriate. Several parallel multipliers have been proposed based on such approaches [10,5]. They all have subquadratic arithmetic complexity, i.e., the number of bit operations is $O(n^{1+\varepsilon})$, where $0 < \varepsilon < 1$, and they are *logarithmic* in time. When such a subquadratic complexity multiplier is implemented in hardware in bit parallel fashion, well known approaches include 2-way split formulas with three recursive multiplications and 3-way split formulas with six recursive multiplications [10,5]. Recently, Bernstein in [1] has proposed a 3-way split formula with only *five* recursive multiplications.

A. Miri and S. Vaudenay (Eds.): SAC 2011, LNCS 7118, pp. 384–398, 2012.

In this paper we also deal with the 3-way splits and propose new formulas for binary polynomial multiplication with five recursive multiplications. We use the extension field $\mathbb{F}_4$ to obtain a sufficient number of elements to be able to apply the multi-evaluation (i.e., evaluation at multiple elements) and interpolation method. This leads to Toom-Cook like formulas. We study the recursive complexity of the proposed formulas and evaluate the delay of the corresponding parallel multiplier.

The remainder of this paper is organized as follows: in Section 2 we review the general method based on multi-evaluation and interpolation to obtain 3-way split formulas. We then review Bernstein's formula and evaluate a non-recursive form of its complexity. In Section 3 we present a new set of 3-way formulas based on field extension. We evaluate the complexity and the delay of a parallel multiplier based on these formulas. Complexity comparison and some concluding remarks are given in Section 4.

2 Review of 3-Way Splitting Methods for Polynomial Multiplication

In this section we review the general approach to the design of 3-way split formulas for binary polynomial multiplication. Then we review the 3-way split methods with five multiplications of [1] and study its complexity. Pertinent lemmas along with their proofs are given in Appendix A.

2.1 General Approach to Design 3-Way Split Multiplier

A classical method to derive Toom-Cook like formulas consists of applying the multi-evaluation and interpolation approach. Let us consider two degree $n-1$ polynomials $A(X) = \sum_{i=0}^{n-1} a_i X^i$ and $B(X) = \sum_{i=0}^{n-1} b_i X^i$ in $\mathcal{R}[X]$, where $\mathcal{R}$ is an arbitrary ring and n a power of 3. We split A and B in three parts: $A = \sum_{i=0}^{2} A_i X^{in/3}$ and $B = \sum_{i=0}^{2} B_i X^{in/3}$, where A_i and B_i are degree $n/3-1$ polynomials. We replace $X^{n/3}$ by the indeterminate Y in these expressions of A and B. We then fix four elements $\alpha_1, \ldots, \alpha_4 \in \mathcal{R}$ plus the infinity element $\alpha_5 = \infty$. Finally we multi-evaluate $A(Y)$ and $B(Y)$ at these five elements and we multiply term by term $A(\alpha_i)$ and $B(\alpha_i)$ for $i = 1, \ldots, 5$, which provides $C(\alpha_i)$ of $C(Y) = A(Y) \times B(Y)$ at those five elements.

These five multiplications can be computed by recursively applying the same process for degree $n/3-1$ polynomial in X. We then interpolate $C(Y)$ to obtain its polynomial expression in Y. Specifically, if we define the Lagrange polynomial as $L_i(Y) = \prod_{j=1, j\neq i}^{4} \left(\frac{Y-\alpha_j}{\alpha_i - \alpha_j}\right)$ for $i = 1, \ldots, 4$ and $L_\infty = \prod_{i=1}^{4}(Y - \alpha_i)$ then we have

$$C(Y) = \sum_{i=1}^{4} L_i(Y) C(\alpha_i) + C(\infty) L_\infty(Y).$$

We obtain the regular expression of C as a polynomial in X by replacing Y by $X^{n/3}$.

2.2 Bernstein's 3-Way Split Formula

In this subsection, first we review the 3-way split formula with five recursive multiplications presented by Bernstein in [1]. We then derive its complexity results. We consider two degree $n-1$ polynomials A and B in $\mathbb{F}_2[X]$ where n is a power of 3. We split these two polynomials in three parts and then replace $X^{n/3}$ by Y and consider them as polynomial in $\mathcal{R}[Y]$ where $\mathcal{R} = \mathbb{F}_2[X]$

$$A = A_0 + A_1 Y + A_2 Y^2 \text{ and } B = B_0 + B_1 Y + B_2 Y^2$$

with $\deg_X A_i, \deg_X B_i < n/3$. Bernstein uses a multi-evaluation and interpolation approach by evaluating the polynomials at these five elements $1, 0, X, X+1$ and ∞ of $\mathcal{R} \cup \{\infty\}$. We denote C as the product of A and B. We then define the pairwise products of the evaluations of $A(Y)$ and $B(Y)$ at $0, 1, X, X+1$ and ∞ as follows

$$\begin{aligned}
P_0 &= A_0 B_0 \quad \text{(eval. at 0)},\\
P_1 &= (A_0 + A_1 + A_2)(B_0 + B_1 + B_2) \quad \text{(eval. at 1)},\\
P_2 &= (A_0 + A_1 X + A_2 X^2)(B_0 + B_1 X + B_2 X^2) \quad \text{(eval. at } X),\\
P_3 &= \big((A_0 + A_1 + A_2) + (A_1 X + A_2 X^2)\big)\\
&\quad \times \big((B_0 + B_1 + B_2) + (B_1 X + B_2 X^2)\big) \quad \text{(eval. at } X+1),\\
P_4 &= A_2 B_2 \quad \text{(eval. at } \infty).
\end{aligned}$$

Bernstein has proposed the following expressions for the reconstruction of C:

$$\begin{aligned}
&U = P_0 + (P_0 + P_1)X \text{ and } V = P_2 + (P_2 + P_3)(X^{n/3} + X), \text{ then}\\
&C = U + P_4(X^{4n/3} + X^{n/3}) + \frac{(U + V + P_4(X^4 + X))(X^{2n/3} + X^{n/3})}{X^2 + X}.
\end{aligned} \tag{1}$$

2.3 Asymptotic Complexity of the Bernstein Method

We evaluate the complexity of the formula of Bernstein when they are applied recursively. This complexity will be expressed in terms of the number of bit addition denoted as $\mathcal{S}_{\oplus}(n)$ and the number of bit multiplication denoted $\mathcal{S}_{\otimes}(n)$. The complexities of the computation of the five products P_0, P_1, P_2, P_3 and P_4 are given in Table 7 in Appendix B. Note that the degrees of R_3, R_3', R_4 and R_4' are all equal to $n/3+1$, while the degrees of A_0, B_0, A_2, B_2, R_1 and R_1' are equal to $n/3-1$. Consequently, the products P_0, P_1 and P_4 have their degree equal to $(2n/3-2)$ and the degrees of P_2 and P_3 are equal to $(2n/3+2)$.

The formulas in Table 7 can be applied only once since the five products involve polynomials of degree $n/3-1$ and $n/3+1$. In order to have a fully recursive method, we express the product of degree $n/3+1$ polynomials in terms of one product of degree $n/3-1$ polynomial plus some additional non-recursive computations.

For this purpose, we consider $P = \sum_{i=0}^{n/3+1} p_i X^i$ and $Q = \sum_{i=0}^{n/3+1} q_i X^i$. We first rewrite P as $P = P' + (p_{n/3}X^{n/3} + p_{n/3+1}X^{n/3+1})$ and $Q = Q' + (q_{n/3}X^{n/3} + q_{n/3+1}X^{n/3+1})$ and then if we expand the product PQ we obtain

$$PQ = \underbrace{P'Q'}_{M_1} + \underbrace{(p_{n/3}X^{n/3} + p_{n/3+1}X^{n/3+1})Q'}_{M_2} + \underbrace{(q_{n/3}X^{n/3} + q_{n/3+1}X^{n/3+1})P'}_{M_3} + \underbrace{(p_{n/3}X^{n/3} + p_{n/3+1}X^{n/3+1})(q_{n/3}X^{n/3} + q_{n/3+1}X^{n/3+1})}_{M_4}. \quad (2)$$

The product M_1 can be performed recursively since P' and Q' are of degree $n/3-1$ each. The other products M_2, M_3 and M_4 can be computed separately and then added to M_1. The computation of M_2 and M_3 is not difficult, each consisting of $2n/3$ bit multiplications and $n/3-1$ bit additions. We compute the product M_4 as follows

$$M_4 = p_{n/3}q_{n/3}X^{2n/3} + (p_{n/3+1}q_{n/3} + p_{n/3}q_{n/3+1})X^{2n/3+1} + p_{n/3+1}q_{n/3+1}X^{2n/3+2}$$

and this requires one bit additions and four bit multiplications. Finally, the complexities $\mathcal{S}_\oplus(n/3)$ and $\mathcal{S}_\otimes(n/3)$ consist of the complexity of each product M_i plus $2n/3+1$ bit additions for the sum of these five products. This results in the following complexity:

$$\begin{cases} \mathcal{S}_\oplus(n/3+2) = \mathcal{S}_\oplus(n/3) + 4n/3, \\ \mathcal{S}_\otimes(n/3+2) = \mathcal{S}_\otimes(n/3) + 4n/3 + 4. \end{cases} \quad (3)$$

Explicit computations of the reconstruction. We now review the sequence of computation proposed by Bernstein in [1] for the reconstruction. This sequence first computes the two polynomials U and V defined in (1) and then computes C. The details are given in Table 8 in Appendix B.

With regard to the division of $W = (U + V + P_4(X^4 + X))(X^{2n/3} + X^{n/3})$ by $X^2 + X$ in the reconstruction (1) (i.e., the computation of W' in Table 8), we remark that W is of degree n, so we can write $W = w_nX^n + \ldots + w_1X + w_0$. Since $X^2 + X = X(X+1)$, the division can be performed in two steps: first we divide W by X which consists of a shift of the coefficients of W and then we divide $W/X = w_nX^{n-1} + \ldots + w_1$ by $X+1$. The result $W' = W/(X^2+X)$ has its coefficients defined as follows:

$$w'_{n-j} = w_n + w_{n-1} + \cdots + w_{n-j+2}.$$

These computations require $n-2$ bit additions: we perform sequentially the additions $w'_i = w'_{i+1} + w_{i+2}$ starting from $w'_{n-2} = w_n$. The corresponding delay is then equal to $(n-2)D_\oplus$ where $D_\oplus$ is the delay of a bit addition.

Overall Arithmetic Complexity Now we evaluate the overall complexity of Bernstein's method (Table 7 and 8 in Appendix B). By adding the number of bit additions listed in the two tables in Appendix B we obtain $\mathcal{S}_\oplus(n) = 3\mathcal{S}_\oplus(n/3) + 2\mathcal{S}_\oplus(n/3+2) + 35n/3 - 12$ and for the bit multiplication we have $\mathcal{S}_\otimes(n) = 3\mathcal{S}_\otimes(n/3) + 2\mathcal{S}_\otimes(n/3+2)$. In order to obtain a recursive expression of the complexity, we replace $\mathcal{S}_\oplus(n/3+2)$ and $\mathcal{S}_\otimes(n/3+2)$ by their corresponding expression in terms of $\mathcal{S}_\oplus(n/3)$ and $\mathcal{S}_\otimes(n/3)$ given in (3). We then obtain the following:

$$\mathcal{C} = \begin{cases} \mathcal{S}_\oplus(n) = 5\mathcal{S}_\oplus(n/3) - \frac{43n}{3} - 12, \\ \mathcal{S}_\otimes(n) = 5\mathcal{S}_\otimes(n/3) + \frac{8n}{3} + 8. \end{cases}$$

Then we apply Lemma 1 from Appendix A and we obtain the following:

$$\mathcal{C} = \begin{cases} \mathcal{S}_{\oplus}(n) = \frac{37}{2}n^{\log_3(5)} - \frac{43n}{2} + 3, \\ \mathcal{S}_{\otimes}(n) = 7n^{\log_3(5)} - 4n - 2. \end{cases} \quad (4)$$

Delay of parallel computation based on Bernstein's method Here we evaluate the delay of a parallel multiplier based on Bernstein's formula. We will denote $\mathcal{D}(n)$ the delay required for a multiplication of two degree $n-1$ polynomial where n is a power of 3. The delay will be expressed in terms of the delay of bit addition denoted as $D_{\oplus}$ and the delay of bit multiplication denoted as $D_{\otimes}$. For this, we have drawn a data-flow graph of the multi-evaluation and the reconstruction part of the computation. These graphs are shown in Figure 1, from which we remark that the critical path delay is $\mathcal{D}(n/3) + (n+8)D_{\oplus}$. For example, this is the delay of the critical path which starts from A_0 or A_1 exiting at R_4 in the multi-evaluation, then goes through a multiplier of polynomial of degree $n/3+1$ which has a delay of $\mathcal{D}(n/3)+1$ (cf. (2)), and finally enters the reconstruction in P_3 and ends at C. Since we have assumed that n is a power of 3, we transform

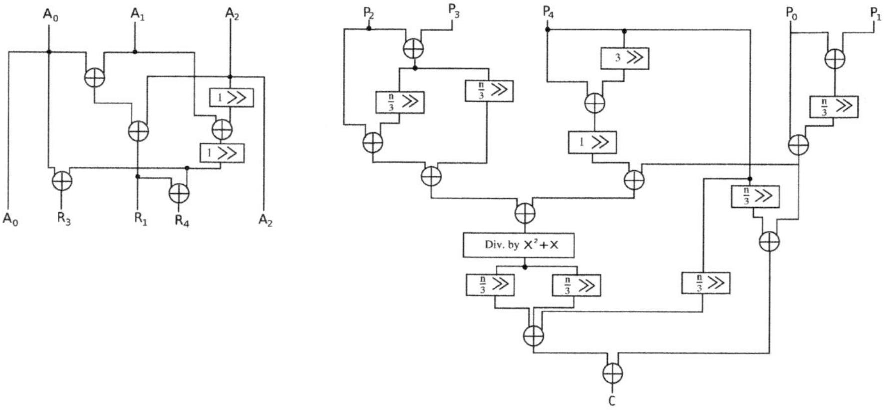

Fig. 1. Multi-evaluation (left) and reconstruction (right) data flow

$\mathcal{D}(n) = \mathcal{D}(n/3) + (n+8)D_{\oplus}$ into a non-recursive expression, by applying it recursively and using $\mathcal{D}(1) = D_{\otimes}$.

$$\begin{aligned} \mathcal{D}(n) &= (n+8)D_{\oplus} + (n/3+8)D_{\oplus} + (n/9+8)D_{\oplus} + \ldots + (3+8)D_{\oplus} + D_{\otimes} \\ &= (8\log_3(n) + \tfrac{3n}{2} - \tfrac{3}{2})D_{\oplus} + D_{\otimes}. \end{aligned} \quad (5)$$

3 Three-Way Formulas Based on Field Extension

In this section we present an approach based on field extension which provides 3-way split formulas with five recursive multiplications. We consider two binary polynomials $A = \sum_{i=0}^{n-1} a_i X^i$ and $B = \sum_{i=0}^{n-1} b_i X^i$ with $n = 3^\ell$. As before, we split A and B in three parts $A = A_0 + A_1X^{n/3} + A_2X^{2n/3}$ and $B = B_0 + B_1X^{n/3} + B_2X^{2n/3}$ where A_i and B_i have degree $< n/3$. We would like to use the approach based on multi-evaluation at five elements reviewed in Subsection 2.1. The problem we faced is that there are not enough elements in $\mathbb{F}_2$: we can only evaluate at the two elements of $\mathbb{F}_2$ and at infinity. Bernstein used the two elements X and $X+1$ in order to overcome this problem. We use here a different approach: in order to evaluate at two more elements we will consider the method proposed in [2,12] which uses a field extension. Specifically, we consider an extension $\mathbb{F}_4 = \mathbb{F}_2[\alpha]/(\alpha^2+\alpha+1)$ of degree 2 of $\mathbb{F}_2$. Afterwards, we evaluate the polynomials at 0, 1, α, $\alpha+1$ and ∞. The resulting evaluations and recursive multiplication are given below:

$$\begin{array}{lll} P_0 = A_0B_0 & \text{in } \mathbb{F}_2[X], \\ P_1 = (A_0+A_1+A_2)(B_0+B_1+B_2) & \text{in } \mathbb{F}_2[X], \\ P_2 = (A_0+A_2+\alpha(A_1+A_2))(B_0+B_2+\alpha(B_1+B_2)), & \text{in } \mathbb{F}_4[X], \\ P_3 = (A_0+A_1+\alpha(A_1+A_2))(B_0+B_1+\alpha(B_1+B_2)), & \text{in } \mathbb{F}_4[X], \\ P_4 = A_2B_2 & \text{in } \mathbb{F}_2[X]. \end{array} \quad (6)$$

The reconstruction of $C = A \times B$ uses the classical Lagrange interpolation. An arranged form of this interpolation is given below

$$\begin{array}{l} C = (P_0 + X^{n/3}P_4)(1+X^n) + (P_1 + (1+\alpha)(P_2+P_3))(X^{n/3}+X^{2n/3}+X^n) \\ \quad +\alpha(P_2+P_3)X^n + P_2X^{2n/3} + P_3X^{n/3} \end{array} \quad (7)$$

Note that if we evaluate a binary polynomial at $0, 1$ or ∞ we obtain a polynomial in $\mathbb{F}_2[X]$ and on the other hand if we evaluate the same polynomial at α or $\alpha+1$ we obtain a polynomial in $\mathbb{F}_4[X]$. These multiplications are performed recursively by splitting and evaluating at the same set of points recursively. We will give a sequence of computations for (6) and (7) dealing with the two following cases: the first case is when the formulas are applied to A and B in $\mathbb{F}_4[X]$ and the second case is when A and B are in $\mathbb{F}_2[X]$.

3.1 Explicit 3-Way Splitting Formulas

In this subsection, we provide a sequence of computations for (6) and (7) when A and B are taken in $\mathbb{F}_4[X]$ or in $\mathbb{F}_2[X]$. We split the computations of (6) and (7) in the three different steps . We first give the formulas for the multi-evaluation, then for the products and finally for the reconstruction.

Multi-evaluation formulas. The proposed steps to compute the multi-evaluation of A and B are detailed in Table 1. The formulas are the same for polynomials in $\mathbb{F}_4[X]$ and in $\mathbb{F}_2[X]$. The only difference between these two cases is the cost of each computation. For the evaluation of the cost of each operation in $\mathbb{F}_4[X]$ we have used the following facts:

- A sum of two elements of $\mathbb{F}_4$ is given by $(a_0+a_1\alpha)+(b_0+b_1\alpha) = (a_0 + b_0) + (a_1+b_1)\alpha$ and requires 2 bit additions. Consequently, the sum of two degree $d-1$ polynomials in $\mathbb{F}_4[X]$ requires $2d$ bit addition.

Table 1. Cost of multi-evaluation for the new three-way split formulas

Computations		Cost in $\mathbb{F}_4$	Cost in $\mathbb{F}_2$
		$\#\oplus$	$\#\oplus$
$R_1 = A_0 + A_1$,	$R'_1 = B_0 + B_1$	$4n/3$	$2n/3$
$R_2 = A_1 + A_2$,	$R'_2 = B_1 + B_2$	$4n/3$	$2n/3$
$R_3 = \alpha R_2$,	$R'_3 = \alpha R'_2$	$2n/3$	0
$R_4 = R_1 + R_3$ $(= A(\alpha+1))$,	$R'_4 = R'_1 + R'_3$	$4n/3$	0
$R_5 = R_4 + R_2$ $(= A(\alpha))$,	$R'_5 = R'_4 + R'_2$	$4n/3$	$2n/3$
$R_6 = R_1 + A_2$ $(= A(1))$,	$R'_6 = R'_1 + B_2$	$4n/3$	$2n/3$
Total		$22n/3$	$8n/3$

Table 2. Cost of products for the new three-way split formulas

Computations	Cost in $\mathbb{F}_4$		Cost in $\mathbb{F}_2$	
	$\#\oplus$	$\#\otimes$	$\#\oplus$	$\#\otimes$
$P_0 = A_0B_0$	$S_{\mathbb{F}_4,\oplus}(n/3)$	$S_{\mathbb{F}_4,\otimes}(n/3)$	$S_{\mathbb{F}_2,\oplus}(n/3)$	$S_{\mathbb{F}_2,\otimes}(n/3)$
$P_1 = R_6R'_6$	$S_{\mathbb{F}_4,\oplus}(n/3)$	$S_{\mathbb{F}_4,\otimes}(n/3)$	$S_{\mathbb{F}_2,\oplus}(n/3)$	$S_{\mathbb{F}_2,\otimes}(n/3)$
$P_2 = R_5R'_5$	$S_{\mathbb{F}_4,\oplus}(n/3)$	$S_{\mathbb{F}_4,\otimes}(n/3)$	$S_{\mathbb{F}_4,\oplus}(n/3)$	$S_{\mathbb{F}_4,\otimes}(n/3)$
$P_3 = R_4R'_4$	$S_{\mathbb{F}_4,\oplus}(n/3)$	$S_{\mathbb{F}_4,\otimes}(n/3)$	$S_{\mathbb{F}_4,\oplus}(n/3)$	$S_{\mathbb{F}_4,\otimes}(n/3)$
$P_4 = A_2B_2$	$S_{\mathbb{F}_4,\oplus}(n/3)$	$S_{\mathbb{F}_4,\otimes}(n/3)$	$S_{\mathbb{F}_2,\oplus}(n/3)$	$S_{\mathbb{F}_2,\otimes}(n/3)$
Total	$5S_{\mathbb{F}_4,\oplus}(\frac{n}{3})$	$5S_{\mathbb{F}_4,\otimes}(\frac{n}{3})$	$3S_{\mathbb{F}_2,\oplus}(\frac{n}{3}) + 2S_{\mathbb{F}_4,\oplus}(\frac{n}{3})$	$3S_{\mathbb{F}_2,\otimes}(\frac{n}{3}) + 2S_{\mathbb{F}_4,\oplus}(\frac{n}{3})$

- The multiplication of an element $a = a_0 + a_1\alpha$ in $\mathbb{F}_4$ by α: it is given by $a\alpha = a_1 + (a_0 + a_1)\alpha$ and thus requires one bit additions. This implies that the multiplication of a degree $d-1$ polynomial of $\mathbb{F}_4[X]$ by α requires d bit additions.

When A and B are taken in $\mathbb{F}_2[X]$, we use the following facts to save some computations

- Since the additions performed for R_1, R_2, R'_1 and R'_2 involve polynomials in $\mathbb{F}_2[X]$ with degree $n/3-1$, they all require $n/3$ bit additions.
- For R_3 (resp. R'_3), the multiplication of R_2 (resp. R'_2) by α is free since the coefficients of the polynomial R_2 (resp. R'_2) are in $\mathbb{F}_2$.
- The addition in R_4 (resp. R'_4) involves a polynomial with coefficients in $\mathbb{F}_2$ and a polynomial with coefficients in $\alpha\mathbb{F}_2$; it is thus free of any bit operation.
- The operation in each of R_5, R'_5, R_6 and R'_6 is an addition of polynomial in $\mathbb{F}_2[X]$ with a polynomial in $\mathbb{F}_4[X]$ and thus no bit additions are required for the coefficient corresponding to α.

Using these facts and also using that A_i and B_i are degree $n/3-1$ polynomials and P_i is a degree $2n/3-2$ polynomial, we evaluate each step of Table 1 and then deduce the complexity of the multi-evaluation by adding the cost of each step.

Recursive products. In Table 2 we give the cost of the five recursive products. In the case of a multiplication in $\mathbb{F}_4[X]$, all the polynomials are in $\mathbb{F}_4[X]$ and

Table 3. Three-way split formulas - Reconstruction

Reconstruction in $\mathbb{F}_4$ Computations	#⊕
$U_1 = P_2 + P_3$	$4n/3 - 2$
$U_2 = \alpha U_1 \quad (= \alpha(P_2 + P_3))$	$2n/3 - 1$
$U_3 = (1+\alpha)U_1 \quad (= (1+\alpha)(P_2 + P_3))$	0
$U_4 = P_1 + U_3 \quad (= P_1 + (1+\alpha)(P_2 + P_3))$	$4n/3 - 2$
$U_5 = U_4(X^{n/3} + X^{2n/3} + X^{3n/3})$	$4n/3 - 4$
$U_6 = P_0 + X^{n/3}P_4 \quad (= P_0 + X^{n/3}P_4)$	$2n/3 - 2$
$U_7 = U_6(1 + X^n) \quad (= P_0 + X^{n/3}P_4)(1 + X^n))$	0
$C = U_7 + U_5 + X^nU_2$ $+P_2X^{2n/3} + P_3X^{n/3}$	$20n/3 - 10$
Total	$36n/3 - 21$

Reconstruction in $\mathbb{F}_2$ Computations	#⊕
$U_1 = P_2 + P_3$	$4n/3 - 2$
$U_2 = [\alpha U_1]_{cte}$	0
$U_3 = [(1+\alpha)U_1]_{cte}$	$2n/3 - 1$
$U_4 = [P_1 + U_3]_{cte}$	$2n/3 - 1$
$U_5 = [U_4(X^{n/3} + X^{2n/3} + X^{3n/3})]_{cte}$	$2n/3 - 2$
$U_6 = [P_0 + X^{n/3}P_4]_{cte}$	$n/3 - 1$
$U_7 = [U_6(1 + X^n)]_{cte}$	0
$C = [U_7 + U_5 + X^nU_2]_{cte}$ $+P_2X^{2n/3} + P_3X^{n/3}]_{cte}$	$10n/3 - 5$
Total	$21n/3 - 12$

thus the cost of the recursive products are $\mathcal{S}_{\mathbb{F}_4,\oplus}(n/3)$ and $\mathcal{S}_{\mathbb{F}_4,\otimes}(n/3)$. For the multiplication in $\mathbb{F}_2[X]$, there are three products which involve polynomials in $\mathbb{F}_2[X]$ incurring a cost of $\mathcal{S}_{\mathbb{F}_2,\oplus}(n/3)$ and $\mathcal{S}_{\mathbb{F}_2,\otimes}(n/3)$; the two other products are in $\mathbb{F}_4[X]$ and thus the corresponding cost is $\mathcal{S}_{\mathbb{F}_4,\oplus}(n/3)$ and $\mathcal{S}_{\mathbb{F}_4,\otimes}(n/3)$.

Reconstruction. In Table 3 we give the sequence of computations for the reconstruction of the product C. For the computation in $\mathbb{F}_4[X]$, we evaluate the cost of each computation by using the same facts as in the multi-evaluation computations. For the computation in $\mathbb{F}_2$, since the resulting polynomial C is in $\mathbb{F}_2[X]$ we can save some computations. We use the following facts:

- P_3 and P_4 are degree $2n/3 - 2$ polynomials in $\mathbb{F}_4[X]$.
- P_1, P_2 and P_5 are degree $2n/3 - 2$ polynomials in $\mathbb{F}_2[X]$; so we don't need to add their bits corresponding to α.
- The polynomial C is in $\mathbb{F}_2[X]$; consequently, we do not need to compute the coefficients corresponding to α. Indeed, if $a = a_0 + a_1\alpha$ and $b = b_0 + b_1\alpha$ we denote $[a + b]_{cte} = a_0 + b_0$ which requires only one bit addition. We use the same notation for the polynomials.

3.2 Complexity Evaluation

We now evaluate the complexity of the formulas given in Tables 1, 2 and 3. We first evaluate the complexity for a multiplication in $\mathbb{F}_4[X]$.

Complexity of the formulas in $\mathbb{F}_4[X]$ We obtain the following complexities in terms of the number of bit additions and multiplications

$$\begin{cases} \mathcal{S}_{\mathbb{F}_4,\oplus}(n) = 5\mathcal{S}_{\mathbb{F}_4,\oplus}(n/3) + 58n/3 - 21, \\ \mathcal{S}_{\mathbb{F}_4,\otimes}(n) = 5\mathcal{S}_{\mathbb{F}_4,\otimes}(n/3). \end{cases} \tag{8}$$

Now, in order to derive a non-recursive expression of the complexity, we need to know the cost of a multiplication in $\mathbb{F}_4$. There are two ways to perform such multiplication:

- The first method computes the product of $a = a_0 + a_1\alpha$ and $b = b_0 + b_1\alpha$ as follows:

$$(a_0 + a_1\alpha) \times (b_0 + b_1\alpha) = a_0b_0 + (a_0b_1 + a_1b_0)\alpha + a_1b_1(1 + \alpha).$$

  This requires 3 bit additions and 4 bit multiplications.
- The second method computes the product of $a = a_0 + a_1\alpha$ and $b = b_0 + b_1\alpha$ as follows:

$$(a_0 + a_1\alpha) \times (b_0 + b_1\alpha) = (a_0 + a_1)(b_0 + b_1)\alpha + (a_0b_0 + a_1b_1)(1 + \alpha).$$

  This requires 4 bit additions and 3 bit multiplications.

The choice among these methods depends on the relative cost of a bit addition compared to that of a bit multiplication. If the bit multiplication is cheaper, then the first method is advantageous, otherwise it is the second method.

Using Lemma 1 for (8) with the initial condition $\mathcal{S}_{\mathbb{F}_4,\oplus}(1) = 3$ and $\mathcal{S}_{\mathbb{F}_4,\otimes}(1) = 4$, the first method leads to the complexity $\mathcal{C}$ below. Similarly, using Lemma 1 for (8) with the initial condition $\mathcal{S}_{\mathbb{F}_4,\oplus}(1) = 4$ and $\mathcal{S}_{\mathbb{F}_4,\otimes}(1) = 3$, the second method leads to the complexity $\mathcal{C}'$ below.

$$\mathcal{C} = \begin{cases} \mathcal{S}_{\mathbb{F}_4,\oplus}(n) = \frac{107}{4}n^{\log_3(5)} - 29n + \frac{21}{4}, \\ \mathcal{S}_{\mathbb{F}_4,\otimes}(n) = 4n^{\log_3(5)}. \end{cases} \mathcal{C}' = \begin{cases} \mathcal{S}_{\mathbb{F}_4,\oplus}(n) = \frac{111}{4}n^{\log_3(5)} - 29n + \frac{21}{4}, \\ \mathcal{S}_{\mathbb{F}_4,\otimes}(n) = 3n^{\log_3(5)}. \end{cases} \tag{9}$$

Complexity of recursive 3-way splitting multiplication in $\mathbb{F}_2[X]$ We evaluate now the overall complexity of the proposed three-way split formulas for polynomials in $\mathbb{F}_2[X]$. If we add the complexity results given in Tables 1, 2 and 3, we obtain the number of bit additions and bit multiplications expressed in terms of $\mathcal{S}_{\mathbb{F}_4,\oplus}(n/3)$ and $\mathcal{S}_{\mathbb{F}_2,\oplus}(n/3)$ as follows

$$\begin{aligned} \mathcal{S}_{\mathbb{F}_2,\oplus}(n) &= 2\mathcal{S}_{\mathbb{F}_4,\oplus}(n/3) + 3\mathcal{S}_{\mathbb{F}_2,\oplus}(n/3) + 29n/3 - 12, \\ \mathcal{S}_{\mathbb{F}_2,\otimes}(n) &= 2\mathcal{S}_{\mathbb{F}_4,\otimes}(n/3) + 3\mathcal{S}_{\mathbb{F}_2,\otimes}(n/3). \end{aligned} \tag{10}$$

We now derive a non-recursive expression from the previous equation. This is done in two steps: we first replace $\mathcal{S}_{\mathbb{F}_4,\otimes}(n/3)$ and $\mathcal{S}_{\mathbb{F}_4,\oplus}(n/3)$ by their corresponding non-recursive expression, then we solve the resulting recursive expression of $\mathcal{S}_{\mathbb{F}_2,\oplus}(n)$ and $\mathcal{S}_{\mathbb{F}_2,\otimes}(n)$. We can replace $\mathcal{S}_{\mathbb{F}_4,\otimes}(n/3)$ and $\mathcal{S}_{\mathbb{F}_4,\oplus}(n/3)$ by the non-recursive expressions $\mathcal{C}$ or $\mathcal{C}'$ given in (9). To this effort, since these computations are essentially identical, we only treat in detail the computation of $\mathcal{S}_{\mathbb{F}_4,\oplus}(n/3)$. In (10), we replace $\mathcal{S}_{\mathbb{F}_4,\oplus}(n/3)$ by its expression given in (9) and we obtain $\mathcal{S}_{\mathbb{F}_2,\oplus}(n) = 3\mathcal{S}_{\mathbb{F}_2,\oplus}(n/3) + \frac{107}{10}n^{\log_3(5)} - \frac{29}{3}n - 3/2$. Then a direct application of Lemma 2 from Appendix A yields a non-recursive expression as follows: $\mathcal{S}_{\mathbb{F}_2,\oplus}(n) = \frac{107}{4}n^{\log_3(5)} - \frac{29}{3}n\log_3(n) - \frac{55n}{2} + \frac{3}{4}$.

We then apply the same method to other complexities. Below we list the final non-recursive expression for each case.

$$\mathcal{C} = \begin{cases} \mathcal{S}_{\mathbb{F}_2,\oplus}(n) = \frac{107}{4}n^{\log_3(5)} - \frac{29}{3}n\log_3(n) \\ \qquad\qquad -\frac{55n}{2} + \frac{3}{4} \\ \mathcal{S}_{\mathbb{F}_2,\otimes}(n) = 4n^{\log_3(5)} - 3n \end{cases}$$
$$\mathcal{C}' = \begin{cases} \mathcal{S}_{\mathbb{F}_2,\oplus}(n) = \frac{111}{4}n^{\log_3(5)} - \frac{29}{3}n\log_3(n) \\ \qquad\qquad -\frac{57n}{2} + \frac{3}{4} \\ \mathcal{S}_{\mathbb{F}_2,\otimes}(n) = = 3n^{\log_3(5)} - 2n \end{cases} \tag{11}$$

3.3 Delay Evaluation

We evaluate the delay of the 3-way split multiplier by drawing the data flow of the 3-way multiplier in $\mathbb{F}_4[X]$ and in $\mathbb{F}_2[X]$. The sequence of operations for these two cases ($\mathbb{F}_4$ and $\mathbb{F}_2$) are essentially the same: their only difference is on the reconstruction: in the $\mathbb{F}_2[X]$ multiplication the operations are restricted to $\mathbb{F}_2$. The data flow shown in Figure 2 is valid for both cases. We now evaluate the critical path delay for the multiplication in $\mathbb{F}_4[X]$ and then for the multiplication in $\mathbb{F}_4[X]$.

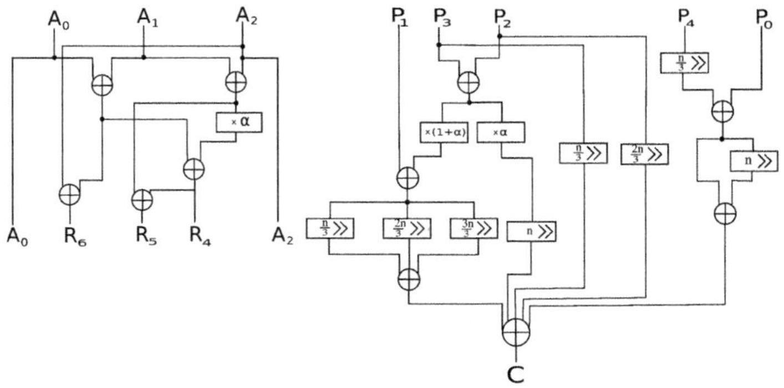

Fig. 2. Multi-evaluation (left) and reconstruction (right) data flow

Delay of the multiplier in $\mathbb{F}_4[X]$. The critical path is made of the following three parts:

- The critical path in the multi-evaluation data-flow begins in A_2, goes through three $\oplus$'s and one multiplication by α and then ends in R_1. Since a multiplication by α consists of one bit addition, the delay of this critical path is $4D_{\oplus}$.
- The path goes through a multiplier for degree $n/3-1$ polynomials with a delay of $\mathcal{D}_{\mathbb{F}_4}(n/3)$.
- Finally, in the reconstruction part, the path enters the reconstruction in P_2 and goes through one multiplication by $(1+\alpha)$ and three additions and then in a multi-input $\oplus$. A careful observation of this last multi-input addition shows that the delay in terms of the 2-input $\oplus$ gate is $2D_{\oplus}$. Consequently, the critical path delay of this part is $6D_{\oplus}$.

By summing up the above three delay components, we obtain a recursive expression of the delay as $\mathcal{D}_{\mathbb{F}_4}(n) = 10D_X + \mathcal{D}_{\mathbb{F}_4}(n/3)$. After solving this inductive relation, we obtain the following non-recursive expression:

$$\mathcal{D}_{\mathbb{F}_4}(n) = (10\log_3(n) + 2)D_{\oplus} + D_{\otimes}. \tag{12}$$

Delay of the multiplier in $\mathbb{F}_2[X]$. The critical path is the same as the critical path for the multiplication in $\mathbb{F}_4[X]$. The only difference is that the multiplication by α and $(1+\alpha)$ does not give any delay since it consists of some permutation of the coefficients. Consequently, the recursive expression of the delay is $\mathcal{D}_{\mathbb{F}_2}(n) = 8D_X + \mathcal{D}_{\mathbb{F}_4}(n/3)$ and this yields the corresponding non-recursive expression to be

$$\mathcal{D}_{\mathbb{F}_2}(n) = 10\log_3(n)D_{\oplus} + D_{\otimes}. \tag{13}$$

4 Complexity Comparison and Conclusion

In this paper, we have first reviewed Bernstein's recently proposed formula for polynomial multiplication using the 3-way split that requires five recursive multiplications. We have carefully evaluated its cost and have provided a non-recursive form of its complexity. We have then presented a new set of 3-way split formulas for binary polynomial multiplication based on field extension. For the proposed formulas, we have computed two non-recursive forms of the complexity: one minimizes the number of bit additions and the other minimizes the number of bit multiplications. We have also evaluated the time delays of parallel multipliers based on the proposed formulas.

Assuming that n is a power of three, the resulting complexities of Bernstein's and the proposed formulas are reported in Table 4. As it can be seen from Table 4, in the asymptotic sense, the ratio of the total number of bit level operations (addition and multiplication combined) of the Bernstein formula and that of either of the proposed formulas is close to $\frac{(18.5+7)}{(26.75+4)} \cong 0.82$. We can also remark that the proposed method are less expensive in term of bit addition, consequently if the cost of a bit multiplication is twice the cost of a bit addition then the complexity of the proposed method become smaller than the one of Bernstein approach. On the other hand, when those formulas are applied to parallel implementation for polynomial multipliers, Bernstein's formula leads to a time delay linear in n, while the proposed ones are logarithmic.

Table 4. Complexities of the three approaches considered in this article

Algorithm	$\mathcal{S}_{\oplus}(n)$	$\mathcal{S}_{\otimes}(n)$	Delay
Bernstein [1]) ($\mathcal{C}$ in (4)	$18.5n^{\log_3(5)} - 21.5n + 3$	$7n^{\log_3(5)} - 4n - 2$	$(1.5n + 8\log_3(n) - 1.5)D_{\oplus}$ $+D_{\otimes}$
$\mathcal{C}$ from (11)	$26.75n^{\log_3(5)} - 9.67n\log_3(n)$ $-27.5n + 0.75$	$4n^{\log_3(5)} - 3n$	$10\log_3(n)D_{\oplus} + D_{\otimes}$
$\mathcal{C}'$ from (11)	$27.75n^{\log_3(5)} - 9.67n\log_3(n)$ $-28.5n + 0.75$	$3n^{\log_3(5)} - 2n$	$10\log_3(n)D_{\oplus} + D_{\otimes}$

Improvement for multiplication of polynomials of size $n = 2^i \cdot 3^j$. Our proposed method can also be used to design efficient multipliers for more generic values of n. To illustrate this point, we now consider the situation where we want to perform $A \times B$ where A and B are of degree $n-1$ where $n = 2 \cdot 3^j$. A direct approach to perform this operation consists of first applying the Karatsuba formula which breaks this multiplication into three multiplications of polynomials of degree $3^j - 1$. If these three multiplications are performed using Bernstein's approach, then the cost of $A \times B$ is 3 times the complexity of one instance of Bernstein's approach plus $7n/2 - 3$ bit additions for Karatsuba.

This can be done more efficiently as follows. We perform this multiplication by first splitting the two polynomials in two parts $A = A_0 + X^{n/2}A_1$ and $B = B_0 + X^{n/2}B_1$. We then perform $A_0 \times (B_0 + \alpha B_1)$ and $A_1 \times (B_0 + \alpha B_1)$ using the proposed formulas for multiplication in $\mathbb{F}_4[X]$ of Subsection 3.1. This provides the four products A_iB_j for $i, j \in \{0, 1\}$. The product $C = A \times B$ is then reconstructed as $C = A_0C_0 + X^{n/2}(A_0B_1 + A_1B_0) + B_1A_1X^n$. The cost of this approach is thus two times the cost a degree $n/3 - 1$ multiplications in $\mathbb{F}_4[X]$ plus $2n$ bit additions for the reconstruction. The resulting complexities are reported in Table 5.

Table 5. Complexities of a multiplication of polynomials of size $n = 2 \cdot 3^j$

Method	$\mathcal{S}_{\oplus}(n)$	$\mathcal{S}_{\otimes}(n)$
Karatsuba and Bernstein [1] ($\mathcal{C}$ in (4))	$20.1n^{\log_3(5)} - 35.75n + 6$	$7.6n^{\log_3(5)} - 6n - 6$
With $\mathcal{C}$ from Subsection 3.1	$19.37n^{\log_3(5)} - 29n + 10.5$	$2.17n^{\log_3(5)} - 3n$
With $\mathcal{C}'$ from Subsection 3.1	$20.1n^{\log_3(5)} - 29n + 10.5$	$2.89n^{\log_3(5)} - 2n$

Explicit complexity for polynomial multiplication with practical size. In Table 6 we give complexity results of polynomial multiplication for $n = 2^i \cdot 3^j$ with cryptographic sizes, specifically, in the range $[160, 500]$. The complexities correspond to the combination of Karatsuba (cf [1]) and the formula of Bernstein or the proposed formulas. To get the complexity based on the proposed formulas in the special case where $i \geq 1$ and $j \geq 1$, we apply Karatsuba recursively up to obtain polynomials of size $2 \cdot 3^j$ and then we apply the strategy presented above to multiply such polynomials. The resulting complexity shows that, for $j \geq 1$ in $n = 2^i \times 3^j$, our approach yields better space and time complexities for the considered fields. The fact that our space complexity is better is due to the terms $-9.67n\log_3(n))$ in $\mathcal{C}$ and $\mathcal{C}'$ in (11) which are non-negligible for the above-mentioned sizes of polynomials.

Table 6. Complexities for polynomial multiplication of size $n = 2^i \cdot 3^j \in [160, 500]$

Method	$162 = 2 \cdot 3^4$			$192 = 2^6 \cdot 3$			$216 = 2^3 \cdot 3^3$		
	#AND	#XOR	Del.	#AND	#XOR	Del.	#AND	#XOR	Del.
Karat. and Bern. [1]	12147	30036	155	15309	35472	29	20655	50397	72
Karat. and $\mathcal{C}$ in (11)	4757	26217	43	7533	30126	28	8271	42765	39
Karat. and $\mathcal{C}'$ in (11)	3588	27386	43	5832	31827	28	6264	44772	39

Method	$243 = 3^5$			$256 = 2^8$			$288 = 2^5 \cdot 3^2$		
	#AND	#XOR	Del.	#AND	#XOR	Del.	#AND	#XOR	Del.
Karat. and Bern. [1]	20901	52591	403	6561	34295	24	33291	79026	43
Karat. and $\mathcal{C}$ in (11)	11771	65167	50	6561	34295	24	14013	65661	35
Karat. and $\mathcal{C}'$ in (11)	8889	68049	50	6561	34295	24	10692	68982	35

Method	$324 = 2^2 \cdot 3^4$			$384 = 2^7 \cdot 3^1$			$432 = 2^4 \cdot 3^3$		
	#AND	#XOR	Del.	#AND	#XOR	Del.	#AND	#XOR	Del.
Karat. and Bern. [1]	36441	91239	158	45927	107757	32	61965	152700	75
Karat. and $\mathcal{C}$ in (11)	14271	79782	46	22599	91719	31	24813	129804	42
Karat. and $\mathcal{C}'$ in (11)	10764	83289	46	17496	96822	31	18792	135825	42

Acknowledgement. This work was supported in part by an NSERC grant awarded to Dr. Hasan.

References

1. Bernstein, D.J.: Batch Binary Edwards. In: Halevi, S. (ed.) CRYPTO 2009. LNCS, vol. 5677, pp. 317–336. Springer, Heidelberg (2009)
2. Cenk, M., Koç, Ç., Özbudak, F.: Polynomial Multiplication over Finite Fields Using Field Extensions and Interpolation. In: 19th IEEE Symposium on Computer Arithmetic, ARITH 2009, pp. 84–91 (2009)
3. ElGamal, T.: A Public-Key Cryptosystem and a Signature Scheme Based on Discrete Logarithms. IEEE Transactions on Information Theory 31(4), 469–472 (1985)
4. Fan, H., Hasan, M.A.: A New Approach to Subquadratic Space Complexity Parallel Multipliers for Extended Binary Fields. IEEE Transactions on Computers 56(2), 224–233 (2007)
5. Fan, H., Sun, J., Gu, M., Lam, K.-Y.: Overlap-free Karatsuba-Ofman Polynomial Multiplication Algorithm (May 2007)
6. Karatsuba, A.A.: The Complexity of Computations. In: Proceedings of the Steklov Institute of Mathematics, vol. 211, pp. 169–183 (1995)
7. Koblitz, N.: Elliptic curve cryptosystems. Mathematics of Computation 48, 203–209 (1987)
8. McGrew, D.A., Viega, J.: The Security and Performance of the Galois/Counter Mode (GCM) of Operation. In: Canteaut, A., Viswanathan, K. (eds.) INDOCRYPT 2004. LNCS, vol. 3348, pp. 343–355. Springer, Heidelberg (2004)

9. Miller, V.: Use of Elliptic Curves in Cryptography. In: Williams, H.C. (ed.) CRYPTO 1985. LNCS, vol. 218, pp. 417–426. Springer, Heidelberg (1986)
10. Sunar, B.: A generalized method for constructing subquadratic complexity GF(2^k) multipliers. IEEE Transactions on Computers 53, 1097–1105 (2004)
11. Toom, A.L.: The Complexity of a Scheme of Functional Elements Realizing the Multiplication of Integers. Soviet Mathematics 3, 714–716 (1963)
12. Winograd, S.: Arithmetic Complexity of Computations. Society For Industrial & Applied Mathematics, U.S. (1980)

A Lemmas and Their Proofs

In this section we provide two lemmas which gives the non-recursive solution to inductive expression. These solutions are required to obtain a non-recursive expression of the complexity of the formula presented in the paper. The proof of Lemma 1 can be found in [4].

Lemma 1. *Let a, b and i be positive integers and assume that $a \neq b$. Let $n = b^i$, $a \neq b$ and $a \neq 1$. The solution to the inductive relation* $\begin{cases} r_1 = e, \\ r_n = ar_{n/b} + cn + d, \end{cases}$ *is as follows*

$$r_n = (e + \frac{bc}{a-b} + \frac{d}{a-1})n^{\log_b(a)} - \frac{bc}{a-b}n - \frac{d}{a-1}. \tag{14}$$

Lemma 2. *Let a, b and i be positive integers. Let $n = b^i$ and $a = b$ and $a \neq 1$. The solution to the inductive relation* $\begin{cases} r_1 = e, \\ r_n = ar_{n/b} + cn + fn^\delta + d, \end{cases}$ *is*

$$r_n = n\left(e + \frac{fb^\delta}{a - b^\delta} + \frac{d}{a-1}\right) - n^\delta\left(\frac{fb^\delta}{a - b^\delta}\right) + cn\log_b(n) - \frac{d}{a-1}. \tag{15}$$

We prove the statement of Lemma 2 by induction on i where $n = b^i$.

- For $i = 1$, i.e., $n = b$ we have

$$r_b = ar_1 + fb^\delta + cb + d = ae + fb^\delta + cb + d \tag{16}$$

Now we compare this value of r_b to the value given by the formula (15)

$$\begin{aligned} r_b &= ae + \tfrac{fb^\delta(b^\delta - a)}{b^\delta - a} + cb\log_b(b) + \tfrac{d(a-1)}{a-1} \\ &= ae + fb^\delta + bc + d. \end{aligned}$$

Consequently, the formula in (15) is correct for $n = b$.
- We assume now that the formula is true for i and we prove its correctness for $i + 1$. We first write

$$r_{b^{i+1}} = ar_{b^i} + fb^{i\delta} + cb^i + d$$

We then use the expression of r_{b^i} given by the induction hypothesis

$$\begin{aligned} r_{b^{i+1}} &= a\left(a^i e + \frac{fb^\delta(b^{\delta i}-a^i)}{b^\delta - a} + cb^i + \frac{d(a^i-1)}{a-1})\right) + fb^{(i+1)\delta} + cb^{i+1} + d \\ &= a^{i+1}e + fb^\delta\left(\frac{ab^{\delta i}-a^{i+1}}{b^\delta - a} + b^{\delta i}\right) + c\left(iab^i + b^{i+1}\right) + d\left(\frac{a^{i+1}-a}{a-1} + 1\right) \\ &= a^{i+1}e + fb^\delta\left(\frac{ab^{\delta(i+1)}-a^{i+1}}{b^\delta - a}\right) + cb^{i+1}\log_b(b^{i+1}) + d\left(\frac{a^{i+1}-1}{a-1}\right) \end{aligned}$$

as required.

B Bernstein's Three-Way Split Formula

In Table 7 we give the multi-evaluation and the products for Bernstein's formula.

Table 7. Cost of multi-evaluation and products for Bernstein's 3-way split formula

Operations	Computations	Cost #⊕	Cost #⊗
Multi-eval.	$R_1 = A_0 + A_1 + A_2$, $R'_1 = B_0 + B_1 + B_2$	$4n/3$	0
	$R_2 = A_1X + A_2X^2$, $R'_2 = B_1X + B_2X^2$	$2n/3 - 2$	0
	$R_3 = A_0 + R_2$, $R'_3 = B_0 + R'_2$	$2n/3 - 2$	0
	$R_4 = R_1 + R_2$, $R'_4 = R'_1 + R'_2$	$2n/3 - 2$	0
Products	$P_0 = A_0B_0$	$S_\oplus(n/3)$	$S_\otimes(n/3)$
	$P_1 = R_1R'_1$	$S_\oplus(n/3)$	$S_\otimes(n/3)$
	$P_2 = R_3R'_3$	$S_\oplus(n/3+2)$	$S_\otimes(n/3+2)$
	$P_3 = R_4R'_4$	$S_\oplus(n/3+2)$	$S_\otimes(n/3+2)$
	$P_4 = A_2B_2$	$S_\oplus(n/3)$	$S_\otimes(n/3)$
	Total	$3S_\oplus(\frac{n}{3}) + 2S_\oplus(\frac{n}{3}+2)$ $+10n/3 - 6$	$3S_\otimes(\frac{n}{3})$ $+2S_\otimes(\frac{n}{3}+2)$

In Table 8 we give explicit computations for the reconstruction of Bernstein's formula.

Table 8. Cost of reconstruction for Bernstein's 3-way split formula

	Computations	#⊕
Reconstruction	$S = P_2 + P_3$,	$2n/3 + 1$
	$U = P_0 + (P_0 + P_1)X^{n/3}$	$n - 2$
	$V = P_2 + S(X^{n/3} + X)$	$n + 4$
	$W = U + V + P_4(X^4 + X)$	$7n/3 - 3$
	$W' = W/(X^2 + X)$	$n - 2$
	$W'' = W(X^{2n/3} + X^{n/3})$	$2n/3 - 1$
	$C = U + P_4(X^{4n/3} + X^{n/3}) + W''$	$5n/3 - 3$
	Total	$25n/3 - 6$

Let us clarify the computation of S in Table 8: the coefficients of $X^{2n/3+2}$ and $X^{2n/3+1}$ in P_2 are the same as the coefficients of the corresponding terms in P_3, therefore the degree of $P_2 + P_3$ is of degree $2n/3$ and this requires only $2n/3 + 1$ bit additions.

Sublinear Scalar Multiplication on Hyperelliptic Koblitz Curves

Hugo Labrande[1] and Michael J. Jacobson Jr.[2,*]

[1] ENS Lyon
46 Allée d'Italie, 69364 Lyon Cedex 07, France
hugo.labrande@ens-lyon.fr
[2] Department of Computer Science, University of Calgary
2500 University Drive NW, Calgary, Alberta, Canada T2N 1N4
jacobs@cpsc.ucalgary.ca

Abstract. Recently, Dimitrov et. al. [5] proposed a novel algorithm for scalar multiplication of points on elliptic Koblitz curves that requires a provably sublinear number of point additions in the size of the scalar. Following some ideas used by this article, most notably double-base expansions for integers, we generalize their methods to hyperelliptic Koblitz curves of arbitrary genus over any finite field, obtaining a scalar multiplication algorithm requiring a sublinear number of divisor additions.

Keywords: Hyperelliptic Koblitz curves, scalar multiplication, double-base expansions.

1 Introduction

Following an idea proposed independently by Koblitz and Miller in 1985 (respectively in [9] and [12]), elliptic and hyperelliptic curves over finite fields are now widely used for cryptographic purposes. Operations are carried out in the finite group of rational points of the elliptic curve; schemes such as ElGamal encryption can be applied in this group. Due to particular properties of the group, cryptography on elliptic curves offers security as strong as other algorithms (such as the RSA algorithm, for instance) with keys of shorter lengths. Hyperelliptic curve cryptosystems are interesting generalizations of elliptic curve cryptosystems. Curves with a too high genus were shown to be cryptographically insecure [7], but if the genus is small hyperelliptic curves can be used in some cryptosystems, and represent an alternative that is as secure and efficient as elliptic curve cryptosystems.

Anomalous binary elliptic curves (elliptic Koblitz curves), first introduced by Koblitz in a 1992 article [10], are of particular interest in cryptographic applications. Cryptographic schemes using elliptic curves are faster on Koblitz curves than on any other type of curves. Moreover, secure Koblitz curves are easy to find: all this make those curves very convenient for cryptography. Those

* Supported in part by NSERC of Canada.

A. Miri and S. Vaudenay (Eds.): SAC 2011, LNCS 7118, pp. 399–411, 2012.

curves can be used for instance in embedded systems, where the computing power and the memory are limited.

The problem we deal with in this article is scalar multiplication, computing m-folds of elements of the group associated to the curve. This problem has practical implications: cryptographic schemes in the group of an elliptic or hyperelliptic curve often require computing m-folds. Thus, by making scalar multiplication more efficient, we improve the speed of curve-based cryptosystems, possibly making them more practical and applicable in a broader set of systems.

In [5] the authors present a method to compute m-folds of points ($m \in \mathbb{Z}$) on elliptic Koblitz curves requiring a sublinear (in the size of m) number of point additions. The method involves finding a suitable triple-base τ-adic expansion for a particular complex number τ. They also design an algorithm using double-base expansions that, while not requiring a provably sublinear number of point additions (although benchmarks and experimental results would let us think it is), is efficient in practice. These represent the first result that breaks the barrier of linearity in number of point additions; all previous algorithms were using a linear number of them, and aimed at improving the O-constant.

In this paper, we generalize the methods of [5] to the case of scalar multiplication on hyperelliptic Koblitz curves of all characteristic and all genera. We present a scalar multiplication algorithm with sublinear complexity (in the number of divisor additions) using triple-base expansions, with carefully chosen bases. Although mostly of theoretical interest due to large constants in the O-notation, our algorithm does prove for the first time the existence of sublinear divisor multiplication on hyperelliptic Koblitz curves. We also present an algorithm using double-base expansions that is conjecturally sublinear and more likely to perform well in practice.

The next two sections provide background on hyperelliptic Koblitz curves and multi-base number systems. The sections that follow contain our results. We first present our algorithm that uses triple-base expansions to achieve a sublinear complexity in number of divisor additions, followed by our practical double-base algorithm.

2 Hyperelliptic Koblitz Curves

More information on hyperelliptic curves can be found, for example, in [2, pp.81-85].

Let $q = p^r$ be a prime power and let $\mathbb{F}_q$ be the finite field with q elements. A (non-singular) hyperelliptic curve of genus g with one point at infinity is defined by the equation

$$C : v^2 + h(u)v = f(u),$$

where $h, f \in \mathbb{F}_q[X]$, $\deg(h) \leq g$, f monic of degree $2g+1$, and if $y^2+h(x)y = f(x)$ for $(x, y) \in \overline{\mathbb{F}_q} \times \overline{\mathbb{F}_q}$, then $2y + h(x) \neq 0$ or $h'(x)y - f'(x) \neq 0$.

Let $\mathrm{Pic}^0(C(\mathbb{F}_q))$ denote the degree zero divisor class group of C over $\mathbb{F}_q$. Elements of $\mathrm{Pic}^0(C(\mathbb{F}_q))$ can be represented uniquely using the Mumford representation, a pair of polynomials $[u, v]$, $u, v \in \mathbb{F}_q[x]$, $\deg v < \deg u \leq g$, u monic, and $u|f - v^2 - hv$. Thus, each divisor can be represented by at most $2g$ elements of $\mathbb{F}_q$. The divisor corresponding to the principal ideals class is denoted div$[1, 0]$. The inverse of $[u, v]$ is $[u, -h - v]$, where the second entry is reduced modulo u, and is thus efficiently computable. The group operation can be done using Cantor's algorithm for any genus; for genus up to 4 more efficient explicit formulas exist.

Hyperelliptic Koblitz curves are hyperelliptic curves defined over $\mathbb{F}_q$ but the group $\mathrm{Pic}^0(C(\mathbb{F}_{q^n}))$ is considered over $\mathbb{F}_{q^n}$ where n is prime. For example, one of the hyperelliptic curves that is studied in [8] is the curve of genus 2

$$C : v^2 + uv = u^5 + u^2 + 1$$

considered over $\mathbb{F}_{2^n}$. Such curves are a generalization of the approach developed in the elliptic case by Koblitz [10]. In a string of articles, some authors successfully generalized Solinas's scalar multiplication method [13] to hyperelliptic curves to get fast algorithms for divisor multiplication on this type of Koblitz curve. An article [8] describes the method for hyperelliptic curves of genus 2, and subsequent work by Lange describes a generalization of the method for hyperelliptic curves of all genera and for every characteristic [11] (see also [2, Sections 15.1.2 and 15.1.3].

As in the elliptic case, one main interest in hyperelliptic Koblitz curves is that scalar multiplication can be sped up by making use of the action of the Frobenius endomorphism on elements in $\mathrm{Pic}^0(C(\mathbb{F}_q))$. The Frobenius endomorphism τ over $\mathbb{F}_{q^n}$ is defined as $x \to x^q$. This operation is inherited by points on the curve and by $\mathrm{Pic}^0(C(\mathbb{F}_q))$. It operates on elements of $\mathrm{Pic}^0(C(\mathbb{F}_q))$ given in Mumford representation by

$$\tau([u(x), v(x)]) = [\tau(u(x)), \tau(v(x))], \quad \text{where } \tau\left(\sum_{i=0}^{d} u_i x^i\right) = \sum_{i=0}^{d} u_i^q x^i \ .$$

In this manner, τ acts as an endomorphism on the group $\mathrm{Pic}^0(C(\mathbb{F}_q)$.

To generalize the methods discussed previously, we have to represent the Frobenius endomorphism as a complex number τ. Let P be the characteristic polynomial of the Frobenius endomorphism:

$$P(T) = T^{2g} + a_1 T^{2g-1} + ... + a_g T^g + a_{g-1} q T^{g-1} + ... + a_1 q^{g-1} T + q^g \ .$$

Let τ be a complex root of P; since the Frobenius endomorphism and τ are both roots of this polynomial, we can consider the Frobenius endomorphism as the complex number τ. For example, in the case of the genus 2 Koblitz curve

$$C_1 : v^2 + uv = u^5 + u^2 + 1 \ ,$$

we may take $\tau = \frac{\mu \pm i\sqrt{4-\mu}}{2}$, where $\mu = \frac{1 \pm \sqrt{17}}{2}$.

The idea to improve scalar multiplication is to compute a base-τ expansion of the scalar, enabling a version of binary exponentiation based on repeated applications of τ as opposed to doublings. As the computation of τ is negligible compared to the cost of a doubling, this yields an especially efficient algorithm.

The problem of finding a τ-adic representation using this set of coefficients is addressed in [11, Algorithm 5.19]. The algorithm attempts to compute a τ-adic expansion of a given scalar using the digit set $R = \{0, \pm 1, ..., \pm\lceil \frac{q^g-1}{2} \rceil\}$. Lange proved [11, Theorem 5.5] that, unlike the elliptic case, the expansions produced by this algorithm are not necessarily finite. Some criteria for non-finiteness are provided in particular cases, and in general it is possible to check for a particular curve whether periodic expansions occur by testing a set of elements in $\mathbb{Z}[\tau]$ of bounded norm. These results use the following norm, which we also use in this paper:

$$\mathcal{N}(\zeta) = \sqrt{\sum_{i=1}^{g} \left| \sum_{j=0}^{2g-1} b_j \tau_i^j \right|^2} \quad ,$$

where $\zeta = b_0 + b_1\tau + \cdots + b_{2g-1}\tau^{2g-1} \in \mathbb{Z}[\tau]$ and $\tau_1, \tau_2, \ldots, \tau_g$ denote g conjugates of τ (one of each conjugate pair).

In the case that expansions are finite, Lange proves [11, Theorem 5.16] that the number of terms is bounded by $n + 4g + 1$. This bound is achieved by first reducing the scalar modulo $\frac{\tau^n - 1}{\tau - 1}$ in $\mathbb{Z}[\tau]$, as in the elliptic case. The expected number of non-zero terms in the expansion is $\frac{q^g-1}{q^g}$, yielding an algorithm that requires the precomputation of $\lceil \frac{q^g-1}{2} \rceil$ divisors and only $\frac{q^g-1}{q^g}(n + 4g + 1)$ divisor additions on average.

When compared to standard methods, Lange's algorithm leads to a speed-up of $1.5g$ as compared to the binary method and $1.3g$ compared to NAF. When compared to a binary window method of width 2 (assuming $q = 2$ and $g = 2$), the speed-up is $11/3$. However, we notice that the asymptotic complexity (in number of divisor additions) is still linear in the size of the scalar m assuming, as is usually the case in cryptographic applications, that $m \in O(q^{ng})$. In the next sections, we give two algorithms that achieve sublinear complexity, one provably so and the other conjecturally.

3 Multi-base Number Systems

As in [5], the main tool we use to achieve sublinearity is multi-base expansions of elements of $\mathbb{Z}[\tau]$.

Definition 1 (double-base expansions). *Let $P, Q, m \in \mathbb{Z}[\tau]$. An expression of the form:*

$$m = \sum_{i=1}^{d} r_i P^{a_i} Q^{b_i} \quad ,$$

where $0 \neq r_i \in R \subset \mathbb{N}$ and $a_i, b_i \in \mathbb{Z}_{\geq 0}$, is called a double-base representation or $\{P, Q\}$-representation of m.

Definition 2 (triple-base expansion). *Let $P, Q, S, m \in \mathbb{Z}[\tau]$. An expression of the form:*

$$m = \sum_{i=1}^{d} r_i P^{a_i} Q^{b_i} S^{c_i} ,$$

where $0 \neq r_i \in R \subset \mathbb{N}$ and $a_i, b_i, c_i \in \mathbb{Z}_{\geq 0}$, is called a triple-base representation or $\{P, Q, S\}$-representation of m.

Our definitions are adapted from [3,5], where integer scalars are considered, and the digit set $R = \{\pm 1\}$.

The motivation of applying multi-base expansions to the scalar multiplication problem is that the number of non-zero terms in such an expansion, when using appropriate bases, is sublinear in the size of the scalar. In the case of integer bases and scalars, we have the following theorem.

Theorem 1. *Given two primes p, q, every integer m has a $\{p, q\}$-representation with a sublinear number of summands, i.e., it can be represented as the sum or difference of at most $O(\frac{\log m}{\log \log m})$ integers of the form $p^a q^b$ for $a, b \in \mathbb{N}$ with $a, b \in O(\log m)$.*

Theorem 1 first appeared with proof in [3, Theorem 1] for bases $p = 2$ and $q = 3$, but generalizes to any number of arbitrary distinct prime bases. The representation can be computed using a greedy algorithm, namely computing the largest integer of the form $p^a q^b$ less than or equal to m and repeating with $m - p^a q^b$. A result of Tijdeman [14] implies that there exists $p^a q^b$ with $m - m/(\log m)^C < p^a q^b < m$ for some absolute constant $C > 0$; this implies the running time and the bound on the exponents a and b occurring in the representation of m.

Tijdeman's result also holds for for complex bases provided that the norm of one base is strictly greater than the other. For elliptic and hyperelliptic Koblitz curves, we would like to use bases that are simple functions of τ, ideally τ and $\tau - 1$, so that the resulting scalar multiplication algorithm requires as few divisor additions as possible. Unfortunately these bases have the same norm, and the theoretical result does not apply. In [5], the authors get around this problem by using a combination of triple-base representations in $\mathbb{Z}[\tau]$ and $\{2, 3\}$-representations of integers, yielding an algorithm requiring only $o(\log m)$ point additions. As that algorithm does not appear to be efficient in practice, an algorithm using $\{\tau, \tau - 1\}$-representations is also presented that works well in practice, despite having only conjectural sublinearity.

4 A Sublinear Divisor Multiplication Algorithm Using Triple-Base Expansions

Our goal is to find a representation of an integer with a sublinear number of summands that leads to a sublinear scalar multiplication algorithm. By sublinear, we mean that the number of divisor additions is sublinear in the size of the integer. Our asymptotic statements in this section assume that the field size q and genus g are fixed, so that the norm of the scalar tends to infinity, although we also give the dominant terns in q and g as well.

In [5], the authors achieve this for elliptic curves by using $\{2,3\}$-expansions of integers and then replacing the 2s and 3s by expressions involving τ using

$$\begin{aligned} 2 &= \tau(\mu - \tau) \\ 3 &= 1 + \mu\tau - \tau^2 \ , \end{aligned}$$

where $\mu \in \{\pm 1\}$ is a parameter indicating which of the two elliptic Koblitz curves over $\mathbb{F}_2$ is used. We use a similar approach. We first select suitable bases for our representation, that is two prime numbers that we can replace by polynomial identities involving τ. Considering the characteristic polynomial of the Frobenius endomorphism τ, we have the following identity:

$$q^g = -\tau^{2g} - a_1\tau^{2g-1} - \ldots - a_1 q^{g-1}\tau = Q(\tau).$$

Consider $i, j \in \mathbb{Z}$ such that $q^g + i$ and $q^g + j$ are prime. By Theorem 1, any integer can be represented with a sublinear number of summands of the form $\pm(Q(\tau)+i)^x(Q(\tau)+j)^y$. For convenience we call $\{\tau, Q(\tau)+i, Q(\tau)+j\}$*-integers* terms of the form $\pm\tau^x(Q(\tau)+i)^y(Q(\tau)+j)^z$, $x, y, z \in \mathbb{Z}$.

First, note that the straightforward approach of computing a $\{q^g + i, q^g + j\}$ representation of the integer scalar m and performing the substitution does not yield a sublinear algorithm. Although the number of terms in the expansion is indeed sublinear, the number of required divisor additions may not be because the required powers of $q^g + i$ and $q^g + j$ may be as large as $\log m$. Instead, we model our approach on that of [5] and obtain the following theorem.

Theorem 2. *Let $\zeta \in \mathbb{Z}[\tau]$, and assume that the τ-adic representation of ζ with coefficients in $R = \{0, \pm 1, \ldots, \pm\lceil \frac{q^g-1}{2} \rceil\}$ is finite. Then, for g and q fixed, ζ can be represented as the sum of at most*

$$O\left(gq^g \frac{\log \mathcal{N}(\zeta)}{\log\log \mathcal{N}(\zeta)}\right)$$

$\{\tau, Q(\tau)+i, Q(\tau)+j\}$-integers such that the largest power of both $Q(\tau)+i$ and $Q(\tau)+j$ is $O(q^g[g+\log \mathcal{N}(\zeta)]^\alpha)$ for any real constant α such that $0 < \alpha < 1/2$.

Proof. Let $\alpha \in (0, 1/2)$. We first determine the τ-adic representation of ζ using coefficients taken in R by using Algorithm 5.19 of [11]. As we assume the length of this expansion is finite, Lemma 5.6 of [11] implies (see the discussion on p.58 of [11]) that its length is $l = O(\log \mathcal{N}(\zeta) + g)$. For convenience, we denote $N_0 = g + \log_q \mathcal{N}(\zeta)$.

Now, we break this representation in $M = \lceil N_0^{1-\alpha} \rceil$ blocks of $O(N_0^\alpha)$ coefficients each such that

$$\zeta = \sum_{i=1}^{l} x_i\tau^i = \sum_{i=0}^{M-1} C_i\tau^{ik} (\text{where } k = \lfloor l/M \rfloor).$$

Using the fact that $P(\tau) = 0$, we see that for $i \in \{0...M\}$, the ith block corresponds to an element of the form

$$C_i = \sum_{j=0}^{2g-1} c_{ij}\tau^i.$$

We note that, since the x_i are in R (and thus bounded by $O(q^g)$) and that there are $O(N_0^\alpha)$ digits in each block, $\log c_{ij}$ is in $O(q^g N_0^\alpha)$.

We represent each c_{ij} in double-base representation using the prime integer bases $q^g + i$ and $q^g + j$. According to Theorem 1, and since both of our bases are prime, these representations can be computed using the greedy algorithm of [3], and have at most

$$O\left(\frac{q^g N_0^\alpha}{\log q^g N_0^\alpha}\right)$$

summands of the form $(q^g + i)^x (q^g + j)^y$ where $x, y \in O(q^g N_0^\alpha)$. Then, since $q^g = Q(\tau)$, we substitute $q^g + i$ by $Q(\tau) + i$ and $q^g + j$ by $Q(\tau) + j$ to obtain a $\{Q(\tau) + i, Q(\tau) + j\}$-expansion of each c_{ij}.

Next, we compute the $\{\tau, Q(\tau)+i, Q(\tau)+j\}$-expansions of C_i by multiplying the expansion of c_{ij} for each $j \in \{0...2g-1\}$ by τ^j, and adding the results. Thus, the expansion of C_i has $O(gq^g N_0^\alpha / \log q^g N_0^\alpha)$ summands of the form $\pm\tau^x(Q(\tau)+i)^y(Q(\tau)+j)^z$, with $x \in \{0...2g-1\}$ and $y, z \in O(q^g N_0^\alpha)$.

The last step is to compute the expansion of ζ from the expansions of the M blocks C_i, by multiplying each C_i by τ^{il}. We obtain a $\{\tau, Q(\tau) + i, Q(\tau) + j\}$-expansion of ζ that has

$$O\left(gq^g \frac{N_0^\alpha}{\log q^g N_0^\alpha} N_0^{1-\alpha}\right) = O\left(gq^g \frac{N_0}{\log q^g N_0^\alpha}\right)$$

terms, and in which the exponents of of $Q(\tau) + i$ and $Q(\tau) + j$ are $O(q^g N_0^\alpha)$. Now, since

$$\begin{aligned}\log q^g N_0^\alpha &= g \log q + \log(g + \log \mathcal{N}(\zeta))^\alpha \\ &\geq \alpha \log(g + \log \mathcal{N}(\zeta)) \\ &\geq \alpha \log\log \mathcal{N}(\zeta)\end{aligned}$$

assuming that g and q are fixed, we get that our number of terms in the end is indeed

$$O\left(gq^g \frac{g + \log \mathcal{N}(\zeta)}{\alpha \log\log \mathcal{N}(\zeta)}\right) = O\left(gq^g \frac{\log \mathcal{N}(\zeta)}{\log\log \mathcal{N}(\zeta)}\right)$$

as required. □

The proof of Theorem 2 is constructive in the sense that it leads immediately to an algorithm to compute a $\{\tau, Q(\tau) + i, Q(\tau) + j\}$-expansion of $\zeta \in \mathbb{Z}[\tau]$.

This leads to the following algorithm for computing ζD using a sublinear number of divisor additions in $\log \mathcal{N}(\zeta)$. The idea is, given the representation of

ζ from Theorem 2, to compute $(Q(\tau)+i)^a(Q(\tau)+j)^b D$ for all powers a, b in the representation, use these to compute each term in the representation multiplied by D, and then to add these together. We will prove that the sublinearity holds for fixed g and q as long α is selected satisfying $0 < \alpha < 1/2$.

Algorithm 1. Divisor multiplication using triple-base expansions

Input: $\zeta = b_0 + b_1\tau + ... + b_{2g-1}\tau^{2g-1}$ and $D \in \mathrm{Pic}^0(C(\mathbb{F}_q))$
Output: ζD

1: Find $i, j \in \mathbb{Z}$ such that $q^g + i$ and $q^g + j$ are prime.
2: Compute a $\{\tau, Q(\tau)+i, Q(\tau)+j\}$-expansion of ζ using Theorem 2 with any α such that $0 < \alpha < 1/2$; store terms in $L = \{s_i\tau^{a_i}(Q(\tau)+i)^{b_i}(Q(\tau)+j)^{c_i}$ with $1 \leq i \leq d$, $s_i = \pm 1, a_i, b_i \in \mathbb{Z}_{\geq 0}$.
3: Compute $A = \max(b_i)$ and $B = \max(c_i)$.
4: Compute in succession for $x \in \{0...A\}$ the divisor classes $D_x = (Q(\tau) + i)D_{x-1}$, with $D_0 = D$.
5: **for** $x \in \{0...A\}$ **do**
6:     Compute in succession for $y \in \{0...B\}$ the divisor classes $F_{x,y} = (Q(\tau)+j)F_{x,y-1}$, with $F(x,0) = D_x$.
7: **end for**
8: $Res \leftarrow \mathrm{div}[1,0]$
9: **for** $i = 1, \ldots, d$ **do**
10:     $Res \leftarrow Res + s_i\tau^{a_i}F_{b_i,c_i}$
11: **end for**
12: **return** Res

Theorem 3. *Algorithm 1 requires $o(gq^g \log \mathcal{N}(\zeta))$ divisor additions for fixed g and q, i.e. the required number of divisor additions is sublinear in $\log \mathcal{N}(\zeta)$.*

Proof. We analyze the algorithm step by step:

1. Step 1: this step does not require any divisor additions. We give here an order of magnitude of i and j. By Chebyschev's theorem, there is a prime number between n and $2n$ for any integer n. Thus, we know there is a prime number between $\lfloor q^g/2 \rfloor$ and q^g, and between q^g and $2q^g$, and we can bound $|i|$ and $|j|$ by q^g.
2. Steps 2-3: these steps also require no divisor additions. Note that the greedy algorithm of [3] can be used to compute the double-base representations of the c_{ij}, and that consequently $A, B \in O(\log^\alpha \mathcal{N}(\zeta))$.
3. Step 4: we compute A divisors, each one being derived from the previous one by applying $Q(\tau) + i$ to it. Applying $Q(\tau) + i$ to a divisor D can be done as follows:
   (a) Compute rD for every $r \leq 2q^g$. Since the absolute value of every coefficient in $Q(\tau)$ is smaller than $2^{2g}q^{g/2}$ (see [15, p.378]) and $|i| \leq q^g$, every coefficient of $Q(\tau)+i$ is bounded by $2q^g$. This step requires $O(q^g)$ divisor additions.

(b) Compute every term in $Q(\tau) + i$ by application of the Frobenius endomorphism and add those terms together. This step requires $O(g)$ divisor additions.

Thus, the complexity of this step is $O(q^g \log^\alpha \mathcal{N}(\zeta))$ divisor additions.

4. Step 5 to 7: we compute AB divisors by repeatedly applying $Q(\tau) + j$ to the divisors computed in the previous step. As discussed in the analysis of previous step (since we have $|j| \leq q^g$ as well), each of those require $O(q^g)$ divisor additions. The complexity of this step is $O(q^g \log^{2\alpha} \mathcal{N}(\zeta))$ divisor additions.
5. Step 8 to 11: Since $s = \pm 1$, the number of point additions is equal to the number of terms of the expansion, which by Theorem 2 is

$$O\left(gq^g \frac{\log \mathcal{N}(\zeta)}{\log \log \mathcal{N}(\zeta)}\right) .$$

Now, since $\alpha < 1/2$, the total number of divisor additions in Steps 4 and 5 is $o(q^g \log \mathcal{N}(\zeta))$. Thus, the number of divisor additions for the entire algorithm is $o(q^g \log \mathcal{N}(\zeta))$. □

Note that, although the number of divisor additions required is sublinear, the overall bit complexity of the algorithm is linear in $q^g \log \mathcal{N}(\zeta)$. This is due to the cost of computing the representation in Step 2. The first step of Theorem 2 is to compute the τ-adic expansion of ζ, which has complexity $O(\log \mathcal{N}(\zeta))$. In addition, double base expansions of the c_{ij} must be computed. From [4], the bit complexity of each of these operations is in $O(\log c_{ij}) = O(q^g N_0^\alpha)$. There are $2g \times M = 2g\lceil N_0^{1-\alpha}\rceil$ of the c_{ij}, so the total bit complexity is in $O(gq^g N_0) = O(gq^g \log \mathcal{N}(\zeta))$.

A straightforward application of this algorithm to $\zeta = m \in \mathbb{Z}$ allows one to compute mP in $o(gq^g \log m)$ divisor additions, as $\log \mathcal{N}(m) = \log \sqrt{gm^2} \in O(\log m)$. However, in the case that m is of the usual size used for cryptographic applications, namely $O((q^n)^g)$, we can do better by first reducing it modulo $\tau^n - 1$, as $\tau^n(D) = D$ in $\mathrm{Pic}^0(C(\mathbb{F}_{q^n}))$. If, as is also usual in cryptographic applications, arithmetic is restricted to a large prime order subgroup of $\mathrm{Pic}^0(C(\mathbb{F}_{q^n}))$, we can reduce the scalar by $\frac{\tau^n-1}{\tau-1}$ (see [11, p.65]). For $M \equiv m \pmod{\frac{\tau^n-1}{\tau-1}}$, we get $\log \mathcal{N}(M) = O(n+2g) = O(\frac{\log m}{g \log q} + 2g)$, as we are assuming that $\log m = \log q^{ng}$. Thus, by applying our algorithm to M instead of m we require the same number of divisor additions asymptotically, but would save a factor of g.

Although our algorithm is sublinear in $\log m$, it depends badly on q and g. However, the most typical applications of Koblitz curves for cryptographic purposes are with small q (to enable easy computation of group orders) and small g (because $g > 3$ is insecure — see, for example, [2, Section 23.2.1]). Note also that our result coincides with that of [5] for the elliptic case, where $q = 2$ and $g = 1$.

We note that this algorithm is asymptotically more efficient than previous methods such as the double-and-add method ($3/2gn \log q$ divisor additions) or

Lange's method using single-base expansion ($(1-1/q^g)n$ divisor additions), since its complexity is sublinear ($o(g^2 q^g n)$). However, the presence of big constants in the asymptotic complexity makes it likely less efficient than those algorithms in practice; we stress that the point of this algorithm was to prove that there exists a scalar multiplication algorithm that only requires a sublinear number of divisor additions. Furthermore, we note that our asymptotics in the case $g = 1$ (elliptic case) and $q = 2$ is the same as in [5] – the primes being used in both methods being 2 and 3.

5 A Practical Scalar Multiplication Algorithm Using Double-Base Expansion

In [5], the authors also devise a scalar multiplication algorithm for elliptic Koblitz curves using $\{\tau, \tau-1\}$-expansions that is designed to work well in practice. Even though these bases have the same norm, and thus cannot be proved to yield sublinear length representations using the results of [14], they were selected because they are as cheap as possible to apply to a given point (0 or 1 addition required). A greedy algorithm to compute representations is too expensive, as it is not known how to efficiently compute the closest $\{\tau, \tau-1\}$ number to a given element in $\mathbb{Z}[\tau]$. Hence, a blocking strategy is used, in which each short block of a τ-adic representation is replaced by a pre-computed optimal $\{\tau, \tau-1\}$ representation. Assuming that these bases do yield sublinear representations, it is proved that the strategy yields a sublinear algorithm, and numerical results were presented demonstrating its efficiency in practice.

We attempt to follow the same strategy with hyperelliptic Koblitz curves, using bases τ and $\tau - 1$, and terms of the form $r_i \tau^{a_i} (\tau - 1)^{b_i}$, with $r \in R = \{0, \pm 1, \ldots, \pm \lceil \frac{q^g-1}{2} \rceil\}$. Our algorithm computes the τ-adic expansion of a given scalar $\zeta \in \mathbb{Z}[\tau]$ using Algorithm 5.19 of [11] and cut this representation into d blocks of fixed size w. Each block corresponds to an element of $\mathbb{Z}[\tau]$, and we can write:

$$\zeta = \sum_{i=0}^{d-1} N_i \tau^{iw}.$$

The complete representation is obtained by replacing each N_i by its optimal $\{\tau, \tau-1\}$-representation obtained from a precomputed table.

We assume the following conjecture:

Conjecture 1. Let τ be a root of the characteristic polynomial of the Frobenius endomorphism of a hyperelliptic Koblitz curve. Every $\zeta \in \mathbb{Z}[\tau]$ with a finite τ-adic representation using digits in R can be represented as the sum of $O(\frac{\log \mathcal{N}(\zeta)}{\log \log \mathcal{N}(\zeta)})$ numbers of the form $r_i \tau^{a_i} (\tau - 1)^{b_i}$, $r_i \in R$.

This conjecture implies that the precomputed optimal representations of the width-w blocks all have a sublinear number of terms. Numerical evidence (see, for example, [5]), suggests that Conjecture 1 holds for elliptic curves. Our belief in the general conjecture for hyperelliptic curves is based on this evidence. Work is underway to produce supporting numerical evidence for genus 2.

Assuming Conjecture 1,we obtain the following theorem.

Theorem 4. *For fixed g and q, and assuming Conjecture 1, every $\zeta \in \mathbb{Z}[\tau]$ with a finite τ-adic expansion using digits in R can be represented as the sum of at most $O(\log \mathcal{N}(\zeta)/\log\log \mathcal{N}(\zeta))$ $\{\tau, \tau-1\}$-integers such that the largest power of $\tau - 1$ is $O(\log \mathcal{N}(\zeta)/\log\log \mathcal{N}(\zeta))$.*

Proof. The method used here is exactly the same as the proof of Theorem 5 of [5]: cut the τ-adic representation of ζ in $\log\log \mathcal{N}(\zeta)$ blocks, each of which is of length $O(\log \mathcal{N}(\zeta)/\log\log \mathcal{N}(\zeta))$. If each block is replaced by a representation with a sublinear number of terms, which is possible by Conjecture 1, then both the total number of terms and the highest power of $\tau-1$ are in $O(\log \mathcal{N}(\zeta)/\log\log \mathcal{N}(\zeta))$. □

The resulting algorithm is presented in Algorithm 2. We note that the bigger the block size, the better our algorithm performs thanks to the optimality of the precomputed table. However, this has to be balanced by the increase storage cost for the larger table.

Algorithm 2. Blocking algorithm for computing $\{\tau, \tau-1\}$-expansions

Input: $\zeta \in \mathbb{Z}[\tau]$, block size w, precomputed table of the minimal $\{\tau, \tau-1\}$-expansion of every $\mu = \sum_{i=0}^{w-1} d_i \tau^i$, $d_i \in R$.

Output: List L of $\{\tau, \tau-1\}$-integers representing the double-base expansion of ζ.

$L \leftarrow \emptyset$
Compute the τ-adic expansion of ζ to get an expression of the form $\zeta = \sum_{i=0}^{d-1} d_i \tau^i$.
for $j = 0$ to $\lceil l/w \rceil$ **do**
    Find minimal $\{\tau, \tau-1\}$-expansion of $\sum_{i=0}^{w-1} d_{i+jw}\tau^i$ from the precomputed table
    Multiply by τ^{jw} and add to L
end for
return L

Our algorithm can be used for scalar multiplication as follows. To simplify the analysis we assume that the $\{\tau, \tau-1\}$-expansion is of the form $\zeta = \sum_{l=0}^{\max(a_i)} (\tau - 1)^l \sum_{i=0}^{\max(a_{i,l})} r_{i,l}\tau^{a_{i,l}}$, where $\max(a_{i,l})$ is the maximal power of τ that is multiplied by $(\tau-1)^l$ in the expansion and $r_{i,j} \in R$. We then denote $r_l(\zeta) = \sum_{i=0}^{\max(a_{i,l})} r_{i,l}\tau^{a_{i,l}}$, and thus $\zeta = \sum_{l=0}^{\max(a_i)} (\tau-1)^l r_l(\zeta)$. The algorithm is presented in Algorithm 3.

The number of divisor additions required to compute ζD is equal to the number of terms in the expansion plus $\max(a_i)\lfloor \frac{q^g-1}{2} \rfloor$. Provided Conjecture 1 holds, Theorem 4 implies that the total number of divisor additions is sublinear in $\log \zeta$. As before, if we assume that integer scalars of size $O(q^{ng})$ are used, then reducing the scalar modulo $(\tau^n - 1)/(\tau - 1)$ and applying the algorithm also requires a sublinear number of divisor additions.

Algorithm 3. Scalar multiplication using $\{\tau, \tau - 1\}$-expansions

Input: $\zeta \in \mathbb{Z}[\tau]$, $D \in \text{Pic}^0(C(\mathbb{F}_q))$
Output: ζD

Compute $r_l(\zeta)$ for $0 \leq l \leq \max(a_i)$ such that $\zeta = \sum_{l=0}^{\max(a_i)} (\tau - 1)^l r_l(\zeta))$ using Algorithm 2.
$D_0 \leftarrow D$
$Q \leftarrow \text{div}[1, 0]$
for $l = 0$ to $\max(a_i)$ **do**
  Compute rD_l for $r \in R$.
  $S \leftarrow r_l(m) D_l$ (τ-adic scalar multiplication using the rD_l)
  $D_{l+1} \leftarrow \tau D_l - D$ (application of $\tau - 1$)
  $Q \leftarrow Q + S$
end for
return Q

6 Conclusion and Future Work

This paper successfully generalizes ideas taken from the elliptic case to achieve improved algorithms for computing m-folds of divisor classes on hyperelliptic Koblitz curves. However, there are still a number of ways this work could be expanded.

As indicated earlier, Algorithm 1 requires provably (and unconditionally) sub-linear number of divisor additions, but only in the asymptotic sense. The O-constants involved are almost certainly too large for it to be efficient in practice. The blocking algorithm, Algorithm 3, is more promising for practical applications, but numerical experiments are required in order to determine its complexity in practice. Most importantly, we need to determine whether sufficiently short $(\tau, \tau - 1)$-representations of all length w τ-adic numbers can be found, i.e., providing numerical evidence in support of Conjecture 1. If such short representations can be found, then the algorithm should compare favorably to the methods in [11], and a careful implementation, possibly generalizing ideas in [6] to compute $(\tau - 1)D$ efficiently, will be required. This is work in progress.

We also base our result on the hypothesis that all τ-adic expansions that we consider are finite. Although this is the case in many hyperelliptic Koblitz curves, the possibility of periods arising can be a concern in practice. We still have to come up with ways to understand those periods better, and devise efficient methods to deal with them or to avoid them completely.

Finally, we note that our double-base algorithm requires a modest amount of storage in order to achieve computational improvements. Although the pre-computed table used can be viewed as part of the domain parameters, for it does not depend on m or on the divisor class D, an efficient memory-free divisor multiplication algorithm, such as that of [1] in the case of elliptic Koblitz curves, is still left to find, as it would allow the most memory-constrained systems to enjoy this speedup as well.

Acknowledgments. The authors wish to thank the anonymous referees for their careful reading and helpful suggestions.

References

1. Avanzi, R., Dimitrov, V., Doche, C., Sica, F.: Extending Scalar Multiplication Using Double Bases. In: Lai, X., Chen, K. (eds.) ASIACRYPT 2006. LNCS, vol. 4284, pp. 130–144. Springer, Heidelberg (2006)
2. Cohen, H., Frey, G., Avanzi, R., Doche, C., Lange, T., Nguyen, K., Vercauteren, F. (eds.): Handbook of elliptic and hyperelliptic curve cryptography. Discrete Mathematics and its Applications (Boca Raton). Chapman & Hall/CRC, Boca Raton (2006); MR2162716 (2007f:14020)
3. Dimitrov, V.S., Jullien, G.A., Miller, W.C.: An algorithm for modular exponentiation. Inform. Process. Lett. 66(3), 155–159 (1998); MR 1627991 (99d:94023)
4. Dimitrov, V.S., Imbert, L., Zakaluzny, A.: Multiplication by a constant is sublinear. In: IEEE Symposium on Computer Arithmetic 2007, pp. 261–268 (2007)
5. Dimitrov, V.S., Järvinen, K.U., Jacobson Jr., M.J., Chan, W.F., Huang, Z.: Provably sublinear point multiplication on Koblitz curves and its hardware implementation. IEEE Trans. Comput. 57(11), 1469–1481 (2008); MR2464687 (2009j:68053)
6. Doche, C., Kohel, D.R., Sica, F.: Double-Base Number System for Multi-scalar Multiplications. In: Joux, A. (ed.) EUROCRYPT 2009. LNCS, vol. 5479, pp. 502–517. Springer, Heidelberg (2009)
7. Enge, A.: Computing discrete logarithms in high-genus hyperelliptic Jacobians in provably subexponential time. Math. Comp. 71(238), 729–742 (2002); (electronic). MR 1885624 (2003b:68083)
8. Günther, C., Lange, T., Stein, A.: Speeding up the Arithmetic on Koblitz Curves of Genus Two. In: Stinson, D.R., Tavares, S. (eds.) SAC 2000. LNCS, vol. 2012, pp. 106–117. Springer, Heidelberg (2001); MR 1895585 (2003c:94024)
9. Koblitz, N.: Elliptic curve cryptosystems. Math. Comp. 48(177), 203–209 (1987); MR 866109 (88b:94017)
10. Koblitz, N.: CM-Curves with Good Cryptographic Properties. In: Feigenbaum, J. (ed.) CRYPTO 1991. LNCS, vol. 576, pp. 279–287. Springer, Heidelberg (1992)
11. Lange, T.: Efficient arithmetic on hyperelliptic curves, Ph.D. thesis, Universität-Gesamthochschule Essen, Essen, Germany (2001)
12. Miller, V.S.: Use of Elliptic Curves in Cryptography. In: Williams, H.C. (ed.) CRYPTO 1985. LNCS, vol. 218, pp. 417–426. Springer, Heidelberg (1986)
13. Solinas, J.A.: Efficient arithmetic on Koblitz curves. Des. Codes Cryptogr. 19(2-3), 195–249 (2000)
14. Tijdeman, R.: On the maximal distance between integers composed of small primes. Compositio. Math. 28, 159–162 (1974); MR 0345917 (49 #10646)
15. Vercauteren, F.: Computing Zeta Functions of Hyperelliptic Curves Over Finite Fields of Characteristic 2. In: Yung, M. (ed.) CRYPTO 2002. LNCS, vol. 2442, pp. 369–384. Springer, Heidelberg (2002)

Faster Hashing to $\mathbb{G}_2$

Laura Fuentes-Castañeda[1], Edward Knapp[2], and Francisco Rodríguez-Henríquez[1]

[1] CINVESTAV-IPN, Computer Science Department
lfuentes@computacion.cs.cinvestav.mx, francisco@cs.cinvestav.mx
[2] University of Waterloo, Dept. Combinatorics & Optimization
edward.m.knapp@gmail.com

Abstract. An asymmetric pairing $e\colon \mathbb{G}_2 \times \mathbb{G}_1 \to \mathbb{G}_T$ is considered such that $\mathbb{G}_1 = E(\mathbb{F}_p)[r]$ and $\mathbb{G}_2 = \tilde{E}(\mathbb{F}_{p^{k/d}})[r]$, where k is the embedding degree of the elliptic curve $E/\mathbb{F}_p$, r is a large prime divisor of $\#E(\mathbb{F}_p)$, and $\tilde{E}$ is the degree-d twist of E over $\mathbb{F}_{p^{k/d}}$ with $r \mid \tilde{E}(\mathbb{F}_{p^{k/d}})$. Hashing to $\mathbb{G}_1$ is considered easy, while hashing to $\mathbb{G}_2$ is done by selecting a random point Q in $\tilde{E}(\mathbb{F}_{p^{k/d}})$ and computing the hash value cQ, where $c \cdot r$ is the order of $\tilde{E}(\mathbb{F}_{p^{k/d}})$. We show that for a large class of curves, one can hash to $\mathbb{G}_2$ in $\mathrm{O}(1/\varphi(k)\log c)$ time, as compared with the previously fastest-known $\mathrm{O}(\log p)$. In the case of BN curves, we are able to double the speed of hashing to $\mathbb{G}_2$. For higher-embedding-degree curves, the results can be more dramatic. We also show how to reduce the cost of the final-exponentiation step in a pairing calculation by a fixed number of field multiplications.

Keywords: Pairing-based cryptography, fast hashing, final exponentiation.

1 Introduction

Let E be an elliptic curve defined over $\mathbb{F}_p$ and let r be a large prime divisor of $\#E(\mathbb{F}_p)$. The embedding degree of E (with respect to r, p) is the smallest positive integer k such that $r \mid p^k - 1$. The Tate pairing on ordinary elliptic curves maps two linearly independent rational points defined over the order-r groups $\mathbb{G}_1, \mathbb{G}_2 \subseteq E(\mathbb{F}_{p^k})$ to the group of r-th roots of unity of the finite field $\mathbb{F}_{p^k}$. In practice, the Tate pairing is computed using variations of an iterative algorithm that was proposed by Victor Miller in 1986 [21]. The result is in the quotient group $\mathbb{F}_{p^k}^*/(\mathbb{F}_{p^k}^*)^r$ and is followed by a final exponentiation in order to obtain a unique representative.

Efficient realizations of the Tate pairing have been intensively pursued in recent years. Using different strategies, that research effort has produced several remarkable algorithm improvements that include: construction of pairing-friendly elliptic curves with prescribed embedding degree [4,8,23], decreases of the Miller loop length [3,13,14,29], and reductions in the associated towering field arithmetic costs [6,11,15,17].

A. Miri and S. Vaudenay (Eds.): SAC 2011, LNCS 7118, pp. 412–430, 2012.

With the increase in efficiency of the Miller loop calculation, the final exponentiation step has become more of a computational bottleneck. Several research works have reported more refined methods for computing the final exponentiation on pairings defined over ordinary elliptic curves [6,12,26]. In particular, the results by Scott *et al.* [26] represent the current state-of-the-art in this topic, as can be verified from the fact that most recent implementations of pairings (see for example [1,5]) have obtained significant accelerations by computing the final exponentiation according to the vectorial addition chain based method described in that work.

Another important task related to pairing computation that has been less studied is the problem of generating random points in $\mathbb{G}_1$ and $\mathbb{G}_2$, known in the literature as *hashing to* $\mathbb{G}_1$ and *hashing to* $\mathbb{G}_2$, respectively. The group $\mathbb{G}_1$ is defined as $E(\mathbb{F}_p)[r]$. Hashing to $\mathbb{G}_1$ is normally seen as a straightforward task, whereas hashing to $\mathbb{G}_2$ is considered more challenging.

The customary method for representing $\mathbb{G}_2$ is as the order-r subgroup of $\tilde{E}(\mathbb{F}_{p^{k/d}})$, where $\tilde{E}$ is the degree-d twist of E over $\mathbb{F}_{p^{k/d}}$ with $r \mid \#\tilde{E}(\mathbb{F}_{p^{k/d}})$; here $\#S$ denotes the cardinality of S. Hashing to $\mathbb{G}_2$ can be accomplished by finding a random point $Q \in \tilde{E}(\mathbb{F}_{p^{k/d}})$ followed by a multiplication by $c = \#\tilde{E}(\mathbb{F}_{p^{k/d}})/r$. The main difficulty of this hashing is that c is normally a relatively large scalar (for example, larger than p). Galbraith and Scott [10] reduce the computational cost of this task by means of an endomorphism of $\tilde{E}$. This idea was further exploited by Scott *et al.* [27], where explicit formulae for hashing to $\mathbb{G}_2$ were given for several pairing-friendly curves.

In this work, we offer improvements in both the final exponentiation and hashing to $\mathbb{G}_2$. We draw on the methods that Vercauteren [29] employed to reduce the cost of the Miller function. Our results for the final exponentiation reduce the cost by a fixed number of operations in several curves, a modest but measurable improvement. Nonetheless, the techniques we use can be applied to increase the speed of hashing as well, saving a fixed number of point additions and doublings. Our framework for fast hashing produces more dramatic results. For example, we estimate that for BN curves [4] at the 128-bit security level, our results yield a hashing algorithm that is at least two times faster than the previous fastest-known algorithm. For higher-embedding-degree curves, the results can be more dramatic.

The rest of this paper is organized as follows. In Section 2 we review Vercauteren's "optimal" pairings. Sections 3 and 4 present our lattice-based method for computing the final exponentiation and exponentiation examples for several emblematic pairing-friendly elliptic curves, respectively. Sections 5 and 6 give our lattice-based approach for hashing to $\mathbb{G}_2$ and hashing for several families of elliptic curves.

2 Background

The Tate pairing is computed in two steps. First, the Miller function value $f = f_{r,P}(Q) \in \mathbb{F}_{p^k}^*$ is computed. This gives a value in the quotient group $\mathbb{F}_{p^k}^*/(\mathbb{F}_{p^k}^*)^r$.

Second, to obtain a unique representative in this quotient group, the value f is raised to the power $(p^k - 1)/r$.

The Miller function is computed using a square-and-multiply algorithm via the following relation

$$f_{a+b,P} = f_{a,P} f_{b,P} \frac{\ell_{aP,bP}}{v_{(a+b)P}}.$$

Using this method, the function $f_{r,P}$ can be computed in $\log r$ steps.

The eta and ate pairings reduces the length of the Miller loop from $\log r$ to $\log |t| \leq \frac{1}{2} \log p$, where t is the trace of the p-power Frobenius acting on E [2,14]. The R-ate pairing [18] provided further improvement, reducing the Miller loop to length $(1/\varphi(k)) \log r$ in some cases. This idea was further generalized by Vercauteren [29] to reduce the Miller loop length to $(1/\varphi(k)) \log r$ for all curves. The idea behind Vercauteren's result lies in the fact that for $h(p) = \sum_{i=0}^{s} h_i p^i$ divisible by r, we have

$$f_{r,P}^{h(p)/r} = g_P \prod_{i=0}^{s} f_{h_i,p^i P} f_{p^i,P}^{h_i},$$

where g_P is the product of s lines. By observing that $f_{r,P}^{(p^k-1)/r}$, $f_{p,P}^{(p^k-1)/r}$, ..., $f_{p^s,P}^{(p^k-1)/r}$ are pairings, it follows that

$$\left(g_P \prod_{i=0}^{s} f_{h_i,p^i P} \right)^{(p^k-1)/r} \tag{1}$$

is a pairing. By choosing a polynomial h with small coefficients, Vercauteren showed that the loop length for each Miller function in (1) can be reduced to at most $(1/\varphi(k)) \log r$.

3 A Lattice-Based Method for Efficient Final Exponentiation

The exponent $e = (p^k - 1)/r$ in the final exponentiation can be broken into two parts by

$$(p^k - 1)/r = [(p^k - 1)/\Phi_k(p)] \cdot [\Phi_k(p)/r],$$

where $\Phi_k(x)$ denotes the k-th cyclotomic polynomial [17]. Computing the map $f \mapsto f^{(p^k-1)/\Phi_k(p)}$ is relatively inexpensive, costing only a few multiplications, inversions, and very cheap p-th powerings in $\mathbb{F}_{p^k}$. Raising to the power $d = \Phi_k(p)/r$ is considered more difficult.

Observing that p-th powering is much less expensive than multiplication, Scott *et al.* [26] give a systematic method for reducing the expense of exponentiating by d. They showed that by writing $d = \Phi_k(p)/r$ in base p as $d = d_0 + d_1 p + \cdots + d_{\varphi(k)-1} p^{\varphi(k)-1}$, one can find short vectorial addition chains to compute $f \mapsto f^d$ much more efficiently than the naive method. For parameterized curves, more concrete results can be given. For instance, Barreto-Naehrig curves [4] are constructed over a prime field $\mathbb{F}_p$, where p is a large prime number that can be parameterized as a fourth-degree polynomial $p = p(x)$, $x \in \mathbb{Z}$. The result of Scott *et al.* gives an algorithm to compute $f \mapsto f^d$, by calculating three intermediate exponentiations, namely, $f^x, (f^x)^x, (f^{x^2})^x$, along with a short sequence of products. By choosing the parameter $x \in \mathbb{Z}$ to have low hamming weight, the total cost of computing $f \mapsto f^d$ is $\frac{3}{4}\log p$ field squarings plus a small fixed-number of field multiplications and squarings.

Using the fact that a fixed power of a pairing is also a pairing, it suffices to raise to the power of any multiple d' of d, with r not dividing d'. Based on this observation, we present a lattice-based method for determining d' such that $f \mapsto f^{d'}$ can be computed at least as efficiently as $f \mapsto f^d$. For Barreto-Naehrig and several other curves, explicit d' polynomials yielding more-efficient final exponentiation computations are reported. However, it is noted that the main bottleneck remains, namely the exponentiation by powers of x.

In the case of parameterized curves, the key to finding suitable polynomials d' is to consider $\mathbb{Q}[x]$-linear combinations of $d(x)$. Specifically, we consider $\mathbb{Q}$-linear combinations of $d(x), xd(x), \ldots, x^{\deg r-1}d(x)$. To see why this set of multiples of $d(x)$ suffices, consider $f \in \mathbb{F}_{p^k}$ with order dividing $\Phi_k(p)$. Since $r(x)d(x) = \Phi_k(p)$, it follows that $f^{r(x)d(x)} = 1$ and so $f^{x^{\deg r}d(x)}$ is the product of $\mathbb{Q}$-powers of f, $f^{xd(x)}, \ldots, f^{x^{\deg r-1}d(x)}$.

Now, consider an arbitrary $\mathbb{Q}$-linear combination $d'(x)$ of the elements $d(x)$, $xd(x), \ldots, x^{\deg r-1}d(x)$. Following the method of Scott *et al.* [26], $d'(x)$ can be written in base $p(x)$ as $d'(x) = d'_0(x) + d'_1(x)p(x) + \cdots + d'_{\phi(k)-1}(x)p(x)^{\phi(k)-1}$, where each d'_i has degree less than the degree of p. Set $d'_i = d_{i,0} + xd_{i,1} + \cdots + x^{\deg p-1}d_{i,\deg p-1}$ and assume that $d_{i,j} \in \mathbb{Z}$ for $0 \le i \le \varphi(k) - 1$, $0 \le j \le \deg(p(x)) - 1$. Then $f^{d'(x)}$ can be computed in two steps as explained next.

First, the exponentiations $f^x, \ldots, f^{x^{\deg p-1}}$ are performed. From these intermediate exponentiations, terms of the form $f^{x^j p^i}$ can be easily calculated. Second, a vectorial addition chain containing the $d_{i,j}$-s is found. This allows to compute $f^{d'(x)}$ from terms of the form $f^{x^j p^i}$ using the work of Olivos [24]. The advantage of allowing multiples of $d(x)$ for this computation is to provide more flexibility in the choices of the exponents $d'(x) = \sum d_{i,j}x^j p^i$ with $d_{i,j} \in \mathbb{Z}$, that can potentially yield shorter addition chains, which in turn means a more-efficient final exponentiation calculation. However the savings are necessarily modest, since as in the method of Scott *et al.* [26], the main expense in this exponentiation process comes from computing the terms $f^x, \ldots, f^{x^{\deg p-1}}$.

In order to find efficient polynomials $d'(x)$, let us construct a rational matrix M' with dimensions $\deg r \times \varphi(k)\deg p$ such that

$$\begin{bmatrix} d(x) \\ xd(x) \\ \vdots \\ x^{\deg r-1}d(x) \end{bmatrix} = M' \left(\begin{bmatrix} 1 \\ p(x) \\ \vdots \\ p(x)^{\varphi(k)-1} \end{bmatrix} \otimes \begin{bmatrix} 1 \\ x \\ \vdots \\ x^{\deg p-1} \end{bmatrix} \right).$$

Here $\otimes$ denotes the Kronecker product and the $(i, u + v \deg p)$-th entry of M' is $d_{u,v}$, where $x^{i-1}d(x) = \sum d_{u,v}x^{v-1}p^{u-1}$.

Elements in the rational lattice formed by the matrix M' correspond to $\mathbb{Q}$-linear combinations $d'(x)$ of $d(x)$, $xd(x)$, ..., $x^{\deg r-1}d(x)$. Short vectorial addition chains can be produced from the elements of M' with small integer entries. The *LLL algorithm* of Lenstra, Lenstra, and Lovasz [19] produces an integer basis of an integer matrix with small coefficients. Let us consider the integer matrix M constructed from M' as the unique matrix whose rows are multiples of the rows of M' such that the entries of M are integers, and the greatest common divisor of the set of entries is 1. Next, the LLL algorithm is applied to M to obtain an integer basis for M with small enties. Finally, small integer linear combinations of these basis elements are examined with the hope of finding short addition chains. It is worth mentioning that even if these results do not yield an advantage over the results of Scott *et al.* [26], since the lattice contains an element corresponding to $d(x)$, the method described in this section includes the results of that work.

In the next section, the main mechanics of our method are explained by applying it to the computation of the final exponentiation step of several pairing-friendly families of curves.

4 Exponentiation Examples

4.1 BN Curves

BN curves [4] have embedding degree 12 and are parameterized by x such that

$$\begin{aligned} r = r(x) &= 36x^4 + 36x^3 + 18x^2 + 6x + 1 \\ p = p(x) &= 36x^4 + 36x^3 + 24x^2 + 6x + 1 \end{aligned}$$

are both prime.

The value $d = \Phi_k(p)/r = (p^4 - p^2 + 1)/r$ can be expressed as the polynomial

$$\begin{aligned} d = d(x) = {} & 46656x^{12} + 139968x^{11} + 241056x^{10} + 272160x^9 \\ & + 225504x^8 + 138672x^7 + 65448x^6 + 23112x^5 \\ & + 6264x^4 + 1188x^3 + 174x^2 + 6x + 1. \end{aligned}$$

At first glance, it appears that exponentiations by multiples of large powers of x are required. However, following the work of Scott *et al.* [26], d can be written in base p such that the degree of the coefficients is at most 3. In particular,

$$\begin{aligned} d(x) = {} & -36x^3 - 30x^2 - 18x - 2 \\ & + p(x)(-36x^3 - 18x^2 - 12x + 1) \\ & + p(x)^2(6x^2 + 1) \\ & + p(x)^3. \end{aligned}$$

Scott *et al.* [26] applied the work of Olivos [24] to compute the map $f \mapsto f^d$ using vectorial addition chains. From the above representation for d, vectorial addition chains can be used to compute $f \mapsto f^d$ using 3 exponentiations by x, 13 multiplications, and 4 squarings.

For the method described in Section 3, consider multiples of d represented in the base p with coefficients in $\mathbb{Q}[x]/(p(x))$.

A 4×16 integer matrix M is found such that

$$\begin{bmatrix} d(x) \\ xd(x) \\ 6x^2d(x) \\ 6x^3d(x) \end{bmatrix} = M \left(\begin{bmatrix} 1 \\ p(x) \\ p(x)^2 \\ p(x)^3 \end{bmatrix} \otimes \begin{bmatrix} 1 \\ x \\ x^2 \\ x^3 \end{bmatrix} \right).$$

The first row in M corresponds to the final exponentiation given by Scott *et al.* [26]. Any non-trivial integer linear combination of the rows corresponds to an exponentiation. For computational efficiency, a linear combination with coefficients as small as possible is desired.

None of the basis vectors returned by the LLL algorithm has an advantage over [26]. However, if small integer linear combinations of the short vectors returned by the LLL algorithm are considered, a multiple of d which corresponds to a shorter addition chain could potentially be found. A brute force search of linear combinations of the LLL basis yields 18 non-zero vectors with maximal entry 12. Among these vectors we consider the vector

$$(1, 6, 12, 12, 0, 4, 6, 12, 0, 6, 6, 12, -1, 4, 6, 12),$$

which corresponds to the multiple $d'(x) = \lambda_0 + \lambda_1 p + \lambda_2 p^2 + \lambda_3 p^3 = 2x(6x^2 + 3x + 1)d(x)$, where

$$\begin{aligned} \lambda_0(x) &= 1 + 6x + 12x^2 + 12x^3 \\ \lambda_1(x) &= 4x + 6x^2 + 12x^3 \\ \lambda_2(x) &= 6x + 6x^2 + 12x^3 \\ \lambda_3(x) &= -1 + 4x + 6x^2 + 12x^3. \end{aligned}$$

The final exponentiation which results can be computed more efficiently without using addition chains.

First, the following exponentiations are computed

$$f \mapsto f^x \mapsto f^{2x} \mapsto f^{4x} \mapsto f^{6x} \mapsto f^{6x^2} \mapsto f^{12x^2} \mapsto f^{12x^3}$$

which requires 3 exponentiations by x, 3 squarings, and 1 multiplication. The terms $a = f^{12x^3} \cdot f^{6x^2} \cdot f^{6x}$ and $b = a \cdot (f^{2x})^{-1}$ can be computed using 3 multiplications. Finally, the result $f^{d'}$ is obtained as

$$[a \cdot f^{6x^2} \cdot f] \cdot [b]^p \cdot [a]^{p^2} \cdot [b \cdot f^{-1}]^{p^3}$$

which requires 6 multiplications.

In total, our method requires 3 exponentiations by x, 3 squarings, and 10 multiplications. [1]

4.2 Freeman Curves

Freeman curves [7] have embedding degree $k = 10$ and are parameterized by x as follows

$$\begin{aligned} r &= r(x) = 25x^4 + 25x^3 + 15x^2 + 5x + 1 \\ p &= p(x) = 25x^4 + 25x^3 + 25x^2 + 10x + 3. \end{aligned}$$

For $d = \Phi_{10}(p)/r = (p^4 - p^3 + p^2 - p + 1)/r$, let us consider a 4×16 integer matrix M such that

$$\begin{bmatrix} d(x) \\ xd(x) \\ 5x^2 d(x) \\ 5x^3 d(x) \end{bmatrix} = M \left(\begin{bmatrix} 1 \\ p(x) \\ p(x)^2 \\ p(x)^3 \end{bmatrix} \otimes \begin{bmatrix} 1 \\ x \\ x^2 \\ x^3 \end{bmatrix} \right).$$

In the lattice spanned by M, there exist two short vectors,

$$\pm(1, -2, 0, -5, -1, -4, -5, -5, 1, 3, 5, 5, 2, 5, 5, 5).$$

Both of these vectors have maximal coefficient 5. Consider the vector corresponding to the multiple

$$d'(x) = (5x^3 + 5x^2 + 3x + 1)d(x) = \lambda_0 + \lambda_1 p + \lambda_2 p^2 + \lambda_3 p^3,$$

where

$$\begin{aligned} \lambda_0(x) &= 1 - 2x - 5x^3 \\ \lambda_1(x) &= -1 - 4x - 5x^2 - 5x^3 \\ \lambda_2(x) &= 1 + 3x + 5x^2 + 5x^3 \\ \lambda_3(x) &= 2 + 5x + 5x^2 + 5x^3, \end{aligned}$$

Now, the map $f \mapsto f^{d'}$ can be computed as

$$f \mapsto f^x \mapsto f^{2x} \mapsto f^{4x} \mapsto f^{5x} \mapsto f^{5x^2} \mapsto f^{5x^3},$$

followed by

$$\begin{aligned} A &= f^{5x^3} \cdot f^{2x}, \qquad & B &= A \cdot f^{5x^2}, \\ C &= f^{2x} \cdot f, & D &= B \cdot f^x \cdot f, \end{aligned}$$

and finally

$$f^{d'} = [A^{-1} \cdot f] \cdot [B^{-1} \cdot C^{-1}]^p \cdot [D]^{p^2} \cdot [C \cdot D]^{p^3},$$

requiring a total of 12 multiplications, 2 squarings, and 3 exponentiations by x.

[1] We ignore the relatively inexpensive p-power Frobenius maps. Since the embedding degree k is even, we have that $f^{-1} = f^{p^{k/2}}$ for all f in the cyclotomic subgroup of $\mathbb{F}_{p^k}$. That is, inversion can be done using a p-power Frobenius. Hence, we ignore inversions as well.

4.3 KSS-8 Curves

KSS-8 curves [16] have embedding degree $k = 8$ and are parameterized by x such that

$$r = r(x) = \frac{1}{450}(x^4 - 8x^2 + 25),$$
$$p = p(x) = \frac{1}{180}(x^6 + 2x^5 - 3x^4 + 8x^3 - 15x^2 - 82x + 125)$$

are both prime. For $d = \Phi_k(p)/r$, we compute an integer matrix M such that

$$\begin{bmatrix} 6d(x) \\ (6/5)xd(x) \\ (6/5)x^2d(x) \\ (6/5)x^3d(x) \end{bmatrix} = M \left(\begin{bmatrix} 1 \\ p(x) \\ p(x)^2 \\ p(x)^3 \end{bmatrix} \otimes \begin{bmatrix} 1 \\ x \\ x^2 \\ x^3 \\ x^4 \\ x^5 \end{bmatrix} \right).$$

Note that since x needs to be chosen as a multiple of 5, the rows of M correspond to integer multiples of $d(x)$. We obtain a short vector corresponding to the multiple

$$d'(x) = \frac{6x}{5}d(x) = \lambda_0 + \lambda_1 p + \lambda_2 p^2 + \lambda_3 p^3$$

of $d(x)$, where

$$\lambda_0 = 2x^4 + 4x^3 + 5x^2 + 38x - 25$$
$$\lambda_1 = -x^5 - 2x^4 - x^3 - 16x^2 + 20x + 36$$
$$\lambda_2 = x^4 + 2x^3 - 5x^2 + 4x - 50$$
$$\lambda_4 = 3x^3 + 6x^2 + 15x + 72.$$

We use addition chains to compute $f^{d'}$. First, write $f^{d'}$ as

$$f^{d'} = y_0^1 y_1^2 y_2^3 y_3^4 y_4^5 y_5^6 y_6^{15} y_7^{16} y_8^{20} y_9^{25} y_{10}^{36} y_{11}^{38} y_{12}^{50} y_{13}^{72}$$

and compute the y_i's. The y_i's can be computed from $f, f^x, \ldots, f^{x^5}$ using only multiplications and Frobenius maps.

Next, we find an addition chain containing all the powers of the y_i's. With the inclusion of the element 10, we obtain

$$\{1, 2, 3, 4, 5, 6, \underline{10}, 15, 16, 20, 25, 36, 38, 50, 72\}.$$

The work of Olivos gives an efficient method for producing a vectorial addition chain from an addition chain and states the computational expense of computing the final result $f^{d'}$ from the y_i's.

The computation of the y_i's requires 5 exponentiations by x, and 6 multiplications. The addition chain requires 7 multiplications and 7 squarings. The conversion to a vectorial addition chain requires 13 multiplications. In total, we require 5 exponentiations by x, 26 multiplications, and 7 squarings to compute the map $f \mapsto f^{d'}$.

4.4 KSS-18 Curves

KSS-18 curves [16] have embedding degree $k = 18$ and a twist of order $d = 6$. These curves are parameterized by x such that

$$\begin{aligned} r = r(x) &= \frac{1}{343}(x^6 + 37x^3 + 343) \\ p = p(x) &= \frac{1}{21}(x^8 + 5x^7 + 7x^6 + 37x^5 + 188x^4 \\ &\quad + 259x^3 + 343x^2 + 1763x + 2401) \end{aligned}$$

are both prime. For $d = \Phi_k(p)/r$, we compute an integer matrix M such that

$$\begin{bmatrix} 3d(x) \\ (3/7)xd(x) \\ (3/49)x^2d(x) \\ (3/49)x^3d(x) \\ (3/49)x^4d(x) \\ (3/49)x^5d(x) \end{bmatrix} = M \left(\begin{bmatrix} 1 \\ p(x) \\ p(x)^2 \\ p(x)^3 \\ p(x)^4 \\ p(x)^5 \end{bmatrix} \otimes \begin{bmatrix} 1 \\ x \\ x^2 \\ x^3 \\ x^4 \\ x^5 \\ x^6 \\ x^7 \end{bmatrix} \right).$$

Since 7 divides x, the rows of M correspond to integer multiples of $d(x)$. We find a short vector corresponding to the multiple $d'(x) = \frac{3x^2}{49}d(x) = \lambda_0 + \lambda_1 p + \lambda_2 p^2 + \lambda_3 p^3 + \lambda_4 p^4 + \lambda_5 p^5$ of $d(x)$, where

$$\begin{aligned} \lambda_0 &= x^6 + 5x^5 + 7x^4 + 21x^3 + 108x^2 + 147x, \\ \lambda_1 &= -5x^5 - 25x^4 - 35x^3 - 98x^2 - 505x - 686, \\ \lambda_2 &= -x^7 - 5x^6 - 7x^5 - 19x^4 - 98x^3 - 133x^2 + 6, \\ \lambda_3 &= 2x^6 + 10x^5 + 14x^4 + 35x^3 + 181x^2 + 245x, \\ \lambda_4 &= -3x^5 - 15x^4 - 21x^3 - 49x^2 - 254x - 343, \\ \lambda_5 &= x^4 + 5x^3 + 7x^2 + 3. \end{aligned}$$

Proceeding as in the KSS-8 example, we construct an addition chain

$$\{1, 2, 3, 5, 6, 7, 10, 14, 15, 19, 21, 25, 35, \underline{38}, 49, \underline{73}, \\ 98, 108, 133, 147, 181, 245, 254, 343, \underline{490}, 505, 686\}.$$

Once again, applying Olivos' method for computing a short vectorial addition chain, we can compute the map $f \mapsto f^d$ using 7 exponentiations by x, 52 multiplications, and 8 squarings.

4.5 A Comparison with Scott et al.

In Table 1, we compare our results against those given by Scott *et al.* [26]. Although operation counts are given for only the vectorial addition portion of

Table 1. A comparison of our final exponentiation method with the method of Scott *et al.* [26]. 'M' denotes a multiplication and 'S' denotes a squaring. Both methods require the same number of exponentiations by x, determined by the curve.

Curve	Scott *et al.*	This work
BN	13M 4S	10M 3S
Freeman	14M 2S	12M 2S
KSS-8	31M 6S	26M 7S
KSS-18	62M 14S	52M 8S

the exponentiation, the total cost can easily be computed from their work. The operation counts are given for field multiplications and squarings only, since the number of exponentiations by x is fixed for each curve and computing p-th powers maps is comparatively inexpensive.

For example, let us consider the case of BN curves parameterized with $x = -2^{62} - 2^{54} + 2^{44}$, which yields a 127-bit security level [5]. Further, assume that the relative cost of a field multiplication compared to a cyclotomic squaring on $\mathbb{F}_{p^k}$ is given as $M \approx 4.5S$ [1,15]. Then, the total cost to perform the exponentiations $f^x, (f^x)^x, (f^{x^2})^x$, is of around $3 \cdot \lfloor \log_2 x \rfloor = 183$ cyclotomic squarings. Using the results reported in Table 1, this gives an approximate cost for the hard part of the final exponentiation of $187S + 13M \approx 245S$ for the method of Scott *et al.* and $186S + 10M \approx 231S$ using our method.

5 A Lattice-Based Method for Hashing to $\mathbb{G}_2$

Let E be an elliptic curve over $\mathbb{F}_p$ with r, a large prime divisor of $n = \#E(\mathbb{F}_p)$, and let $k > 1$ be the embedding degree of E. Let q be an arbitrary power of p. An elliptic curve $\tilde{E}$ defined over $\mathbb{F}_q$ is said to be a *degree-d twist of E over* $\mathbb{F}_q$, if d is the smallest integer such that $\tilde{E}$ and E are isomorphic over $\mathbb{F}_{q^d}$. If $p \geq 5$, the only possible degrees of twists are those integers d which divide either 4 or 6. Since our examples deal only with curves where the degree of the twist divides the embedding degree k, we assume that d divides k and set $q = p^{k/d}$. However, with some modifications, the preliminary discussion and results apply to curves where d does not divide k.

Hess *et al.* [14] show that there exists a unique non-trivial twist $\tilde{E}$ of E over $\mathbb{F}_q$ such that r divides $\#\tilde{E}(\mathbb{F}_q)$. If $d = 2$, then $\#\tilde{E}(\mathbb{F}_q) = q + 1 + \hat{t}$, where $\hat{t}$ is the trace of the q-power Frobenius of E. In fact, the order of any twist can be found by first determining the trace $\hat{t}$ of the q-power Frobenius of E from the trace t of the p-power Frobenius of E via the Weil Theorem and then using a result given by Hess *et al.*[14].

The trace t_m of the p^m-power Frobenius of E for an arbitrary m can be determined using the recursion $t_0 = 2$, $t_1 = t$, and $t_{i+1} = t \cdot t_i - p \cdot t_{i-1}$ for all $i > 1$ [20]. After computing the trace $\hat{t}$ of the q-power Frobenius of E, the possible values for the trace $\tilde{t}$ of the q-power Frobenius of $\tilde{E}$ over $\mathbb{F}_q$ can be determined using Table 2 [14], where D is the discriminant of E and $\hat{f}$ satisfies $\hat{t}^2 - 4q = D\hat{f}^2$.

Table 2. Possible values for the trace $\tilde{t}$ of the q-power Frobenius of a degree-d twist $\tilde{E}$ of E

d	2	3	4	6
$\tilde{t}$	$-\hat{t}$	$(\pm 3\hat{f} - \hat{t})/2$	$\pm\hat{f}$	$(\pm 3\hat{f} + \hat{t})/2$

The group $\mathbb{G}_2$ can be represented as $\tilde{E}(\mathbb{F}_q)[r]$. In order to hash to $\mathbb{G}_2$, it suffices to hash to a random point $Q \in \tilde{E}(\mathbb{F}_q)$ followed by a multiplication by the cofactor $c = \#\tilde{E}(\mathbb{F}_q)/r$, to obtain the element $cQ \in \tilde{E}(\mathbb{F}_q)[r]$. Let $\phi\colon \tilde{E} \to E$ be an efficiently-computable isomorphism defined over $\mathbb{F}_{q^d}$ and let π be the p-th power Frobenius on E. Scott *et al.* [27] observed that the endomorphism $\psi = \phi^{-1} \circ \pi \circ \phi$ can be used to speed up the computation of $Q \mapsto cQ$. The endomorphism ψ satisfies

$$\psi^2 P - t\psi P + pP = \infty \tag{2}$$

for all $P \in \tilde{E}(\mathbb{F}_q)$ [9, Theorem 1]. The cofactor c can be written as a polynomial in p with coefficients less than p. Scott *et al.* use this representation of c and reduce using (2) so that c is expressed as a polynomial in ψ with coefficients less than p. For parameterized curves, the speedup in the cost of computing $Q \mapsto cQ$ can become quite dramatic. For example, MNT curves have embedding degree $k = 6$ and are parameterized by x such that

$$\begin{aligned} p(x) &= x^2 + 1 \\ r(x) &= x^2 - x + 1 \end{aligned}$$

are both prime. It can be shown that

$$\begin{aligned} c(x)P = (x^4 + x^3 + 3x^2)P &= (p^2 + (x+1)p - x - 2)P \\ &= \psi(2xP) + \psi^2(2xP). \end{aligned}$$

It suffices to multiply by a multiple c' of c such that $c' \not\equiv 0 \pmod r$. Combining this observation with a new method of representing c in base ψ, we prove the following theorem.

Theorem 1. *Suppose that $\tilde{E}(\mathbb{F}_q)$ is cyclic and $p \equiv 1 \pmod d$. Then there exists a polynomial $h(z) = h_0 + h_1 z + \cdots + h_{\varphi(k)-1} z^{\varphi(k)-1} \in \mathbb{Z}[z]$ such that $h(\psi)P$ is a multiple of cP for all $P \in \tilde{E}(\mathbb{F}_q)$ and $|h_i|^{\varphi(k)} \le \#\tilde{E}(\mathbb{F}_q)/r$ for all i.*

The proof of Theorem 1 is divided into two parts. We first prove a technical lemma and then show how the polynomial h can be obtained using an integer-lattice technique. Let f, $\tilde{f}$ be such that $t^2 - 4p = Df^2$ and $\tilde{t}^2 - 4q = D\tilde{f}^2$, where D is the discriminant. It also holds that $n + t = p + 1$ and $\tilde{n} + \tilde{t} = q + 1$, where $\tilde{n} = \#\tilde{E}(\mathbb{F}_q)$.

Recall that the endomorphism $\psi\colon \tilde{E} \to \tilde{E}$ is defined over $\mathbb{F}_{q^d}$. In the following lemma, it is proved that ψ fixes $\tilde{E}(\mathbb{F}_q)$ as a set.

Lemma 1. *If $p \equiv 1 \pmod{d}$, then $\psi P \in \tilde{E}(\mathbb{F}_q)$ for all $P \in \tilde{E}(\mathbb{F}_q)$.*

Proof. From the work of Hess *et al.* we have that the twist is defined by first selecting $\gamma \in \mathbb{F}_{q^d}$ such that $\gamma^d \in \mathbb{F}_q$. The map ϕ is then defined by $\phi(x, y) = (\gamma^2 x, \gamma^3 y)$ and hence ψ is defined by $\psi(x, y) = (\gamma^{2(p-1)} x^p, \gamma^{3(p-1)} y^p)$. Now, $\gamma^d \in \mathbb{F}_q$ and $p - 1 \equiv 0 \pmod{d}$ yield $\gamma^{p-1} \in \mathbb{F}_q$, which in turn implies that $\psi(x, y) \in \tilde{E}(\mathbb{F}_q)$ for $(x, y) \in \tilde{E}(\mathbb{F}_q)$. □

The following lemma illustrates the effect of ψ on elements in $\tilde{E}(\mathbb{F}_q)$.

Lemma 2. *If $p \equiv 1 \pmod{d}$, $\gcd(\tilde{f}, \tilde{n}) = 1$, and $\tilde{E}(\mathbb{F}_q)$ is a cyclic group, then $\psi P = aP$ for all $P \in \tilde{E}(\mathbb{F}_q)$, where a is one of $(t + f(\tilde{t}-2)/\tilde{f})/2$, $(t - f(\tilde{t}-2)/\tilde{f})/2$.*

Proof. Since $\tilde{E}(\mathbb{F}_q)$ is cyclic and ψ fixes $\tilde{E}(\mathbb{F}_q)$, there exists an integer a such that $\psi P = aP$ for all $P \in \tilde{E}(\mathbb{F}_q)$. By solving for a in (2) and using the fact that $t^2 - 4p = Df^2$, we obtain

$$a \equiv \frac{1}{2}(t \pm \sqrt{t^2 - 4p}) \equiv \frac{1}{2}(t \pm \sqrt{Df^2}) \equiv \frac{1}{2}(t \pm f\sqrt{D}) \pmod{\tilde{n}}.$$

Working modulo $\tilde{n}$, we observe that $D\tilde{f}^2 = \tilde{t}^2 - 4q = \tilde{t}^2 - 4\tilde{t} + 4 = (\tilde{t} - 2)^2$ and so $\sqrt{D} \equiv \pm(\tilde{t} - 2)/\tilde{f} \pmod{\tilde{n}}$. Without loss of generality, let f, $\tilde{f}$ be such that $a = \frac{1}{2}(t + f\sqrt{D})$ and $\sqrt{D} \equiv (\tilde{t} - 2)/\tilde{f} \pmod{\tilde{n}}$. Then, since $P \in \tilde{E}(\mathbb{F}_q)$ has order dividing $\tilde{n}$, it follows that

$$\psi P = aP = \left(\frac{1}{2}(t + f\sqrt{D})\right) P = \left(\frac{1}{2}(t + f(\tilde{t} - 2)/\tilde{f})\right) P.$$

□

In the space of polynomials $h \in \mathbb{Q}[z]$ such that $h(a) \equiv 0 \pmod{c}$, we wish to find an h with small integer coefficients. Ignoring the small coefficient requirement for the moment, $h(z) = c$ and $h(z) = z^i - a^i$ satisfy the required condition for all integers i. Furthermore, any linear combination of these polynomials satisfies this condition.

Since π acting on $E(\mathbb{F}_{p^k})$ has order k and ψ is an automorphism when restricted to the cyclic group $\tilde{E}(\mathbb{F}_q)$, the automorphism ψ acting on $\tilde{E}(\mathbb{F}_q)$ has order k. Hence, the integer a satisfies $\Phi_k(a) \equiv 0 \pmod{\tilde{n}}$. Therefore, the polynomial $h(z) = z^i - a^i$ with $i \geq \varphi(k)$ can be written as a linear combination (modulo c) of $z - a, \ldots, z^{\varphi(k)-1} - a^{\varphi(k)-1}$. For this reason, the polynomials of higher degree are excluded in the following construction.

Notice that polynomials $h \in \mathbb{Z}[z]$ such that $h(a) \equiv 0 \pmod{c}$ correspond to points in the integer lattice generated by the matrix

$$\left[\begin{array}{c|c} c & \mathbf{0} \\ \hline \mathbf{a} & I_{\varphi(k)-1} \end{array}\right],$$

where $\mathbf{a}$ is the column vector with i-th entry $-a^i$. Consider the convex set $C \subseteq \mathbb{R}^{\varphi(k)}$ generated by all vectors of the form $(\pm|c|^{1/\varphi(k)}, \ldots, \pm|c|^{1/\varphi(k)})$. The volume of C is $2^{\varphi(k)}|c|$ and the lattice above has volume $|c|$. By Minkowski's Theorem [22], the region C contains a lattice point. Hence, there exists a non-zero polynomial h with coefficients at most $|c|^{1/\varphi(k)}$ such that $h(a) \equiv 0 \pmod{c}$. This concludes the proof of Theorem 1. □

6 Hashing Examples

6.1 BN Curves

BN curves are parameterized by

$$\begin{aligned} p(x) &= 36x^4 + 36x^3 + 24x^2 + 6x + 1 \\ r(x) &= 36x^4 + 36x^3 + 18x^2 + 6x + 1 \\ t(x) &= 6x^2 + 1 \\ f(x) &= 6x^2 + 4x + 1 \end{aligned}$$

where

$$\begin{aligned} t(x)^2 - 4p(x) &= -3f(x)^2 \\ r(x) + t(x) &= p(x) + 1 \\ q(x) &= p(x)^2. \end{aligned}$$

After computing the trace $\hat{t}$ of the q-power Frobenious of E, we compute $\hat{f}$ such that $4q - \hat{t} = -3\hat{f}^2$. Using $\hat{t}$ and $\hat{f}$, we find the twist $\tilde{E}(\mathbb{F}_q)$ is parameterized by

$$\begin{aligned} \tilde{n}(x) &= q(x) + 1 - (3\hat{f}(x) + \hat{t}(x))/2 \\ &= (36x^4 + 36x^3 + 18x^2 + 6x + 1)(36x^4 + 36x^3 + 30x^2 + 6x + 1) \\ \tilde{t}(x) &= 36x^4 + 1 \end{aligned}$$

We have that $c(x) = p(x) + t(x) - 1$ is such that $\tilde{n}(x) = r(x)c(x)$. Using Lemma 2, we obtain

$$\begin{aligned} a(x) &= \frac{1}{2}(t + f(\tilde{t} - 2)/\tilde{f}) \\ &= -\frac{1}{5}(3456x^7 + 6696x^6 + 7488x^5 + 4932x^4 + 2112x^3 + 588x^2 + 106x + 6). \end{aligned}$$

As a sobriety check, note that $a(x) \equiv p(x) \pmod{r}$ and thus $\psi Q = a(x)Q = p(x)Q$ for all $Q \in \tilde{E}(\mathbb{F}_q)[r]$.

We construct the following lattice and reduce the $-a(x)^i$ entries modulo $c(x)$:

$$\left[\begin{array}{c|ccc} c(x) & 0 & 0 & 0 \\ -a(x) & 1 & 0 & 0 \\ -a(x)^2 & 0 & 1 & 0 \\ -a(x)^3 & 0 & 0 & 1 \end{array}\right] \rightarrow \left[\begin{array}{c|ccc} 36x^4 + 36x^3 + 30x^2 + 6x + 1 & 0 & 0 & 0 \\ 48/5x^3 + 6x^2 + 4x - 2/5 & 1 & 0 & 0 \\ 36/5x^3 + 6x^2 + 6x + 1/5 & 0 & 1 & 0 \\ 12x^3 + 12x^2 + 8x + 1 & 0 & 0 & 1 \end{array}\right].$$

From this lattice, we find the polynomial $h(z) = x + 3xz + xz^2 + z^3$. Working modulo $\tilde{n}(x)$, we have that

$$h(a) = -(18x^3 + 12x^2 + 3x + 1)c(x)$$

and since $\gcd(18x^3 + 12x^2 + 3x + 1, r(x)) = 1$, the following map is a homomorphism of $\tilde{E}(\mathbb{F}_q)$ with image $\tilde{E}(\mathbb{F}_q)[r]$:

$$Q \mapsto xQ + \psi(3xQ) + \psi^2(xQ) + \psi^3(Q).$$

We can compute $Q \mapsto xQ \mapsto 2xQ \mapsto 3xQ$ using one doubling, one addition, and one multiply-by-x. Given Q, xQ, $3xQ$, we can compute $h(a)Q$ using three ψ-maps, and three additions. In total, we require one doubling, four additions, one multiply-by-x, and three ψ-maps. As seen in Table 3 on page 428, the previous fastest-known method of computing such a homomorphism costs two doublings, four additions, two multiply-by-x's, and three ψ-maps.

6.2 Freeman Curves

Freeman curves [7] have embedding degree $k = 10$ and are parameterized by x as follows

$$r = r(x) = 25x^4 + 25x^3 + 15x^2 + 5x + 1$$
$$p = p(x) = 25x^4 + 25x^3 + 25x^2 + 10x + 3.$$

Since Freeman curves do not have a fixed discriminant, the algorithm given in the proof of Lemma 2 does not directly apply. However, we are able to apply the techniques of Scott *et al.* on $c(x)$, $xc(x)$, $x^2c(x)$, $x^3c(x)$ and then use our method from Section 3.

We find a short vector corresponding to the multiple $h(a) = \lambda_0 + \lambda_1 a + \lambda_2 a^2 + \lambda_3 a^3$ of c, where $\lambda = (\lambda_0, \lambda_1, \lambda_2, \lambda_3, \lambda_4)$ is such that

$$\lambda_0(x) = 10x^3 + 5x^2 + 4x + 1$$
$$\lambda_1(x) = -3x$$
$$\lambda_2(x) = -10x^3 - 10x^2 - 8x - 3$$
$$\lambda_3(x) = -5x^3 - 5x^2 - x$$
$$\lambda_4(x) = -5x^3 + 2.$$

Using the addition chain $\{1, 2, 3, 4, 5, 8, 10\}$, we can compute $h(a)Q$ using fourteen additions, four doublings, three multiply-by-x's, and four ψ maps.

6.3 KSS-8

KSS-8 curves [16] have embedding degree $k = 8$ and are parameterized by x such that

$$r = r(x) = \frac{1}{450}(x^4 - 8x^2 + 25)$$
$$p = p(x) = \frac{1}{180}(x^6 + 2x^5 - 3x^4 + 8x^3 - 15x^2 - 82x + 125)$$

are both prime. Set $q = p^{k/d} = p^2$. There exists a degree-4 twist $\tilde{E}(\mathbb{F}_q)$ of order

$$\tilde{n}(x) = \frac{1}{72}(x^8 + 4x^7 + 6x^6 + 36x^5 + 34x^4 - 84x^3 + 486x^2 + 620x + 193)r(x).$$

Set $c(x) = \tilde{n}(x)/r(x)$. After some work, we discover that ψ is such that $\psi Q = aQ$ for all $Q \in \tilde{E}(\mathbb{F}_q)$ where

$$\begin{aligned} a = \frac{1}{184258800}\big(&- 52523x^{11} - 174115x^{10} + 267585x^9 - 193271x^8 \\ &- 325290x^7 + 15093190x^6 - 29000446x^5 - 108207518x^4 \\ &+ 235138881x^3 + 284917001x^2 - 811361295x - 362511175\big). \end{aligned}$$

As we've done previously, we find a short basis for the lattice generated by the matrix

$$\left[\begin{array}{c|ccc} c(x) & 0 & 0 & 0 \\ -a(x) & 1 & 0 & 0 \\ -a(x)^2 & 0 & 1 & 0 \\ -a(x)^3 & 0 & 0 & 1 \end{array}\right]$$

and discover a short vector corresponding to the multiple

$$h(a) = \frac{1}{75}(x^2 - 25)c(x) = \lambda_0 + \lambda_1 a + \lambda_2 a^2 + \lambda_3 a^3$$

of c such that $\lambda = (\lambda_0, \lambda_1, \lambda_2, \lambda_3) = (-x^2 - x, x - 3, 2x + 6, -2x - 4)$.

For an element $Q \in \tilde{E}(\mathbb{F}_q)$, we can compute $h(a)Q$ with the following sequence of calculations. We compute $Q \mapsto xQ \mapsto (x+1)Q \mapsto (x^2 + x)Q$ and $Q \mapsto 2Q \mapsto 4Q$ which requires one addition, two doublings, and two multiply-by-x's. Then we compute

$$\begin{aligned} \lambda_0 Q &= -(x^2 + x)Q \\ \lambda_1 Q &= (x+1)Q - 4Q \\ \lambda_2 Q &= 2(x+1)Q + 4Q \\ \lambda_3 Q &= -2(x+1)Q - 2Q \end{aligned}$$

which requires three more additions and another doubling. Finally, we compute

$$h(a)Q = \lambda_0 Q + \psi(\lambda_1 Q) + \psi^2(\lambda_2 Q) + \psi^3(\lambda_3 Q)$$

which requires three more additions and three ψ maps.

In total, we require seven additions, three doublings, two multiply-by-x's, and three ψ maps to compute $Q \mapsto h(a)Q$.

6.4 KSS-18

KSS-18 curves [16] have embedding degree $k = 18$ and a twist of order $d = 6$. These curves are parameterized by x such that

$$\begin{aligned} r = r(x) &= \frac{1}{343}(x^6 + 37x^3 + 343) \\ p = p(x) &= \frac{1}{21}(x^8 + 5x^7 + 7x^6 + 37x^5 + 188x^4 \\ &\qquad + 259x^3 + 343x^2 + 1763x + 2401) \end{aligned}$$

are both prime. We find that

$$\begin{aligned} c(x) = \frac{1}{27}\big(&x^{18} + 15x^{17} + 96x^{16} + 409x^{15} + 1791x^{14} + 7929x^{13} + 27539x^{12} \\ &+ 81660x^{11} + 256908x^{10} + 757927x^9 + 1803684x^8 \\ &+ 4055484x^7 + 9658007x^6 + 19465362x^5 + 30860595x^4 \\ &+ 50075833x^3 + 82554234x^2 + 88845918x + 40301641\big). \end{aligned}$$

Constructing our lattice, we obtain the vector corresponding to the multiple

$$h(a) = -\frac{3}{343}x(8x^3 + 147)c(x) = \lambda_0 + \lambda_1 a + \lambda_2 a^2 + \lambda_3 a^3 + \lambda_2 a^4 + \lambda_3 a^5$$

of $c(x)$, where

$$\begin{aligned} \lambda_0 &= 5x + 18 \\ \lambda_1 &= x^3 + 3x^2 + 1 \\ \lambda_2 &= -3x^2 - 8x \\ \lambda_3 &= 3x + 1 \\ \lambda_4 &= -x^2 - 2 \\ \lambda_5 &= x^2 + 5x. \end{aligned}$$

We construct the addition chain $\{1, 2, 3, 5, 8, \underline{10}, 18\}$, from which we can compute $Q \mapsto h(a)Q$ using sixteen additions, two doublings, three multiply-by-x's, and five ψ maps.

6.5 Comparison with Previous Work

In Table 3, we compare our results to the work of Scott *et al.* [27,28]. In the proceedings version [27] of their work, the authors assume that the identity $\Phi_k(\psi)P = \infty$ holds for all points P in $\tilde{E}(\mathbb{F}_q)$. However, there exist concrete examples showing that this identity does *not* hold for some curves. In particular, MNT and Freeman curves do not satisfy this identity in general. On the

Table 3. A comparison of our hashing algorithm with the hashing algorithm of Scott *et al.* 'A' denotes a point addition, 'D' denotes a point doubling, 'X' denotes a multiplication by x, and 'ψ' denotes an application of the map ψ.

Curve	Scott *et al.*	This work
BN	4A 2D 2X 3ψ	4A 1D 1X 3ψ
Freeman	20A 5D 3X 4ψ	14A 4D 3X 4ψ
KSS-8	22A 5D 5X 2ψ	7A 3D 2X 3ψ
KSS-18	59A 5D 7X 4ψ	16A 2D 3X 5ψ

other hand, the identity $\psi^{k/2}P = -P$ is critically used in the eprint version [28] of their work. Fortunately, all curves except the MNT curve can be explicitly shown to satisfy the identity $\psi^{k/2}P = -P$. In practice, we've found that MNT curves also satisfy this property. More work needs to be done to determine the structure of the twist and the action of ψ on various subgroups of the twist.

We use the eprint version [28] to represent Scott *et al.*'s operation counts on Freeman curves. We have verified that the identity $\Phi_k(\psi)P = \infty$ holds for BN, KSS-8, and KSS-18 curves and use the counts from the proceedings version [27] of their work for those curves in Table 3. Since the multiplications by x dominate the other operations, it can be seen that our hash algorithm is approximately twice as fast as that of Scott *et al.* for BN curves. For the KSS-8 curve we see a $\frac{5}{2}$-fold improvement, and for the KSS-18 curves, we see a $\frac{7}{3}$-fold improvement.

7 Conclusion

We shown that both the final exponentiation and hashing to $\mathbb{G}_2$ tasks can be efficiently performed by adapting the lattice-based framework that Vercauteren utilized in [29] for finding optimal pairings. Let us recall that an optimal pairing as defined in [29] computes the Miller loop in just $log_2 r/\phi(k)$ iterations.

Scott *et al.* [26] showed that by writing $d = \Phi_k(p)/r$ in base p as $d = d_0 + d_1 p + \cdots + d_{\varphi(k)-1}p^{\varphi(k)-1}$, one can find short vectorial addition chains to efficiently compute the hard part of the final exponentiation $f \mapsto f^d$. This work presents a lattice-based method for determining a multiple d' of d, with r not dividing d' such that $f \mapsto f^{d'}$ can be computed at least as efficiently as $f \mapsto f^d$ and where $d'(x)$ is written in base $p(x)$ as $d'(x) = d'_0(x) + d'_1(x)p(x) + \cdots + d'_{\phi(k)-1}(x)p(x)^{\phi(k)-1}$. In theorem 1 it was proved that there exists a polynomial $h(z) = h_0 + h_1 z + \cdots + h_{\varphi(k)-1}z^{\varphi(k)-1} \in \mathbb{Z}[z]$ such that every point $P \in \tilde{E}(\mathbb{F}_q)$, can be hashed to $\mathbb{G}_2$ by computing $h(\psi)P$, where $|h_i|^{\varphi(k)} \leq \#\tilde{E}(\mathbb{F}_q)/r$ for all i.

Vercauteren's lattice-based framework reveals the crucial role that $\phi(k)$ plays for defining upper bounds on the optimal length of the Miller loop and on the final exponentiation and hashing to $\mathbb{G}_2$ computational efforts. This makes us conclude that the optimal solutions of these three problems are tightly related on an eternal golden braid.

Acknowledgments. The authors would like to express their deepest thanks to Professor Alfred Menezes for valuable discussions and constructive criticism related to this work and for the careful proof-reading of the technical sections of this paper.

References

1. Aranha, D.F., Karabina, K., Longa, P., Gebotys, C.H., López, J.: Faster Explicit Formulas for Computing Pairings over Ordinary Curves. In: Paterson, K.G. (ed.) EUROCRYPT 2011. LNCS, vol. 6632, pp. 48–68. Springer, Heidelberg (2011)
2. Barreto, P.S.L.M., Galbraith, S., ÓhÉigeartaigh, C., Scott, M.: Efficient pairing computation on supersingular Abelian varieties. Designs, Codes and Cryptography 42(3), 239–271 (2007)
3. Barreto, P.S.L.M., Kim, H.Y., Lynn, B., Scott, M.: Efficient Algorithms for Pairing-Based Cryptosystems. In: Yung, M. (ed.) CRYPTO 2002. LNCS, vol. 2442, pp. 354–368. Springer, Heidelberg (2002)
4. Barreto, P.S.L.M., Naehrig, M.: Pairing-Friendly Elliptic Curves of Prime Order. In: Preneel, B., Tavares, S. (eds.) SAC 2005. LNCS, vol. 3897, pp. 319–331. Springer, Heidelberg (2006)
5. Beuchat, J.-L., González-Díaz, J.E., Mitsunari, S., Okamoto, E., Rodríguez-Henríquez, F., Teruya, T.: High-speed Software Implementation of the Optimal Ate Pairing over Barreto–Naehrig Curves. In: Joye, M., Miyaji, A., Otsuka, A. (eds.) Pairing 2010. LNCS, vol. 6487, pp. 21–39. Springer, Heidelberg (2010)
6. Devegili, A.J., Scott, M., Dahab, R.: Implementing Cryptographic Pairings over Barreto-Naehrig Curves. In: Takagi, T., Okamoto, T., Okamoto, E., Okamoto, T. (eds.) Pairing 2007. LNCS, vol. 4575, pp. 197–207. Springer, Heidelberg (2007)
7. Freeman, D.: Constructing Pairing-Friendly Elliptic Curves with Embedding Degree 10. In: Hess, F., Pauli, S., Pohst, M. (eds.) ANTS 2006. LNCS, vol. 4076, pp. 452–465. Springer, Heidelberg (2006)
8. Freeman, D., Scott, M., Teske, E.: A Taxonomy of Pairing-Friendly Elliptic Curves. Journal of Cryptology 23(2), 224–280 (2010)
9. Galbraith, S.D., Lin, X., Scott, M.: Endomorphisms for Faster Elliptic Curve Cryptography on a Large Class of Curves. In: Joux, A. (ed.) EUROCRYPT 2009. LNCS, vol. 5479, pp. 518–535. Springer, Heidelberg (2009)
10. Scott, M., Benger, N., Charlemagne, M., Dominguez Perez, L.J., Kachisa, E.J.: On the Final Exponentiation for Calculating Pairings on Ordinary Elliptic Curves. In: Shacham, H., Waters, B. (eds.) Pairing 2009. LNCS, vol. 5671, pp. 78–88. Springer, Heidelberg (2009)
11. Granger, R., Scott, M.: Faster Squaring in the Cyclotomic Subgroup of Sixth Degree Extensions. In: Nguyen, P.Q., Pointcheval, D. (eds.) PKC 2010. LNCS, vol. 6056, pp. 209–223. Springer, Heidelberg (2010)
12. Hankerson, D., Menezes, A., Scott, M.: Software Implementation of Pairings. In: Identity-Based Cryptography, ch.12, pp. 188–206 (2009)
13. Hess, F.: Pairing Lattices. In: Galbraith, S.D., Paterson, K.G. (eds.) Pairing 2008. LNCS, vol. 5209, pp. 18–38. Springer, Heidelberg (2008)
14. Hess, F., Smart, N., Vercauteren, F.: The Eta Pairing Revisited. IEEE Transactions on Information Theory 52(10), 4595–4602 (2006)
15. Karabina, K.: Squaring in Cyclotomic Subgroups (2010) (manuscript), `http://eprint.iacr.org/2010/542`

16. Kachisa, E.J., Schaefer, E.F., Scott, M.: Constructing Brezing-Weng Pairing-Friendly Elliptic Curves Using Elements in the Cyclotomic Field. In: Galbraith, S.D., Paterson, K.G. (eds.) Pairing 2008. LNCS, vol. 5209, pp. 126–135. Springer, Heidelberg (2008)
17. Koblitz, N., Menezes, A.: Pairing-Based Cryptography at High Security Levels. In: Smart, N.P. (ed.) Cryptography and Coding 2005. LNCS, vol. 3796, pp. 13–36. Springer, Heidelberg (2005)
18. Lee, E., Lee, H.-S., Park, C.-M.: Efficient and Generalized Pairing Computation on Abelian Varieties. IEEE Transactions on Information Theory 55(4), 1793–1803 (2009)
19. Lenstra, A.K., Lenstra Jr., H.W., Lovasz, L.: Factoring Polynomials with Rational Coefficients. Mathematische Annalen 261(4), 515–534 (1982)
20. Menezes, A.: Elliptic Curve Public Key Cryptosystems. Kluwer Academic Publishers (1993)
21. Miller, V.S.: The Weil Pairing, and Its Efficient Calculation. Journal of Cryptology 17(4), 235–261 (2004)
22. Minkowski, H.: Geometrie der Zahlen, Leipzig und Berlin, Druck ung Verlag von B.G. Teubner (1910)
23. Miyaji, A., Nakabayashi, M., Takano, S.: New Explicit Conditions of Elliptic-Curve Traces for FR-reduction. IEICE Trans. Fundamentals E84, 1234–1243 (2001)
24. Olivos, J.: On Vectorial Addition Chains. Journal of Algorithms 2(1), 13–21 (1981)
25. Pereira, G.C.C.F., Simplcio Jr., M.A., Naehrig, M., Barreto, P.S.L.M.: A Family of Implementation-Friendly BN Elliptic Curves. Journal of Systems and Software (to appear, 2011)
26. Scott, M., Benger, N., Charlemagne, M., Dominguez Perez, L.J., Kachisa, E.J.: On the Final Exponentiation for Calculating Pairings on Ordinary Elliptic Curves. In: Shacham, H., Waters, B. (eds.) Pairing 2009. LNCS, vol. 5671, pp. 78–88. Springer, Heidelberg (2009)
27. Scott, M., Benger, N., Charlemagne, M., Dominguez Perez, L.J., Kachisa, E.J.: Fast Hashing to G_2 on Pairing-Friendly Curves. In: Shacham, H., Waters, B. (eds.) Pairing 2009. LNCS, vol. 5671, pp. 102–113. Springer, Heidelberg (2009)
28. Scott, M., Benger, N., Charlemagne, M., Dominguez Perez, L.J., Kachisa, E.J.: Fast Hashing to $\mathbb{G}_2$ on Pairing-Friendly Curves, `http://eprint.iacr.org/2008/530`
29. Vercauteren, F.: Optimal Pairings. IEEE Transactions on Information Theory 56(1), 455–461 (2010)

Author Index

Ågren, Martin 213
Akishita, Toru 278
Andreeva, Elena 37

Bertoni, Guido 320
Bouillaguet, Charles 243

Cenk, Murat 384
Chatterjee, Sanjit 293
Chen, Jiazhe 185
Costello, Craig 92

Daemen, Joan 320
Demirci, Hüseyin 169
Dunkelman, Orr 243

Fouque, Pierre-Alain 243
Fuentes-Castañeda, Laura 412
Fuhr, Thomas 230

Gilbert, Henri 230

Hamann, Matthias 134
Harmancı, A. Emre 169
Hasan, M. Anwar 384
Hiwatari, Harunaga 278

Izu, Tetsuya 260

Jacobson Jr., Michael J. 399
Jakimoski, Goce 356
Jean, Jérémy 19
Jia, Keting 185

Karakoç, Ferhat 169
Khajuria, Samant 356
Knapp, Edward 412
Knellwolf, Simon 200
Krause, Matthias 134
Kunihiro, Noboru 260

Labrande, Hugo 399
Lauter, Kristin 92
Leurent, Gaëtan 243
Loftus, Jake 55

Maitra, Subhamoy 151
May, Alexander 55
Meier, Willi 200
Menezes, Alfred 293
Mennink, Bart 37

Naito, Yusuke 338
Naya-Plasencia, María 19, 200
Negre, Christophe 384

Paul, Goutam 151
Peeters, Michaël 320
Plût, Jérôme 373

Reinhard, Jean-René 230
Rodríguez-Henríquez, Francisco 412

Saarinen, Markku-Juhani O. 118
Sarkar, Palash 293
Sarkar, Santanu 151
Sasaki, Yu 1
Schläffer, Martin 19
Sen Gupta, Sourav 151
Shinohara, Naoyuki 260
Slamanig, Daniel 73
Smart, Nigel P. 55

Van Assche, Gilles 320
Vercauteren, Frederik 55
Videau, Marion 230

Wang, Meiqin 185
Wang, Xiaoyun 185

GPSR Compliance

The European Union's (EU) General Product Safety Regulation (GPSR) is a set of rules that requires consumer products to be safe and our obligations to ensure this.

If you have any concerns about our products, you can contact us on ProductSafety@springernature.com

In case Publisher is established outside the EU, the EU authorized representative is:

Springer Nature Customer Service Center GmbH
Europaplatz 3
69115 Heidelberg, Germany

Batch number: 10844619

Printed by Printforce, the Netherlands